# MACROECONOMIC

# READINGS

*JOHN LINDAUER* Editor

# MACROECONOMIC

# READINGS

THE FREE PRESS
*New York*

COLLIER-MACMILLAN LIMITED
*London*

# *Preface*

**M**ore than three decades have passed since the epic work of Lord Keynes brought macroeconomics into the economic limelight as a separate field of study. Since that time, refinements, extensions, and policy recommendations have increasingly poured forth to expand the material covered by macroeconomic textbooks and lectures. As a result, most students have little opportunity during the initial stages of their educations to become familiar with the articles which macroeconomists typically use to report their ideas and research.

The purpose of this book is to introduce undergraduates to those articles and thus to the type of work which is done by macroeconomists. It contains forty-four selections. Most of them are from the post-1960 era, although some of the more important earlier milestones, such as Evsey Domar's "Expansion and Employment," are also included. In addition to the pre-1960 milestones, the collection includes representative works from each topic area as well as those articles most often cited in macroeconomic texts. Each of the articles is related to a topic which is typically considered in a macroeconomic theory class.

The articles are grouped in nine sections on the basis of their subject matter. A brief introduction precedes each section to provide a frame of reference for the reader.

The editor is particularly indebted to the authors and original publishers of this material for their permission to anthologize it in this manner.

*JOHN LINDAUER*

v

# Contents

## Part 4    Income and employment

## Part 5    Income fluctuations and growth

## Part 6    Inflation

## Part 7    General policy considerations

*Part 8 Monetary policy*

*Part 9 Fiscal policy*

# Contents by Author

# *Consumption*

*THE CONCEPT OF* a consumption function is accepted by a great many economists as being one of Lord Keynes's most important theoretical contributions. As a result of the importance which the Keynesian and subsequent analyses assigned to them, consumption functions have received substantial research emphasis, and there are now more than a few explanations of the levels of consumption purchasing which have occurred in economies such as that of the United States.

Two articles are included in this section. The first is an early article by James S. Duesenberry in which he presents an explanation of the short-run and long-run relationship between consumption and income. In the second article, Saul Hyman examines the behavior of consumers during different stages of the business cycle.

*Part*

*1*

*J A M E S   S .   D U E S E N B E R R Y*

# Income-Consumption Relations and Their Implications

*1* Of all the new ideas introduced by Keynes in *The General Theory*, the concept of the "consumption function" was the easiest to accept. Few wished to deny that consumption expenditures are primarily determined by income; Keynes' arguments for the stability of the relationship were cogent enough to convince a great number of economists. The opportunities for empirical work opened up by the introduction of the new concept were at once apparent. Here, for once, was a theoretical relationship which involved magnitudes which could be measured not merely theoretically but practically. Econometricians went to work with a will and their efforts were amply rewarded. They were not only able to find a relationship between income and consumption, but they found that virtually all of the variation in consumer expenditures was explained by variations in income.

Yet, in spite of these empirical successes, the consumption function is a more controversial subject today than it was ten years ago. For

Reprinted from *Income, Employment and Public Policy*, Essays in Honor of Alvin H. Hansen (New York: Norton, 1948), pp. 54-81. James Duesenberry is a Professor at Harvard University.

empirical investigation has yielded not one consumption function but many, and each of them explains all the variations in consumption.

Like most economic magnitudes the literature on the consumption function seems to grow according to the compound-interest law. This would be easy to understand if the literature appeared as the result of the discovery of new data. But no fundamental changes in our knowledge of the facts about income and consumption have occurred in the past five years.

Most of the articles on the consumption function present hypotheses about the relation between consumption, income, and some other variable such as time, the price level, or the degree of unemployment. The hypothesis is presented in the form of an equation which makes consumption a function of the other variables. The appropriate regression is fitted to the data, and the correlation between the observed and calculated values of consumption or saving is computed. The correlation is invariably high, and most writers seem to be satisfied that a high correlation coefficient provides an adequate test of their hypothesis. But a test which is passed by so many different hypotheses is not a very satisfactory one. Before any more consumption functions are introduced it seems desirable to give some consideration to our methods of testing hypotheses.

In Section I it is shown that aggregate hypotheses cannot be adequately tested by the use of correlation analysis. The general principles on which appropriate testing methods can be developed are then discussed. Section II is devoted to a consideration of the possibility that the relation between saving and income is different at different points of the trade cycle. A test based on the principles developed in Section I shows that we must reject the hypothesis that the saving-income relation is invariant with respect to measures of position in the trade cycle.

In Section III hypotheses which explain both cyclical and secular movements of savings are developed. It is shown that these hypotheses are consistent with: (1) the long-run data on income and consumption given by Kuznets, (2) the annual data on income and consumption in the period 1923–40, (3) the budget study data collected in 1935–36 and 1941. These hypotheses lead to the conclusion that aggregate saving out of disposable income can be estimated by the equation

$$\frac{s_t}{y_t} = .165 \frac{y_t}{y_0} - .066,$$

where $s_t$ = current savings, $y_t$ = current disposable income, $y_0$ = highest disposable income ever attained, with all variables corrected for population and price changes.[1]

## I. Tests of Aggregate Hypothesis

When we deal with a problem in aggregate economics we usually seek for relationships which are, in some sense, invariant. By invariance we do not mean a historical invariance like the Pareto law. Rather, we mean that the relationship between a certain set of variables is unaffected by changes in some other variables. The concept of an invariant relationship is therefore a relative one; a relation may be invariant with respect to one set of variables, but not with respect to some others. Indeed it might be said that hardly any economic relationship can be regarded as completely invariant. For no economic relation is likely to continue to hold good both before and after a fundamental change in social organization. In fact, one of the objects of economic policy

is the modification of social organization in such a way as to produce relations of a desirable type among economic variables.

Our idea of invariance is somewhat as follows: We conceive that at any one moment certain variables within the control of households or firms are related in a definite way to certain other variables not within their control. For example, we suppose that the consumption expenditure of families depends on their income. The form of these relations is governed by the behaviour characteristics of individuals and by institutional factors such as laws or customs. The relations we seek are invariant with respect to all variables except these psychological or institutional factors. A relation which satisfies that criterion may be said to be more or less stable according as these factors are more or less constant. We can make satisfactory predictions if we can find invariant relations of this type which are highly stable.[2]

If an invariant relation of this type holds for the variables associated with individual households or firms, then a corresponding invariant relation must hold among some functions (not necessarily sums) of all the household or firm variables of the same kind. If we can write

[2] Finding invariant relations of this sort actually helps in only one kind of policy problem. We may conceive of the "structure" of the economy as being described by a certain set of invariant relations. Then one kind of policy consists in fixing the values of certain of the variables which enter into these equations without otherwise disturbing any of the relations. Fixing an interest rate or tax rate is a policy of this sort. If we know all the invariant relations necessary to describe the structure, we can predict the effect of this sort of policy (at least in the sense that we can assign a probability to any values of any economic variable at each point in the future).

On the other hand, many of the most important policies involve changes in the structure. If a law is changed which has never been changed before, then we may know that certain structural equations will be changed, but we may not be able to foretell exactly what the new equations will be like. Or, to take a simple example, if the Treasury undertakes a campaign to get people to save more, it will be difficult to know what its effect will be. For this is an attempt to induce changes in behaviour patterns, and we have comparatively little experience with this kind of change. The kind of data with which economists deal is not likely to reveal anything about the possible effects of the Treasury's campaign. On the other hand, a sufficiently general theory of behaviour ought to make a prediction possible, but this would be entirely a question of social psychology.

As a matter of fact, it seems probable that most of the economic policies of really fundamental importance involve structural changes of this sort. To the extent that this is true, economists can be regarded as competent to judge the effect of these policies only by default on the part of the social psychologists.

[1] Part of this paper was presented at the meeting of the Econometric Society in January, 1947. At the same meeting Prof. Franco Modigliani presented a paper containing an almost identical income-saving relation.

$y_i = f_i(x_i)$ for every household (when $x_i$ and $y_i$ are variables applying to the ith household), then we can write $\Phi(x_1, x_2 \ldots x_n, y_1, y_2, \ldots y_n) = 0$. The invariance of the second relation will depend on the constancy of the behaviour characteristics and institutional elements which determine the invariance of the original relations, and in some cases on the constancy of the distribution of the $x$'s. Aggregate relations which can be deduced from household or firm relations, I shall call fundamental aggregate relations. (There are of course some additional fundamental aggregate relations which are definitional and need not be deduced from anything.)

Now consider a pair of such fundamental aggregate relations:

$$\Phi_1(x_1 x_2 \ldots x_n) = \psi_1(y_1 y_2 \ldots y_n) \quad (1)$$

$$\Phi_2(x_1 x_2 \ldots x_n) = \psi_2(z_1 z_2 \ldots z_n) \quad (2)$$

where the $x$'s are exogenous variables.

It is clear that a further relation

$$x_1(y_1 y_2 \ldots y_n) = x_2(z_1 z_2 \ldots z_n) \quad (3)$$

may be derived from the first two. Further, this relation will be invariant so long as (1) and (2) are invariant. This type of relation I shall call a derived aggregate relation.[3]

Now suppose that we observe the historical invariance of the relation (3) and conclude that it is a fundamental relation. We might then conclude that by changing the $z$'s we could manipulate the $y$'s. But we might find instead that we had merely invalidated the relation (2) without having any effect at all on the $y$'s or $x$'s. Derived relations like (3) may break down either as a consequence of policy changes or of structural changes in the economy. In addition there is an important class of derived relations which are likely to hold good only during the course of a single trade cycle. For example, a certain variable $z$ may be partly dependent on the level of unemployment. Within the course of a single trade cycle, income is very closely associated with the level of unemployment. If we have data covering only a single trade cycle, we might conclude from the empirical evidence that $z$ is determined by income. Actually we have a derived relation between $z$ and income, which is bound to break up because the upward trend in income will ultimately change the association between income and unemployment. It is clear from these considerations that many of the relations observed empirically may be only

[3] Cf. T. Haavelmo, "The Probability Approach to Econometrics," *Econometrica*, July, 1944, Supplement.

derived relations which will break down because of a structural change in one of the fundamental relations on which they are based. This is particularly true of relations whose existence has been tested against the data of only a single trade cycle. Whether we are concerned with policy or with prediction, we shall often make errors if we treat derived relations as though they were fundamental ones. The difficulty of distinguishing between these two kinds of relations is one of the fundamental difficulties in testing economic hypotheses.

Let us now return to a consideration of the adequacy of correlation methods of hypothesis testing. Suppose we have a hypothesis which asserts that total consumer expenditure is dependent on disposable income. We can fit a regression to the data for income and consumption and compute the correlation coefficient. When we find a significant correlation, what, exactly, have we found? We have not shown that the "data are consistent with the hypothesis." We have merely disproved the null hypothesis. That is, we have shown that the association between income and consumption was too strong to allow us to ascribe it to chance. Then we should be reasonably confident in asserting that we have found either (a) a fundamental relation between income and consumption, or (b) a derived relation between them. We might exploit our results a little further. If it could be shown that the lower confidence limit on the correlation was (say) .95, we could assert that during the period income was linearly related to all the variables fundamentally related to consumption. But this is about as far as we can safely go. It can be argued, of course, that a derived relation will tend to produce lower correlations than a fundamental relation. But, when our data cover only short periods, the connections between economic variables may be so close that the differences in correlations between the two sorts of relations may be too small to be statistically significant. Moreover, if the variables in a derived relation have a lower observational error than those in the fundamental relations, the correlation in the derived relation may be the higher one.

A very simple example of a derived relation is that which appears to have existed between consumer expenditures in dollars and disposable income in dollars during the period 1929–40. Just as good a correlation is obtained by using undeflated as deflated data. This can be true only because the price level was related to income during the period. If real consumption is fundamentally related to real income, the money relationship is a derived one and will break down in the postwar period. Conversely, if money consumption is fundamentally related to money income the relation between the real variables is a derived one and will break down. Now it is obviously of vital importance to know which is the fundamental relation, but the correlation test is not very helpful.

The difficulties we have just been discussing arise because of the existence of derived relations among aggregate variables. But, ordinarily, such derived relations will not hold for individual firms or households. This suggests that in testing hypotheses we ought to operate on the following principles. First, every hypothesis ought to be stated in terms of the behaviour of individual firms or households, even when we are only interested in aggregate results. This does not, of course, prevent us from considering interactions among individuals, any more than the use of the theory of the firm in analysis of monopolistic competition prevents us from dealing with interactions among firms. Second, in so far as it is possible, we ought to test our hypotheses against data which indicate the behaviour of individual households or firms. This does not mean that we ought to abandon statistical procedures. Nearly every hypothesis has to allow for random elements in behaviour so that in making tests we have to measure the average behaviour of groups. But by dealing with relatively small groups we may escape the net of interrelations which makes it impossible to test aggregate hypotheses.

Suppose we are faced with the following situation: One hypothesis asserts that saving varies with income and the price level, another asserts that saving depends on income alone. Aggregate income and the price level are related in the period for which data are available. Then, if one of these hypotheses is true, it will be impossible to disprove the other by means of aggregate data alone. But, while movements of aggregate income may have been correlated with those of the price level, there are certainly some individuals whose incomes moved in a different way. By studying the behaviour of those individuals it will be possible to disprove one of the hypotheses. When this has been done the parameters in the chosen relation may be fitted by the use of aggregate data (though in some cases this may still be difficult because of multi-collinearity).

Of course it will not always be possible to find the data necessary to test every hypothesis. But there is a great deal of microeconomic data, which has never been properly exploited because of the tendency of econometricians to emphasize

parameter fitting rather than hypothesis testing. Actually it is much more important to work with a true hypothesis than to make extremely precise estimates of parameters.

## II. Changes in Income and the Rate of Saving

In this section we shall apply the method just suggested to some questions about the consumption function. In the view of a number of writers, notably Smithies and Mosak,[4] consumer expenditures are essentially dependent on the prevailing level of disposable income. The effect on consumption of an increase in income is supposed to be the same whether the increase comes about through a rise of employment during recovery from a depression or through a rise in productivity in a period of sustained full employment like that of the twenties. Professor Hansen[5] and Professor Samuelson[6] have maintained for some time that the relation between income and consumption varies through the trade cycle. Mr. Woytinski[7] and Mr. Bean[8] have made similar statements and have tried to test them empirically. They obtained correlations just as good as the others but no better, and certainly cannot claim to have disproved the alternative hypothesis. There is, however, some evidence which proves nearly conclusively that the consumption function is cyclically variable though not quite in the ways suggested by Bean or Woytinski.

This evidence is provided by the budget studies made in 1935–36[9] and 1941.[10] One of the remarkable results of the Study of Consumer Purchases of 1935–36 was that a great number of families reported expenditures in excess of income for the year. The average deficit of the

[4] "Forecasting Postwar Demand, I, III," *Econometrica*, January, 1945.

[5] *Business Cycles and Fiscal Policy*, New York, W. W. Norton & Company, 1941, pp. 225–249.

[6] "Full Employment after the War," in *Postwar Economic Problems*, edited by S. E. Harris, New York, McGraw Hill, 1943.

[7] "Relationship between Consumer's Expenditure, Savings and Disposable Income," *Review of Economic Statistics*, January, 1946.

[8] "Relationship of Disposable Income and the Business Cycle to Expenditure," *Review of Economic Statistics*, November, 1946.

[9] Summarized by the National Resources Committee in *Consumer Expenditures in the United States*, Washington, 1938; *Consumer Incomes in the United States*, Washington, 1939; *Family Expenditures in the United States*, Washington, 1941.

[10] Bureau of Labor Statistics, Bulletins 723 and 724.

## Table 1. White Urban and Rural Non-Farm Families with Incomes under $1000 in 1935–36

| | Relief | Non-relief |
|---|---|---|
| Retired | 600,000 | 600,000 |
| Independent Business and Professional | 100,000 | 600,000 |
| Partially or Fully Unemployed | 2,100,000 | 1,900,000 |
| Fully Employed | — | 2,400,000 |
| Total | 2,800,000 | 5,500,000 |

under $500 a year group amounted to 50 per cent of income, while the average deficit of the $500–$1000 group was 10 per cent of income.[11] The results of the 1935–36 study are not above criticism, of course, but the fact that deficits were reported in every city and every area, together with the independent evidence of studies like those of Gilboy, Clague and Powell, makes it clear that very substantial deficits did occur during the depression.[12]

The total deficits of urban and rural non-farm families (who were white and not on relief) alone amounted to 593 million dollars for 1935–36. Since total net savings of consumers during the twenties and thirties varied from $7.6 to $2.0 billion, an explanation of the deficits can contribute a good deal to our understanding of variations in saving.

But the real significance of the deficits does not lie in their magnitude but in what they reveal about the relations between income and saving. We shall first show that the deficits arose largely because families whose income fell in the depression tried to preserve their pre-depression living standards. Families in the higher income groups did the same thing but accomplished it by reducing their rate of saving rather than by dissaving. The analysis of the deficits is important chiefly because it helps us to analyze variations in the positive savings of higher income groups.

Let us first consider what kind of people were in the low income groups in 1935–36. While there is little direct information about the low income families in 1935–36, a rough estimate of their composition can be made from the data on income and employment in 1939 contained in the Census of 1940. Table 1 shows the result of this estimate.[13]

In the nature of the case this estimate can be only a rough one since it has to be based on a number of unverified assumptions. Yet there does not seem to be much doubt that the non-relief low-income families included a high proportion of families whose incomes were low because of unemployment and whose incomes were much higher in periods of full employment. Moreover, some of the families in the independent business and professional group would have higher incomes in more prosperous periods. Finally, some of the fully employed wage and salary workers were down-graded from higher wage jobs so that their normal incomes were higher than the incomes reported in 1935–36.

(1) Keeping these considerations in mind, let us now ask what is the significance of the deficits for the theory of saving. A supporter of the view that saving depends on real income would say, presumably, that $c/y = f(y)$ and that $c/y$ exceeds 1 for some positive value of $y$ (where $y$ is in constant prices). When that value of $y$ is reached, those who have assets or credit will have deficits; the others will have to be content with spending all of their income.

In its simple form this position is untenable, for the break-even point (the income at which consumption just equals income) stood at about $800 in 1917 and $1500 in 1935–36, using 1941 prices in both cases.[14] If consumption were merely a function of current income the break-even level of income should have remained the same. To this the sophisticated Keynesian will reply by introducing a trend factor. Consumption at a given level of income can be changed by the introduction of new goods (this is about the only factor likely to cause a trend in the consumption of urban families, and these are the families included in the budget studies in

[11] *Family Expenditures in the United States*, p. 1.

[12] Elizabeth Gilboy, *Applicants for Work Relief*, Cambridge, Harvard University Press, 1940. E. Clague and W. Powell, *Ten Thousand Out of Work*, Philadelphia, University of Pennsylvania, 1933.

[13] This estimate was obtained by reconciling the data given by the National Resources Committee on numbers of families with incomes under $1000 in 1935–36 with the data in the Census of 1940 on the

family wage and salary income and employment in 1939. See *Family Expenditures in the United States*, pp. 123, 127, 130 and Census of 1940, *The Labor Force (Sample Statistics)*, *Wage or Salary Income in 1939* and *Family Wage or Salary Income in 1939*.

[14] See G. Cornfield, W. D. Evans, and M. Hoffenberg, "Full Employment Patterns in 1950, Part I," *Monthly Labor Review*, February, 1947, p. 181.

question). For the sake of the argument let us agree that introduction of new goods in itself increases consumption at a given level of income. We know too that families in the low income groups were driving automobiles and using various recently introduced household appliances. This does not advance the argument much, however, for the families in question were for the most part using these things rather than buying them. We can turn to other new goods, movies and silk stockings (say), which were also consumed by the low-income groups in the thirties. Let us grant that a family with an $800 income did not buy these things in 1917 and did in 1935. Then it follows that at least part of the deficits in the thirties were due to the fact that low income families bought new goods which did not exist in the earlier period. But this is not the whole story. We can say on the one hand that families at an $800 income level in the thirties spent more than families with that income in 1917 because they had become used to a high standard of living (including silk stockings and movies) in the twenties and found it difficult to give up. Or we can say that even if income had remained constant from 1917 to 1935 the attraction of these new goods was so irresistible that they incurred deficits to get them (or at least that they would have done so if they had had the necessary assets or credit). The latter position seems to be a somewhat untenable one. But, if we argue that consumption depends on current real income and trend, that is the position which must be maintained in order to explain the facts. For, if we write $c/y = f(y,t)$, nothing has been said about the influence of past living standards on current consumption.

This does not disprove the proposition that consumption at a given moment is dependent on real income alone; but it does require the supporters of that proposition to subscribe to some very strong propositions about the influence of new products and similar trend factors.

(2) We can make a further test if we compare the deficits reported in 1935–36 with those reported in 1941. Deficits at given levels of income were much smaller in 1941 than in 1935–36. At every level deficits were less than one half as great in 1941 as in 1935–36. How is this shift to be explained? Suppose the deficits, in both cases, were due to the fact that families whose incomes had fallen as a result of unemployment found it hard to reduce their living standards. Then the explanation is easy. The low income group consists primarily of two subgroups: families whose earners are normally fully employed at

low wages, and families whose incomes have been reduced by unemployment. The second group will run deficits to protect the high living standard attained when they were fully employed. The first group balances its budget. Suppose now that we have complete data on families in the $1000 income group in two periods. Suppose that the situation is as follows:

|  | NUMBER | DEFICIT |
|---|---|---|
| Fully Employed Families (with normal incomes) | 5000 | 0 |
| Partially Employed Families | 5000 | $300 |
| Average |  | $150 |

Suppose that in a second period we obtain reports from the same group but that half of the families in the $1000 group have increased their incomes. The situation in the $1000 group now is as follows:

|  | NUMBER | DEFICIT |
|---|---|---|
| Fully Employed Families | 5000 | 0 |
| Partially Employed Families | 2500 | $300 |
| Average |  | $100 |

Now suppose that instead of subdividing the families in this way our report had shown only the average deficit of the $1000 income families. We would have observed a reduction in the average deficit from $150 to $100 per family without knowing why. The differences in the 1935–36 and 1941 studies seem to correspond very clearly to the examples just given. In 1935–36 there were about 8 million unemployed, in 1941 there were only 3 million. In 1935–36 a much higher proportion of families in the low income groups were there because of unemployment than in 1941. If, therefore, we accept the proposition that the deficits were due to unemployment, or to incomes low by comparison with previous ones, the difference between the two studies is easily explained.

If we try to support the view that consumption depends on absolute income, how shall we explain the difference? The trend explanation cannot be used in this case. For the break-even point moves in the wrong direction.

We can suppose that the families left in the low income groups would like to have run deficits but were unable to do so because they lacked the necessary assets or credit. But we have argued that a higher proportion of the low income group in 1941 were permanent members of that group than in 1935–36. It follows that the higher deficits in 1935–36 must have been incurred by the group whose incomes had fallen. For those permanently in the low income group were in more or less the same position in both years. Then we have to explain the differences in the reactions of the two groups. There are three possible explanations. (1) The families with temporarily low incomes were technically in a better position to have deficits. That is, they were not more willing to run deficits, but more able to get the resources to do so. (2) The families with temporarily low incomes had expectations of reëmployment and higher income in the future. (3) These families had had higher living standards in the past and were therefore more willing to have deficits to protect their living standards.

If either of the last two factors is influential, then consumption must depend on past income (since this governs the expected level of income at full employment) as well as on current income. In this case a general rise in income to levels above the 1929 peak followed by a fall would bring about a recurrence of the deficits, for the standard of living and expectations of income would be based on the new peak. If income declined from this peak by the same percentage as 1935 income had declined from the 1929 peak, deficits of a relative magnitude as large as those of 1935 would occur. This would be true even if the absolute level of income were as high as the 1929 level. On the other hand if the break-even point is independent of past levels of income no deficits would occur unless income were absolutely low.

The budget study data do not tell us anything directly about which of the three factors just mentioned are actually relevant. We must leave the question open for the moment. However, it should be noted that the hypothesis that consumption depends on past as well as on current income is consistent with all the data discussed so far. The alternative hypothesis that consumption depends only on current income can be made consistent with the data only if we are willing to accept some rather doubtful subsidiary propositions.

(3) One further piece of evidence is available for testing these two hypotheses. The 1941 budget study reported income for the first quarter of 1942 as well as for 1941. Families at each income level were classified by the changes in their income. Savings for the first quarter of 1942 were separately reported for those whose incomes had changed less than 5 per cent, for those whose incomes had increased more than 5 per cent, and those whose incomes had decreased more than 5 per cent from the 1941 level. The results are shown in Table 2. Families whose incomes rose had about the same savings or deficits as those whose incomes stayed the same.

On the other hand, families whose incomes fell had much smaller savings or larger deficits than those whose incomes stayed constant. Now these facts can be interpreted in two ways. On the one hand we can say that they show that a rate of change factor is important in the determination of saving. That is, we write $c/y = f(y,y')$ where $y'$ is the rate of change of income. On the other hand we can say that saving is low when income is low relative to past income. The two explanations are not the same. In a year when income is declining, either explanation would lead to the same result. But suppose that income declines and then remains at a (more or less constant) low level. After the decline has stopped, the rate of change is zero but income is still low relative to its pre-depression level.

It is fairly easy to tell which of the two hypotheses is correct. If the rate of change of income is an important factor it should show up in regressions of aggregate data. But it is well known that when the equation $c = f(y,t,y')$ is fitted to aggregate data for the twenties and thirties the addition of the factor $y'$ contributes

## Table 2. Average Yearly Savings in 1942 for City Families by Income Change from 1941 to 1942

| | CONSUMERS WHOSE INCOMES IN 1942 | | |
|---|---|---|---|
| Money Income Class in 1942[a] | Decreased over 5 per cent | Changed less than 5 per cent | Increased over 5 per cent |
| 0 to $1000 | —337 | —35 | —15 |
| $1000 to $1500 | —181 | —34 | 62 |
| $1500 to $2000 | — 81 | 126 | 157 |
| $2000 to $3000 | 0 | 242 | 290 |
| $3000 and over | 143 | 1228 | 1059 |

*Source:* Based on B.L.S. Bulletin 724
a Annual rate for 1942 based on first quarter

very little to the correlation. In the face of the budget study data this is difficult to explain unless we accept relative income instead of rate of change as the explanation of the differences in saving at the same level of income.

The asymmetry in the results is also important. If we take the view that rate of change of income is a determinant of saving, then there are strong reasons for supposing that the adjustment lag works in both directions. On the other hand, if we argue that people whose incomes are low relative to their past incomes reduce saving to protect their living standard, the asymmetry is easy to understand. Those whose incomes rose were for the most part getting back to levels of incomes which they had previously experienced. In these circumstances they merely returned to the expenditure patterns of the past and no adjustment lag is involved.

The data just discussed seem to show fairly conclusively that consumption at a given level of income does depend on past income. This hypothesis is consistent with the existence of deficits in 1935–36 and 1941, with the changes in deficits (at given levels of income) from 1935–36 to 1941, with the upward movement of the break-even point from 1917 to 1935–36 and 1941, and with the differences in saving among families whose incomes had changed in different ways. It is difficult to explain all of these facts on any other hypothesis.

### Psychological Foundation

So far our argument has been a strictly empirical one. But it must be clear that it also has a strong psychological foundation. The fundamental psychological postulate underlying our argument is that it is harder for a family to reduce its expenditures from a high level than for a family to refrain from making high expenditures in the first place. Consider two families who have incomes of $1000 per year at a particular time. Now suppose one of these families has an income of $1000 per year for ten years thereafter. Suppose the other family gets an increase in income from $1000 to $1500, retains this position for nine years, and then has its income reduced to $1000 so that in the last year it is in the same position as the other family. Initially both families might have exactly balanced their budgets at $1000, and the first family might continue in this way for the whole ten-year period. But when the second family had its income increased it would increase its consumption by (say) $400 and its saving by $100.

When the reduction in income occurred it would certainly find it difficult to cut its consumption to the $1000 level. The first family had only to refrain from increasing its consumption expenditures to balance its budget. The second family had actually to give up consumption of $400 per year to achieve the same result. It would be surprising if a family in these circumstances succeeded in reducing its consumption sufficiently to balance its budget after the loss in income.

Since all of the data are consistent with the view that this does happen, there does not seem to be much doubt that past income has an influence on current consumption and saving.

The argument so far has been devoted to explaining the deficits reported in the budget studies. But the significant result of this argument is not the conclusion that deficits will occur when income falls below previously attained levels but the more general proposition that families are willing to sacrifice saving in order to protect their living standard. This proposition applies to all income groups who have suffered losses in income. We can argue in the following way. If a family has a certain income $y_0$ and this income is higher than any previously attained, it will save some amount. This amount will be a function of income $s_0 = f(y_0)$. If its income increases the same function will hold. But if after an increase income falls to the original level its saving will be less than $f(y_0)$. If the family's income and saving are low throughout, it will have a deficit after the fall in income. If the family is in a higher bracket it will simply save less after the fall in income than it did before the increase. This view is checked by the fact that savings in the last five years of the twenties averaged 10.2 per cent of disposable income while from 1936 to 1940 they averaged only 9.0 per cent. Real disposable income per capita was almost the same in the two periods.

### A Base Year for Downward Adjustments of Consumption

We have now shown that consumption is dependent on current income relative to past income as well as on the absolute level of current income. The problem now is to find just which past incomes are relevant. In view of the argument just given we appear to be safe in supposing that past incomes lower than the current one are not very relevant. This is pretty well demonstrated by the 1941–42 budget figures cited above. Families whose incomes rose to a given level saved about the same amount as those whose incomes had been at that level in the previous year. At first glance then it would seem reasonable to suppose that current consumption depends on the ratio of current income to some weighted average of past higher incomes, with weights decreasing as the time interval involved grows longer. There are, however, some fairly strong arguments against this position. The declines in income which occur in the depression are not uniformly distributed even though the size distribution of income remains more or less unchanged.

Income losses will be of three kinds: (1) reductions in property incomes, (2) reductions in wage rates, (3) losses due to underemployment. Since real wage rates do not decline very much in the depression (and were even higher in the late years of the depression than in the twenties), losses of income are mostly of types (1) and (3). (A fourth class results from downgrading of workers either within or between industries, but for our purposes this can be regarded as underemployment.)

Let us first consider the effect of losses of income in the upper income groups. It is not important here whether the losses are due to reductions in property incomes or to salary reductions. It can be assumed, however, that unemployment among the upper income groups is not important. The upper 10 per cent of the income distribution produces almost all of the positive saving for the whole economy. Moreover, families in this group save a high proportion of their income. This means that they have a good deal of leeway in maintaining consumption standards without running into deficits; also they have more free (non-contractual) saving. When high income families suffer a loss in income, therefore, they continue to live in the same kind of neighborhoods and maintain their contacts with others of the same socio-economic status. In general they maintain the way of life which was established before the onset of the depression. They will, of course, cut expenditures on some lines, particularly on durable goods. But in view of the high rate of savings maintained in prosperity they can absorb a considerable reduction of income by reducing saving without cutting consumption too deeply. Moreover, there is no reason why they should not continue in this position for several years. Suppose now that income falls sharply from a cyclical peak and then remains constant for several years. The peak year's consumption sets the standard from which cuts are made (provided the peak did not represent a mere spurt in income). The

higher the peak consumption, the more difficult it will be to reduce consumption to any given level. After the initial reductions are made the situation becomes static. The peak year does not lose its influence because the consumption of the following years depends on the peak consumption. Of course, if income began to fall again further consumption cuts would take place, and the intermediate level of income would be important in determining the extent of the cuts as well as the previous peak income. But if the depression consists in a fall of income lasting only a couple of years followed by a rise or a low plateau, the consumption of the peak year is likely to have very heavy weight in determining consumption in the depression. The influence of the peak consumption will not "fade away" unless income continues to fall steadily.

All of the above argument applies only to the upper income groups. Those who were in the lower 90 per cent of the distribution in prosperity are in a different situation. For this group, reductions in individual income are usually associated with unemployment. These people probably save very little even in prosperous times. In a depression they can only influence saving by having deficits. A considerable number of families in this group go nearly unscathed by the depression. Their real wages do not fall and they never have serious losses of employment. These we may leave out of account since their savings are simply zero throughout. The remaining families suffer serious loss of employment at some point during the depression. These may also be divided into two groups. Some will remain employed up to a certain point, then lose their jobs and never get steady employment again until a high level of prosperity is reached. These families will presumably run substantial deficits immediately after they become unemployed, but as their assets become smaller they will have to adjust to the new situation and presumably balance budgets in which relief is the principal source of income. They may continue to have deficits for a long time, but in any case the influence of the prosperity living standard will certainly "fade away" as time passes. However, it should be noted that not all of the persons who will eventually constitute the "hard core" of unemployment get there at once. The result is that a certain number of families are going through the initial stages of long-term unemployment at any time during the depression. Presumably, however, there are rather more families in this position during the downturn in the early years than later on. We should expect, therefore, to find somewhat greater deficits and lower aggregate savings at a given income in the downturn than in the upturn. However, the total number of families in this group was not very large in the thirties, and the differences in the numbers entering cannot have been great enough to cause numerically important reductions in aggregate savings.

· The remainder of the unemployment is widely spread so that a large number of workers "take turns" being unemployed. Families lose income through unemployment and accordingly cut consumption; they also run a deficit. When they get reëmployed they may return to something very close to the prosperity consumption standard. Sometimes later unemployment may reoccur and the process repeats. Those families who are very frequently in and out of employment will presumably gradually reduce consumption (even when employed) because of the decrease in their assets and the accumulation of debt. The influence of the peak standard will therefore gradually lose its effect. But a great part of the total unemployment can be accounted for by families who have only one or two stretches of prolonged unemployment during the depression. For these families the influence of the peak consumption standard will not fade away because it renews itself with each stretch of full employment.

We can conclude then that the income or consumption of the last cyclical peak will carry a special and very heavy weight in determining consumption at a given (lower) level of income during a depression. In principle a weighted average of all the incomes from the peak year to the current year ought to be used. But with only a few observations it would be impossible to estimate the weights. In what follows we shall consider the relation of current consumption to the ratio

$$\frac{\text{current income}}{\text{highest previously attained income}}$$

but the results are to be taken as an approximation to the true relation.

If the argument just given is correct, then there is a cyclical component in the explanation of saving. Savings at a given level of income, when income is the highest ever attained, as in the late twenties, will be higher than savings at a similar income level reached in a decline from a still higher level. I conclude, therefore, that in a general way at least the propositions of those who have argued that saving varies with the trade cycle as well as with income are supported by the evidence of the budget studies.

## III. Aggregate Income-Saving Relationships

So far it has been shown that saving depends on the level of current incomes relative to higher incomes in previous years. But saving also depends on the absolute level of income. We may write then, $s_t = f(y_t, \ y_t/y_0)$ where $y_0$ is the highest income attained previous to the year $t$. Then

$$\frac{ds_t}{dy_t} = \frac{df}{dy_t} + \frac{df}{d(y_t)/y_0} \cdot \frac{d(y_t/y_0)}{dy_t}$$

If we plot out the long period relation of saving and income considering only periods of approximately full employment, the term $(dy_t/y_0)/dy_t$ will be 0 so that $ds_t/dy_t = df/dy_t$. But, with data covering a trade cycle, $(dy_t/y_0)/dy_t$ will have a positive value, and, if we use cyclical data to estimate the secular marginal propensity to consume, our estimates will be too high.

If data covering a number of cycles were available, we could take the regression on saving on $y_t/y_0$ and $y_t$ and estimate simultaneously the secular and cyclical components in saving. Unfortunately the period 1923–40 covers only one major cycle, so that we are forced to estimate the influence of the two factors separately. First, it should be noted that there are strong grounds for supposing that (in the absence of cyclical fluctuations) aggregate saving remains a constant proportion of aggregate income.

This position can be best understood by a consideration of the apparent contradictions in the relations between saving and income. On the one hand, we have the Keynesian dictum that "apart from short period changes in the level of income, it is also obvious that a higher absolute income will tend to widen the gap between income and consumption. For the satisfaction of the immediate primary needs of a man and his family is usually a stronger motive than the motives toward accumulation, which only acquire effective sway after a margin of comfort has been attained. These reasons will lead as a rule to a greater proportion of income being saved as income increases."[15] This argument which, at first glance at any rate, appears very plausible, has had wide acceptance. Moreover, it seems to be supported by important empirical evidence. Every budget study supports the view that families with high incomes save a greater pro-

[15] J. M. Keynes, *The General Theory of Employment, Interest, and Money*, New York, Harcourt, Brace and Co., 1937, p. 97. Reprinted by permission.

portion of income than those with low incomes. It is also known that, in the period 1923–40, saving fluctuated more than in proportion to income. On the other hand, the data given by Kuznets indicate that aggregate saving has been an approximately constant proportion of income for a long time.[16]

From a psychological viewpoint, Keynes' argument about the relative importance of saving and accumulation at different income levels does not throw much light on the situation to which it is supposed to apply. It is no doubt true that a family will not save when its income is so low that it cannot satisfy its immediate primary needs. But in the United States, at least, the problem of getting an income high enough to maintain physical existence has hardly existed (for families whose workers are employed) for many years. The problem is not one of saving vs. consuming enough to maintain existence. It is one of choosing between an immediate comfort and security. Any psychological theory of saving must give an explanation of the resolution of the conflict between the desire for security and the desire for comfort. When the problem is put in this way the conclusion that saving rises more than in proportion to income is not at all obvious. Moreover, in view of the paucity and ambiguity of the empirical evidence a psychological basis is necessary if an adequate theory of saving is to be constructed.

Such a theory already exists in the form of marginal utility and "indifference map" analysis, but it is hardly adequate for our purposes. The whole structure of preference analysis is based on the assumption that one individual's preferences are independent of the actual consumption patterns of another individual's. It is this assumption which permits us to add up the demand functions of individuals to get a market-demand function.

Yet consumption preferences can hardly be regarded as innate characteristics of individuals. Nor can they be regarded, in a society as dynamic as ours, as being determined by tradition. There is a great deal of evidence to show that consumer tastes are socially determined. This does not mean that consumer tastes are governed by considerations of conspicuous consumption. Rather, it means that any individual's desire to increase his expenditure is governed by the extent to which the goods consumed by others

are demonstrably superior to the ones which he consumes. If we can assume that the degree of superiority of one set of goods over another is highly correlated with the relative costs of obtaining these goods, we are led to the following proposition. The strength of any individual's desire to increase his consumption expenditure is a function of the ratio of his expenditure to some weighted average of the expenditures of others with whom he comes in contact. The weights are determined by the social character of these contacts. If the distribution of income is constant (in the Lorenz curve sense) this weighted average can be regarded as a function of an individual's percentile position in the income distribution. The proportion of income saved is set by balancing the desire to increase current consumption against the desire to increase assets relative to current consumption (that is, to have a greater assurance of continued maintenance of the existing standard). We may therefore conclude that if the strength of the desire to increase consumption is a function of percentile position in the income distribution, the proportion of income saved will be a function of the same variable. It is also easy to see that it will be a rising function.[17]

This hypothesis leads to the following conclusions:

(a) At any one moment the proportion of income saved will be higher for the higher income groups than for low income groups.

(b) If income increases, while the proportional distribution remains constant, the ratio of aggregate saving to aggregate income will be constant.

Both of these conclusions are in accord with known facts.

If we accept the hypothesis just given, then secularly consumer saving will be a constant proportion of disposable income.

This hypothesis, together with the cyclical relation, considered in Section II, should give a complete explanation of variations in saving.

If the secular relation between savings and income makes for a constant income-saving ratio, the *proportion* of income saved will depend only on cyclical factors.[18] Then we may write $s_t/y_t = F(y_t/y_0)$. There is not much basis for selecting any particular functional form for $F(y_t/y_0)$. However, a linear approximation, which

---

[16] Simon Kuznets, *Uses of National Income in Peace and War*, New York, National Bureau of Economic Research, 1942, p. 30.

[17] In a paper of this length it is impossible to go too deeply into the theory of consumer behaviour underlying the above propositions. This theory together with some empirical tests of its adequacy will be developed more fully in a forthcoming paper.

fits the data well, is always satisfactory, provided that we do not have to make predictions involving values of the variable outside the range of the data used in fitting the approximation. In the period 1923–40 values of $y_t/y_0$ ranged from about 1.1 to .5. It seems unlikely that income will ever decline to less than 50 per cent of full employment levels, so that we can be safe in using a linear form for $F(y_t/y_0)$ for prediction. When the relation

$$\frac{s_t}{y_t} = a\frac{y_t}{y_0} + b$$

is fitted to the data for the period 1923–40, we obtain $a = .165$, $b = .066$.[19] The correlation is .9, which is as good as that usually obtained for relations between savings and income.

However, the correlation is not the test of the adequacy of the relation. The test is based on the fact that the secular average propensity to consume is predicted by the relation just given. In a period when income is slowly rising with only minor cyclical fluctuations, each year's income should be slightly above that of the preceding year. $y_t/y_0$ should be about 1.02 in each year. If we put $y_t/y_0 = 1.02$ in the relation

$$\frac{s_t}{y_t} = .165\frac{y_t}{y_0} - .066$$

we obtain $s_t/y_t = .102$ which is very close to Kuznets' estimate of the (stable) savings ratio in the period 1879–1919. Since the regression was based on the period 1923–40 we may say that the regression "predicted" the Kuznets' results.

All three major sources of data about income and consumption are consistent with the two hypotheses, (1) that secularly an individual's propensity to consume is a function of his position in the income distribution (which implies that aggregate saving tends in the long run to be a constant proportion of income) and (2) that, cyclically, the aggregate propensity to consume depends on the ratio of current income to the highest income previously achieved. They are also consistent with the internal evidence of the budget studies and with the results of inter-temporal comparisons of budget studies. So far as I am aware there are no data about saving and income which are inconsistent with these hypotheses.

There is, however, another important class of hypotheses which has not been considered here. These are the hypotheses which introduce variables other than income into the consumption function. In particular it has been suggested that saving may vary with the price level (when the price level is considered as a separate variable and not as a mere deflator) and with the value of assets. There is, of course, no real conflict between these hypotheses and the ones presented here. The two variables just mentioned are highly correlated with income, so that it is quite possible that they may be important contributors to the variance of saving, even though a high correlation can be obtained without considering them. These hypotheses will have to be tested by methods similar to those used in Section II of this paper.

The implications of the hypotheses developed here are fairly obvious. We may expect that, when the transition period is completed, consumer savings will fall to around 10 per cent of disposable income. This may be compared with the estimate of 14 per cent given by Smithies for consumer savings out of a disposable income of 158.2 billion dollars in 1943 prices.[20] The volume of offsets to savings required to maintain full employment is therefore considerably smaller than would be expected from estimates based on simple income-consumption regressions.

The relation

$$\frac{s_t}{y_t} = .166\frac{y_t}{y_0} - .066$$

has the property that the marginal propensity to save out of disposable income is fairly high with respect to cyclical movements of income, but the average propensity to save is much lower and does not tend to rise with secular increases in income. During the trough of a cycle (from the time income falls below the peak value for one cycle until it rises above that value in the next cycle) $y_t/y_0$ is dependent entirely on $y_t$ (since $y_0$ is constant). We have then

---

[18] If we accept the proposition that the high marginal propensity to consume indicated by linear income consumption relationships is largely due to cyclical factors, there is no *evidence* of the existence of any powerful trend in consumption. Various factors which might have caused either an upward or a downward trend can be cited. But when we have a hypothesis which explains all the data there is no point in introducing a trend unless some evidence of its operation can be given.

[19] The data used are those given by E. G. Bennion, "The Consumption Function Cyclically Variable," *Review of Economic Statistics*, November, 1946. Disposable income and savings are both corrected for price and population changes.

$$s_t = \frac{.166}{y_0}y_t{}^2 - .066y_t; \text{ then } \frac{ds_t}{dy_t} = .332\frac{y_t}{y_0} - .066.$$

[20] *Vide* A. Smithies, "Forecasting Postwar Demand," *Econometrica*, January, 1945.

The marginal propensity to save with respect to decreases in income is therefore about .26 at the peak of a cycle. As income declines $ds_t/dy_t$ falls until it reaches zero at an income equal to one-fifth that of the last cyclical peak.

On the other hand, the average propensity to save does not rise as income rises secularly. For in the upswing of a cycle after full employment is reached, $y_0$ and $y_t$ move together. If income increases steadily at an annual rate of 3 per cent, $y_t/y_0$ is constant at a value of 1.03. The long-run savings function is therefore $s_t = .166(1.03) \, y_t - .066y_t$ or simply $S_t = .102 \, y_t$. Thus the cyclical marginal propensity to save is (in the relevant range) higher than the long-run propensity to save, and the use of cyclical data to estimate the long-period relationship leads to invalid conclusions.

*SAUL H. HYMANS*

# The Cyclical Behavior of Consumers' Income and Spending: 1921-61

2    The American economy is not yet fully insulated from the distortions caused by cycles of prosperity and depression. Nonetheless, there is considered to be much evidence which points toward our increasing ability to resist deep depressions.[1] This much-discussed mitigation of cyclical excesses has frequently been attributed to monetary reforms, the growth of "automatic stabilizers," the

improvement of data collection systems, and so on. In this study we focus attention on personal consumption, in an attempt to judge whether any environmental or behavioral changes which may have occurred in the past four decades have acted to reduce the cyclical sensitivity of this important component of GNP.

In an attempt to draw inferences about the cyclical behavior of consumption over time, we take the business cycle itself as our "unit of observation." We shall make liberal use of the National Bureau of Economic Research's reference cycle methodology,[2] a descriptive technique specifically designed for the purpose of inter-cycle comparisons.[3] Our data, then, will be a set of reference cycle patterns for each of a considerable number of variables whose behavior affects personal consumption. Most of the series extend

---

[1] Many of the postwar business cycle studies of the National Bureau of Economic Research deal with one or another aspect of this subject. There is a useful list of such publications in Moore [15; pp. 736–44], and further work in this area is being carried on by Burns and Moore. See also Burns [2], and Moore [16; pp. 292–308]. Other very useful works are: B. G. Hickman [10], J. S. Duesenberry [7], and R. A. Gordon [9; especially Chapters 8 and 11].

Reprinted from the *Southern Economic Journal,* vol. XXXII (1965), pp. 23–34, by permission of the author and publisher. Saul H. Hymans is a professor at the University of Michigan. He is currently on leave of absence to the Council of Economic Advisors. This study is an extension of part of the author's doctoral dissertation [11]. The author wishes to acknowledge the most generous aid of Professors R. A. Gordon, D. W. Jorgenson, and I. M. Lee, all of the University of Caliifornia, Berkeley. The author, of course, assumes total responsibility for any remaining errors.

[2] The reference cycle technique is by now a well-known business cycle tool. A convenient explanatory source is Gordon [9; Chapter 10]. For a more detailed treatment, the standard reference is Burns and Mitchell [1].

[3] We feel that this method of analysis—despite some obvious and well-known limitations [12] [18]—is capable of providing valuable economic insights as the result of its concentration on patterns of behavior during cyclical stages.

## Table 1. Dates and Duration of Business Cycle Expansions and Contractions, 1921–61

| | BUSINESS CYCLE REFERENCE DATES | | DURATION (MONTHS) | |
| Initial trough | Peak | Terminal trough | Expansion | Contraction |
|---|---|---|---|---|
| July        1921 | May        1923 | July        1924 | 22 | 14 |
| July        1924 | October    1926 | November   1927 | 27 | 13 |
| November    1927 | August     1929 | March      1933 | 21 | 43 |
| March       1933 | May        1937 | June       1938 | 50 | 13 |
| June        1938 | February   1945 | October    1945 | 80 | 8 |
| October     1945 | November   1948 | October    1949 | 37 | 11 |
| October     1949 | July       1953 | August     1954 | 45 | 13 |
| August      1954 | July       1957 | April      1958 | 35 | 9 |
| April       1958 | May        1960 | February   1961 | 25 | 9 |
| | Average: 1921–27 | | 24.3 | 13.5 |
| | Average: 1921–29 | | 23.3 | — |
| | Average: 1945–61 | | 35.5 | 10.4 |

*Sources:* (15; pp. 670–71) through the 1957–58 contraction and the National Bureau for the 1958–61 cycle.

over the period of 1921–61, excluding the war cycle 1938–45.[4] Table 1 presents the basic chronological information on the cycles used in this study.

## I. Consumption and Personal Income

Proceeding to the data, Figure 1 presents the reference cycle patterns for consumption for each cycle individually during the period 1921–61 (omitting the war cycle, 1938–45). The four postwar patterns are strikingly similar, being characterized by reasonably long expansions, short contraction phases, and a clear lead at the terminal trough. Only the first postwar cycle —1945–49—displays a substantial decline between stages V and VI,[5] a fact attributable to the unusually rapid price decline following the

[4] I would like to express gratitude to the National Bureau of Economic Research for their most generous provision of data. The Bureau supplied most of the data and computed nearly all the reference cycle patterns for the period 1921–58. The patterns for the 1958–61 cycle were computed by the author, using the Bureau's reference dates. Actual data and sources are available from the author upon request.

[5] The reference cycle chronology distinguishes nine cyclical stages. Stages I, V, and IX are respectively the initial trough, reference peak, and terminal trough of the cycle. Each of the latter stages is composed of a three month period. The expansion and contraction phases are each divided into thirds and the standings at each such third are labelled stages II, III, and IV for the expansion and VI, VII, and VIII for the contraction.

early postwar inflation. The 1924–27 pattern is remarkably like those of 1945–61, though the pattern for 1921–24 does not conform as well. In particular, the latter cycle shows a decline from stage I to stage II and a strong two-stage lag at the reference peak. The earlier lag is partially due to a continued fall in prices—still part of the period of price adjustment following

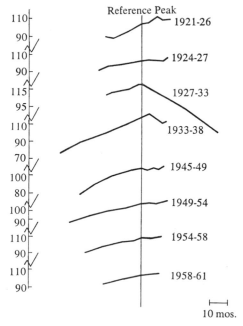

Figure 1. Reference Cycle Patterns, Consumers' Expenditures, 1921–61.

## Table 2. Percentage Change in Consumers' Expenditures and Income During Interwar and Postwar Reference Contractions[a]

| REFERENCE CONTRACTION | PERCENTAGE CHANGE DURING REFERENCE CONTRACTION | | | |
| --- | --- | --- | --- | --- |
| | GNP | Personal Income | Disposable Income | Consumers' Expenditures |
| 1. 1923–24 | −2.3 | 0.0 | − −[b] | 3.8 |
| 2. 1926–27 | 0.3 | 0.8 | − − | 0.3 |
| 3. Average, (1) + (2) | −1.0 | 0.4 | − − | 2.0 |
| 4. 1948–49 | −3.4 | −3.2 | −2.4 | 1.8 |
| 5. 1953–54 | −1.9 | −0.1 | 1.6 | 2.3 |
| 6. 1957–58 | −3.0 | −0.2 | 0.5 | 0.9 |
| 7. 1960–61 | −0.7 | 1.1 | 1.4 | 0.3 |
| 8. Average, (4) − (7) | −2.3 | −0.6 | 0.3 | 1.3 |
| 9. 1929–33 | −49.6 | −49.7 | − − | −45.8 |
| 10. 1929–30[c] | −7.5 | −8.1 | − − | −8.0 |
| 11. 1937–38 | −11.9 | −11.2 | − − | −5.6 |

[a]With the exception of line (10) in the table, all changes are measured from stage V to stage IX of each reference cycle. Changes are taken from original quarterly data in current dollars.
[b] The double dash indicates "not available."
[c] In the case of line (10) changes are measured from stage V to stage VI of the 1929–33 reference contraction.

World War I. The most distinctive feature of 1921–24, the rapid rise from VI to VII, mirrors precisely the rise in personal income which occurred simultaneously. It is interesting to note that the depression phase of the 1933–38 cycle is qualitatively the same as those corresponding to far less severe downturns—a lag at the reference peak and a lead at the terminal trough.

With respect to intra-cycle movements, a secular increase in consumption is apparent for both the 1920's and the postwar period, although correction for price changes (see Figure 2) reveals a stronger upward trend in the 'twenties than in the more recent period.

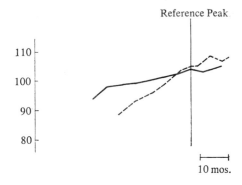

Figure 2. Average Reference Cycle Patterns, Deflated Consumers' Expenditures, 1921–27 (– – – –) and 1945–61 (———).

### Consumption During Recession and Depression

There are several points to be made about the comparative behavior of consumers' expenditures during interwar and postwar business declines. (Table 2.)

(1) In all postwar recessions and during the interwar minor recessions (1923–24 and 1926–27) consumers' spending showed a slight net increase. The average increase in the 'twenties amounted to 2 per cent, that of the postwar period to 1.3 per cent. There is little difference whether one measures in current or constant dollars.

(2) In the 'twenties consumers' spending did not fall in recession partly because personal income (and presumably disposable income) did not decline; but consumers' buying—on the average—increased relatively more than personal income. In postwar recessions consumers' spending generally seemed to be even more buoyant relative to personal income, though the relation between consumption and disposable income since the war is much like that of consumption and personal income in the 1920's.[6] In the

[6] Clearly the postwar income tax structure accounts for a large part of the current discrepancy between personal and disposable income. For the 1920's, however, it is reasonable to assume (particularly for small changes in personal income) that personal and disposable income moved quite closely together.

recession of 1948–49, however, consumption seems to have been more than merely buoyant. Indeed, it seems to have been an autonomous force for expansion since it rose in the face of a noticeable decline in disposable income. Undoubtedly, this was still part of the aftermath of war. Nearly all of the increase in consumption can be accounted for by consumer durables, the "pipelines" for which opened rather slowly after the war so that there was still a strong real demand which did not abate under the influence of a 2.4 per cent decline in disposable income. The existence of a still high level of consumers' liquid assets and the easing of instalment credit both favored a continued increase in the purchase of durables.[7] In the most recent recession, 1960–61, consumption did indeed rise during the contraction, but by a good deal less than either personal or disposable income. Further, consumption initially declined slightly in the first recession stage despite a small rise in personal income. It is difficult to pin the cause down precisely, although several possibilities suggest themselves. First, during the lethargic expansion following the 1958 trough and into the early stages following the 1960 peak monetary conditions were extremely tight [4]. In addition, fiscal policy was definitely not expansionary, particularly toward the end of the 1958–60 upswing [13, especially p. 241]. Second, the cyclical peak of personal income generated in the manufacturing sector nearly always coincides with the reference cycle peak; in the 1958–60 expansion, this source of personal income reached a peak three months prior to the reference peak and declined rather rapidly following the peak.[8] Lastly, automobile purchases reached a very high peak in the first quarter of 1960 following the 1959 steel strike and then led consumer durables purchases into a rather sharp drop.

(3) Consumer behavior was obviously far different during the severe declines following 1929 and 1937, than during either the 'twenties or the postwar period.

Taking all these findings together, the postwar recession behavior of consumers' expenditures does not look radically different from the behavior of such expenditures during the two minor cycles of the 1920's. In both periods consumer spending helped to support the economy during recession, largely because consumers' incomes were so well maintained.[9] However, the net buoyancy of consumption in the minor recessions of the 'twenties provided no basis for predicting how such spending would react in the face of a serious decline in income. The same is true for the postwar data. The behavior of consumption in 1929–33 and 1937–38 in particular imply that consumption is more sensitive to falling income the larger is the amplitude of the fall and, for a given amplitude, the more rapid the fall—indeed, a not very surprising conclusion.

Investigating further, Table 3 relates stage-to-stage changes in the cycle relatives for consumption and personal income during various periods since the 'twenties.

In the 1929–33 contraction, for example, the ratio of the changes in consumption to the changes in personal income varied between .85 and 1.10.[10] If consumption tends to be buoyant in a downswing, we should expect to find very low ratios in the early stages of the contraction in personal income: either negative ratios indicating that consumption rose in the face of a decline in personal income, or small positive ratios indicating that consumption fell relatively a good deal less than income. If we look at the contraction phases corresponding to 1921–27 and 1933–38, we find the smallest ratios in the first stage of contraction, when indeed the ratios are negative. Again in 1953–54 and 1957–58 consumers' spending rose relative to personal income in the early stages of income contraction. For the first stage of the 1960–61 recession a decline in consumption coincided with a slight rise in personal income, a fact which has already been noted.

Turning to late recession behavior, it is clear that, with the exception of 1929–33, consumption has led at all terminal troughs—including that of 1938. One can, however, make an even stronger statement than this. When consumption and income are compared, it becomes clear that consumption leads at the trough whether or not personal income leads, and in fact consumption

---

[7] These points are all discussed in great detail in Hickman [10; Chapter 4, especially pp. 72–73].

[8] In the quarter following the 1957 peak, for example, income from manufacturing sources fell only 0.7 per cent. From the quarter preceding to the quarter following the 1960 peak, income from this same source declined nearly 1.4 per cent. See U.S. Department of Commerce, *Business Statistics*, 1963, p. 7, and 1961, p. 5.

[9] The maintenance of consumers' incomes is discussed below.

[10] A ratio smaller (larger) than 1.00 means that the change in consumption as a percentage of its average over the cycle, was smaller (larger) than the change in income, also as a percentage of its average over the cycle.

## Table 3. Relation of Stage-to-Stage Changes in Consumers' Expenditures to Those in Personal Income in Interwar and Postwar Reference Cycles

(Changes are measured in reference-cycle relatives)

| REFERENCE CYCLE[a] | CHANGES BETWEEN STAGES | | | | | | | | | | |
|---|---|---|---|---|---|---|---|---|---|---|---|
| | I–II | II–III | III–IV | IV–V | V–VI | VI–VII | VII–VIII | VIII–IX | I–V | V–IX | I–IX |
| *Average: 1921–27* | | | | | | | | | | | |
| ΔC | 2.30 | 3.95 | 6.80 | 2.40 | 0.45 | 2.95 | −2.20 | 0.95 | 15.45 | 2.15 | 17.60 |
| ΔY | 3.60 | 5.70 | 6.15 | 2.80 | −0.65 | 1.50 | −1.00 | 0.60 | 18.25 | 0.45 | 18.70 |
| ΔC/ΔY | .64 | .69 | 1.11 | .86 | −.69 | 1.97 | 2.20 | 1.58 | .85 | 4.78 | .94 |
| *1927–33* | | | | | | | | | | | |
| ΔC | 2.5 | 2.6 | 5.9 | 1.0 | −9.6 | −16.3 | −20.0 | −9.1 | 12.0 | −55.0 | −43.0 |
| ΔY | 0.4 | 4.3 | 6.8 | 1.9 | −10.1 | −18.7 | −23.6 | −8.3 | 13.4 | −60.7 | −47.3 |
| ΔC/ΔY | 6.25 | .60 | .87 | .53 | .95 | .87 | .85 | 1.10 | .90 | .91 | .91 |
| *1933–38* | | | | | | | | | | | |
| ΔC | 8.9 | 12.2 | 13.1 | 7.8 | 2.7 | −5.7 | −4.3 | 0.7 | 42.0 | −6.6 | 35.4 |
| ΔY | 9.4 | 13.4 | 18.8 | 10.9 | −0.3 | −6.8 | −5.6 | −1.5 | 52.5 | −14.2 | 38.3 |
| ΔC/ΔY | .95 | .91 | .70 | .72 | −9.00 | .84 | .77 | −.47 | .80 | .46 | .92 |
| *Average: 1945–61* | | | | | | | | | | | |
| ΔC | 5.32 | 7.20 | 5.63 | 3.20 | −0.23 | 0.18 | 0.60 | 0.90 | 21.35 | 1.45 | 22.80 |
| ΔY | 4.53 | 7.66 | 6.61 | 3.10 | −0.42 | −0.43 | −0.19 | 0.40 | 21.90 | −0.64 | 21.26 |
| ΔC/ΔY | 1.17 | .94 | .85 | 1.03 | .55 | −0.42 | −3.16 | 2.25 | .97 | −2.27 | 1.07 |
| *Average: 1949–61* | | | | | | | | | | | |
| ΔC | 3.80 | 5.87 | 4.83 | 3.44 | 0.00 | −0.10 | 0.73 | 0.67 | 17.94 | 1.30 | 19.24 |
| ΔY | 4.37 | 7.95 | 5.71 | 3.06 | 0.07 | −0.35 | 0.06 | 0.52 | 21.09 | 0.30 | 21.39 |
| ΔC/ΔY | .87 | .74 | .85 | 1.12 | .00 | .29 | 12.17 | 1.29 | .85 | 4.33 | .90 |

[a]ΔC stands for changes in consumers' expenditures, measured in reference cycle relatives, between the stages indicated. ΔY refers to changes in personal income, measured the same way. Current dollars are used throughout.

rises relative to income between stages VIII and IX. It was, in fact, during the 1937–38 cycle that consumption displayed a lead despite a continued decline in personal income. The one exception to this conclusion occurred during the Great Depression. In the 1929–33 decline consumption did not lead at the trough in general business. Indeed, consumption fell most rapidly relative to income in precisely the last stage of contraction.[11]

With respect to the expansion phases of the cycles in Table 3, there is indeed very little basis for distinguishing between any of them. The only exceptional features are the extremely small change in personal income between stages I and II of the 1927–33 cycle and the war-induced

[11] Part of this behavior was apparently due to the changing relation between disposable and personal income. Unfortunately, we do not have quarterly data for disposable income prior to 1939. On an annual basis, the ratio of the change in disposable income to the change in personal income was: 1929–30, .985; 1930–31, .942; 1931–32, .974; 1932–33, 1.003. The increase in these ratios after 1930–31 suggests the exhaustion of whatever stabilizing effects there were in the personal income tax. More important than this consideration, however, is the fact that the

rates of increase of consumption in the 1945–48 upswing.

To summarize, in nearly all cases with the clear exception of the 1929–33 depression the behavior patterns of consumers' spending during business contractions were extremely similar in their essential features: a significant lead at the terminal trough and, generally, buoyancy at the peak. In the case of 1937–38, when personal income fell all during the depression consumption displayed a very significant net "ratchet" (i.e., the ratio $\Delta C/\Delta Y$ for the net change V-IX was only .46. In original units, the ratio is .50; see Table II above). There appears to be little justification for the view that consumption is currently very different in its sensitivity to changes in disposable income than it was prior to World War II.

federal Revenue Act of 1932 introduced higher and more steeply progressive income tax rates in order to stem the mounting federal deficit! The effect of this was a decline in federal income tax receipts between stages VIII and IX which was negligible compared to the rates of decline earlier in the depression, and also negligible compared to the rate of decline of personal income in the final contraction phase. See Firestone [8; pp. 53–54 and p. 88].

## II. The Stability of Personal Income

It is clear that if we take personal income as given, then consumers' spending during mild or short contractions behaves much as one would expect on the basis of either "ratchet" or "Permanent Income" theories. Such behavior will be a more powerful stabilizer for the economy, however, the more stable is personal or disposable income relative to GNP (Figure 3).

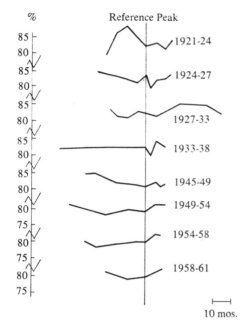

Figure 3. Reference Cycle Patterns, Personal Income as Percent of GNP (Units: one percent), 1921–61.

We can distinguish at least three important sources of stability in consumers' incomes:

(1) The behavior of corporate dividend payments relative to corporate earnings.
(2) Government Stabilizers.
(3) Secular shifts in the personal income structure.

Before discussing each of these, we take note briefly of a relevant conclusion put forth by Hickman [10]. His results are particularly appropriate here since they refer almost precisely to the periods with which we are concerned. Finding near-constancy in the rate of change of business savings with respect to GNP over the period since the 1920's, Hickman is led to conclude "that the great bulk of the increase in the strength of the governmental stabilizers since the 1920's represents a net addition to the

stabilizing potential of gross business savings."[12] We feel that the latter statement must be qualified. We shall show that there is evidence for the belief that gross business savings imparted greater cyclical stability to personal income in the interwar than in the postwar period.[13]

### Internal Stability: Dividends and Business Savings

In his study of business savings policies, Dobrovolsky [5] arrives at the following conclusions:

(1) Generally, net income retention did not begin until a certain minimum level of net income—approximately 5 per cent of net worth—had been attained. Below the critical level of income, dividend payments exceed current earnings.
(2) Above the critical income-level corporate savings appears, and the corporate marginal propensity to save (hence also the marginal propensity to pay dividends) is about constant during periods of steadily rising earnings.
(3) Past dividend payments are extremely important in the determination of current payments. In general, dividend payments have first priority in the disposition of net income.[14]

In obvious agreement with the implications of Dobrovolsky's conclusions, Figures 4 and 5 display the very substantial stability of dividends relative to corporate income for the minor cycles since the 1920's. The recessions, in fact, show an inverse movement of the two variables: a net fall in corporate profits and a net rise in dividend

---

[12] Hickman [10; p. 227]. We must caution, of course, that stability is a two-sided coin. The stabilizers prevent disposable income and consumption from falling rapidly in recession and also retard the rise during expansion. It is quite conceivable that a good part of the increase in stability which Hickman's regression analysis detects for the postwar period is the result of the expansion years in the 1947–58 sample. This seems likely in view of the statements which Hickman makes on pp. 229, 232, and 237 which we refer to below.

[13] We discuss this fully in the next section. Hickman notes that ". . . corporate profits taxes and after-tax corporate profits tend to absorb relatively more of a fall than of a rise in gross national income" [10; p. 229] and that "net corporate saving not only acted as a personal income stabilizer before the government stabilizers became important, but that it was sufficiently effective to raise disposable personal income substantially relative to gross national product during the two mild contractions of the 1920's" [10; p. 232].

[14] Dobrovolsky [5; pp. 1–6]. These conclusions are supported by aggregate data for "all manufacturing companies" and by samples of corporations by size classes. See also Lintner [14] for substantially the same conclusions.

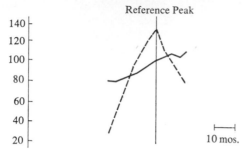

Figure 4. Average Reference Cycle Patterns, Dividend Payments (——) and Corporate Profits after Taxes (– – – –), 1921–27.

payments. It is also interesting to note that dividends were larger for five consecutive months after the 1929 peak than they had been at the peak month, and precisely the same was true following the 1937 peak.[15] Most significantly, the average patterns clearly show a far greater net increase in dividend payments during the minor contractions of the 'twenties than during

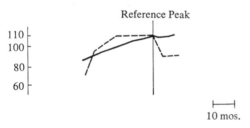

Figure 5. Average Reference Cycle Patterns, Dividend Payments (——) and Corporate Profits after Taxes (– – – –), 1945–61.

those of the postwar period. Figure 6 compares dividends and personal income directly for the postwar and prewar minor cycles.[16] It is evident from these data—and the individual cycle patterns are quite consistent with the average patterns—that dividend payments constituted an important stabilizing component of personal

income during the recessions of the 1920's. In relative terms, this has been far less true since World War II. In addition, dividends currently have less effect on the path of personal income since they constitute a far smaller proportion of personal income than was true in the earlier period.

The quantitative importance of these changes in both buoyancy and relative size can be illustrated with the hypothetical data of Table 4. During the hypothesized recession of the 'twenties

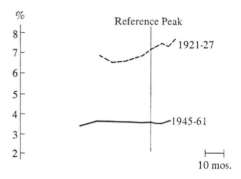

Figure 6. Average Reference Cycle Patterns, Dividend Payments as Percent of Personal Income (Units: one percent), 1921–27 and 1945–61.

the net rise in dividend payments is 8 per cent; the corresponding figure for the 'fifties is 6.7 per cent. When this is coupled with the fact that dividends in the earlier period are a larger fraction of personal income, the net effect is for dividends to offset 40 per cent of the 1920's decline in GNP and only 25.6 per cent of the 1950's decline in GNP. Even if dividends had remained constant during the latter recession 23.2 per cent of the fall in GNP would have been offset.

The mere fact that dividends rise *relative* to profits constitutes a stabilizing effect, whether or not dividends actually rise in absolute amount. It is thus clear that a lag relationship in the payment of dividends has an important stabilizing effect on personal income during a recession. The latter is exactly the point made in the Duesenberry-Eckstein-Fromm study and others.[17] In comparing interwar and postwar recessions, however, the evidence favors the view that dividend behavior was a more powerful influence

[15] See [11; Chapter 4, especially pp. 84–87].

[16] This is a more meaningful comparison than that between dividends and disposable income (aside from the fact that the latter is not available for the 'twenties except as annual data). The latter comparison would result in an identification problem due to the large difference in the government stabilizers in the two periods. Since the tax rate stabilizer operates on the relation of personal to disposable income, we are examining the stabilizing effects of dividend payments while holding the other main stabilizer—the government—more nearly constant.

[17] Duesenberry, Eckstein, Fromm [6; especially pp. 762–63], Gordon [9; especially pp. 480, 489, 498], Creamer [3; pp. 68–69]. See also Creamer [3; pp. 64–65] where he notes that "the average lag (in dividend payments relative to the reference peak) tends to decrease as we approach the most recent period."

## Table 4. Stabilizing Potential of Dividend Payments 1920's vs. 1950's: Hypothetical Data[a]

|  | 1920's | | 1950's | |
|---|---|---|---|---|
|  | Peak | Trough | Peak | Trough |
| GNP | 400 | 350 | 400 | 350 |
| Less: Corporate Profits after Taxes | 50 | 30 | 50 | 35 |
|  | 350 | 320 | 350 | 315 |
| Plus: Dividend Payments | 25 | 27 | 15 | 16 |
| Personal Income | 375 | 347 | 365 | 331 |
| Dividends as % of Personal Income | 6.7% | 7.8% | 4.1% | 4.8% |
| % Change in GNP | −12.5% | | −12.5% | |
| % Change in Personal Income | −7.5% | | −9.3% | |

a (1) We have made corporate profits fall relative to GNP during both recessions, but more so in the 1920's. This is in agreement with the actual data for the two periods. (2) We have made the ratio of corporate profits to GNP the same for both the 1920's peak and the 1950's peak. This accords with actual data; though the ratio we have used is too large. (3) Dobrovolsky's data for 1922–28 indicates an average ratio of dividends to after-tax earnings of .69 [5; p. 109]. For the years 1950–57 the ratio is .51 [*Economic Report of the President*, January 1959, p. 203]. Accordingly, we show dividends to be a larger share of profits at the peak of the 1920's than at the peak of the 1950's.

on the course of personal income in the earlier period. Its effect has waned since the 1920's because dividends have failed to grow secularly as much as personal income[18] and because recent recessions have resulted in nearly a net cessation of the growth of dividend payments rather than merely a slight net retardation in the rate of growth as occurred in the 'twenties.[19]

### Government Stabilizers

Figures 7 and 8 compare the paths of GNP, personal, and disposable income during the

[18] The lagging secular growth of dividends relative to personal income may in part be due to the higher corporate tax rates of the postwar period. These higher rates could have the effect of reducing the base out of which dividends are paid and hence the level of dividend payments relative to personal income. I am grateful to Warren L. Smith for discussion on this point.

[19] Two qualifications are in order. First, the hypothetical data of Table 4 exaggerate the absolute stabilizing potential of dividend payments (Duesenberry-Eckstein-Fromm find that dividend stability currently offsets between nine and eighteen per cent of a decline in GNP, depending on the amplitude and duration of the decline) but not the relative potential for the 1920's vs the 1950's. Second, as with consumption "ratchets," dividend stability weakens as the recession wears on in either severity or length. As one might expect, the government stabilizers dominate as the downswing becomes more pronounced.

postwar cycles. In all cases disposable income increases relative to personal income during recession.[20] For several stages into the recession (i.e., 5–6 months) the net rise in the ratio of disposable to personal income is generally small.[21] As the down-swing progresses, the combined effects of transfer payments (which

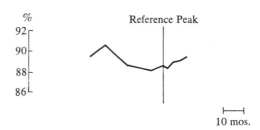

Figure 7. Average Reference Cycle Pattern, Disposable Personal Income as Percent of Personal Income (Units: one percent), 1945–61.

[20] Again, it must be noted that stability is two-sided. During most of the expansion disposable income falls relative to personal income. This is particularly true between stages II and IV when personal income rises vigorously and higher tax brackets take hold.

[21] This can be explained by the fact that tax rates change discretely with income, not continuously. There is therefore little change in the average effective tax rate for small initial declines in personal income.

operate with a lag) and progressive tax rates take hold so that personal income is at least maintained relative to GNP and the ratios of disposable income to GNP and personal income rise rapidly.[22]

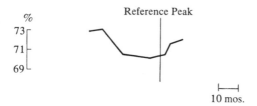

%
73
71
69

Reference Peak

10 mos.

Figure 8. Average Reference Cycle Pattern, Disposable Personal Income as Percent of GNP (Units: one percent), 1945–61.

With respect to the relative strength of progressive tax rates and government transfers, Hickman's conclusions run as follows:

> . . . the induced changes in personal income tax receipts during the recent recessions have been quite unimportant compared with the induced changes in corporate income tax receipts and with the substantial and growing influence of transfer payments. . . .

and

> it would be easy to exaggerate the extent to which the multiplier has been diminished (by government tax and transfer stabilizers) . . . since business saving exerted a substantial stabilizing influence over personal income before the government stabilizers became important. . . . the value of the multiplier was already quite small for mild contractions during the 1920's.[23]

In view of the findings of the previous section, it would seem that the stabilizing potential of the postwar growth of transfer payments, increase in tax rates, and broadening of the tax base cannot simply be added to the stability which already existed in the 'twenties. With respect to the kinds of downswings which have been experienced since World War II, the stability added by the federal government has amounted to little more than a replacement for that which has been lost due to the less contracyclical course of dividend payments and the reduction of the

normal ratio of dividends to personal income.[24] On the other hand, although we have had no recent depressions severe enough to permit a definitive judgment, it does seem quite clear that the automatic stabilizers represent a most significant addition to the economy's ability to resist serious depressions. The primary reasons for this would be the progressivity of personal tax rates and especially the fact that the government's unemployment compensation payments need not be effectively hampered by a budget constraint[25] as are corporate dividend payments.[26]

## Secular Changes in the Composition of Personal Income

Historical observation has shown that the components of total personal income which are cyclically most volatile are those associated with agricultural sources. The most stable components have typically been transfer payments, government payrolls, and interest payments [3; pp. 29–31].

Detailed studies [3], [11; especially pp. 97–102] have turned up several obvious changes in the composition of personal income over the period since about 1910. The following stabilizing changes are clearly evident:

(1) The share of Farm Proprietors' Net Income has declined since the 1920's.

(2) The share of Transfer Payments has increased greatly since the 'twenties.

(3) Government wage and salary payments have increased significantly since the interwar period (and tend to be extremely stable in recession).

The following destabilizing shifts are noticeable:

(1) Dividends and net rent have lost ground since the 'twenties.

(2) Interest payments have declined relative to personal income, but—offsetting this movement—there has been a clear upward trend since World War II.

[24] Note that this discussion is not meant to reflect on discretionary fiscal policy. For the latter, see Lewis [13].

[25] This was actually demonstrated in the 1957–58 recession when the period of payments of unemployment compensation was extended.

[26] Charles L. Schultze [17] stresses that "the share of declines in total income absorbed by corporate profits tends to be quite large, *but* this absorption rate decreases the faster the rate of decline in income." And "The ratio of corporate profit change to income change tends to become smaller as the magnitude of the decline in GNP increases." Quotations from [17; pp. 15 and 23 respectively].

[22] It must be pointed out that these data are not detailed enough to separate federal from state and local tax effects, though of course the former clearly dominate in the data.

[23] Hickman [10; Chapter 9. Quotes from pp. 232 and 237 respectively, parenthesis added]. See also footnote 15 above.

Balancing such shifts in composition is indeed difficult. It does seem clear, however, that the more serious is the precipitating cause of a downturn (say, a serious decline in fixed investment), the more important will the stabilizing shifts be relative to the destabilizing shifts. This is in the nature of the categories involved. Thus, in considering the composition of personal income we seem to arrive at a conclusion closely akin to that already arrived at in the previous two sections on dividend policy and government stabilizers.[27]

## III. Summary and Conclusions

In analyzing consumption behavior since the 1920's we have found striking similarities between the postwar and interwar periods. During expansionary phases, the only discernible difference between the two periods was the more rapid growth of consumption in the interwar period, particularly beyond the initial expansion stages.[28] Some of this can surely be ascribed to the generally less rapid growth of output during the postwar expansions.[29] On the other hand, it is also true that the higher and more progressive personal tax rates which have existed since World War II have tended to retard the growth of disposable income relative to personal income and GNP during business cycle upswings.

With respect to business contractions, consumers' expenditures have—with the clear exception of 1929–33—been noticeably resistant to deflationary pressures. In most cases this resistance was manifested in the form of an extremely small marginal propensity to consume during the initial contraction phases[30] and a clear lead of consumption relative to both personal income and GNP at the business cycle trough. Even during the severe decline of 1937–38 consumption exhibited marked stability by first expanding during the initial stage of depression and ultimately declining by only half as much as personal income over the entire downswing.

With the fiscal "automatic stabilizers" incontrovertibly more powerful in the postwar period, why have consumers' expenditures seemed no more stable during recent downswings than they were during the prewar minor recessions? The answer comes in two parts.

First, the stability resulting from discontinuously progressive tax rates becomes more noticeable the larger the change in income. In postwar expansions, incomes have risen long enough and far enough to make the depressing effects of rising marginal tax rates quite noticeable; in periods of contraction the converse effect has indeed occurred, but it has been small relative to the effects felt during expansions because the changes in income have also been correspondingly smaller. It is fair to say that no postwar decline has been severe enough to permit observation of the maximum effects of the built-in anti-recession stabilizers.

Second, the postwar stabilizers have not operated under *ceteris paribus* conditions with respect to the 1920's. The composition of personal income has altered in such a way that personal income is probably more resistant to powerful destabilizing shocks currently than was true in the period before World War II. Largely, this is due to a relative decrease in agricultural sources of personal income and an increase in governmental sources. From the point of view of recessions as mild as those of the 'twenties and the postwar period, however, an extremely important destabilizing shift in composition has occurred. Corporate dividend payments have, since the 1920's, fallen from seven to three and one-half per cent of personal income. Further, in the earlier period mild recessions served—at most—to bring about a slight retardation in the rate of growth of dividend payments. In the postwar period, dividend payments have nearly ceased to rise during recessions; i.e., the recession rate of growth has fallen to about zero. Before World War II, dividend payments played a powerful anti-cyclical role during mild recessions and even during the early months of quite severe contractions. Since World War II, this source of short run stability has weakened considerably.[31]

In sum, then, the fiscal stabilizers have in a very real sense replaced much of the dividend stabilizer that has been lost since the interwar period. Given a contraction more severe than any experienced yet in the postwar period, the American Economy would probably receive

---

[27] A similar conclusion is offered by Hickman [10; p. 242].

[28] This was observable for consumption in current prices but was especially prominent with respect to real consumption (Figure 2).

[29] This aspect of the two periods is treated in [11; especially Chapter 3]. For example, real GNP rose 67 per cent between 1921 and 1929 and only 39 per cent between 1949 and 1957.

[30] In very many cases, the MPC was in fact negative in early contraction phases as consumption continued to rise in the face of a decline in personal income.

[31] It is still an important stabilizer of personal income in any absolute sense, but far less so than in the 1920's.

substantial net benefit from the "automatic stabilizers" vis-à-vis the interwar period. On the other hand, in the kinds of recessions actually experienced, the postwar behavior pattern of consumers' incomes has been strikingly similar to that of the interwar minor cycles.

## REFERENCES

[1] A. F. Burns and W. C. Mitchell, *Measuring Business Cycles* (N.B.E.R., 1946).

[2] A. F. Burns, "Progress Towards Economic Stability," *American Economic Review*, March, 1960.

[3] D. Creamer, *Personal Income During Business Cycles* (N.B.E.R., 1956).

[4] J. M. Culbertson, "The Use of Monetary Policy," *Southern Economic Journal*, October, 1961.

[5] S. P. Dobrovolsky, *Corporate Income Retention, 1915–43* (N.B.E.R., 1951).

[6] J. S. Duesenberry, O. Eckstein, and G. Fromm, "A Simulation of the United States Economy in Recession," *Econometrica*, October, 1960.

[7] J. S. Duesenberry, *Business Cycles and Economic Growth* (McGraw-Hill, 1958).

[8] J. M. Firestone, *Federal Receipts and Expenditures During Business Cycles, 1879–1958* (N.B.E.R., 1960).

[9] R. A. Gordon, *Business Fluctuations*, 2nd edition (Harper, 1961).

[10] B. G. Hickman, *Growth and Stability of the Postwar Economy* (Brookings Institution, 1960).

[11] S. H. Hymans, *American Business Cycles: Interwar and Postwar*, Unpublished Ph.D. Dissertation, University of California, Berkeley, 1964.

[12] T. C. Koopmans, "Measurement Without Theory," *Review of Economics and Statistics*, August, 1947.

[13] W. Lewis, *Federal Fiscal Policy in the Postwar Recessions* (Brookings Institution, 1962).

[14] J. V. Lintner, "Distribution of Incomes of Corporations Among Dividends, Retained Earnings, and Taxes," *American Economic Review*, May, 1956.

[15] G. H. Moore, ed., *Business Cycle Indicators* (Princeton, 1960).

[16] G. H. Moore, "The 1957–58 Business Contraction: New Model or Old?" *American Economic Review*, May, 1959.

[17] C. L. Schultze, *Short Run Movements of Income Shares*, Preliminary (N.B.E.R., 1961).

[18] E. S. Shaw, "Burns and Mitchell on Business Cycles," *Journal of Political Economy*, August, 1947.

# Investment and Capital

*T*HE STOCK OF useful capital assets in an economy continually tends to be consumed through its employment in the productive process and reduced by destruction and obsolescence. Simultaneously, the stock tends to be expanded as the economy's producers acquire new capital assets with their investment purchasing. A host of factors determine the level of investment purchasing which will occur in an economy during a given time period and the optimum size of the economy's stock of capital. Some of these aspects are discussed in the next three selections.

In the first selection, John W. Kendrick considers some of the problems inherent in any attempt to measure the size of an economy's stock of capital. Then Paul Wells examines the demand for capital and rate of investment purchasing and Abba Lerner discusses some past and present developments in capital theory.

*JOHN W. KENDRICK*

# Some Theoretical Aspects of Capital Measurement

3  There are few areas of economic statistics in which progress is needed more and would be more valuable than in the measurement of capital. Capital measures are essential for analysis of investment demand, factor prices and inputs, production functions, and productivity. They are thus requisite to empirical study of economic fluctuations and growth generally and as a background for stabilization policy and development planning.

In this paper, I shall first pick out what appear to me to be the chief points in capital theory which are relevant to capital measurement. Then I shall examine critically what I believe to be false paths that have been taken in the direction of quantification.

## Basic Characteristics of Capital Relevant to Estimation

### Capital as a Stock

The earlier classical economists tended to mix the notions of wealth as a fund and as a flow of goods. As Schumpeter points out, "... the classics were not very clear concerning the differences between funds and flows, and between

wealth and the services of wealth."[1] He credits Irving Fisher in *Nature of Capital and Income* with nailing down the distinction and clearly defining capital as the stock of wealth of all kinds that exists at any moment. Fisher himself showed that the definitions of most classical writers really came to this. Most economists have continued to view capital as a stock, but not necessarily so comprehensively as Fisher.

The stock approach links the economist's capital concept with the accountant's capital account. This link has operational significance analagous to that provided by the Commerce Department's "rule" that national product consists of final goods and services defined as products which are not resold during the accounting period. The Fisher approach does not necessarily identify capital with those items included in balance sheets of operating units, but the notion of capital as a stock of goods which can be

[1] Joseph A. Schumpeter, *History of Economic Analysis*, pp. 627–28.

Reprinted from the *American Economic Review: Papers and Proceedings*, Vol. LI (1961), pp. 102–111, by permission of the author and publisher. John W. Kendrick is a professor at George Washington University.

inventoried and valued at successive points in time has obvious operational significance.

The inventory approach makes statistically irrelevant the Austrian concept of capital as an "intermediate product" temporarily embodying land and labor en route to ultimate consumption. The analysis of Boehm-Bawerk and his followers stemmed from a laudable desire to look beneath the surface and find a truly "genetic" explanation. But Schumpeter has observed that the Austrian theory is not relevant (as well as being non-operational) "as soon as we realize that all economic theory is a theory of planning and inevitably has to accept the results of the past—plant, equipment, and stocks all included—*as data*. We shall then cease to try to construct an economic process *ab ovo* and, looking forward only, to consider instead the 'amount of investment of capital.' "[2]

The role of capital must be distinguished from that of intermediate products that are themselves used up rather than just used in production during an accompanying period. As Haavelmo has pointed out, "the trouble with the idea of capital as something that 'goes into' the product is . . . the result of a difficulty that perhaps most of us have of understanding how something can be used and render a yield in a process without itself being destroyed or depleted."[3]

To the extent that producers' durables are depleted in a period, in the sense of losing value, such capital consumption must be classed with intermediate product input.[4] The input of capital (human or nonhuman) must be thought of as a time-rate of use of stocks, valued in terms of their marginal contributions to revenue per time period. Even today, there is confusion between capital input and capital consumption.

### The Scope and Structure of Capital

Some economists, like Fisher, would identify capital with wealth, including human resources. Others would confine capital to those resources or "factors" used in production. In common usage, many economists restrict the term capital to the produced means of production, on a par with land and labor as one of the productive factors.

Any broad groupings of wealth, or capital, particularly the notion of a triad of factors, are misleading if the groupings are thought of as homogeneous quantities with unambiguous meaning rather than as "complex quantities." It was with this in mind that Frank Knight called the factor notion an "incubus on economic analysis." It is certainly true that there are many individual types of capital goods—and this goes for land and labor, despite the superficial appearance of homogeneity of acres and men. More fundamentally, all types of capital are really the same, economically, in that each provides a flow of productive services, and is valued thereby. Thus, in terms of valuation, capital is homogeneous; in terms of underlying physical characteristics, there are myriad varieties of capital goods which gradually change form in a dynamic economy.

Nevertheless, there is no inherent objection for purposes of theory or measurement in grouping capital into general categories possessing similar characteristics and exhibiting significant interrelationships. Most basic is the distinction between human and nonhuman factors (or capital). As Knight himself has pointed out, the distinction is fundamental in a free society in which men can sell their services but not themselves; whereas nonhuman capital goods are bought and sold, although owners may also lease the services of the durable goods. Because of the inevitability man-centered interests of man, we are also interested in the distinction with regard to the distribution of the national income, as conditioned by the relative inputs and rates of compensation of the two factors.

Certainly the distinction between human and nonhuman capital is essential for measurement. Records are available relating to the services and compensation of labor, but not to the value of the human labor stock since this is irrelevant in our type of society; records of both the compensation and value of the stock of nonhuman capital are available.

Within the classification of producers' capital the old distinction between land and produced capital has gradually broken down. The two are inextricably mixed physically and land can be "produced" when profit prospects warrant. More importantly, the two types of assets are valued in the same way.[5]

Construed broadly, capital should also include

---

[2] *Ibid.*, p. 908.

[3] Trygve Haavelmo, *A Study in the Theory of Investment*, p. 93.

[4] If the accounting period were very long, all "durable" but nonpermanent goods would become intermediate products. F. Hayek restricts the term capital to such goods (*The Pure Theory of Capital*, p. 54).

[5] Cf. Tibor Scitovsky, *Welfare and Competition*, p. 228: "From every point of view, therefore, land may be regarded as a capital good and the rent of land as similar in every respect to the gross earnings of a produced factor."

consumer durables and household inventories which also furnish a stream of services, although these are not generally valued through market processes except in the case of rentals of houses and a few other durables. Further, the required stocks in the business and household sectors are interdependent. Inventory fluctuations in the two sectors are obviously related, and the ownership of durables by households is reduced as leasing from the business sector expands.

This broad view of capital is inconsistent with the present U.S. national accounts which measure current consumption in terms of purchases rather than the rate of disappearance of goods or their services. Adaptation of the accounts would involve a household investment account, the corresponding balance-sheet items of durable stocks and inventories, and estimates of the value of household capital services (including depreciation) to be included in the current consumption account.

There has been unnecessary argument as to the inclusion of social capital with private. As long as publicly-owned stocks contribute to the productivity of the private economy or furnish direct services to consumers, they must be counted. Otherwise, the amount of the community's capital will vary depending purely on the relative extent of public ownership. One of the criteria in national income measurement is that the flows should be invariant to purely institutional changes. The same rule is applicable to capital.

Finally, the concept of "intellectual capital" advanced by Adam Mueller, Friedrich List, and other early economists[6] has retained its vitality. This "intangible capital" comprises the technical knowledge or know-how of men as expressed in their activities, forms of organization, and tangible capital goods. It is the result of investments in the discovery and spread of productive knowledge.

Note that intangible capital is embodied in tangible capital both physically and in value terms. Factor compensation stems from both the physical and qualitative aspects of productive agents. It would require major statistical surgery to try to value intangible separately from tangible capital. The notion of intangible capital is an important one, as eloquently developed by Professor Schultz in his Presidential address, but I am skeptical as to whether it can be usefully measured.

[6] In England, Bentham, Senior, and Sidgwick, *et al.*, developed this approach.

## Capital Value

Monetary values furnish the common denominator for diverse types of capital goods. Since the works of Boehm-Bawerk and Fisher, capital has generally been regarded as the discounted value of the future stream of revenue expected from capital goods. Thus it becomes possible to regard capital as a fund of abstract productive power. J. B. Clark, for instance, compared capital with a waterfall, which remains essentially the same even though the constituent drops of water are continually changing, just as the stock of capital, when maintained, remains a source of productive power in perpetuity, even though the capital is embodied in a succession of physical instruments.

Of course, any value aggregate can be thought of as representing physical goods or other "real" variables. The trick in converting a value fund to real terms lies in specifying the appropriate deflator which meaningfully corrects current values. It is here that a second aspect of the valuation process comes in: the prices of the underlying capital goods, as established in markets or imputed by owners, can be appropriately combined (with variable quantity weights) to provide a deflator to convert capital values into physical volumes of the various types of underlying capital goods at base-period prices. Or, the result can be achieved directly by weighting quantities by constant prices.

As I view it, this is the most meaningful way to measure "real capital stock," since the weighted aggregate measures the physical complex of capital goods in terms of its estimated ability to contribute to production as of the base period. Or, assuming that relative prices also approximate relative costs of production, the aggregate stock measures changes in real costs of capital goods at base-period levels of factor productivity.

The real stock estimates so conceived make possible comparisons with associated real output to obtain average productivity estimates indicating savings of capital per unit of output over time as a result of changing productivity efficiency and factor combinations. They also make possible the estimation of production functions and "total productivity" ratios indicating the net saving of resources per unit of output and thus changes in productive efficiency net of the effects of factor substitutions.[7]

[7] These concepts are developed in more detail in the author's study for the National Bureau of Economic Research, *Productivity Trends in the United States*.

Implementation of our concept of real capital stock, in a dynamic economy, requires working solutions to a number of difficult conceptual problems such as quality change, depreciation, and weighting. In view of these complexities, certain analysts have suggested alternative methods of measuring the physical volume of capital. Some of these less direct methods have been promoted as being not only simpler, but also more profound. As Joan Robinson has noted: "The human mind is naturally poetic and thinks in terms of mystic essences. The proposition that everything is what it is and not another thing, has to be accepted, but it goes against the grain."[8] We shall now critically review several indirect approaches to measurement of real capital stocks.

## Indirect Approaches to Real Capital Measurement

### Capital as Embodied Labor, or Real Cost

Many economists have been led by the deceptively homogeneous appearance of the worker, or man-hour, to try to measure capital (as well as output) in terms of the labor time embodied, or commanded.[9] Despite the statement by Mrs. Robinson just quoted, rather than measure capacity directly in terms of what it is, she prefers to express it in terms of labor-time. She thinks this is easier than trying to measure "an enormous who's who of miscellaneous items that can be treated as a quantity only when it is measured according to some more or less arbitrary convention. . . . We can divide the value in terms of commodities of the stock of capital in any economy by the wage per man-hour in terms of commodities ruling in that economy and so obtain the quantity of capital in terms of labor time. This is in some ways the most significant way of measuring capital, for the essence of the productive process is the expenditure of labor time . . . capital goods in existence today can be regarded as an embodiment of past labor time to be used up in the future."[10]

The first weakness to note in Mrs. Robinson's argument is that not just capital but most economic aggregates comprise many heterogeneous and qualitatively changing types of units. With respect to labor force and labor time there are thousands of different types of occupational specialties, with different levels and changes in rates of compensation. To develop an average wage rate with which to deflate asset values, labor time weights are needed which immediately poses the index number problem. Thus Mrs. Robinson's procedure does not avoid the ambiguity of a weighting convention any more than did Keynes's attempt to state national product and its components in terms of wage units. For to convert man-hours of all types into common labor hours requires choice of relative wage rates, which differ somewhat depending on the period used.[11]

The more fundamental objection to this approach is theoretical. The original factors involved in producing capital may be labor working on natural resources, but, since Adam, man-made capital has also been used in the process, giving rise to capital compensation reflecting its productivity and scarcity. Even from the viewpoint of embodied resources, the man-hours commanded by the capital compensation part of asset values has no meaning and in a dynamic economy certainly does not show the same movement as the underlying capital stocks and input.

This leads to the final objection to this type of measure, whether looked on as an artificial conversion of asset values to man-hours or as the total real cost of producing the capital stock with current technology. In a progressive economy, the embodied man-hours or total real factor input will rise less than the real capital stock measured in its own units. This is enlightening when we wish to measure the changed productivity in capital goods production; but is real cost a meaningful measure if we wish to learn the extent to which changing technology has been capital-saving (or using)? By relating capital-as-input to output, the effects of partial productivity advance are double-counted: once in the use of capital stocks as such to produce output and again in the use of labor (or total input) to produce the capital.

It is analogous, in measuring man-hours per unit of output, not to count the man-hours actually expended but rather the man-hours that

[8] Joan Robinson, *The Accumulation of Capital*, p. 20.

[9] "Embodied" and "commanded" labor differ in movement insofar as wage rates in the capital goods sector move differently from those in the whole economy, and as the ratio of labor to total cost changes.

[10] *Ibid.*, pp. 22, 121.

[11] Cf. Alvin Hansen, *A Guide to Keynes*, p. 44: "Keynes' analysis could have proceeded quite as well had he adopted the price index as his deflator instead of his wage unit. . . . On balance, Keynes readers would probably have preferred constant-value dollars to constant-wage-unit dollars."

would be required to produce a standard subsistence for the workers involved.[12]

### Capital as Capacity

It is useful to have measures of output capacity, and some theorists have suggested measuring capital stocks in these terms, assuming "an appropriate amount of employment."[13] This approach has been seen as a possible way of handling the problem of quality change, since if a new model of a machine can produce twice as much output as the old model, it can be counted as twice as "much" capital. A more sophisticated version of this approach would relate the quantity of a capital good to its real marginal value product. We shall look at this variant later.

For the economy as a whole, or broad sectors, it is obvious that the index number problem is not avoided by the average capacity approach, since the real capital would be approximated by estimates of the capacity of capital goods to produce a heterogeneous collection of outputs. There would be further measurement problems in a realistic situation in which part of capital resources were idle at times: An estimate of output capacity would involve guessing the average productivity of the unused resources, which would depend on the composition of the required additional demand in relation to the composition of the unused capacity.

Even if total output capacity of the capital stock of the economy were estimated as the sum of capacity of individual producing units at the most efficient rates of utilization—regardless of whether the capacity fully meshed, sufficient complementary resources were available, or whether capacity conformed to the actual structure of demand—there would be other problems. In particular, the "most efficient rate" of operations is an economic concept, depending on relative prices of inputs. This means that capacity output is difficult to estimate in the first instance, and that, in a dynamic economy, capacity (at the most efficient rate) changes as relative prices change.

Useful though capacity estimates would be in their own right, much would be lost by substituting them for estimates of real capital as such. By this convention, output-capital ratios would

merely indicate changes in rates of utilization of capacity, and the marginal capital coefficient by definition would be unity. Further, as Edward Denison has pointed out, the results for capital formation are absurd.[14]

The alternative of measuring the quantity of capital in terms of the capacity of the capital goods to contribute to real income does take account of the freeing of other resources. That is, not only would the gross output capacity of the equipment be considered, but also the real non-capital costs of operation, the difference representing the contribution to real value-added. The real value of the capital goods would, of course, involve a discounting of the future annuities as defined.

Despite virtually insuperable estimation problems, this approach has been considered theoretically attractive. On this basis, a constant capital stock and zero net capital formation would maintain the productive capacity of the economy and thus provide a way to implement the notion of "keeping capital intact."[15] Essentially this method of measuring the quantity of capital goods, as a means of allowing for quality change, has also been suggested as the proper basis for pricing.[16]

The associated prices would, however, be quite artificial. After all, prices of capital goods in a progressive economy, assuming constant output prices, do not represent the present value of the future net income stream based on constant prices of inputs as well as outputs, but rather on a net income stream being narrowed with time as input prices rise relative to output prices as a result of technological progress. In other words, the capacity of new capital goods to produce real value-added (at constant output and input prices) is greater than their ability to produce real net revenue at constant output prices but with input prices rising as is typical in a progressive economy. Furthermore, since competition among sellers and buyers of the capital goods tends to push their prices and capitalized values down to equality with average cost, real costs are a better basis upon which to estimate relative physical volumes and prices.

As Denison stressed, "the idea of a 'capital saving invention,' for example, would have only the most limited applicability if the measurement

---

[12] The same problem is also present, although less acutely, under conditions of unchanging technology, so long as the law of variable proportions operates. This provides another objection to Keynes's wage-unit.

[13] Robinson, *op. cit.*, p. 119.

[14] Edward F. Denison, "Theoretical Aspects of Quality Change, Capital Consumption, and Net Capital Formation," *Problems of Capital Formation*, Vol. 19, *Studies in Income and Wealth*, p. 229.

[15] *Ibid.*, p. 231.

[16] Preliminary Report of the Price Statistics Review Committee, NBER.

of the quantity of capital were tied to its productive ability."[17] By this approach, the capital-output ratio would rise if, as is usual, innovations were laborsaving. Yet the physical volume of capital defined as standard units in terms of base-period cost might well be falling relative to output.

Other indirect methods of measuring capital stocks have been suggested, such as dividing the value of capital assets by an index of consumer goods prices in order to measure the volume of consumption foregone to provide capital.[18] But none of the indirect approaches avoids the complexities of the problem, and all suffer from the defect of measuring something other than capital inventory as such.

## Conclusion

All the alternative measures we have discussed would show the same rates of change in a hypothetical state of competitive equilibrium, with perfect knowledge, with technology and tastes constant, assuming proportionate and steady growth of the real capital stock and labor force. As soon as technological progress is introduced, the measures diverge. The physical capital stock rises more rapidly than the volume of labor or total inputs required to reproduce it at current technology; the physical stock rises less rapidly than its average ouput capacity or its capacity to contribute to real value-added; and physical stock rises either more or less rapidly than its real value in terms of consumption goods and services depending on relative productivity changes in the two sectors.

Measurement of capital as a weighted physical stock, which we consider the most useful general approach for reasons noted earlier, raises several major conceptual problems discussed elsewhere.[19]

The first is the problem of measuring physical volumes of various types in standard units over time, when in fact the characteristics of most capital goods gradually change, new goods are introduced, and some goods have no standard unit. The second problem, distinctive to reproducible durables, is how to handle the depreciation or "consumption" of capital goods as they age. In addition, interpretation of the meaning of capital stocks in either current or constant dollars is clouded somewhat by the fact that in the real economy the meaning of price deviates from its meaning under competitive equilibrium with perfect knowledge.

There is little to add to the discussion of the index number problem. The movement of any price of quantity aggregate will be affected by choice of weight base so long as relative changes in prices and in quantities are correlated. Since the correlation is generally negative in the U.S. economy, recent price weights tend to produce a smaller increase in an aggregate of physical volume than earlier period weights. Since this is true of both capital stocks and output, ratios of the two variables are less affected by alternative weighting systems than is either variable alone. Nevertheless, it is desirable in comparing changes in real stocks between two points in time to use the prices of each as weights in order to bracket the difference in change.

Procedures used to cope with the various measurement problems are inevitably conventional, but if they are basically reasonable they result in meaningful measures. As Simon Kuznets has put it, "all concepts in the field of national income are, in one way or another, non-operational. They are goals that forever elude measurement and for which measurable approximations are substituted. . . . All these operational measures assume meaning only because they are approximations to the 'purer,' non-operational concepts behind them."[20]

[17] Denison, *op. cit.*, p. 223.

[18] Robinson, *op. cit.*, pp. 119–21.

[19] See John W. Kendrick, "Measurement of Real Product," in *A Critique of the U.S. Income and Product Accounts*, Vol. 22 of *Studies in Income and Wealth*.

[20] Simon Kuznets, "Comment" on Edward F. Denison, *op. cit.*, p. 272.

*PAUL WELLS*

# Output and the Demand for Capital in the Short Run

4 This paper develops a short, simple macroeconomic model of the economy. The primary reason for constructing this model is to provide an efficient framework for the study of both the aggregate demand for capital and the rate of investment from an elementary point of view. The analysis begins in Section I with the development of a new and rather different version of Keynes's theory of short run equilibrium; a version which is based squarely on an aggregate supply function as well as on an aggregate demand function. After explaining the way in which the equilibrium value of the real and the monetary aggregates of the economy are determined, the model is applied, in Section II, to derive a relation between the level of output and the aggregate amount of capital needed to minimize the cost of producing each level of output. From this "needed" stock we subtract society's present, or existing stock of capital to obtain a function which states the demand for *additional* capital associated with each level of output.

Reprinted from the *Southern Economic Journal*, Vol. XXXII (1965), pp. 146–152, by permission of the author and publisher. Paul Wells is a professor at the University of Illinois.

The presence of this latter function focuses attention on the central problem of aggregate investment theory; that of explaining the rate at which firms, *in toto*, accumulate the additional capital they demand. In this paper we shall prove the important, though unhappy, fact that for single commodity macroeconomic models of the Hicks-Samuelson-Lange-Modigliani type,[1] the traditional argument that the level of investment is determined by the rate of interest and the marginal efficiency of investment is false. Instead, it is shown that these variables explain the demand for additional capital only, rather than the rate at which additional capital accumulated. Because the literature has not succeeded in constructing a theory which determines the level of aggregate investment we conclude that more work needs to be done on this subject at the most fundamental level of investigation.

## I. A Model of Supply and Demand

The aggregate supply function is defined to be a relation between real output, $Q$, and the volume of total receipts, $Y_s$, which firms in the aggregate

[1] "Single commodity macroeconomic models are those models which have a single aggregate production function producing a single final good, part of which is consumed, and the remainder invested."

must realize if total output is to remain unchanged. To develop this relation we need the following assumptions and definitions:

1. $Q = F(N, K_0)$ is the aggregate production function of the economy, where $N$ denotes the level of employment, and $K_0$ the given short run stock of capital. We shall suppose that $F$ is a linear homogenous function and that its first and second partial derivatives with respect to both arguments (denoted by $F_N$, $F_K$, $F_{NN}$, and $F_{KK}$) are positive and negative respectively. Furthermore, in order to reduce the mathematical complexity of the model, we shall assume that the third partial derivative of $F$ with respect to $N$ is zero.

2. Perfect competition prevails in the commodity market.

3. A given money wage rate, $w_0$, obtains as long as there is any unemployment.

Under conditions of perfect competition firms adjust their rates of output until short run, or labor, marginal cost equals the price of output, $P$. Since labor marginal cost equals the money wage rate divided by the marginal product of labor, $F_N$, we may write the following short run microeconomic equilibrium condition:

$$P = \frac{w_0}{F_N}. \qquad (1.1)$$

From this equality[2] it follows that when the economy is in equilibrium, the sum total of receipts of all producers will be equal to the product of aggregate output and labor marginal cost. Thus we have the following macroeconomic condition:

$$Y_s = \frac{w_0}{F_N} Q. \qquad (1.2)$$

This is the equation of the aggregate supply function. It states the total receipts, $Y_s$, firms must receive from the sale of aggregate output if they are to continue their rates of production unchanged. If, for example, actual revenues from the sale of output $Q$ exceeded $(w_0/F_N)Q$, price would be greater than marginal cost, and firms would increase their rates of output until equations (1.1) and (1.2) were satisfied. This function does not, of course, state the total revenues firms will in fact receive from the sale of output.

[2] If price should exceed (fall short of) marginal costs, firms would employ more (less) labor and produce more (less) real output. As a result, marginal cost would rise (fall) and, in the market place, the price of output would fall (rise). In this way the labor marginal cost of output is brought into equality with the price of output and equations (1.1) and (1.2) satisfied.

To determine this variable an aggregate demand relation is needed.

Before we specify the demand function to be used in this paper, let us investigate briefly the slope and curvature of the supply function. Differentiating equation (1.2) with respect to $Q$ yields:

$$\frac{dY_s}{dQ} = w_0 \left[ \frac{F_N^2 - QF_{NN}}{F_N^3} \right]. \qquad (1.3)$$

Because $Q$ and $F_N$ are positive while $F_{NN}$ is negative, $dY_s/dQ$ is positive, as we should expect. Furthermore, differentiating (1.3), and keeping in mind that $F_{NNN} = 0$, we find that $d^2Y_s/dQ^2$ is positive also. Accordingly, the aggregate supply function is drawn concave to the abscissa in Fig. 1. The positive slope and curvature of this function means that successive increments in total spending would produce successively smaller increments in output up to $Q^*$, the full employment level of production. When full employment is reached, supply becomes perfectly inelastic and additional spending would only force the money wage rate and the price of output to rise in proportion.

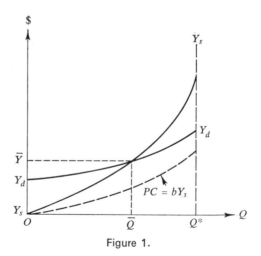

Figure 1.

The aggregate demand function is defined to be a relation between real output and the sum of consumption and investment spending measured in dollars. Our method of deriving this relation will be first to state the two elements of demand in real terms, and then deduce their corresponding monetary expressions.

Suppose that real consumption, $C$, is a constant proportion $b$ of real output.

$$C = bQ; \qquad 0 < b < 1. \qquad (1.4)$$

Multiplying on the left hand side by the price of

output and on the right hand side by its equilibrium equivalent, labor marginal cost, gives consumption expenditures in dollars.

$$PC = b \left[\frac{w_0}{F_N}\right] Q = bY_s. \qquad (1.5)$$

Our reason for multiplying on the right hand side by $(w_0/F_N)$ instead of by $P$ is to emphasize the fact that variations in output exert both a direct and an indirect effect on dollar consumption spending. The direct effect is given by equation (1.4). The indirect effect is due to the fact that when output changes, so also does the price of output, and thus consumption spending in dollar terms. Because $PC = bY_s$, the graph of the consumption function is drawn in proportion to the supply function (Fig. 1).

For the present let us suppose that real investment spending is fixed at some given value, $I_0$.[3] Even so, investment spending in dollars will vary with the level of output because of induced changes in the price of output. Hence the equation of the investment function is:

$$PI_0 = \left(\frac{w_0}{F_N}\right) I_0. \qquad (1.6)$$

The aggregate demand relation $Y_d$ can now be found by summing equations (1.5) and (1.6). This summation yields equation (1.7) which has, as Fig. 1 shows, both a positive slope, $dY_d/dQ$, and curvature, $d^2 Y_d/dQ^2$.

$$Y_d = \frac{w_0}{F_N} (I_0 + bQ). \qquad (1.7)$$

The equations of aggregate supply, (1.2), and aggregate demand, (1.7), together with the market clearing condition that supply equals demand, suffice to determine the equilibrium values of national income, aggregate demand, and real output. The solution values for these variables are shown in Fig. 1 by the intersection of the demand and supply functions. Their precise values, though, are given by the following two equations:

$$\bar{Y} = \frac{w_0}{F_N} I_0 \left(\frac{1}{1-b}\right) \qquad (1.8a)$$

$$\bar{Q} = I_0 \left(\frac{1}{1-b}\right), \qquad (1.8b)$$

where $\bar{Y}$ denotes the equilibrium value of both national income and aggregate demand, and $\bar{Q}$ of real output.

[3] In Section II below we shall no longer treat investment as a given exogenous variable, but will attempt to establish a relation between the aggregate demand for real capital and the level of investment.

The price of output also is determined by supply and demand; the supply of output and the demand for it.

$$P = \frac{Y_d}{Q}. \qquad (1.9)$$

Finally, the level of employment can be found by substituting $\bar{Q}$ into the equation of the aggregate production function and solving for $N$.

This completes our short run model of the economy. We have accounted for all the major aggregates of the economy with the exception of real investment and the rate of interest. Section II deals with the problem of investment, and there we shall see that the rate of interest does not play a very important role in single commodity models. For this reason additional supply and demand equations will not be introduced to solve for this variable. Instead, we shall assume that the monetary authority has fixed the rate of interest at $r_0$.

Before going to investigate the demand for capital and the rate of investment we shall briefly list the equations and unknowns of the system. They are:

$$Q = F(N, K) \qquad (1.10)$$

$$Y_s = (w_0/F_N)Q \qquad (1.11)$$

$$Y_d = (w_0/F_N)(I_0 + bQ) \qquad (1.12)$$

$$Y_s = Y_d \qquad (1.13)$$

$$C = bQ, 0 < b < 1 \qquad (1.14)$$

$$P = Y_d/Q. \qquad (1.15)$$

These six equations together with the information that $w = w_0$,[4] $I = I_0$, and $K = K_0$, determine the equilibrium values of real output, employment, national income, aggregate demand, real consumption, and the price of output. Additional information about consumption measured in dollars, real and money savings, the real wage rate, labor's share of national income, and so forth, can easily be obtained from the above equations.

The main properties of this model are worked out in the appendix of this paper. There it is

[4] The assumption of a rigid money wage rate, so long as there is any unemployment in the economy, serves to establish $w$ as the numeraire of the system. This fact can be seen by differentiating equation (1.1) of the text with respect to $w$, and then dividing the resulting expression by the price of output. By performing these two operations we find that $dP/P = dw/w$, which states that a given percentage change in the money wage rate will cause an equal percentage change in the price of output.

shown that: (a) the equilibrium of the system is stable, (b) employment, output, and the price of output all rise as demand increases but the increments in output and employment will be smaller, and that of the price of output larger, the closer the economy is to full employment, and (c) an increase in real demand will, short of full employment, produce the same increase in real output no matter what the level of employment happens to be, but that the increase in the money value of output will vary directly with the level of employment.

## II. The Demand for Capital

We can most easily begin our analysis of the demand for capital and the rate of investment by comparing the aggregate supply function with a relation which values output at average total cost ($ATC$). The graph of this function is shown in Fig. 2 by the locus of points labeled "$Y_a = ATC \cdot Q$." To obtain the equation of this relation

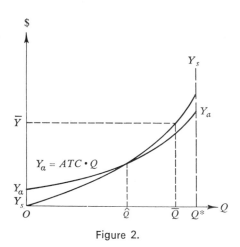

Figure 2.

assume, for the sake of simplicity, that capital has an infinite life. If so, then $(w_0/F_N)K_0$ is the dollar value of the capital stock, and $r_0(w_0/F_N)K_0$ is the current dollar cost of having or operating this stock.[5] Adding current labor costs of $w_0N$ to this figure gives the total cost of output, or output valued at average total cost.

$$Y_a = w_0N + r_0\left(\frac{w_0}{F_N}\right)K_0 = ATC \cdot Q. \quad (2.1)$$

[5] For a thorough discussion of the subject of current capital costs see Vernon L. Smith, *Investment and Production* (Cambridge, Mass., 1961), Chapters III and IV.

Differentiating with respect to $Q$ yields the slope of this equation:

$$\frac{dY_a}{dQ} = w_0\left[\frac{F_N{}^2 - r_0K_0F_{NN}}{F_N{}^3}\right]. \quad (2.2)$$

Because $dY_a/dQ$, though positive, is less than $dY_s/dQ$, and because $Y_a$ has a positive intercept, the graph of output valued at average total cost intersects the supply function from above at a positive output, $\hat{Q}$.

If the market were to establish $\hat{Q}$ as the equilibrium rate of output, average total cost would equal labor marginal cost, and the aggregate demand for additional capital (capital in addition to the existing stock of $K_0$) on the part of producers would be nil. If, however, the market established an output in excess of (less than) $\hat{Q}$, labor marginal cost would exceed (be less than) average total cost, and the demand for additional capital would be positive (negative). This is because the cost of producing any given output can be reduced by substituting capital for labor when average total cost is less than labor marginal cost, or by substituting labor for capital when average total cost exceeds labor marginal cost.

The exact relation between output and the demand for additional capital, $\Delta K$, can be constructed by finding the amounts of capital and labor needed to minimize the cost of producing a particular output $\bar{Q}$, say, and then subtracting $K_0$ from the solution value obtained for $K$. This subtraction yields the value of $\Delta K$ which "belongs" to $\bar{Q}$. The entire relation between $\Delta K$ and $Q$, as shown in Fig. 3 by the locus of points labeled $\Delta K \Delta K'$, can then be obtained by repeating this process for all values of $Q$.

To find those values of $K$ and $N$ which minimize the total cost of producing $\bar{Q}$ we form the following Lagrange equation:

$$\Phi = w_0N + r_0PK - \lambda[F(N, K) - \bar{Q}]. \quad (2.3)$$

Differentiating with respect to $N$, $K$, and $\lambda$, and setting the results equal to zero yields:

$$\frac{\partial \Phi}{\partial N} = w_0 - \lambda F_N = 0 \quad (2.4a)$$

$$\frac{\partial \Phi}{\partial K} = r_0P - \lambda F_K = 0 \quad (2.4b)$$

$$\frac{\partial \Phi}{\partial \lambda} = F(N, K) - \bar{Q} = 0. \quad (2.4c)$$

These three equations suffice to determine the amounts of capital and labor needed to minimize the cost of producing $\bar{Q}$, and the value of $\lambda$, the common labor and capital marginal cost of output. That $\lambda$ is indeed the common marginal cost of output can be seen by combining equations (2.4a) and (2.4b) into:

$$\lambda = \frac{w_0}{F_N} = \frac{r_0 P}{F_K}. \qquad (2.5)$$

This equation states that the labor marginal cost of output will equal the capital marginal cost of output if total cost has been minimized. When

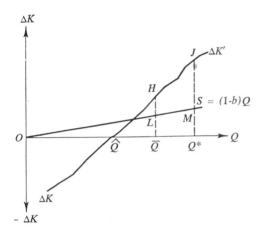

Figure 3.

this equality obtains, any substitution of one input for the other will raise, rather than lower, costs. Figure 3 illustrates the fact that the demand for additional capital is an increasing function of output. At $\bar{Q}$, for example, demand would be equal to $\bar{Q}H$, while at the full employment rate of output, $Q^*J$ units of additional capital would be demanded. In addition to this dependence however, inspection of equations (2.4) shows that $\Delta K$ varies with the rate of interest as well.[6] Thus we may write:

$$\Delta K = G(Q, K, r) \qquad (2.6)$$

with partial derivatives having the following signs:

$$\frac{\partial G}{\partial Q} > 0, \quad \frac{\partial G}{\partial K} < 0, \quad \frac{\partial G}{\partial r} < 0. \quad (2.7)$$

Suppose now we fix the level of output along with the stock of capital and the technical conditions of production. Then the demand for additional capital will be a function of the rate of interest alone. Figure 4 illustrates this conclusion. In this diagram the curve labeled "$F_K(\bar{Q})$" represents the marginal productivity of additional

---

[6] $\Delta K$ does not vary with $w$ because a change in the money wage rate will produce a proportionate change in $r_0(w_0/FF)$, the per-unit current cost of capital equipment.

capital "belonging" to $\bar{Q}$. This function, together with the rate of interest determines the amount, $OH$, of additional capital needed to minimize the total costs of producing $\bar{Q}$. This follows because if $OH$ units of additional capital were added to the present stock of $K_0$ then $r_0 = F_K$. Multiplying the left hand member of this equality by $P$, and the right hand member by $(w_0/F_N)$, and rearranging terms gives $(r_0 P)/F_K = w_0/F_N$, the cost of minimization condition specified by equation (2.5). Similarly, $F_K(\hat{Q})$ and $F_K(Q^*)$ are marginal productivity functions belonging to $\hat{Q}$ and $Q^*$ respectively.[7] They show that zero and $OJ$[8] amounts of additional capital would be needed to minimize the costs of producing these two outputs. From this discussion we may conclude that in the short run, the rate of interest and the marginal productivity of capital determine for each level of output a demand for additional capital.

We shall now prove that $F_K(\bar{Q})$, the marginal productivity of capital function belonging to $\bar{Q}$, is also the marginal efficiency of investment (*MEI*) function for $\bar{Q}$. With this done, our contention

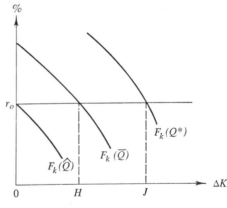

Figure 4.

that the rate of interest and the *MEI* determine the demand for additional capital, rather than the rate of investment, will be established. To prove that $F_K$ is the *MEI* we recall that the marginal efficiency of investment is defined to be

---

[7] The reason $F_K$ is an increasing function of $Q$ is because in the short run $Q$ can be increased only if more labor is employed. However, when more labor is employed, the capital-labor ratio falls. As a result of the fall in this ratio, $F_K$ rises, and $F_N$ falls. These results follow from the assumption that $F(N, K)$ is a linear homogenous function.

[8] $OJ$ and $OH$ of Fig. 4 are equal to $Q^*J$ and $\bar{Q}H$ of Fig. 3.

that rate of discount, $\rho$, which equates the present value of the stream of future benefits yielded by an additional unit of capital with the supply price of capital. The benefit per unit of time to be obtained from substituting a unit of capital for labor in the production of a given output is $w_0(F_K/F_N)$, the savings in wage payments over the same time span. Combining this benefit with the definition of the marginal efficiency we have:

$$P = w_0 \left(\frac{F_K}{F_N}\right) \int_0^\infty e^{-\rho t} dt = \frac{w_0}{\rho} \frac{F_K}{F_N}. \quad (2.8)$$

Dividing the left hand side by $P$, and the right hand side by $(w_0/F_N)$ yields:

$$1 = \frac{F_K}{\rho}. \quad (2.9)$$

From this we have that $F_K = \rho$. Thus for single commodity macroeconomic models, the marginal product of capital and the marginal efficiency of investment are identical.

We may now conclude that because investment spending is *not* determined by the rate of interest and the *MEI*, single commodity models which are based on this belief are incomplete and unable to solve for the short run equilibrium position of the economic systems they attempt to describe.

In the model developed in Section I of this paper, investment was determined by the fact that in the aggregate firms decided to purchase $I_0$ units of newly produced capital equipment. This decision established $\bar{Q}$ as the level of output, and generated savings of $(1 - b)\bar{Q} = \bar{Q}L$ (Fig. 3), an amount just equal to investment. However, we have seen that at $\bar{Q}$ firms will want more new capital ($\bar{Q}H$) than they are presently buying ($\bar{Q}L$). Since it would be more profitable for them to have the entire amount of new capital they want as soon as possible, rather than some of it now and the rest later, we look to the theory of aggregate investment to explain why firms do not, or cannot, purchase all the additional capital they demand in the immediate short run period. Unfortunately, the theory of aggregate investment as it now stands is not capable of providing an answer to this question.

It has been argued, in more broadly conceived contexts, by Keynes, Lerner, and Scitovsky[9] that

[9] J. M. Keynes, *The General Theory of Employment, Interest and Money* (London, 1936), p. 136; A. P. Lerner, *The Economics of Control* (New York, 1944), pp. 334–38; and T. Scitovsky, *Welfare and Competition* (Chicago, 1951), pp. 221–24. See also James G. Witte Jr., "The Microfoundations of the Social Investment Function," *The Journal of Political Economy*, LXXI, pp. 441–56.

it is the rising marginal costs of the capital goods industries which limits the rate of capital accumulation. As the demand for capital rises, the costs and prices of these goods rise in relation to the prices of all other goods. The then higher prices of capital goods reduces the profitability of substituting capital for labor and this serves to limit the rate of investment.

In any single commodity model, however, the price of the capital cannot rise in relation to the price of the consumer good. Hence a higher rate of investment does not by itself reduce the marginal return to capital and thus limit the rate at which capital can profitably be substituted for labor. For this reason the rate of investment, though limited by full employment savings, cannot be determined analytically within the confines of a single commodity macroeconomic model. This suggests that to make investment a genuine dependent variable, a two commodity model is needed at the very least.

## Appendix

For the system and its solution to be stable, the slope of the aggregate supply function must be greater than the slope of the aggregate demand function. Equation (1.3) expresses the gradient of the supply function. It is:

$$\frac{dY_s}{dQ} = \frac{w_0}{F_N{}^3} (F_N{}^2 - Q F_{NN}). \quad (A.1)$$

Differentiating (1.7) with respect to $Q$ yields the slope of the demand function.

$$\frac{dY_d}{dQ} = \frac{w_0}{F_N{}^3} [b(F_N{}^2 - Q F_{NN}) - I_0 F_{NN}). \quad (A.2)$$

An algebraic comparison shows $dY_s/dQ$ to be greater than $dY_d/dQ$.

In view of the fact that supply equals demand when equilibrium obtains, we may write $Y_d = (w_0/F_N)Q$. From this equation we find that:

$$\frac{dN}{dY_d} = \frac{1}{w_0} \left[\frac{F_N{}^2}{F_N{}^2 - Q F_{NN}}\right]. \quad (A.3)$$

This function is positive, but its derivative, $d^2N/dY_d{}^2$, is negative. Thus employment increases with demand, but at a decreasing rate. The change in output produced by a change in demand is:

$$\frac{dQ}{dY_d} = \frac{1}{w_0} \left[\frac{F_N{}^3}{F_N{}^2 - Q F_{NN}}\right]. \quad (A.4)$$

Again, this variable is positive and its derivative, $d^2Q/dY_d{}^2$, is negative.

The derivative price with respect to demand is:

$$\frac{dP}{dY_d} = \frac{-F_{NN}}{F_N{}^2 - QF_{NN}}. \qquad \text{(A.5)}$$

Both this function and its derivative, $d^2P/dY_d{}^2$, are positive so that the rate at which the price of output rises increases with the level of output.

Differentiating (1.8*b*) with respect to I produces the "real" multiplier of the system.

$$\frac{dQ}{dI} = \left(\frac{1}{1 - b}\right). \qquad \text{(A.6)}$$

Differentiating (1.8*a*) with respect to I then yields the "monetary" multiplier.

$$\frac{dY}{dI} = \frac{w_0}{F_N(1 - b)}\left\{1 - \left[\frac{IF_{NN}}{F_N{}^2(1 - b)}\right]\right\}. \qquad \text{(A.7)}$$

Inspection shows that this multiplier varies directly with the level of output.

*ABBA P. LERNER*

# On Some Recent Developments
# in Capital Theory

5

I

In 1936 Keynes introduced the term "marginal efficiency of capital," substituting the word "efficiency" for the word "productivity." His declared purpose was to obtain a measure that could be compared with the rate of interest, $i$. He did this by considering values rather than physical quantities [4].

At least as important was the undeclared shift from considering the stock of capital to considering the flow of investment and its influence on the level of employment. This led me to substitute "marginal efficiency of investment" for his marginal efficiency of capital, leaving the term "marginal productivity of capital" to represent the effects on output of having a greater stock of capital [5]. I would now like to suggest a slight change in terminology which would clearly show both distinctions, using four terms instead of two: the marginal productivity

Reprinted from the *American Economic Review: Paper and Proceedings*, LV (1965), pp. 284–295, by permission of the author and publisher. Abba Lerner is a professor at the University of California, Berkeley. Comments and questions by Jack Hirshleifer, Dale Jorgenson, Arthur Lerner, and Robert Solow are responsible for some significant clarifications.

of capital ($mpK$), the marginal productivity of investing ($mpI$), the marginal efficiency of capital ($meK$) and the marginal efficiency of investing ($meI$).

$MpK$ is the extra flow of output resulting from a unit increase in the stock of capital. But this is not comparable with $i$ because the units of output may not be the same as the units of capital. It is possible to make $mpK$ commensurable with $i$ by measuring both the capital and the output by their value either in dollars or in output, which we can call apples, but this would obscure the distinction between the effects of a change in the size of the capital stock ($K$) and a change in the rate of investing ($I$).

We can isolate these different influences by distinguishing between apples and apple trees, so that $mpK$ stands for the extra potential apples per annum from one extra tree. This diminishes with $K$, the number of trees already in existence, because the more trees there are the less favorable is the best site remaining available for planting yet another tree.

$MpI$ is the extra capital produced by diverting resources from making one unit of consumption goods to making capital goods. It is also not comparable with $i$. The greater is $I$, investment, the rate at which trees are being planted (or $S$, saving, the rate at which apples are being sacrificed) the smaller will be $MpI$ because more use will have to be made of resources that are relatively less efficient at planting new trees than at coaxing apples out of the already existing trees. $MpK$, too, will diminish as $I$ increases because fewer resources are left to help trees produce more apples.

We get a rate of return to compare with $i$ by multiplying together the two marginal productivities. If a tree yields 100 apples per annum (net), $mpK$ is

$$\frac{100 \text{ apples per annum}}{1 \text{ tree}}.$$

If it takes the sacrifice of 1,000 potential apples to plant an additional tree, $mpI$ is

$$\frac{1 \text{ tree}}{1{,}000 \text{ apples}}.$$

The product is

$$\frac{100 \text{ per annum}}{1{,}000}$$

or 10 per cent per annum.

$MeI$ is the rate of return which in (perfectly competitive) equilibrium will be equal to $i$. A positive $I$ will then indicate that $K$ is less than that appropriate to $i$; namely, that $meK$ is greater than $i$. In long-period equilibrium $K$ would be adjusted, $meK$ would be equal to $i$, and $I$ would be zero. $MeK$ may, therefore, be defined as $meI$ when $I = 0$.

These relationships are illustrated in Figure 1 and Table 1, in which position (1) represents an initial long-period equilibrium, position (2) a new short-period equilibrium following a reduction in $i$, (3) a long-period equilibrium corresponding to that lower $i$, and (4) a new short-period equilibrium following a further reduction of $i$. The $meI$ curves are downward sloping because $meI = mpI \times mpK$ and both of these diminish as $I$ increases.

The downward slope of the $meK$ curve may seem to be more questionable. While $mpK$ may be expected to fall as the ratio of capital to other factors increases, $mpI$ is as likely to rise as to fall in response to an increase in $K$. If $mpK$ falls less in making capital goods than in making consumption goods, giving up a unit of consumption sets free enough resources to make more extra capital goods than it did before the increase in $K$. $MpI$ will have increased!

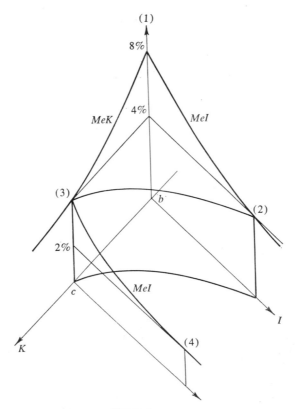

Figure 1.

## Table 1

| | | (1) | (2) | (3) | (4) |
|---|---|---|---|---|---|
| $i$ | Rate of interest | 8% | 4% | 4% | 2% |
| $K$ | Capital stock (number of trees) | 2,000 | 2,000 | 6,000 | 6,000 |
| $O$ | Output (potential apples per annum) | 1,000,000 | 1,000,000 | 2,100,000 | 2,100,000 |
| $C$ | Consumption (apples produced and consumed per annum) | 1,000,000 | 700,000 | 2,100,000 | 1,500,000 |
| $S$ | Saving ($O-C$) (potential apples sacrificed per annum to produce trees) | 0 | 300,000 | 0 | 600,000 |
| $I$ | Investing (trees produced per annum, net) | 0 | 40 | 0 | 48 |
| $O/K$ | Average productivity of capital (potential apples per annum per tree) | 500 | 500 | 350 | 350 |
| $mpK$ | Marginal productivity of capital (extra potential apples per annum per extra tree) | 400 | 400 | 240 | 240 |
| $I/S$ | Average productivity of investing (trees planted (per annum) per apple sacrificed (per annum)) | — | 1/7,500 | — | 1/12,500 |
| $mpI$ | Marginal productivity of investing (extra trees planted (per annum) per extra apple sacrificed (per annum)) | 1/5,000 | 1/10,000 | 1/6,000 | 1/12,000 |
| $pk$ | Price of capital goods ($=1/mpI$ in short period equilibrium) (price of a tree in apples) | 5,000 | 10,000 | 6,000 | 12,000 |
| $meI$ | Marginal efficiency of investing or rate of return ($\equiv mpK \times mpI$) ($=i$ in short period equilibrium) (extra apples per annum per extra apple sacrificed from consumption) | 8% | 4% | 4% | 2% |
| $meK$ | Marginal efficiency of capital or rate of return in long period equilibrium ($\equiv meI$ when $I=0$) | 8% | 8% | 4% | 4% |
| $K'$ | Value of the capital stock (value of the trees in apples) | 10,000,000 | 20,000,000 | 36,000,000 | 72,000,000 |
| $K'/O$ | "Capital-Output Ratio" | 10 | 20 | $17\frac{1}{7}$ | $34\frac{2}{7}$ |
| $\Delta K'/\Delta O$ | "Marginal Capital-Output Ratio" | $\infty$ | $14\frac{6}{11}$ | $\infty$ | |

But the new capital goods will suffer exactly the same decline in their $mpK$ in making consumption goods. The greater number of trees that can be planted when 1,000 potential apples are sacrificed is exactly offset by the greater decline in yield of potential apples per annum per extra tree. As long as there is any decline in $mpK$ in making capital goods, as $K$ increases, $meK$ will be downward sloping.

## II

The peculiar nature of capital in relation to time in the productive process and how this applies just as much to the services of capital as to land or labor services is shown in Figure 2. Time is measured along $AB$. The increasing distance from $AB$ of a point moving along the line $AC$ represents the cumulative application of "original" or "noncapital" factors of production —land-labor services (hereafter called "labor"), beginning at $A$ and concluding at $B$. The line $BC$ represents the emergence of the product at time $B$. The total length of the process is $AB$ and the average time between the application of the factor and the emergence of the product is $LB$. If $AC$ is a straight line, $LB$ will be half of $AB$. The total quantity of capital, measured by its labor content, will be represented by the area of the triangle $ABC$ or the rectangle $LMCB$.

If $i > 0$, the values of the flow of consumption

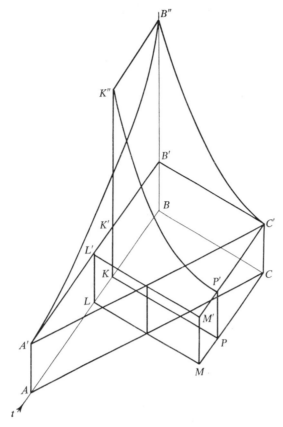

Figure 2.

goods and of the stock of capital goods will exceed the values of the labor services incorporated in them. If we represent the value of a unit of land-labor by the vertical distance $AA'$ we can show its growth as, with the passage of time, it turns into a unit of output. In equilibrium this growth in value must correspond to the rate of interest or discount. The unit of labor applied at time $A$ has an initial value $AA'$ which grows at a rate equal to $i$, reaching $B''$ at the end of the process. The other units of labor, since they are applied later, do not reach so high a value. The values they do reach are traced out by the curve $B''C'$. The growth in value may be conceived of as due to inputs of capital services; i.e., as resulting from the reinvesting from moment to moment of the continuous increase in the value of the goods in process during the production period. The causal influence is, of course, the other way around. All inputs are put in only because of the expectation of a greater value of future outputs.

The total value of output is represented by the area $BB''C'C$ at the further end of the figure, of which the rectangle $BB'CC'$ represents the

payment for land-labor, the remainder $B'B''C'$ being the return to capital. The value of the capital stock is represented by the complete solid figure $ABCB''$. $AA'BB'CC'$, the lower slice of this figure, represents the land-labor incorporated in the stock of capital. It may be considered as corresponding to the "wages fund," or "rent and wages fund," and we may call this "land-labor capital." The rest of the figure, the upper part $A'B'C'B''$, represents capital that must be invested in addition to the initial payment for the land-labor because it is impossible for the capital providers to start consuming all the interest on these (wages and rent) payments from the moment they make them. We may call this part of the capital the "interest fund" or "capital capital."

The average period of production is now represented by $KB$. The point $K$ is obtained by moving the plane figure at the end of the diagram back along $BA$ towards $A$ up to $K$, where the volume it will have moved through, the slice between the congruent parallel planes $BB''C$ and $KK''P$, will be just equal to $ABCB''$. $KB$ will be less than $LB$ because the greater weight of capital services comes closer to the end of the process when there are more capital earnings that must be reinvested as capital services.

It should be noted that the average period of production, which is also the capital-output ratio and the measure of capital intensity, is not independent of the rate of interest or the price of waiting, just as it is not independent of the relative prices of land and of labor. Without the relative prices it would be impossible to have a single measure of input.

## III

I now turn to "post-Keynesian" capital theory —the development, mostly in Cambridge, England, of models of economic growth centering largely, in its present presumably introductory efforts, on steady states, often called "golden ages," in which everything grows at the same rate so that all the current ratios are steady. The "Keynesian" element is the direction of influence from investing to saving rather than the other way around, as in Keynes's insistence on this direction of influence via employment and the multiplier. The difference which makes it post-Keynesian is that full employment is usually assumed. $I$ influences $S$ by increasing not employment but profits. The additional spending that constitutes the investing is received and saved by the capitalists. If they spend some of this, no less is saved, because that only increases their income enough to make the $S$ seem appropriate.

As one who certainly has spilled not too little ink in the "saving equals investment" spree of the 1930's and 1940's, I should have had no difficulty with this kind of argument. But I experienced severe discomfort which I traced to an unreadiness to accept the implied reduction in real wages. The rather startling response to my expression of these difficulties in Cambridge was "of course, if you bring in the inflation barrier the whole process is stopped and we just have inflation." The trouble was clearly that my own post-Keynesianism rests essentially on the belief that most economies today are at or beyond the inflation barrier. Nevertheless, it seemed incumbent on me to try to overcome my provincialism and make the assumptions necessary to follow the analysis.

This was not easy. One difficulty was the reversal of the roles of capital and investment. I tend to consider as natural a short-period model

in which the quantity of capital is given by history. Together with the current techniques it governs the current investment opportunities. The problem is to achieve the desired level of employment, perhaps with some consideration, among other social objectives, of a desired rate of growth.

Post-Keynesian capital theory does all this the other way around. The rate of growth of everything is set by the rate of growth of population and the technical progress, since it is only when everything else has been completely adjusted to these that a steady state can be achieved. A greater degree of thrift—meaning that a larger fraction of the output is saved and invested—thus does not show itself in a more rapid rate of accumulation of capital or of economic growth. It shows itself only in a higher level of capital stock in relation to output which just absorbs the higher rate of saving and investing in growing at the predetermined steady rate of growth of everything.

But after many painful exercises have got one into the swing of thinking in terms of states of steady growth, some interesting things begin to emerge. It now makes sense to isolate the effects of an increase in $K$ from the effects of an increase in $I$ by holding $I$, or rather $I/K$, constant not at zero but at $g$ the rate of growth of a steady state. In particular, what may justify the pains is that technical progress can be incorporated in the main structure of the model instead of being dragged in as an afterthought.

## IV

If technical progress is neutral as between the use of capital and the use of labor, it fits into $g$, the steady state rate of growth, in exactly the same way as an increase in labor. A 1 per cent per annum rate of such neutral technical progress means that each succeeding year the same number of men working with 1 per cent more machinery can produce 1 per cent more output including the 1 per cent greater output of machines required by the 1 per cent increase in the number of machines operated per working man. It is just as if the working population grew at an additional 1 per cent per annum, except that per capita wages and incomes now rise.

However, some interesting questions arise as to how it is appropriate to define neutrality of technical progress—the line between capital-using and capital-saving technical progress. Here the field has been narrowed to competition between J. R. Hicks and R. F. Harrod.

Hick's definition is enticingly neat, "equiproportional increases in the marginal productivities of capital and labor" [1] and works ideally for an individual producer who can freely change the number of men he hires or the number of machines he rents or buys and will not be induced by Hicks-neutral technical progress to change the ratio in which he combines them.

But society as a whole cannot vary the ratio between the quantities of capital and labor. It can only vary the uses to which they are put. If the marginal productivities of labor and of machines both increase by 10 per cent, an additional unit of labor used in the production of machines produces 10 per cent more of these, and each machine in turn produces 10 per cent more of its product. The marginal product of labor used indirectly is then increased twice by 10 per cent; i.e., by 21 per cent. Labor will, therefore, be shifted from direct use, where its marginal product increases by only 10 per cent, to indirect use, where the technical progress—the increase in marginal productivity—is "multiplied" by the number of stages in the economic process. Similarly, labor will be shifted from indirect uses to still more indirect uses. This is what constitutes the substitution of capital for labor.[1]

Harrod's definition of neutral technical progress—"technical progress that results in no change in the capital-output ratio for the same rate of interest" [2]—gives us neutrality with respect to the substitution between direct and indirect labor. By avoiding any reference either to the marginal productivity of capital or to physical quantities of capital, it avoids the traps that surround these concepts. If the marginal productivity of direct labor increases by 10 per cent, Harrod-neutrality would be satisfied by a 10 per cent increase in the productivity of men making machines with no increase in the marginal productivity of machines; by an unchanged marginal productivity of men or machines in making machines with a 10 per cent increase in the marginal productivity of machines making final goods, or by some intermediate changes that add up to a 10 per cent increase of productivity in the indirect manufacture of final goods just as in the first two cases.

In all three cases, $K'$ the value of the capital stock $K$ (measured in terms of output) will increase in the same proportion as output. In the first case, each batch of 100 retired machines is replaced by 110 of the new kind, each new machine having the same capacity and the same marginal cost as one of the old machines. In the second case, the number of machines does not change, but each new machine has a 10 per cent greater capacity and a 10 per cent greater marginal cost. The third case is intermediate between these two. The only difference between the three cases is in the degree to which the 10 per cent increase in the value of the stock of capital goods is due to a change in the number of machines and the degree to which it is due to a change in the value of each machine. The increase, decrease, or stationariness of the capital output ratio—the Harrod criterion—will correctly indicate capital-using, capital-saving, or neutral technical progress.

## V

Harrod, feeling that a measure of technical progress should hold "the quantity of capital in some sense" constant if it is not to "ascribe to technical progress some element of the increase of output which is better ascribed to capital accumulation," suggests that the proper measure of the quantity of capital for this purpose is not its value in terms of consumption goods but "the length of the productive process" defined as "the average time of waiting multiplied by the number of man hours (or other non-capital factors of production as currently valued in terms of man hours) in respect of which there is waiting" [3]. This means the average period of production of our "labor."

But technical progress can also affect the productivity of capital services, changing the structure of production and altering the value of the capital stock, the average period of production and the capital output ratio, even though the average period of production of labor has not changed.

This is shown in Figure 3 (which reproduces part of Figure 2). The broken lines show a shift in the input stream from the middle to both ends of the production process, the added area $Q$ being just equal to the subtracted area $R$, and $BB'CC'$, the labor content of the output, and $AA'BB'CC'$, that of the capital stock, are unchanged and so is $LB$ labor's average period of production. But the value of the output is in-

---

[1] Hicks may not have intended to identify the marginal productivity of capital with the marginal productivity of capital goods, but only on this interpretation is Hick's neutrality different in content from Harrod-neutrality.

creased because the addition $S$ (the accumulated value of $Q$) must exceed the subtraction $T$ (the accumulated value of $R$), while the value of the whole capital stock, including the "capital capital," must increase still more since it must grow in the same proportion as $B'B''C'$, the interest on it. Since that increases by the same absolute amount as total output $BB''C'C$, it will increase in a greater proportion. The overall average production and the capital output ratio will therefore increase from $KB$ to say $K*B$. Harrod's restriction of "the average time of waiting" to "noncapital" factors of production is unjustified. We must recognize that at any moment the capital goods and their services are just as "given" as the labor force and the land and their services.

## VI

I have so far followed the convention of treating capital as a stock and labor as a flow. But the legitimization of capital services on a par with labor opens the way to a more pleasingly

general approach which treats every flow of a productive service as yielded by a stock of the source of that flow, and also reduces the differences between the Hicks and Harrod neutrality to a difference between the private and the social points of view that lie behind them.

In microeconomics we consider a producer who buys or hires his factors of production on the market. If he uses only flows of services to produce a flow of output, he simply gets the difference between the two flows of payments for these as the payment for the flow of his personal services. He requires no capital to run such a business.

Capital comes into the picture only if the producer wants to own some of the sources of the flows of services. Even if he lets others own all the buildings and machines, etc., and buys their services (or rents the sources) he will normally find it necessary to own some goods in process which incorporate past services which will contribute to future output. They constitute working capital and must also be considered as sources of flows of productive services. We may then define private capital as sources owned.

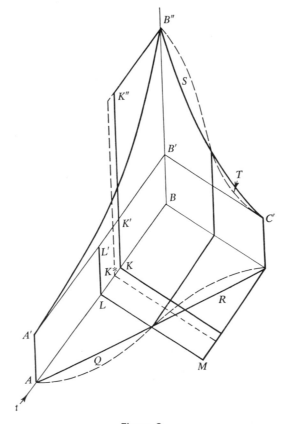

Figure 3.

The more of the sources he is to own, the greater the amount of capital he must have or borrow. A capital-using invention from his point of view is one that induces him to shift from the use of services that he buys to the use of services from sources that he owns, for which he needs capital. This will happen whenever the marginal productivities of the services of owned sources rise relatively to those of bought services. This fits Hicks's formula that a capital-using invention raises the marginal productivity of capital relatively to the marginal productivity of labor, etc., remembering that by capital we mean any sources that the producer owns and that by labor we mean any productive services that he buys.

But the economy as a whole cannot change the proportions between sources owned and sources rented. It can only change the uses to which the given flows of services from the given stock of sources are directed. In particular, it can and will shift them away from the manufacture of producible sources whose marginal productivity relatively to their marginal cost has fallen and toward the manufacture of producible sources where this has risen.

From the macroeconomic point of view, the significant distinction is not between services flowing from sources owned and services bought from others but between sources that are producible and sources that are not. Producible sources may then be called "social capital." From the social point of view a technical improvement is capital using if it diverts current services from producing current consumption goods to increasing the stock of producible sources, capital saving if it diverts current services in the opposite direction, and neutral if it does neither. Harrod's device—his use of the capital-output ratio (for a given $i$) as an indicator of the bias in technical progress—accurately reflects the initial direction of movement of the marginal productivity of indirect relative to that of direct use of resources.

# VII

There is, however, a third and more natural, because more direct, indicator of the bias in technical progress. This is none other than a change of our *meI*, the marginal efficiency of investing.

*MeI* has been defined in terms of potential consumption goods: the future flow of consumption goods made possible per unit reduction of current consumption via the shifting of current services from making current consumption goods to making (producible) sources. A change in *meI* is, therefore, a change in the relative marginal productivity of indirect as compared to direct use of services flowing from all kinds of sources: labor, land or capital, producible or non-producible. It may even be read as the marginal efficiency of indirectness in the use of productive services of all kinds.

An increase in *meI* (which $= mpK \times mpI$) may be the result of an increase in *mpK*, the marginal productivity of (the services of) producible sources in making consumption goods. But it may also come about from an increase in *mpI* by virtue of an increase in the *mp* of services in general (including nonproducible sources) in making producible sources relatively to their productivity in making consumption goods. In the first case, *meI* takes the form of an increase in the prices of producible sources: the tree is worth more because it produces more apples. In the second case it takes the form of a reduction in their marginal cost: it takes a smaller sacrifice in apples to get an extra tree. Combinations of these are, of course, also possible. In all cases an increase, decrease, or absence of change in *meI* (for a given ratio of $I$ to $C$) is a proper indicator of whether an improvement is capital using, capital saving, or neutral in the fundamental sense of how it affects the marginal efficiency of indirectness in the use of the currently available flow of services yielded by the currently existing stock of sources of all kinds.

# REFERENCES

[1] J. R. Hicks, *The Theory of Wages* (London: Macmillan, 1935), p. 123.
[2] R. F. Harrod, *Towards a Dynamic Economics* (London: Macmillan, 1948), p. 23.
[3] ———, "The Neutrality of Improvements," *Econ. J.*, June, 1961.
[4] J. M. Keynes, *The General Theory of Employment, Interest and Money* (London: Macmillan, 1936), p. 138.
[5] A. P. Lerner, "Capital, Investment and Interest," *Proceedings, Manchester Statistical Society*, 1936–37.
[6] ———, "Alternative Formulations of the Theory of Interest," *Econ. J.*, June, 1938.

[7] A. P. Lerner, "Equilibrium and Dynamic Concepts in the Theory of Employment," *Economica*, Apr., 1939.

[8] ———, *The Economics of Control* (London: Macmillan, 1944), Chaps. 20 and 25.

[9] ———, "Money," *Encyclopaedia Britannica*, 1946.

[10] ———, "Investment, Economic Aspects," *Encyclopaedia Britannica*, 1947.

[11] ———, *The Economics of Employment* (McGraw-Hill, 1951), Chap. 6.

[12] ———, "The Essential Properties of Interest and Money," *Q.J.E.*, May, 1952.

[13] ———, "On the Marginal Product of Capital and the Marginal Efficiency of Investment," *J.P.E.*, Feb., 1953.

# Money and Interest

*T*HE FIRST SELECTION in this group is Sir John Hicks's well-known 1937 article, "Mr. Keynes and the 'Classics'; a Suggested Interpretation." Here Hicks contrasts the work of Keynes to those of earlier economists and demonstrates the interrelationship between an economy's money market and its commodity market. In article seven Robert Mundell uses a hybrid form of the Hicksian analysis and suggests that the nature of equilibrium in an economy is affected in the short run by both stocks and flows of capital, securities, and money. The Mundell article is followed by the John G. Gurley and Edward S. Shaw discussion of the role of financial intermediaries such as insurance companies and savings and loan associations in the saving-investment process. Then Lawrence S. Ritter discusses the role of money in Keynesian theory, and H. Laurence Miller considers the transaction costs associated with liquid assets. Finally, Karl Brunner discusses some of the aspects of money-supply theory, and E. Ray Canterbery describes the behavior of the United States money supply during a recent period of time.

*Part*

*3*

J. R. HICKS

# Mr. Keynes and the "Classics"; A Suggested Interpretation

*6*

I

It will be admitted by the least charitable reader that the entertainment value of Mr. Keynes' *General Theory of Employment* is considerably enhanced by its satiric aspect. But it is also clear that many readers have been left very bewildered by this Dunciad. Even if they are convinced by Mr. Keynes' arguments and humbly acknowledge themselves to have been "classical economists" in the past, they find it hard to remember that they believed in their unregenerate days the things Mr. Keynes says they believed. And there are no doubt others who find their historic doubts a stumbling block, which prevents them from getting as much illumination from the positive theory as they might otherwise have got.

Reprinted from *Econometrica*, Vol. V (1937), pp. 147–159, by permission of the author and publisher. Sir John Hicks is a professor at All Souls College, Oxford.

Based on a paper which was read at the Oxford meeting of the Econometric Society (September, 1936) and which called forth an interesting discussion. It has been modified subsequently, partly in the light of that discussion, and partly as a result of further discussion in Cambridge.

One of the main reasons for this situation is undoubtedly to be found in the fact that Mr. Keynes takes as typical of "Classical economics" the later writings of Professor Pigou, particularly *The Theory of Unemployment*. Now *The Theory of Unemployment* is a fairly new book, and an exceedingly difficult book; so that it is safe to say that it has not yet made much impression on the ordinary teaching of economics. To most people its doctrines seem quite as strange and novel as the doctrines of Mr. Keynes himself; so that to be told that he has believed these things himself leaves the ordinary economist quite bewildered.

For example, Professor Pigou's theory runs, to a quite amazing extent, in real terms. Not only is his theory a theory of real wages and unemployment; but numbers of problems which anyone else would have preferred to investigate in money terms are investigated by Professor Pigou in terms of "wage-goods." The ordinary classical economist has no part in this *tour de force*.

But if, on behalf of the ordinary classical economist, we declare that he would have preferred to investigate many of those problems in money terms, Mr. Keynes will reply that there is no classical theory of money wages and employment. It is quite true that such a theory cannot easily be found in the textbooks. But this is only because most of the textbooks were written at a time when general changes in money wages in a closed system did not present an important problem. There can be little doubt that most economists have thought that they had a pretty fair idea of what the relation between money wages and employment actually was.

In these circumstances, it seems worth while to try to construct a typical "classical" theory, built on an earlier and cruder model than Professor Pigou's. If we can construct such a theory, and show that it does give results which have in fact been commonly taken for granted, but which do not agree with Mr. Keynes' conclusions, then we shall at last have a satisfactory basis of comparison. We may hope to be able to isolate Mr. Keynes' innovations, and so to discover what are the real issues in dispute.

Since our purpose is comparison, I shall try to set out my typical classical theory in a form similar to that in which Mr. Keynes sets out his own theory; and I shall leave out of account all secondary complications which do not bear closely upon this special question in hand. Thus I assume that I am dealing with a short period in which the quantity of physical equipment of all kinds available can be taken as fixed. I assume homogeneous labour. I assume further that depreciation can be neglected, so that the output of investment goods corresponds to new investment. This is a dangerous simplification, but the important issues raised by Mr. Keynes in his chapter on user cost are irrelevant for our purposes.

Let us begin by assuming that $w$, the rate of money wages per head, can be taken as given.

Let $x$, $y$, be the outputs of investment goods and consumption goods respectively, and $N_x$, $N_y$, be the numbers of men employed in producing them. Since the amount of physical equipment specialised to each industry is given, $x = f_x(N_x)$ and $y = f_y(N_y)$, where $f_x$, $f_y$, are *given* functions.

Let $M$ be the *given* quantity of money.

It is desired to determine $N_x$ and $N_y$.

First, the price-level of investment goods = their marginal cost = $w(dN_x/dx)$. And the price-level of consumption goods = their marginal cost = $w(dN_y/dy)$.

Income earned in investment trades (value of investment, or simply Investment) = $wx(dN_x/dx)$. Call this $I_x$.

Income earned in consumption trades = $wy(dN_y/dy)$.

Total Income = $wx(dN_x/dx) + wy(dN_y/dy)$. Call this $I$.

$I_x$ is therefore a given function of $N_x$, $I$ of $N_x$ and $N_y$. Once $I$ and $I_x$ are determined, $N_x$ and $N_y$ can be determined.

Now let us assume the "Cambridge Quantity equation"—that there is some definite relation between Income and the demand for money. Then, approximately, and apart from the fact that the demand for money may depend not only upon total Income, but also upon its distribution between people with relatively large and relatively small demands for balances, we can write

$$M = kI.$$

As soon as $k$ is given, total Income is therefore determined.

In order to determine $I_x$, we need two equations. One tells us that the amount of investment (looked at as demand for capital) depends upon the rate of interest:

$$I_x = C(i).$$

This is what becomes the marginal-efficiency-of-capital schedule in Mr. Keynes' work.

Further, Investment = Saving. And saving depends upon the rate of interest and, if you like, Income. $\therefore$ $I_x = S(i, I)$. (Since, however, Income is already determined, we do not need to bother about inserting Income here unless we choose.)

Taking them as a system, however, we have three fundamental equations,

$$M = kI, \quad I_x = C(i), \quad I_x = S(i, I),$$

to determine three unknowns, $I$, $I_x$, $i$. As we have found earlier, $N_x$ and $N_y$ can be determined from $I$ and $I_x$. Total employment, $N_x + N_y$, is therefore determined.

Let us consider some properties of this system. It follows directly from the first equation that as soon as $k$ and $M$ are given, $I$ is completely determined; that is to say, total income depends directly upon the quantity of money. Total employment, however, is not necessarily determined at once from income, since it will usually depend to some extent upon the proportion of income saved, and thus upon the way production is divided between investment and consumption-goods trades. (If it so happened that the elasticities of supply were the same in each of these trades, then a shifting of demand between them would produce compensating movements in

$N_x$ and $N_y$, and consequently no change in total employment.)

An increase in the inducement to invest (i.e., a rightward movement of the schedule of the marginal efficiency of capital, which we have written as $C(i)$) will tend to raise the rate of interest, and so to affect saving. If the amount of saving rises, the amount of investment will rise too; labour will be employed more in the investment trades, less in the consumption trades; this will increase total employment if the elasticity of supply in the investment trades is greater than that in the consumption-goods trades—diminish it if *vice versa*.

An increase in the supply of money will necessarily raise total income, for people will increase their spending and lending until incomes have risen sufficiently to restore $k$ to its former level. The rise in income will tend to increase employment, both in making consumption goods and in making investment goods. The total effect on employment depends upon the ratio between the expansions of these industries; and that depends upon the proportion of their increased incomes which people desire to save, which also governs the rate of interest.

So far we have assumed the rate of money wages to be given; but so long as we assume that $k$ is independent of the level of wages, there is no difficulty about this problem either. A rise in the rate of money wages will necessarily diminish employment and raise real wages. For an unchanged money income cannot continue to buy an unchanged quantity of goods at a higher price-level; and, unless the price-level rises, the prices of goods will not cover their marginal costs. There must therefore be a fall in employment; as employment falls, marginal costs in terms of labour will diminish and therefore real wages rise. (Since a change in money wages is always accompanied by a change in real wages in the same direction, if not in the same proportion, no harm will be done, and some advantage will perhaps be secured, if one prefers to work in terms of real wages. Naturally most "classical economists" have taken this line.)

I think it will be agreed that we have here a quite reasonably consistent theory, and a theory which is also consistent with the pronouncements of a recognizable group of economists. Admittedly it follows from this theory that you may be able to increase employment by direct inflation; but whether or not you decide to favour that policy still depends upon your judgment about the probable reaction on wages,

and also—in a national area—upon your views about the international standard.

Historically, this theory descends from Ricardo, though it is not actually Ricardian; it is probably more or less the theory that was held by Marshall. But with Marshall it was already beginning to be qualified in important ways; his successors have qualified it still further. What Mr. Keynes has done is to lay enormous emphasis on the qualifications, so that they almost blot out the original theory. Let us follow out this process of development.

## II

When a theory like the "classical" theory we have just described is applied to the analysis of industrial fluctuations, it gets into difficulties in several ways. It is evident that total money income experiences great variations in the course of a trade cycle, and the classical theory can only explain these by variations in $M$ or in $k$, or, as a third and last alternative, by changes in distribution.

(1) Variation in $M$ is simplest and most obvious, and has been relied on to a large extent. But the variations in $M$ that are traceable during a trade cycle are variations that take place through the banks—they are variations in bank loans; if we are to rely on them it is urgently necessary for us to explain the connection between the supply of bank money and the rate of interest. This can be done roughly by thinking of banks as persons who are strongly inclined to pass on money by lending rather than spending it. Their action therefore tends at first to lower interest rates, and only afterwards, when the money passes into the hands of spenders, to raise prices and incomes. "The new currency, or the increase of currency, goes, not to private persons, but to the banking centers; and therefore, it increases the willingness of lenders to lend in the first instance, and lowers the rate of discount. But it afterwards raises prices; and therefore it tends to increase discount."[1] This is superficially satisfactory; but if we endeavoured to give a more precise account of this process we should soon get into difficulties. What determines the amount of money needed to produce a given fall in the rate of interest? What determines the length of time for which the low rate will last? These are not easy questions to answer.

(2) In so far as we rely upon changes in $k$, we

[1] Marshall, *Money, Credit, and Commerce*, p. 257.

can also do well enough up to a point. Changes in $k$ can be related to changes in confidence, and it is realistic to hold that the rising prices of a boom occur because optimism encourages a reduction in balances; the falling prices of a slump because pessimism and uncertainty dictate an increase. But as soon as we take this step it becomes natural to ask whether $k$ has not abdicated its status as an independent variable, and has not become liable to be influenced by others among the variables in our fundamental equations.

(3) This last consideration is powerfully supported by another, of more purely theoretical character. On grounds of pure value theory, it is evident that the direct sacrifice made by a person who holds a stock of money is a sacrifice of interest; and it is hard to believe that the marginal principle does not operate at all in this field. As Lavington put it: "The quantity of resources which (an individual) holds in the form of money will be such that the unit of money which is just and only just worth while holding in this form yields him a return of convenience and security equal to the yield of satisfaction derived from the marginal unit spent on consumables, and equal also to the net rate of interest."[2] The demand for money depends upon the rate of interest! The stage is set for Mr. Keynes.

As against the three equations of the classical theory,

$$M = kI, \quad I_x = C(i), \quad I_x = S(i, I),$$

Mr. Keynes begins with three equations,

$$M = L(i), \quad I_x = C(i), \quad I_x = S(I).$$

These differ from the classical equations in two ways. On the one hand, the demand for money is conceived as depending upon the rate of interest (Liquidity Preference). On the other hand, any possible influence of the rate of interest on the amount saved out of a given income is neglected. Although it means that the third equation becomes the multiplier equation, which performs such queer tricks, nevertheless this second amendment is a mere simplification, and ultimately insignificant.[3] It is the liquidity preference doctrine which is vital.

[2] Lavington, *English Capital Market*, 1921, p. 30. See also Pigou, "The Exchange-value of Legal-tender Money," in *Essays in Applied Economics*, 1922, pp. 179–181.

[3] This can be readily seen if we consider the equations

$$M = kI, \quad I_x = C(i), \quad I_x = S(I),$$

For it is now the rate of interest, not income, which is determined by the quantity of money. The rate of interest set against the schedule of the marginal efficiency of capital determines the value of investment; that determines income by the multiplier. Then the volume of employment (at given wage-rates) is determined by the value of investment and of income which is not saved but spent upon consumption goods.

It is this system of equations which yields the startling conclusion, that an increase in the inducement to invest, or in the propensity to consume, will not tend to raise the rate of interest, but only to increase employment. In spite of this, however, and in spite of the fact that quite a large part of the argument runs in terms of this system, and this system alone, *it is not the General Theory*. We may call it, if we like, Mr. Keynes' *special theory*. The General Theory is something appreciably more orthodox.

Like Lavington and Professor Pigou, Mr. Keynes does not in the end believe that the demand for money can be determined by one variable alone—not even the rate of interest. He lays more stress on it than they did, but neither for him nor for them can it be the only variable to be considered. The dependence of the demand for money on interest does not, in the end, do more than qualify the old dependence on income. However much stress we lay upon the "speculative motive," the "transactions" motive must always come in as well.

Consequently we have for the General Theory

$$M = L(I, i), \quad I_x = C(i), \quad I_x = S(I).$$

With this revision, Mr. Keynes takes a big step back to Marshallian orthodoxy, and his theory becomes hard to distinguish from the revised and qualified Marshallian theories, which, as we have seen, are not new. Is there really any difference between them, or is the whole thing a sham fight? Let us have recourse to a diagram (Figure 1).

Against a given quantity of money, the first equation, $M = L(I, i)$, gives us a relation between Income ($I$) and the rate of interest ($i$).

which embody Mr. Keynes' second amendment without his first. The third equation is already the multiplier equation, but the multiplier is shorn of his wings. For since $I$ still depends only on $M$, $I_x$ depends only on $M$, and it is impossible to increase investment without increasing the willingness to save or the quantity of money. The system thus generated is therefore identical with that which, a few years ago, used to be called the "Treasury View." But Liquidity Preference transports us from the "Treasury View" to the "General Theory of Employment."

This can be drawn out as a curve (*LL*) which will slope upwards, since an increase in income tends to raise the demand for money, and an increase in the rate of interest tends to lower it. Further, the second two equations taken together give us another relation between Income and interest. (The marginal-efficiency-of-capital schedule determines the value of investment at any given rate of interest, and the multiplier tells us what level of income will be necessary to make savings equal to that value of investment.) The curve *IS* can therefore be drawn showing the relation between Income and interest which must be maintained in order to make saving equal to investment.

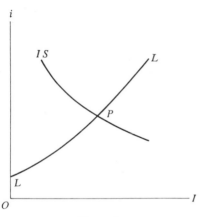

Figure 1.

Income and the rate of interest are now determined together at *P*, the point of intersection of the curves *LL* and *IS*. They are determined together; just as price and output are determined together in the modern theory of demand and supply. Indeed, Mr. Keynes' innovation is closely parallel, in this respect, to the innovation of the marginalists. The quantity theory tries to determine income without interest, just as the labour theory of value tried to determine price without output; each has to give place to a theory recognising a higher degree of interdependence.

## III

But if this is the real "General Theory," how does Mr. Keynes come to make his remarks about an increase in the inducement to invest not raising the rate of interest? It would appear from our diagram that a rise in the marginal-efficiency-of-capital schedule must raise the curve *IS*; and, therefore, although it will raise Income

and employment, it will also raise the rate of interest.

This brings us to what, from many points of view, is the most important thing in Mr. Keynes' book. It is not only possible to show that a given supply of money determines a certain relation between Income and interest (which we have expressed by the curve *LL*); it is also possible to say something about the shape of the curve. It will probably tend to be nearly horizontal on the left, and nearly vertical on the right. This is because there is (1) some minimum below which the rate of interest is unlikely to go, and (though Mr. Keynes does not stress this) there is (2) a maximum to the level of income which can possibly be financed with a given amount of money. If we like we can think of the curve as approaching these limits asymptotically (Figure 2).

Therefore, if the curve *IS* lies well to the right (either because of a strong inducement to invest or a strong propensity to consume), *P* will lie upon that part of the curve which is decidedly upward sloping, and the classical theory will be a good approximation, needing no more than the qualification which it has in fact received at the hands of the later Marshallians. An increase in the inducement to invest will raise the rate of interest, as in the classical theory, but it will also have some subsidiary effect in raising income, and therefore employment as well. (Mr. Keynes in 1936 is not the first Cambridge economist to have a temperate faith in Public Works.) But if the point *P* lies to the left of the *LL* curve, then the *special* form of Mr. Keynes' theory becomes valid. A rise in the schedule of the marginal efficiency of capital only increases employment, and does not raise the rate of

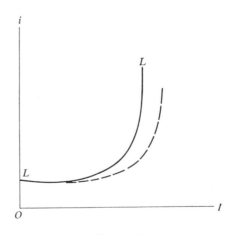

Figure 2

interest at all. We are completely out of touch with the classical world.

The demonstration of this minimum is thus of central importance. It is so important that I shall venture to paraphrase the proof, setting it out in a rather different way from that adopted by Mr. Keynes.[4]

If the costs of holding money can be neglected, it will always be profitable to hold money rather than lend it out, if the rate of interest is not greater than zero. Consequently the rate of interest must always be positive. In an extreme case, the shortest short-term rate may perhaps be nearly zero. But if so, the long-term rate must lie above it, for the long rate has to allow for the risk that the short rate may rise during the currency of the loan, and it should be observed that the short rate can only rise, it cannot fall.[5] This does not only mean that the long rate must be a sort of average of the probable short rates over its duration, and that this average must lie above the current short rate. There is also the more important risk to be considered, that the lender on long term may desire to have cash before the agreed date of repayment, and then, if the short rate has risen meanwhile, he may be involved in a substantial capital loss. It is this last risk which provides Mr. Keynes' "speculative motive" and which ensures that the rate for loans of indefinite duration (which he always has in mind as *the* rate of interest) cannot fall very near zero.[6]

It should be observed that this minimum to the rate of interest applies not only to one curve *LL* (drawn to correspond to a particular quantity

of money) but to any such curve. If the supply of money is increased, the curve *LL* moves to the right (as the dotted curve in Figure 2), but the horizontal parts of the curve are almost the same. Therefore, again, it is this doldrum to the left of the diagram which upsets the classical theory. If *IS* lies to the right, then we can indeed increase employment by increasing the quantity of money; but if *IS* lies to the left, we cannot do so; merely monetary means will not force down the rate of interest any further.

So the General Theory of Employment is the Economics of Depression.

## IV

In order to elucidate the relation between Mr. Keynes and the "Classics," we have invented a little apparatus. It does not appear that we have exhausted the uses of that apparatus, so let us conclude by giving it a little run on its own.

With that apparatus at our disposal, we are no longer obliged to make certain simplifications which Mr. Keynes makes in his exposition. We can reinsert the missing *i* in the third equation, and allow for any possible effect of the rate of interest upon saving; and, what is much more important, we can call in question the sole dependence of investment upon the rate of interest, which looks rather suspicious in the second equation. Mathematical elegance would suggest that we ought to have *I* and *i* in all three equations, if the theory is to be really General. Why not have them there like this:

$$M = L(I, i), \quad I_x = C(I, i), \quad I_x = S(I, i)?$$

Once we raise the question of Income in the second equation, it is clear that it has a very good claim to be inserted. Mr. Keynes is in fact only enabled to leave it out at all plausibly by his device of measuring everything in "wage-units," which means that he allows for changes in the marginal-efficiency-of-capital schedule when there is a change in the level of money wages, but that other changes in Income are deemed not to affect the curve, or at least not in the same immediate manner. But why draw this distinction? Surely there is every reason to suppose that an increase in the demand for consumers' goods, arising from an increase in employment, will often directly stimulate an increase in investment, at least as soon as an expectation develops that the increased demand will continue. If this is so, we ought to include *I* in the second equation, though it must be

---

[4] Keynes, *General Theory*, pp. 201–202.

[5] It is just conceivable that people might become so used to the idea of very low short rates that they would not be much impressed by this risk; but it is very unlikely. For the short rate may rise, either because trade improves, and income expands; or because trade gets worse, and the desire for liquidity increases. I doubt whether a monetary system so elastic as to rule out both of these possibilities is really thinkable.

[6] Nevertheless something more than the "speculative motive" is needed to account for the system of interest rates. The shortest of all short rates must equal the relative valuation, at the margin, of money and such a bill; and the bill stands at a discount mainly because of the "convenience and security" of holding money—the inconvenience which may possibly be caused by not having cash immediately available. It is the chance that you may want to discount the bill which matters, not the chance that you will then have to discount it on unfavourable terms. The "precautionary motive," not the "speculative motive," is here dominant. But the prospective terms of rediscounting are vital, when it comes to the *difference* between short and long rates.

confessed that the effect of $I$ on the marginal efficiency of capital will be fitful and irregular.

The Generalized General Theory can then be set out in this way. Assume first of all a given total money Income. Draw a curve $CC$ showing the marginal efficiency of capital (in money terms) at that given Income; a curve $SS$ showing the supply curve of saving at that *given* Income (Figure 3). Their intersection will determine the

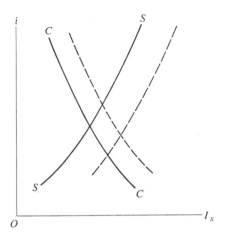

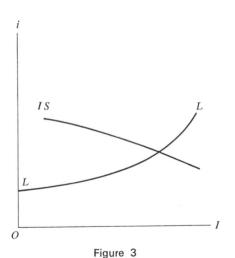

Figure 3

rate of interest which makes savings equal to investment at that level of income. This we may call the "investment rate."

If Income rises, the curve $SS$ will move to the right; probably $CC$ will move to the right too. If $SS$ moves more than $CC$, the investment rate of interest will fall; if $CC$ more than $SS$, it will rise. (How much it rises and falls, however, depends upon the elasticities of the $CC$ and $SS$ curves.)

The $IS$ curve (drawn on a separate diagram) now shows the relation between Income and the corresponding investment rate of interest. It has to be confronted (as in our earlier constructions) with an $LL$ curve showing the relation between Income and the "money" rate of interest; only we can now generalise our $LL$ curve a little. Instead of assuming, as before, that the supply of money is given, we can assume that there is a given monetary system—that up to a point, but only up to a point, monetary authorities will prefer to create new money rather than allow interest rates to rise. Such a generalised $LL$ curve will then slope upwards only gradually —the elasticity of the curve depending on the elasticity of the monetary system (in the ordinary monetary sense).

As before, Income and interest are determined where the $IS$ and $LL$ curves intersect—where the investment rate of interest equals the money rate. Any change in the inducement to invest or the propensity to consume will shift the $IS$ curve; any change in liquidity preference or monetary policy will shift the $LL$ curve. If, as the result of such a change, the investment rate is raised above the money rate, Income will tend to rise; in the opposite case, Income will tend to fall; the extent to which Income rises or falls depends on the elasticities of the curves.[7]

When generalised in this way, Mr. Keynes' theory begins to look very like Wicksell's; this is of course hardly surprising.[8] There is indeed one special case where it fits Wicksell's construction absolutely. If there is "full employment" in the sense that any rise in Income immediately calls forth a rise in money wage rates; then it is *possible* that the $CC$ and $SS$ curves may be moved to the right to exactly the same extent, so that $IS$ is horizontal. (I say possible, because it is not unlikely, in fact, that the rise in the wage level may create a presumption that wages will rise again later on; if so, $CC$ will probably be shifted more than $SS$, so that $IS$ will be upward sloping.) However that may be, if $IS$

[7] Since $C(I, i)$,
$$\frac{dI}{di} = -\frac{\partial S/\partial i - \partial C/\partial i}{\partial S/\partial I - \partial C/\partial I}$$
The savings investment market will not be stable unless $\partial S/\partial i + (-\partial C/\partial i)$ is positive. I think we may assume that this condition is fulfilled.

If $\partial S/\partial i$ is positive, $\partial C/\partial i$ negative, $\partial S/\partial I$ and $\partial C/\partial I$ positive (the most probable state of affairs), we can say that the $IS$ curve will be more elastic, the greater the elasticities of the $CC$ and $SS$ curves, and the larger is $\partial C/\partial I$ relatively to $\partial S/\partial I$. When $\partial C/\partial I > \partial S/\partial I$, the $IS$ curve is upward sloping.

[8] Cf. Keynes, *General Theory*, p. 242.

is horizontal, we do have a perfectly Wicksellian construction;[9] the investment rate becomes Wicksell's *natural rate*, for in this case it may be thought of as determined by real causes; if there is a perfectly elastic monetary system, and the money rate is fixed below the natural rate, there is cumulative inflation; cumulative deflation if it is fixed above.

This, however, is now seen to be only one special case; we can use our construction to harbour much wider possibilities. If there is a great deal of unemployment, it is very likely that $\partial C/\partial I$ will be quite small; in that case $IS$ can be relied upon to slope downwards. This is the sort of Slump Economics with which Mr. Keynes is largely concerned. But one cannot escape the impression that there may be other conditions when expectations are tinder, when a slight inflationary tendency lights them up very easily. Then $\partial C/\partial I$ may be large and an increase in Income tend to *raise* the investment rate of interest. In these circumstances, the situation is unstable at *any* given money rate; it is only an imperfectly elastic monetary system—a rising $LL$ curve—that can prevent the situation getting out of hand altogether.

These, then, are a few of the things we can get out of our skeleton apparatus. But even if it may claim to be a slight extension of Mr. Keynes' similar skeleton, it remains a terribly rough and ready sort of affair. In particular, the concept of "Income" is worked monstrously hard; most of our curves are not really determinate unless something is said about the distribution of Income as well as its magnitude. Indeed, what they express is something like a relation between the price-system and the system of interest rates; and you cannot get that into a curve. Further, all sorts of questions about depreciation have been neglected; and all sorts of questions about the timing of the processes under consideration.

The *General Theory of Employment* is a useful book; but it is neither the beginning nor the end of Dynamic Economics.

[9] Cf. Myrdal, "Gleichgewichtsbegriff," in *Beitrage zur Geldtheorie*, ed. Hayek.

# A Fallacy in the Interpretation of Macroeconomic Equilibrium

*7*

## I. Dimensions and Magnitudes

The problem of determining the conditions of monetary equilibrium admits of a comparatively simple solution so long as those terms heretofore considered of the second order of magnitude are neglected. If stock and flow demands for goods, money, and securities balance stock and flow supplies, the interest rate and money income are in equilibrium. It is generally admitted that the equilibrium is not a complete one, since positive savings-investment implies a growing stock of wealth and capital goods and a positive rate of growth of output.

Reprinted from the *Journal of Political Economy*, Vol. LXXIII (1965), pp. 61–66, by permission of the author and the University of Chicago Press. Copyright 1965 by the University of Chicago. Robert Mundell is a professor at the University of Chicago. The author is grateful to Alan Day, H. G. Johnson, and J. C. Weldon for helpful discussion of some of the issues raised in this paper but they are not responsible for any errors which remain.

But the growth effects are usually dismissed as magnitudes of the second order in the time interval relevant to the short-run equilibrium under consideration.

There does not appear in the literature, however, an explicit justification for the demarcation between magnitudes of the first order and magnitudes of the second order, a distinction that should be an implication, not an assumption, of theory. The implicit rationale for the neglect of rates of change in the context of macroeconomic theory appears to derive from the misuse of a dimensionality argument. Investment, for example, is dimensionally different from the capital stock; it involves, whereas the capital stock does not, a time dimension. Now if the time interval is made sufficiently short, increments in the stock become negligible in relation to the stock itself. The capital stock grows over time according to the equation

$$K = K_0 e^{(I/K)t},$$

where $I \equiv dK/dt$. Clearly, as $t \to 0$, $K \to K_0$, the initial capital stock. Hence, for short-run analysis, the flow of investment can be disregarded in relation to the capital stock and, by a similar argument, the flows of securities and money can be ignored in relation to the stocks of these assets; the flows are of a second order in relation to the stocks themselves.

I shall demonstrate in this paper that, despite the logic of the above argument, flows of capital goods, securities, and money must be explicitly introduced into macroeconomic analysis in order to determine the short-run equilibrium of the interest rate and money income. It is a fallacy to suppose that because flows are infinitesimal in relation to stocks they are of a second order of magnitude with respect to variables incommensurate with the stocks, such as the rate of interest. The rates of change of the capital stock, financial assets, and the money supply are dimensionally equivalent to the rate of interest and cannot be disregarded. Neglect of them in the literature has led to a one-sided and erroneous approach to monetary policy and has concealed theoretical results of great interest.

## II. Monetary Equilibrium and Growth

The classification of variables implicit in the Keynesian system affords a good point of departure for a demonstration of the importance to the equilibrium position of flows of money and securities. Consider an economy with three types of assets—goods, securities (bonds and equities), and money—held by a consolidated private sector (firms and households) and a consolidated public sector (banks and government). Stock equilibrium requires that the public be willing to hold the existing capital stock; that banks and households be willing to hold the net stock of securities issued by firms and government; and that firms, households and the government be willing to hold the stock of money issued by the banks. Flow equilibrium requires that any excess of saving over investment of the private sector be matched by an equivalent budget deficit (including net interest payments) of the public sector; that banks and households accumulate the new securities offered by firms and government; and that the public and government hoard the new money created by the banks.

In the Keynesian system, stock equilibrium is assured by equality of the demand and supply of money explicit in the theory of liquidity preference, and by equality of demand and supply of capital goods implicit in the theory of investment;[1] while flow equilibrium is insured by the equality of investment and savings (after adjustment for the public sector) and by the equality of new-money creation and hoarding that is a direct implication of equality between the stocks of money demanded and supplied. Together, these conditions imply equality between stocks and flows of securities demanded and supplied.

The important issue is the nature of the equilibrium that is implied by these conditions and whether or not the economic sense of the specific functional relationships making up the system is violated. In the Keynesian system, the demand for money is assumed to depend on the interest rate and money income. Positive investment implies a growing capital stock and (presumably) rising output. If the stock of money is constant and output is rising monetary equilibrium requires that the price level be falling or that the interest rate be rising. The point at issue is therefore whether falling prices or rising interest rates affect the demand for money or whether they are merely terms of the second order of magnitude.

Suppose that the demand for money varies in direct proportion to money income and in inverse proportion to the interest rate.[2] Monetary equilibrium, together with growth and a constant stock of money, then implies that interest rates are rising or prices are falling at a rate equal to the rate of growth of output. But rates of growth are pure numbers per day, month, or year and have dimensions equivalent to the interest rate. An asset-holder would therefore have to weight the importance of a rate of decrease in bond prices equally with the interest rate itself in making portfolio decisions involving choices between money and securities; he would similarly have to take into account the rate of inflation in making portfolio decisions involving the choice between commodities or equities on the one hand, and bonds and money on the other.

It follows that rates of change in commodity and security prices have a first-order impact on the general equilibrium of the system. If monetary equilibrium is established by falling commodity

---

[1] Whereby the stock demand-supply price of capital goods, equal to the marginal discounted product, is brought into equilibrium, at any given rate of interest, with the flow-supply price of capital goods.

[2] This slightly restrictive assumption simplifies the exposition without fundamentally altering the conclusions; the analysis can be made general by allowing for interest and income elasticities of demand for money differing from unity.

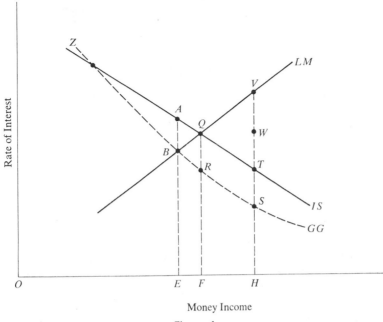

Figure 1

prices, the money interest rate (the nominal yield on bonds and bills) will differ from the real interest rate (the return on equities and the marginal efficiency of capital); whereas if it is established by falling bond prices, the cost of holding money will differ from the nominal return on bonds by the rate at which bond prices are falling. In both cases the discrepancy between the cost of holding money and the real interest rate causes a shift in the demand for money.

## III. A Geometric Solution

We can illustrate one solution to the problem of determining equilibrium income by making use of a famous geometric interpretation of macroeconomic equilibrium. The lines *LM* and *IS* (Fig. 1) are the familiar Hicksian schedules portraying the loci of interest rates and money incomes at which, respectively, money demand equals money supply and real investment equals real saving. I shall use the configuration to refer to both full-employment and unemployment situations; in the full-employment case real saving can be assumed to rise with money income because of the (negative) wealth effect of an increased price level on real-money balances; whereas in the unemployment case the Keynesian saving function can be assumed. My results do not depend upon any particular theory underlying

the schedules,[3] so I have drawn them with the conventional slopes.

Growth can be introduced explicitly on the diagram because the growth rate and the interest rate have identical dimensions. A growth schedule *GG* can be constructed such that the vertical distance between *GG* and *IS* measures the rate of growth of output corresponding to each level of saving and investment on *IS*. At some sufficiently high interest rate and low income level saving and investment (and therefore the growth rate) are zero and *GG* intersects

[3] For a given employment of the capital stock the ratio of labor to capital rises with the level of output, raising the marginal productivity of capital and hence the rate of growth, for any fraction of income saved, a factor that should be taken into account in constructing the investment schedule. David Meiselman, in a paper forthcoming in the *Journal of Political Economy*, explores this theme and discusses its implications for the slope of *IS*; related arguments were made back in 1956 by J. A. Stockfisch and A. J. Steigmann.

There are numerous theoretical difficulties associated with the use of the *IS–LM* configurations involving the possible interdependence of the schedules, the implicit role of the relative price of consumption and investment goods, and the role of expectations in deriving the investment schedule. Since, however, my paper is restricted to a consideration of the correct equilibrium position itself, it seems legitimate to ignore these difficulties, which are, in any case, common to virtually all of modern macroeconomic theory.

*IS* (at *Z*). At lower interest rates and higher incomes the growth rate is positive. Thus, at the point *A* the rate of growth is (assumed to be) *AB*, at *Q* it is *QR*, and at *T* it is *TS*.

Consider now the point at the intersection of *IS* and *LM*. *Q* is usually taken to be the equilibrium point. At *Q*, however, the rate of growth of output is *QR*, so that the demand for money can equal the supply of money only if the price level is falling or the interest rate is rising. In both cases the interest rate appropriate for saving-investment decisions will no longer reflect the cost of holding money.

There are three essentially equivalent techniques by means of which the equilibrium can be found (they are analogous to the three techniques used for partial equilibrium analysis of an excise tax). The first is to regard the ordinate as the marginal efficiency of capital (on the basis of which investment decisions are made) so that the *IS* schedule remains in position while the *LM* schedule shifts upward by any discrepancy between the real rate of interest and the cost of holding money. The second method is to regard the ordinate as the cost of holding money so that the *LM* schedule is fixed while the *IS* schedule shifts downward by any discrepancy between the money rate of interest and the marginal efficiency of capital. In the first case the intersection of the *IS* schedule and the shifted *LM* schedule determines the marginal efficiency of capital; and in the second case the intersection of the *LM* schedule and the shifted *IS* schedule determines the cost of holding money.

The third method, and the one I shall use, is to regard the ordinate, for purposes of deriving the *LM* schedule, as the cost of holding money, so that *LM* remains fixed; and to regard the ordinate, for purposes of deriving the *IS* schedule, as the marginal efficiency of capital, so that *IS* too remains fixed. The equilibrium is then discovered by finding the level of money income at which the vertical distance between the *IS* and *LM* schedules equals the difference between the cost of holding money and the marginal efficiency of capital.

The true equilibrium is most easily interpreted if we analyze the extreme cases where commodity prices fall and where bond prices fall separately. If at *Q* commodity prices were falling at a rate sufficient for the real quantity of money to increase at the same rate as output, that is, at the rate *QR*, the cost of holding money would be *FR*, not *FQ*, since the rate of decline in the

prices of commodities and equities (*QR*) would reduce the cost of holding money with respect to commodities and equities by an equal amount. At *Q* asset-holders would sell equities and try to acquire more money and bonds, and this would raise the real rate of interest and lower the money rate of interest to the point where the commodity value of yields on all assets were equalized. Equilibrium, therefore, requires a discrepancy between the real and money rates of interest equal to the rate of deflation, which in turn must equal the rate of growth. This is possible only at the point where *GG* intersects *LM* at *B*. At this equilibrium the level of income is *OE*, the money rate of interest is *EB*, the real rate of interest is *EA*, and both the rate of growth and the rate of deflation are *AB*.

A similar analysis holds if interest rates, instead of commodity prices, adapt to preserve equality between money demand and supply. *Q* cannot be the equilibrium point because at *Q* bond prices would be falling, reducing the opportunity cost of holding money. If bond prices fall at the same rate that output is growing, the cost of holding money is again *FR*, not *FQ*, and true equilibrium is again at the income level *OE*.

The interpretation of the new equilibrium in the case of falling bond prices (rising interest rates) is somewhat different from the preceding example of falling commodity prices. There is no gap between the real and money rates of interest since all rates of interest are expressed, when the price level is constant, in real terms. *EA* represents the bond rate of interest (and the return on equities) while *EB* represents the bond rate of interest less the rate at which the interest rate is rising. The gap between the bond rate and the cost of holding money arises from the capital losses associated with holding bonds.

The interest rate *EB* can be interpreted as the short-term rate of interest. It is the yield on bills of (virtually) zero duration because the price of bills must reflect both the nominal bond interest rate and the depreciation capital value of bonds. At the equilibrium income *OE*, therefore, the short-term interest rate is lower and the long-term interest rate is higher than at *Q*. Instead of a gap between money and real rates of interest there is a gap between short-term and long-term rates of interest.[4]

---

[4] The link between a changing interest rate or price level and the demand for assets (including real-money balances) is of course expectational: asset-holders are assumed to expect current rates of

## IV. Alternative Rates of Monetary Expansion

It has now been established that if the rate of monetary expansion is zero, the price of goods or bonds must fall, under the assumed conditions, at a rate equal to the rate of growth of output, $AB$, and the equilibrium income is $OE$, not $OF$. Similar reasoning shows that there is a different position of equilibrium for each (given) rate of monetary expansion. When the latter is negative equilibrium income is less than $OE$, and when it is positive income is greater than $OE$.

The position of equilibrium is in all cases at the level of income where the rate of monetary expansion is equal to the vertical distance between $LM$ and $GG$. With a rate of monetary expansion equal to $QR$ (the rate of growth at the income level $OF$) equilibrium is at $Q$ and the price level and the interest rate are constant. The point $Q$, the conventional interpretation of equilibrium, can therefore be regarded as the true equilibrium if the rate of monetary expansion equals the rate of growth of output. In other words, the traditional exposition of macroeconomic equilibrium can be used provided it is specified that the money supply is growing rapidly enough to satisfy the (growing) demand for money.

Consider now a situation in which the rate of monetary expansion exceeds the rate of growth of output. If the rate of monetary expansion is $SV$ (greater than the rate of growth $TS$), the equilibrium income is $OH$. Then, regardless of whether commodity prices are fixed or flexible, $HV$ will reflect the short-term rate of interest (the cost of holding money) and $VT$ the excess of the rate of monetary expansion over the rate of growth. But if prices are flexible, $HV$ can also be identified with both the long-term rate of interest and the money rate of interest,

and $VT$ with both the rate of inflation and the excess of the money rate of interest over the real rate of interest.[5] If, however, the price level is fixed, $HT$ will be the long-term rate of interest, and $VT$ both the rate at which the long-term rate of interest is falling and the excess of the short-term interest rate over the existing long-term rate. In both cases the rate of monetary expansion $SV$ establishes the equilibrium income $OH$.[6]

Equilibrium would probably, in the real world, be preserved by movements in both bond prices, and commodity and equity prices the division between which is intimately bound up with anticipations, the state of employment, and the conjuncture of the business cycle. For example, the rate of monetary expansion $VS$ at the equilibrium income $OH$ might be divided between the rate of growth equal to $ST$, a rate of inflation equal to $WT$, and a rate of increase in bond prices equal to $WV$; in that case the nominal return on equities would be $HT$, on bonds $HW$, and on bills $HV$, despite the fact that bonds, bills, and equities all yield the same commodity rate of return of $HT$.

The essential conclusion to be drawn, however, concerns not the determination of the precise pattern of real and money rates of interest on short- and long-term securities to which the rate of monetary expansion gives rise, but rather the central role of the rate of monetary expansion itself, operating through its influence on anticipations and asset prices, in determining the equilibrium level of money income. This role is entirely distinct from concepts of the role of monetary policy which attach sole importance to alterations in the stock of monetary assets.

[5] In "Inflation and Real Interest," *Journal of Political Economy*, LXXI (June, 1963), 282, I analyzed this case, noting (correctly) that "the inflation itself is generated by monetary expansion *in excess of growth*." It was, in fact, the conclusions of that paper which led me to suspect there must be an analogous result in the "Keynesian" unemployment case.

[6] Notice that this analysis has been concerned solely with various *states* of growth equilibrium and not with the comparative dynamics problem of actually moving from one state of growth equilibrium to another, a problem which is complicated by the entangling of two basically different types of expectation, namely, those engendered by the extrapolation of various rates of expansion at a state of growth equilibrium and those generated by the actual (finite) changes in the level of equilibrium income in the transition from one growth equilibrium to another.

change to continue. The *duration* of the expectation is, however, crucial in determining the prevailing crescendo of interest rates since, obviously, a given rate of change of commodity, equity, or bond prices that is expected to persist for only, say, a few months would produce a structure of rates higher at the short end of the maturity scale relative to the structure produced by rates of change expected to persist for several years. In order to draw sharper lines in this discussion, I have assumed, implicitly in the text, that rates of change are expected to persist indefinitely in which case the "short-term rate" reflects the instantaneous rate of interest and the "long-term rate" reflects that rate on consols.

*JOHN G. GURLEY AND EDWARD S. SHAW*

# Financial Intermediaries and the Saving-Investment Process

8      It is fashionable these days to speak of the growing institutionalization of saving and investment. Rapid advances in recent years by pension funds, open-end investment companies, credit unions, and savings and loan associations, among others, have caught our eye. But the advance has been going on at least since the Civil War, and, as Raymond Goldsmith has recently shown, it was quite pronounced during the first three decades of this century. It is with these three decades that our paper is primarily concerned. Our method of analyzing financial data, however, requires explanation since it is based on unconventional theory. Accordingly, the first portions of the paper are largely theoretical. After that, we get down to brass tacks.

---

Reprinted from the *Journal of Finance*, Vol. II (1956), pp. 257–276, by permission of the authors and publisher. John Gurley and Edward Shaw are professors at Stanford University. This paper (was) presented at a joint meeting of the American Finance Association and the American Statistical Association held in New York City on December 27, 1956. The program was under the chairmanship of Robert V. Roosa, Federal Reserve Bank of New York.

## Deficits, Security Issues, and GNP

It is easy to imagine a world in which there is a high level of saving and investment, but in which there is an unfavorable climate for financial intermediaries. At the extreme, each of the economy's spending units—whether of the household, business, or government variety—would have a balanced budget on income and product account. For each spending unit, current income would equal the sum of current and capital expenditures. There could still be saving and investment, but each spending unit's saving would be precisely matched by its investment in tangible assets. In a world of balanced budgets, security issues by spending units would be zero, or very close to zero.[1] The same would be true of the accumulation of financial assets. Consequently, this world would be a highly uncongenial one for financial intermediaries; the saving-investment process would grind away without them.

[1] Securities might be issued by spending units to build up their financial assets or their holdings of existing real assets. However, in a world of balanced budgets, no spending unit would have a *net* accumulation of these assets, positive or negative.

Financial intermediaries are likely to thrive best in a world of deficits and surpluses, in a world in which there is a significant division of labor between savers and investors. In the ideal world for financial intermediaries, all current and capital expenditures would be made by spending units that received no current income, and all current income would be received by spending units that spent nothing. One group of spending units would have a deficit equal to its expenditures, and the other group would have a surplus equal to its income. And, of course, the *ex post* deficit would necessarily be equal to the *ex post* surplus. In this setting, the deficit group would tend to issue securities equal to its deficit, and the other group would tend to accumulate financial assets equal to its surplus. Security issues and financial-asset accumulations, therefore, would tend to approximate GNP or the aggregate of expenditures. No more congenial world than this could exist for financial intermediaries.

Unfortunately for these intermediaries, our own economy has been much closer to the first than to the second world. With some exceptions during the past half-century, the annual security issues of spending units over complete cycles have averaged somewhat below 10 per cent of GNP in current prices. These issues include government securities, corporate and foreign bonds, common and preferred stock, farm and non-farm mortgages, and consumer and other short-term debt. We shall call these primary security issues. Thus, at the turn of the century when GNP was around $20 billion, primary security issues ran a bit less than $2 billion per annum. In the late 1940's, with a GNP of approximately $250 billion, primary issues hovered around $20 billion per annum. Dividing the half-century into thirteen complete cycles, we find that the average annual ratio of primary issues to GNP was between 7 and 10 per cent in nine of the cycles. The exceptional cases include World War I, when the ratio reached 20 per cent, the 1930's, when the ratio fell to 3 or 4 per cent, and World War II, when it climbed to 25 per cent. However, if we consider longer phases, 1897–1914, 1915–32, and 1933–49, the ratio was between 9 and 10 per cent in each phase. There is sufficient strength, then, in the link between borrowing and GNP to make the relationship useful for financial analysis. And while the ratio lies closer to zero than to 100 per cent, still it is high enough to permit financial intermediation to be a substantial business.

## The Role of Financial Intermediaries

What is the business of financial intermediaries? They lend at one stratum of interest rates and borrow at a lower stratum. They relieve the market of some primary securities and substitute others—indirect securities or financial assets—whose qualities command a higher price. This margin between yields on primary and indirect securities is the intermediaries' compensation for the special services they supply.

The financial institutions that fit these specifications are savings and loan associations, insurance companies, mutual savings banks, Postal Savings banks, investment companies, common trust funds, pension funds, government lending agencies, and others. In addition, we count the monetary system, including commercial banks, as one among many intermediaries. It is a vitally important intermediary, in view of its functions and its size. But its elevated rank among intermediaries does not alter the principle that the monetary system, like other intermediaries, transmits loanable funds by issues of indirect financial assets to surplus units and purchases of primary securities from deficit units. The indirect financial assets, deposits and currency that it issues or creates, are, like the indirect financial assets issued or created by other intermediaries, substitutes for primary securities in the portfolios of spending units. We shall return to this point in a few moments.

## Internal and External Finance of Expenditures

In a world of balanced budgets, each spending unit's current and capital expenditures would be financed entirely from its current income. Thus, aggregate expenditures in the economy would be self-financed or internally financed. Internal finance would be equal to GNP.

In a world of deficits and surpluses, some expenditures would be financed externally. The extent of such financing is measured by the sum of the deficits (or surpluses) run by spending units. If at a GNP of $400 billion, the sum of all spending units' deficits as $40 billion, then 10 per cent of GNP is financed externally and 90 per cent is financed internally.

External finance may take two forms: direct finance and indirect finance. The distinction is based on the changes that occur in the financial accounts of surplus units' balance sheets. The finance is indirect if the surplus units acquire claims on financial intermediaries.[2] It is direct if surplus units acquire claims on debtors that are not financial intermediaries.[3]

While the proportion of GNP that is externally financed has not changed much over the past half-century, the proportion that is indirectly financed has risen and, of course, the proportion that is directly financed has fallen. In short, a growing share of primary issues has been sold to financial intermediaries.[4] But the relative gainers have been the non-monetary intermediaries and the relative loser has been the monetary system. Now, if we look at these trends from the standpoint of surplus spenders, we have the following picture: the surplus units have accumulated financial assets in annual amounts that, over long periods, have been a fairly steady percentage of GNP. However, these accumulations have been relatively more and more in the form of indirect financial assets, and relatively less and less in the form of primary securities Moreover, the accumulations of indirect financial assets have swung toward the non-monetary types and away from bank deposits and currency. Commercial banks and the monetary system have retrogressed relative to financial intermediaries generally.

[2] In our empirical work, we exclude from indirect finance some kinds of claims on intermediaries, such as accrued expenses or even stockholder equities, that are essentially like debt issues of non-financial spending units.

[3] It may help to illustrate these financing arrangements. Suppose that at a GNP of $400 billion the sum of all spending units' deficits is $40 billion. Suppose further that $40 billion of primary securities, such as corporate bonds and mortgages, are issued to cover the deficits. The primary securities may be sold directly to surplus spending units whose aggregate surplus will also be equal to $40 billion, looking at it *ex post*. In this case direct finance will take place, with surplus spenders acquiring various types of primary securities. Alternatively, if the primary securities are sold to financial intermediaries, surplus spenders will accumulate claims on these intermediaries, indirect financial assets instead of primary securities. In this event we say that the expenditures represented by the primary securities have been indirectly financed. If indirect finance occurs through commercial banks, surplus spenders accumulate bank deposits; if through savings and loan associations, they acquire savings and loan shares; if through life insurance companies, policyholder equities; and so on.

[4] This growth has not been steady. Indeed, it is shown later that there was retrogression in intermediation from 1898 to 1921. The share of issues going to intermediaries rose in the 1920's, rose further in the 1930's, and remained high in the 1940's.

## A Reconsideration of Banking Theory

A traditional view of the monetary system is that it determines the supply of money: it determines its own size in terms of monetary debt and of the assets that are counterparts of this debt on the system's balance sheet. Other financial intermediaries transfer to investors any part of this money supply that may be deposited with them by savers. Their size is determined by the public's choice of saving media.

As we see it, on the contrary, the monetary system is in some significant degree competitive with other financial intermediaries. The growth of these intermediaries in terms of indirect debt and of primary security portfolios is alternative to monetary growth and inhibits it. Their issues of indirect debt displace money, and the primary securities that they hold are in some large degree a loss of assets to the banks.

Bank deposits and currency are unique in one respect: they are means of payment, and holders of money balances have immediate access to the payments mechanism of the banking system. If money were in demand only for immediate spending or for holding in transactions balances, and if no other financial asset could be substituted as a means of payment or displace money in transactions balances, the monetary system would be a monopolistic supplier exempt from competition by other financial intermediaries.

But money is not in demand exclusively as a means of payment. It is in demand as a financial asset to hold. As a component of balances, money does encounter competition. Other financial assets can be accumulated preparatory to money payments, as a precaution against contingencies, or as an alternative to primary securities. For any level of money payments, various levels of money balances will do and, hence, various sizes of money supply and monetary system.

The more adequate the non-monetary financial assets are as substitutes for money in transactions, precautionary, speculative, and—as we shall see— diversification balances, the smaller may be the money supply for any designated level of national income. For any level of income, the money supply is indeterminate until one knows the degree of substitutability between money created by banks and financial assets created by other intermediaries. How big the monetary system is depends in part on the intensity of competition from savings banks, life insurance companies, pension funds, and other intermediaries.

Financial competition may inhibit the growth of the monetary system in a number of ways.

Given the level of national income, a gain in attractiveness of, say, savings and loan shares vis-à-vis money balances must result in an excess supply of money. The monetary authority may choose to remove this excess. Then bank reserves, earning assets, money issues, and profits are contracted. This implies that, at any level of income, the competition of non-monetary intermediaries may displace money balances, shift primary securities from banks to their competitors, and reduce the monetary system's requirement for reserves. In a trend context, bank reserves cannot be permitted to grow as rapidly as otherwise they might, if non-monetary intermediaries become more attractive channels for transmission of loanable funds.

Suppose that excess money balances, resulting from a shift in spending units' demand away from money balances to alternative forms of indirect financial assets, are not destroyed by central bank action. They may be used to repay bank loans or to buy other securities from banks, the result being excess bank reserves. At the prevailing level of security prices, spending units have rejected money balances. But cannot banks force these balances out again, resuming control of the money supply? They can do so by accepting a reduced margin between the yield of primary securities they buy and the cost to them of deposits and currency they create. But this option is not peculiar to banks: other intermediaries can stimulate demand for their debt if they stand ready to accept a reduced markup on the securities they create and sell relative to the securities they buy. The banks can restore the money supply, but the cost is both a decline in their status relative to other financial intermediaries and a reduction in earnings.

The banks may choose to live with excess reserves rather than pay higher prices on primary securities or higher yields on their own debt issues. In this case, as in the previous two, a lower volume of reserves is needed to sustain a given level of national income. With their competitive situation improved, non-monetary intermediaries have stolen away from the banking system a share of responsibility for sustaining the flow of money payments. They hold a larger share of outstanding primary securities; they owe a larger share of indirect financial assets. They have reduced the size of the banking system at the given income level, both absolutely and relatively to their own size, and their gain is at the expense of bank profits.[5]

[5] We may mention a few additional issues in banking theory. As intermediaries, banks buy primary securities and issue, in payment for them, deposits and currency. As the payments mechanism, banks transfer title to means of payment on demand by customers. It has been pointed out before, especially by Henry Simons, that these two banking functions are at least incompatible. As managers of the payments mechanism, the banks cannot afford a shadow of insolvency. As intermediaries in a growing economy, the banks may rightly be tempted to wildcat. They must be solvent or the community will suffer; they must dare insolvency or the community will fail to realize its potentialities for growth.

All too often in American history energetic intermediation by banks has culminated in collapse of the payments mechanism. During some periods, especially cautious regard for solvency has resulted in collapse of bank intermediation. Each occasion that has demonstrated the incompatibility of the two principal banking functions has touched off a flood of financial reform. These reforms on balance have tended to emphasize bank solvency and the viability of the payments mechanism at the expense of bank participation in financial growth. They have by no means gone to the extreme that Simons proposed, of divorcing the two functions altogether, but they have tended in that direction rather than toward indorsement of wildcat banking. This bias in financial reform has improved the opportunities for non-monetary intermediaries. The relative retrogression in American banking seems to have resulted in part from regulatory suppression of the intermediary function.

Turning to another matter, it has seemed to be a distinctive, even magic, characteristic of the monetary system that it can create money, erecting a "multiple expansion" of debt in the form of deposits and currency on a limited base of reserves. Other financial institutions, conventional doctrine tells us, are denied this creative or multiplicative faculty. They are merely middlemen or brokers, not manufacturers of credit. Our own view is different. There is no denying, of course, that the monetary system creates debt in the special form of money: the monetary system can borrow by issue of instruments that are means of payment. There is no denying, either, that non-monetary intermediaries cannot create this same form of debt. They would be monetary institutions if they could do so. It is granted, too, that non-monetary intermediaries receive money and pay it out, precisely as all of us do: they use the payments mechanism.

However, each kind of non-monetary intermediary can borrow, go into debt, issue its own characteristic obligations—in short, it can create credit, though not in monetary form. Moreover, the non-monetary intermediaries are less inhibited in their own style of credit creation than are the banks in creating money. Credit creation by non-monetary intermediaries is restricted by various qualitative rules. Aside from these, the main factor that limits credit creation is the profit calculus. Credit creation by banks also is subject to the profit condition. But the monetary system is subject not only to this restraint and to a complex of qualitative rules. It is committed to a policy restraint, of avoiding excessive expansion or contraction of credit for the community's welfare, that is not imposed explicitly on non-monetary intermediaries. It is also held in check by a system

## A Reconsideration of Interest Theory

It is clear from the foregoing remarks that this way of looking at financial intermediaries leads to a reconsideration of interest theory. Yields on primary securities, the terms of borrowing available to deficit spenders, are influenced not only by the amount of primary securities in the monetary system—that is, by the supply of money—but also by the amount of these securities in non-monetary intermediaries—that is, by the supply of indirect financial assets created by these intermediaries. Suppose that savings and loan shares become more attractive relative to bank deposits, resulting in an excess supply of money. Now, if we suppose that the monetary system chooses and manages to keep the money supply constant under these circumstances, the excess supply of money will cause yields on primary securities to fall. The activities of non-monetary financial intermediaries, then, can affect primary yields. The same money supply and national income are compatible with various interest rate levels, depending upon the size of non-monetary intermediaries and upon the degree to which their issues are competitive with money.[6]

of reserve requirements. The legal reserve requirement on commercial banks is a "sharing ratio"; it apportions assets within the monetary system. The share of assets allocated to the commercial banks varies inversely with the reserve requirement. The proportion of the commercial banks' share to the share of the central bank and Treasury is the "multiple of expansion" for the commercial banking system. The "multiple of expansion" is a remarkable phenomenon not because of its inflationary implications but because it means that bank expansion is anchored, as other financial expansion is not, to a regulated base. If credit creation by banks is miraculous, creation by other financial institutions is still more a cause for exclamation.

[6] We can reach the same conclusion by looking at the supply of and the demand for primary securities. The shift in demand to savings and loan shares reduces spending units' demand for bank deposits by, say, an equivalent amount. Consequently, the demand by spending units for primary securities is unchanged at current yields. Also, there is no change in this demand by the monetary system, since we have assumed the money supply constant. However, there is an increase in demand for primary securities by savings and loan associations. So, for the economy as a whole, there is an excess demand for primary securities at current yields, which is the counterpart of the excess supply of money.

Downward pressure on primary yields is exerted as long as the indirect debt of non-monetary intermediaries is to some degree competitive with money and as long as the additional demand for primary securities by these intermediaries is roughly equivalent to their creation of indirect debt.

The analysis is only a bit more complicated when we allow for issues of primary securities and the growth of income. Let us take these one at a time. At any income level, some spending units will have deficits and others surpluses. During the income period, the deficit spenders will tend to issue primary securities in an amount equal to their aggregate deficits. Now, if the surplus spenders are willing to absorb all of the issues at current yields on these securities, there will be no tightening effect on security markets. Surplus spenders will accumulate financial assets, all in the form of primary securities, and financial intermediaries will purchase none of the issues.

But this is an unlikely outcome. Ordinarily, surplus spenders can be expected to reject some portion of the primary securities emerging at any level of income and demand indirect financial assets instead, unless their preference for the latter is suppressed by a fall in prices of primary securities and a corresponding rise in interest rates charged to deficit spenders. This incremental demand for indirect financial assets is in part a demand for portfolio diversification. The diversification demand exists because there is generally no feasible mixture of primary securities that provides adequately such distinctive qualities of indirect securities as stability of price and yield or divisibility. The incremental demand for indirect assets, however, reflects not only a negative response, a partial rejection of primary securities, but also a positive response, an attraction to the many services attached to indirect assets, such as insurance and pension services and convenience of accumulation. Part of the demand is linked to the flow of primary security issues, but another part is linked more closely to the level of income.

For these reasons, then, ordinarily some portion of the primary issues must be sold to financial intermediaries if present yields on these securities are to be defended. Assuming for the moment that the monetary system is the only financial intermediary, the increase in the money supply must be equal to the portion of primary issues that spending units choose not to accumulate at current yields. If the monetary system purchases less than this, spending units will accumulate the residual supply at rising interest rates to deficit spenders. The emergence of security issues and a diversification demand for money based on these issues means that the money supply must rise at a given income level to maintain current yields on primary securities.

Still retaining the assumption that the monetary system is the only financial intermediary, we now permit income to grow. As money income gains, spending units demand additions to their active or transactions balances of means of payment. An upward trend in money payments calls for an upward trend in balances too. The income effect also applies to contingency or precautionary balances. If spending units are increasingly prosperous in the present, they feel able to afford stronger defenses against the hazards of the future.[7]

The combination of the income and diversification effects simply means that, when income is rising, a larger share of the issues must be purchased by the monetary system to prevent a rise in primary yields. The system must supply money for both diversification and transactions, including contingency, balances.

We may now introduce non-monetary intermediaries. The growth of these intermediaries will ordinarily, to some extent, reduce the required growth of the monetary system. We have already presented the reasons for this, so it suffices to say that primary yields may be held steady under growth conditions even with a monetary system that is barely growing, provided other intermediaries take up the slack.

In summary, primary security issues depend on aggregate deficits, and the latter in turn are related to the income level. At any income level, the diversification effect of these issues means that financial intermediaries must grow to hold primary yields steady. If income is rising, too, there is an incremental demand for money and perhaps for other indirect assets for transactions and contingency balances, requiring additional intermediary growth. To the extent that the issues of non-monetary intermediaries are competitive

with money balances of whatever type, the required growth of the monetary system is reduced by the expansion of other intermediaries.

## Financial Aspects of Output Growth, 1898–1930

We turn now to the task of attaching empirical content to this theoretical structure.[8] Our period runs from about 1898 through 1930. It starts with an upturn in economic activity, following the depression of the 1890's. It then traces the especially high rate of growth in real output through 1906, the Panic of 1907 and the ensuing depression, and the continuance of output growth, at a reduced pace, from 1909 to World War I. It covers the accelerated activity of the war and postwar years and the sharp downturn in 1920–21. Finally, the homestretch of the period is characterized by fairly steady output growth, with minor setbacks in 1924 and 1927. Over the entire period, GNP in current prices rose by more than 500 per cent, while GNP in 1929 prices grew by almost 200 per cent, at an average annual rate of about 3.5 per cent.

### Primary security issues

From 1898 to 1930, the annual ratio of primary security issues to GNP in current prices averaged just a bit more than 10 per cent.[9] However, the range of fluctuation in the annual ratios was large, from about 2 to 20 per cent. During years of rapid acceleration in GNP, the ratio was relatively high, and this was especially true during the war years. During years of retarded growth, the ratio dipped below its average value, but there was no year when primary security issues were negative.

A steadier picture, then, is obtained when the years are grouped into complete cycles as Table 1 shows. Each of these subperiods of which there are nine commences with a recovery year and ends with either a recession or a depression year. These subperiods are: 1898–1900, 1901–4, 1905–8,

---

[7] For periods longer than the Keynesian short run, it is hardly safe to assume that transactions and contingency demands for additional money balances are proportional to increments in the level of money income. They may be elastic to interest rates on such primary securities as Treasury bills and brokers' loans. For any increment in money income, they may rise with real income. As a larger share of national income involves market transactions, as population moves from farms to cities, as a dollar of income is generated with more or fewer dollars of intermediate payments, as credit practices change, as checks are collected more efficiently or as deposits cease to bear interest and bear service charges instead, one expects the marginal ratio of active balances to income to vary. And incremental demand for contingency balances must be sensitive not only to income, and perhaps to interest rates, but to the evolution of emergency credit facilities, to job security and social security, to an array of circumstances that is largely irrelevant in short-period analysis.

[8] Our empirical work was made possible by Raymond W. Goldsmith's significant contributions, especially his *A Study of Saving in the United States* (Princeton, N.J.: Princeton University Press, 1955).

[9] The flow of securities is measured in issue prices. The issues are net of retirements. The average for the full period is the cumulated flow of securities divided by cumulated GNP. For the entire period, this flow was about $180 billion. In 1898, the current value of outstanding primary securities was between $35 and $40 billion.

## Table 1. Primary Security Issues and GNP
## 1898–1930, by Subperiods

*(in millions of dollars; percentages)*

|           | Total Net Issues[a] | GNP     | Ratio of Net Issues to GNP | Alternative Ratio[b] |
|-----------|---------------------|---------|----------------------------|----------------------|
| 1898–1900 | 4,731               | 50,812  | 9.3                        | 9.3                  |
| 1901–1904 | 8,603               | 86,174  | 10.0                       | 10.0                 |
| 1905–1908 | 10,117              | 110,141 | 9.2                        | 9.2                  |
| 1909–1911 | 9,126               | 98,081  | 9.3                        | 9.3                  |
| 1912–1914 | 9,557               | 109,170 | 8.8                        | 8.8                  |
| 1915–1921 | 67,595              | 479,394 | 14.1                       | 14.1                 |
| 1922–1924 | 17,197              | 244,207 | 7.0                        | 7.1                  |
| 1925–1927 | 26,497              | 282,652 | 9.4                        | 9.5                  |
| 1928–1930 | 23,196              | 291,878 | 7.9                        | 8.2                  |

[a] Unadjusted for mortgage write-downs and foreclosures
[b] Net issues adjusted for mortgage write-downs and foreclosures

1909–11, 1912–14, 1915–21, 1922–4, 1925–7, and 1928–30. In this way, nine ratios are obtained, each of which is equal to the cumulated primary issues divided by cumulated GNP during a subperiod. Leaving aside the exceptional years from 1915 to 1921, the ratios fall within the range of 7.1 per cent and 10.0 per cent with six of them between 8.8 per cent and 10.0 per cent. The "exceptional" ratio was 14.1 per cent. All in all, the series shows remarkable stability with no evidence of an upward or downward trend.[10]

### Direct and Indirect Finance

The primary security issues were directly financed through spending units or indirectly

[10] This is somewhat surprising in view of the large changes during the period in the proportion of total issues represented by each of the several types of issue. For example, at the turn of the century, mortgage issues were about 10 per cent of total issues, but the proportion grew rapidly to 25 per cent a decade later, and then to 35 per cent at the end of the period. On the other hand, consumer and other debt, mainly short-term consumer and business borrowing, moved in exactly the opposite way, from 35 per cent to about 10 per cent. United States government securities fluctuated widely as a percentage of total issues. Except for the first subperiod, the ratio was negligible to 1914. It was 33 per cent from 1915 to 1921, and then averaged over minus 10 per cent for the remainder of the period. Common and preferred stock issues, with two exceptions, were either a bit below or above 20 per cent of total issues during each subperiod. In the 1915–21 phase, the proportion was about 12 per cent, and it was 44 per cent from 1928 to 1930. State and local government securities gained relative to the others during the period while corporate and foreign bonds, if anything, lost some ground.

financed through financial intermediaries. In terms of the nine cycles the indirect finance ratio—the ratio of primary securities purchased by intermediaries to total primary issues—commenced at 56 per cent and then fell slowly and steadily with a single interruption until it reached 36 per cent in 1915–21. In the next phase, 1922–4, the ratio leaped to almost 80 per cent, and then fell to 65 per cent in 1925–7, and finally to 50 per cent in 1928–30. There were two downward sweeps in the series. The first covered the initial two decades of the period. The second, starting from a fantastically high level, covered most of the third decade. Because of this high starting-point, the indirect finance ratio was unusually high, on the average, during most of the 1920's. From 1922 to 1929, for example, the ratio averaged about 65 per cent. This compares to 47 per cent from 1898 to 1914, and 36 per cent from 1915 to 1921.

The direct finance ratio—the proportion of total issues purchased by non-financial spending units—naturally behaved in the opposite fashion. In 1898–1900 it began a long upward sweep, which carried to the subperiod 1915–21. In the following cycle, it fell to an extremely low level, and then rose during the remainder of the period. Table 2 records these trends.

The significant finding here is the steady retrogression of financial intermediation during the first two decades and its resurgence during the 1920's. The counterpart of the retrogression was the growing share of primary issues absorbed by spending units, and the counterpart of the resurgence was the relatively low share of issues absorbed by spending units.

## Table 2. Direct and Indirect Finance Ratios 1898–1930, by Subperiods

(*in percentages*)

| | DIRECT FINANCE RATIOS | | | INDIRECT FINANCE RATIOS | | |
| | Ia | IIb | IIIc | Ia | IIb | IIIc |
|---|---|---|---|---|---|---|
| 1989–1900 | 43.7 | 43.7 | 45.2 | 56.3 | 56.3 | 54.8 |
| 1901–1904 | 46.0 | 46.0 | 45.9 | 54.0 | 54.0 | 54.1 |
| 1905–1908 | 56.7 | 56.7 | 55.0 | 43.3 | 43.3 | 45.0 |
| 1909–1911 | 53.5 | 53.5 | 49.7 | 46.5 | 46.5 | 50.3 |
| 1912–1914 | 58.5 | 58.5 | 58.3 | 41.5 | 41.5 | 41.7 |
| 1915–1921 | 63.5 | 63.5 | 64.5 | 36.5 | 36.5 | 35.5 |
| 1922–1924 | 20.7 | 21.2 | 18.8 | 79.3 | 78.8 | 81.2 |
| 1925–1927 | 35.1 | 35.3 | 34.5 | 64.9 | 64.7 | 65.5 |
| 1928–1930 | 49.7 | 49.4 | 47.5 | 50.3 | 50.6 | 52.5 |

a Unadjusted for mortgage write-downs and foreclosures
b Adjusted for mortgage write-downs and foreclosures
c Above adjustment plus adjustment for foreign purchases of primary securities

### Indirect Finance and Financial Intermediaries

The principal intermediary during the period was the monetary system, including Federal Reserve Banks after 1914. Up to World War I, life insurance companies, mutual savings banks, and savings and loan associations dominated the non-monetary intermediary group. After the war, land banks, management investment companies, and federal agencies and trust funds became important.

The main responsibility for the retrogression of financial intermediation during the first two decades, or at least up to 1915, must be laid at the door of the monetary system, that is, commercial banks. In 1898–1900, the system absorbed over 40 per cent of the primary issues. By 1912–14, it was purchasing less than 25 per cent of the issues. This relatively low share was not raised during the subperiod 1915–21, even with the addition of the Federal Reserve Banks to the monetary system. However, this perhaps is not surprising in view of the abnormally heavy issues of securities during these years. But the performance of the system did not improve from 1922 to 1930, on the average, when security issues were normal relative to GNP. In fact, during these years, the average annual share of issues taken by the system fell to 21 per cent.[11]

The group of non-monetary intermediaries

[11] The share was a great deal higher than this, though from 1922 to 1924 and somewhat higher from 1925 to 1927. The system purchased only 0.2 per cent of the issues from 1928 to 1930. However, excluding the "bad" years of 1929 and 1930, the system purchased only 29 per cent of the issues (from 1922 through 1928), which is much lower than its share from 1898 to 1904.

purchased 15 per cent of total issues in 1898–1900. The share rose very slowly to 17 per cent just before the war, and then fell to 11 per cent in the face of the heavy issues of the war period. After that, the activity of these intermediaries was phenomenal. During 1922–24, their share jumped to 40 per cent, remained at about this level in the following sub-period, and then hit 50 per cent during the final three years of the period. The high indirect finance ratio during most of the 1920's, therefore, was due principally to the growth of non-monetary intermediation. These and the monetary trends are shown in Table 3.

In short, the monetary system retrogressed up to World War I and it participated very little in the resurgence of intermediation after that date.

### Direct Finance Ratios and Long-Term Yields

Our theoretical framework suggests that there should be a positive relationship between the direct finance ratio and changes in interest rates on primary securities. We should expect interest rates to rise whenever a large share of primary issues is absorbed by spending units; in the opposite case, when intermediation is heavy, we should expect falling rates.

The direct finance ratio may be a crude indicator of changes in primary yields. This may be most easily seen in terms of a simple financial growth model. Assuming that non-monetary indirect assets are competitive only with money, spending units' incremental demand for primary securities is: $e(abY - tdY)$. $abY$ is primary security issues, where $a$ is the ratio of issues to aggregate deficits of spending units, $b$ is the ratio of deficits to GNP in current prices, and $Y$ is GNP

### Table 3. Indirect Finance Ratios of Selected Intermediaries, 1898–1930, by Subperiods

(*in percentages*)

|           | Monetary System[a] | Life Insurance Companies | Mutual Savings Banks | Savings and Loan Assn's | Mngm't Invest. Co's | All Others |
|-----------|------|------|------|------|------|------|
| 1898–1900 | 41.3 | 6.7  | 7.7  | −0.8 | —    | 1.4  |
| 1901–1904 | 38.3 | 8.1  | 5.3  | 0.5  | —    | 1.8  |
| 1905–1908 | 25.6 | 9.7  | 4.2  | 1.6  | —    | 2.2  |
| 1909–1911 | 28.0 | 8.0  | 5.5  | 2.2  | —    | 2.8  |
| 1912–1914 | 24.4 | 8.2  | 4.0  | 2.7  | —    | 2.2  |
| 1915–1921 | 24.5 | 4.3  | 2.7  | 1.9  | 0.1  | 3.0  |
| 1922–1924 | 39.3 | 12.8 | 7.8  | 8.0  | 0.1  | 11.3 |
| 1925–1927 | 26.3 | 13.6 | 6.2  | 7.7  | 1.8  | 9.3  |
| 1928–1930 | 0.2  | 17.2 | 5.0  | 4.7  | 17.1 | 6.1  |

a Includes Federal Reserve banks after 1914

in current prices. $tdY$ expresses spending units' incremental demand for transactions and contingency balances. At given interest rates, spending units will desire to purchase the proportion, $e$, of the residual supply of primary securities. The remainder of the issues, $1 - e$, they will want sold to financial intermediaries so that an equivalent amount of indirect assets for diversification balances may be accumulated. Thus, $e(abY - tdY)$ is the desired incremental demand of spending units for primary securities. Interest rates will remain steady if the incremental realized supply of the securities to spending units is equal to this demand.

Now, dividing through by $abY$, we have:

Realized Direct   Desired Direct
Finance Ratio = Finance Ratio = $e - g$ (et/ab),

where $g$ is the annual growth rate of GNP. When the realized exceeds the desired ratio, interest rates will rise. When the desired ratio is the larger, interest rates will fall. If we assume that the desired ratio moves within relatively narrow limits, a high realized ratio will generally indicate upward pressure on yields, and a low realized ratio will generally mean downward pressure on yields. With this assumption, then, we can compare the realized ratio to changes in interest rates.

Before doing this, though, we should take a moment to comment on the last assumption. Is it likely that the desired ratio will move within narrow limits? The answer is almost certainly "no" when we are dealing with annual data. To begin with, as we have seen, $ab$ fluctuated between 2 per cent and 20 per cent during the period. Second, the annual growth rate of GNP was highly unstable.[12] Third, speculative demand

reflected in $e$, was undoubtedly quite high in some years and quite low in others. Finally, even annual $t$ may have been unstable. Consequently, a high realized ratio, for example, may not indicate upward pressure on interest rates because the desired ratio may be just as high or higher.

But, in some large degree, these problems disappear when we work with annual averages during complete cycles. We have previously observed that, in these terms, $ab$ was remarkably stable. In addition, fluctuations in speculative demand are likely to be smoothed out when annual data are averaged over a cycle. Moreover, the growth rate of GNP is less unstable when it is expressed as an average annual rate during a cycle, and the same is probably true of $t$. The assumption, then, that the desired ratio fluctuates within relatively narrow limits would appear to be reasonable, provided that annual averages for our subperiods are used. Nevertheless, there is nothing to prevent the desired ratio from showing an upward or downward drift over long periods of time. Our results should be checked against this possibility.

There is one more problem to straighten out. The interest rate used in this paper is the long-term yield on high-grade corporate bonds. This series, extending from 1900 to 1950, was recently compiled by W. Braddock Hickman.[13] For our period, it is probably the best series available. However, we have experimented with other long-term yields and with unweighted averages of several, and the results are substantially the same in every case. On the other hand, our results

---

[12] The first two factors may partly cancel. When $g$ is high, $ab$ tends to be high, too, and the reverse is also true.

[13] W. Braddock Hickman, *Trends and Cycles in Corporate Bond Financing*, National Bureau of Economic Research, Occasional Paper 37 (1952), pp. 34–35. The use of the series carries a disadvantage, since our initial subperiod, 1898–1900, cannot be used in the correlation analysis.

## Table 4

| | | | |
|---|---|---|---|
| 1901–1904 | +0.017 | 1915–1921 | +0.189 |
| 1905–1908 | +0.068 | 1922–1924 | −0.313 |
| 1909–1911 | −0.037 | 1925–1927 | −0.143 |
| 1912–1914 | +0.073 | 1928–1930 | +0.040 |

are much less satisfactory when short-term rates are used. There are some obvious reasons for this, and probably others not so obvious, but there is no time to explore them here.

We may now return to the heart of the matter. We have seen that the (realized) direct finance ratio,[14] starting at 44 per cent, rose almost without interruption through the sixth subperiod, 1915–21, at which time it was 64 per cent. It then fell sharply to 20 per cent, moved up to the still relatively low level of 35 per cent, and ended the period a little below 50 per cent. On the basis of these movements, we should expect growing upward (or diminishing downward) pressures on the long rate lasting through the phase 1915–21. We should then expect the rate to fall sharply in 1922–24, fall again but less sharply in 1925–27, and perhaps rise a little (or fall a little) in 1928–30.

rise in the direct finance ratio during the first two decades came in the phase 1909–11. Over the same period, the only interruption to the upward trend of interest rates also came in this phase. With this exception, each increase in rates up to the 1920's was larger than the preceding one. This conforms exactly to movements in the direct finance ratio. The sharpest fall in rates came in 1922–24, and the next sharpest in the following subperiod. Again, this is in conformity with the ratio. Finally, there was a small upward movement in yields, as we would expect, during the final years of the period.

Using the direct finance ratio as the independent variable and the average annual change in bond yield as the dependent one, the coefficient of correlation is 97.5 per cent, with a standard error of about one-tenth of 1 per cent. A direct finance

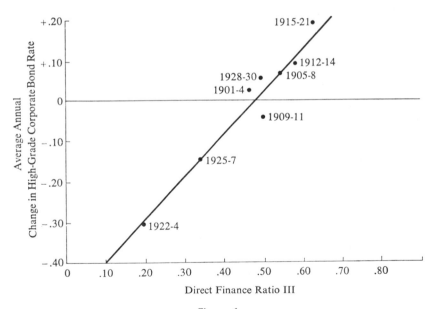

Figure 1

In a way it is embarrassing to find that the actual world is almost identical to this mental image of it. The average yearly changes in the long rate during the eight subperiods were as shown in Table 4. The sole interruption to the

ratio of 48 per cent was sufficient to hold the yield almost constant. Anything higher raised it, and anything lower reduced it. A change in the ratio of 5 percentage points changed the yield by 0.05[15] (see Figure 1).

[14] The ratio used here is corrected for net foreign purchases of primary securities (see Table 2, ratio III).

[15] The estimating equation is: average annual change in bond yield = − 0.50 + 1.04049 (direct finance ratio).

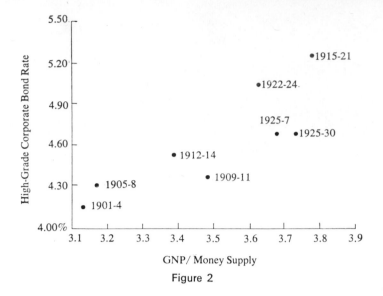

Figure 2

## Some Alternative Models

An alternative model frequently used is that which relates the income velocity of the money supply to interest rates. Aside from some basic difficulties with this model, which we have discussed elsewhere, it is not likely to be useful under growth conditions, especially when non-monetary intermediation is important. For one thing, under ordinary circumstances, the money supply has to grow relative to national income to keep interest rates stable. This is because primary security issues tend to force rates up unless a portion of the issues is sold to the monetary system. Moreover, the money supply growth required to stabilize interest rates depends

on the growth of other indirect assets that are competitive with money. If non-monetary intermediaries are growing rapidly, it is perfectly possible for money supply growth to lag behind income growth without any adverse effects on security markets.

There is a good example of this in our period, from 1922 to 1929 or 1930. In the subperiod, 1922–24, income velocity averaged 3.63. It was 3.67 in the next phase, and 3.74 from 1928 to 1930. Over these years, income velocity was higher than it was during any other phase of the full period with the exception of the war years. And yet these high and rising velocities were compatible with downward trends in interest rates over most of this decade. The reason is simply

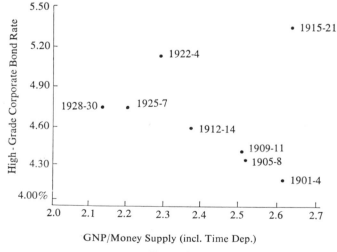

Figure 3

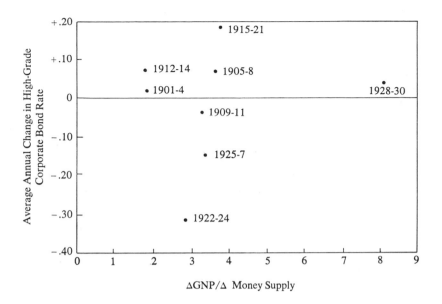

Figure 4

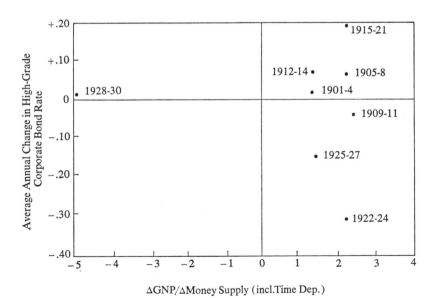

Figure 5

that non-monetary intermediaries grew so rapidly that the required growth of the monetary system was sharply reduced. Financial analysis cannot stop with the money supply when other indirect assets are of growing importance.

Nevertheless, as other investigators have discovered, there was a fairly good relationship between income velocity and interest rates during the period 1900 to 1930, in spite of the negative correlation between the two variables during most of the 1920's. But the relationship is much less impressive than the one presented above, especially when one views the 1920's as the crucial decade, the decade of rapid growth in non-monetary intermediation (see Figure 2).

The link between velocity and yields is weakened, moreover, when time deposits are included in the money supply. In fact, in this case, a negative correlation for most of the period is evident (see Figure 3). Finally, the relationship between marginal velocity and the change in yields is not very close, whether time deposits are included in or excluded from the money supply (see Figures 4 and 5).

Briefly, then, we have obtained the best results when account is taken of primary security issues and the growth of all intermediaries, including the monetary system. The two familiar variables, the money supply and national income, form only a part of the total picture.

*LAWRENCE S. RITTER*

# The Role of Money in Keynesian Theory

*9*   In recent years it has frequently been asserted, primarily by Quantity theorists, that the main characteristic of Keynesian theory is that "money does not matter."[1] The view that "money matters" is held to be the exclusive province of the Quantity theory, and extensive statistical tests are thereupon conducted to demonstrate that the supply of money has had an important influence on the level of economic activity. On this basis, Keynesian theory is, *ipso facto*, declared fallacious.

The purpose of this essay is to examine carefully the role of money in Keynesian theory, in order to evaluate the thesis that in the Keynesian system "money does not matter." It turns out that the validity of this point of view depends in

large part on which version of Keynesian theory one has in mind, just as the validity of many Keynesian criticisms of the Quantity theory depend on which version of the latter one has in mind.

## I. Keynes Without Money

The most familiar version of Keynesian economics, which we will call Model A, is the elementary simplification of Keynes in which the only determinants of the level of national income are the consumption function and a given volume of investment (including government) spending. Consumption spending is seen as depending mainly upon income, and investment spending is assumed to be given, determined autonomously. Occasionally, in order to include an accelerator effect, investment spending may also be made to depend partly upon income. Within this context, the equilibrium level of national income is found where realized income, resulting from consumption plus investment expenditures, equals anticipated income, on the basis of which spending decisions are made. Alternatively, equilibrium income is that level

[1] See, for example, Milton Friedman's statements in *Studies in the Quantity Theory of Money* (Chicago: University of Chicago Press, 1956), p. 3; *Employment, Growth, and Price Levels*, Hearings before the Joint Economic Committee, U.S. Congress, 1959, pp. 606–7; and *A Program for Monetary Stability* (New York: Fordham University Press, 1960), p. 1.

Reprinted from *Banking and Monetary Studies* Dean Carson (editor), (Chicago: Irwin, 1963) pp. 134–150, by permission of the author and publisher. Lawrence Ritter is a professor at New York University.

of income at which planned investment equals planned saving.

It is this simplified model which has been popularized by the widely known "Keynesian cross" diagram, in which either consumption and investment or saving and investment are plotted on the vertical axis, and anticipated income is plotted on the horizontal axis. Equilibrium income is determined where aggregate demand equals anticipated income or, alternatively, where planned investment equals planned saving.[2] This particular analytical system has also been the basis for the bulk of orthodox Keynesian multiplier theory: a sustained increase in autonomous spending is assumed to raise equilibrium income by a multiple of the initial increment in spending. The specific value of the multiplier is determined solely by the size of the marginal propensity to consume. Such an uncomplicated formula for the value of the multiplier can only be derived from an equally uncomplicated frame of reference, such as that outlined above.[3] For if the value of the multiplier depends solely on the size of the marginal propensity to consume, it must be assumed, implicitly or explicitly, that spending is insensitive to such increases in interest rates and tightening of credit availability as would normally accompany an expansion in income.

On the basis of this model, countless public policy recommendations, dealing almost exclusively with the implications of alternative fiscal policies, have been advanced over the years in the name of Keynesian economics. In this scheme of things, the Quantity theory's characterization of the Keynesian system as one in which "money does not matter" is quite accurate: national income is determined without any reference whatsoever to either the supply of or the demand for money, and public policy prescriptions are confined to the area of fiscal policy. Monetary policy is completely extraneous. That this model evidently commands considerable allegiance, even today, is attested to by the great

amount of attention paid in 1962 and 1963 to alternative forms of tax reduction, and to the size of the resulting budget deficit, as compared with the relative lack of interest in how such a deficit should be financed i.e. whether by monetary creation or otherwise.

## II. Keynes With Money

Although Model A is probably the most popular version of Keynesian economics, it is not the same economics to be found in Keynes' *The General Theory of Employment, Interest, and Money*. As far as Keynes himself was concerned, and as the title of his major work indicates, money plays a significant role in the determination of income and employment. Let us call the orthodox Keynesian system, as advanced in *The General Theory* and much subsequent literature, Model B.

Most important, Keynes did not assume that investment spending is exogenous, a given datum, but rather that it depends on relationships *within* the system, namely on comparisons between the expected rate of profit and the rate of interest. The rate of interest, in turn, depends on the supply of and demand for money. The demand for money, or liquidity preference, is viewed as consisting of two parts, the demand for idle money balances (with the amount demanded increasing as the rate of interest falls) and the demand for active or transaction balances (with the amount demanded increasing as the level of income rises).

In contrast to the partial Keynesian system, represented by Model A, the complete Keynesian system, Model B, requires that *two* conditions be fulfilled before income can be said to be in equilibrium. Not only must planned investment equal planned saving, as before, but in addition at any moment in time the amount of money people want to hold must equal the supply of money, the amount that is available for them to hold. If the second condition is not satisfied, the rate of interest will rise or fall, thereby altering the volume of investment and consequently changing the equilibrium level of income.[4]

[2] This has been a standard textbook diagram for well over a decade. See Paul A. Samuelson, *Economics* (5th ed.; New York: McGraw-Hill Book Co., Inc., 1961), chap. xiii, or Abba P. Lerner, *Economics of Employment* (New York: McGraw-Hill Book Co., Inc., 1951), chap. v.

[3] See Paul A. Samuelson, "The Simple Mathematics of Income Determination," in *Income, Employment, and Public Policy* (New York: W. W. Norton & Co., Inc., 1948), pp. 133–55; and L. S. Ritter, "Some Monetary Aspects of Multiplier Theory and Fiscal Policy," *Review of Economic Studies*, Vol. XXIII, No. 2 (1956), pp. 126–31.

[4] The diagrammatics of the complete Keynesian system thus are not contained in the "Keynesian cross," but rather in Hicks' *IS* and *LM* curves. See J. R. Hicks, "Mr. Keynes and the Classics: A Suggested Interpretation," *Econometrica*, Vol. V (1937), pp. 147–59, reprinted in *Readings in the Theory of Income Distribution* (Philadelphia: The Blakiston Co., 1946), pp. 461–76. Also see Alvin H. Hansen, *Monetary Theory and Fiscal Policy* (New York:

If, at a given interest rate and income, planned investment equals planned saving but the amount of money desired exceeds (falls short of) the supply, the interest rate will rise (fall), thereby reducing (increasing) investment spending and lowering (raising) the level of income. As the interest rate rises, the desired amount of idle balances contracts, and as income falls the desired amount of active balances contracts, until the amount of money demanded is reduced to the point where it is equal to the given supply. Thus, the equilibrium level of income eventually is reached, with both planned investment equal to planned saving and the demand for money equal to the supply, but the interest rate is now higher and income now lower than initially postulated.

Here there is room for monetary policy to operate: if the monetary authorities want to prevent upward pressure on the interest rate, and the consequent drop in income, they can increase the supply of money enough to satisfy the demand at the initial interest rate and income level. On the other hand, if they want to permit money income to fall, they can sit back and let nature take its course. Both of these are rather passive policies. More aggressive actions would call for increasing the money supply even more than enough to satisfy the initial demand, in order to stimulate an increase in income rather than merely prevent a decrease; or actually reducing the money supply, even though it is already less than the demand, to provide added impetus to the decline in income.

It is obvious that a policy of doing nothing is but one alternative among a spectrum of possibilities. The Federal Reserve at times seems to suggest that those changes in interest rates which occur when the central bank is passive are none of its doing. It is implied that changes in interest rates which take place when the central bank is holding the money supply constant are solely the result of "free market forces," and are in some sense preferable to changes which result from more active monetary policies. But as long as interest rates could be different if the central bank did something rather than nothing, it follows that interest rates are what they are in part because the central bank prefers them that way.

McGraw-Hill Book Co., Inc., 1949), chap. v, and his *A Guide to Keynes* (New York: McGraw-Hill Book Co., Inc., 1953), chap. vii. For a concise exposition see Joseph P. McKenna, *Aggregate Economic Analysis* (New York: Holt, Rinehart and Winston, Inc., 1955), chap. viii.

All this does not mean that the monetary authorities are omnipotent. In the orthodox Keynesian system, monetary policy is important but not always in the same degree. As a general principle, monetary policy is likely to be *less* effective the more interest-elastic the demand for idle balances (for then a change in the money supply will not succeed in altering the interest rate) and the less interest-elastic the investment and consumption schedules (for then a change in the interest rate will not induce a change in spending). This has typically been construed by most Keynesians to mean that monetary policy is likely to be less effective in combating depression than in stopping inflation. In a severe depression, the public may prefer to hold additional amounts of money at low interest rates rather than lend it out or buy securities, so that the rate of interest may reach a floor below which it will not fall; investment prospects may appear so bleak that reductions in interest rates become of negligible importance; and job prospects may appear so dismal that consumer spending on durable goods is severely inhibited, despite such additions to the public's wealth as are brought about by expanding the stock of money.

In formal Keynesian terms, during severe depressions the interest-elasticity of liquidity preference may become so great as to prevent increases in the supply of money from reducing the interest rate, as they normally would. And investment and consumer spending may become so unresponsive to changes in interest rates and in wealth as to preclude what would be expected to be their normal reactions. In terms of the equation of exchange, $MV = PT$, increases in the money supply would be offset by proportionate reductions in the velocity of money. Under such circumstances, money again "does not matter" in the Keynesian system, in the sense that increases in the money supply beyond a certain point will not affect the volume of spending, and for all practical purposes we are back in the world of Model A above.

It is important to realize, however, that severe depression is only a special case in the general Keynesian system. And even then, *decreases* in the money supply would not be looked upon as trivial. In other instances, the supply of money may be of crucial importance. From the beginning, for example, it has been a basic tenet of Keynesian doctrine that inflation cannot proceed very far without an increase in the supply of money. Rising incomes are seen as leading to larger demands for transactions balances, which in the absence of increases in the money supply must be drawn from formerly idle balances, inducing a rise in interest rates. This process can continue until idle balances are depleted, or perhaps somewhat further if there is some interest-elasticity in the demand for active balances at high interest rates. But, unless the money supply is increased, the expansion in spending is viewed as having to grind to a halt before too long, because rising interest rates and tightening monetary conditions in general will sooner or later choke off investment spending.[5] Indeed, so strongly has this position been held by some orthodox Keynesians that they have at times objected to the use of monetary policy to stop inflation because of the fear that it is likely to be *too* effective.[6] In brief, in the orthodox Keynesian system sometimes the supply of money is not very important, sometimes it is critically important, and most of the time it is somewhere in between, depending in each instance on the circumstances at hand.

It is rather ironic that Keynes should be the target of a blanket charge by Quantity theorists that he is responsible for propagating the view that "money does not matter." For in Keynes' own mind he was enlarging the scope of monetary theory, not narrowing it.[7] Before Keynes prevailing monetary theory in the form of the Quantity theory of money had been concerned almost exclusively with the determination of the general level of prices, to the neglect of the influence of money on real output and employment. As expressed by Jean Bodin in 1569, through John Locke, David Hume, David Ricardo, John Stuart Mill, and Irving Fisher, the Quantity theory had always stressed that the supply of money determined primarily the absolute price level. The velocity of money was

held to be an institutional datum and aggregate real output was assumed at the full employment level by virtue of Say's Law. In terms of the equation of exchange, $MV = PT$, $V$ and $T$ were assumed to be given so that changes in the money supply would result in proportionate changes in prices.[8]

The policy implications of the pre-Keynesian Quantity theory were simple and paralyzing. Increases in the supply of money, even in periods of substantial unemployment, could never achieve any permanent benefit. They could only be harmful, by raising prices proportionately—a view that is deeply imbedded in popular folklore to this day. It is this framework, rather than the Keynesian, which in a fundamental sense views money as unimportant. Here money is seen as "neutral," a veil behind which "real" forces work themselves out just about as they would in the absence of money. In the Keynesian approach, on the other hand, money also plays a role in the determination of real output. For the first time money becomes more than merely a veil, and a monetary economy is seen as behaving very differently from a barter economy.

## III. New Departures

Model C is a lineal descendant of Model B, but comes to rather different conclusions. Although Model C uses most of the orthodox Keynesian apparatus, it is so unorthodox in its handling of selected parts of that apparatus as to make it debatable whether it should be classified as a version of Keynesian theory. Perhaps it should be given a category of its own and called Radcliffism, since it has been most closely associated with the work of the Radcliffe Committee and Professors Gurley and Shaw.[9] In any case, in this model changes in

5 "A rise in prices and incomes leads to an increase in requirements for money balances in active circulation. This tends to reduce the amount available for inactive balances and so causes the rate of interest to rise, which checks investment. The rope which holds the value of money is a limitation on its supply. If the monetary authorities are compelled to increase the supply of money, the rope frays and snaps in their hands." Joan Robinson, *Essays in the Theory of Employment* (Macmillan, 1937), pp. 17–21 (spliced quotation). Also see J. R. Hicks, *op. cit.*, p. 470.

6 See Alvin H. Hansen, *Monetary Theory and Fiscal Policy*, pp. 161–63. For a closely related view see Keynes, *op. cit.*, pp. 322–23.

7 See *The General Theory*, Preface, chap. xvii, and pp. 292–94. On this point see also Dudley Dillard, "The Theory of a Monetary Economy," in Kenneth Kurihara (ed.), *Post-Keynesian Economics* (New Brunswick, N.J.: Rutgers University Press, 1954), pp. 3–30.

8 As expressed by Irving Fisher, in the most widely accepted pre-Keynesian statement of the Quantity theory: "Since a doubling in the quantity of money will not appreciably affect either the velocity of circulation or the volume of trade, it follows necessarily and mathematically that the level of prices must double. There is no possible escape from the conclusion that a change in the quantity of money must normally cause a proportional change in the price level." Irving Fisher, *The Purchasing Power of Money* (Macmillan, 1911), pp. 156–57 (spliced quotation).

9 *Report* of the Committee on the Working of the Monetary System (London, 1959), and J. G. Gurley and E. S. Shaw, *Money in a Theory of Finance* (Washington, D.C.: The Brookings Institution, 1960). See also J. G. Gurley, *Liquidity and Financial Institutions in the Postwar Economy*, Study Paper 14, Joint

the money supply are seen as no more likely to be effective against inflation than they were against depression in Model B!

The analysis of Model C differs from both previous models in that it does not ignore the liquidity preference function, as A does, nor does it stress the significance of its interest-elasticity, as B does. Rather than being ignored, the liquidity preference function is an integral part of Model C, *but the demand for liquidity is no longer viewed as identical with the demand for money*. And rather than stressing the importance of the interest-elasticity of the demand schedule for money, attention is directed instead to the likelihood of *shifts* in that schedule. While the orthodox Keynesian literature has a great deal to say about shifts in the investment demand function, through the influence of changes in expectations, it tends to ignore the possibility of shifts in the demand for money, and instead concentrates almost exclusively on its interest-elasticity.

In the orthodox Keynesian system, Model B, the demand for liquidity is synonymous with the demand for money. The ready availability of interest-yielding money substitutes, however, destroys that equation. Such near monies as time deposits, savings and loan shares, and Treasury bills are virtually as liquid as cash and in addition yield an interest return. Thus, the demand for money (demand deposits plus currency) may contract even though the demand for liquidity broadly conceived remains stable. Liquidity preference, in other words, may be satisfied partially by holdings of money substitutes in place of money itself.

There are two reasons for the demand for money in the orthodox Keynesian system. In the first place, active money balances are needed for transactions purposes. The demand for active balances is assumed to bear a more or less constant ratio to income, so that an expansion in income will lead to a proportionate increase in the amount of active balances desired. In the second place, idle cash is demanded because of uncertainties regarding the future course of interest rates. Idle cash is held primarily because of the fear that interest rates might rise (bond prices fall), imposing capital losses on bondholders. This is the main reason why Keynes

believed that the amount of idle cash desired would increase as the rate of interest falls.[10] The lower the rate of interest, the more it is likely to drop below what are considered "safe" or "normal" levels, leading to the expectation that its future course is likely to be upward, with consequent losses in capital values. Under such circumstances, it is prudent to get out of bonds and into a more liquid asset. In *The General Theory* the only liquid asset available is cash.

The existence of short-term money substitutes, however, provides an alternative to holding money for both of these purposes. With respect to *active* balances, there is no reason to assume that these need be held solely in the form of money. For immediate transactions purposes, there is little alternative to possessing the medium of exchange itself. But for payments scheduled for several months in the future, there are many assets available which can serve as a substitute for holding cash without diminishing liquidity, and which at the same time provide an interest income. Firms with scheduled payments to make at particular dates in the future can hold Treasury bills, sales finance company paper, or repurchase agreements with government securities dealers, for example—all of which can easily be arranged to come due when the cash is needed. The very purpose of tax anticipation bills is to fill just such a need. Similarly, households can hold time deposits, paying interest from date of deposit to date of withdrawal, pending anticipated payments. For possible emergencies, lines of credit can be arranged on a standby basis in place of holding idle cash.

Many other methods exist through which both households and business firms can economize on their average holdings of transactions cash without impairing their liquidity positions. Indeed, there is ample evidence that high short-term interest rates in the postwar period have stimulated the expenditure of considerable ingenuity in the economical management of cash balances, with consequent reductions in the required ratio of active money balances to income. To the extent that this is accomplished, an expansion in income will not lead to a proportionate increase in the amount of transactions cash desired.

With respect to *idle* balances, the existence of short-term money substitutes also provides an alternative to holding cash when it is feared

Economic Committee, U.S. Congress (1960); R. S. Sayers, "Monetary Thought and Monetary Policy in England," *Economic Journal*, Vol. LXX, No. 280 (December, 1960), pp. 710–24; and A. B. Cramp, "Two Views on Money," *Lloyds Bank Review*, No. 65 (July, 1962), pp. 1–15.

[10] See *General Theory*, pp. 201–2. Also see Day and Beza, *Money and Income* (New York: Oxford University Press, Inc., 1960), pp. 17–20.

that long-term interest rates might rise (bond prices fall). If it is thought that long-term rates are too low (bond prices too high) for safety, investors need not increase their holdings of idle cash to get liquidity, but instead can purchase Treasury bills or other interest-bearing liquid assets. With highly liquid money substitutes, the concept of a "safe" yield level is almost meaningless and the chance of suffering a capital loss close to nil; indeed, the very definition of a liquid asset is one which can be turned into cash on short notice with little or no loss in dollar value.

The concept of a "safe" yield level is crucial in decisions as to whether or not to buy *long-term* securities, because the existence of uncertainty regarding future long rates gives rise to the fear of taking substantial capital losses (or the hope of making capital gains). But the rationale behind buying *short-term* liquid assets is that if yields rise no loss need be suffered. The securities will mature shortly anyway, and thereby turn into cash at their face value. And, in any event, even if one has no choice but to dispose of them before maturity, the resulting capital losses (or gains) are likely to be small. Unlike long-terms, a rather large change in yields on short-term instruments involves but a small change in their price.[11]

In brief, the amount of money desired may not increase when the rate of interest falls, even though the amount of liquidity desired does increase. At least part of the accumulation of

[11] A rise in yields from 4 per cent to 5 per cent on a $1,000 face value 30-year bond bearing a 4 per cent coupon involves a fall in price from $1,000 to $845. A similar rise in yield on a 3-month security of similar coupon involves a fall in price from $1,000 to only $997.

The point can be made even more dramatically. Assume, not too unrealistically, that at the extreme long-term yields on government securities might be expected to vary between 2 per cent and 6 per cent in the forseeable future, and short-term yields between 1 per cent and 7 per cent. The holder of a $1,000 30-year bond bearing a 4 per cent coupon might then anticipate, at the extreme, that its price might possibly vary between the limits of $723 and $1,450. For a 3-month security of similar coupon, however, the possible range of price variation would be only from $992 to $1,008. In one case possible range of price variation is $727 on a $1,000 security, and in the other case it is only $16. Safety of principal is tenuous in the former, and practically assured in the latter.

These figures can be calculated from any bond basis book. See also Burton G. Malkiel, "Expectations, Bond Prices, and the Term Structure of Interest Rates," *Quarterly Journal of Economics*, Vol. LXXVI, No. 2 (May, 1962), pp. 197–218.

liquidity is likely to take the form of interest-bearing near monies instead of nonearning cash. In comparison with Model B, the demand for idle cash balances will have contracted throughout the range of interest rates, even though the liquidity preference function may have remained stable. Under these circumstances, with both segments of the demand for money susceptible to leftward shifts, monetary policies confined to regulating the supply of money are not likely to be as successful in stemming inflation as orthodox Keynesian theory believes. Since the significant variable is not the supply of money, per se, but rather the supply relative to the demand, the flexibility of demand makes control of the supply, alone, an unreliable instrument through which to affect the level of economic activity. These results do not depend, as in orthodox Keynesian theory, on the short-run interest-elasticity of the demand for money, but rather on shifts in that demand.

In Model B, for example, if the economy is initially in equilibrium, with planned investment equal to planned saving and the demand for money equal to the supply, an exogenous increase in spending will raise money income and increase the amount of transactions cash desired proportionately. Limitation of the money supply—holding it constant—will then automatically result in an excess demand for money, which will raise interest rates, check investment, and thereby bring the expansion in income to a halt. There will probably be some slippage, as the rise in interest rates attracts some funds out of idle cash holdings into transactions balances, with the degree of slippage depending on the interest-elasticity of the demand for idle balances and the specific ratio between active cash and income. But that same rise in interest rates, and the related tightening of monetary conditions in general, will tend to discourage some expenditures. In any event, sooner or later idle balances will be depleted. If the monetary authorities want to accelerate the process, they can provide added impetus by actually reducing the money supply rather than merely holding it stable.

In the world envisaged by Model C, on the other hand, these results are not as likely to be realized. If the required ratio of transactions cash to income contracts as income rises, the expansion in income will not lead to a proportionate increase in the amount of active cash desired. It may not even lead to an absolute increase. Limitation of the money supply then may not produce very much of an excess demand for money, so that upward pressure on interest rates will be negligible, investment will not be checked, and the rise in spending will proceed unhindered. If, at the same time, the demand for idle balances has also shifted to the left, then—regardless of its interest-elasticity—formerly idle balances will become available for transactions use, again with minimal increases in interest rates. Instead of an excess demand for money, there might conceivably be an excess supply, with consequent *downward* pressure on interest rates. Even if the monetary authorities were to actually reduce the supply of money, they might be hard put to keep pace with the contraction in demand. And although idle balances must sooner or later be depleted, this will pose no obstacle to the continued rise in spending if the desired active cash to income ratio continues to contract.

Of course, the process need not be this straightforward. Models B and C need not be mutually exclusive, but may be combined over several cycles. Interest rates may indeed rise during periods of cyclical expansion, especially if the expansion is vigorous, as spending increases more rapidly than can be accommodated by contractions in the demand schedules for money. However, rising interest rates are likely to stimulate new financial techniques for economizing on cash balances.[12] These techniques for cash management, introduced during periods of tight money, are not likely to be abandoned when rates recede in the subsequent recession. As a result, the contraction in the demand for money may not be clearly evident until the *next* upturn in business conditions. When that upturn comes, the supply of money may be more than ample to finance it, even though, by past standards, it would appear to be less than adequate. In effect, liquidity is accumulated during the recession, in the form of money substitutes instead of money, and is then released when needed to finance expenditures when economic activity revives.

Presumably, the central bank could always reduce the money supply drastically enough to counteract the decline in the demand for money, and thereby produce the results it wants. But with business prospects cloudy, as they generally

are, and with past guidelines unreliable indicators of the current adequacy of the money supply, the monetary authorities are usually not sure enough of where they stand to take decisive action in *any* direction. This inaction is then rationalized by the invocation of moral principles, as ethical values are attributed to the determination of interest rates by "free market forces" and to "minimum intervention" in general.

It is for these reasons that Model C shifts attention away from the money supply narrowly defined to the significance of liquidity broadly conceived. Traditional monetary policy, which is confined to the control of the money supply, is seen as having to give way to a more broadly based liquidity policy if it is to successfully influence economic activity within the context of the present-day financial environment.[13] It is thus Radcliffe monetary theory, rather than orthodox Keynesian theory, which poses the most fundamental challenge to the modern Quantity theory of money.

## IV. Summary and Conclusions

The differences between orthodox Keynesian theory (Model B), Radcliffe theory (Model C), and the modern Quantity theory of money can be summarized most conveniently in terms of their implications for the behavior of velocity. This simultaneously affords a comparison of their respective evaluations of the effectiveness of monetary policy. For if monetary policy is to be effective—i.e., if changes in the money supply are to produce changes in aggregate spending, and thus in income—then velocity must either remain more or less stable or else move in the same direction as the money supply.

If the phrase "money matters" is to have any operational meaning, it must imply the existence of such conditions. In terms of the equation of exchange, if changes in $M$ are to produce changes in $MV$ and thus in $PT$, then $V$ must necessarily remain rather stable or else reinforce the change in $M$. On the other hand, to the extent that velocity falls when the money supply is increased, or rises when the money supply is decreased, or changes in the absence of changes in the money supply, the effectiveness of monetary policy is

[12] See Hyman P. Minsky, "Central Banking and Money Market Changes," *Quarterly Journal of Economics*, Vol. LXXI, No. 2 (May, 1957), pp. 171–87; and L. S. Ritter, "The Structure of Financial Markets, Income Velocity, and the Effectiveness of Monetary Policy," *Schweizerische Zeitschrift für Volkswirtschaft und Statistik*, Vol. XCVIII, No. 3 (September, 1962), pp. 276–89.

[13] In the words of the Radcliffe Report (paragraph 981, p. 337): "The factor which monetary policy should seek to influence or control is something that reaches far beyond what is known as 'the supply of money.' It is nothing less than the state of liquidity of the whole economy."

correspondingly reduced. If these offsetting changes in velocity are so great that the influence of monetary policy is negligible, then "money does not matter." In between these two extremes lies a continuum of possibilities.

It should be noted that the modern Quantity theory is not precisely the same as the pre-Keynesian Quantity theory. As presented by Milton Friedman, the present-day version of the Quantity theory is no longer strictly an explanation of what determines the price level. Friedman uses the Quantity theory to explain major depressions as well as inflations, so that it is now, like the Keynesian approach, essentially a theory of income determination.[14]

In addition, Friedman accepts variations in velocity as consistent with the Quantity theory. Unlike Irving Fisher, Friedman does not view velocity as an institutional datum, nor as a numerical constant, but rather as a functional relationship in which the demand for money is a function of a number of variables within the system, such as interest rates, income, wealth, and expected changes in the price level. Depending on movements in these variables, velocity may vary both cyclically and secularly. This also represents a major shift in emphasis by the Quantity theory in the direction of the Keynesian approach, wherein velocity has *always* been functionally related to such variables.

Nevertheless, the two are still rather far apart. In Friedman's view, under normal circumstances the demand-for-money function is so stable and inelastic that such changes in velocity as do occur will not be very bothersome. Velocity may fall somewhat when the money supply is increased, or rise somewhat when the money supply is decreased, or even change to some extent in the absence of changes in the money supply so as to produce minor fluctuations in income despite stability in the stock of money. But these changes in velocity are assumed to be small. Velocity is no longer seen as constant, but it *is* seen as

fluctuating only very moderately.[15] Thus, changes in velocity are not likely to appreciably offset changes in the money supply, and major fluctuations in income are not likely to take place in the absence of major fluctuations in the stock of money. As a result, the modern Quantity theory views monetary policy as highly effective. Aside from minor short-run fluctuations in income, monetary policy is seen as both necessary *and sufficient* for the attainment of economic stability.

Radcliffe monetary theory, on the other hand, looks upon monetary policy in a rather different light: "Though we do not regard the supply of money as an unimportant quantity, we view it as only part of the wider structure of liquidity in the economy. It is the whole liquidity position that is relevant to spending decisions, and our interest in the supply of money is due to its significance in the whole liquidity picture. The fact that spending is not limited by the amount of money in existence is sometimes argued by reference to the velocity of money. It is possible, for example, to demonstrate statistically that during the last few years the volume of spending has greatly increased while the supply of money has hardly changed: the velocity of money has increased. We have not made more use of this concept because we cannot find any reason for supposing, or any experience in monetary history indicating, that there is any limit to velocity."[16]

---

[14] In terms of the equation of exchange, $T$ is no longer assumed as given by virtue of Say's Law, so that changes in the supply of money can affect output and employment as well as the price level. See Milton Friedman, "The Quantity Theory of Money—A Restatement," in *Studies in the Quantity Theory of Money*, and Chapter 1 in *A Program for Monetary Stability*. Friedman prefers to view the Quantity theory as a theory of the demand for money rather than a theory of income determination, with the addition of the supply of money necessary before income can be determined. However, this is a purely semantic matter. In the same sense, neither is orthodox Keynesian theory a theory of income determination until the supply of money is given.

[15] In Friedman's words: "It is, of course, true that velocity varies over short periods of time. The fact of the matter, however, is that these variations are in general relatively small." *Monetary Policy and Management of the Public Debt*, Hearings before the Joint Economic Committee, U.S. Congress, 1952, p. 720. From the same source, p. 743: "Income velocity is a reasonably stable magnitude. It has been declining over the last century . . . however, the decline appears to have been rather gradual, and income velocity is relatively stable over short periods." From *Studies in the Quantity Theory of Money* (p. 21): "There is an extraordinary empirical stability and regularity to such magnitudes as income velocity that cannot but impress anyone who works extensively with monetary data. This very stability and regularity contributed to the downfall of the Quantity theory, for it was overstated and expressed in unduly simple form. The numerical value of velocity itself, whether income or transactions, was treated as a natural 'constant.' Now this it is not; and its failure to be so, first during and after World War I and then, to a lesser extent, after the crash of 1929, helped greatly to foster the reaction against the Quantity theory. The studies in this volume are premised on a stability and regularity in monetary relations of a more sophisticated form than a numerically constant velocity."

[16] Radcliffe, *Report*, pp. 132–33.

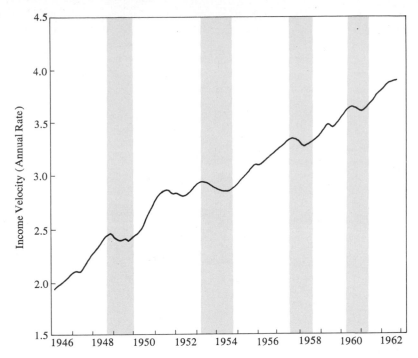

Figure 1. Income Velocity, Quarterly, 1946–62. (Income velocity is the quotient of gross national product divided by the average money supply over the period, both seasonally adjusted. The money supply is defined as demand deposits, adjusted, plus currency outside banks. Shaded areas indicate periods of recession in general business conditions.)

While the Quantity theory views traditional monetary policy as both necessary and sufficient, and Radcliffe views it as too narrowly conceived to be of much use, Keynesian theory lies in between these two extremes. Sometimes changes in velocity are seen as nullifying changes in the money supply, sometimes they are seen as reinforcing,[17] and most of the time they are seen as somewhere in between. The crucial determinants of the behavior of velocity in the orthodox Keynesian system are the interest and wealth-elasticities of the spending and liquidity preference functions, and these are likely to vary depending on the particular historical, institutional, and expectational circumstances at hand. Since velocity is not something the monetary authorities can depend upon, in the sense of being able to reliably anticipate its behavior,

monetary policy emerges from the Keynesian system as usually necessary but rarely sufficient for the attainment of national economic objectives.

Although it is not the purpose of this paper to evaluate the implications of the empirical evidence, a brief look, in closing, at the postwar movements in velocity would not be inappropriate. As Figure 1 indicates, velocity has fluctuated between an annual rate of 1.93 in the first quarter of 1946 and 3.87 in the fourth quarter of 1962.[18] Over the period as a whole, velocity has shown a marked upward trend, with fluctuations about that trend coinciding with cyclical fluctuations in general business conditions. Each cyclical peak in velocity has typically been accompanied by rising interest rates and other signs of monetary stringency, leading observers to believe that velocity could not rise much further, that it was close to its

[17] "In conditions like those of the last decade, it seems unwise to expect that induced changes in $V$ will largely undo the effects of central bank operations; at times they could be reinforcing. The Radcliffe Report seems to me to give misleading impressions in this regard, whatever its other merits." Paul A. Samuelson, "Reflections on Monetary Policy," *Review of Economics and Statistics*, Vol. XLII, No. 3 (August, 1960), pp. 268.

[18] In the first quarter of 1963, the latest data available at the time of writing, velocity reached a post-1929 high of 3.88. It should be noted that with our present money supply of about $150 billion, even so small an absolute change in velocity as 0.1 would correspond to a change in gross national product of $15 billion.

upper limit.[19] But then, after a slight decline during recession periods, velocity has promptly resumed its upward climb as soon as business conditions have turned up again. Not only has velocity risen to successively higher peaks from cycle to cycle, but in each period of business recovery it has equaled or exceeded its prior-cycle peak *within only two quarters* after recovery has begun.

How much higher can velocity rise? Recent levels of velocity, approaching a turnover rate of 4 times per annum, are comparable to previous peaks of 4 reached in 1919 and again in 1929. This has once again revived speculation that velocity is approaching its upper limit. However,

as of late 1962 and early 1963, liquidity has appeared to be ample throughout the economy, no upward pressure has been evident on interest rates, and the money and capital markets have been characterized more by ease than by tightness. There is thus less evidence today that velocity is approaching a ceiling than there was six years ago, when velocity was around 3.3. Recent increases in velocity would appear to stem from a decrease in the demand for money, rather than a scarcity of supply, indicating that there is probably considerable room for further advance still remaining.

The "extraordinary empirical stability" that Quantity theorists find in the behavior of velocity is revealed only to the disciples. But whether the Radcliffe Report is correct, that for all practical purposes velocity has no upper limit whatsoever, remains to be seen.

---

[19] See, for example, L. S. Ritter, "Income Velocity and Anti-Inflationary Monetary Policy," *American Economic Review*, Vol. XLIX, No. 1 (March, 1959), pp. 120–29.

*H. LAURENCE MILLER, JR.*

# On "Liquidity" and "Transaction Costs"[1]

*10* The term "liquidity" appears constantly in the literature. Yet, as Johnson notes in his recent survey of monetary theory and policy, the term is "slippery and ill-defined."[2] A less pronounced but somewhat similar situation prevails in the case of "transaction costs." This paper attempts to clarify the concept of liquidity in one basic sense while investigating the relationship between the two phenomena. In many respects it simply reexamines and reorganizes ideas already present somewhere in the literature with the aim of eliminating irrelevancies. But some of the ideas advanced—including the fact that the time element in liquidity is "comparable to and reflects" transaction cost—are believed to be new.

## Various Usages and Definitions of "Liquidity"

It is sometimes said that liquid means "easily cashable" or something equivalent. Any asset is immediately convertible to cash, of course, if the owner is in contact with anyone who will pay any price above zero for the item. "Easily converted to cash" may be regarded as a (possibly confusing) short cut.

In the *Treatise on Money*, Keynes takes liquid to mean "more certainly realizable at short notice without loss." In a recent examination of Keynes' definition, Hicks suggests that the "without loss" could refer to the loss suffered in buying and selling, but that the time it takes to sell an item is a more relevant characteristic. He then argues that the quality of being convertible at short notice at a price that is high relative to the one attainable in a longer period constitutes

[1] I am indebted to Armen A. Alchian for some stimulating suggestions and criticisms of ideas advanced in conversations. He bears no responsibility for the result. Acknowledgment is gratefully made to the Division of Research, Graduate School of Business Administration, U.C.L.A., for research support. I have made some minor stylistic alterations and added footnotes 10 and 15 to include some references to newer material, while leaving the basic discussion unchanged. Harold Demsetz has done some excellent work recently on property rights and transaction costs. See, especially, his forthcoming paper, "The Costs of Transacting," which will appear in the *Quarterly Journal of Economics*.

[2] H. G. Johnson, "Monetary Theory and Policy," *American Economc Review*, June 1962, p. 348.

This is a revised version of an article by the same title which initially appeared in the *Southern Economic Journal*, Vol. XXXII (1965), pp. 43–48, reprinted by permission of the author and publisher. H. Laurence Miller, Jr., is a professor at Carleton College.

"marketability" rather than "liquidity." Liquidity is something possessed only by those marketable assets (if I understand his discussion) whose value is relatively certain with no possibility of highly unfavorable outcomes, this last being what is meant by "without loss."[3] There is no point in disputing word usage. But many economists clearly do not rule out degrees of marketability and include some of the other factors in discussing liquidity as a characteristic of assets. Thus, writers like Marschak and Patinkin treat "having non-zero transaction cost" and "illiquid" as equivalent terms, where transaction cost refers to the cost of effecting exchanges.[4] Similarly, Bronfenbrenner treated liquidity some years ago as a function of the three factors: fraction of cost lost in buying and subsequently selling, the time element, and relative certainty of value, or price stability.[5] The often used term "reversibility" presumably includes the last as well as the first of these three characteristics.

"Liquidity" is utilized in some fundamentally different, though related, senses than the one so far at issue. As everyone knows, it is used to designate a variable influencing spending, liquidity being supplied by some roughly defined entity identified as "liquid assets." That the Radcliffe Committee Report makes liquidity in this sense the crucial monetary variable is also well known. And, the term is employed to designate relative liquidity or safety, a state or situation relative to certain risks, as assessed by the quick asset test, the current ratio, and such.

More usages, and variations on the ones already presented, could perhaps be cited,[6] but adequate attention has been directed to the diversity and character of present practice. What follows will be almost exclusively concerned with

liquidity as a descriptive characteristic of assets and its relationship to transaction costs. Clarification of this subject is desirable in itself and a first step toward clarification of the liquidity concept in all of its usages.

## Liquidity and the Cost of Effecting Exchanges Rapidly

In considering the results of buying and subsequently selling an asset, a number of matters merit attention.[7] Three have already been noted: (1) the cost of effecting exchanges, or of finding sellers and buyers, (2) how rapidly one can obtain a good price—$100,000 in Treasury bills and a building "worth $100,000" may both be immediately convertible to cash, but it usually takes longer to sell a building than a Treasury bill at a price that is high relative to the one obtainabie after a period of time—and (3) the probability of obtaining various prices for the asset given the expenditures and search undertaken. When considering all possible assets, other matters can also be relevant. In selling a building, some preparation cost, for example, paint for the building, may be economic, but this can be ignored here. It is also worth observing, perhaps, that irreversibility can result from more than the already noted costs if certain kinds of assets (seldom or never held to satisfy "the demand for liquidity") are considered. Assets like a specialized machine or painting bought for the top price which are worth more to the buyer than they are worth to others illustrate the point.

Now let us look carefully at the time element in liquidity (or at marketability?). Consider someone putting a building up for sale. The seller may very well think in terms of having to wait for a while for the top buyer or a reasonably good buyer to come along, and expect that he will have to wait longer on the average for a high price than a low price. But why does it take longer to realize a relatively high price for some assets than others, for example, buildings as compared to Treasury bills? There are two ways of responding to this question.

The existence or non-existence of highly organized markets for the asset obviously explains a large part of the difference. Then, for any given set of institutions, several factors influence the rapidity with which one can sell at a good price. Legal obstacles work against easy liquidation. Observance of "business hours" has

[3] J. R. Hicks, "Liquidity," *Economics Journal*, December 1962, pp. 787–802. See esp., p. 790.

[4] J. Marschak, "The Rationale of the Demand for Money and of 'Money Illusion,' " *Metroeconomica*, August 1950, pp. 87–100. Patinkin intoduces liquidity for bonds by allowing them to be used for payments at the cost of "certain unspecified inconveniences." (D. Patinkin, *Money, Interest, and Prices* [Evanston, Ill.: Row Peterson and Co., 1956], p. 80).

[5] M. Bronfenbrenner, "Some Fundamentals in Liquidity Theory," *Quarterly Journal of Economics*, May 1945, pp. 405–26. Bronfenbrenner's development of the subject is not easily summarized. It suffices to note that Bronfenbrenner includes deflated values in the formulation, and to refer the interested reader to the paper itself.

[6] E.g., some interesting but, I think, unsuccessful definitions are advanced by W. T. Newlyn in *Theory of Money* (Oxford: Clarendon Press, 1962), pp. 119–32.

[7] For a complementary list see *ibid.*, pp. 51–55.

a similar consequence. And it necessarily takes time to search out prospective buyers or sellers.

In a different vein, the answer is that—though some finite amount of time is required to effect any activity—beyond this, it does not have to take longer. A sufficient expenditure of resources would always put the seller in touch almost at once with all potential buyers. The "reason" it takes longer to realize a good price for some assets is that it is economic to do so.

It is important to understand that time can be overcome for a price. It can be bought by selling the asset to a lower price buyer, by selling to someone who will take the time to find a better buyer, or by expending resources to overcome time as just suggested. Thus, not only is any loss on the same footing as searching expenditures in reducing net worth of the seller, any time loss is suffered *because* it would be even costlier to spend resources to find buyers more rapidly.

In general, "time is valuable" in at least three senses or contexts. It is valuable in the time preference sense (the Böhm Bawerk-Fisher value of time). It is valuable in situations where getting something rapidly is more important than it usually is. I am concerned with this commonplace of business here only in connection with liquidity. Finally, one's time is itself a scarce resource with alternative uses. As is noted below, the fact that nothing can be accomplished in zero time, i.e., that some costly time must be utilized in all activities, is a fundamental factor underlying transaction costs.[8]

Whether the best action is to sell to an accessible buyer, to sell to someone who will take the time to find a better buyer, or to spend more in an effort to find a good buyer, one can estimate (1) the cost that will be incurred in acquiring and disposing of the asset—or simply of disposing of it, if viewed after the fact of purchase—when there is no time pressure, and (2) the additional loss that would be suffered when time is

crucial. The sum would account in an operational manner[9] for all elements in the discussion other than uncertainty or price stability. And assets could be ranked on the basis of the ratio of this sum to price (or a related measure). Of course, the cost depends upon the time allowed for liquidation, and could vary with economic conditions. The time cost might be greater in a depression than in a prosperous period. These facts can be ignored as relatively less significant matters which could be formally dealt with at the cost of greater complexity.

That the cost of selling rapidly is an important descriptive characteristic of assets, and a key matter to consider in assessing "liquidity" in one relevant sense, is surely beyond argument. Hicks makes "perfect marketability" a necessary condition for liquidity. Our practice combines the reversibility element associated with transaction costs and marketability to form one characteristic which, in turn, is a matter of degree.[10] Moreover, it is evident that in many contexts low liquidation cost is all that is meant by liquidity, that a highly marketable government security and a highly marketable equity would be said to be equally liquid. But it is an almost universal—and, obviously relevant—practice to include relative certainty of value or price stability (Hicks emphasizes absence of quite unfavorable outcomes) in the concept as well. This leaves an unresolved problem. If one says that assets are liquid only if they have both low liquidation cost, which reduces expected value, and little uncertainty in terms of money prices, liquid assets resemble money in both respects. But no one has suggested a satisfactory way as yet to rank two assets' liquidity, defined in this fashion, if one is superior on one

[8] The role time plays in transaction costs is emphasized in J. C. Gilbert, "The Demand for Money: The Development of an Economic Concept," *Journal of Political Economy*, April 1953, esp. pp. 147, 149–54. Gilbert's interesting paper relates a positive demand for money (including bank savings deposits) to the presence of one or both of two fundamental factors (only): the fact that human action takes time, which introduces transaction costs, and uncertainty about future rates of interest. An as yet unpublished paper by Gary Becker examines the mostly neglected area of the economics of time in consumption (e.g. leisurely as opposed to less leisurely dinners) and other behavior.

[9] The distinction being made here between searching plus time cost, or transaction cost in the broadest sense, on the one hand, and relative certainty of value, on the other, is not completely satisfactory, since it neglects uncertainty associated with searching endeavors. In a pathbreaking paper, Stigler explicitly allows for this uncertainty in looking into the question of how much searching of the present set of buyers is economic ("The Economics of Information," *Journal of Political Economy*, June 1961, pp. 213–25, esp. pp. 214–19).

[10] In the paper on transaction costs cited earlier, Demsetz tests a number of hypotheses with data on ask-bid spreads in New York Stock Exchange transactions (the study gives less attention to brokerage commissions). All of the securities included in his samples—even those not traded on certain days—are highly liquid in this sense, with zero or close to zero time loss. They thus (presumably) meet Hicks's requirement of perfect marketability, but differ in brokerage commission and ask-bid spread. How and why? Demsetz's paper addresses itself to this question.

count and the other is superior on the second. Money is the perfectly liquid asset in both respects relative to claims payable in money. But money cannot be "sold" for a car at once on the best possible terms. Nor is its value certain in terms of goods.

It is worth observing that, in principle, low non-time cost might counterbalance high time cost to make an asset relatively liquid. Also worth notice is the fact that a time loss is suffered only when liquidation is not anticipated at a point in time sufficiently prior to the desire for cash. Some liquid assets, including money, are demanded when the date and amount of future liquidation are certain. Duesenberry has described this as the "float" component in total demand for liquid assets (others may also have used the phrase). If liquidation is fully anticipated, the time cost need not be borne. Thus, two assets could be perfect substitutes for a given individual in satisfying the demand for assets available for rapid liquidation, but not perfect substitutes in satisfying float demand, and *vice versa*. These possibilities may have little practical import in ordinary circumstances since the time loss is virtually zero for many assets and will usually be highly correlated with transaction cost in the narrow sense. A highly organized market simultaneously lowers the cost of contacting a given number of potential buyers and makes it possible to reach most potential buyers rapidly. This does not reduce the need for careful identification of the two elements and recognition of the fact that liquidity in the time sense depends upon and reflects the presence of transaction costs.

## Transaction Costs of Money

The term "transaction cost" ("transaction friction" appears to be a virtually if not wholly equivalent concept) is used throughout the literature to refer to costs incurred in effecting exchanges. The cost is often equated with the difference between the price at which an asset can be bought and the (stable) price for which it can be resold, or the loss of wealth suffered in moving from money to some other asset and back, adjusted for any other costs or benefits associated with the activity other than any yield paid on the asset.[11]

It is sometimes said that money has zero transaction costs. Of course, no costs are incurred in getting from money into money. But transaction costs are incurred in transactions utilizing money, for example, in going to the store to buy steak, and there is no apparent basis for associating such costs with the item that is not money rather than with money or both. Furthermore, one does not have to utilize money in indirect exchanges. These considerations are reflected in the practice that associates the cost with the transaction, which cost equals the loss of wealth suffered in moving from one good to another via an intermediate good where the intermediate good may or may not be money.[12] This practice incorporates the others but does not rule out transaction costs for money. Money can subsequently be said to minimize costs or to have zero transaction costs if this is understood to mean as measured from the base of the transaction cost when using money.

One also sometimes encounters statements to the effect that transaction costs are the result of illiquidity. For example, in *Money, Interest, and Prices*, Patinkin favorably cites a statement of this sort made by Hicks in *Value* and *Capital*, namely, that the cost and bother of converting bonds into money and *vice versa* is the result not the cause of illiquidity, that if bonds were perfectly liquid, they could themselves be used to make payments.[13] Given that an efficient money exists, and one is considering ways to hold wealth, the substantive point is obviously correct. Costs must be borne in converting any asset which is not money into money. On the other hand, as was argued above, transaction costs underlie both the "fraction of cost" and "time element" in liquidity. And transaction costs

---

[11] This is the practice followed, for example in Hicks's well-known paper, "A Suggestion for Simplifying the Theory of Money," *Economica*, N.S.,

February 1935, pp. 6–7. Also, see the Marschak paper cited in note 3.

Implicit in these remarks is purchase of a single unit of something, or that the cost applies to all units purchased. As is well understood, there are important economies of scale in most transactions, i.e., in cost per unit. See, e.g., J. S. Duesenberry, "The Portfolio Approach to the Demand for Money and Other Assets," *Review of Economics and Statistics*, Supplement, February 1963, pp. 9–24, and the comment by Arrow.

[12] A. A. Alchian and K. Brunner have been discussing "the transaction costs of money" in these terms for some time. Essentially the same idea underlies a statement in Marschak, *op. cit.*, p. 92. Recently, K. Brunner and A. Meltzer have made some use of this approach in "Some Further Investigations of Demand and Supply Functions for Money," *Journal of Finance*, May 1964, pp. 258–61.

[13] D. Patinkin, *op. cit.*, p. 85.

would be incurred utilizing completely liquid bonds to buy other things.[14]

## The Nature of Transaction Costs

So far as the writer knows, the nature of transaction costs has received little attention, although it has been pointed out frequently that there are important economies of scale in conducting transactions.[15] A number of factors underlie these costs.[16] These are the fact that it takes time to accomplish anything, that people are dispersed in space, that they have "imperfect information"—enclosed in quotation marks to call attention to the fact that a world with perfect information would differ from any known world —and that, though it is advantageous to have records, legal titles, etc., costs are encountered both in keeping and changing them.

The first fundamental factor giving rise to transaction costs is the fact that it takes time to accomplish anything. Of course, one can always hire resources to substitute for time, as has been emphasized here, but only down to some point, and at a cost. And nothing can be accomplished

in zero time, even in a room where all potential exchangers are publicly displaying their goods, bids, and offers.

Distance is a second factor. Someone who is not at the bank and wants to change a savings deposit into cash has no problem of finding out who will buy or sell what and at what price. His problem is simply one of expending time and/or other resources to go to the bank and effect the exchange. Or, put more carefully, this is his only problem so long as he gives no thought to the possibility of selling the deposit to an intermediary. When this possibility is introduced, he must then consider the fact that there may be higher and lower price buyers.

Some writers like Gilbert (see note 8) might question the suggestion that dispersion in space is a fundamental factor in explaining transaction costs, saying that it is costly to overcome distance because it takes time, and that distance would not introduce costs if activities could be effected in zero time. What it would mean to be able to traverse space in zero time is unclear, but it is evident that it costs more to traverse a greater than a smaller distance for any value of time, and that dispersion in space increases transaction costs.

If transactions could be effected instantaneously throughout space in zero time, perhaps everyone would have perfect information about everything. In fact, an effort must be made to find buyers and sellers, and to acquire, and to impart, information of all types. This subject has received scant attention from economists, the major contribution to one aspect of the subject itself a beginning, being the paper by Stigler already cited. For the present purpose, it suffices to identify lack of information, for both the seller and the buyer, as a factor in transaction costs. Similarly, only brief mention need be made of the fact that keeping and changing records, legal fees, etc., contribute to these costs.

The subject undoubtedly merits much more investigation. My chief concern has been to indicate the principal factors underlying transaction costs while advancing the view that the time element in liquidity is not only comparable to but reflects the existence of these costs.

---

[14] What are the characteristics of good monies? The traditional discussion ran in terms of identifiability, durability, portability, divisibility, etc. An asset which rates high in all of these respects clearly will be less costly to use than one less favorably situated. For a related but not, I think, identical suggestion which emphasizes information about characteristics of assets, see Brunner and Meltzer, *op. cit.*, pp. 258–61. As an example of one difference, a can of beer made by a well-known manufacturer is not likely to serve as means of payment, though easily identified, widely utilized within the community, etc., since, in most circumstances, other more durable and portable items will be less costly to use. Also, see the remarks in the next section.

[15] Demsetz's conclusions are likely to be applicable to a much wider variety of phenomena than stock exchange transactions. In any event, one of his conclusions is that the marginal costs of trading on the exchange decline as the time rate of transactions increases but only up to approximately five transactions per day. At that point they level off.

[16] I have profited from a conversation with Jack Melitz on this subject, who is absolved of responsibility for the outcome.

*KARL BRUNNER*

# Some Major Problems in Monetary Theory[1]

# 11

## I

Monetary policy operates directly on the Federal Reserve's portfolio of government securities, the requirement ratios, and the rediscount rate. The transmission of the desired effects to the target variables (income, employment, and prices) presupposes a systematic connection between policy and target variables crucially mediated by a set of monetary magnitudes. It therefore appears convenient to subdivide the monetary mechanisms into two branches: one relates policy and monetary variables and the other associates monetary variables with income or prices. Money supply theory explicates the first subrelation and money demand theory together with aggregate demand theory defines the second subrelation. Existence and nature of these subrelations form the central issue of recent policy discussions. An evaluation of the degree of effectiveness of monetary policy consequently involves a comparative appraisal of rival theories concerning the properties of the two subrelations. Such appraisal has barely begun, particularly as many conceptions advanced still require a translation into properly formulated hypotheses. This situation explains the emergence of abundant references to observable patterns which actually possess no evidential significance or discriminating power but are diligently adduced to support contentions concerning the usefulness of monetary policy.[2]

[2] Three observation statements, one referring to the relative growth of nonbanking financial intermediaries, another referring to large or increasing excess reserves in a deflationary environment and a third to a systematic association between restrictive policy and rising velocity, whose truth we may concede, have been advanced in support of the contention that monetary policy is decreasingly effective. The fallacy involved is revealed by constructing a hypothesis which implies the three observation statements together with a statement about an unreduced or even increasing degree of effectiveness for policy actions. Logical analysis thus exhibits the three observation statements to be consistent with a theory which implies continued usefulness of monetary policy.

[1] This paper forms part of a research project on monetary theory and monetary policy, financed by the Bureau of Economic Research at U.C.L.A. I wish to thank Armen A. Alchian, Alan Meltzer, and Harold Demsetz for extensive discussions on the subject.

Reprinted from the *American Economic Review: Papers and Proceedings*, Vol. LI (1961), pp. 47–54, by permission of the author and publisher. Karl Brunner is a professor at The Ohio State University.

Analysis of these patterns indicates that they are equally consistent with alternative hypotheses which imply opposite statements about the effectiveness of monetary policy. Explication of vague conceptions into empirically significant theories thus forms a necessary step in the resolution of conflicting ideas. The construction and comparative assessment of such theories alone assures "cognitive respectability" to policy discussions.

## II

Long neglected, money supply theory has recently attracted more attention, and a variety of promising leads have been developed. A rough outline of a potentially fruitful formulation follows.

The institutional arrangements of our financial system suggest that the money stock, assets, and liabilities of all financial institutions are jointly determined by the operation of the credit markets. The banks' net flow demand for earning assets is determined by the banks' wealth (balance-sheet) position and pertinent market prices; i.e., an index of interest rates formed on the bank oriented credit market. The public's net flow supply of assets to the banks depends on the public's wealth position, the index rate, interest rates on related credit markets, and current income. The equilibrium of net demand and supply determines the index rate as a function of the public's and the banks' wealth position, interest on other credit markets, and income. This flow equilibrium is consistent with continuous changes in the banks' wealth position, in particular with changes in the portfolio of earning assets. A determination of this stock magnitude is obtained with a condition of stock equilibrium, equating the banks' net flow demand to zero. The banks' net borrowing from the Federal Reserve banks is explained by a flow demand function with balance-sheet position, index rate, and rediscount rate as arguments. The optimal stock of outstanding discounts and advances to commercial banks is again determined by a condition of stock equilibrium equating net borrowing to zero. All equilibrium conditions, stock or flow, can be justified in terms of a rapid adjustment of interest rates and bank positions relative to time units implicit in the definition of observable magnitudes associated with the hypothesis. More significant is the cognitive function of such equilibrium conditions: They imply that variations in exogenous variables are a necessary condition for the occurrence of variations in endogenous variables.

The construction is completed by specifying the processes changing the banks' volume of "free" cash assets. Money stock, the banks' portfolio of earning assets, the index rate, the volume of reserves, the volume of excess reserves, and the amount of indebtedness to Federal Reserve banks are jointly explained by this formulation in terms of the (adjusted) monetary base[3] plus the cumulated sum of reserves liberated (or frozen in) by past changes in the requirement ratios, the rediscount rate, two parameters expressing specific asset preferences of the public, an index of interest rates on related credit markets, the outstanding stock of government securities, and income.[4]

The "money supply function" is thus obtained as a solution of the formal structure describing the operation of the bank oriented credit market. The function defines a relation between policy variables and the money stock. Partial correlation analysis based on monthly data or on quarterly averages of monthly data and covering very differently situated sample periods confirms this connection between the monetary base, the reserve requirements, and the money supply. It appears that the monetary base is the most important magnitude explaining the behavior of the money stock. Explanations which disregard the base yield thoroughly unreliable results or factually erroneous conclusions.[5] The relative importance of the base does not signify irrelevance of other explanatory magnitudes. Variations in reserve requirements contribute substantially to the behavior of the money stock as do the shifts in parameters expressing the public's asset preferences between currency and deposits, or between demand and time deposits.

A useful operation of monetary policy depends on the effective transmission of policy actions

---

[3] The adjusted monetary base is equal to the monetary base minus discounts and advances. The monetary base is the amount of money directly issued by the authorities. Its precise definition depends on the institutional arrangements.

[4] See Appendix A for a concise formal statement, together with a few observational results. [Appendix A has not been included in this reprinting.—Ed.]

[5] The Radcliffe *Report* apparently misses the significance of the base. The report complains that the money supply grew during the last decade in spite of a constant cash ratio and concludes that the money supply was evidently uncontrolled. The report neglects completely that the base is the most important determinant of the money stock and that the base grew continuously and at an accelerating rate since 1949 by courtesy of U.K. policy.

to the money stock and, conceivably, to other monetary variables. Existence or absence of such a transmission, particularly in a deflationary environment, is still under consideration. The hypothesis outlined enables a systematic inquiry into crucial links of the monetary mechanism which endanger a persistent connection between policy and monetary variables. With a vanishing interest elasticity of the public's net supply of assets to banks, a vanishing elasticity of the banks' net demand for assets with respect to an accrual of excess reserves, and an indefinitely large interest elasticity of the banks' asset acquisition, the monetary variables would respond to neither open market nor to requirement policy. Experience indicates that a direct evaluation of the public's and the banks' behavior properties yields, at best, tenuous and unclear evidence. The hypothesis eliminates this difficulty by a transformation of not directly assayable propositions into statements to which we may associate a meaningful appraisal procedure. The hypothesis implies that each of the three specified elasticities is a sufficient condition for the money supply function to have a derivative not exceeding unity with respect to the base and a zero derivative with respect to the requirement ratios and with respect to the parameters expressing the public's pertinent asset preferences. Consequently, any evidence bearing directly on the properties of the money supply function contributes indirectly to assay propositions about the crucial elasticities in the structure of the bank oriented credit market. Estimates derived from observations generated under radically different economic conditions consistently yield values of the "monetary multiplier" (i.e., the derivative of the money supply function with respect to the base) in the range 1.5 to 3.5 and confirm the significance, expected sign, and expected relative order of magnitude of other derivatives. The persistent pattern of the results obtained under deflationary and inflationary "economic climates" is incompatible with the indicated behavior elasticities blocking the transmission of policy actions to the monetary variables.

Discussions about monetary policy frequently assign to bank reserves a crucial significance in the money supply mechanism. The precise meaning of these statements is often ambiguous, and their formulation permits the following three alternative explications: the volume of bank reserves is a policy variable; the volume of bank reserves is immediately and completely controlled by policy variables; and the volume of bank reserves is a target variable; it is chosen by the authorities as a signal for appropriate policy actions. The first interpretation can be immediately dismissed. The third interpretation admits bank reserves as an endogenous magnitude determined by the total interaction of all pertinent relations. The important issue under this interpretation bears on the rational choice of signs by the monetary authorities, and I contend that to include bank reserves among the signs to be watched raises the likelihood of inappropriate actions, measured in terms of income stabilization. The second interpretation raises a substantive issue. It usually involves a dismissal of the public's asset preferences as a determinant of money supply behavior and, in particular, a dismissal of the public's marginal propensity to hold currency. Its logical structure appears to exhibit a causal ordering of money stock, reserves, and monetary base which conflicts with the causal ordering determined by the theory outlined. The second interpretation implies a linear ordering from $B$ over $R$ to $M$; whereas, the theory specifies both $M$ and $R$ as jointly dependent on $B$. This latter formulation permits an evaluation of the issue with the aid of partial correlation analysis, and we observe that the results are more compatible with the theory outlined than with the second interpretation.[6]

## III

An effective connection between policy variables and monetary variables is a necessary but not a sufficient condition for the transmission of policy actions to the relevant target variables. A useful operation of monetary policy requires, in addition, an effective causal connection between monetary and target variables. Observations of high correlations between income or prices and the money stock affirm the significant existence of the second subrelation. However, this correlation conveys no information about the causal ordering of the underlying structure which generates the relation. We are yet confronted by rival interpre-

[6] The partial Kendall coefficients for the period 1947–57, computed from quarterly averages of seasonally unadjusted monthly values, are:

$$M, B/R = +.581 \qquad M, R/B = .058$$

It should be noted that the hypothesis outlined can be extended to cover related credit markets and thus to incorporate the behavior patterns of nonbanking financial institutions. A preliminary investigation of the comparative usefulness of the hypothesis yielded an average error of 1.8 per cent in predicting ten observations not contained in the sample underlying the coefficient estimates.

tations of this relation. One interpretation recognizes, in the observed correlation, the demand for money and denies the existence of any significant feedback from monetary variables to aggregate demand for output. Another interpretation explains the second subrelation in terms of the joint interaction of a "demand pull" for money and an "asset push on" aggregate demand. Under the first interpretation monetary policy would be useless, unless we acknowledge a substantial interest elasticity of aggregate demand; whereas, the second interpretation provides a theoretical basis for policy actions.

Both interpretations admit the notion of a demand function for money, and the suitable formulation of the substantive issue concerning the causal nexus of the monetary variables requires explicit consideration of this demand function. The Keynesian analysis generalized the Cambridge demand schedule by relating the desired money balance to both interest rate and current income. A demand function of this type can be derived from a number of higher level hypotheses. Such analytical formulation may exhibit the theory under consideration as a connected part of a more general structure, but it cannot justify the theory's empirical content. Quarterly observations drawn from the period 1939–57 and annual observations covering the period 1929–59 yield coefficient estimates which are statistically significant and also possess the expected sign. The results thus confirm the basic idea, expressed by the Keynesian demand function, viz., that desired balances are systematically associated with interest rates and a major component of current transactions. Purely "associative laws" form a considerable part of our systematic knowledge, and they contribute usefully to elucidate a number of broad policy problems. Nevertheless, the usefulness of a theory rises with our ability to specify relatively stable orders of magnitude. Stability of the quantitative properties permits a successful application of the hypothesis to more detailed policy situations. Unfortunately, the demand hypothesis under consideration does not satisfy these more stringent requirements.

A diligent search for more fruitful hypotheses is under way. Promising modifications are suggested by an errant tradition which relates desired balances primarily to "wealth" and interest rates. The success of these modifications depends decisively on a useful specification of the term wealth. One line of investigations, opened by Professor Friedman, determines an index of wealth with the aid of a functional containing current income's time function as an argument. This demand theory explains the desired balances in terms of the wealth index per capita (labeled "permanent" income), population and permanent prices. The Friedman hypothesis yields an explanation of velocity which consistently subsumes both secular and cyclic behavior and to this extent at least, appears more highly corroborated than the Keynesian demand function. Yet, the demand theory formulated by Friedman has to prove its mettle under a more detailed quantitative appraisal. A casual inspection of the data, particularly for the thirties and fifties, reveals quite substantial differences between actual and estimated velocities, and the signs of the deviations seem broadly related to the comparative levels of interest rates in the two periods. Two modifications of the Friedman theory were therefore tentatively considered, both of which maintain the advance gained in the explanation of velocity. Each modification incorporates an index of interest rates; one replaces permanent prices by current price, and the other replaces permanent prices by transitory income in current prices. Estimates were based on annual data drawn from the period 1919 to 1959 and computed for a number of subperiods. With one exception, having a very small power of discrimination, the interest elasticities are significantly negative; the elasticity of desired balances with respect to "permanent income" dominates persistently; its value exceeds considerably the value of interest elasticity and is approximately three times the elasticity with respect to current prices or transitory income.[7]

The concept of a demand for money helps clarify the nature of the chain linking monetary variables and current output. The demand function for money reveals an aspect of the public's allocation pattern for wealth. The optimal composition is determined by the "inherited" portfolio, the price-constellation, and the preferences between types of assets and liabilities. Variations in prices and the inherited position induce, in general, readjustments in the optimal portfolio. These rearrangements and the

---

[7] The modification of the Friedman hypothesis involving current prices was estimated for the total period and four subperiods. Only the subperiod 1919–34 yielded a positive and nonsignificant interest elasticity. The modification involving transitory income was estimated for the total period and two subperiods. The estimated interest elasticities are all significantly negative and cluster closely in the range −.27 to −.22. See furthermore Appendix B. [Appendix B has not been included in this reprinting. —Ed.]

associated price movements are an essential feature of the monetary mechanism which transmits changes in policy variables to national income or current output. Deviations of actual from desired balances induce readjustments in the public's balance-sheet position involving the whole range of assets and liabilities. These readjustments in asset portfolios spill over into the markets for current output. Three links of the chain are of particular significance: bonds are not the only substitute for money, for substitutability permeates the whole spectrum of assets, production of assets is a close substitute for the existing assets, and many services are close substitutes for the holding of assets. An increase in the public's money balances generated by suitable policy actions thus triggers a substitution chain in the public's portfolio which spills over to new production of assets and services and thus affects aggregate demand for output.

This general argument can be represented by an extensive class of formal structures. These formalizations explicate the idea that optimal stocks and flows (i.e., purchases) depend simultaneously on prices and wealth. The money stock affects the demand decisions for assets and output as a component of the inherited wealth position, and the usefulness of monetary policy hinges on the circumstance that such action simultaneously modifies the market situation confronting the public and its inherited portfolio. The precise incorporation of wealth into the demand function, particularly into the components of aggregate demand for output, still requires investigation. One view holds that net worth completely summarizes the relation between a portfolio position and demand behavior. This view implies that variations in the composition of a constant net worth exert no effect on demand. Another view contends that both net worth and its composition affect demand behavior. A particularly important aspect of this problem concerns the comparative order of asset and liability effects. The net worth hypothesis, for instance, assigns equal significance to both. The resolution of this issue has far-reaching ramifications. Our interpretation of nonbanking financial intermediaries, of changes in their portfolio composition exemplified by a loan expansion balanced by a sale of government securities, and of new issues of government securities depends substantially on the existence and order of magnitude of the liability effects.

The degree of inflation resulting from a reallocation of resources to the government financed by an injection of base money is independent, under a net worth hypothesis, of the monetary multiplier. This multiplier would be significant in case the asset effects exceed the liability effects, and demand behaviour depends on the composition of net worth.

The general idea of a balance-sheet reaction process with eventual spill-over to current production of assets and services appears to explain without difficulties a number of observable patterns. A broad range of observations is consistent with hypotheses based on this idea and difficult to reconcile with theories which neglect or explicitly deny the chain of interdependent balance-sheet adjustments. Among the pertinent observations we may note the following four: A constant deficit financed by new issues of base money has been associated without exception with a rising price level, and stabilization occurred only when the relation between deficit and the rate of change of the base was broken. The elimination of controls after a large accrual of money balances permits a delayed adjustment of actual to desired wealth positions, and the usually occurring increase in prices reveals the operation of this process. Furthermore, cross-section data seem to indicate that money balances are not erratically distributed among economic units relative to other components of wealth. In particular, larger balances are associated, in the average, with greater values of most other important types of assets and liabilities. Lastly, the operation of the portfolio adjustment mechanism implies that, at least in periods exhibiting sufficiently large variations in the money stock, hypotheses which incorporate this monetary variable as an argument of the aggregate demand function for output yield better results than hypotheses which eliminate any reference to monetary variables.[8] These remarks do not justify a particular class of monetary theories—but they do constitute a case for considerable investment of resources to further a detailed investigation of the chain connecting monetary and target variables.

[8] Some evidence bearing on this problem was presented in the paper by K. Brunner and A. Balbach, "An Evaluation of Two types of Monetary Theories," *Proceedings of the Western Econ. Asso.*, 1959.

E. RAY CANTERBERY

# A Note on Recent Money Supply Behavior

*12*  By the end of April 1965,
the U.S. commercial banking system had had
no free reserves, in terms of daily averages, for
two consecutive months. During this time net
borrowed reserves exceeded a daily average of
minus $100 million. This "reserve position" of
the banking system was at its lowest level in
five years. It is not uncommon for the Federal
Reserve System to restrict credit when prices
rise or when the economy experiences a boom
of "unsustainable" proportions. But the industrial production index had been on a plateau
since November 1964, and Fed officials were
applauding the "balanced nature" of the economic expansion.

The intentional contraction of the money
supply during this period of stable production
and prices reflected the continuation of a System
policy of placing a "floor" under short-term
interest rates, attempting to slow the outflow of
short-term capital in the international balance
of payments. This interest rate policy was

Reprinted from the *Western Economic Journal*,
Vol. IV (1965), pp. 91–98, by permission of the
author and publisher. E. Ray Canterbery is a professor
at the University of Maryland.

initiated by a new FOMC directive to the New
York Federal Reserve Bank's trading desk on
October 25, 1960. At that time the lower limit
to short-term interest rate movements was
pegged. The purpose of this note is to explain
the effect of this policy upon seasonal-cyclical
changes in the money supply and upon the
domestic stabilization goal of monetary policy.

## The Impact on the Money Supply, Beginning Mid-1960

Even the most casual observation suggests
that setting an interest rate target will cause
the money supply (demand deposits plus currency
in circulation) to behave differently from what
it otherwise would. Normally the rate of interest
is thought of as a price determined by the demand
for and supply of money. Through open-market
operations the central bank can alter the quantity
of outstanding bank credit and thus influence
the money supply. In turn, interest rates are
pushed one direction or the other. But setting
an interest rate goal first results in the money
supply doing essentially what the interest rate
requires rather than vice versa. While the exact

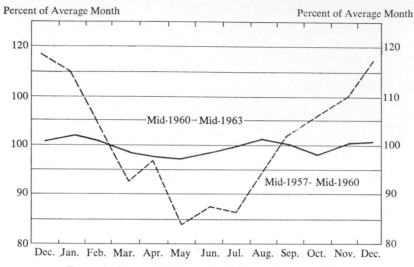

Figure 1. Seasonal Patterns in Yields on Treasury Bills.

response in economic activity to a given change in the money supply and interest rates is uncertain, it is generally presumed that lower rates and a more rapidly expanding money supply are more expansionary in terms of GNP and employment than a slower growth in credit (and money) and higher interest rates.

But in view of balance-of-payments "considerations," the Federal Reserve placed a "floor" under the short-term Treasury bill rate from mid-1960 through most of 1961. The shift to an upward movement came late in 1961 and prompted a new FOMC policy declaration to the New York Trading Desk on December 19, 1961, calling for less expansive monetary con-

ditions, higher short-term rates, and slower additions to banking reserves. It also was necessary for the Federal Reserve to interfere with free market forces during periods of seasonal slow-downs in business activity.

This new policy contributed to a behavior of short-term interest rates and the money supply which can best be described as "unorthodox." Prior to mid-1960, there was a definite seasonal pattern in short-term rates. When commercial and industrial loan demand is slack in mid-summer, short-term interest rates normally are lower than in the winter or fall. From mid-1960 to mid-1963, however, as Figures 1 and 2 illustrate, there was only a moderate seasonal

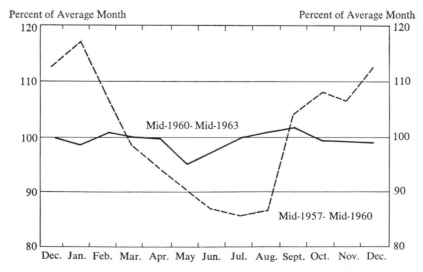

Figure 2. Seasonal Patterns in Rates on Bankers' Acceptances.

## Table 1. Changes in the Money Supply

| Year | ANNUAL RATES OF CHANGE[a] | |
|---|---|---|
| | January–August | August–January |
| 1960 | −1.1% | +1.0% |
| 1961 | +1.7 | +5.0 |
| 1962 | −0.9 | +6.0 |
| 1963 | +2.1 | +6.9 |
| Average 1960–63 | +0.5 | +4.7 |
| Average 1951–59 | +2.4 | +1.9 |

*Source:* Research Department, Federal Reserve Bank of St. Louis.
[a] Demand deposits plus currency in circulation, seasonally adjusted by Board of Governors of the Federal Reserve System.

movement in yields on Treasury bill rates and on bankers' acceptances.[1]

This unseasonal interest rate pattern could not be sustained without changing the behavior of the money supply. From 1951 through 1959, the average annual rate of increase in money (seasonally adjusted) from January to August was about the same as in the remainder of each year. But from 1960 through 1963 the average annual rate of advance was only 0.5 per cent during the first half-year, while the rate rose to 4.7 per cent in the last half (see Table 1). This new pattern began to emerge in 1960.

It is unlikely that the weather suddenly reversed itself, starting in 1960. Farm crops are still largely harvested and marketed in the fall, while retailers continue to build inventories for the Christmas season. Although there is more construction activity in winter months currently than in the distant past, building patterns did not abruptly change in mid-1960.

It is more reasonable to conclude that this change in the intra-yearly movement of the money stock was a consequence of the "pegging" and pushing of the short-term Treasury bill rate. In the early months of the year the monetary authorities supported higher yields by selling securities in the open market. During the fall and winter, when seasonal credit demands were strong, the System allowed the money supply to expand without endangering the support level for Treasury bill yields. The net result has been a marked alteration in seasonal movements of the money supply.

A continuation of this program means a slow addition to bank reserves and the money supply during seasonal lulls, regardless of the stage of the business cycle. Moreover, this policy has

permanently changed the behavior of one of the seasonally adjusted indicators used in evaluating monetary policy, that is, the money supply itself. While the import of the latter is not altogether clear at this point, the use of the standard seasonal adjustment factors causes the money supply, between April and November of each year, to appear to have expanded faster than it actually did. The Federal Reserve Bank of St. Louis has computed alternative seasonal adjustment factors based on money supply data since mid-1960. While the number of years used in this calculation may not be sufficient for accuracy, four years is adequate for noting that a definite change has occurred in the magnitude of the seasonal factors. These alternatively adjusted data appear in Table 2.

There is also a longer-run impact from this policy. After remaining on a plateau, three-month Treasury bill rates fluctuated near 2.70 per cent during the first five months of 1962, rising to a range of 2.75 to 2.90 per cent in the remaining months of that year. This range was near the level prevailing in the early months of 1959 and is historically high. Meanwhile, long-term interest rates drifted slightly lower during 1962, but began to move upward in early 1963. And business borrowing costs fluctuated near their average for the previous three years.

Because the bond market is thinner, yields can be easily changed (in the short run) with a relatively moderate volume of transactions in the capital market by the Fed. This is not, however, the case with the money market which has a much larger number of buyers, sellers, and dealers. In short, interest rates are much more elastic in the Treasury bill than in the bond markets.[2]

---

[1] This documentation of a change in seasonal patterns appears in the April 1964 *Federal Reserve Bank of St. Louis Monthly Review*. The Reserve Bank, of course, accepts no responsibility for the conclusions drawn from these data.

[2] It is extremely difficult, of course, to maintain a "floor" under interest rates during a period when the demand function for business loans shifts downward. This leads to an increased demand by banks for excess reserves and a rise in their demand for short-term

## Table 2. Money Supply (Monthly averages of daily figures seasonally adjusted)

| | 1960 | 1961 | *(BILLIONS OF DOLLARS)*<br>1962 | 1963 | 1964 |
|---|---|---|---|---|---|
| **January** | | | | | |
| Standard[a] | | 141.5 | 145.9 | 148.7 | 154.8 |
| Alternative[b] | | 140.7 | 145.1 | 147.8 | 153.8 |
| **February** | | | | | |
| Standard | | 141.8 | 145.5 | 148.6 | 154.4 |
| Alternative | | 141.6 | 145.3 | 148.3 | 154.1 |
| **March** | | | | | |
| Standard | | 142.2 | 145.7 | 148.9 | 154.8 |
| Alternative | | 142.2 | 145.5 | 148.7 | 154.8 |
| **April** | | | | | |
| Standard | | 142.5 | 146.1 | 149.4 | |
| Alternative | | 142.4 | 146.1 | 149.4 | |
| **May** | | | | | |
| Standard | | 142.9 | 145.7 | 149.4 | |
| Alternative | | 143.1 | 145.9 | 149.7 | |
| **June** | | | | | |
| Standard | | 142.8 | 145.6 | 149.8 | |
| Alternative | | 143.3 | 146.0 | 150.3 | |
| **July** | | | | | |
| Standard | 140.4 | 143.0 | 145.7 | 150.7 | |
| Alternative | 140.5 | 143.2 | 145.9 | 151.1 | |
| **August** | | | | | |
| Standard | 140.9 | 142.9 | 145.1 | 150.5 | |
| Alternative | 141.6 | 143.6 | 145.8 | 151.2 | |
| **September** | | | | | |
| Standard | 141.0 | 143.5 | 145.3 | 150.9 | |
| Alternative | 141.3 | 144.0 | 145.9 | 151.4 | |
| **October** | | | | | |
| Standard | 141.1 | 144.2 | 146.1 | 152.1 | |
| Alternative | 141.2 | 144.4 | 146.4 | 152.3 | |
| **November** | | | | | |
| Standard | 140.8 | 144.9 | 146.9 | 153.4 | |
| Alternative | 140.8 | 144.9 | 146.7 | 153.3 | |
| **December** | | | | | |
| Standard | 141.2 | 145.7 | 147.9 | 153.5 | |
| Alternative | 140.3 | 144.9 | 147.0 | 152.7 | |

a Board of Governors seasonal adjustment based on data from 1947 through 1961.
b Seasonally adjusted at Federal Reserve Bank of St. Louis by link-relative method based on data since mid-1960.

## The Economic Implications

### The Monetary Contraction of 1962

In Federal Reserve efforts to accommodate its international objective of moderating short-term capital outflows and its avowed domestic goal of moderate monetary expansion, the period between the end of 1961 and the start of 1963 was most difficult. In the first quarter of 1962

marketable securities. For discussion of this process and a model describing it, see Leroy J. Grossman, "An Evaluation of the Consistency of the Defensive and Dynamic Objectives of Federal Reserve Policy." Unpublished Ph.D. Dissertation, Vanderbilt University, 1963, pp. 68–73.

the Open Market Committee had to sell, on balance, $528 million of its security holdings in order to nudge the Treasury bill rate higher (see Table 3). In the same quarter the United States lost $291 million in gold, setting the stage for a possible monetary contraction of a multiple of $819 million. Indeed, during the period January through September 1962, Open Market net purchases amounted to only $823 million, failing to offset the loss of $827 million in U.S. gold.

These open-market operations and gold losses, plus lesser factors affecting bank reserves, resulted in an extremely sharp contraction in member-bank reserves available for private demand

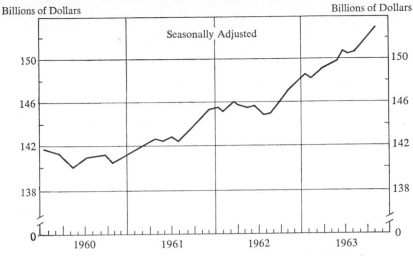

Figure 3. Money Supply (Monthly Averages of Daily Figures).

deposits.[3] In turn, the nation's money supply (demand deposits plus currency) declined slightly between January and May (see Figure 3). Some analysts would say this monetary contraction contributed to the plateau in employment and

### Table 3. Open-Market Operations and the Gold Outflow, 1962

*(millions of dollars, unadjusted)*

| Quarter | Net purchases or Sales (—) of Securities[a] | Gold Losses (—) |
|---------|---------------------------------------------|-----------------|
| I       | − 528                                       | − 291           |
| II      | 998                                         | − 102           |
| III     | 353                                         | − 434           |
| IV      | 625                                         | − 6             |

*Source:* Figures based on data released by Board of Governors of the Federal Reserve System.
[a] Includes net repurchase agreements.

industrial production from May through the end of 1962. In any case, Federal Open Market Operations clearly were not expansionary preceding a period—May 1962 to January 1963—when the FRB Industrial Production Index and the total number of employed workers remained virtually unchanged.

### The Policy in Theory

Available theory supports the view that monetary policy since late 1960 has tended to

be destabilizing for domestic income and employment. It has been noted herein that Federal Reserve policy has placed a "floor" under short-term interest rates and pushed (or allowed) rates to move upward when the money market has firmed. Irrespective of whether the cause is seasonal or cyclical, if the demand for money declines, the Federal Reserve has to reduce the level of the money supply. On the other hand, it can allow the money supply to expand somewhat if the demand for money rises. This is illustrated in the simple Hicksian liquidity-preference model.[4]

Hypothetically, if real income drops seasonally, credit demands for sustaining business inventories would decline and the transactions demand for money by both consumers and producers would descend. As the monetary authorities have "pegged" the interest rate at $i_0$, the demand for idle money would remain unchanged; but the demand for money balances would drop. To prevent the interest rate from falling to, say, $i_1$—which is below the support level—the central bank must take actions to destroy enough demand deposits to contract the money supply. This process of monetary contraction would continue so long as the transactions demand for money slumped.

Under the same policy arrangements, let us suppose that real income is rising and credit demands are stimulated by rising consumer sales. Initially, the demand schedule for money jumps upwards. With no change in the money supply the new rate of interest rises sharply to, say, $i_2$.

[3] During this period total member-bank reserves increased at a 3 per cent annual rate, but this advance was more than absorbed by a fast growth in time deposits and, hence, required reserves behind time deposits.

[4] See John R. Hicks, "Mr. Keynes and the 'Classics,' A Suggested Interpretation," *Econometrica*, Vol. V, 1937, pp. 147–59. [Reprinted in this volume.]

However, this accelerated demand for money balances enables the authorities to augment the money supply without greatly depressing the interest rate. Hence the money supply is allowed to expand, the interest rate stabilizing at, say, $i_3$.

This model and its more modern versions[5] describe the general seasonal and cyclical behavior of the money supply since mid-1960. Beyond this, it yields several other interesting results. First, the Hicksian *LM* curve derived herein is perfectly elastic prior to that point where the transactions demand for money ascends. This resultant curve bears a remarkable resemblance to John R. Hicks's original graph of J. M. Keynes's interest rate theory.[6] The Monetary authorities apparently have created their own "liquidity trap"! But, whereas Keynes

envisaged a level below which the money market would not allow the interest rate to fall, the System has imposed its own minimum.

Second, the money supply is behaving proseasonally and procyclically. It rises when persons demand more liquidity and declines when they demand less. With central-bank policy dictated by these whims of the public, Federal Reserve actions parallel those of commercial banks rather than compensate for changes in commercial bank portfolios. Hence, continuing the policy into recession—when the general public and business desire to spend less—liquidity is diminished and a falling propensity to consume is reinforced. The resultant higher rate of interest and lesser availability of loanable funds also may induce businesses to curb their borrowing for inventory needs and invest in government securities, thus perhaps contributing to a slower growth in national income. Finally, it is a curious consequence of this process that, when interest rates do move up with market forces, ostensibly to slow capital outflows, this policy results in a slightly lower rate of interest than would prevail in an undisturbed money market.

[5] See especially George Horwich, *Money, Capital, and Prices* (Homewood, Illinois: Richard D. Irwin & Co., 1964), p. 369; and Franco Modigliani, "Liquidity Preference and the Theory of Interest and Money," *Econometrica*, Vol. XII, 1944, pp. 45–88, and "The Monetary Mechanism and Its Interaction with Real Phenomena," *The Review of Economics and Statistics*, Vol. XLV, 1963 supplement, pp. 79–107.

[6] Hicks, *op. cit.*, p. 153.

# Income and Employment

*T*HIS GROUP OF selections contains several "classics" in the field of macroeconomics. The first is A. W. Phillips' widely read work which introduces the "Phillips curve" and suggests that the rate of increase in money wages in the United Kingdom has been greatest when the rate of unemployment was lowest. The Phillips' article is followed by Don Patinkin's highly theoretical discussion of the effects of changes in the level of an economy's prices. In the final two articles of this section, E. J. Mishan and Edwin Kuh consider various factors which might affect the wage and employment conditions existing in an economy's labor market.

*Part*

*4*

*A. W. PHILLIPS*

# The Relation Between Unemployment and the Rate of Change of Money Wage Rates in the United Kingdom, 1861-1957[1]

*13*

## I. Hypothesis

When the demand for a commodity or service is high relatively to the supply of it we expect the price to rise, the rate of rise being greater the greater the excess demand. Conversely when the demand is low relatively to the supply we expect the price to fall, the rate of fall being greater the greater the deficiency of demand. It seems plausible that this principle should operate as one of the factors determining the rate of change of money wage rates, which are the price of labour services. When the demand for labour is high and there are very few unemployed we should expect employers to bid wage rates up quite rapidly, each firm and each industry being continually tempted

to offer a little above the prevailing rates to attract the most suitable labour from other firms and industries. On the other hand it appears that workers are reluctant to offer their services at less than the prevailing rates when the demand for labour is low and unemployment is high so that wage rates fall only very slowly. The relation between unemployment and the rate of change of wage rates is therefore likely to be highly non-linear.

It seems possible that a second factor influencing the rate of change of money wage rates might be the rate of change of the demand for labour, and so of unemployment. Thus in a year of rising business activity, with the demand for labour increasing and the percentage unemployment decreasing, employers will be bidding more vigorously for the services of labour than they would be in a year during which the average percentage unemployment was the same but the demand for labour was not increasing. Conversely in a year of falling business activity, with the demand for labour decreasing and the percentage unemployment increasing, employers will be less inclined to grant wage increases, and workers

[1] This study is part of a wider research project financed by a grant from the Ford Foundation. The writer was assisted by Mrs. Marjory Klonarides. Thanks are due to Professor E. H. Phelps Brown, Professor J. E. Meade and Dr. R. G. Lipsey for comments on an earlier draft.

Reprinted from *Economica*, Vol. XXV (1958), pp 283–300, by permission of the author and publisher. A. W. Phillips is a professor at the London School of Economics.

will be in a weaker position to press for them, than they would be in a year during which the average percentage unemployment was the same but the demand for labour was not decreasing.

A third factor which may affect the rate of change of money wage rates is the rate of change of retail prices, operating through cost of living adjustments in wage rates. It will be argued here, however, that cost of living adjustments will have little or no effect on the rate of change of money wage rates except at times when retail prices are forced up by a very rapid rise in import prices (or, on rare occasions in the United Kingdom, in the prices of home-produced agricultural products). For suppose that productivity is increasing steadily at the rate of, say, 2 per cent per annum and that aggregate demand is increasing similarly so that unemployment is remaining constant at, say, 2 per cent. Assume that with this level of unemployment and without any cost of living adjustments wage rates rise by, say, 3 per cent per annum as the result of employers' competitive bidding for labour and that import prices and the prices of other factor services are also rising by 3 per cent per annum. Then retail prices will be rising on average at the rate of about 1 per cent per annum (the rate of change of factor costs minus the rate of change of productivity). Under these conditions the introduction of cost of living adjustments in wage rates will have no effect, for employers will merely be giving under the name of cost of living adjustments part of the wage increases which they would in any case have given as a result of their competitive bidding for labour.

Assuming that the value of imports is one fifth of national income, it is only at times when the annual rate of change of import prices exceeds the rate at which wage rates would rise as a result of competitive bidding by employers by more than five times the rate of increase of productivity that cost of living adjustments become an operative factor in increasing the rate of change of money wage rates. Thus in the example given above a rate of increase of import prices of more than 13 per cent per annum would more than offset the effects of rising productivity so that retail prices would rise by more than 3 per cent per annum. Cost of living adjustments would then lead to a greater increase in wage rates than would have occurred as a result of employers' demand for labour and this would cause a further increase in retail prices, the rapid rise in import prices thus initiating a wage-price spiral which would continue until the rate of increase of import prices dropped significantly

below the critical value of about 13 per cent per annum.

The purpose of the present study is to see whether statistical evidence supports the hypothesis that the rate of change of money wage rates in the United Kingdom can be explained by the level of unemployment and the rate of change of unemployment, except in or immediately after those years in which there was a very rapid rise in import prices, and if so to form some quantitative estimate of the relation between unemployment and the rate of change of money wage rates. The periods 1861–1913, 1913–48 and 1948–57 will be considered separately.

## II. 1861–1913

Schlote's index of the average price of imports[2] shows an increase of 12.5 per cent in import prices in 1862 as compared with the previous year, an increase of 7.6 per cent in 1900 and in 1910, and an increase of 7.0 per cent in 1872. In no other year between 1861 and 1913 was there an increase in import prices of as much as 5 per cent. If the hypothesis stated above is correct the rise in import prices in 1862 may just have been sufficient to start up a mild wage-price spiral, but in the remainder of the period changes in import prices will have had little or no effect on the rate of change of wage rates.

A scatter diagram of the rate of change of wage rates and the percentage unemployment for the years 1861–1913 is shown in Figure 1. During this time there were 6½ fairly regular trade cycles with an average period of about 8 years. Scatter diagrams for the years of each trade cycle are shown in Figures 2 to 8. Each dot in the diagrams represents a year, the average rate of change of money wage rates during the year being given by the scale on the vertical axis and the average unemployment during the year by the scale on the horizontal axis. The rate of change of money wage rates was calculated from the index of hourly wage rates constructed by Phelps Brown and Sheila Hopkins,[3] by expressing the first central difference of the index for each year as a percentage of the index for the same year. Thus the rate of change for 1861 is taken to be half the difference between the index for 1862 and the index for 1860 expressed as a percentage of

---

[2] W. Schlote, *British Overseas Trade from 1700 to the 1930's*, Table 26.

[3] E. H. Phelps Brown and Sheila Hopkins, "The Course of Wage Rates in Five Countries, 1860–1939," *Oxford Economic Papers*, June, 1950.

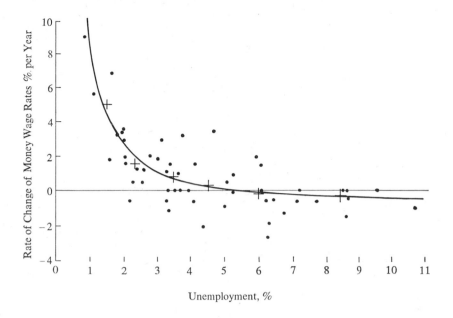

**Figure 1. 1861–1913.**

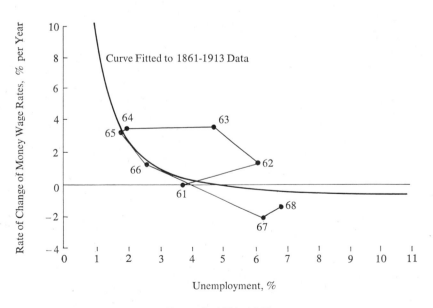

**Figure 2. 1861–1868.**

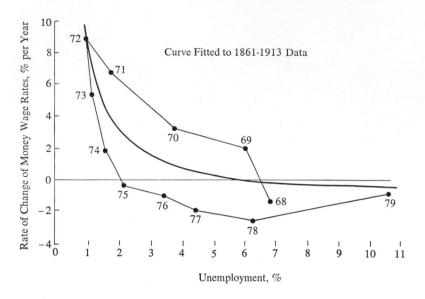

Figure 3. 1868–1879.

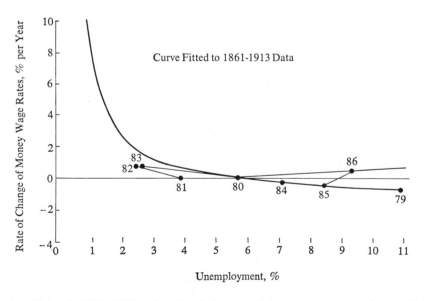

Figure 4. 1879–1886, using Bowley's wage index for the years 1881 to 1886.

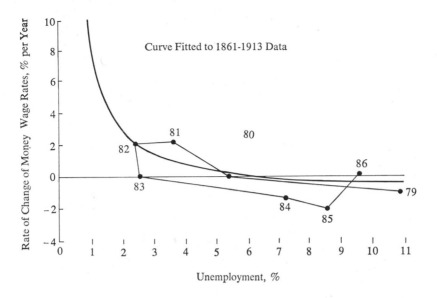

Figure 4a. 1879–1886.

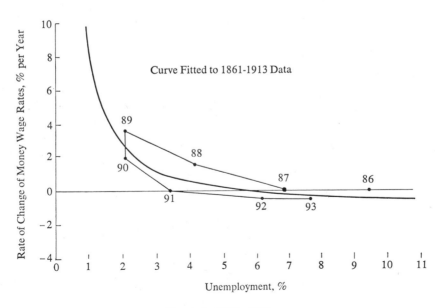

Figure 5. 1886–1893.

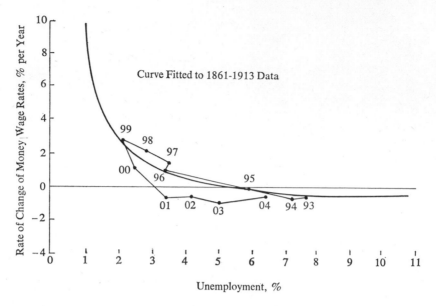

Figure 6. 1893–1904.

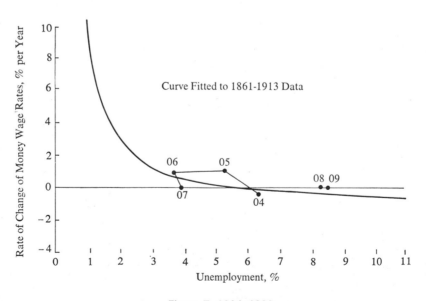

Figure 7. 1904–1909.

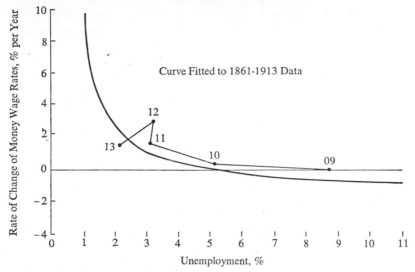

Figure 8. 1909–1913.

the index for 1861, and similarly for other years.[4] The percentage unemployment figures are those calculated by the Board of Trade and the Ministry of Labour[5] from trade union returns. The corresponding percentage employment figures are quoted in Beveridge, *Full Employment in a Free Society*, Table 22.

It will be seen from Figures 2 to 8 that there is a clear tendency for the rate of change of money wage rates to be high when unemployment is low and to be low or negative when unemployment is high. There is also a clear tendency for the rate of change of money wage rates at any given level of unemployment to be above the average for that level of unemployment when unemployment is decreasing during the upswing of a trade cycle and to be below the average for that level of unemployment when unemployment is increasing during the downswing of a trade cycle.

The crosses shown in Figure 1 give the average values of the rate of change of money wage rates and of the percentage unemployment in those years in which unemployment lay between 0 and 2, 2 and 3, 3 and 4, 4 and 5, 5 and 7, and 7 and 11

[4] The index is apparently intended to measure the average of wage rates during each year. The first central difference is therefore the best simple approximation to the average absolute rate of change of wage rates during a year and the central difference expressed as a percentage of the index number is an appropriate measure of the average percentage rate of change of wage rates during the year.

[5] *Memoranda upon British and Foreign Trade and Industrial Conditions* (Second Series) (Cd. 2337), B.P.P. 1905, Vol. 84; *21st Abstract of Labour Statistics, 1919–33* (Cd. 4625), B.P.P. 1933–34, Vol. 26.

per cent respectively (the upper bound being included in each interval). Since each interval includes years in which unemployment was increasing and years in which it was decreasing the effect of changing unemployment on the rate of change of wage rates tends to be cancelled out by this averaging, so that each cross gives an approximation to the rate of change of wages which would be associated with the indicated level of unemployment if unemployment were held constant at that level.

The curve shown in Figure 1 (and repeated for comparison in later diagrams) was fitted to the crosses. The form of equation chosen was

$$y + a = bx^c$$

or

$$\log(y + a) = \log b + c \log x$$

where $y$ is the rate of change of wage rates and $x$ is the percentage unemployment. The constants $b$ and $c$ were estimated by least squares using the values of $y$ and $x$ corresponding to the crosses in the four intervals between 0 and 5 per cent unemployment, the constant $a$ being chosen by trial and error to make the curve pass as close as possible to the remaining two crosses in the intervals between 5 and 11 per cent unemployment.[6] The equation of the fitted curve is

$$y + 0.900 = 9.638x^{-1.394}$$

or

$$\log(y + 0.900) = 0.984 - 1.394 \log x.$$

[6] At first sight it might appear preferable to carry out a multiple regression of $y$ on the variables $x$ and $dx/dt$. However, owing to the particular form of the relation between $y$ and $x$ in the present case it is not

Considering the wage changes in individual years in relation to the fitted curve, the wage increase in 1862 (see Figure 2) is definitely larger than can be accounted for by the level of unemployment and the rate of change of unemployment, and the wage increase in 1863 is also larger than would be expected. It seems that the 12.5 per cent increase in import prices between 1861 and 1862 referred to above (and no doubt connected with the outbreak of the American civil war) was in fact sufficient to have a real effect on wage rates by causing cost of living increases in wages which were greater than the increases which would have resulted from employers' demand for labour and that the consequent wage-price spiral continued into 1863. On the other hand the increases in import prices of 7.6 per cent between 1899 and 1900 and again between 1909 and 1910 and the increase of 7.0 per cent between 1871 and 1872 do not seem to have had any noticeable effect on wage rates. This is consistent with the hypothesis stated above, about the effect of rising import prices on wage rates.

Figure 3 and Figures 5 to 8 show a very clear relation between the rate of change of wage rates and the level and rate of change of unemployment,[7] but the relation hardly appears at all in the cycle shown in Figure 4. The wage index of Phelps Brown and Sheila Hopkins from which the changes in wage rates were calculated was based on Wood's earlier index,[8] which shows the same stability during these years. From 1880 we have also Bowley's index of wage rates.[9] If the rate of change of money wage rates for 1881 to

1886 is calculated from Bowley's index by the same method as was used before, the results shown in Figure 4a are obtained, giving the typical relation between the rate of change of wage rates and the level and rate of change of unemployment. It seems possible that some peculiarity may have occurred in the construction of Wood's index for these years. Bowley's index for the remainder of the period up to 1913 gives results which are broadly similar to those shown in Figures 5 to 8, but the pattern is rather less regular than that obtained with the index of Phelps Brown and Sheila Hopkins.

From Figure 6 it can be seen that wage rates rose more slowly than usual in the upswing of business activity from 1893 to 1896 and then returned to their normal pattern of change; but with a temporary increase in unemployment during 1897. This suggests that there may have been exceptional resistance by employers to wage increases from 1894 to 1896, culminating in industrial strife in 1897. A glance at industrial history[10] confirms this suspicion. During the 1890's there was a rapid growth of employers' federations and from 1895 to 1897 there was resistance by the employers' federations to trade union demands for the introduction of an eight-hour working day, which would have involved a rise in hourly wage rates. This resulted in a strike by the Amalgamated Society of Engineers, countered by the Employers' Federation with a lock-out which lasted until January 1898.

From Figure 8 it can be seen that the relation between wage changes and unemployment was again disturbed in 1912. From the monthly figures of percentage unemployment in trade unions[11] we find that unemployment rose from 2.8 per cent in February 1912 to 11.3 per cent in March, falling back to 3.6 per cent in April and 2.7 per cent in May, as the result of a general stoppage of work in coal mining. If an adjustment is made to eliminate the effect of the strike on unemployment the figure for the average percentage unemployment during 1912 would be reduced by about 0.8 per cent, restoring the typical pattern of the relation between the rate of change of wage rates and the level and rate of change of unemployment.

From a comparison of Figures 2 to 8 it appears that the width of loops obtained in each trade cycle has tended to narrow, suggesting a reduc-

---

easy to find a suitable linear multiple regression equation. An equation of the form $y + a = bx^c + k [(1/x^m) \cdot (dx/dt)]$ would probably be suitable. If so the procedure which has been adopted for estimating the relation that would hold between $y$ and $x$ if $dx/dt$ were zero is satisfactory, since it can easily be shown that $(1/x^m) \cdot (dx/dt)$ is uncorrelated with $x$ or with any power of $x$ provided that $x$ is, as in this case, a trend-free variable.

[7] Since the unemployment figures used are the averages of monthly percentages, the first central difference is again the best simple approximation to the average rate of change of unemployment during a year. It is obvious from an inspection of Fig. 3 and Figs. 5 to 8 that in each cycle there is a close relation between the deviations of the points from the fitted curve and the first central differences of the employment figures, though the magnitude of the relation does not seem to have remained constant over the whole period.

[8] See Phelps Brown and Sheila Hopkins, *loc. cit.*, pp. 264–5.

[9] A. L. Bowley, *Wages and Income in the United Kingdom since 1860*, Table VII, p. 30.

[10] See B. C. Roberts, *The Trades Union Congress, 1868–1921*, Chapter IV, especially pp. 158–162.

[11] *21st Abstract of Labour Statistics, 1919–1933*, *loc. cit.*

tion in the dependence of the rate of change of wage rates on the rate of change of unemployment. There seem to be two possible explanations of this. First, in the coal and steel industries before the first world war sliding scale adjustments were common, by which wage rates were linked to the prices of the products.[12] Given the tendency of product prices to rise with an increase in business activity and fall with a decrease in business activity, these agreements may have strengthened the relation between changes in wage rates and changes in unemployment in these industries. During the earlier years of the period these industries would have fairly large weights in the wage index, but with the greater coverage of the statistical material available in later years the weights of these industries in the index would be reduced. Second, it is possible that the decrease in the width of the loops resulted not so much from a reduction in the dependence of wage changes on changes in unemployment as from the introduction of a time lag in the response of wage changes to changes in the level of unemployment, caused by the extension of collective bargaining and particularly by the growth of arbitration and conciliation procedures. If such a time lag existed in the later years of the period the wage change in any year should be related, not to average unemployment during that year, but to the average unemployment lagged by, perhaps, several months. This would have the effect of moving each point in the diagrams horizontally part of the way towards the point of the preceding year and it can easily be seen that this would widen the loops in the diagrams. This fact makes it difficult to discriminate at all closely between the effect of time lags and the effect of dependence of wage changes on the rate of change of unemployment.

## III. 1913–1948

A scatter diagram of the rate of change of wage rates and percentage unemployment for the years 1913–48 is shown in Figure 9. From 1913 to 1920 the series used are a continuation of those used for the period 1861–1913. From 1921 to 1948 the Ministry of Labour's index of hourly wage rates at the end of December of each year[13] has been used, the percentage change in the index each year being taken as a measure of the average rate of change of wage rates during

that year. The Ministry of Labour's figures for the percentage unemployment in the United Kingdom[14] have been used for the years 1921–45. For the years 1946–48 the unemployment figures were taken from the *Statistical Yearbooks* of the International Labour Organisation.

It will be seen from Figure 9 that there was an increase in unemployment in 1914 (mainly due to a sharp rise in the three months following the commencement of the war). From 1915 to 1918 unemployment was low and wage rates rose rapidly. The cost of living was also rising rapidly and formal agreements for automatic cost of living adjustments in wage rates became widespread, but it is not clear whether the cost of living adjustments were a real factor in increasing wage rates or whether they merely replaced increases which would in any case have occurred as a result of the high demand for labour. Demobilization brought increased unemployment in 1919 but wage rates continued to rise rapidly until 1920, probably as a result of the rapidly rising import prices, which reached their peak in 1920, and consequent cost of living adjustments in wage rates. There was then a sharp increase in unemployment from 2.6 per cent in 1920 to 17.0 per cent in 1921, accompanied by a fall of 22.2 per cent in wage rates in 1921. Part of the fall can be explained by the extremely rapid increase in unemployment, but a fall of 12.8 per cent in the cost of living, largely a result of falling import prices, was no doubt also a major factor. In 1922 unemployment was 14.3 per cent and wage rates fell by 19.1 per cent. Although unemployment was high in this year it was decreasing, and the major part of the large fall in wage rates must be explained by the fall of 17.5 per cent in the cost of living index between 1921 and 1922. After this experience trade unions became less enthusiastic about agreements for automatic cost of living adjustments and the number of these aggreements declined.

From 1923 to 1929 there were only small changes in import prices and in the cost of living. In 1923 and 1924 unemployment was high but decreasing. Wage rates fell slightly in 1923 and rose by 3.1 per cent in 1924. It seems likely that if business activity had continued to improve after 1924 the changes in wage rates would have shown the usual pattern of the recovery phase of earlier trade cycles. However, the decision to check demand in an attempt to force the price level down in order to restore the gold standard at the pre-war parity of sterling prevented the

---

[12] I am indebted to Professor Phelps Brown for pointing this out to me.
[13] *Ministry of Labour Gazette*, April, 1958, p. 133.

[14] *Ibid.*, January, 1940 and subsequent issues.

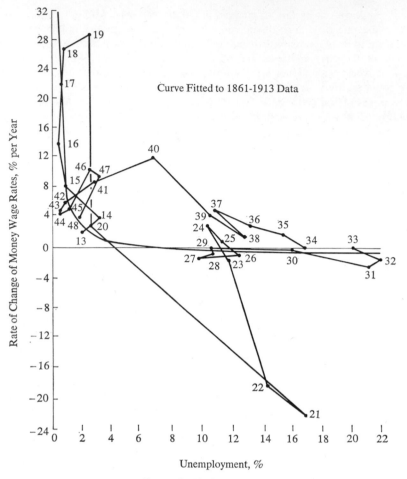

Curve Fitted to 1861-1913 Data

Figure 9. 1913–1948.

recovery of business activity and unemployment remained fairly steady between 9.7 per cent and 12.5 per cent from 1925 to 1929. The average level of unemployment during these five years was 10.94 per cent and the average rate of change of wage rates was −0.60 per cent per year. The rate of change of wage rates calculated from the curve fitted to the 1861–1913 data for a level of unemployment of 10.94 per cent is −0.56 per cent per year, in close agreement with the average observed value. Thus the evidence does not support the view, which is sometimes expressed, that the policy of forcing the price level down failed because of increased resistance to downward movements of wage rates. The actual results obtained, given the levels of unemployment which were held, could have been predicted fairly accurately from a study of the pre-war data, if anyone had felt inclined to carry out the necessary analysis.

The relation between wage changes and unemployment during the 1929–37 trade cycle

follows the usual pattern of the cycles in the 1861–1913 period except for the higher level of unemployment throughout the cycle. The increases in wage rates in 1935, 1936 and 1937 are perhaps rather larger than would be expected to result from the rate of change of employment alone and part of the increases must probably be attributed to cost of living adjustments. The cost of living index rose 3.1 per cent in 1935, 3.0 per cent in 1936 and 5.2 per cent in 1937, the major part of the increase in each of these years being due to the rise in the food component of the index. Only in 1937 can the rise in food prices be fully accounted for by rising import prices; in 1935 and 1936 it seems likely that the policies introduced to raise prices of home-produced agricultural produce played a significant part in increasing food prices and so the cost of living index and wage rates. The extremely uneven geographical distribution of unemployment may also have been a factor tending to increase the rapidity of wage changes

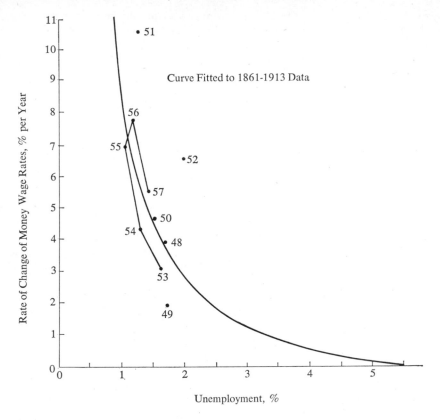

Figure 10. 1948–1957.

during the upswing of business activity between 1934 and 1937.

Increases in import prices probably contributed to the wage increases in 1940 and 1941. The points in Figure 9 for the remaining war years show the effectiveness of the economic controls introduced. After an increase in unemployment in 1946 due to demobilization and in 1947 due to the coal crisis, we return in 1948 almost exactly to the fitted relation between unemployment and wage changes.

## IV. 1948–1957

A scatter diagram for the years 1948–57 is shown in Figure 10. The unemployment percentages shown are averages of the monthly unemployment percentages in Great Britain during the calendar years indicated, taken from the *Ministry of Labour Gazette*. The Ministry of Labour does not regularly publish figures of the percentage unemployment in the United Kingdom; but from data published in the *Statistical Yearbooks* of the International Labour Organization it appears that unemployment in

the United Kingdom was fairly consistently about 0.1 per cent higher than that in Great Britain throughout this period. The wage index used was the index of weekly wage rates, published monthly in the *Ministry of Labour Gazette*, the percentage during each calendar year being taken as a measure of the average rate of change of money wage rates during the year. The Ministry does not regularly publish an index of hourly wage rates;[15] but an index of normal weekly hours published in the *Ministry of Labour Gazette* of September 1957 shows a reduction of 0.2 per cent in 1948 and in 1949 and an average annual reduction of approximately 0.04 per cent from 1950 to 1957. The percentage changes in hourly rates would therefore be greater than the percentage changes in weekly rates by these amounts.

It will be argued later that a rapid rise in import prices during 1947 led to a sharp increase in retail prices in 1948 which tended to stimulate wage increases during 1948, but that this tendency

[15] An index of hourly wage rates covering the years considered in this section is, however, given in the *Ministry of Labour Gazette* of April, 1958.

was offset by the policy of wage restraint introduced by Sir Stafford Cripps in the spring of
1948; that wage increases during 1949 were
exceptionally low as a result of the policy of
wage restraint; that a rapid rise in import prices
during 1950 and 1951 led to a rapid rise in retail
prices during 1951 and 1952 which caused cost
of living increases in wage rates in excess of the
increases that would have occurred as a result of
the demand for labour, but that there were no
special factors of wage restraint or rapidly rising
import prices to affect the wage increases in 1950
or in the five years from 1953 to 1957. It can be
seen from Figure 10 that the point for 1950 lies
very close to the curve fitted to the 1861–1913
data and that the points for 1953 to 1957 lie
on a narrow loop around this curve, the direction
of the loop being the reverse of the direction of
the loops shown in Figures 2 to 8. A loop in this
direction could result from a time lag in the
adjustment of wage rates. If the rate of change
of wage rates during each calendar year is related
to unemployment lagged seven months, i.e. to
the average of the monthly percentages of unemployment from June of the preceding year
to May of that year, the scatter diagram shown
in Figure 11 is obtained. The loop has now dis-

appeared and the points for the years 1950 and
1953 to 1957 lie closely along a smooth curve
which coincides almost exactly with the curve
fitted to the 1861–1913 data.

In Table 1 below the percentage changes in
money wage rates during the years 1948–57 are
shown in column (1). The figures in column (2)
are the percentage changes in wage rates calculated from the curve fitted to the 1861–1913 data
corresponding to the unemployment percentages
shown in Figure 11, i.e. the average percentages
of unemployment lagged seven months. On the
hypothesis that has been used in this paper, these
figures represent the percentages by which wage
rates would be expected to rise, given the level
of employment for each year, as a result of
employers' competitive bidding for labour, i.e.
they represent the "demand pull" element in
wage adjustments.

The relevant figure on the cost side in wage
negotiations is the percentage increase shown by
the retail price index in the month in which the
negotiations are proceeding over the index of
the corresponding month of the previous year.
The average of these monthly percentages for
each calendar year is an appropriate measure of
the "cost push" element in wage adjustments,

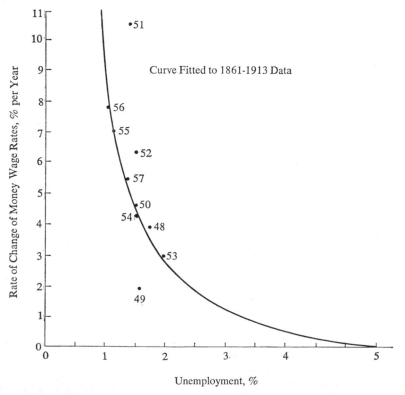

Figure 11. 1948–1957, with unemployment lagged 7 months.

and these averages[16] are given in column (3). The percentage change in the index of import prices[17] during each year is given in column (4).

From Table 1 we see that in 1948 the cost push element was considerably greater than the demand pull element, as a result of the lagged effect on retail prices of the rapid rise in import prices during the previous year, and the change in wage rates was a little greater than could be accounted for by the demand pull element. It would probably have been considerably greater but for the co-operation of the trade unions in Sir Stafford Cripps' policy of wage restraint. In 1949 the cost element was less than the demand element and the actual change in wage rates was also much less, no doubt as a result of the policy of wage restraint which is generally acknowledged to have been effective in 1949. In 1950 the cost

exactly equal to the demand element. Thus in these five years, and also in 1950, there seems to have been pure demand inflation.

## V. Conclusions

The statistical evidence in Sections II to IV above seems in general to support the hypothesis stated in Section I, that the rate of change of money wage rates can be explained by the level of unemployment and the rate of change of unemployment, except in or immediately after those years in which there is a sufficiently rapid rise in import prices to offset the tendency for increasing productivity to reduce the cost of living.

Ignoring years in which import prices rise

## Table 1

| | (1) Change in Wage Rates | | (2) Demand Pull | | (3) Cost Push | | (4) Change in Import Prices | |
|---|---|---|---|---|---|---|---|---|
| 1947 | — | | — | | — | | 20.1 | . |
| 1948 | 3.9 | . | 3.5 | . | 7.1 | . | **10.6** | . |
| **1949** | **1.9** | . | **4.1** | . | **2.9** | . | **4.1** | . |
| **1950** | **4.6** | . | **4.4** | . | **3.0** | . | 26.5 | . |
| 1951 | 10.5 | . | 5.2 | . | 9.0 | . | **23.3** | . |
| **1952** | **6.4** | . | **4.5** | . | **9.3** | . | −11.7 | . |
| 1953 | 3.0 | . | 3.0 | . | 3.0 | . | −4.8 | . |
| 1954 | 4.4 | . | 4.5 | . | 1.9 | . | 5.0 | . |
| 1955 | 6.9 | . | 6.8 | . | 4.6 | . | 1.9 | . |
| 1956 | 7.9 | . | 8.0 | . | 4.9 | . | 3.8 | . |
| 1957 | 5.4 | . | 5.2 | . | 3.8 | . | −7.3 | . |

element was lower than the demand element and the actual wage change was approximately equal to the demand element.

Import prices rose very rapidly during 1950 and 1951 as a result of the devaluation of sterling in September 1949 and the outbreak of the Korean War in 1950. In consequence the retail price index rose rapidly during 1951 and 1952 so that the cost element in wage negotiations considerably exceeded the demand element. The actual wage increase in each year also considerably exceeded the demand element so that these two years provide a clear case of cost inflation.

In 1953 the cost element was equal to the demand element and in the years 1954 to 1957 it was well below the demand element. In each of these years the actual wage increase was almost

rapidly enough to initiate a wage-price spiral, which seem to occur very rarely except as a result of war, and assuming an increase in productivity of 2 per cent per year, it seems from the relation fitted to the data that if aggregate demand were kept at a value which would maintain a stable level of product prices the associated level of unemployment would be a little under $2\frac{1}{2}$ per cent. If, as is sometimes recommended, demand were kept at a value which would maintain stable wage rates the associated level of unemployment would be about $5\frac{1}{2}$ per cent.

Because of the strong curvature of the fitted relation in the region of low percentage unemployment, there will be a lower average rate of increase of wage rates if unemployment is held constant at a given level than there will be if unemployment is allowed to fluctuate about that level.

These conclusions are of course tentative. There is need for much more detailed research into the relations between unemployment, wage rates, prices and productivity.

---

[16] Calculated from the retail price index published in the *Monthly Digest of Statistics*. The figure for 1948 is the average of the last seven months of the year.

[17] *Board of Trade Journal.*

*DON PATINKIN*

# Price Flexibility and Full Employment[1]

*14* At the core of the Keynesian polemics of the past ten years and more is the relationship between price flexibility and full employment. The fundamental argument of Keynes is directed against the belief that price flexibility can be depended upon to generate full employment automatically. The defenders of the classical tradition, on the other hand, still insist upon this automaticity as a basic tenet.

[1] In the process of writing this paper the author acknowledges having benefited from stimulating discussions with Milton Friedman, University of Chicago, and Alexander M. Henderson, University of Manchester.

Reprinted from *Readings in Monetary Theory* (New York: Blakiston, 1951), pp. 252–283, by permission of the author and publisher. This is a revised version of an article which appeared in the *American Economic Review*, Vol. XXXVIII, (1948), pp. 543–564. The major changes are the following: the addition of the latter part of the last paragraph of § 5, as a result of discussions with Milton Friedman; the addition of paragraphs three and four of § 6, as a result of comments by Donald Gordon, Franco Modigliani, and Norman Ture; the correction of the last paragraph of § 6 and Table 1 of § 11 in accordance with Herbert Stein's comment on the original article in the *American Economic Review*, XXXIX (1949), 725–26; and the addition of the last three paragraphs of § 14, in the attempt to clarify some points left ambiguous in the original article. (All significant additions are enclosed in brackets.)

Don Patinkin is a professor at The Hebrew University, Jerusalem.

During the years of continuous debate on this question, the issues at stake have been made more precise. At the same time, further material on the question of flexibility has become available. This paper is essentially an attempt to incorporate this new material, and, taking advantage of the perspective offered by time, to analyze the present state of the debate.

In Part I, the problem of price flexibility and full employment is presented from a completely static viewpoint. Part II then goes on to discuss the far more important dynamic aspects of the problem. Finally, in Part III, the implications of the discussion for the Keynesian-classical polemic are analyzed. It is shown that over the years these two camps have really come closer and closer together. It is argued that the basic issue separating them is the rapidity with which the economic system responds to price variations.

## I. Static Analysis

1. The traditional interpretation of Keynesian economics is that it demonstrates the absence of an automatic mechanism assuring the equality of desired savings and investment at full employment. The graphical meaning of this interpretation is presented in a simplified form in Figure 1. Here desired real savings ($S$) and investment ($I$) are each assumed to depend only

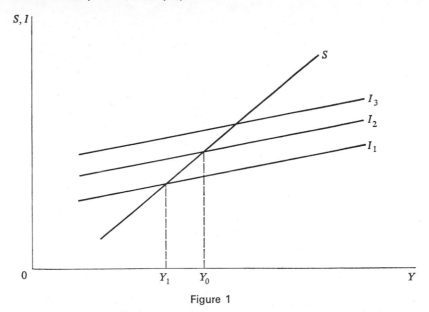

Figure 1

on the level of real income ($Y$). $I_1$, $I_2$, and $I_3$ represent three possible positions of the investment schedule. $Y_0$ is the full employment level of real income. If the investment desires of individuals are represented by the curve $I_1$, desired savings at full employment are greater than desired investment at full employment. This means that unemployment will result: the level of income will drop to $Y_1$, at which income desired savings and investment are equal. Conversely, if $I_3$ is the investment curve, a situation of overemployment or inflation will occur: people desire to invest more at full employment than the amount of savings will permit. Only if the investment schedule happened to be $I_2$ would full employment, desired investment and savings be equal. But since investment decisions are independent of savings decisions, there is no reason to expect the investment schedule to coincide with $I_2$. Hence there is no automatic assurance that full employment will result.

2. The classical answer to this attack is that desired savings and investment depend on the rate of interest, as well as the level of real income; and that, granted flexibility, variations in the interest rate serve as an automatic mechanism insuring full employment.

The argument can be interpreted as follows: the savings and investment functions (representing what people desire to do) are written as

$$S = \Omega(r, Y)$$
$$I = \Psi(r, Y)$$

where $r$ represents that rate of interest.

Consider now Figure 2. On this graph there

can be drawn a whole family of curves relating savings and investment to the rate of interest —one pair for each level of real income. In Figure 2, these pairs of curves are drawn for the full employment income, $Y_0$, and for the less than full employment income, $Y_1$. On the assumption that for a given rate of interest people will save and invest more at a higher level of income, the investment curve corresponding to $Y = Y_0$ is drawn above that corresponding to $Y = Y_1$; similarly for the two savings curves. The curves also reflect the assumption that, for a given level of real income, people desire to save more and invest less at higher rates of interest.

Consider now the pair of curves corresponding to the full employment income $Y_0$. If in Figure 2 the interest rate were $r_1$, then it would be true that individuals would desire to save more at full employment than they would desire to invest. But, assuming no rigidities in the interest rate, this would present no difficulties. For if the interest rate were to fall freely, savings would be discouraged, and investment stimulated until finally desired full employment savings and investment would be equated at the level $S_0 = I_0$. Similarly, if at full employment desired investment is greater than desired savings, a rise in the interest rate will prevent inflation. In this way variations in the rate of interest serve automatically to prevent any discrepancy between desired full employment investment and savings, and thus to assure full employment.

This argument can also be presented in terms of Figure 1: assume for simplicity that desired

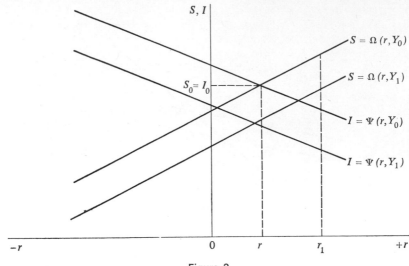

Figure 2

investment depends on the rate of interest as well as the level of real income, while desired savings depends only on the latter. Then downward variations in the interest rate can be counted on to raise the investment curve from, say, $I_1$ to $I_2$. That is, at any level of income people can be encouraged to invest more by a reduction in the rate of interest. Similarly, upward movements of the interest rate will shift the investment curve from, say, $I_3$ to $I_2$. Thus desired full employment savings and investment will always be equated.

3. The Keynesian answer to this classical argument is that it greatly exaggerates the importance of the interest rate. Empirical evidence has accumulated in support of the hypothesis that variations in the rate of interest have little effect on the amount of desired investment. (That savings are insensitive to the interest rate is accepted even by the classical school.) This insensitivity has been interpreted as a reflection of the presence of widespread uncertainty.[2] The possible effect of this insensitivity on the ability of the system automatically to generate full employment is analyzed in Figure 3. For simplicity the savings functions corresponding to different levels of income are reproduced from Figure 2. But the investment functions are now represented as being much less interest-sensitive than those in Figure 2. If the situation in the real world were such as represented in Figure 3,

it is clear that interest rate variations could never bring about full employment. For in an economy in which there are negligible costs of storing money, the interest rate can never be negative.[3] But from Figure 3 we see that the only way the interest rate can equate desired full employment savings and investment is by assuming the negative value $r_2$. Hence it is impossible for the full employment national income $Y_0$ to exist: for no matter what (positive) rate of interest may prevail, the amount people want to save at full employment exceeds what they want to invest. Instead there will exist some less than full employment income (say) $Y_1$ for which desired savings and investment can be brought into equality at a positive rate of interest, (say) $r_3$ (cf. Figure 3).

Thus once again the automaticity of the system is thrown into question. Whether the system will generate full employment depends on whether the full employment savings and investment functions intersect at a positive rate of interest. But there is no automatic mechanism to assure that the savings and investment functions will have the proper slopes and positions to bring about such an intersection.[4]

4. Sometimes attempts are made to defend the classical position by arguing that the invest-

[2] Cf. Oscar Lange, *Price Flexibility and Employment* (Bloomington, Indiana, Principia Press, 1945), p. 85 and the literature cited there. For an excellent theoretical discussion of this insensitivity, cf. G. L. S. Shackle, "Interest Rates and the Pace of Investment," *Economic Journal*, Vol. LVI (1946), pp. 1–17.

[3] Note that in a dynamic world of rising prices, the effective rate of interest may become negative. But even here the *anticipated* effective rate cannot be negative. For in that event there would again be an infinite demand for money.

[4] [I have discussed this whole question of the contrast between the classical and Keynesian positions in greater detail elsewhere. Cf. "Involuntary Unemployment and the Keynesian Supply Function," *Economic Journal* LIX (1949), 376–78.]

ment function is really higher (or the savings function lower) than represented by the Keynesians—so that desired full employment savings and investment can be equated at a positive rate of interest (*cf.* Figure 3). But this is beside the point. [The fundamental disagreement between Keynesian and classical economics lies in the former's denial of the automaticity of full employment posited by the latter.] Hence a successful restatement of the classical position must demonstrate the existence of some automatic mechanism which will always bring about

argument of § 1 was answered by introducing a new variable—the rate of interest—into the savings function, so the more refined argument of § 3 is countered by the introduction of yet another variable—the real value of cash balances held by the individuals in the economy. Thus, denoting the amount of money in the economy $M_1$ (assumed to remain constant) and the absolute price level by $p$, Pigou's saving schedule is written as

$$S = \Gamma\left(r, Y, \frac{M_1}{p}\right).]$$

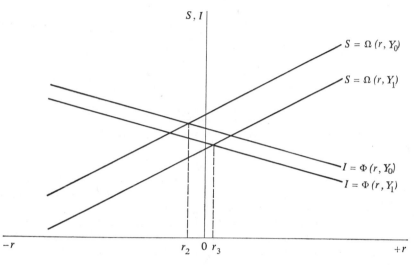

Figure 3

full employment. Thus to argue that *if* the investment or saving function is at a certain level, full employment will be brought about is irrelevant; what must be shown is that there exist forces which will *automatically* bring the investment or saving functions to the required level. In other words, the issue at stake is not the *possible*, but the *automatic*, generation of full employment.

5. [To the Keynesian negative interest rate argument replies have been made by both Haberler and Pigou.[5] Just as the crude Keynesian

His argument is as follows: if people would refuse to save anything at negative and zero rates of interest, then the desired savings schedule would intersect the desired investment schedule at a positive rate of interest regardless of the level of income (*cf.* Figure 3). The willingness to save even without receiving interest, or even at a cost, must imply that savings are not made solely for the sake of future income (*i.e.*, interest) but also for "the desire for possession as such, conformity to tradition or custom and so on."[6] But the extent to which an individual wishes to save out of current income for reasons other than the desire of future income is inversely related to the real value of his cash balances.[7] If this is sufficiently large, all his secondary desires for saving will be fully satisfied. At this point the only reason he will continue to save

[5] [G. Haberler, *Prosperity and Depression* (League of Nations, Geneva, 1941), 3rd ed., pp. 242, 389, 403, 491–503.]

A. C. Pigou, "The Classical Stationary State," *Economic Journal*, LIII (1943), 343–51; "Economic Progress in a Stable Environment," *Economica*, n. s. XIV (1947), 180–90. Although these articles deal only with a stationary state, their basic argument can readily be extended to the case in which net investment is taking place.

[In the subsequent text, I shall follow the exposition of Pigou; but the argument holds also with respect to Haberler.]

[6] *Ibid.*, p. 346.

[7] And all his other assets too. But the introduction of these other assets does not change Pigou's argument; while concentration on money assets brings out its (the argument's) basic aspect. *Cf.* below, § 6.

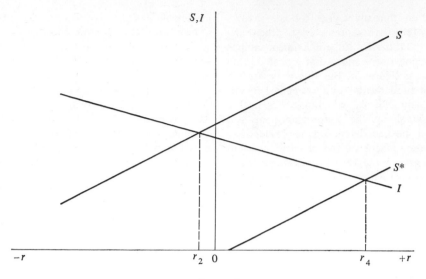

Figure 4

out of current income is the primary one of anticipated future interest payments. In other words, if the real value of cash balances is sufficiently large, the savings function becomes zero at a positive rate of interest, regardless of the income level.

A graphical interpretation of this argument is presented in Figure 4. Here $S$ and $I$ are the full-employment savings and investment curves of Figure 3 (*i.e.*, those corresponding to $Y = Y_0$), and $r_2$ is again the negative rate of interest at which they are equal. Pigou then argues that by increasing the real value of cash balances, the full employment savings curve shifts to the right until it is in such a position that no savings are desired except at positive rates of interest. This is represented by the savings curve $S^*$, which becomes zero for a positive rate of interest. (In fact, $S^*$ shows dissaving taking place for sufficiently low rates of interest.) The full employment savings curve $S^*$ clearly intersects the full employment investment curve I at the positive rate of interest $r_4$. Thus by changing the real value of cash balances, desired full employment savings and investment can always be equated at a positive rate of interest.

How can we be sure that real cash balances will automatically change in the required direction and magnitude? Here Pigou brings in his assumptions of flexible wage and price levels, and a constant stock of money in circulation. If full employment saving exceeds investment, national income begins to fall, and unemployment results. If workers react to this by decreasing their money wages, then the price level will also

begin to fall. As the latter continues to fall, the real value of the constant stock of money increases correspondingly. Thus, as the price level falls, the full employment saving function continuously shifts to the right until it intersects the full employment investment function at a positive rate of interest.[8]

This is the automatic mechanism on which Haberler and Pigou rely to assure full employment. It is essential to note that it will operate regardless of the interest-elasticities of the savings

[8] The exact price level is determined when to our preceding four equations is added the liquidity preference equation, $M_0 = (r, Y, p)$, where $M_0$ represents the given amount of money in the system. (As will be shown in the next section, the "stock of money" relevant for the liquidity equation is completely different from the "stock of money" relevant for the Pigou analysis of the savings function; hence the use of two different symbols—$M_0$ and $M_1$.) We then have the complete system of five equations in five variables:

$$I = \Phi(r, Y)$$
$$S = \Gamma\left(r, Y, \frac{M_1}{p}\right)$$
$$I = S$$
$$Y = Y_0$$
$$M_0 = \Lambda(r, Y, p).$$

Under the Pigovian assumptions this system is consistent; its equations are satisfied for a positive rate of interest.

[The workings of a more general system of equations under the Pigovian assumption are described in detail in Parts IV and V of the reference cited in footnote 4 above. In this more detailed treatment, the full employment level, $Y_0$, is not arbitrarily defined—as is done in the present paper—but emerges instead from the economic behavior functions themselves.]

and investment functions—provided they are not both identically zero. [It should also be emphasized, as Haberler does, that although this argument has been presented above as an answer to Keynes, it is of much older origin. In particular, it is implicit in classical theorizing on the quantity theory of money. The crucial step in this analysis, it will be recalled, comes at the point where it is argued that as a result of increasing the amount of money in the economy, individuals' cash balances are larger than desired at the existing price level, so that they will attempt to reduce these real balances by increasing their money expenditures. The main contribution of Haberler and Pigou is to show how this set of forces must, and can, be introduced into the Keynesian analytical apparatus.]

6. The inner mechanism and distinctive characteristic of the Pigou analysis can be laid bare by considering it from a larger perspective. It is obvious that a price reduction has a stimulating effect on creditors. But, restricting ourselves to the private sector of a closed economy, to every stimulated creditor there corresponds a discouraged debtor. Hence from this viewpoint the net effect of a price reduction is likely to be in the neighbourhood of zero. The neatness of the Pigou approach lies in its utilizing the fact that although the private sector considered in isolation is, on balance, neither debtor nor creditor, when considered in its relationship to the government, it *must be* a net "creditor." This is due to the fact that the private sector always holds money, which is a (non-interest bearing) "debt" of government. If we assume that government activity is not affected by the movements of the absolute price level,[9] then the net effect of a price decline must always be stimulatory.[10] The community gains at the "expense" of a gracious government, ready, willing, and able to bear the "loss" of the increased value of its "debt" to the public.

More precisely, not every price decline need have this stimulating effect. For we must consider the effect of the price decline on the other assets held by the individual. If the decline reduces the real value of these other assets (*e.g.*, houses and other forms of consumer capital; stock shares; etc.) to an extent more than off-

setting the increased value of real cash balances,[11] then the net effect will be discouraging. But the important point is that no matter what our initial position, *there exists* a price level sufficiently low so that the total real value of assets corresponding to it is greater than the original real value. Consider the extreme case in which the value of the other assets becomes arbitrarily small.[12] Clearly even here the real value of the fixed stock of money can be made as large as desired by reducing the price level sufficiently. Thus, to be rigorous, the statement in the preceding paragraph should read: "There always exists a price decline such that its effect is stimulatory." From this and the analysis of the preceding section, we can derive another statement which succinctly summarizes the results of the Pigou analysis: "In the static classical model, regardless of the position of the investment schedule, there always exists a sufficiently low price level such that full employment is generated." In any event, it is clearly sufficient to concentrate (as Pigou has done) on cash balances alone.[13]

[This analysis is subject to at least two reservations, neither one of which has been considered by Haberler or Pigou. First of all, we have tacitly been assuming that the depressing effect of a price decline on a debtor is roughly offset by its stimulating effect on a creditor; hence the private sector, being on balance a creditor with respect to the government, can ultimately be stimulated by a price decline. But allowance must be made for the possibility of a differential reaction of debtors and creditors. That is, if debtors are discouraged by a price decline much more than creditors are encouraged, it may be possible that there exists no price decline which would have an encouraging effect on expenditures. In brief, the Keynesian aggregative analysis followed by Pigou overlooks the possibility of microeconomic "distribution effects."

Secondly we have so far considered only the effects of a change in real balances on household behavior; that is on the consumption (or its

---

[9] Pigou makes this assumption when he writes the investment function (which presumably also includes government expenditure) as independent of the absolute price level. *Cf.* footnote 8 above.

[10] It must be emphasized that I am abstracting here from all dynamic considerations of the effect on anticipations, etc. These will be discussed in Part II of the paper.

[11] A necessary (but not sufficient) condition for this to occur is that the price level of assets falls in greater proportion than the general price level.

[12] I am indebted to M. Friedman for this example.

[13] *Cf.* above, footnote 7. Another possible reason for Pigou's emphasis on cash balances to the exclusion of other assets is that the relative illiquidity of the latter makes them less likely to be used as a means of satisfying the "irrational" motives of saving. Hence the inverse relationship between other assets and savings out of current income might not be so straightforward as that between real cash balances and savings.

counterpart the savings) function. It seems only natural to extend the analysis to include the influence of real cash balances on firms and, hence, on the investment function as well. However, this extension cannot be made automatically, inasmuch as the respective motivations of firms and households are not necessarily the same. Nevertheless, it does seem reasonable to assume that investment decisions of firms are favorably influenced by a higher level of real balances. Once we take account of firms, the differential reactions mentioned in the preceding paragraph become increasingly significant. If firms are, on balance, debtors with respect to households and government, then a persistent price decline will cause a wave of bankruptcies. This will have a seriously depressing effect upon the economy which may not be offset by the improved status of creditors. Furthermore, in most cases of bankruptcy the creditors also lose. For these reasons it is not at all certain that a price decline will result in a positive net effect on the total expenditures (consumption plus investment) function. On this point much further investigation—of a theoretical as well as an empirical nature—is required.]

From the preceding analysis we can also see just exactly what constitutes the "cash balance" whose increase in real value provides the stimulatory effect of the Pigou analysis. This balance clearly consists of the net obligation of the government to the private sector of the economy. That is, it consists primarily of the total interest- and non-interest-bearing government debt held outside the treasury and central bank, [plus the net amount owed by the central bank to member banks]. Thus, by excluding demand deposits and including government interest-bearing debt and member bank reserves, it differs completely from what is usually regarded as the stock of money.

These same conclusions can be reached through a somewhat different approach. Begin with the ordinary concept of the stock of money as consisting of hand-to-hand currency and demand deposits. Consider now what changes must be made in order to arrive at the figure relevant for the Pigou analysis. Clearly, government interest-bearing debt must be added, since a price decline increases its value. Now consider money in the form of demand deposits. To the extent that it is backed by bank loans and discounts, the gains of deposit holders are offset by the losses of bank debtors.[14] Thus the net

effect of a price decline on demand deposits is reduced to its effect on the excess of deposits over loans, or (approximately) on the reserves of the banks held in the form of hand-to-hand currency [and deposits in the central bank]. Finally, hand-to-hand currency held by individuals outside the banking system is added in, and we arrive at exactly the same figure as in the preceding paragraph.

For convenience denote the stock of money relevant for the Pigou analysis by $M_1$. Note that this is completely different from $M_0$ of footnote 8: for $M_0$ is defined in the usual manner as hand-to-hand currency plus demand deposits. This distinction is of fundamental importance. [One of its immediate implications is that central bank open market operations which do not change the market price of government bonds affect the economic system only through the liquidity preference equation.] Since such operations merely substitute one type of government debt (currency) for another (bonds), they have no effect on $M_1$ and hence no direct effect on the amount of savings. [Even when open market purchases do cause an increase in the price of government bonds, the changes in $M_0$ and $M_1$ will not, in general, be equal. The increase in $M_0$ equals the total amount of money expended for the purchase of the bonds; the increase in $M_1$ equals the increase in the value of bonds (both of those bought and those not bought by the central bank) caused by the open-market operations.[15] Corresponding statements can be made for open-market sales.]

7. How does the Pigou formulation compare with the original classical theory?[16] Although both Pigou and the "classics" stress the importance of "price flexibility," they mean by

---

14 *Cf.* M. Kalecki, "Professor Pigou on 'The Classical Stationary State'—A Comment," *Economic Journal,* LIV (1944), 131–32.

15 [It might be argued that through its effect on the interest rate, open-market purchases affect the value of assets other than government securities; hence, this change in value should also be included in the change in $M_1$. This is a point which deserves further investigation. The main question is whether there exists an offset to this improvement in the position of bondholders of private corporations.]

16 Pigou, of course, introduces the absolute price level into the analysis of the real sector of the economy, whereas classical economics insists that this sector must be considered on the basis of relative prices alone. [As I have shown elsewhere, on this point classical economics is definitely wrong. For, in a money economy, the demand for any good must, in general, depend on the absolute price level, as well as on relative prices. This is a direct result of utility maximization. *Cf.* "Money in General Equilibrium Theory: Critique and Reformulation," *Econometrica,* XVIII (1950), and references cited there.]

this term completely different things. The "classics" are talking about flexibility of relative prices; Pigou is talking about flexibility of absolute prices. The classical school holds that the existence of long-run unemployment is *prima facie* evidence of rigid wages. The only way to eliminate unemployment is, then, by reducing *real* wages. (Since workers can presumably accomplish this end by reducing their *money* wage, this position has implicit in it the assumption of a constant price level—[or at least one falling relatively less than wages].) Pigou now recognizes that changing the relative price of labor is not enough, and that the absolute price level itself must vary. In fact, a strict interpretation of Pigou's position would indicate that unemployment can be eliminated even if real wages remain the same or even rise (namely, if the proportionate fall in prices is greater than or equal to that of wages); for in any case the effect of increased real value of cash balances is still present.[17]

The Pigou analysis also differs from those interpretations of the classical position which, following Keynes, present the effect of a wage decrease as acting through the liquidity preference equation, to increase the real value of $M_0$ and thereby reduce the rate of interest; this in turn stimulates both consumption and investment expenditures—thus generating a higher level of national income. To this effect, Pigou now adds the direct stimulus to consumption expenditures provided by the price decline and the accompanying increase in real balances. Consequently, even if the savings and investment functions are completely insensitive to changes in the rate of interest (so that the effect through the liquidity equation is completely inoperative), a wage decrease will still be stimulatory through its effect on real balances and hence on savings.

8. Before concluding this part of the paper, one more point must be clarified. The explicit assumption of the Pigou analysis is that savings are directly related to the price level, and therefore inversely related to the size of real cash balances. This assumption by itself is, on *a priori* grounds, quite reasonable; [indeed, in a money economy it is a direct implication of utility maximization (above, note 16)]. But it must be emphasized that even if we disregard the reser-

vations mentioned in the preceding sections, this assumption is insufficient to bring about the conclusion desired by Pigou. For this purpose he *implicitly* makes an additional, and possibly less reasonable, assumption. Specifically, in addition to postulating explicitly the direction of the relationship between savings and the price level, he also implies something about its *intensity*.

The force of this distinction is illustrated by Figure 5. Here $S$ and $I$ are the full employment savings and investment curves of Figure 3 (*i.e.*, those corresponding to $Y = Y_0$) for a fixed price level, $p_0$. The other savings curves, $S_1$, $S_2$, $S_3$, $S_4$, represent the full employment savings schedules corresponding to the different price levels $p_1$, $p_2$, $p_3$, $p_4$, respectively. In accordance with the Pigou assumption, as the price level falls, the savings function shifts over to the right. (That is $p_1$, $p_2$, $p_3$, $p_4$, are listed in descending order.) But it may well be that as the real value of their cash balances continues to increase, people are less and less affected by this increase. That is, for each successive increase in real balances (for each successive price level decline) the savings function moves less and less to the right, until eventually it might respond only infinitesimally, no matter how much prices fall. In graphical terms, as the price decline continues, the savings function might reach $S_3$ as a limiting position. That is, no matter how much the price level might fall, the savings function would never move to the right of $S_3$.[18] In such an event the declining price level would fail to bring about full employment. The validity of the Pigou argument thus depends on the additional assumption that the intensity of the inverse relationship between savings and real cash balances is such that it will be possible to shift over the savings function to a position where it will intercept the

---

[17] The role of real wages in Pigou's system is very ambiguous. At one point (p. 348, bottom) he assumes that reduced money wages will also decrease real wages. At another (p. 349, lines 20–38) no such assumption seems to be involved. "As money wage-rates fall . . . prices fall and go on falling." *Ibid.*

[18] Mathematically this may be stated as follows. Write the savings function as

$$S = \Gamma(r, p, Y).$$

(*Cf.* footnote 8 above.) Pigou's explicit assumption is

$$\Gamma_p(r, p, Y) > 0$$

where $\Gamma_p$ is the partial derivative of $S$ with respect to $p$. Let $Y = Y_0$ represent the full employment income. Then the argument here is that the savings function, $\Gamma$, may still be of a form such that

$$\lim_{p \to 0} \Gamma(r, p, Y_0) = \Gamma^*(r, Y_0)$$

for any fixed $r$—where $\Gamma^*$ is any curve which intersects the investment curve at a negative rate of interest. (In the argument of the text, $\Gamma^*$ is taken to be $S_3$ in Figure 5.) Pigou tacitly assumes that the savings function approaches no such limit; or that if it does, the limiting function intersects the investment function at a positive rate of interest.

investment function at a positive rate of interest: say, $S_4$ (*cf.* Figure 5).

What is at issue here is the reaction of individuals with already large real balances to further increases in these balances. Consider an individual with a cash balance of a fixed number of dollars. As the price falls, the increased real value of these dollars must be allocated between the alternatives of an addition to either consumption and/or real balances.[19] How the individual will actually allocate the increase clearly depends on the relative marginal utilities of these two alternatives. If we are willing to assume that the marginal utility of cash balances approaches zero with sufficient rapidity relative to that of consumption, then we can ignore the possibility of the savings curve reaching a limiting

(made available by the price decline) to add to his balances. In this event, the situation of Figure 5 may well occur.

9. I do not believe we have sufficient evidence either of an *a priori* or empirical[20] nature—to help us answer the question raised in the preceding paragraph. The empirical evidence available is consistent with the hypothesis that the effect of real balances on savings is very weak. But even granted the truth of this hypothesis, it casts no light on the question raised here. What we want to know is what happens to the effect of real balances on savings as these real balances increase in size. Even if the effect were arbitrarily small, but remained constant regardless of the size of real balances, there could be no convergence of savings functions like that pictured

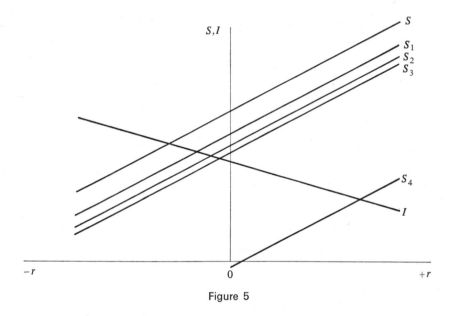

Figure 5

position such as in Figure 5. That is, we would be maintaining the position that by increasing the individual's balances sufficiently, he will have no further incentive to add to these balances; hence he will spend any additional real funds on consumption, so that we can make him consume any amount desired. If on the other hand, we admit the possibility that, for sufficiently large consumption, the decrease in the marginal utility of cash balances is accompanied by a much faster decrease in the marginal utility of consumption, then the individual will continuously use most of the additional real funds

in Figure 5. In the face of this lack of evidence, we have to be satisfied with the conclusion that, subject to the [reservations of §§ 6 and 8, Haberler and Pigou have] demonstrated the automaticity of full employment within the framework of the classical static model[21]—the

[20] Empirical studies on the effect of real balances on savings have been made by L. R. Klein, "The Use of Econometric Models as a Guide to Economic Policy," *Econometrica*, Vol. XV (1947), pp. 122–25. Klein's procedure was incorrect in that he used a series for $M_0$, instead of $M_1$ in fitting his equations (*cf.* last paragraph of § 6 above).

[21] It must be re-emphasized that this conclusion holds only for static analysis. The modifications that must be introduced once dynamic factors enter are discussed in Part II.

[19] I am abstracting here from the possible third alternative, investment.

main mechanism by which this is brought about being the effect of a price decline on cash balances.

The statement of this conclusion immediately raises the interesting question of how this set of forces, [emphasized by Haberler and Pigou,] could have been overlooked by Keynesian economists, in general, and Keynes himself, in particular. Questions of this type can rarely be answered satisfactorily—and perhaps should not even be asked. Nevertheless, I think it is both possible and instructive to trace through the exact chain of errors in Keynes's reasoning which caused him to overlook these factors.

I submit the hypothesis that Keynes recognized the influence of assets on saving (consumption), but unfortunately thought of this influence only in terms of physical capital assets. This was his fundamental error.[22] From it immediately followed that in his main discussion of the (short-run) consumption function, where he assumed a *constant* stock of capital, the possible influence of assets was not (and could not) even be considered.[23] But as soon as Keynes discussed a period sufficiently long for noticeable capital growth, the influence of assets on savings was immediately recognized.[24] Even here, Keynes could not come to the same conclusion as Pigou. For Keynes restricted himself to physical assets, and thus rightfully pointed out that it would be "an unlikely coincidence" that just the correct amount of assets should exist—*i.e.*, that amount which would push over the savings function to such a position where full employment could be generated. Compare this with the determinate process by which just exactly the "correct amount" of real cash balances is brought into existence in the Pigou analysis. (See above, § 5, paragraph 4.)

This exclusion of physical assets from the short-run consumption function was subconsciously extended to all kinds of assets. Here was the last link in the chain of errors. For later when Keynes began to examine the effects of

increased real cash balances (brought about either by price declines or increases in the amount of money), he did not even consider their possible influence on consumption. Instead, he concentrated exclusively on their tendency, through the liquidity function, to lower interest rates.[25] (*Cf.* above, § 7, last paragraph.)

Looking back on the nature of these errors, we cannot but be struck by the irony that they should have emanated from the man who did most to demonstrate the fundamental inseparability of the real and monetary sectors of our economy.

## II. Dynamic Analysis: The Question of Policy

10. [The Haberler-Pigou analysis discussed in Part I makes two contributions. First, in its emphasis on the effects of a price on savings *via* its effects on real balances, it introduces into the Keynesian analytical apparatus a set of forces hitherto overlooked by the latter. (For convenience this will be referred to as the Pigou effect —though as mentioned at the end of § 5 above, it is of much older origin.) Secondly, it proceeds to draw the implications of this set] of forces for static analysis, and summarizes its results in the following theorem (*cf.* §§ 5 and 6): *There always exists a sufficiently low price level such that, if expected to continue indefinitely,*[26] *it will generate full employment.*[27] (For convenience this will be referred to as the Pigou Theorem.) The purpose of this part of the paper is to accomplish a third objective: *viz.* to draw the implications of the Pigou effect for dynamic analysis and policy formulation. It must be emphasized that the Pigou Theorem tells us nothing about the dynamic and policy aspects

---

[22] Note that there are really two distinct errors involved here. The first is the obvious one of the exclusion of monetary assets. The second is that what is relevant for the influence on saving is not the *physical* asset, but its *real* value in terms of some general price level.

[23] J. M. Keynes, *The General Theory of Employment, Interest, and Money* (New York, Harcourt, Brace, and Co., 1936), Chap. 8. See especially pp. 91–5, where Keynes considers the possible influence of other factors besides income on consumption, and does not even mention assets.

[24] *Ibid.*, p. 218, second paragraph.

[25] *Ibid.*, pp. 231–34, 266. The following passage is especially interesting: "It is, therefore, on the effect of a falling wage- and price-level on the *demand for money* that those who believe in the self-adjusting quality of the economic system must rest the weight of their argument; though I am not aware that they have done so. If the quantity of money is itself a function of the wage and price-level, there is, indeed, nothing to hope for in this direction. But if the quantity of money is virtually fixed, it is evident that its quantity in terms of wage-units can be indefinitely increased by a sufficient reduction in money wage...." (*Ibid.*, p. 266. Italics not in original.)

[26] This qualifying phrase incorporates in it the restriction of the Pigou argument to static analysis.

[27] I am overlooking here the reservations discussed in §§ 6 and 8 above.

## Table 1

| Year | Money in Circulation Outside Treasury and Federal Reserve System | Market Value of Government Interest-bearing Debt Held Outside Government Agencies and the Federal Reserve System | Member Bank Deposits in the Federal Reserve System | Nonmember Bank Deposits in the Federal Reserve System | Other Federal Reserve Accounts | Reserve Bank Credit Outstanding Excluding that Based on Reserve Bank Holdings of U.S. Government Securities | Treasury Deposits in Member and Nonmember Banks | Postal Savings | Net Balances ($M_1$) $(1) + (2)$ $+ (3) + (4)$ $+ (5) - (6)$ $- (7) + (8)$ | Cost of Living Index ($p$) | Net Real Balances $\frac{M_1}{p}$ $(9) - (10)$ | Real National Income |
|------|------|------|------|------|------|------|------|------|------|------|------|------|
|      | (1)  | (2)  | (3)  | (4)  | (5)  | (6)  | (7)  | (8)  | (9)  | (10) | (11) | (12) |
| 1929 | 4.5  | 14.5 | 2.4  | 0.0  | 0.4  | 1.3  | 0.4  | 0.2  | 20.2 | 1.22 | 16.6 | 89.9 |
| 1930 | 4.2  | 13.9 | 2.4  | 0.0  | 0.4  | 0.5  | 0.3  | 0.2  | 20.4 | 1.19 | 17.1 | 76.3 |
| 1931 | 4.7  | 15.1 | 2.3  | 0.1  | 0.4  | 0.6  | 0.4  | 0.6  | 22.1 | 1.09 | 20.3 | 66.3 |
| 1932 | 5.3  | 16.0 | 2.1  | 0.1  | 0.4  | 0.6  | 0.4  | 0.9  | 23.7 | .98  | 24.2 | 54.2 |

All money figures are in billions of dollars.

Data for series (1), (3), (4), (5), (6) were obtained from *Banking and Monetary Statistics*, p. 368. On pp. 360–67 of this book their interrelationships are discussed. For (7) see *ibid.*, pp. 34-5. For (8) see *Statistical Abstract of the United States*, 1947, p. 419.

Being unable to find an official series for (2), I used the following procedure: Total outstanding government debt at face value was classified according to maturities (0–5 years, 5–10, and over 10) on the basis of *Banking and Monetary Statistics*, p. 511. These classifications were multiplied by price indexes for government bonds with maturities of more than 3 and less than 4 years, more than 6 and less than 9, and more than 10, respectively (Standard and Poor, *Statistics: Security Price Index Record*, 1948 edition, pp. 139–44). The sum of these products was used as an estimate of the market value of the total government debt. The ratio of this to the face value of the total debt was computed, and this ratio applied to the face value of government debt held outside the Treasury and Federal Reserve System (*Banking and Monetary Statistics*, p. 512) to yield an estimate of the required series.

Series (10): Bureau of Labor Statistics, cost of living index, *Survey of Current Business*, Supplement, 1942, p. 16.

Series (12): National income in billions of 1944 dollars. J. Dewhurst and Associates, *America's Needs and Resources* (New York, The Twentieth Century Fund, 1947), p. 697.]

which interest us in this third objective. (This point is discussed in greater detail in § 12.)

Specifically consider a full employment situation which is suddenly terminated by a downswing in economic activity. The question I now wish to examine is the usefulness of a policy which consists of maintaining the stock of money constant, allowing the wage and price levels to fall, and waiting for the resulting increase in real balances to restore full employment.

At the outset it must be made clear that the above policy recommendation is *not* to be attributed to Pigou. His interest is purely an intellectual one, in a purely static analysis. As he himself writes: "The puzzles we have been considering ... are academic exercises, of some slight use perhaps for clarifying thought, but with very little chance of ever being posed on the chequer board of actual life."[28]

In reality, Pigou's disavowal of a deflationary policy (contained in the paragraph from which the above quotation is taken) is not nearly as thoroughgoing as might appear on the first reading. The rejection of a price decline as a practical means of combatting unemployment may be due to: (a) the conviction that dynamic considerations invalidate its use as an immediate policy, regardless of its merits in static analysis; (b) the conviction that industrial and labor groups, sometimes with the assistance of government, prevent the price flexibility necessary for the success of a deflationary policy. A careful reading of Pigou's disclaimer indicates that he had only the second of these alternatives in mind; *i.e.*, that he felt that the policy would not work because it would not be permitted to work. What I hope to establish in this part of the essay is the first alternative: namely, that even granted full flexibility of prices, it is still highly possible that a deflationary policy will not work, due to the dynamic factors involved.

Nevertheless, nothing in this part of the paper is intended (or even relevant) as a criticism of Pigou, since the latter has clearly abstained from the problem of policy formulation. If sometimes the terms "Pigou effect" and "Pigou Theorem" are used in the following discussion, they should be understood solely as shorthand notations for the concepts previously explained.

11. The analysis of this section is based on the following two assumptions: (a) One of the prerequisites of a successful anti-depression policy is that it should be able to achieve its objective

rapidly (say, within a year). (b) Prices cannot fall instantaneously; hence, the larger the price level fall necessary to bring about full employment *via* the Pigou effect, the longer the time necessary for the carrying out of the policy. (If no price fall can bring about full employment, then we can say that an infinite amount of time is necessary for the carrying out of the policy.)

There are at least two factors which act toward lengthening the period necessary to carry out a policy based on the Pigou effect. The first is the possibility that the effect of an increase in cash balances on consumption is so small, that very large increases (very great price declines) will be necessary. [Certainly there is a burden of proof on the supporters of a policy of absolute price flexibility to show that this is not so;] that the economic system is sufficiently responsive to make the policy practical. So far no one has presented the required evidence.

The second factor is a result of the price decline itself. In dynamic analysis we must give full attention to the role played by price expectations and anticipations in general. It is quite possible that the original price decline will lead to the expectation of further declines. Then purchasing decisions will be postponed, aggregate demand will fall off, and the amount of unemployment increased still more. In terms of Figures 1 and 3, the savings function will rise (consumption will be decreased) and the investment function fall, further aggravating the problem of achieving full employment. This was the point on which Keynes was so insistent.[29] Furthermore, the uncertainty about the future generated by the price decline will increase the liquidity preference of individuals. Thus if we consider an individual possessing a fixed number of dollars, and confronted with a price decline which increases the real value of these dollars, his uncertainty will make him more inclined to employ these additional real funds to increase his real balances, than to increase his expenditures.[30] In other words, the uncertainty created by the price decline might cause people to accumulate indefinitely large real cash balances, and to increase their expenditures very little if at all. [Finally, the bankruptcies caused by the inability of creditors to carry the increased real burden of their debt (above, § 6) will strengthen the pessimistic outlook for the future. The simultaneous

---

[28] "Economic Progress in a Stable Environment," *Economica*, n. s. XIV (1947), 188.

[29] See his discussion of changes in money wages, *op. cit.*, pp. 260–69, especially p. 263. *Cf.* also J. R. Hicks, *Value and Capital* (Oxford, Oxford University Press, 1939), and O. Lange, *op. cit.*

[30] *Cf.* above, § 8, last paragraph.

interaction of these three forces] will further exacerbate these difficulties. For as the period of price decline drags itself out, anticipations for the future will progressively worsen, and uncertainties further increase. The end result of letting the Pigou effect work itself out may be a disastrous deflationary spiral, continuing for several years without ever reaching any equilibrium position. Certainly our past experiences should have sensitized us to this danger.

Because of these considerations I feel that it is impractical to depend upon the Pigou effect as a means of policy: the required price decline might be either too large (factor one), or it might be the initial step of an indefinite deflationary spiral (factor two).

On this issue, it may be interesting to investigate the experience of the United States in the 1930's. In Table 1, net balances are computed for the period 1929–32 according to the definition in § 6. As can be seen, although there was a 19 per cent *increase* in real balances from 1930 to 1931, real national income during this period *decreased* by 13 per cent. Even in the following year, when a further increase of 19 per cent in real balances took place, real income proceeded to fall by an additional 18 per cent. For the 1929–32 period as a whole there was an increase in real balances of 46 per cent, and a decrease in real income of 40 per cent.

It will, of course, be objected that these data reflect the presence of "special factors," and do not indicate the real value of the Pigou effect. But the pertinent question which immediately arises is: To what extent were these "special factors" necessary, concomitant results of the price decline itself! If the general feeling of uncertainty and adverse anticipations that marked the period is cited as one of these "special factors," the direct relationship between this and the decline in price level itself certainly cannot be overlooked. Other proposed "special factors" must be subjected to the same type of examination. The data of the preceding table are not offered as conclusive evidence. But they are certainly consistent with the previously stated hypothesis of the impracticability of using the Pigou effect as a means of policy; and they certainly throw the burden of proof on those who argue for its practicality.

12. The argument of the preceding section requires further explanation on at least one point. In the discussion of the "second factor" there was mentioned the possibility of an indefinitely continuing spiral of deflation and unemployment. But what is the relation between this possibility

and the Pigou Theorem (*cf.* § 10) established in Part I? The answer to this question may be expressed as follows:

On the downswing of the business cycle it might be interesting to know that there exists a sufficiently low price level which, if it were expected to continue existing indefinitely, would bring about full employment. Interesting, but, for policy purposes, irrelevant. For due to perverse price expectations and the dynamics of deflationary spirals, it is impossible to reach (or, once having reached, to remain at) such a position.

The implication of these remarks can be clarified by consideration of the cobweb theorem for the divergent case. Assume that a certain market can be explained in terms of the cobweb theorem. It is desired to know whether (assuming unchanged demand and supply curves) the designated market will ever reach a stationary position; that is, whether it will settle down to a unique price that will continue indefinitely to clear the market. This question is clearly divided into two parts: (a) does there exist such a price, and (b) if it does exist, will the market be able to attain it. In the case of the cobweb presented in Figure 6 it is clear that such a price does exist. For if the price $p_0$ had always existed and were expected to exist indefinitely, it would continuously clear the market. But Figure 6 represents the case of a divergent cobweb; hence the market will never be able to reach the price $p_0$. In brief, even though $p_0$ exists, it is irrelevant to the workings of the market. The analogy to the argument of the preceding paragraph is obvious.[31]

---

[31] The distinction of this section can be expressed in rigorous mathematical form using the dynamic system which has become familiar through the work of Samuelson and Lange (P. A. Samuelson, "The Stability of Equilibrium: Comparative Statics and Dynamics," *Econometrica*, Vol. IX [1941], pp. 97–120; Lange, *op. cit.*, pp. 91 ff.). Consider a single market and let $D$, $S$, and $p$ represent the demand, supply and price of the particular good, respectively. Let $t$ represent time. Then we can write this system as

(a)  $D = f(p)$       demand function
(b)  $S = g(p)$       supply function
(c)  $\dfrac{dp}{dt} = h(D\text{-}S)$       market adjusting function

The last equation has the property that

(d)  $\text{sign } \dfrac{dp}{dt} = \text{sign } (D\text{-}S)$

*i.e.*, price rises with excess demand and falls with excess supply. Consider now the static system identical with (a) − (c), except that it replaces (c) by

(e)  $D = S$

As long as (e) is not satisfied, we see from (d) that the

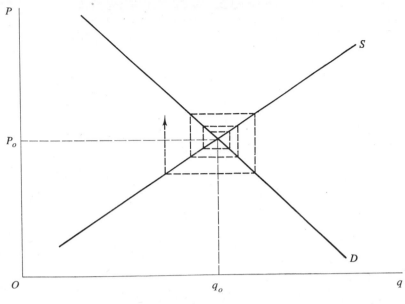

Figure 6

## III. Conclusions

13. The conclusions of this paper can be summarized as follows: in a static world with a constant stock of money,[32] price flexibility assures full employment. (I abstract here again from the difficulties raised in §§ 6 and 8.) But in the real dynamic world in which we live, price flexibility with a constant stock of money might generate full employment only after a long period; or might even lead to a deflationary spiral of continuous unemployment. On either of these grounds, a full employment policy based

on a constant stock of money and price flexibility does not seem to be very promising.

All that this means is that our full employment policy cannot be the fairly simple one of maintaining a constant stock of money and waiting for the economic system to generate full employment automatically through price declines. Other policies will be required. One possible alternative policy can be inferred from the Haberler-Pigou analysis itself: there are two ways to increase real balances. One is to keep the money stock constant and permit prices to fall. An equally effective way is to maintain the price level constant, and increase the stock of money by creating a government deficit.[33] This method of increasing real balances has the added advantage of avoiding one of the difficulties encountered previously (§ 11), for a policy of stabilizing the price level by increasing money stocks avoids some of the dangers of uncertainty and adverse anticipation accompanying general price declines. Nevertheless, there still remains the other difficulty—that individuals may not be very sensitive to increases

---

system will not be in stationary equilibrium, but will continue to fluctuate. Thus the existence of a solution to the static system (a), (b), (e) (*i.e.*, the consistency of (a), (b), (e) is a *necessary* condition for the existence of a stationary solution for the dynamic system (a), (b), (c). But this is not a sufficient condition. For the static system (a), (b), (e) may have a consistent solution which, if the dynamic system is not convergent, will never be reached.

Thus Pigou has completed only half the task. Setting aside the difficulties of § 8, we can accept his proof of the *consistency* of the *static* classical system. But that still leaves completely unanswered the question of whether the classical *dynamic* system will converge to this consistent solution. In this and the preceding section I have tried to show why such convergence may not occur in the real world. (I have discussed these issues in greater detail elsewhere. *Cf.* footnote 4, above.)

[32] Throughout Part III, unless otherwise indicated, "stock of money" is to be understood in the $M_1$ sense of the last paragraph of § 6.

[33] Considered from this perspective, the Pigou analysis presents in a rigorous fashion part of the theoretical framework implicit in the fiscal-monetary policy of the Simons-Mints position. *Cf.* the recently published collection of essays of Henry C. Simons, *Economic Policy for a Free Society* (Chicago, University of Chicago Press, 1948); and Lloyd W. Mints, "Monetary Policy," *Revue of Economic Statistics*, Vol. XXVIII (1946), pp. 60–9.

in real balances. If this turned out to be true, we would have to seek still other policies.

14. [On the basis of the analysis presented in this paper it is possible to re-examine the question which has been a favorite one of economists these past years: namely,] What is the distinctive characteristic of Keynesian analysis? It certainly cannot be the claim to have demonstrated the possibility of the coexistence of underemployment equilibrium and flexible prices. This, in its day, served well as a rallying cry. But now it should be definitely recognized that this is an indefensible position. For flexibility means that the money wage falls with excess supply, and rises with excess demand; and equilibrium means that the system can continue on through time without change. Hence, *by definition*, a system with price flexibility cannot be in equilibrium if there is any unemployment;[34] [but, like any other proposition that must be true by definition, this one, too, is uninteresting, unimportant, and uninformative about the real problems of economic policy].

Nor should Keynesian economics be interpreted as asserting that just as an underemployment equilibrium is impossible, so, too, in a static system may a full-employment equilibrium be impossible. That is, the static system may be at neither an underemployment equilibrium, nor a full-employment equilibrium. In other words, the static system may be inconsistent. (This is the negative interest rate argument of § 3.) For Pigou's and Haberler's discussion of the effect of a declining price level on real balances shows how this inconsistency is removed. It is, of course, still possible to maintain this interpretation of Keynes on the basis of the reservations of §§ 6 and 8. But I think this is neither necessary nor advisable. For the real significance of the Keynesian contribution can be realized only

within the framework of *dynamic* economics. Whether or not an underemployment equilibrium exists; whether or not full employment equilibrium always will be generated in a static system—all this is irrelevant. The fundamental issue raised by Keynesian economics is the *stability of the dynamic system*: its ability to return automatically to a full-employment equilibrium within a reasonable time (say, a year) if it is subjected to the customary shocks and disturbances of a peacetime economy. In other words, what Keynesian economics claims is that the economic system may be in a position of underemployment *dis*equilibrium (in the sense that wages, prices, and the amount of unemployment are continuously changing over time) for long, or even indefinite, periods of time.

But this is not sufficient to characterize the Keynesians. Everyone agrees that there exist dynamic systems which will not automatically generate full employment. What distinguishes one economic school from the other is the system (or systems) to which this lack of automaticity is attributed. If the Keynesian message is applied to an economic system with no monetary policy (if such a thing is possible to define), then it is purely trivial. For few would claim automaticity of full employment for such a system. Keynesian theory acquires meaning only when applied to systems with more intelligent monetary policies. Here an element of arbitrariness is introduced; for what is termed "Keynesian" depends entirely on the choice of the monetary policy to be used as a criterion.

On the basis of Keynes' writings, I believe it is clear that he was primarily interested in attacking the policy of assuring full employment by manipulation of the interest rate through open market operations.[35] But to Keynes, this policy was equivalent to one of wage flexibility;[36] for (he erroneously thought) the only effect of a wage decline was to increase the real value of the stock of money (in the $M_0$, not $M_1$, sense; *cf.* above, last paragraph of § 6) and thereby decrease the rate of interest—just as in open market operations. As we have pointed out above (end of §§ 6 and 7), these policies are really not equivalent. For open market operations may

---

[34] This can be expressed mathematically in the following way: let $N^S$ and $N^D$ be the amounts of labor supplied and demanded, respectively; $w$, the money wage rate; and $t$, time. Then a flexible dynamic system will, by definition, contain an equation of the general type

$$\frac{dw}{dt} = f(N^D - N^S)$$

where

$$\text{sign } \frac{dw}{dt} = \text{sign } (N^D - N^S).$$

If by equilibrium is meant a situation such that

$$\frac{dw}{dt} = 0$$

then clearly this system cannot be in equilibrium unless

$$N^D - N^S = 0$$

*i.e.*, unless there is full employment.

[35] *Cf.* Keynes, *op. cit.*, pp. 231–34; 266–67.

[36] "There is, therefore, no ground for the belief that a flexible wage policy is capable of maintaining a state of continuous full employment;—any more than for the belief that an open market monetary policy is capable, unaided, of achieving this result. The economic system cannot be made self-adjusting along these lines." (*Ibid.*, p. 267.)

change only $M_0$, whereas a wage and price decline change the real value of $M_1$ as well. Hence, open market operations may act only through the liquidity preference equation, whereas a policy of price flexibility acts also through the savings function (*cf.* above, footnote 8 and end of §§ 6 and 7).

Let us now assume that even if Keynes had recognized the distinction between open market and wage flexibility policies (*i.e.*, if he had recognized the Pigou effect) he still would have continued to reject the latter as a means of assuring full employment. This is not an unreasonable assumption; for most of the objections cited above (§ 11) against the use of a policy based on the Pigou effect, are the very same ones that Keynes uses in arguing against open market operations.[37]

Granted this assumption, I believe it is useful to identify the Keynesian position against one which maintains that full employment can be automatically achieved *via* the Pigou effect by maintaining a constant stock of money, and providing for wage and price flexibility. It is now possible to delineate three distinct theoretical formulations of the Keynesian position—differing in varying degrees from the classical one: (a) Most opposed to the classical position is the Keynesian one which states that even if there were no problem of uncertainty and adverse anticipations (that is, even if there were a static system), and even if we were to allow an infinite amount of time for adjustment, a policy of price flexibility would still not assure the generation of full employment. (This is the negative interest rate argument of §§ 3 and 8; [or the argument based on differential creditor-debtor responses of § 6].)

(b) Then there is the position which states that, in a static world, price flexibility would always assure full employment. But in a dynamic world of uncertainty and adverse anticipations, even if we were to allow an infinite adjustment period, there is no certainty that full employment will be generated. That is, we may remain indefinitely in a position of underemployment disequilibrium. (c) Finally, there is the Keynesian position, closest to the "classics," which states that even with uncertainty full employment would eventually be generated by a policy of price inflexibility; but the length of time that might be necessary for the adjustment makes the policy impractical.

Although these positions are quite distinct theoretically, their policy implications are very

similar. (In what way would the policies of a man advocating position (a) differ from those of a man advocating (c) and stating that the adjustment would take ten years?) The policies would in general be directed at influencing the consumption and investment functions themselves, in addition to manipulating the amount of money. Thus the policies may advocate tax reductions to stimulate consumption and investment (the Simons-Mints school); or may insist on direct government investment to supplement private investment (Hansen, *et al.*). In this way we could classify Keynesian positions according to their advocated policies, as well as their theoretical foundations.

[Finally, it should be noted that none of the preceding formulations of the Keynesian position is dependent upon the assumption of wage rigidities. This assumption is frequently, and erroneously, attributed to Keynesian economics as a result of two related misconceptions as to its nature. First of all, as we have seen, the attempt to interpret Keynes' analysis of unemployment within a static equilibrium framework makes it mandatory, by definition, to assume the existence of wage rigidities. The dynamic approach followed in this paper obviates this necessity.

A second implication of restricting ourselves to static equilibrium analysis is that *involuntary* unemployment can, *by definition*, exist only if there are wage rigidities. For if there were no rigidities, the wage level could assume any value; and for each such value there would be a corresponding, and presumably different, amount of labor supplied. Thus at the intersection point of the demand and supply curves—the only point of interest in static equilibrium analysis—workers are providing all the labor they wish to at the equilibrium wage. There can be no question of involuntary unemployment. Only if there are wage rigidities—a minimum wage $w_0$, below which the workers refuse to go—can the situation be different. For then the supply curve of labor is parallel to the quantity axis at the height $w_0$ until a certain point (say) $N_1$, is reached; only afterwards does the curve begin to rise. If the demand curve is now assumed to intersect the supply curve in its horizontal portion at, say, the quantity $N_0$, then we can say that *involuntary* unemployment to the extent $N_1 - N_0$ exists; for at the equilibrium wage rate, $w_0$, workers desire to provide a maximum of $N_1$ units of labor, and are instead providing only $N_0$.

However, once we throw off the restrictions of static equilibrium analysis, we also free ourselves of the necessity of assuming wage rigidity as a

[37] *Cf.* the passages cited in footnote 35, above.

necessary precondition of involuntary unemployment. For, during any given period of time, the dynamic workings of the system may well keep the workers at a point *off their supply curve*. In this departure from the supply curve lies the *involuntariness* of the unemployment. The important point here is that this situation can exist regardless of the shape of the supply curve; that is, even if wages are not rigid. One's view on the length of time such a situation can continue

clearly depends on one's choice of the three alternative Keynesian positions delineated above. All this has been dealt with at length elsewhere,[38] and there is no need for any further repetition here.[39]

wage rigidities are *not* an *assumption* of Keynes' analysis, but rather a policy conclusion that follows from his investigation of the probable effects of *wage flexibility*.

Further explicit evidence that Keynes, in his theory of unemployment, was concerned with a regime of flexible prices is provided by the following passage from the *General Theory* (p. 191): "in the extreme case where money wages are assumed to fall without limit in face of involuntary unemployment . . . there will, it is true, be only two possible long period positions—full employment and the level of employment corresponding to the rate of interest at which liquidity preference becomes absolute (in the event of this being less than full employment)."

[38] *Cf.* reference cited in footnote 4, above.

[39] It might be added that in the light of Chapter 19 of the *General Theory*—the chapter which provides the climax to Keynes' argument, and which explicitly examines the effects of wage flexibility—it is difficult to understand how wage rigidities can be considered a basic assumption of the Keynesian theory of unemployment. From this chapter it is quite clear that

*E. J. MISHAN*

# The Demand for Labor in a Classical and Keynesian Framework

*15* The principal aim of the first section of this paper is to demonstrate that, contrary to current opinion and teaching,[1] the marginal product of labor can no more be regarded as representing the demand curve for labor in a "classical" monetary framework—one in which the rate of interest alone brings into equilibrium current saving and investment plans —than in a Keynesian framework: indeed, that such a demand curve is, like that in a Keynesian system, primarily derivable from the effective demand for goods.

Section II illustrates a geometric device for tracing the effects on the aggregate demand and

supply of labor of changes in the exogenous variables under the usual technological and market assumptions. The final section briefly reconsiders the operation of the cash-balance effect and its irrelevance to the homogeneity postulate.

## I

The justification for treating the marginal product of labor curve as a demand curve for labor appears to rest on two popular simplifications: (*a*) perfect competition and, as an ostensible corollary, (*b*) diminishing marginal product. And this alleged demand curve has been interpreted to yield either or both of the following propositions: (1) that, since the amount of labor employed is uniquely associated with a given marginal product and, therefore, in perfect competition with a given real wage, this amount of labor is the maximum demanded by the economy at that real wage; (2) that any fall in the real wage—since it implies a fall in money wages relative to prices —acts to increase the demand for labor.

These two simplifications, though obviously convenient in the formal treatment of macroeconomic systems, are not necessary, as we shall

[1] To mention just a few writers, D. Patinkin, *Money, Interest and Prices* (Evanston, Ill.: Row, Peterson, & Co., 1956), p. 128; Gardner Ackley, *Macroeconomic Theory* (New York: Macmillan Co. 1963), pp. 131 ff.; T. Durnburg and D. McDougall, *Macroeconomics* (New York: McGraw-Hill Book Co., 1960), p. 139 ff. See also A. C. Pigou, *The Theory of Unemployment* (London: Macmillan & Co., 1933), esp. chap. ii, Part III.

Reprinted from the *Journal of Political Economy,* Vol. LXXII (1964), pp. 610-16, by permission of the author and the University of Chicago Press. Copyright 1964 by The University of Chicago. E. J. Mishan is at the London School of Economics.

see later. Even if we adopt them, however, propositions (1) and (2) do not follow. The first casts the marginal productivity relation, essentially $q$–$p$, or quantity-into-price, relation into a $p$–$q$, or price-into-quantity, form. And while it is true that perfect competition implies that price equals marginal cost and, therefore, that—since a common wage prevails—marginal physical product equals the real wage, this condition holds not only in some full-employment equilibrium but for any amount of labor that happens to be employed. The most we could say of the marginal product curve in this connection is that it traces a locus of all possible equilibrium positions in which this condition obtains. But such a downward sloping locus is not to be reconciled with proposition (2), a decline in the real wage being properly regarded as the *result* of an expansion of aggregate demand, an expansion which has yet to be explained; the wage decline is not the "cause" of the expansion. In perfect competition, an initial expansion in aggregate effective demand takes on immediate shape as a rise in price above marginal cost (and therefore a fall in the real wage) at the *existing* output (before any expansion takes place) and *irrespective* of the shape of the marginal product curve. Only as firms respond to this initial differential by expanding output is marginal cost equated to price again, and only if the marginal product is *diminishing* will the resulting real wage be lower than before.

The question of the shape of the marginal product curve turns our attention once again to simplifications (*a*) and (*b*). As suggested above, neither is a necessary part of the classical, or any, monetary system. The Cambridge monetary equation,[2] $M^s = kpY^*$ is, like the fundamental Keynesian equation $Y = C + I$, no less true for a monopolistic economy than for a competitive one. Moreover, the validity of either hypothesis does not depend upon a particular production function.

Thus, if we happened to believe that perfect competition was formally consistent, in the short period, only with rising supply price,[3] there would be nothing to prevent us from considering short-period constant or decreasing cost for the

economy if we introduce a non-competitive structure of industry. True, maximizing firms now set price above marginal cost, but this implies only that the locus of real wages against amounts of labor employed will lie at all points below the corresponding locus of the marginal product of labor while following its general shape. This locus of real wages can now also be constant or upward-sloping. In the former, the customary interpretation of such a locus would entail an infinitely elastic demand for labor at a given real wage.[4] If the latter, the demand curve for labor increases with a *rise* in the real wage. This real-wage locus, then, makes little sense regarded as a demand curve for labor in these technological conditions. But it makes perfectly good sense if such a locus is regarded as indicating no more than a real wage (equals marginal product in perfect competition) corresponding to any output that may be produced—the output itself, and the level of employment necessary to produce it, being determined by effective demand to which concept we now turn.

Within a classical monetary system in which the prices of different sorts of securities are determined, like any other good, by current demand and supply (equal, respectively, to current saving and current investment), there can be no liquidity trap. Provided all income is spent—that is, no hoarding or dishoarding—the division of expenditure between commodities and services on the one hand, and securities on the other, makes no difference to aggregate effective demand $E$, which, then, always remains equal to income. If, for any reason, such as trade union control, money wages and therefore the price level are held constant over the period in question, the equilibrium level of money income within that period may entail underemployment; that is, at the existing real wage, the supply of labour exceeds the current demand for it.[5] If we begin with some underemployment equilibrium, by referring .to the quantity equation $M^s = kpY^*$, any increase of the stock of money $M^s$ with unchanged price level, or any reduction in the price

---

[2] $Y^*$ is real income, by definition equal to real output, $X$.

[3] If, on the other hand, we allow for external economies of scale, then each firm can face an upward-sloping marginal cost curve while, for the economy as a whole, the marginal cost curve can be constant or declining—that is, for the economy as a whole, the marginal product of labor can be constant or increasing.

[4] Full employment would still be determined by the intersection of the upward-sloping supply curve of labor with the real-wage curve. But, regarding this wage curve as a demand curve for labor, it would also imply that, regardless of effective demand, industry would be prepared to employ an infinite amount of labor at the given real wage.

[5] Keynes's definition of involuntary unemployment on p. 15 of *The General Theory* is close to the above. The reversed L-shaped supply curve of labor, which is more frequently associated with the Keynesian system, is adumbrated later on, on p. 26.

level $p$, increases the real effective demand $E^*$ and therefore real income $Y^*$. If we hold $M^s$ constant, real effective demand $E^*$ may be constructed as a rectangular hyperbola against the price level: halving the price level doubles the effective demand. And it is from this effective demand for goods that the effective demand for labor is derived.

It will be noticed that it is the absolute, or money, level of prices that is the operative factor in determining the demand for goods and therefore for labor. Since we are dealing with monetary systems, this is as it should be. For all markets respond, in the first instance, to money prices. If, for example, there happens to be an excess supply of labor on the market at the existing wage, the assumption of "flexible wages," by definition,[6] entails a fall in the *money* wage. It is then an *implication* of this flexibility assumption— one of the possible assumptions within the classical framework[7]—that the equilibrium level of income must be one of full employment. In other words, full-employment equilibrium is not only an "essential" property of the basic monetary model, but something that may be inferred as resulting from the monetary-operated effective demand, on the one hand, which *is* an "essential" component of the classical system, and, on the other, the posited flexibility of money wages.

## II

The attempt has been made to establish the proposition that the demand curve for labor is derived *primarily* from the effective demand for goods in a monetary system in which the quantity theory is central. The word "primarily" has been italicized, for it now remains to effect a synthesis by bringing into the picture the marginal product curve and the supply curve of labor. These curves can be of any shape, but we may begin with the more familiar diminishing marginal product of labor and rising supply curve of labor against real wages in a perfectly competitive economy. It is now simple to show that, although the effective demand for goods against the price level is of

unit elasticity, that for the labor has an elasticity greater than unity. If, for example, we increase the aggregate demand for goods by 10 per cent, by reducing the price level 10 per cent, the more rapidly returns to additional labor diminish—the less effective, therefore, being additional labor— the greater, proportionally, is the labor required to produce the increase in goods required.[8] As for the derived *supply* curve of labor against the price level, this will in general have an elasticity different from the supply curve against the real wage. If having the price level (doubling the quantity of goods demanded and, given diminishing marginal product, more than doubling the demand for labor) happens to result in an exact halving of the marginal product, or real wage, the elasticity of the supply of labor against the price level will be the same as that against the real wage. If, however, the marginal product is more than halved, the supply of labor against the price level has a higher elasticity than that of the supply curve against real wages; and a lower elasticity if the marginal product is less than halved. In the limiting case of an unchanged marginal product of labor, and therefore unchanged real wage, there is a zero response in the supply of labor to alterations in the price level. Finally, a rising marginal product of labor would imply a negative relation between the price level and the supply of labor.

The exact derivation of the demand and supply curves for labor against the price level can be illustrated in the four-quadrant Figure 1. In quadrant *I* we have a set of rectangular hyperbolas indicating the equilibrium relation between the price level $p$ and the demand for output $X$, the successive curve to the right being associated with larger stocks of money $M$. In quadrant *II* we plot three things: (a) the $F(X)$ curve, or Knightian curve, relating *total* product $X$ to labor employed $L^d$; (b) the $F'(X)$ curve, or *marginal* product curve; and (c) the supply curve of labor, $S$, against the real wage, $w^*$. Quadrant *III* is largely a dummy quadrant and is used to transfer the quantities of labor demanded and supplied, $L^d$ and $L^s$, from the vertical axis of quadrant *II* to the horizontal axis of quadrant *IV*. Quadrant *IV* shows the derived demand and supply curves of labor against the price level.

---

[6] See Patinkin, *op. cit.*, p. 214.

[7] Pigou, working within the classical framework in his *Theory of Unemployment*, in fact attributed the existing unemployment primarily to the prevailing inflexibility of money wages, not to too high a real-wage rate (as one might infer from reading Keynes's interpretation of Pigou's argument in chap. ii of *The General Theory*.)

[8] We are for the present, constructing the demand for labor against the money price, *not* the money wage. With diminishing marginal product, money wage falls relative to price as output increases, so that the elasticity of demand for labor against money wages becomes smaller than it is against the price level.

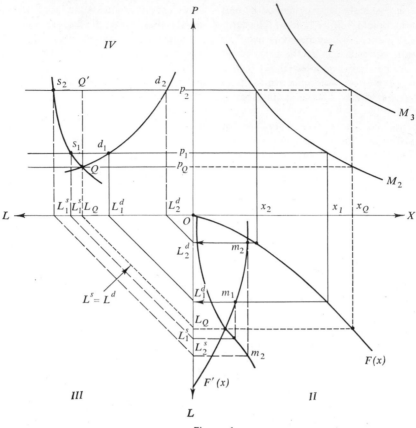

Figure 1

Hold the stock of money constant at $M_2$. With price level $p_2$, $X_2$ goods will be demanded. From the $F(X)$ curve, we demand the labor requirements $L_2^d$ which, through quadrant *III*, are projected on to the horizontal axis of quadrant IV. The coordinates of $L_2^d$ and $p_2$ give us the point $d_2$ on the demand curve for labor in *IV*. Beginning now with $p_1$, with $X_1$, demanded, the $F(X)$ curve requires $L_1^d$ labor, and we determine another point $d_1$ on the demand curve for labor. Consider now the derivation of the supply curve for labor against the price level. Once more we begin with price $p_2$ with $X_2$ demanded and therefore $L_2^d$ of labor required. The real wage is therefore given by the $F'(X)$ curve as $L_2^d m_2$ ($= L_2^s m_2$). From the $S$ curve in the same quadrant the amount of labor offered at this real wage is $OL_2^s$, this being projected via *III* on to the horizontal axis of quadrant *IV*. The coordinates of $L_2^s$ and $p_2$ give the point $s_2$ on the supply curve of labor. If we take another price, $p_1$, associated with effective demand for $X_1$, and therefore for $L_1^d$ labor, we have a real wage of $L_1^d m_1$ and, from the $S$ curve, an offer of labor equal to $OL_1^s$; hence another point $s_1$ on the

supply curve in quadrant *IV*.[9] Finally, there is some price level $P_Q$ at which the amounts of labor demanded and offered are equal, indicated by $L_Q$ in the figure. The coordinates of $L_Q$ and $p_Q$ in quadrant *IV* are given by $Q$, the point of intersection of the demand and supply curves for labor. This "full-employment" route is traced through the four quadrants by the dotted line.

At any price level above $p_Q$, $L^s$ exceeds $L^d$, indicating the prevalence of "involuntary unemployment." At a price level below $p_Q$ there is excess demand for labor, that is, "involuntary vacancies." The assumption of flexible wages implies a reduction in money wages whenever there is an excess supply of labor, and con-

[9] The more monopolistic is production, the more price exceeds marginal cost and the further below the marginal product curve is the real wage paid corresponding to any employment. With an upward-sloping supply curve for labor against real wages, monopoly has the effect of shifting inward the supply curve for labor against the price level, so reducing the full-employment equilibrium quantities of labor used, and goods produced, and raising the full-employment price level.

versely; the only position of rest being at $p_Q$, the "full-employment" equilibrium.

It should be noted in passing that since, in perfect competition, the money wage is equal to the marginal physical product times the product price, we can transfer these price demand and supply schedules into money-wage demand and supply schedules.

Using this basic construction several implications are worth noticing.

1. If in the initial situation with $M_2$, the price level is fixed at $p_2$, involuntary unemployment being measured by $L_2{}^s - L_2{}^d$, full-employment equilibrium may be restored by increasing the stock of money to $M^3$, which has the effect of shifting upward the demand and supply schedules for labor to intersect at $Q'$, associating $L_Q$ with $p_2$. If, on the other hand, money wages, and hence prices, are flexible, and we begin with the full-employment price $p_Q$ (corresponding to $M_2$ stock of money) increases in the stock of money raise the demand and supply schedules and the full-employment price level *pari passu* without altering the employment level $L_Q$ or aggregate real income $X_Q$.[10]

2. If the supply of labor is fixed independently of the real wage, it will be fixed independently of the price level and, therefore, of the money wage also. (The full-employment equilibrium is here determined irrespective of the degree of monopoly.)[11]

3a. If there are constant returns to labor, the $F(X)$ curve is a ray through the origin, and the $F'(X)$ curve a straight line parallel to $OL$ in quadrant *II*. The demand for labor curve in quadrant *IV*, like the $X^d$ curve in quadrant *I*, is then a rectangular hyperbola. Since, however, the real wage remains unchanged regardless of output produced, the supply schedule of labour in *IV* becomes a vertical line—the supply of labor being unresponsive to movements in the price level or money wage. (Monopoly results in some inward movement of this vertical supply curve.)

3b. If returns to labor are increasing, however, the curvature of $F(X)$ is reversed and the demand

curve for labor in *IV* has an elasticity below unity (ignoring the negative sign). The $F'(X)$ curve is now upward-sloping and, with the same real supply curve (and regardless of the degree of monopoly), the supply curve of labor in *IV* becomes downward-sloping. If the upward-sloping supply curve in *IV* is less steep than the demand curve, the equilibrium employment position is unstable in the Hicksian sense.[12] This is possible where the elasticity of labor supply against the real wage is high and increasing marginal product of labor is marked. However, since the supply of labor must become increasingly inelastic against the real wage, and the returns to labor must eventually diminish, there will exist a stable full-employment equilibrium at a higher output.

4. Finally, if instead of plotting the price level against aggregate output $X$ in the *I* quadrant, we plot the popular Keynesian diagram, measuring vertically aggregate real demand (instead of price level), we can use the same quadrants *II* and *III* to derive in quadrant *IV* demand and supply schedules of labor against aggregate output. The simplest case is that in which the marginal consumption propensity is less than unity and the rate of interest is perfectly stabilized —changes in the quantity of money making no difference to aggregate effective demand, which depends only on exogenous investment in a closed system. The more investment, the higher we are in our 45° line through the origin of quadrant *I*.[13] As we move along this line (as investment increases) we trace out the demand curve for labor against aggregate output in *IV*. In the familiar case of diminishing marginal product and the upward-sloping curve of labor against real wages, the demand curve in *IV* is positively correlated with aggregate output, the two schedules yielding a stable full-employment equilibrium. At any other aggregate demand we

---

[10] If, at the other extreme, the supply curve of labor is infinitely elastic at some real wage, then whatever the price level corresponding to the real wage (as indicated in perfect competition by the $F'[X]$ curves), the supply schedule in *IV* is horizontal at that price level. At any price level above this, unemployment is "infinitely" large; below it, employment is zero.

[11] Again, however, the higher the degree of monopoly the more inward-shifted is the supply curve in *IV*.

[12] Hicksian stability requires that at a price just below the equilibrium there is excess demand.

[13] Thus the Keynesian model may be regarded as a "real" (non-monetary) theory insofar as the assumption of perfect interest-rate stability (infinite liquidity preference) implies that no changes in the real stock of money, either direct or through falling prices, can dislodge us from the intersection reached on a 45° line. Insofar as an increase in money can—by lowering interest rates and increasing investment— move this equilibrium income up the 45° line, then it is to that extent also a monetary theory. But it is only when an increase in the stock of money increases effective demand by flowing *directly* into the circulating medium that we are back in our classical system, in which the determination of the level of income is purely a monetary phenomenon.

can measure the extent of the involuntary un-employment (or over-employment) from these quadrant $IV$ schedules. No recourse need be had to "money illusion" or to any special assumptions about the shape of the labor supply curve.[14]

## III

In this simplest of classical monetary models we may briefly indicate the operation of the cash balance effect. The hyperbolas in quadrant $I$ of Figure 1 illustrate equilibrium relations only, those in which $M^s = M^d$, where $M^d = kpY^*$. Consider disequilibrium positions: (1) beginning from underemployment real income $X_1$ and price $p_1$ corresponding to stock of money $M_2$, introduce an institutional rise in price to $p_2$. $M^s < kpY^*$ until real income has fallen to $X_2$; (2) beginning with full-employment equilibrium income $X_q$ and price $p_q$, an autonomous increase in the money stock from $M_2$ to $M_3$ results in $M^s > kpY^*$ until price has been re-established at $p_2$. The mechanism which is in operation during the disequilibrium periods generates the cash-balance effect. The exact path of adjustment to the new equilibrium is a matter for dynamics, but the direction imparted to aggregate money income is given by the rule, known as the cash-balance effect—operative only in monetary dis-equilibrium—that an excess stock of cash tends to raise money income, and vice versa. In general, then, aggregate effective demand $E$ in the simple classical model is best represented by the equation $E = Y + f(M^s - M^d)$, where $Y$ is the existing money income. When the Cambridge monetary equilibrium is met, $M^s = M^d$, and effective demand is exactly equal to income. If for any reason $M^s > M^d$, a positive cash-balance effect is in operation, and effective demand exceeds income by some rate of dishoarding determined by the function.

We conclude by comparing the real and mone-tary models of a classical flexible-wage full-

employment economy. Provided the equilibrium condition in the real model is that aggregate real expenditure equals real income, there are no in-consistencies in the respective equilibrium re-sponses of real quantities demanded to changes in the price level, the stock of money, or the demand to hold cash balances.

There is no need to consider a change in $p$ alone since in the Cambridge equation such a change is not possible without a change in $M$ or $k$.[15] If $k$ increases, with $M$ constant, $p$ falls and, in the Cambridge equation aggregate real quantities demanded and supplied remain un-altered as they do also in the real system. If $M$ increases with $k$ constant, $p$ increases in the same proportion, real quantities again being unaltered as in the real system. Both in the equilibrium money and real systems, then, real quantities are homogeneous of degree zero in the stock of money and prices. And it is in this sense that the real variables—the amounts demanded—are "independent of money," a sense which seems to warrant the procedural dichotomy between the real and the monetary systems.

[14] As, for example, in Modigliani's well-known paper "Liquidity Preference and the Theory of Interest and Money," *Econometrica*, 1944.

[15] To assert that, in the real system, the real (quantity) variables are homogeneous of degree zero with respect to money prices *alone* would certainly appear to disclose an inconsistency between the money and the real system. For a rise, say, in prices alone, being incompatible with the Cambridge equilibrium equation, generates a *disequilibrium* in the money system, the demand to hold money exceeding the stock; and in consequence—according to $f(M^s - M^d)$—there would be an excess current supply of goods which (dynamic conditions permitting) would tend to restore the original level of prices. But it is not legitimate to complain of inconsistency if we compare the implications of a real model in equi-librium with a money model in *disequilibrium*. The inferred budget constraint of a long-run equilibrium real system (aggregate expenditure exactly = aggre-gate earnings), such as that of Walras, itself excludes the favored experiment of, say, doubling all prices alone and, therefore, throwing the economy into dis-equilibrium. In order to meet the condition that the real system remain in equilibrium irrespective of the level of money prices, any level of money prices must be associated with the corresponding equilibrium stock of money: in the simple quantity equation, a scaling-up of all prices entails a proportional scaling-up of the stock of money.

*EDWIN KUH*

# Unemployment, Production Functions, and Effective Demand

*16* The hegemony of neo-classical theory was destroyed in 1936 by Keynes, who nevertheless retained much neoclassical analysis. Now, thirty years later, most economists have two separate tool kits to deal with interdependent systems—one relating to effective demand and unemployment and the other to microeconomic behavior under assumed conditions of full employment. Indeed, within four years of publication, one of the *General Theory*'s major neoclassical microeconomic suppositions—that the real wage should decline as employment increased—was brought into question by the empirical articles of Dunlop (1938) and Tarshis (1939). Econometric model builders and others concerned with empirical reality dropped most of the production-function-labor-market elements of the *General Theory* and concentrated their efforts on a better understanding of demand-expenditure equations.

In this paper I will sketch out a modest reformulation of effective demand, labor-market relations, and production functions. This will serve to link in a more observable fashion neoclassical supply-and-demand considerations at full employment and effective demand at less than full employment. Involuntary unemployment, according to this approach, depends mostly on production-function attributes in a manner first suggested by Vanek (1963)[1] and the Keynes-Lerner hypothesis about price-wage adjustment, having little to do with the Keynesian "money-illusion" labor-supply schedule. The important elements are familiar and straightforward.

## A. Short-Run Production and the Level of Output

One new but widely accepted characterization of the production process is the following. It is now fashionable to posit that ex ante investment decisions are made according to standard neo-

Reprinted from the *Journal of Political Economy*, Vol. LXXIV (1966), pp. 238–346, by permission of the author and the University of Chicago Press. Copyright 1966 by the University of Chicago. Edwin Kuh is a professor at the Massachusetts Institute of Technology.

[1] Vanek's main purpose was to provide a systematic rationale of an investment-acceleration model based on fixed technical coefficients for an earlier business-cycle model proposed by Kaldor.

classical production-function and capital-theory analysis. Relative factor scarcity, both actual and expected, will determine the optimal factor proportions for new investment goods according to a variable proportion production function.[2] Once built, though, a machine is used with labor in fixed proportions, since most machine designs severely restrict possibilities for ex post variation of factor proportions.

This general approach of ex ante substitutability and ex post fixed proportions has been made the basis of growth models by Johannsen (1959) and Phelps (1962) as well as providing the point of departure for a capital theoretic article by Solow (1962). Since my objective is to study short-run and not asymptotic long-run behavior, the growth models cited do not provide much guidance. Solow's model provides the most convenient point of departure even though it postulates full employment. In models such as this, employment of the labor force will be determined by the level of output. If the real wage is not malleable in the short run (which as a matter of fact it does not appear to be), fluctuations in output will determine variations in employment exactly according to the fixed coefficients relating capital and labor to each other and to output. The actual pattern of employment depends on the composition of technical coefficients embodied in the existing stock of capital. In turn, the composition of technologies depends upon the neoclassical determinants of expected future wages and interest rates at the time that investment decisions were made.

Thus effective demand determines the level of output, and a fixed coefficient technology determines employment of labor and capital in use, provided that the real wage is at a level that will permit non-negative profits on the marginal piece of equipment in use.[3] This pro-

vides an obvious parallel to acceleration-principle reasoning used to explain the steady-date dynamics of fixed plant and equipment and of inventory investment. While few economists believe that nature has immutably fixed desired capital-output ratios, many accept the notion that changes in the technology itself, and new factor combinations induced by relative price changes are intrinsically slow moving compared to variations in output and capacity utilization during a business cycle.

Short-run fluctuations around the desired capital-output or labor-output ratio depend upon distributed lags in the process of adjusting factor inputs to different levels of output. A complete statement embodying both the neoclassical elements and distributed lags for capital assets can be found in Jorgenson (1963, 1965). More recently, attention has been devoted to the short-term lagged adjustments of labor requirements to output levels by Nield (1963), Soligo (1963), Solow (1963), Eckstein and Wilson (1964). Brechling (1965), and myself (1965a, 1965b). The lags depend primarily on the quasi-fixed or overhead nature of numerous types of labor and on the costs associated with changes in employment, according to the propositions of Holt, Modigliani, Muth, and Simon (1960). Since these lags are quantitatively much shorter and less central to the theory under discussion, this particular similarity in behavior of capital and labor will not be pursued further.

## B. Real Wages and Fixed Coefficient Intramarginal Technology

The full employment analysis of Solow (1962) requires further exposition. He makes the assumption that no labor can be redundant at a non-negative real wage because an insufficient number of machines are in existence. Thus machinery is either fully used or, in an essentially Ricardian way, it is idle because it cannot earn non-negative profits at the going real-wage rate. On this (labor) "non-redundancy" assumption, a homogeneous stock of labor is supplied inelastically to the market, the real wage being set by the intersection of the (vertical) labor supply and a declining step function demand-for-labor schedule which depends on the capital stock's labor intensity.

It is interesting to note that the reverse assumption has been used by Richard S. Eckaus (1955) to explain the massive unemployment observed in under-developed countries such as India. But

[2] The proper curvature conditions for an interior solution to cost minimization in the context of a present value maximization criterion for capital decisions will be assumed, but none of the standard and more restrictive assumptions (for example, constant returns) need be assumed at this stage of the argument.

[3] It has been suggested that the propositions concerning labor unemployment developed here are compatible with smooth factor substitution in a neo-classical production function, only provided that the real wage is fixed. This suggestion, however, is not compatible with the simultaneous occurrence of idle capital and idle labor. In short, I believe that the framework used here is much more capable of explaining reality than the alternative possibility of a rigid real wage in the context of a neoclassical production function.

in most industrially advanced countries, including the United States, the prevalence of
single-shift operations and spare-plant capacity,
except during wartime or postwar booms,
suggests that the labor non-redundancy assumption is most relevant here.

However, the labor-supply equation cannot
be used to explain unemployment, which cannot
exist by virtue of assumptions about: (1) labor
demand, (2) labor non-redundancy, and (3) real-
wage inelastic supply. Retaining the first two
assumptions while dropping the third clearly
offers the greatest promise of reconstructing a
labor-market supply equation which permits
unemployment when demand is deficient, yet
which also is compatible with full employment.
A number of behavorial assumptions are possible,
including the Keynesian money-illusion supply
schedule. However ingenious this assumption is
in providing one theoretical transition admitting
involuntary unemployment in an otherwise fully
classical mold, it does not seem especially compelling in the context of the short-run fixed
proportions technology, which appears to be
the dominant element in short-run employment
fluctuations. In substance, then, involuntary
unemployment ought to depend primarily on
fixed coefficient production functions and not
upon questionable assumptions about the true
labor-supply function.

An examination of real-wage data in manufacturing recorded in an Appendix below indicates that over long stretches of time the real
wage moves upward rather steadily with occasional acceleration or retardation; there appears
to be slight systematic relation between the real
wage and short-term fluctuations in output and
employment. If our identification on the demand
site is correct, it then follows that the existing
total labor force can be hired at the going real
wage but not for less until the total labor force is
fully employed. Then the total labor force will
behave in a more nearly classical mode. The
horizontal (up to full employment) relation
between employment and the real wage should
be thought of as an "as if" supply schedule. In
actuality, money wages depend upon prices (and
other things as well), while prices depend upon
wages (and other determinants as well) with
quite complicated lag structures. The upshot,
however, is that wide variations in the quantity
of labor supplied are compatible with small
deviations the given real wage (trend).[4]

## C. Short-Run Labor Supply and Real Wages

There are several reasons why a valid approximation to a real short-run labor supply, real-
wage relation should be pictured as infinitely
elastic with respect to the real wage, rather than
assuming unemployment away by postulating a
totally inelastic function or even a horizontal
supply curve with a fixed money wage the crucial
element. The most important reason is the highly
restricted ability of labor to affect its real wage
because prices will move approximately in
proportion to money wages in competitive
markets, as Keynes long ago pointed out. Imperfectly competitive product markets where
prices are set according to markups, and labor
is the main component of variable costs, yield
equivalent results. Most emphasis should be
given to the imperfect competition aspect since
most industrial prices do not decline rapidly
even when massive idle capacity appears to
exist.[5] As an evident additional imperfection
arising in labor markets, it is improbable that
strong trade unions would tolerate substantial
reductions in real wages, since they are aware that
the real-wage demand elasticity for labor is likely
to be small. Even when trade unions were weak in
the early 1930's, however, real wages were considerably more stable than money wages. In the
prevailing circumstances, which I believe to be
highly unfavorable to large-scale short-run
substitution, trade unions would be quite
rational to opt against cyclical reductions in real
wages. At best, such cuts would result in some
slight increase in employment but only at the
expense of a drastic adverse shift in the distribution of income. Irrespective of trade union
behavior, however, fixed technical coefficients
will largely determine employment decisions,
since empirical observations of relatively stable
real wages accompanied by large fluctuations in
employment in the short run are broadly similar
before and after strong trade union organization.

A correlative point concerns the nature of
expectations. Suppose the demand for labor on
new machines is determined by the usual marginal
productivity considerations in a standard capital
model setting. Furthermore, labor productivity
is expected to rise in a steady way, much as it has
done historically. Downward real-wage rigidity of
labor supply can then rationally be based on the
belief that the decline in labor demand is viewed

[4] Observations concerning real and money wages
are based on historical time series presented in the
Appendix, Section B (Not reprinted).

[5] These points are elaborated in Section E of this
paper.

as temporary and that even competitive wage bargains should be based on long-run determinants.

The operative employment, real-wage relation is closely akin to but differs from the usual conception of a free-market labor-supply relation. The supply curve is the lower bound of the wage-employment combinations open to employers. Even though the unemployed would accept a lower real wage, this is prevented by market behavior of the sort described, so that the observed combination of employment and real wages in depressions lies above the supply curve.[6]

I have raised various questions in regard to the real or monetary arguments of short-run labor supply and speculated on the motivation and influence of trade unions on real wages. In most respects the answers cannot be crucial to the principal argument of this paper, according to which employment is determined by effective demand through fixed coefficient production relations, so that involuntary unemployment, strictly speaking, is the difference between the (given) labor force and employment thus determined. Involuntary unemployment is, therefore, independent of the precise nature of the labor-supply function.[7] As a side condition, however, the real wage cannot be at such a high level that the expected profitability of operating capital goods becomes negative.

There are, however, matters of genuine analytical interest which do hinge on the nature of the labor-supply function. Large short-run variations in output and employment do take place at nearly constant or rising real wages, so that it is worth asking whether observed labor-supply relations might in fact have a rather different motivation than the Keynesian money-illusion variant. If the operative employment, wage relation can sensibly be interpreted as being in real terms, which I believe it can, it will greatly facilitate construction of operational macro models with detailed labor-market equations

that embody both unemployment and full employment. Until now, labor supply and in many cases labor demand as well have been ignored or treated in the most *ad hoc* fashion in effective demand models, while growth models assume full employment in order to concentrate on resource-allocation problems and thereby precluding effective demand considerations from interacting with long-run growth determinants. The proposed labor-supply construction should go some distance toward bridging this gap.[8] At the same time, more detailed future study of the short-run dynamics of wage and price determination will almost certainly modify the strong assumption of a fixed real wage for even major variations in employment. This position was adopted in order to present the sharpest contrast with alternative postulates about labor behavior which, I believe, need revision in the directions indicated.

### D. Basic Aggregate Model: Unemployment Version

At this point it seems useful to present a symbolic summary of the preceding discussion. The symbols are as follows:

$X$ = aggregate real output, in constant dollars
$E$ = employment
$L$ = labor force
$K$ = capital, in constant dollars
$C$ = real consumption, in constant dollars
$I$ = real investment, in constant dollars
$\pi$ = real profit rate on marginal capital stock
$w$ = real wage

The equations (and comments on them) are as follows:

$$X = \min(aE, bK) \qquad (1)$$

$$X = aE \qquad (1a)$$

(by labor non-redundancy assumption there is more than enough capital),

---

[6] A. Rees (1951) earlier suggested that an explanation of involuntary unemployment in part depends on employer unwillingness to cut money wages. This, in turn, causes the wage-employment relation to lie above the true supply curve, even in the absence of trade union actions. Such non-competitive behavior, Rees believes, might be important; it would reinforce oligopolistic reluctance to cut price, discussed in Section E of this paper.

[7] Recent findings about cyclical variations in labor-force participation, especially by women and teenagers, provide an important qualification to the assumption of a fixed labor force. See especially Strand and Dernberg (1964), Tella (1964), and Mincer (1965).

[8] After completing the first draft of this paper, I reread an excellent piece by Tobin (1948), who argued exactly the reverse proposition: "his [Keynes's] denial of the 'homogeneity postulate' for the labor supply function constitutes a belated theoretical recognition of the facts of economic life" (p. 581). He also argues that, through cash balance and other price inhomogeneities of decisions taken elsewhere, labor can affect its real wage through variations in its money wage. Since Tobin was analyzing situations of comparative macrostatics as Keynes did in the *General Theory*, rather than short-run cyclical fluctuations in output and employment, the conflict in viewpoint regarding "Pigou effects" need not be especially sharp.

$$C = C(X) \qquad (2)$$

(consumption function),

$$I = I \qquad (3)$$

(investment treated as autonomous),

$$X = C + I \qquad (4)$$

(definition of total output),

$$E < L \qquad (5)$$

(employment cannot exceed labor force),

$$\pi(w) \geqslant 0 \qquad (6)$$

(marginal profit rate, which depends on real wage, must be non-negative).

The basic equations are (1a)–(4). In their simplest forms, (2)–(4) determine total output demanded and (1a) determines employment. Inequality (5) restricts feasible solutions of (1a) and (4) to employment levels less than the labor force in this unemployment version. Inequality (6) involves the real wage implicitly; since the real wage does not adjust during periods of unemployment, it must be thought profitable to operate machinery, or the labor non-redundancy assumption, which implies that there always exists enough physical capital to assure full employment, will be overridden by the economic criterion of profitability.

Those parts of the model which are least novel in this context have been suppressed. To have described them would require more space than a single article permits and would also obscure the points which I now seek to emphasize.

## E. Price Policy, Money Wages, and Real Wages

An apparently innocuous though basic assumption in the previous analysis concerns the nature of business price policy. The condition in equation (6) requiring that profits from operations expected on the marginal price of equipment in use should be non-negative implies that the most profitable machine(s) out of uses could earn non-negative profits as well. Why would a profit-maximizing business keep out of production a machine that could earn positive profits if a decline in product price could induce increased output while at the same time profits still remain positive?

These competitive actions would, I believe, be frustrated by two different mechanisms. The first reason relates to the Keynes-Lerner hypothesis about wage-price adjustment but pertains to the opposite side of the bargaining table to that originally envisaged by Keynes. Suppose price cuts were put into effect in accord with the motivation sketched in the preceding paragraph. Under these conditions the money wage could then be adjusted downward in approximately the same proportion, so that the original competitive efforts would have been frustrated.

It must then be asked whether an underemployment equilibrium with falling prices could persist in the presence of real cash balance effects. As Don Patinkin suggested some years ago (1948), the correlation of adverse expectations with falling prices could realistically be expected to cancel or outweigh the expectationally static Pigou effect on consumption. Evidence to the contrary is not readily obtainable. In any event, my major concern is not with underemployment equilibrium but with a theory of involuntary unemployment in a cyclical context, so that deriving equilibrium conditions in money prices and wages is peripheral to the central thesis.

Reinforcing the Keynes-Lerner effect, rather than in lieu of it, is the presence of important market imperfections in many industrial product markets. The widespread existence of oligopoly requires no documentation here. Even though the lack of a unified theory of oligopoly behavior also must be noted, one often-made empirical observation concerns the use of stable price markups on variable costs even under a variety of demand conditions, a subject on which the best empirical research still remains that of Richard Ruggles (1955). Thus widespread resort to price policies of this nature suggests that maintenance of "market discipline" in the interests of long-run profits (share, size, or stability) will dominate short-run profit maximizing, which is denied when marginal equipment is idle even though it could earn a profit. We do not observe an endless downward spiral of product prices when there is large-scale idle equipment. Instead, we observe money prices and wages declining together, although prices do so at a greater trend rate in light of the historically observed trend increase in the real wage.[9]

[9] According to Frisch's (1950) extremely careful exposition, Alfred Marshall thought that short-period supply functions in competitive industrial markets would deviate from marginal cost pricing at low levels of output: "When the price falls below the point at which all costs are covered . . . many firms will begin to react according to a different strategy than when they were above this critical point. Most firms will then, according to Marshall, consider a stronger curtailment of production than that indicated by the marginal cost curve" (p. 502).

As indicated by various quantitative studies of long-run behavior, the real wage appears to be determined by long-run considerations closely geared to productivity considerations. Approximately stable profit shares imply that the real wage will be approximately proportional to average productivity. Rees (1959) presents a convincing case that standard price theory, in terms of relative factor scarcities, can explain much of the historically observed variations in real wages, while trade unions can also be given some but not a dominant share in the total explanation.

Supposing that marginal productivity is strongly correlated with average productivity (it is strictly proportional for the ubiquitous Cobb-Douglas function), we can, and I believe we should, rely upon full or near-full employment factor scarcities to provide the basic explanation for the level and the rate of change of real wages. The main point, however, is that long-run adjustments in factor proportions are largely independent of the short-run output and employment fluctuations of the sort experienced by the United States and other capitalist countries.

One further implication of the comparatively steady trend behavior of the real wage should be noted. Real-wage changes during an ordinary business cycle do not appear to be closely related to the various cycle phases. Actual changes usually lie in the range of 2–4 per cent per year. It thus follows that the historical possibilities of cyclically substituting capital for labor at a rate different from the trend rate have been slight. This is both a restatement of an empirical support for the assertions of this paper relating to the dominance of input-output relations compared to real-wage, labor-supply behavior in the determination of involuntary unemployment.

## F. Income Distribution

Income distribution under the assumptions of this paper would behave in a manner that contradicts casual observations of cyclical movements in factor shares. While the profit share drops in a typical depression, the model presented implies that the most labor-intensive units would be withdrawn from production first as output declines, so that the profit share would tend to increase under a regime of constant real wages.

Reconciliation of the theory with the facts depends on cyclical variations in labor productivity alluded to in Section A and the existence of increasing returns to scale. While the steady-state behavior of profits could accord with the theory, lagged adjustments of labor to output cause a cyclical decline in labor productivity when output falls, which, however, would be reversed if output stabilized at a lower level. The earlier papers cited (Nield, 1963; Soligo, 1963; Solow, 1963; Eckstein and Wilson, 1964; Brechling, 1965; and Kuh, 1965a, 1965b) provide theoretical foundations as well as ample quantitative evidence on the extent and nature of these cyclical labor-productivity swings which obscure observations of actual steady-state behavior of profits.

The possibility that there are decreasing short-run unit costs should not be excluded on grounds of fact or analytical convenience. In this situation, the steady-state profit share would be lower at low levels of output, thereby reinforcing the cyclical dynamics for quite other reasons. Should this phenomenon be of primary importance, the constant returns to scale assumption of this paper (which, in the manner employed here, does not preclude oligopoly or monopoly) regarding technology would require modification. A closely related source of positive profits on the marginal item of equipment in use could arise from discreteness in technology. Where technological units of production are not small relative to output, the neoclassical "no-profit" maximizing condition should be replaced by an inequality of the sort advanced here.

## G. Conclusion

I have sketched hypotheses about the demand for labor and its relation to the demand for output which shift the emphasis of Keynesian unemployment theory from the combination of effective demand and a "money-illusion" labor-supply schedule to the combination of effective demand, technical conditions of production and imperfect competition.

In the *General Theory*, Keynes asserts

that, in general, an increase in employment can only occur to the accompaniment of a decline in the rate of real wages. Thus I am not disputing this vital fact which the classical economists have (rightly) asserted as indefeasible [p. 17].

We have shown that when effective demand is deficient there is underemployment of labor in the sense that there are men unemployed who would be willing to work at less than the existing real wage. Consequently, as effective demand increases, employment increases, though at a real wage equal to or less than the existing one, until a point comes at which there is no surplus of labor at the then existing real wage [p. 289].

As an analytical device for obtaining a theory of unemployment equilibrium while jettisoning the least amount of the neoclassical apparatus, the *General Theory* is truly a tour de force. But however essential the insistence on retaining most of the neoclassical analysis might have been at one time, it does seem to obscure a proper understanding of short-run fluctuations in employment. While it seems highly sensible to retain the neoclassical cost-minimization rationale to obtain a proper understanding of long-run behavior, it appears more questionable to do so for the short run. Furthermore, pure-competition, constant-returns assumptions seem inappropriate when a great many important industrial markets are dominated by several large firms.[10] A more correct perspective does not insist on instantaneous maintenance of the neoclassical equalities, primarily because in the short run approximately fixed labor-output proportions will cause employment to vary in proportion to output, provided it is desirable in the sense of being profitable to produce at all.

[10] One argument sometimes voiced against imperfect competition models is that "anything can happen." It can be argued with equal plausibility that "not enough can happen" in constant-returns, pure-competition models. In short, this level of discourse does not permit overwhelming methodological persuasiveness.

# Income Fluctuations
# and Growth

*C*HANGES IN THE levels of income in economies have always intrigued economists. There is, as a result, a tremendous amount of literature dealing with income fluctuations and growth. Five representative articles are included in this section. The first is an early article by Paul Samuelson which brings together the Keynesian multiplier concept and the accelerator analysis of investment purchasing and the level of income. Evsey Domar's "Expansion and Employment" follows the Samuelson article. In this selection Domar considers the dual role of investment purchasing and derives, on the basis of some simplifying assumptions, the rate at which an economy's investment purchasing must grow from one time period to the next if full-employment levels of income are to be maintained without inflation. The next article is Robert M. Solow's well-known 1957 attempt to determine the extent to which the growth of gross output per worker was caused by capital accumulation as opposed to changes in the techniques of production.

The section concludes with William Fellner's discussion of rapid economic growth as a policy objective and Edward F. Denison's discussion of the various ways in which the United States rate of growth could be increased by one percentage point.

*PAUL A. SAMUELSON*

# Interactions Between the Multiplier Analysis and the Principle of Acceleration

*17*     Few economists would deny that the "multiplier" analysis of the effects of governmental deficit spending has thrown some light upon this important problem. Nevertheless, there would seem to be some ground for the fear that this extremely simplified mechanism is in danger of hardening into a dogma, hindering progress and obscuring important subsidiary relations and processes. It is highly desirable, therefore, that model sequences, which operate under more general assumptions, be investigated, possibly including the conventional analysis as a special case.[1]

In particular the "multiplier," using this term in its usual sense, does *not* pretend to give the

[1] The writer, who has made this study in connection with his research as a member of the Society of Fellows at Harvard University, wishes to express his indebtedness to Professor Alvin H. Hansen of Harvard University at whose suggestion the investigation was undertaken.

Reprinted from the *Review of Economics and Statistics,* Vol. XXI (1939), pp. 75–78, by permission of the author and publisher, Harvard University Press. Copyright 1939, 1967 by the President and Fellows of Harvard College. Paul Samuelson is a professor at the Massachusetts Institute of Technology.

relation between total national income induced by governmental spending and the original amount of money spent. This is clearly seen by a simple example. In an economy (not necessarily our own) where any dollar of governmental deficit spending would result in a hundred dollars less of private investment than would otherwise have been undertaken, the ratio of total induced national income to the initial expenditure is overwhelmingly negative, yet the "multiplier" in the strict sense must be positive. The answer to the puzzle is simple. What the multiplier does give is the ratio of the total increase in the national income to the total amount of investment, governmental and private. In other words, it does *not* tell us how much is to be multiplied. The effects upon private investment are often regarded as tertiary influences and receive little systematic attention.

In order to remedy the situation in some measure, Professor Hansen has developed a new model sequence which ingeniously combines the multiplier analysis with that of the *acceleration* principle or *relation*. This is done by making additions to the national income consist of three components: (1) governmental deficit spending, (2) private consumption expenditure induced by previous public expenditure, and (3) induced private investment, assumed according to the familiar acceleration principle to be proportional

**Table 1. The Development of National Income as a Result of a Continuous Level of Governmental Expenditure When the Marginal Propensity to Consume Equals One-Half and the Relation Equals Unity**

*(unit: one dollar)*

| Period | Current governmental expenditure | Current consumption induced by previous expenditure | Current private investment proportional to time increase in consumption | Total national income |
|---|---|---|---|---|
| 1 | 1.00 | 0.00 | 0.00 | 1.00 |
| 2 | 1.00 | 0.50 | 0.50 | 2.00 |
| 3 | 1.00 | 1.00 | 0.50 | 2.50 |
| 4 | 1.00 | 1.25 | 0.25 | 2.50 |
| 5 | 1.00 | 1.25 | 0.00 | 2.25 |
| 6 | 1.00 | 1.125 | −0.125[a] | 2.00 |
| 7 | 1.00 | 1.00 | −0.125 | 1.875 |
| 8 | 1.00 | 0.9375 | −0.0625 | 1.875 |
| 9 | 1.00 | 0.9375 | 0.00 | 1.9375 |
| 10 | 1.00 | 0.96875 | 0.03125 | 2.00 |
| 11 | 1.00 | 1.00 | 0.03125 | 2.03125 |
| 12 | 1.00 | 1.015625 | 0.015625 | 2.03125 |
| 13 | 1.00 | 1.015625 | 0.00 | 2.015625 |
| 14 | 1.00 | 1.0078125 | −0.0078125 | 2.00 |
| .. | .... | .......... | .......... | .......... |

[a] Negative induced private investment is interpreted to mean that for the system as a whole there is *less* investment in this period than there otherwise would have been. Since this is a marginal analysis, superimposed implicitly upon a going state of affairs, this concept causes no difficulty.

to the time increase of consumption. The introduction of the last component accounts for the novelty of the conclusions reached and also the increased complexity of the analysis.

A numerical example may be cited to illuminate the assumptions made. We assume governmental deficit spending of one dollar per unit period, beginning at some initial time and continuing thereafter. The marginal propensity to consume, $\alpha$, is taken to be one-half. This is taken to mean that the consumption of any period is equal to one-half the national income of the previous period. Our last assumption is that induced private investment is proportional to the increase in consumption between the previous and the current period. This factor of proportionality or *relation*, $\beta$, is provisionally taken to be equal to unity; i.e., a time increase in consumption of one dollar will result in one dollar's worth of induced private investment.

In the initial period when the government spends a dollar for the first time, there will be no consumption induced from previous periods, and hence the addition to the national income will equal the one dollar spent. This will yield fifty cents of consumption expenditure in the second period, an increase of fifty cents over the consumption of the first period, and so according to the *relation* we will have fifty cents worth of induced private investment. Finally, we must add the new dollar of expenditure by the government. The national income of the second period must therefore total two dollars. Similarly, in the third period the national income would be the sum of one dollar of consumption, fifty cents induced private investment, and one dollar current governmental expenditure. It is clear that given the values of the marginal propensity to consume, $\alpha$, and the *relation*, $\beta$, all succeeding national income levels can be easily computed in succession. This is done in detail in Table 1 and illustrated in Figure 1. It will be noted that the introduction of the acceleration principle causes our series to reach a peak at the 3rd year, a trough at the 7th, a peak at the 11th, etc. Such oscillatory behavior could not occur in the conventional model sequences, as will soon become evident.

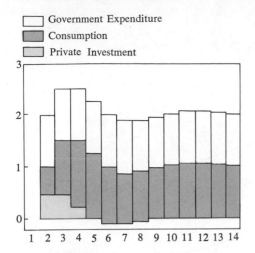

Figure 1. Graphic Representation of Data in Table 1 (Unit: One Dollar).

For other chosen values of $\alpha$ and $\beta$ similar model sequences can be developed. In Table 2 national income totals are given for various selected values of these coefficients. In the first column, for example, the marginal propensity to consume is assumed to be one-half, and the *relation* to be equal to zero. This is of special interest because it shows the conventional multiplier sequences to be special cases of the more general Hansen analysis. For this case no oscillations are possible. In the second column the oscillations in the national income are undamped and regular. In column three things are still worse; the oscillations are explosive, becoming larger and larger but always fluctuating around an "average value." In the fourth column the behavior is no longer oscillatory but is explosive

upward approaching a compound interest rate of growth.

By this time the investigator is inclined to feel somewhat disorganized. A variety of qualitatively different results emerge in a seemingly capricious manner from minor changes in hypotheses. Worse than this, how can we be sure that for still different selected values of our coefficients new and stronger types of behavior will not emerge? Is it not even possible that if Table 2 were extended to cover more periods, new types of behavior might result for these selected coefficients?

Fortunately, these questions can be given a definite negative answer. Arithmetical methods cannot do so since we cannot try all possible values of the coefficients nor compute the endless terms of each sequence. Nevertheless, comparatively simple algebraic analysis can be applied which will yield all possible qualitative types of behavior and enable us to unify our results.

The national income at time $t$, $Y_t$, can be written as the sum of three components: (1) governmental expenditure, $g_t$, (2) consumption expenditure, $C_t$, and (3) induced private investment, $I_t$.

$$Y_t = g_t + C_t + I_t.$$

But according to the Hansén assumptions

$$C_t = \alpha Y_{t-1}$$

$$I_t = \beta[C_t - C_{t-1}] = \alpha\beta Y_{t-1} - \alpha\beta Y_{t-2}$$

and

$$g_t = 1$$

Therefore, our national income can be rewritten

$$Y_t = 1 + \alpha[1+\beta]Y_{t-1} - \alpha\beta Y_{t-2}.$$

## Table 2. Model Sequences of National Income for Selected Values of Marginal Propensity to Consume and Relation

*(unit: one dollar)*

| Period | $\alpha = .5$ $\beta = 0$ | $\alpha = .5$ $\beta = 2$ | $\alpha = .6$ $\beta = 2$ | $\alpha = .8$ $\beta = 4$ |
|---|---|---|---|---|
| 1 | 1.00 | 1.00 | 1.00 | 1.00 |
| 2 | 1.50 | 2.50 | 2.80 | 5.00 |
| 3 | 1.75 | 3.75 | 4.84 | 17.80 |
| 4 | 1.875 | 4.125 | 6.352 | 56.20 |
| 5 | 1.9375 | 3.4375 | 6.6256 | 169.84 |
| 6 | 1.9688[a] | 2.0313 | 5.3037 | 500.52 |
| 7 | 1.9844 | .9141 | 2.5959 | 1,459.592 |
| 8 | 1.9922 | − .1172 | − .6918 | 4,227.704 |
| 9 | 1.9961 | .2148 | −3.3603 | 12,241.1216 |
| .. | ........ | ......... | .......... | ............ |

a Table is correct to four decimal places.

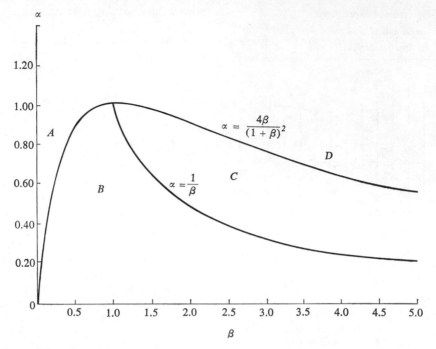

Figure 2. Diagram Showing Boundaries of Regions Yielding Different Qualitative Behavior of National Income.

In words, if we know the national income for two periods, the national income for the following period can be simply derived by taking a weighted sum. The weights depend, of course, upon the values chosen for the marginal propensity to consume and for the *relation*.

This is one of the simplest types of difference equations, having constant coefficients and being of the second order. The mathematical details of its solution need not be entered upon here. Suffice it to say that its solution depends upon the roots —which in turn depend upon the coefficients $\alpha$ and $\beta$—of certain equation.[2] It can be easily shown that the whole field of possible values of $\alpha$ and $\beta$ can be divided into four regions, each of which gives qualitatively different types of behavior. In Chart 2 these regions are plotted. Each point in this diagram represents a selection of values for the marginal propensity to consume and the *relation*. Corresponding to each point

there will be a model sequence of national income through time. The qualitative properties of this sequence depend upon whether the point is in Region A, B, C, or D.[3] The properties of each region can be briefly summarized.

### Region A (Relatively Small Values of the Relation)

If there is a constant level of governmental expenditure through time, the national income will approach asymptotically a value $1/(1-\alpha)$ times the constant level of governmental expenditure. A single impulse of expenditure, or any amount of expenditure followed by a complete cessation, will result in a gradual approach to the original zero level of national income. (It will be noted that the asymptote approached is identically that given by the Keynes-Kahn-Clark formula. Their analysis applies to points along the $\alpha$ axis and is subsumed under the more general Hansen analysis.) Perfectly periodic net governmental expenditure will result eventually in perfectly periodic fluctuations in national income.

[2] Actually, the solution can be written in the form

$$Y_t = \frac{1}{1-\alpha} + a_1[x_1]^t + a_2[x_2]^t$$

where $x_1$ and $x_2$ are roots of the quadratic equation

$$x^2 - \alpha[1+\beta]x + \alpha\beta = 0,$$

and $a_1$ and $a_2$ are constants dependent upon the $\alpha$'s and $\beta$'s chosen.

[3] Mathematically, the regions are demarcated by the conditions that the roots of the equation referred to in the previous footnote be real or complex, greater or less than unity in absolute value.

### Region B

A constant continuing level of governmental expenditure will result in damped oscillatory movements of national income, gradually approaching the asymptote $1/(1-\alpha)$ times the constant level of government expenditure. (Cf. Table 2.) Governmental expenditure in a single or finite number of periods will result eventually in damped oscillations around the level of income zero. Perfectly regular periodic fluctuations in government expenditure will result eventually in fluctuations of income of the same period.

### Region C

A constant level of governmental expenditure will result in *explosive*, ever increasing oscillations around an asymptote computed as above. (Cf. column 3 of Table 2.) A single impulse of expenditure or a finite number of expenditure impulses will result eventually in explosive oscillations around the level zero.

### Region D (Large Values of the Marginal Propensity to Consume and the *Relation*)

A constant level of governmental expenditure will result in an ever increasing national income, eventually approaching a compound interest rate of growth. (Cf. column 4 of Table 2.) A single impulse of net investment will likewise send the system up to infinity at a compound interest rate of growth. On the other hand, a single infinitesimal unit of disinvestment will send the system ever downward at an increasing rate. This is a highly unstable situation, but corresponds most closely to the pure case of pump-priming, where the total increase in national income bears no finite ratio to the original stimulus.

The limitations inherent in so simplified a picture as that presented here should not be overlooked.[4] In particular, it assumes that the marginal propensity to consume and the *relation* are constants; actually these will change with the level of income, so that this representation is strictly a *marginal* analysis to be applied to the study of small oscillations. Nevertheless, it is more general than the usual analysis. Contrary to the impression commonly held, mathematical methods properly employed, far from making economic theory more abstract, actually serve as a powerful liberating device enabling the entertainment and analysis of ever more realistic and complicated hypotheses.

---

[4] It may be mentioned in passing that the formal structure of our problem is identical with the model sequences of Lundberg, and the dynamic theories of Tinbergen. The present problem is so simple that it provides a useful introduction to the mathematical theory of the latter's work.

EVSEY D. DOMAR

# Expansion and Employment[1]

## 18

"A slow sort of a country," said the Queen.
"Now, *here*, you see, it takes all the running *you*
can do, to keep in the same place. If you want to
get somewhere else, you must run at least twice
as fast as that."

Lewis Carroll: *Through the Looking Glass*

In these days of labor
shortages and inflation a paper dealing with
conditions needed for full employment and with
the threat of deflation may well appear out of
place. Its publication at this time is due partly
to a two-year lag between the first draft and the
final copy; also to the widely held belief that the
present inflation is a temporary phenomenon, and
that once it is over, the old problem of deflation
and unemployment may possibly appear before
us again.

[1] This paper forms a sequence to my earlier article
on "The 'Burden' of the Debt and the National
Income," published in this *Review,* Vol. XXXIV,
No. 5 (Dec., 1944), pp. 798–827. Though their titles
seem different, the two papers are based on the same
logical foundation and treat a common subject: the
economic rôle of growth.

Reprinted from the *American Economic Review*,
Vol. XXXVII (1947), pp. 34—55, by permission of the
author and publisher. Evsey Domar is a professor at
the Massachusetts Institute of Technology.

Our comfortable belief in the efficacy of Say's
Law has been badly shaken in the last fifteen
years. Both events and discussions have shown
that supply does not automatically create its own
demand. A part of income generated by the productive process may not be returned to it; this
part may be saved and hoarded. As Keynes put
it, "Unemployment develops . . . because people
want the moon; men cannot be employed when
the object of desire (*i.e.*, money) is something
which cannot be produced. . . ."[2] The core of
the problem then is the public's desire to hoard.
If no hoarding takes place, employment can
presumably be maintained.

This sounds perfectly straight and simple; and
yet it leaves something unexplained. Granted that
absence of hoarding is a *necessary* condition for
the maintenance of full employment, is it also a
*sufficient* condition? Is the absence of hoarding

[2] John M. Keynes, *The General Theory of Employment Interest and Money* (New York, 1936), p. 235.

all that is necessary for the avoidance of unemployment? This is the impression *The General Theory* gives. And yet, on a different plane, we have some notions about an increasing productive capacity which must somehow be utilized if unemployment is to be avoided. Will a mere absence of hoarding assure such a utilization? Will not a continuous increase in expenditures (and possibly in the money supply) be necessary in order to achieve this goal?

The present paper deals with this problem. It attempts to find the conditions needed for the maintenance of full employment over a period of time, or more exactly, *the rate of growth of national income* which the maintenance of full employment requires. This rate of growth is analyzed in Section I. Section II is essentially a digression on some conceptual questions and alternative approaches. It may be omitted by the busy reader. Section III is concerned with the *dual* character of the investment process; that is, with the fact that investment not only generates income but also increases productive capacity. Therefore the effects of investment on employment are less certain and more complex than is usually supposed. In Section IV a few examples from existing literature on the subject are given, and Section V contains some concluding remarks. The most essential parts of the paper are presented in Sections I and III.

As in many papers of this kind, a number of simplifying assumptions are made. Most of them will become apparent during the discussion. Two may be noted at the outset. First, events take place simultaneously, without any lags. Second, income, investment and saving are defined in the *net* sense, *i.e.*, over and above depreciation. The latter is understood to refer to the cost of replacement of the depreciated asset by another one of *equal* productive capacity. These assumptions are not entirely essential to the argument. The discussion could be carried out with lags, and, if desired, in gross terms or with a different concept of depreciation. Some suggestions along these lines are made in Section II. But it is better to begin with as simple a statement of the problem as possible, bearing in mind of course the nature of assumptions made.

## I. The Rate of Growth

It is perfectly clear that the requirement that income paid out should be returned to the productive process, or that savings be equal to investment, or other expressions of the same idea,

are simply formulas for the retention of the income *status quo*. If underemployment was present yesterday, it would still remain here today. If yesterday's income was at a full employment level, that *income level* would be retained today. It may no longer, however, correspond to full employment.

Let yesterday's full employment income equal an annual rate of 150 billion dollars, and let the average propensity to save equal, say, 10 per cent. If now 15 billions are annually invested, one might expect full employment to be maintained. But during this process, capital equipment of the economy will have increased by an annual rate of 15 billions—for after all, investment *is* the formation of capital.[3] Therefore, the productive capacity of the economy has also increased.

The effects of this increase on employment will depend on whether or not *real income* has also increased. Since money income has remained, as assumed, at the 150 billion annual level, an increase in real income can be brought about only by a corresponding fall in the general price level. This indeed has been the traditional approach to problems of this kind, an approach which we shall have to reject here for the following reasons:

1. The presence of considerable monopolistic elements (in industry and labor) in our economy makes unrealistic the assumption that a falling *general* price level could be achieved without interfering with full employment. This of course does not exclude *relative* changes among prices. As a matter of fact, if industries subject to a faster-than-average technological progress do not reduce their prices to some extent, a constant general price level cannot be maintained.

2. For an economy saddled with a large public debt and potentially faced (in peacetime) with serious employment problems, a falling price level is in itself undesirable.

3. A falling price level can bring about a larger income only in the special case when prices of

---

[3] The identification of investment with capital formation is reasonably safe in a private economy where only a small part of resources is disposed of by the government. When this part becomes substantial, complications arise. This question will be taken up again in Section II. Meanwhile, we shall disregard it and divide total national income, irrespective of source, into investment (*i.e.*, capital formation) and consumption.

The term "national income" is understood here in a broad sense, as total output minus depreciation, and does not touch on current controversies regarding the inclusion or exclusion of certain items. Perhaps "net national product" would be more appropriate for our purposes.

consumers' goods fall more rapidly than those of investment goods. For otherwise (with a constant propensity to save) money income will be falling as fast or faster than the price level, and real income will be falling as well. To prevent money income from falling so rapidly, the volume of real investment would have to keep rising—a conclusion which will be presently reached in the more general case.

4. Finally, the assumption of a falling general price level would obscure—and I believe quite unnecessarily—the main subject we are concerned with here.

For these reasons, a *constant general price level* is assumed throughout this paper. But, from a theoretical point of view, this is a convenience rather than a necessity. The discussion could be carried on with a falling or a rising price level as well.

To come back to the increase in capacity. If both money and real national income thus remain fixed at the 150 billion annual level, the creation of the new capital equipment will have one or more of the following effects: (1) The new capital remains unused; (2) The new capital is used at the expense of previously constructed capital, whose labor and/or markets the new capital has taken away; (3) The new capital is substituted for labor (and possibly for other factors).

The first case represents a waste of resources. That capital need not have been constructed in the first place. The second case—the substitution of new capital for existing capital (before the latter is worn out, since investment is defined here in the net sense)—takes place all the time and, in reasonable magnitudes, is both unavoidable and desirable in a free dynamic society. It is when this substitution proceeds on a rather large scale that it can become socially wasteful; also, losses sustained or expected by capital owners will make them oppose new investment—a serious danger for an economy with considerable monopolistic elements.

Finally, capital may be substituted for labor. If this substitution results in a *voluntary* reduction in the labor force or in the length of the work week, no objections can be raised. Such a process has of course been going on for many years. But in our economy it is very likely that at least a part of this substitution—if carried on at an extensive scale—will be involuntary, so that the result will be unemployment.

The tools used in this paper do not allow us to distinguish between these three effects of capital formation, though, as will appear later, our concepts are so defined that a voluntary reduction in the number of man-hours worked is excluded. In general, it is not unreasonable to assume that in most cases all three effects will be present (though not in constant proportions), and that capital formation not accompanied by an increase in income will result in unemployed capital and labor.

The above problems do not arise in the standard Keynesian system because of its explicit assumption that employment is a function of national income, an assumption which admittedly can be justified only over short periods of time. Clearly, a full employment income of 1941 would cause considerable unemployment today. While Keynes' approach—the treatment of employment as a function of income—is a reasonable first approximation, we shall go a step further and assume instead that *the percentage of labor force employed is a function of the ratio between national income and productive capacity*. This should be an improvement, but we must admit the difficulties of determining productive capacity, both conceptually and statistically. These are obvious and need not be elaborated. We shall mean by productive capacity the total output of the economy at what is usually called full employment (with due allowance for frictional and seasonal unemployment), such factors as consumers' preferences, price and wage structures, intensity of competition, and so on being given.

The answer to the problem of unemployment lies of course in a growing income. If after capital equipment has increased by (an annual rate of) 15 billions an income of 150 billions leaves some capacity unused, then a higher magnitude of income can be found—say 155 or 160 billions—which will do the job. There is nothing novel or startling about this conclusion. The idea that a capitalist economy needs growth goes back, in one form or another, at least to Marx. The trouble really is that the idea of growth is so widely accepted that people rarely bother about it. It is always treated as an afterthought, to be added to one's speech or article if requested, but very seldom incorporated in its body. Even then it is regarded as a function of some abstract technological progress which somehow results in increasing productivity per man-hour, and which takes place quite independently of capital formation. And yet, our help in the industrialization of undeveloped countries will take the form not only of supplying technical advice and textbooks, but also of actual machinery and goods. Certainly the 80 odd billion dollars of net capital formation created in the United States in the period 1919–29 had a considerable effect on our productive capacity.[4]

A change in productive capacity of a country is a function of changes in its natural resources (discovery of new ones or depletion of others), in its labor force (more correctly, man-hours available), capital and the state of technique.[5] Since changes in natural resources and technique are very difficult concepts, we can express changes in total capacity via changes in the quantity and productivity of labor or of capital. The traditional approach builds around labor. The several studies of the magnitude of total output corresponding to full employment, made in the last few years, consisted in multiplying the expected labor force (subdivided into several classes) by its expected average productivity.[6] This procedure did not imply that the other three factors (natural resources, technology and capital) remained constant; rather that their variations were all reflected in the changes in productivity of labor.

It is also possible to put capital in the center of the stage and to estimate variations in total capacity by measuring the changes in the quantity of capital and in its productivity, the latter reflecting changes currently taking place in natural resources, technology and the labor force. From a practical point of view, the labor approach has obvious advantages, at least in some problems, because labor is a more homogeneous and easily measurable factor. But from a theoretical point of view, the capital approach is more promising and for this reason: the appearance of an extra workman or his decision to work longer hours *only* increases productive capacity without, however, generating any income to make use of this increase. But the construction of a new factory has a *dual* effect: *it increases productive capacity and it generates income.*

The emphasis on this dual character of the investment process is the essence of this paper's approach to the problem of employment. If investment increases productive capacity and also creates income, what should be the magnitude of investment, or at what rate should it grow, in order to make the increase in income equal to that of productive capacity?[7] Couldn't an equation be set up one side of which would represent the increase (or the rate of increase) of productive capacity, and the other—that of income, and the solution of which would yield the required *rate of growth*?

We shall attempt to set up such an equation. It will be first expressed in symbolic form, and later (on pp. 162–163) illustrated by a numerical example.

Let investment proceed at an annual rate of $I$, and let annual productive capacity (net value added) per dollar of newly created capital be equal on the average to $s$. Thus if it requires, say, 3 dollars of capital to produce (in terms of annual net value added) one dollar of output, $s$ will equal one-third or 33.3 per cent per year. It is not meant that $s$ is the same in all firms or industries. It depends of course on the nature of capital constructed and on many other factors. Its treatment here as a given magnitude is a simplification which can be readily dispensed with.

The productive capacity of $I$ dollars invested will thus be $Is$ dollars per year. But it is possible that the operation of new capital will take place, at least to some extent, at the expense of previously constructed plants, with which the new capital will compete both for markets and for factors of production (mainly labor). If as a result, the output of existing plants must be curtailed, it would be useless to assert that the productive capacity of the *whole economy* has increased by $Is$ dollars per year.[8] It has actually increased by a smaller amount which will be indicated by $I\sigma$.[9] $\sigma$ may be called the *potential social average productivity of investment.* Such a long name calls for an explanation.

1. As stated above, $\sigma$ is concerned with the increase in productive capacity of the whole society and not with the productive capacity per dollar invested in the new plants taken by themselves, that is with $s$. A difference between $s$ and $\sigma$ indicates a certain misdirection of investment, or —more important—that investment proceeds at

---

[4] This figure, in 1929 prices, is taken from Simon Kuznets, *National Income and Its Composition*, Vol. I (New York, 1941), p. 268. The actual figure was 79.1 billion dollars.

[5] Taking other conditions listed on p. 160 as given.

[6] See for instance E. E. Hagen and N. B. Kirkpatrick, "The National Output at Full Employment in 1950," *Amer. Econ. Rev.*, Vol. XXXIV, No. 4 (Sept., 1944), pp. 472–500.

[7] This statement of the problem presupposes that full employment has already been reached and must only be maintained. With a small extra effort we could begin with a situation where some unemployment originally existed.

[8] These comparisons must of course be made at a full employment level of national income. See also pp. 164–165.

[9] We are disregarding here external economies obtained by existing plants from the newly constructed ones.

too rapid a rate as compared with the growth of labor and technological progress. This question will be taken up again in Section II.

2. σ should not be confused with other related concepts, such as the traditional marginal productivity of capital. These concepts are usually based on a *caeteris paribus* assumption regarding the quantity of other factors and the state of technique. It should be emphasized that the use of σ does not imply in the least that labor, natural resources and technology remain fixed. It would be more correct therefore to say that σ indicates the increase in productive capacity which *accompanies* rather than which is caused by each dollar invested.

3. For our purposes, the most important property of σ is its *potential character*. It deals not with an increase in national income but with that of the *productive potential* of the economy. A high σ indicates that the economy *is capable* of increasing its output relatively fast. But whether this increased capacity will actually result in greater output or greater unemployment, depends on the behavior of money income.

The expression $I\sigma$ is the supply side of our system; it is the increase in output which the economy *can* produce. On the demand side we have the multiplier theory, too familiar to need any elaboration, except for the emphasis on the obvious but often forgotten fact that, with any given marginal propensity to save, to be indicated by α, an increase in national income is not a function of investment, but of the *increment* in investment. If investment today, however large, is equal to that of yesterday, national income of today will be just equal and not any larger than that of yesterday. All this is obvious, and is stressed here to underline the lack of symmetry between the effects of investment on productive capacity and on national income.

Let investment increase at an absolute annual rate of $\Delta I$ (*e.g.*, by two billion per year), and let the corresponding absolute annual increase in income be indicated by $\Delta Y$. We have then

$$\Delta Y = \Delta I \frac{1}{\alpha}, \qquad (1)$$

where $1/\alpha$ is of course the multiplier.

Let us now assume that the economy is in a position of a full employment equilibrium, so that its national income equals its productive capacity.[10] To retain this position, income and capacity should increase at the same rate. The annual increase in potential capacity equals $I\sigma$.

[10] See note 7.

The annual increase in actual income is expressed by $\Delta I(1/\alpha)$. Our objective is to make them equal. This gives us the fundamental equation

$$\Delta I \frac{1}{\alpha} = I\sigma. \qquad (2)$$

To solve this equation, we multiply both sides by α and divide by $I$, obtaining

$$\frac{\Delta I}{I} = \alpha\sigma. \qquad (3)$$

The left side of expression (3) is the absolute annual increase (or the absolute rate of growth) in investment—$\Delta I$—divided by the volume of investment itself; or in other words, it is the relative increase in investment, or the annual percentage rate of growth of investment. Thus the maintenance of full employment requires that investment grow at the annual percentage rate $\alpha\sigma$.

So much for investment. Since the marginal propensity to save—α—is assumed to be constant, an increase in income is a constant multiple of an increase in investment (see expression [1]). But in order to remain such a constant multiple of investment, income must also grow at the same annual percentage rate, that is at $\alpha\sigma$.

To summarize, the maintenance of a continuous state of full employment requires that *investment and income grow at a constant annual percentage (or compound interest) rate* equal to the product of the marginal propensity to save and the average (to put it briefly) productivity of investment.[11]

This result can be made clearer by a numerical example. Let $\sigma = 25$ per cent per year, $\alpha = 12$ per cent, and $Y = 150$ billions per year. If full employment is to be maintained, an amount equal to $150 \times \frac{12}{100}$ should be invested. This will raise productive capacity by the amount invested times σ, *i.e.*, by $150 \times \frac{12}{100} \times \frac{25}{100}$, and national income will have to rise by the same annual amount. But the relative rise in income will equal the absolute increase divided

[11] The careful reader may be disturbed by the lack of clear distinction between increments and rates of growth here and elsewhere in the text. If some confusion exists, it is due to my attempt to express these concepts in non-mathematical form. Actually they all should be stated in terms of rates of growth (derivatives in respect to time). For a more serious treatment of this point, as well as for a more complete statement of the logic of the paper, see my article "Capital Expansion, Rate of Growth, and Employment," *Econometrica*, Vol. XIV (Apr., 1946), pp. 137–47.

by the income itself, *i.e.*,

$$\frac{150 \times \dfrac{12}{100} \times \dfrac{25}{100}}{150} = \frac{12}{100} \times \frac{25}{100} \quad (4)$$

$$= \alpha\sigma = 3 \text{ per cent.}$$

These results were obtained on the assumption that $\alpha$, the marginal propensity to save, and $\sigma$, the average productivity of investment, remain constant. The reader can see that this assumption is not necessary for the argument, and that the whole problem can be easily reworked with variable $\alpha$ and $\sigma$. Some remarks about a changing $\alpha$ are made on pp. 166–167.

The expression (3) indicates (in a very simplified manner) conditions needed for the maintenance of full employment over a period of time. It shows that it is not sufficient, in Keynesian terms that savings of yesterday be invested today, or, as it is often expressed, that investment offset saving. Investment of today must always exceed savings of yesterday. A mere absence of hoarding will not do. An injection of new money (or dishoarding) must take place every day. Moreover, this injection must proceed, in absolute terms, at an accelerated rate. The economy must continuously expand.[12]

## II. The Argument Reexamined

The busy reader is urged to skip this section and proceed directly to Section III. The present section is really a long footnote which reexamines the concepts and suggests some alternative approaches. Its purpose is, on the one hand, to indicate the essential limitations of the preceding discussion, and on the other, to offer a few suggestions which may be of interest to others working in this field.

It was established in Section I that the maintenance of full employment requires income and investment to grow at an annual compound interest rate equal to $\alpha\sigma$. The meaning of this result will naturally depend on those of $\alpha$ and $\sigma$. Unfortunately neither of them is devoid of ambiguity.

The marginal propensity to save—$\alpha$—is a relatively simple concept in a private economy where only a small part of resources is handled by the government. National income can be divided, without too much trouble, into investment and consumption, even though it is true that the basis for this distinction is often purely formal.[13] But on the whole it sounds quite reasonable to say that if marginal propensity to save is $\alpha$, then an $\alpha$ fraction of an increase in income is saved by the public and invested in income-producing assets.

When a substantial part of the economy's resources is disposed of by the government, two interpretations of the marginal propensity to save, or of savings and investment in general, appear possible. The first is to continue dividing the total output, whether produced by government or by private business, into consumption and investment. This method was implicitly followed in this paper. But a question arises regarding the meaning and stability of $\alpha$. It makes sense to say that a person or the public save, in accordance with the size of their incomes, their habits, expectations, etc., a certain, though not necessarily constant, fraction of an increment in their *disposable* (*i.e.*, after income and social security taxes) income, but can a similar statement be made regarding total national income, a good part of which is not placed at the disposal of the public? Also it is not easy to divide government expenditures into consumption and investment.

The other method would limit $\alpha$ to disposable income only, and then provide for government expenditures separately. It would be necessary then to find out the effects of these expenditures on productive capacity.

Depreciation raises another problem. Since all terms are defined here in the net sense, the meaning and magnitude of $\alpha$ will also depend on those of depreciation, irrespective of the choice between the above two methods. Depreciation has been defined here (see page 159) as the cost of replacement of a worn out asset by another one with an equal productive capacity. While this approach is about as bad or as good as any other, the difficulty still remains that businesses ordinarily do not use this definition, and therefore arrive at a different estimate of their net incomes, which in turn determine their propensity to save.

I do not have ready answers to these questions, though I do not consider them insurmountable. I am mentioning them here partly in order to indicate the limitations of the present argument,

---

[12] After this paper was sent to the printer, I happened to stumble on an article by R. F. Harrod, published in 1939, which contained a number of ideas similar to those presented here. See "An Essay in Dynamic Theory," *Econ. Jour.*, Vol. XLIX (Apr., 1939), pp. 14–33.

[13] Thanks are due to George Jaszi for his persistent efforts to enlighten me on this subject. The division of national income into investment and consumption is really a more difficult task than my text might imply.

and also as obstacles which will have to be overcome if a more exact analysis is undertaken.

$\sigma$ is even more apt to give rise to ambiguities. $s$, from which it springs, has been used, in one form or another, in economic literature before, particularly in connection with the acceleration principle.[14] Here it indicates the annual amount of income (net value added) which can be produced by a dollar of newly created capital. It varies of course among firms and industries, and also in space and time, though a study recently made seems to indicate that it has been quite stable, at least in the United States and Great Britain, over the last 70 years or so.[15] Whether $s$ has or has not been relatively stable is not essential for our discussion. The real question is whether such a concept has meaning, whether it makes sense to say that a given economy or a plant has a certain capacity. Traditional economic thinking would, I fear, be against such an approach. Unfortunately, it is impossible to discuss this question here. I believe that our actual experience during the last depression and this war, as well as a number of empirical studies, show that productive capacity, both of a plant and of the whole economy is a meaningful concept, though this capacity, as well as the magnitude of $s$, should be treated as a *range* rather than as a single number.

In some problems $s$ may be interpreted as the minimum annual output per dollar invested which will make the investment worth undertaking. If this output falls below $s$, the investor suffers a loss or at least a disappointment, and may be unwilling to replace the asset after it has depreciated.

All these doubts apply to $\sigma$ even more than to $s$. As explained on pages 161–162, $\sigma$ differs from $s$ by indicating the annual increment in capacity of the *whole economy* per dollar invested, rather than that of the newly created capital taken by itself. The possible difference between $s$ and $\sigma$ is due to the following reasons:

1. The new plants are not operated to capacity because they are unable to find a market for their products.

2. Old plants reduce their output because their markets are captured by new plants.

As productive capacity has no meaning except in relation to consumers' preferences, in both of the above cases productive capacity of the country is increased by a smaller amount than could be produced by the new plants; in the limiting case it is not increased at all, and $\sigma = 0$, however high $s$ may be. But it must be made clear that the test of whether or not $\sigma$ is below $s$ can be made only under conditions (actual or assumed) of full employment. If markets are not large enough because of insufficiency of effective demand due to unemployment, it cannot yet be concluded that $\sigma$ is below $s$.

3. The first two cases can take place irrespective of the volume of current investment. A more important case arises when investment proceeds at such a rapid rate that a shortage of other factors relative to capital develops. New plants may be unable to get enough labor, or more likely, labor (and other factors) is transferred to new plants from previously constructed ones, whose capacity therefore declines. In its actual manifestation, case 3 can hardly be separated from cases 1 and 2, because to the individual firm affected the difference between $s$ and $\sigma$ always takes the form of a cost-price disparity. The reason why we are trying to separate the first two cases from the third lies in the bearing of this distinction on practical policy. The first two cases arise from an error of judgment on the part of investors (past or present) which is, at least to some extent, unavoidable and not undesirable. The struggle for markets and the replacement of weaker (or older) firms and industries by stronger (or newer) ones is the essence of progress in a capitalist society. The third case, on the other hand, may result from poor fiscal policy. It constitutes an attempt to invest too much, to build more capital than the economy can utilize even at full employment. Such a situation can develop if an economy with a high propensity to save tries to maintain full employment by investing all its savings into capital goods. But it should be made clear that the expressions "too much capital" or "high propensity to save" are used in a relative sense—in comparison with the growth of other factors, that is natural resources, labor and technology.

The use of $\sigma$ certainly does not imply that these factors remain fixed. As a matter of fact, it would be very interesting to explore the use of a more complex function as the right side of expression (2) instead of $I\sigma$, a function in which the growth of labor, natural resources, and technology

[14] See for instance Paul A. Samuelson, "Interactions between the Multiplier Analysis and the Principle of Acceleration," *Rev. Econ. Stat.*, Vol. XXI (May, 1939), pp. 75–79; also R. F. Harrod, *The Trade Cycle* (Oxford, 1936). These authors, however, used not the ratio of income to capital, but of consumption to capital, or rather the reciprocal of this ratio.

[15] See Ernest H. Stern, "Capital Requirements in Progressive Economies," *Economica*, n.s. Vol. XII (Aug., 1945), pp. 163–71.

would be presented explicitly, rather than through their effects on $\sigma$.[16] I did not attempt it because I wished to express the idea of growth in the simplest possible manner. One must also remember that in the application of mathematics to economic problems, diminishing returns appear rapidly, and that the construction of complex models requires so many specific assumptions as to narrow down their applicability.

And yet it may be interesting to depart in another direction, namely to introduce lags. In this paper both the multiplier effect and the increase in capacity are supposed to take place simultaneously and without any lag. Actually, the multiplier may take some time to work itself out, and certainly the construction of a capital asset takes time. In a secular problem these lags are not likely to be of great importance, but they may play an essential rôle over the cycle. We shall return to this question on pages 167–168.

Finally, it is possible to approach the problem of growth from a different point of view. It was established here that the rate of growth required for a full employment equilibrium to be indicated by $r$ is equal to

$$r = \alpha\sigma, \qquad (5)$$

so that if $\alpha$ and $\sigma$ are given, the rate of growth is determined. But the equation (5) can also be solved for $\alpha$ in terms of $r$ and $\sigma$, and for $\sigma$ in terms of $r$ and $\alpha$. Thus if it is believed that $r$ should be treated as given (for instance by technological progress), and it is also decided to keep $\sigma$ at a certain level, perhaps not too far from $s$, then it is possible to determine $\alpha = r/\sigma$, as being that marginal propensity to save which can be maintained without causing either inflation or unemployment. This approach was actually used by Ernest Stern in his statistical study of capital requirements of the United Kingdom, the United States and the Union of South Africa.[17] I also understand from Tibor de Scitovszky that he used the same approach in a study not yet published.

It is also possible to treat $r$ and $\alpha$ as given and then determine what $\sigma = r/\alpha$ would have to be. Each approach has its own advantages and the choice depends of course on the nature of the problem in hand. The essential point to be noticed is the relationship between these three variables $r$, $\alpha$, and $\sigma$, and the fact that if any two

of them are given, the value of the third needed for the maintenance of full employment is determined; and if its actual value differs from the required one, inflation in some cases and unused capacity and unemployment in others will develop.

## III. The Dual Nature of the Investment Process

We shall continue the discussion of growth by returning to expression (2) on page 162.

$$\Delta I \frac{1}{\alpha} = I\sigma,$$

which is fundamental to our whole analysis. As a matter of fact, the statement of the problem in this form (2) appears to me at least as important as its actual solution expressed in (3). To repeat, the left part of the equation shows the annual increment in national income and is the demand side; while the right part represents the annual increase in productive capacity and is the supply side. Alternatively, the left part may be called the "multiplier side," and the right part the "$\sigma$ side."

What is most important for our purposes is the fact that investment appears on both sides of the equation; that is, it has a *dual effect*: on the left side it generates income via the multiplier effect; and on the right side it increases productive capacity—the $\sigma$ effect. The explicit recognition of this dual character of investment could undoubtedly save much argument and confusion. Unless some special assumptions are made, the discussion of the effects of investment on profits, income, employment, etc., cannot be legitimately confined to one side only. For the generation of income and the enlargement of productive capacity often have diametrically opposed effects, and the outcome in each particular case depends on the special circumstances involved.[18]

Analyzing expression (2) further, we notice

---

[16] Some work along these lines has been done by J. Tinbergen. See his "Zur Theorie der langfristigen Wirtschaftsentwicklung" in the *Weltwirtschaftliches Archiv*, Vol. LV (May, 1942), pp. 511–49.

[17] Stern, *Economica*, n.s. Vol. XII, pp. 163–71.

[18] The effects of labor saving machinery on employment of labor is a good case in point. Some economists, particularly those connected with the labor movement, insist that such machines displace labor and create unemployment. Their opponents are equally sure that the introduction of labor saving devices reduces costs and generates income, thus increasing employment. Both sides cite ample empirical evidence to prove their contentions, and neither side is wrong. But both of them present an incomplete picture from which no definite conclusion can be derived.

that even though investment is present on both its sides, it does not take the same form: for on the $\sigma$ side we have the *amount* of investment as such; but on the multiplier side we have not the amount of investment but its annual increment, or its absolute *rate of increase*.

The amount of investment (always in the net sense) may remain constant, or it may go up or down, but so long as it remains positive (and except for the rare case when $\sigma \leqq 0$) productive capacity increases. But if income is to rise as well, it is not enough that just any amount be invested: *an increase in income is not a function of the amount invested*; *it is the function of the increment of investment*. Thus the whole body of investment, so to speak, increases productive capacity, but only its very top—the increment—increases national income.

In this probably lies the explanation why inflations have been so rare in our economy in peacetime, and why even in relatively prosperous periods a certain degree of underemployment has usually been present. Indeed, it is difficult enough to keep investment at some reasonably high level year after year, but the requirement that it always be rising is not likely to be met for any considerable length of time.

Now, if investment and therefore income do not grow at the required rate, unused capacity develops. Capital and labor become idle. It may not be apparent why investment by increasing productive capacity creates unemployment of labor. Indeed, as was argued on page 160, this need not always be the case. Suppose national income remains constant or rises very slowly while new houses are being built. It is possible that new houses will be rented out at the expense of older buildings and that no larger rents will be paid than before; or that the new houses will stand wholly or partly vacant with the same result regarding the rents.[19] But it is also possible, and indeed very probable, that the complete or partial utilization of the new buildings which are usually better than the old ones, will require the payment of larger rents, with the result that less income will be left for the purchase of, say clothing; thus causing unemployment in the clothing trades. So the substitution or capital for labor need not take the obvious form of labor-saving machinery; it may be equally effective in a more circuitous way.

----

[19] It is worth noticing that in both cases the construction of the new houses represents a misdirection of resources, at least to some extent. But a complete avoidance of such misdirection is perfectly impossible and even undesirable.

The unemployment of men is considered harmful for obvious reasons. But idle buildings and machinery, though not arousing our humanitarian instincts, can be harmful because their presence inhibits new investment. Why build a new factory when existing ones are working at half capacity? It is certainly not necessary to be dogmatic and assert that no plant or house should ever be allowed to stand idle, and that as soon as unused capacity develops the economy plunges into a depression. There is no need, nor is it possible or desirable, to guarantee that every piece of capital ever constructed will be fully utilized until it is worn out. When population moves from Oklahoma to California, some buildings in Oklahoma will stand idle; or when plastics replace leather in women's handbags, the leather industry may suffer. Such changes form the very life of a free dynamic society, and should not be interfered with. The point is that there be no vacant houses while prospective tenants are present but cannot afford to live in them because they are unemployed. And they are unemployed because income and investment do not grow sufficiently fast.

The extent to which unused capacity, present or expected, inhibits new investment greatly depends on the structure of industry and the character of the economy in general. The more atomistic it is, the stronger is competition, the more susceptible it is to territorial, technological and other changes, the smaller is the effect of unused capacity on new investment. One firm may have an idle plant, while another in the same industry builds a new one; steel may be depressed while plastics are expanding. It is when an industry is more or less monopolized, or when several industries are financially connected, that unused capacity presents a particularly serious threat to new investment.

Strictly speaking, our discussion so far, including equation (2), was based on the assumption that $\alpha$ remained constant. If $\alpha$ varies within the time period concerned, the relation between investment and income becomes more involved. What the left side of the equation (2) requires is that *income* increase; and investment must grow only in so far as its growth is necessary for the growth of income. So if $\alpha$ declines sufficiently fast, a growing income can be achieved with a constant or even falling investment. But years of declining $\alpha$ have evidently been offset by others of rising $\alpha$, because whatever information is available would indicate that over the last seventy years or so prior to this war the percentage of income saved was reasonably constant, possibly with a slight downward trend.[20] Therefore, in the absence of direct government interference, it would seem better not to count too much on a falling $\alpha$, at least for the time being.

In general, a high $\alpha$ presents a serious danger to the maintenance of full employment, because investment may fail to grow at the required high rate, or will be physically unable to do so without creating a substantial difference between $s$ and $\sigma$. This difference indicates that large numbers of capital assets become unprofitable and their owners suffer losses or at least disappointments (see page 164). Space does not permit me to develop this idea at greater length here.[21] But it must be emphasized that what matters is not the magnitude of $\alpha$ taken by itself, but its relation to the growth of labor, natural resources, and technology. Thus a country with new resources, a rapidly growing population, and developing technology is able to digest, so to speak, a relatively large $\alpha$, while absence or at least a very slow growth of these factors makes a high $\alpha$ a most serious obstacle to full employment.[22] But the problem can be attacked not only by lowering $\alpha$, but also by speeding up the rate of technological progress, the latter solution being much more to my taste. It must be remembered, however, that technological progress makes it *possible* for the economy to grow, without guaranteeing that this growth will be realized.

In a private capitalist society where $\alpha$ cannot be readily changed, a higher level of income and employment at any given time can be achieved only through increased investment. But investment, as an employment creating instrument, is a mixed blessing because of its $\sigma$ effect. The economy finds itself in a serious dilemma: if sufficient investment is not forthcoming today, unemployment will be here today. But if enough is invested today, still more will be needed tomorrow.

It is a remarkable characteristic of a capitalist economy that while, on the whole, unemployment is a function of the difference between its actual income and its productive capacity, most of the measures (*i.e.*, investment) directed towards raising national income also enlarge productive capacity. It is very likely that the increase in national income will be greater than that of capacity, but the whole problem is that the increase in income is temporary and presently peters out (the usual multiplier effect), while capacity has been increased for good. So that as far as unemployment is concerned, investment is at the same time a cure for the disease and the cause of even greater ills in the future.[23]

## IV. An Economic Excursion

It may be worth while to browse through the works of several economists of different schools of thought to see their treatment of the $\sigma$ and of the multiplier effects of investment. It is not suggested to make an exhaustive study, but just to present a few examples.

Thus in Marshall's *Principles* capital and investment are looked upon as productive instruments (the $\sigma$ effect), with little being said about monetary (that is, income or price) effects of investment.[24] The same attitude prevails in Fisher's *Nature of Capital and Income*,[25] and I presume in the great majority of writings not devoted to the business cycle. It is not that these writers were unaware of monetary effects of investment (even though they did not have the multiplier concept as such), but such questions belonged to a different field, and the problem of aggregate demand was supposed to be taken care of by some variation of Say's Law.

In the business cycle literature we often find exactly an opposite situation. The whole Wicksellian tradition treated economic fluctuations as a result of monetary effects of excessive investment. It is curious that all this investment did not lead to increased output which would counteract its inflationary tendencies. Indeed, as one reads

[20] See Simon Kuznets, *National Product since 1869*, National Bureau of Economic Research (mimeo., 1945), p. II–89. I do not mean that we must always assume a constant $\alpha$; rather that we lack sufficient proof to rely on a falling one.

[21] See my paper, *Econometrica*, Vol. XIV, particularly pp. 142–45.

[22] *Cf.* Alvin H. Hansen, *Fiscal Policy and the Business Cycle* (New York, 1941), particularly Part IV.

[23] That income generating effects of investment are temporary and that new and larger amounts must be spent to maintain full employment, has been mentioned in economic and popular literature a number of times. Particular use has been made of this fact by opponents of the so-called deficit financing, who treat government expenditures as a "shot in the arm" which must be administered at an ever increasing dose. What they fail to realize is that exactly the same holds true for private investment.

[24] Marshall was very careful, however, to distinguish between the substitution of a particular piece of machinery for particular labor, and the replacement of labor by capital in general. The latter he regarded impossible, because the construction of capital creates demand for labor, essentially a sort of a multiplier effect. See *Principles of Economics*, 8th ed. (London, 1936), p. 523.

[25] Irving Fisher, *The Nature of Capital and Income* (New York, 1919).

Hayek's *Prices and Production*, one gets an impression that these investment projects never bear fruit and are, moreover, abandoned after the crisis. The σ effect is entirely absent, or at least appears with such a long lag as to make it inoperative. Prosperity comes to an end because the banking system refuses to support inflation any longer.[26]

σ fares better in the hands of Aftalion.[27] His theory of the cycle is based upon, what I would call, a time lag between the multiplier and the σ effects. Prosperity is started by income generated by investment in capital goods (the multiplier effect), while no increase in productive capacity has taken place as yet. As investment projects are completed, the resulting increase in productive capacity (the σ effect) pours goods on the market and brings prosperity to an end.

A similar approach is used by Michal Kalecki. The essence of his model of the business cycle consists in making profit expectations, and therefore investment, a function (with appropriate lags) of the relation between national income and the stock of capital. During the recovery, investment and income rise, while the accumulation of capital lags behind. Presently, however, due to the structure of the model, the rise of income stops while capital continues to accumulate. This precipitates the downswing.[28]

Space does not allow us to analyze the works of other writers on the subject, among whom Foster and Catchings should be given due recognition for what is so clumsy and yet so keen an insight.[29] I am also omitting the whole Marxist literature, in which capital accumulation plays such an important rôle, because that would require a separate study. The few remaining pages of this section will be devoted to Hobson and Keynes.

Hobson's writings contain so many interesting ideas that it is a great pity he is not read more often.[30] Anti-Keynesians probably like him not much more than they do Keynes, while Keynesians are apt to regard the *General Theory* as the quintessence of all that was worth while in economics before 1936, and may not bother to read earlier writings. I may say that Keynes's own treatment of Hobson, in spite of his generous recognition of the latter's works, may have substantiated this impression.[31]

Even though both Keynes and Hobson were students of unemployment, they actually addressed themselves to two different problems. Keynes analyzed what happens when savings (of the preceding period) are not invested. The answer was—unemployment, but the statement of the problem in this form might easily give the erroneous impression that if savings were invested, full employment would be assured. Hobson, on the other hand, went a step further and stated the problem in this form: suppose savings are invested. Will the new plants be able to dispose of their products? Such a statement of the problem was not at all, as Keynes thought, a mistake.[32] It was a statement of a different, and possibly also a deeper problem.

Hobson was fully armed with the σ effect of investment, and he saw that it could be answered only by growth. His weakness lay in a poor perception of the multiplier effect and his analysis lacked rigor in general. He gave a demonstration rather than a proof. But the problem to which he addressed himself is just as alive today as it was fifty and twenty years ago.[33]

This discussion, as I suspect almost any other, would be obviously incomplete without some

[26] Friedrich A. Hayek, *Prices and Production* (London, 1931). I don't mean to say that Professor Hayek is not aware that capital is productive; rather that he did not make use of this fact in his theory of the business cycle. See, however, his "The 'Paradox' of Saving," *Economica*, Vol. XI (May, 1931), pp. 125–69.

[27] Albert Aftalion, "The Theory of Economic Cycles Based on the Capitalistic Technique of Production," *Rev. Econ. Stat.*, Vol. IX (Oct., 1927), pp. 165–70. This short article contains a summary of his theory.

[28] Michal Kalecki, *Essays in the Theory of Economic Fluctuations* (New York, 1939). See particularly the last essay "A Theory of the Business Cycle," pp. 116–49. What Mr. Kalecki's model shows in a general sense is that accumulation of capital cannot proceed for any length of time in a trendless economy (*i.e.*, an economy with a secularly constant income). His other results depend upon the specific assumptions he makes.

[29] William T. Foster and Waddill Catchins, *Profits* (Boston and New York, 1925). This book is the most important of their several published works. It is interesting to note that they did come to the conclusion that " . . . as long as capital facilities are created at a sufficient rate, there need be no deficiency of consumer income. To serve that purpose, however, facilities must be increased at a constantly accelerating rate" (p. 413). This they regarded quite impossible.

[30] I am particularly referring to his *Economics of Unemployment* (London, 1922) and *Rationalization and Unemployment* (New York, 1930).

[31] See *The General Theory*, pp. 364–71.

[32] *Ibid.*, pp. 367–68.

[33] Contrary to popular impression, Hobson does not advocate a maximum reduction in the propensity to save. What he wants is to reduce it to a magnitude commensurable with requirements for capital arising from technological progress—an interesting and reasonable idea.

mention of Keynes's treatment of the $\sigma$ and of the multiplier effects. Keynes's approach is very curious: as a matter of fact, he has two: the familiar short-run analysis, and another one which may be called a long-run one.[34]

Keynes's short-run system (later expressed so admiringly by Oscar Lange[35]) is based on "... given the existing skill and quantity of available labor, the existing quality and quantity of available equipment, the existing technique, the degree of competition, the tastes and habits of the consumer ..."[36] Productive capacity thus being given, employment becomes a function of national income, expressed, to be sure, not in money terms but in "wage units." A wage unit, the remuneration for "an hour's employment of ordinary labor" (page 41), is of course a perfect fiction, but some such device must be used to translate real values into monetary and *vice versa*, and one is about as good or as bad as another. The important point for our purposes is the assumption that the amount of equipment (*i.e.*, capital) in existence is given.

Now, the heart of Keynesian economics is the argument that employment depends on income, which in turn is determined by the current volume of investment (and the propensity to save). But investment (in the net sense) is nothing else but the rate of change of capital. Is it legitimate then first to assume the quantity of capital as given, and then base the argument on its rate of change? If the quantity of capital changes, so does (in a typical case) productive capacity, and if the latter changes it can be hardly said that employment is solely determined by the size of national income, expressed in wage units or otherwise. Or putting it in the language of this paper, is it safe and proper to analyze the relation between investment and employment without taking into account the $\sigma$ effect?

The answer depends on the nature of the problem in hand. In this particular case, Keynes could present two reasons for his disregard of the $\sigma$ effect. He could assume that the latter operates with at least a one period lag, the period being understood here as the whole time span

covered by the discussion.[37] Or he could argue that over a typical year the net addition (*i.e.*, net investment) to the stock of capital of a society, such as England or the United States, will hardly exceed some 3 or 5 per cent; since this increment is small when compared with changes in income, it can be disregarded.[38]

Both explanations are entirely reasonable provided of course that the period under consideration is not too long. A five-year lag for the $\sigma$ effect would be difficult to defend, and an increase in the capital stock of some 15 to 20 per cent can hardly be disregarded. I am not aware that Keynes did present either of these explanations; but there is just so much one can do in four hundred pages at any one time.

It would be perfectly absurd to say that Keynes was not aware of the productive qualities of capital. In the *long run* he laid great stress on it, possibly too great. All through the *General Theory* we find grave concern for the diminishing marginal efficiency of capital due, in the long run, to its increasing quantity.[39] There is so much of this kind of argument as to leave the reader puzzled in the end. We are told that marginal efficiency of capital depends on its scarcity. Well and good. But scarcity relative to what? It could become less scarce relative to other factors, such as labor, so that the marginal productivity of capital in the real sense (*i.e.*, essentially our $\sigma$) declined. But then on page 213 we read: "If capital becomes less scarce, the excess yield will diminish, without its having become less productive—at least in the physical sense."

Why then does the marginal efficiency of capital fall? Evidently because capital becomes less scarce relative to income.[40] But why cannot income grow more rapidly if labor is not the limiting factor? Could it be only a matter of poor fiscal policy which failed to achieve a faster growing income? After all we have in investment an income generating instrument; if investment grows more rapidly, so does income. This is *the* multiplier effect of investment on which so much of the *General Theory* is built.

[34] This whole discussion is based on *The General Theory* and not on Keynes's earlier writing.

[35] Oscar Lange, "The Role of Interest and the Optimum Propensity to Consume," *Economica*, n.s. Vol. V (Feb., 1938), pp. 12–32. This otherwise excellent paper has a basic defect in the assumption that investment is a function of consumption rather than of the rate of change of consumption.

[36] *The General Theory*, p. 245. See also pp. 24 and 28.

[37] This again is not quite safe unless some provision for investment projects started in preceding periods and finished during the present period is made.

[38] The second assumption is specifically made by Professor Pigou in his *Employment and Equilibrium* (London, 1941), pp. 33–34.

[39] See for instance pp. 31, 105–106, 217, 219, 220–21, 324, and 375.

[40] There is a third possibility namely that income is redistributed against the capitalists, but Keynes makes no use of it.

I don't have the answer. Is it possible that, while Keynes disregarded the $\sigma$ effect in the short-run analysis, he somehow omitted the multiplier effect from the long-run?

## V. Concluding Remarks

A traveller who sat in the economic councils of the United States and of the Soviet Union would be much impressed with the emphasis placed on investment and technological progress in both countries. He would happily conclude that the differences between the economic problems of a relatively undeveloped socialist economy and a highly developed capitalist economy are really not as great as they are often made to appear. Both countries want investment and technological progress. But if he continued to listen to debates, he would presently begin to wonder. For in the Soviet Union investment and technology are wanted in order to enlarge the country's productive capacity. They are wanted essentially as labor-saving devices which would allow a given task to be performed with less labor, thus releasing men for other tasks. In short, they are wanted for their $\sigma$ effects.

In the United States, on the other hand, little is said about enlarging productive capacity. Technological progress is wanted as the creator of investment opportunities, and investment is wanted because it generates income and creates employment. It is wanted for its multiplier effect.

Both views are correct and both are incomplete. The multiplier is not just another capitalist invention. It can live in a socialist state just as well and it has been responsible for the inflationary pressure which has plagued the Soviet economy all these years, since the first five-year plan. And similarly, $\sigma$ is just as much at home in one country as in another, and its effect—the enlarged productive capacity brought about by accumulation of capital—has undoubtedly had much to do with our peacetime unemployment.

But what is the solution? Shall we reduce $\sigma$ to zero and also abolish technological progress thus escaping from unemployment into the "nirvana" of a stationary state? This would indeed be a defeatist solution. It is largely due to technology and savings that humanity has made the remarkable advance of the last two hundred years, and now when our technological future seems so bright, there is less reason to abandon it than ever before.

It is possible that $\alpha$ has been or will be too high as compared with the growth of our labor force, the utilization of new resources, and the development of technology. Unfortunately, we have hardly any empirical data to prove or disprove this supposition. The fact that private investment did not absorb available savings in the past does not prove that they could not be utilized in other ways (*e.g.*, by government), or even that had private business invested them these investments would have been unprofitable; the investing process itself might have created sufficient income to justify the investments. What is needed is a study of the magnitudes of $s$, of the difference between $s$ and $\sigma$ which can develop without much harm and then of the value of $\alpha$ which the economy can digest at its full employment rate of growth.

Even if the resulting magnitude of $\alpha$ is found to be considerably below the existing one, a reduction of $\alpha$ is only one of the two solutions, the speeding up of technological progress being the other. But it must be remembered that neither technology, nor of course saving, guarantee a rise in income. What they do is to place in our hands the *power* and the ability of achieving a growing income. And just as, depending upon the use made of it, any power can become a blessing or a curse, so can saving and technological progress, depending on our economic policies, result in frustration and unemployment or in an ever expanding economy.

*ROBERT M. SOLOW*

# Technical Change and the Aggregate Production Function[1]

*19* In this day of rationally designed econometric studies and super-input-output tables, it takes something more than the usual "willing suspension of disbelief" to talk seriously of the aggregate production function. But the aggregate production function is only a little less legitimate a concept than, say, the aggregate consumption function, and for some kinds of long-run macro-models it is almost as indispensable as the latter is for the short-run. As long as we insist on practicing macro-economics we shall need aggregate relationships.

Even so, there would hardly be any justification for returning to this old-fashioned topic if I had no novelty to suggest. The new wrinkle I want to describe is an elementary way of segregat-

ing variations in output per head due to technical change from those due to changes in the availability of capital per head. Naturally, every additional bit of information has its price. In this case the price consists of one new required time series, the share of labor or property in total income, and one new assumption, that factors are paid their marginal products. Since the former is probably more respectable than the other data I shall use, and since the latter is an assumption often made, the price may not be unreasonably high.

Before going on, let me be explicit that I would not try to justify what follows by calling on fancy theorems on aggregation and index numbers.[2] Either this kind of aggregate economics appeals

[1] I owe a debt of gratitude to Dr. Louis Lefeber for statistical and other assistance, and to Professors Fellner, Leontief, and Schultz for stimulating suggestions.

Reprinted from the *Review of Economics and Statistics*, Vol. XXXIX (1957), pp. 312–320, by permission of the author and publisher, Harvard University Press. Copyright 1957 by the President and Fellows of Harvard College. Robert Solow is a professor at the Massachusetts Institute of Technology.

[2] Mrs. Robinson in particular has explored many of the profound difficulties that stand in the way of giving any precise meaning to the quantity of capital ("The Production Function and the Theory of Capital," *Review of Economic Studies*, Vol. 21, No. 2), and I have thrown up still further obstacles (*ibid.*, Vol. 23, No. 2). Were the data available, it would be better to apply the analysis to some precisely defined production function with many precisely defined inputs. One can at least hope that the aggregate analysis gives some notion of the way a detailed analysis would lead.

or it doesn't. Personally I belong to both schools. If it does, I think one can draw some crude but useful conclusions from the results.

## Theoretical Basis

I will first explain what I have in mind mathematically and then give a diagrammatic exposition. In this case the mathematics seems simpler. If $Q$ represents output and $K$ and $L$ represent capital and labor inputs in "physical" units, then the aggregate production function can be written as:

$$Q = F(K,L;t). \tag{1}$$

The variable $t$ for time appears in $F$ to allow for technical change. It will be seen that I am using the phrase "technical change" as a short-hand expression for *any kind of shift* in the production function. Thus slowdowns, speed-ups, improvements in the education of the labor force, and all sorts of things will appear as "technical change."

It is convenient to begin with the special case of *neutral* technical change. Shifts in the production function are defined as neutral if they leave marginal rates of substitution untouched but simply increase or decrease the output attainable from given inputs. In that case the production function takes the special form

$$Q = A(t) f(K,L) \tag{1a}$$

and the multiplicative factor $A(t)$ measures the cumulated effect of shifts over time. Differentiate (1a) totally with respect to time and divide by $Q$ and one obtains

$$\frac{\dot{Q}}{Q} = \frac{\dot{A}}{A} + A\frac{\partial f}{\partial K}\frac{\dot{K}}{Q} + A\frac{\partial f}{\partial L}\frac{\dot{L}}{Q}$$

where dots indicate time derivatives. Now define

$$w_k = \frac{\partial Q}{\partial K}\frac{K}{Q} \quad \text{and} \quad w_L = \frac{\partial Q}{\partial L}\frac{L}{Q}$$

the relative shares of capital and labor, and substitute in the above equation (note that $\partial Q/\partial K = A\,\partial f/\partial K$, etc.) and there results:

$$\frac{\dot{Q}}{Q} = \frac{\dot{A}}{A} + w_K\frac{\dot{K}}{K} + w_L\frac{\dot{L}}{L}. \tag{2}$$

From time series of $\dot{Q}/Q$, $w_k$, $\dot{K}/K$, $w_L$ and $\dot{L}/L$ or their discrete year-to-year analogues, we could estimate $\dot{A}/A$ and thence $A(t)$ itself. Actually an amusing thing happens here. Nothing has been said so far about returns to scale. But if all factor inputs are classified either as $K$ or $L$, then the available figures always show $w_K$ and $w_L$ adding up to one. Since we have assumed that factors are paid their marginal products, this amounts to assuming the hypotheses of Euler's theorem. The calculus being what it is, we might just as well assume the conclusion, namely that $F$ is homogeneous of degree one. This has the advantage of making everything come out neatly in terms of intensive magnitudes. Let $Q/L = q$, $K/L = k$, $w_L = 1 - w_K$; note that $\dot{q}/q = \dot{Q}/Q - \dot{L}/L$ etc., and (2) becomes

$$\frac{\dot{q}}{q} = \frac{\dot{A}}{A} + w_K\frac{\dot{k}}{k}. \tag{2a}$$

Now all we need to disentangle the technical change index $A(t)$ are series for output per man hour, capital per man hour, and the share of capital.

So far I have been assuming that technical change is neutral. But if we go back to (1) and carry out the same reasoning we arrive at something very like (2a), namely

$$\frac{\dot{q}}{q} = \frac{1}{F}\frac{\partial F}{\partial t} + w_k\frac{\dot{k}}{k}. \tag{2b}$$

It can be shown, by integrating a partial differential equation, that if $\dot{F}/F$ is independent of $K$ and $L$ (actually under constant returns to scale only $K/L$ matters) then (1) has the special form (1a) and shifts in the production function are neutral. If in addition $\dot{F}/F$ is constant in time, say equal to $a$, then $A(t) = e^{at}$ or in discrete approximation $A(t) = (1 + a)^t$.

The case of neutral shifts and constant returns to scale is now easily handled graphically. The production function is completely represented by a graph of $q$ against $k$ (analogously to the fact that if we know the unit-output isoquant, we know the whole map). The trouble is that this function is shifting in time, so that if we observe points in the $(q,k)$ plane, their movements are compounded out of movements along the curve and shifts of the curve. In Figure 1, for instance, every ordinate on the curve for $t = 1$ has been multiplied by the same factor to give a neutral upward shift of the production function for period 2. The problem is to estimate this shift from knowledge of points $P_1$ and $P_2$. Obviously it would be quite misleading to fit a curve through raw observed points like $P_1$, $P_2$ and others. But if the shift factor for each point of time can be estimated, the observed points can be corrected for technical change, and a production function can then be found.[3]

The natural thing to do, for small changes, is to approximate the period 2 curve by its tangent at $P_2$ (or the period 1 curve by its tangent at $P_1$). This yields an approximately corrected point $P_{12}$, and an estimate for $\Delta A/A$, namely $\overline{P_{12}P_1}/q_1$. But $k_1P_{12} = q_2 - \partial q/\partial k\, \Delta k$ and hence $\overline{P_{12}P_1} = q_2 - q_1 - \partial q/\partial k\, \Delta k = \Delta q - \partial q/\partial k\, \Delta k$ and $\Delta A/A = \overline{P_{12}P_1}/q_1 = \Delta q/q - \partial q/\partial k\,(k/q)\,\Delta k/k = \Delta q/q - w_k\,\Delta k/k$ which is exactly the content of (2a). The not-necessarily-neutral case is a bit more complicated, but basically similar.

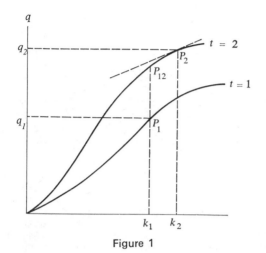

Figure 1

## An Application to the U.S.: 1909–49

In order to isolate shifts of the aggregate production function from movements along it, by use of (2a) or (2b), three time series are needed: output per unit of labor, capital per unit of labor, and the share of capital. Some rough and ready figures, together with the obvious computations, are given in Table 1.

The conceptually cleanest measure of aggregate output would be real net national product. But long NNP series are hard to come by, so I have used GNP instead. The only difference this makes is that the share of capital has to include depreciation. It proved possible to restrict the experiment to private non-farm economic activity. This is an advantage (a) because it skirts the problem of

measuring government output and (b) because eliminating agriculture is at least a step in the direction of homogeneity. Thus my $q$ is a time series of real private non-farm GNP per man hour, Kendrick's valuable work.

The capital time series is the one that will really drive a purist mad. For present purposes, "capital" includes land, mineral deposits, etc. Naturally I have used Goldsmith's estimates (with government, agricultural, and consumer durables eliminated). Ideally what one would like to measure is the annual flow of capital services. Instead one must be content with a less utopian estimate of the stock of capital goods in existence. All sorts of conceptual problems arise on this account. As a single example, if the capital stock consisted of a million identical machines and if each one as it wore out was replaced by a more durable machine of the same annual capacity, the stock of capital as measured would surely increase. But the maximal flow of capital services would be constant. There is nothing to be done about this, but something must be done about the fact of idle capacity. What belongs in a production function is capital in use, not capital in place. Lacking any reliable year-by-year measure of the utilization of capital I have simply reduced the Goldsmith figures by the fraction of the labor force unemployed in each year, thus assuming that labor and capital always suffer unemployment to the same percentage. This is undoubtedly wrong, but probably gets closer to the truth than making no correction at all.[4]

The share-of-capital series is another hodgepodge, pieced together from various sources and ad hoc assumptions (such as Gale Johnson's guess that about 35 per cent of non-farm entrepreneurial income is a return to property). Only after these computations were complete did I learn that Edward Budd of Yale University has completed a careful long-term study of factor shares which will soon be published. It seems unlikely that minor changes in this ingredient would grossly alter the final results, but I have no doubt that refinement of this and the capital time-series would produce neater results.

In any case, in (2a) or (2b) one can replace the time-derivatives by year-to-year changes and calculate $\Delta q/q - w_k\,\Delta k/k$. The result is an estimate of $\Delta F/F$ or $\Delta A/A$, depending on whether these relative shifts appear to be neutral or not.

---

[3] Professors Wassily Leontief and William Fellner independently pointed out to me that this "first-order" approximation could in principle be improved. After estimating a production function corrected for technical change (see below), one could go back and use it to provide a second approximation to the shift series, and on into further iterations.

[4] Another factor for which I have not corrected is the changing length of the work-week. As the work-week shortens, the intensity of use of existing capital decreases, and the stock figures overestimate the input of capital services.

## Table 1. Data for Calculation of $A(t)$

| Year | % labor force employed (1) | Capital stock ($ mill.) (2) | Col. 1 x Col. 2 (3) | Share of property in income (4) | Priv. nonfarm GNP per manhour (5) | Employed capital per manhour (6) | $\Delta A/A$ (7) | $A(t)$ (8) |
|---|---|---|---|---|---|---|---|---|
| 1909 | 91.1 | 146,142 | 133,135 | .335 | $.623 | $2.06 | −.017 | 1.000 |
| 1910 | 92.8 | 150,038 | 139,235 | .330 | .616 | 2.10 | .039 | .983 |
| 1911 | 90.6 | 156,355 | 141,640 | .335 | .647 | 2.17 | .002 | 1.021 |
| 1912 | 93.0 | 159,971 | 148,773 | .330 | .652 | 2.21 | .040 | 1.023 |
| 1913 | 91.8 | 164,504 | 151,015 | .334 | .680 | 2.23 | .007 | 1.064 |
| 1914 | 83.6 | 171,513 | 143,385 | .325 | .682 | 2.20 | −.028 | 1.071 |
| 1915 | 84.5 | 175,371 | 148,188 | .344 | .669 | 2.26 | .034 | 1.041 |
| 1916 | 93.7 | 178,351 | 167,115 | .358 | .700 | 2.34 | −.010 | 1.076 |
| 1917 | 94.0 | 182,263 | 171,327 | .370 | .679 | 2.21 | .072 | 1.065 |
| 1918 | 94.5 | 186,679 | 176,412 | .342 | .729 | 2.22 | .023 | 1.142 |
| 1919 | 93.1 | 189,977 | 176,869 | .354 | .767 | 2.47 | −.076 | 1.157 |
| 1920 | 92.8 | 194,802 | 180,776 | .319 | .721 | 2.58 | .072 | 1.069 |
| 1921 | 76.9 | 201,491 | 154,947 | .369 | .770 | 2.55 | .032 | 1.146 |
| 1922 | 81.7 | 204,324 | 166,933 | .339 | .788 | 2.49 | .011 | 1.183 |
| 1923 | 92.1 | 209,964 | 193,377 | .337 | .809 | 2.61 | .016 | 1.196 |
| 1924 | 88.0 | 222,113 | 195,460 | .330 | .836 | 2.74 | .032 | 1.215 |
| 1925 | 91.1 | 231,772 | 211,198 | .336 | .872 | 2.81 | −.010 | 1.254 |
| 1926 | 92.5 | 244,611 | 226,266 | .327 | .869 | 2.87 | −.005 | 1.241 |
| 1927 | 90.0 | 259,142 | 233,228 | .323 | .871 | 2.93 | −.007 | 1.235 |
| 1928 | 90.0 | 271,089 | 243,980 | .338 | .874 | 3.02 | .020 | 1.226 |
| 1929 | 92.5 | 279,691 | 258,714 | .332 | .895 | 3.06 | −.043 | 1.251 |
| 1930 | 88.1 | 289,291 | 254,865 | .347 | .880 | 3.30 | .024 | 1.197 |
| 1931 | 78.2 | 289,056 | 226,042 | .325 | .904 | 3.33 | .023 | 1.226 |
| 1932 | 67.9 | 282,731 | 191,974 | .397 | .879 | 3.28 | .011 | 1.198 |
| 1933 | 66.5 | 270,676 | 180,000 | .362 | .869 | 3.10 | .072 | 1.211 |
| 1934 | 70.9 | 262,370 | 186,020 | .355 | .921 | 3.00 | .039 | 1.298 |
| 1935 | 73.0 | 257,810 | 188,201 | .351 | .943 | 2.87 | .059 | 1.349 |
| 1936 | 77.3 | 254,875 | 197,018 | .357 | .982 | 2.27 | −.010 | 1.429 |
| 1937 | 81.0 | 257,076 | 208,232 | .340 | .971 | 2.71 | .021 | 1.415 |
| 1938 | 74.7 | 259.789 | 194,062 | .331 | 1.000 | 2.78 | .048 | 1.445 |
| 1939 | 77.2 | 257,314 | 198,646 | .347 | 1.034 | 2.66 | .050 | 1.514 |
| 1940 | 80.6 | 258,048 | 207,987 | .357 | 1.082 | 2.63 | .044 | 1.590 |
| 1941 | 86.8 | 262,940 | 228,232 | .377 | 1.122 | 2.58 | .003 | 1.660 |
| 1942 | 93.6 | 270,063 | 252,779 | .356 | 1.136 | 2.64 | .016 | 1.665 |
| 1943 | 97.4 | 269,761 | 262,747 | .342 | 1.180 | 2.62 | .071 | 1.692 |
| 1944 | 98.4 | 265,483 | 261,235 | .332 | 1.265 | 2.63 | .021 | 1.812 |
| 1945 | 96.5 | 261,472 | 252,320 | .314 | 1.296 | 2.66 | −.044 | 1.850 |
| 1946 | 94.8 | 258,051 | 244,632 | .312 | 1.215 | 2.50 | −.017 | 1.769 |
| 1947 | 95.4 | 268,845 | 256,478 | .327 | 1.194 | 2.50 | .016 | 1.739 |
| 1948 | 95.7 | 276,476 | 264,588 | .332 | 1.221 | 2.55 | .024 | 1.767 |
| 1949 | 93.0 | 289,360 | 269,105 | .326 | 1.275 | 2.70 | ... | 1.809 |

*Notes and Sources:*

Column (1): Percentage of labor force employed. 1909-26, from Douglas, *Real Wages in the United States* (Boston and New York, 1930), 460. 1929-49, calculated from *The Economic Almanac*, 1953-54 (New York, 1953), 426-28.

Column (2): Capital Stock. From Goldsmith, *A Study of Saving in the United States*, Vol. 3 (Princeton, 1956), 20-21, sum of columns 5, 6, 7, 9, 12, 17, 22, 23, 24.

Column (3): (1) x (2).

Column (4): Share of property in income. Compiled from *The Economic Almanac*, 504-505; and Jesse Burkhead, "Changes in the Functional Distribution of Income," *Journal of the American Statistical Association*, Vol. 48 (June 1953), 192-219. Depreciation estimates from Goldsmith, 427.

Column (5): Private nonfarm GPN per man hour, 1939 dollars. Kendrick's data, reproduced in *The Economic Almanac*, 490.

Column (6): Employed capital per man hour. Column (3) divided by Kendrick's man hour series, *ibid*.

Column (7): $\Delta A/A = \Delta(5)/(5) - (4) \times \Delta(6)/(6)$.

Column (8): From (7).

Such a calculation is made in Table 1 and shown in Figure 2. Thence, by arbitrarily setting $A(1909) = 1$ and using the fact that $A(t + 1) = A(t)[1 + \Delta A(t)/A(t)]$ one can successively reconstruct the $A(t)$ time series, which is shown in Figure 3.

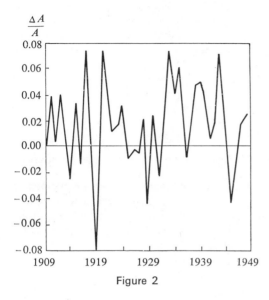

Figure 2

I was tempted to end this section with the remark that the $A(t)$ series, which is meant to be a rough profile of technical change, at least looks reasonable. But on second thought I decided that I had very little prior notion of what would be "reasonable" in this context. One notes with satisfaction that the trend is strongly upward; had it turned out otherwise I would not now be writing this paper. There are sharp dips after each of the World Wars; these, like the sharp rises that preceded them, can easily be rationalized. It is more suggestive that the curve shows a distinct levelling-off in the last half of the 1920's. A sustained rise begins again in 1930. There is an unpleasant sawtooth character to the first few years of the $\Delta A/A$ curve, which I imagine to be a statistical artifact.

## The Outlines of Technical Change

The reader will note that I have already drifted into the habit of calling the curve of Figure 2 $\Delta A/A$ instead of the more general $\Delta F/F$. In fact, a scatter of $\Delta F/F$ against $K/L$ (not shown) indicates no trace of a relationship. So I may state it as a formal conclusion that over the period 1909–49, shifts in the aggregate production function netted out to be approximately neutral. Perhaps I should recall that I have defined

neutrality to mean that the shifts were pure scale changes, leaving marginal rates of substitution unchanged at given capital/labor ratios.

Not only is $\Delta A/A$ uncorrelated with $K/L$, but one might almost conclude from the graph that $\Delta A/A$ is essentially constant in time, exhibiting more or less random fluctuations about a fixed mean. Almost, but not quite, for there does seem to be a break at about 1930. There is some evidence that the average rate of progress in the years 1909–29 was smaller than that from 1930–49. The first 21 relative shifts average about 9/10 of one per cent per year, while the last 19 average $2\frac{1}{4}$ per cent per year. Even if the year 1929, which showed a strong downward shift, is moved from the first group to the second, there is still a contrast between an average rate of 1.2 per cent in the first half and 1.9 per cent in the second. Such *post hoc* splitting-up of a period is always dangerous. Perhaps I should leave it that there is some evidence that technical change (broadly interpreted) may have accelerated after 1929.

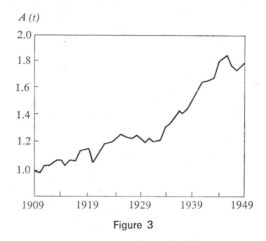

Figure 3

The over-all result for the whole 40 years is an average upward shift of about 1.5 per cent per year. This may be compared with a figure of about .75 per cent per year obtained by Stefan Valavanis-Vail by a different and rather less general method, for the period 1869–1948.[5] Another possible comparison is with the output-per-unit-of-input computations of Jacob Schmookler[6] which show an increase of some 36 per cent in output per unit of input between the decades 1904–13 and 1929–38. Our $A(t)$ rises 36.5 per cent

[5] S. Valavanis-Vail, "An Econometric Model of Growth, U.S.A. 1869–1953," *American Economic Review, Papers and Proceedings*, XLV (May 1955), 217.
[6] J. Schmookler, "The Changing Efficiency of the American Economy, 1869–1938," this REVIEW (August 1952), 226.

between 1909 and 1934. But these are not really comparable estimates, since Schmookler's figures include agriculture.

As a last general conclusion, after which I will leave the interested reader to his own impressions, over the 40 year period output per man hour approximately doubled. At the same time, according to Figure 2, the cumulative upward shift in the production function was about 80 per cent. It is possible to argue that about one-eighth of the total increase is traceable to increased capital per man hour, and the remaining seven-eighths to technical change. The reasoning is this: real GNP per man hour increased from \$.623 to \$1.275. Divide the latter figure by 1.809, which is the 1949 value for $A(t)$, and therefore the full shift factor for the 40 years. The result is a "corrected" GNP per man hour, net of technical change, of \$.705. Thus about 8 cents of the 65 cent increase can be imputed to increased capital intensity, and the remainder to increased productivity.[7]

Of course this is not meant to suggest that the observed rate of technical progress would have persisted even if the rate of investment had been much smaller or had fallen to zero. Obviously much, perhaps nearly all, innovation must be embodied in new plant and equipment to be realized at all. One could imagine this process taking place without net capital formation as old-fashioned capital goods are replaced by the latest models, so that the capital-labor ratio need not change systematically. But this raises problems of definition and measurement even more formidable than the ones already blithely ignored. This whole area of interest has been stressed by Fellner.

For comparison, Solomon Fabricant[8] has estimated that over the period 1871–1951 about 90 per cent of the increase in output per capita is attributable to technical progress. Presumably this figure is based on the standard sort of output-per-unit-of-input calculation.

It might seem at first glance that calculations of output per unit of resource input provide a relatively assumption-free way of measuring productivity changes. Actually I think the implicit load of assumptions is quite heavy, and if anything the method proposed above is considerably more general.

---

[7] For the first half of the period, 1909–29, a similar computation attributes about one-third of the observed increase in GNP per man-hour to increased capital intensity.

[8] S. Fabricant, "Economic Progress and Economic Change," *34th Annual Report of the National Bureau of Economic Research* (New York, 1954).

Not only does the usual choice of weights for computing an aggregate resource-input involve something analogous to my assumption of competitive factor markets, but in addition the criterion output ÷ a weighted sum of inputs would seem tacitly to *assume* (a) that technical change is neutral and (b) that the aggregate production function is *strictly* linear. This explains why numerical results are so closely parallel for the two methods. We have already verified the neutrality, and as will be seen subsequently, a strictly linear production function gives an excellent fit, though clearly inferior to some alternatives.[9]

## The Aggregate Production Function

Returning now to the aggregate production function, we have earned the right to write it in the form (1a). By use of the (practically unavoidable) assumption of constant returns to scale, this can be further simplified to the form

$$q = A(t)f(k,1), \qquad (3)$$

which formed the basis of Figure 1. It was there noted that a simple plot of $q$ against $k$ would give a distorted picture because of the shift factor $A(t)$. Each point would lie on a different member of the family of production curves. But we have now provided ourselves with an estimate of the successive values of the shift factor. (Note that this estimate is quite *independent* of any hypothesis about the exact shape of the production function.) It follows from (3) that by plotting $q(t)/A(t)$ against $k(t)$ we reduce all the observed points to a *single* member of the family of curves in Figure 1, and we can then proceed to discuss the shape of $f(k,1)$ and reconstruct the aggregate production function. A scatter of $q/A$ against $k$ is shown in Figure 4.

Considering the amount of *a priori* doctoring which the raw figures have undergone, the fit is

---

[9] For an excellent discussion of some of the problems, see M. Abramovitz "Resources and Output Trends in the U.S. since 1870," *American Economic Review, Papers and Proceedings*, XLVI (May 1956), 5–23. Some of the questions there raised could in principle be answered by the method used here. For example, the contribution of improved quality of the labor force could be handled by introducing various levels of skilled labor as separate inputs. I owe to Prof. T. W. Schultz a heightened awareness that a lot of what appears as shifts in the production function must represent improvement in the quality of the labor input, and therefore a result of real capital formation of an important kind. Nor ought it be forgotten that even straight technical progress has a cost side.

remarkably tight. Except, that is, for the layer of points which are obviously too high. These maverick observations relate to the seven last years of the period, 1943–49. From the way they lie almost exactly parallel to the main scatter, one is tempted to conclude that in 1943 the aggregate production function simply shifted. But the whole earlier procedure was designed to purify those points from shifts in the function, so that way out would seem to be closed. I suspect the explanation may lie in some systematic incomparability of the capital-in-use series. In particular during the war there was almost certainly a more intensive use of capital services through two- and three-shift operation than the stock

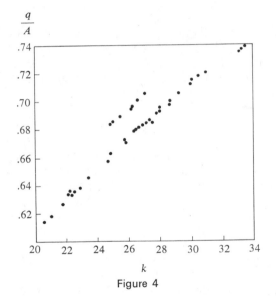

$$\frac{q}{A}$$

Figure 4

figures would show, even with the crude correction that has been applied. It is easily seen that such an underestimate of capital inputs leads to an overestimate of productivity increase. Thus in effect each of the affected points should really lie higher and toward the right. But further analysis shows that, for the orders of magnitude involved, the net result would be to pull the observations closer to the rest of the scatter.

At best this might account for 1943–1945. There remains the postwar period. Although it is possible that multi-shift operation remained fairly widespread even after the war, it is unlikely that this could be nearly enough to explain the whole discrepancy.[10] One might guess that

accelerated amortization could have resulted in an underestimate of the capital stock after 1945. Certainly other research workers, notably Kuznets and Terborgh, have produced capital stock estimates which rather exceed Goldsmith's at the end of the period. But for the present, I leave this a mystery.[11]

In a first version of this paper, I resolutely let the recalcitrant observations stand as they were in a regression analysis of Figure 4, mainly because such casual amputation is a practice I deplore in others. But after some experimentation it seemed that to leave them in only led to noticeable distortion of the results. So, with some misgivings, in the regressions that follow I have omitted the observations for 1943–1949. It would be better if they could be otherwise explained away.

Figure 4 gives an inescapable impression of curvature, of persistent but not violent diminishing returns. As for the possibility of approaching capital-saturation, there is no trace on this gross product level, but even setting aside all other difficulties, such a scatter confers no particular license to guess about what happens at higher $K/L$ ratios than those observed.

As for fitting a curve to the scatter, a Cobb-Douglas function comes immediately to mind, but then so do several other parametric forms, with little to choose among them.[12] I can't help feeling that little or nothing hangs on the choice of functional form, but I have experimented with several. In general I limited myself to two-parameter families of curves, linear in the parameters (for computational convenience), and at least capable of exhibiting diminishing returns (except for the straight line, which on this account proved inferior to all others).

---

[10] It is cheering to note that Professor Fellner's new book voices a suspicion that the postwar has seen a substantial increase over prewar in the prevalence of multi-shift operation. See *Trends and Cycles in Economic Activity* (New York, 1956), 92.

[11] Walter P. Hogan explains the seven maverick observations in "Technical Progress and Production Functions," *Review of Economics and Statistics*, Vol. XL (1958), p. 407. They are the result of inaccurate computations. The correct figures are

|      | $A(t)$ | $q/A$ |
|------|--------|-------|
| 1943 | 1.733  | .681  |
| 1944 | 1.856  | .682  |
| 1945 | 1.895  | .684  |
| 1946 | 1.812  | .671  |
| 1947 | 1.781  | .670  |
| 1948 | 1.810  | .675  |
| 1949 | 1.853  | .688  |

[—Ed.]

[12] A discussion of the same problem in a different context is to be found in Prais and Houthakker, *The Analysis of Family Budgets* (Cambridge, England, 1955), 82–88. See also S. J. Prais, "Non-Linear Estimates of the Engel Curves," *Review of Economic Studies*, No. 52 (1952–53), 87–104.

The particular possibilities tried were the following:

$$q = \alpha + \beta k \qquad (4a)$$
$$q = \alpha + \beta \log k \qquad (4b)$$
$$q = \alpha - \beta/k \qquad (4c)$$
$$\log q = \alpha + \beta \log k \qquad (4d)$$
$$\log q = \alpha - \beta/k. \qquad (4e)$$

Of these, (4d) is the Cobb-Douglas case; (4c and e) have upper asymptotes; the semi-logarithmic (4b) and the hyperbolic (4c) must cross the horizontal axis at a positive value of $k$ and continue ever more steeply but irrelevantly downward (which means only that some positive $k$ must be achieved before any output is forthcoming, but this is far outside the range of observation); (4e) begins at the origin with a phase of increasing returns and ends with a phase of diminishing returns—the point of inflection occurs at $k = \beta/2$ and needless to say all our observed points come well to the right of this.

The results of fitting these five curves to the scatter of Figure 4 are shown in Table 2.

### Table 2

| Curve | $\alpha$ | $\beta$ | $r$ |
|-------|----------|---------|------|
| 4a | .438 | .091 | .9982 |
| b | .448 | .239 | .9996 |
| c | .917 | .618 | .9964 |
| d | −.729 | .353 | .9996 |
| e | −.038 | .913 | .9980 |

The correlation coefficients are uniformly so high that one hesitates to say any more than that all five functions, even the linear one, are about equally good at representing the general shape of the observed points. From the correlations alone, for what they are worth, it appears that the Cobb-Douglas function (4d) and the semilogarithmic (4b) are a bit better than the others.[13]

[13] It would be foolhardy for an outsider (or maybe even an insider) to hazard a guess about the statistical properties of the basic time series. A few general statements can be made, however. (a) The natural way to introduce an error term into the aggregate production function is multiplicatively: $Q = (1 + u) F(K,L;t)$. In the neutral case it is apparent that the error factor will be absorbed into the estimated $A(t)$. Then approximately the error in $\Delta A/A$ will be $\Delta u/1 + u$. If $u$ has zero mean, the variance of the estimated $\Delta A/A$ will be approximately $2(1 - \rho)$ var $u$, where $\rho$ is the first autocorrelation of the $u$ series. (b) Suppose that marginal productivity distribution doesn't hold exactly, so that $K/Q \partial Q/\partial K = w_k + v$, where now $v$ is a random deviation and $w_k$ is the share of property income. Then the error in the estimated $\Delta A/A$ will be $v \Delta k/k$, with variance $(\Delta k/k)^2$ var $v$. Since $K/L$ changes slowly, the multiplying factor will be very small. The effect is to bias the estimate of

Since all of the fitted curves are of the form $g(y) = \alpha + \beta h(x)$, one can view them all as linear regressions and an interesting test of goodness of fit proposed by Prais and Houthakker (*ibid.*, page 51) is available. If the residuals from each regression are arranged in order of increasing values of the independent variable, then one would like this sequence to be disposed "randomly" about the regression line. A strong "serial" correlation in the residuals, or a few long runs of positive residuals alternating with long runs of negative residuals, would be evidence of just that kind of smooth departure from linearity that one would like to catch. A test can be constructed using published tables of critical values for runs of two kinds of elements.

This has been done for the linear, semilogarithmic and Cobb-Douglas functions. The results strongly confirm the visual impression of diminishing returns in Figure 4 by showing the linear function to be a systematically poor fit. As between (4b) and (4d) there is little to choose.[14]

### A Note on Saturation

It has already been mentioned that the aggregate production function shows no signs of levelling off into a stage of capital-saturation. The two curves in Table 2 which have upper asymptotes (c and e) happen to locate that asymptote at about the same place. The limiting values of $q$ are respectively .92 and .97. Of course these are both true asymptotes approached but not reached for any finite value of $k$. It could not be otherwise: no analytic function can suddenly level off and become constant unless it has always been constant. But on the other hand there is no reason to expect nature to be infinitely differentiable. Thus any conclusions extending beyond the range actually observed in Figure 4 are necessarily treacherous. But tongue in cheek, if we take .95 as a guess at the saturation level of $q$, and use the *linear* function (4a) (which will get there first) as a lower-limit guess at the saturation level for $k$, it turns out to be about 5.7 more than twice its present value.

$\Delta A/A$ in such a way as to lead to an overestimate when property receives less than its marginal product (and $k$ is increasing). (c) Errors in estimating $A(t)$ enter in a relatively harmless way so far as the regression analysis is concerned. Errors of observation in $k$ will be more serious and are likely to be large. The effect will of course be to bias the estimates of $\beta$ downward.

[14] The test statistic is $R$, the total number of runs, with small values significant. For (4a), $R = 4$; for (4b), $R = 13$. The 1% critical value in both cases is about 9.

But all this is in terms of *gross output*, whereas for analytic purposes we are interested in the *net* productivity of capital. The difference between the two is depreciation, a subject about which I do not feel able to make guesses. If there were more certainty about the meaning of existing estimates of depreciation, especially over long periods of time, it would have been better to conduct the whole analysis in terms of net product.

However, one can say this. Zero net marginal productivity of capital sets in when gross marginal product falls to the "marginal rate of depreciation," i.e. when adding some capital adds only enough product to make good the depreciation on the increment of capital itself. Now in recent years NNP has run a bit over 90 per cent of GNP, so capital consumption is a bit under 10 per cent of gross output. From Table 1 it can be read that capital per unit of output is, say, between 2 and 3. Thus annual depreciation is between 3 and 5 per cent of the capital stock. Capital-saturation would occur whenever the gross marginal product of capital falls to .03–.05. Using (4b), this would happen at $K/L$ ratios of around 5 or higher, still well above anything ever observed.[15]

[15] And this is under relatively pessimistic assumptions as to how technical change itself affects the rate of capital consumption. A warning is in order here: I have left Kendrick's GNP data in 1939 prices and Goldsmith's capital stock figures in 1929 prices. Before anyone uses the $\beta$'s of Table 2 to reckon a yield on capital or any similar number, it is necessary to convert $Q$ and $K$ to a comparable price basis, by an easy calculation.

## Summary

This paper has suggested a simple way of segregating shifts of the aggregate production function from movements along it. The method rests on the assumption that factors are paid their marginal products, but it could easily be extended to monopolistic factor markets. Among the conclusions which emerge from a crude application to American data 1909–49 are the following:

1.  Technical change during that period was neutral on average.

2.  The upward shift in the production function was, apart from fluctuations, at a rate of about one per cent per year for the first half of the period and 2 per cent per year for the last half.

3.  Gross output per man hour doubled over the interval, with $87\frac{1}{2}$ per cent of the increase attributable to technical change and the remaining $12\frac{1}{2}$ per cent to increased use of capital.

4.  The aggregate production function, corrected for technical change, gives a distinct impression of diminishing returns, but the curvature is not violent.

*WILLIAM J. FELLNER*

# Rapid Growth as an Objective of Economic Policy

*20*

## I. Capital Formation and Technological Progress

It is revealing, even if conventional, to attribute the long-run growth of output to population growth, to the growth of the capital stock, and to technological-organizational improvements ("innovations"). Within the same framework the growth of per capita output and the rise of living standards should be explained by the increase in the capital-labor ratio and by technological-organizational progress.

A few words of caution are required to bring out the fact that labor does not have an unqualified interest (an interest "without constraint") in an ever increasing capital-labor ratio or in technological-organizational progress, although labor does have this interest, provided that we can take innovating activity of the proper kind for granted. The reason why a constraint pointing to innovational requirements enters here is that

the growth process itself will stop and unemployment is apt to develop if the rate of return on investment declines too far; that is, to a floor level set by risk premium requirements. If a low rate of return on investment merely stopped the growth process but did not also create unemployment, then labor would still have an unqualified or unconstrained interest in a rising capital-labor ratio, because the real wage rate rises monotonically with the ratio of capital to labor. But if the level of money wage rates and of prices does not possess unlimited downward flexibility, then it is not possible to count on the "real-balance effect" (Pigou-Patinkin effect) to assure full employment—in other words Say's Law is put out of commission—and in this case sufficient lowering of the rate of return on investment may not merely put an end to the growth process but is apt also to create the "Keynesian" variety of unemployment. It is true that this type of unemployment can be eliminated—at least "in principle"—through government investment or through deficit-financed transfer payments to

Reprinted from the *American Economic Review: Papers and Proceedings*, Vol L (1960), pp. 93–105, by permission of the author and publisher. William Fellner is a professor at Yale University.

consumers, but it is questionable whether under large-scale programs of this sort the essentials of a decentralized market economy and of its political institutions could be preserved.

This means that rather general social interest attaches to the avoidance of "excessive" capital formation, such as lowers the rate of return on investment to a floor level. But if the innovations of a period satisfy certain requirements, then a significant increase in the capital-labor ratio may take place without resulting in any excessive capital formation in the foregoing sense. An appreciable lowering of the rate of return on investment will be avoided if the quantity of innovating activity (i.e., its over-all product-raising effect), and the distribution of its labor-saving, capital-saving, and land-saving effects develop in such a way that the marginal productivity of capital is reasonably well maintained. This implies that innovations must not become excessively capital-saving. The available evidence shows that in the Western economies innovating activity has satisfied these requirements in the long run and that at the same time innovations have not become so strongly laborsaving as to prevent a steep up-trend in real wage rates. As for cyclical disturbances and the consequences of temporary saturation, it should be possible to prevent these from becoming too severe by compensatory monetary and fiscal policies. It seems quite reasonable to assume that somewhat accelerated capital formation would accelerate growth without giving rise in the predictable future to long-run Keynesian difficulties (which would develop only if innovating activity were to become quantitatively insufficient or excessively capital-saving in character).

Furthermore, growth would of course be accelerated by increased technological-organizational progress. But the technological progress we have had, and shall continue to have, mostly requires the acquisition of new capital goods. Therefore, a policy aiming at high rates of technological progress must do its best to promote capital formation, along with research and education.

In summary, we may conclude that, given the population of a country and its rate of population increase, the growth rate of output depends both on the rate of capital formation and the rate of technological progress; and that an effort to raise the growth rate of output is likely to be successful if it concentrates on promoting that kind of capital formation which incorporates technological advance.

## II. Inflationary Difficulties

The postwar experience of Western nations has convinced many economists of the significance of a further problem which previously it was not usual to stress in the context of growth theory. Sufficiently high degrees of resource utilization— at which there does not yet exist an aggregative excess demand—are apt to cause cost inflation, perhaps primarily cost inflation of the "wage-push" variety. The main characteristic of inflation of this sort is that even in the long run a desirable degree of utilization cannot be maintained without letting unit costs rise. Or to put it somewhat differently, the main characteristic of cost-inflation is that restraining demand by monetary-fiscal measures does not merely flatten the price trend but that such a policy of demand restraints results in a reduced degree of utilization even in the long run; that is, even aside from a loss of output during a period of adjustment. This is because noncompetitive forces on the supply side of factor markets are powerful enough to raise unit costs for given outputs as soon as the factor markets become sufficiently tight. The post-Korean period in the United States illustrates these propositions, which should be supplemented by the statement that similar price increases may originate also in the monopoly power of producers.

Recently there has been quite a bit of controversy on the question of whether the inflation of the post-Korean years should not after all be interpreted (at least in part) as demand inflation, with a lag between the earlier excess demand and the subsequent inflationary effects. I do not deny that models of this sort have proved revealing, but I believe that such formulations or formulations based on the existence of sectoral excess demand bypass the issue with which I am concerned. The essential fact, it seems to me, is that in the post-Korean period a policy aiming at approximate general price stability has rarely been compatible with high employment and adequate growth. The effective demand required for high utilization at a stable price level was used up for underutilization at rising prices. I do not see how this fact could be interpreted without relying heavily in one's interpretation on noncompetitive forces on the supply side; that is, on forces of cost-push that produce general price increases even in periods with no aggregative excess demand (indeed in periods of excess supply). Thus even if we recognize the possible causal role of past excess demand or of simultaneous sectoral excess demand, the proper inter-pretation of generalized inflation must in such cases emphasize the "monopolistic" cost be-havior through which the past excess demand, or the simultaneous sectoral excess demand, touches off price increases in periods or in sectors with no excess demand.

The fact that economic systems show consider-able resistance to price-level stabilization at high degrees of utilization (but even in the absence of aggregative excess demand) suggests that specific power groups can get away with an inflationary type of redistribution in their own favor for long enough to make such action rewarding, while they presumably could not get away with an orderly redistribution which could be carried out at a constant price level. This in turn suggests that the essence of the matter is that claims to real income exceed the available real income, and that in each stage of the process certain groups in the economy catch other groups by surprise. Subsequently, the other groups whose claims to real income have stayed unsatisfied engage in a move to catch up. This is the reason why an inflationary process of the cost-push variety carries a serious threat of acceleration. I do not believe that this reasoning is contradicted by the interesting studies which Charles Schultze, Otto Eckstein and Gary Fromm, and Thomas A. Wilson undertook for the Joint Economic Committee; or by the results of Ruth Mack's research which were published in the August, 1959, issue of the *Review of Economics and Statistics*. These studies throw a good deal of light on various important aspects of the recent inflation; they do not, however, contradict the proposition that the generalization and perpetuation of this type of inflation is a phenomenon rooted in the concentration of market power.

We cannot be sure just how sensitive these inflationary forces are to small changes in the employment or unemployment ratio. It is possible that most of the forces of cost-push inflation will become significantly weakened by monetary-fiscal restraints compatible with an average degree of employment which is still tolerably high. These inflationary forces may prove very sensitive to the job situation with which the individual worker is faced whenever he wants a new job. In this event it will not take too much statistically observable aggregate unemployment--and it might take very little unemployment of extended duration—to remove any serious threat of inflation. This is the objective of the experiment in which some Western nations—including the United States—are engaged at the present writing: an experiment

to keep cost-inflation in bounds by monetary-fiscal means. The experiment will prove successful if the resulting unemployment rates will prove tolerable per se and if long-run growth rates will hold up reasonably well at the degrees of utiliza-tion which become established. I think it is con-ceivable that the experiment will be successful, but this can of course not be taken for granted.

If this type of experiment should prove un-successful and if, whenever our employment ratio and our growth rates are not seriously deficient, we should again become faced with a real threat of appreciable and accelerating inflation, then we would have to choose between two lines of policy.

One line of policy is that of direct wage and price controls. Political controls of this sort would render the price and wage structure, and thus the allocation of resources, thoroughly arbitrary. It would be unconvincing to defend comprehensive controls with the argument that noncompetitive forces have introduced a great deal of arbitrari-ness in the price and cost structure all along. Where the degree of deviation from competitive norms has not shown a rising tendency, Western cost and price structures have at least responded properly to changes in technological conditions and in relative demands. Even this would, I think, cease to be the case in the event of comprehensive political wage and price setting. The farm-price policy and some other illustrations give us a taste of what might be in store in such circumstances. Furthermore, comprehensive direct controls would very greatly increase the power of the executive branch of the government. Accelerating cost-push inflation could of course not be left un-controlled, but administrative wage and price controls are an unattractive remedy. Let me add that, in my opinion, those proposing reliance on friendly agreements between the governments, the representatives of labor, and the representa-tives of management are using a euphemism for direct controls.

The other possibility would be to weaken the market power of unions and of corporations by reducing their size sufficiently to make sure that in each major industry there should be a fair number of independent bargaining pairs. This of course would not imply "atomization" of our major industries but it would imply that in some of these industries it does not take the largest observable sizes to utilize practically all the real economies of scale. Each bargaining pair would then consist of a union and a firm, and each pair would be under appreciable competitive pressure from other pairs. Broadened antitrust acts would have to be enforced against collusive behavior.

Under such conditions monetary-fiscal policy could approximate full employment closely without getting us into an inflationary situation. The bargaining pairs in the various industries would know that rapid loss of competitive position is the penalty which inflicts itself upon a union and a firm concluding a bargain with inflationary implications. A reasonable monetary-fiscal policy could then stabilize the price level without creating appreciable unemployment. As for the general trend in real wage rates, this could be trusted to take care of itself in accordance with productivity trends, as long as a high level of employment were maintained with the support of monetary-fiscal policy. Whenever such a monetary-fiscal policy would have to run a deficit or would be accumulating a budgetary surplus is unpredictable a priori.

These solutions involving a reduction of market power are of course politically very difficult. It is conceivable that the growth of foreign economies and (let us hope) free trade will help to reduce the degree of market power in the United States. If, for this or any other reason, the effort of Western nations to get reasonable degrees of employment and satisfactory growth rates without appreciable inflation will prove successful, then it will not be necessary to face the great political difficulties of significantly extended and intensified antimonopoly action. But in the contrary case we will have to choose between broadening the scope of our antimonopoly policies on the one hand and resorting to comprehensive direct controls on the other. I would like to suggest that it would be a mistake to plunge into a policy of extensive direct market controls simply because at first this might appear to be the line of least political resistance. This, I think, would be a mistake, and a mistake we would be quite likely to make.

We now have arrived at the conclusion that strengthening our growth rates requires promoting capital formation of the kind which embodies technological advance; and that a policy aiming at this objective can prove successful only if it is able to remove the threat of accelerating cost-push inflation along the path of economic growth. What is involved in a policy aiming at increased capital formation?

## III. Aiming for Higher Sustainable Rates of Growth

Programs for accelerating the rate of capital formation imply the value judgment that a higher rate of saving would be desirable. This is not quite the same thing as to say that a policy aiming for more rapid growth must violate the time-preference scales of the public. A substantial (more than "marginal") increase of the rate of saving has some effects which are in the nature of "external economies." Hence bringing about a bulky increase in capital formation may prove justified in terms of individual preference scales, even if political measures are needed to raise the rate of saving. This is because in his saving decisions the individual saver leaves out of account the benefits which develop as external economies of bulky incremental saving—benefits which accrue partly to the savers themselves qua wage earners and citizens. Such external economies would develop even in an eternally peaceful world, largely because of the connection between capital formation and technological progress.

Still, in a genuinely peaceful or unified world many of us might refuse to make the judgment that the general social interest is served by raising the rate of private saving beyond the rates establishing themselves through atomistic individual decisions. On the other hand, it should be remembered that in a genuinely peaceful or unified world the ratio of saving to consumption would in all probability be higher than it is now, because it is reasonable to assume that high government expenditures—mainly high defense expenditures—have on balance increased the tax burden of corporations and of high-income recipients in a greater proportion than that of the relatively low-income groups. Therefore by providing inducements to save and by raising the present rate of capital formation we would merely undo (or partly undo) an "artificial" lowering of capital formation. Quite aside from this, the fact that we do not live in a genuinely peaceful or unified world implies also that a vital Western interest attaches to growth rates such as will prevent a gradual rise to economic supremacy of the Communist block. These are rather general value judgments underlying the public concern with the problem of stepping up our rate of growth—a growth rate which has recently been weak. I happen to share this concern. The logical purist may object that the growth rate of the GNP is a statistical concept to which not much "ultimate meaning" can be attached. My answer would be that so far this type of growth rate has proved a pretty good "proxy" for changes that were indeed of very great historical significance.

The rate of saving and of capital formation could doubtless be increased by means of tax policy. Here again political difficulties would be encountered, but it is very likely that a good many difficulties could be overcome by determined effort. What could be accomplished by reducing taxes that have an adverse effect on savings and investment?

It is obviously impossible to try to answer this question without making subjective judgments. These I shall have to make, but I will comment on alternatives subsequently. I will begin my discussion on the postulate that we find it desirable to provide additional incentives for private saving and capital formation, and that we wish to engage in adequate government expenditures of the kind which support growth tendencies.

There is a possibility that gradually we will be able to reduce tax rates as the economy grows. This is because tax revenue at given tax rates tends to grow—indeed tends to grow at a somewhat higher rate than the GNP—creating a leeway for gradual tax reductions whenever there is no urgent need for increasing the sum total of fiscal expenditures in the same proportion as that in which the tax revenue rises. It may not be too optimistic to assume a lesser rate of increase in aggregate fiscal expenditures, considering that this aggregate includes such items as farm subsidies, veterans benefits, and interest on the debt. These at present make up almost one-fourth of the federal budgetary expenditures. If along the growth path of the economy aggregate government expenditures will rise in a lesser proportion than does the revenue at given tax rates, there will be room for a reduction of tax rates. But these possibilities depend on future defense needs about which nothing is known.

So far as possible, I would like to avoid speculations about future defense needs. It is a fact that over the past few years our defense expenditures have risen in a smaller proportion than the GNP and in a much smaller proportion than that in which the GNP would have risen if its rate of growth had been adequate. This has left many of us with an uncomfortable feeling. At present there is much talk about stabilizing or even reducing armament expenditures. Let us assume, however, for a moment that we shall in the long run raise defense expenditures at a rate corresponding to reasonably adequate growth rate of the GNP, say, at about 4 per cent per annum. In this case the potential budgetary surplus should be rising more or less continuously at an annual rate of, say 4 billion dollars (as expressed in terms of present numerical proportions). Of these 4 billions, say, 2 billions would be absorbed by a continuous rise in defense needs (at constant prices and on very speculative as-

sumptions). If now government expenditures other than those for defense, farmers, veterans, and interest were to be raised on the average by about 10 per cent per annum, this would absorb perhaps one to one and one half of the remaining 2 billions. Annually there would remain perhaps 500 million dollars or a little more, which could accumulate for a gradual, slow reduction of those taxes which bear on investment. This assumes a balanced budget, which will not necessarily prove the target most consistent with growth objectives. It also disregards the possibility of having to raise defense expenditures suddenly at a significant rate, since this would call for a reorientation of tax policy, involving conceivably an increase rather than a reduction in some tax rates. (I will add here that if from 1955 to 1959 we had had an average GNP growth rate of 4-4.5 per cent per annum and had been raising defense spending in proportion to the GNP, we would now be spending almost 10 billions more for defense than the amount we are actually spending. Consequently, here too the long-run problem is very largely that of the GNP growth rate, even if relative allocations are not changed much.)

Whenever we get around to tax reductions, I would suggest giving the reduction of the 52 per cent corporate rate high priority rating. This would strengthen incentives, and much of the tax saving would go into capital formation (largely through reinvestment). I believe that attention should be given also to the possibility of setting a lower tax rate on the undistributed proportion of corporate profits than on the part which serves for dividend payments, even though a change of this sort would presumably require qualifying provisions so as not to stimulate an actual reduction of dividend payments below previously attained levels, and so as not even to stimulate the reinvestment of all profit increments. After all, ploughed-back profits are already receiving preferential treatment, even though not on the level of corporate taxation but by not becoming subjected to the individual income tax. Maintenance of dividend payments in recessions is a stabilizing factor; and an unduly high marginal corporate reinvestment ratio could bring irrational investment decisions and a further concentration of economic power. Therefore, while preferential corporate rates on ploughed-back profits would provide a welcome stimulus to investment and growth, it would I think be a mistake to go all out for this type of reform without using safeguards.

However, growth oriented tax reform could be put into effect, not merely along a gradual growth path, but promptly, without a loss of revenue. Recognizing that we are now moving into increasingly controversial territory, I will nevertheless point out the following facts. Reducing all successive bracket rates in the individual income tax by 15 per cent of the rates themselves and increasing exemptions by $100 (i.e., each exemption from $600 to $700) would cost about 9 billion dollars a year, which is no more than the yield of a very limited sales tax. Without going into details I will merely say that a sales tax of such yield might, for example, be levied on a volume corresponding to merely 40 per cent of the aggregate national "consumption expenditure," in which case the rate of the tax would have to be about 7 per cent on the retail level. It is my guess that most of us would not consider this an antisocial reform, since foods and drugs, housing, and practically all other items, which even the poorest must continuously acquire, could be wholly exempted. In essence, I am suggesting here giving consideration to a package which would substitute a moderate and selective sales tax—or luxury tax—for part of the present income tax burden of all income classes. The objective would be not to harm the taxpayers of any income class if they persist in their present spending habits, and to give them an advantage if they decide to save more. It seems to me that a growth oriented tax policy should move at least to some extent toward taxing luxury goods rather than income in general.

Alternatively, one could of course move from the taxation of income toward the taxation of consumption in general, for example by using the device of the expenditure tax. The disadvantage of this device would I think be that all families that are atypical in the sense of having to spend more than is implied (as a norm) in the rate schedule of the expenditure tax would be hard hit.[1] The sales taxation of nonnecessities would I think have the advantage of leaving an outlet for the consumption of untaxed necessities. But I am sure that this, too, belongs among the controversial points.

[1] For illustration, consider the following. Say for example that a household with an income of $x$ dollars "typically" spends precisely its income on consumption. Then $x$ dollars would presumably be the consumption level on which the expenditure tax would levy the same rate as does at present the income tax on $x$ dollars of income. But a family which is atypical in having good reasons to dissave for a good many years, in addition to spending $x$ dollars, would be hard hit by such a rate schedule of an expenditure tax. Leaving an outlet for the untaxed consumption of necessities would I think make a big difference in a great many cases.

A further alternative measure for raising the amount of savings and of capital formation would be to run all the time a surplus in the social security account. This, however, would amount to financing government expenditures or private investment by means of compulsory deductions from wages and by means of the employment tax. I do not consider this method particularly desirable and, therefore, I am inclined to the view that the package which I have been describing is on the whole more advantageous.

It is of course possible to object that the sales tax with exemptions which is contained in this package would bring undesirable selectivity in the sense of penalizing and subsidizing different types of market behavior. This objection I would not regard as decisive because the income tax burden, for part of which this package would substitute a sales tax, also has undesirable selectivity effects as between different types of market behavior. Indeed, while high marginal income tax rates impose a penalty on attitudes conducive to growth, the selectivity of a limited sales tax would have the contrary characteristics. The sales tax burden which we are considering would be conditional—i.e., every household could at any time avoid most of it by not spending on taxed items—and hence it would probably have a smaller disincentive effect than the unconditional income tax. Furthermore, savings would be stimulated.

In the language of welfare economics, both an income tax and a sales tax of the luxury tax variety carry an excess burden. They possess undesirable selectivity (expressing itself in substitution effects) and this is accepted because it inevitably comes in a package with the desired selectivity by which we wish to protect the low-income groups. The undesirable selectivity of all practically feasible taxes pushes the taxpayer around, so to speak. But various taxes push the taxpayer in different directions. A growth oriented tax policy should, I think, push the taxpayer more in the directions in which a luxury tax pushes him and less in the direction in which an income tax pushes him than does our present tax structure. I am arguing that this could be done without appreciably changing the desired selectivity of the tax structure; that is, without placing additional burdens on the low-income groups.

I will mention the question of so-called "punitive" rates here only tangentially. Whether bracket rates in excess of 50 per cent are justified or not depends exclusively on whether they serve the purpose of a reasonable "political equilibrium." This is a hazy question about which the economist cannot have a professional opinion one way or the other. But we know that the yield of these rates is negligible (less than 1 per cent of the total federal tax revenue), and that the existence of these rates leads to irrational decisions of various sorts, prominently including decisions to find means of tax avoidance. The number of taxpayers in those brackets is very small, but most of the strategically located persons in the business life of the country fall in these brackets with part of their incomes. On the other hand, very large incomes from wealth can easily be given the form of capital gains, and for various reasons (some of which are good reasons) the preferential treatment of capital gains will hardly be abolished. Economically the top rates in the income tax structure are "irrational." By closing some "loopholes"—business expenditures for entertainment, overgenerous depletion allowances, etc.—it might be possible to raise more revenue than by leaving the largely nominal top rates on the statute books.

My preceding observations relate mainly to the revenue side of the budget, although they include critical comments on expenditures for agricultural subsidies. It is necessary to add, however, that growth oriented fiscal policy would have to pay a great deal of attention to the expenditure side too. Very much will depend on whether we shall select the areas of thrift and the areas of adequately rising budgetary expenditure in a way consistent with our growth objectives. Research, education, public health, and specific types of public construction should be regarded as belonging among the high-priority areas. It would be difficult to say what can contribute more to healthy growth: research and education or capital formation. All three are vitally important. On the other hand, we should at least be able to prevent the sum total of interest-on-the-debt, farm subsidies, and veteran's payments from rising along with the GNP.

A last word on credit policy. I believe that in recent years the case against selective credit controls has been overstated. Our tax policies and our general credit policies are so strongly selective against capital formation and growth that it would be desirable to take part of the burden off investment and shift it to consumption. I believe that in periods of tight credit we should rely in part on consumer credit control and thus to a correspondingly smaller extent on general credit control.

In summary, it seems to me that growth could be speeded up by gradually reducing, along the growth path of the economy, the tax burden on corporations and particularly the tax on ploughed-back profits; by substituting a moderate sales tax with exemptions for part of the income tax burden, where the exemptions could make a sufficiently simple household budget almost completely tax free; by relying in part on selective credit controls when confronted with an inflationary situation; and last but not least by orienting fiscal expenditures more toward the objective of growth rather than that of pleasing pressure groups. It is obvious that this sort of reform would rest on specific value judgments which others may take or leave. But I think it is possible to claim for such a package that it would promote growth without placing additional burdens on the low-income groups.

I have come to the end of my illustrations. It would be too hazardous to make a guess about the proportion in which per capita growth could be speeded up by measures of this general character. But there is evidence to suggest that recently the leading continental Western European countries have allocated a higher proportion of their output to capital formation than has the United States. There is evidence to suggest also that recently some of the Western European per capita growth rates have been appreciably higher than ours. The investment-to-output ratio is obviously not the only factor on which growth rates depend. But there exists a strong presumption that by stimulating research as well as capital formation and by increasing economic incentives, one can work toward accelerated growth. It seems to me that a comparison of our own recent growth rates with those of various overseas areas suggests that it would be wise to remove some of the growth reducing bias from our public policies.

## IV. The Alternatives

I will finish by adding a word about my guess concerning the future course of events. As for the near future, I do not believe that the cost-push problem will actually be met by 'policies of deconcentration, or even that tax reform of the sort here suggested will soon be enacted. My reluctant guess is that whenever we wake up fully to the fact of having deficient growth rates, we might have to go through a phase of administrative controls instead of turning directly to measures which would strengthen a freer market economy. But sooner or later these trends towards centralization will be reversed. I believe that in retrospect the present period will rather generally be interpreted as one in which we have failed to fight a harmful concentration of market power and have failed to provide sufficient incentives for capital formation. At present we are not giving the "principles of a free market economy" a fair enough chance and we might be pushed toward more centralization, involving more direction of the wage and price mechanism, and more central regulation of the allocational system. If this is what should happen, the question of incentives for private saving and investment will of course be of considerably smaller significance.

But Western nations have had a very good record of keeping ideas alive—even ideas which temporarily seemed outmoded. My paper was not written with the intention to argue that if during one or the other phase of our development we should attempt to solve our problems along different lines than those here considered, then our civilization will have received an irreparable blow. As the European experience shows, one can have a much more socialistic growth policy than that which I have discussed here and subsequently one may witness a renaissance of more individualistic values. Worse things than that have happened in history. But I do believe that, in principle at least, the detour over greater centralization could be avoided without giving up on growth and thus without abandoning the Western position in the world. This is what I have tried to express in this paper.

*EDWARD F. DENISON*

# How to Raise the High-Employment Growth Rate by One Percentage Point

*21* My assignment is to devise a package of proposals that can raise the growth rate over the next twenty years by one percentage point. The package was put together for this session, but my estimate of the contribution each ingredient of the package would make to growth rests upon a study which is about to be published by the Committee for Economic Development.

I was asked to talk about ways of altering the growth of the economy's productive potential, when success in maintaining fairly full utilization of labor and other resources is assumed. We must also find ways to validate the high-employment assumption, but that is outside the present discussion.

Next, I shall be concerned with ways to raise the growth rate of real national income or product as defined and measured by the Department of Commerce. Certain characteristics of these output measures somewhat limit the ways available to raise their growth rate. They preclude raising the growth rate by shifting resources so as to produce things that are more urgently wanted; for ex-

ample, by eliminating distortions in the pattern of output introduced by excise taxes, monopoly or farm programs. Again, the treatment of quality change in the price indexes bars raising the future high-employment growth rate of measured output by developing new or better final products more rapidly.

I omit from my discussion steps that would increase the satisfactions derived from output without changing its amount as measured. However, I shall not consider shifts of resources that would increase measured output while leaving unchanged or reducing a "truer" output measure. Real national income or product may be thought of as an index with certain biases that may be fairly uniform over time so long as steps are not taken deliberately to "rig" the index.

The specific series I shall use to measure economic growth is the index of real national income, which is the same thing as the index of real net national product except that components are weighted by factor cost rather than market price. It is *net* income or product, not GNP, that economic policy properly seeks to maximize. Factor cost valuation is more appropriate and convenient than market price valuation for examination of changes in productivity or inputs.

Reprinted from the *American Economic Review: Papers and Proceedings*, Vol. LII (1962), pp. 67–75, by permission of the author and publishers. Edward Denison is at The Brookings Institution.

However, the conclusions I shall reach would be little changed if references were to net or even gross national product.

Next, the assigned topic concerns means of changing the growth rate over a twenty-year period. This is a reasonable period to consider, but it should be understood that the length of the period greatly affects my results. Because most ways of changing output, and hence affecting the growth rate, are in the one-shot category, it is easier to raise the growth rate by a given amount for twenty years than for a hundred. Suppose, for example, some obstacle to efficient production costs us 1 per cent of the national income. If the obstacle were eliminated, which could be done only once, the level of national income thereafter would be 1 per cent higher than if the obstacle remained. The effect on the growth rate is approximately 1 per cent divided by the number of years over which the growth rate is computed. Thus elimination of the obstacle would raise the growth rate computed over a twenty-year period by one-twentieth of a percentage point, and the growth rate computed over a hundred-year period by one-hundredth of a percentage point. Some measures, on the other hand, would not have their maximum effect in a period as short as twenty years. Provision of additional education to the young and an increase in the saving rate are examples.

I shall use 1960 to 1980 as my twenty-year period, as if it were now 1960, because the calculations I draw on were based on those twenty years. But nothing would be changed materially by substituting 1961 to 1981, or 1962 to 1982.

Next, this paper is not directed to the question of how we can raise the growth rate from what it was in the past. The question posed for this session by Edward Mason is how the growth rate can be raised by one percentage point from "whatever the speaker thinks it will be" if unemployment is low, and in other respects we continue existing policies. I project a 1960-80 growth rate of $3\frac{1}{3}$ per cent in potential national income, starting from a 1960 high-employment level. The amount by which this projected rate exceeds the actual rate in the past is not part of the one percentage point increment my prescription must provide. My task is to indicate how to raise the high-employment growth rate from $3\frac{1}{3}$ per cent to $4\frac{1}{3}$ per cent. Let me also stress that the topic is not whether $3\frac{1}{3}$ per cent is a correct projection given existing policies, but how the rate can be raised one percentage point from whatever it would be if we do nothing special to affect it.

So much for ground rules. Now for some general observations. First, the difference between a $3\frac{1}{3}$ per cent rate and a $4\frac{1}{3}$ per cent rate is big. One implies an increase in per capita income from 1960 to 1980 of 33 per cent, the other of 61 per cent. Thus, a prescription to raise the growth rate of total income by one percentage point must be powerful enough to nearly double the anticipated increase in per capita real income. This conclusion must be modified insofar as the growth rate is to be stimulated by more immigration.

Second, I can hardly stress enough that, as I use the term, economic growth refers only to output. Quite aside from defects in measures of output, aggregate output is anything but a complete measure of economic welfare or economic progress, even less of total welfare or progress. To talk about changing even economic welfare, we would have also to consider, at the very least, real costs of production and the distribution of income and output.

In the present context this no small caveat. It is the heart of the matter. The output we get, aside from involuntary underuse of resources, is determined by individual and collective decisions as to what is or is not worth doing.

I stress that to accelerate growth requires that someone act differently than he would otherwise, that this action usually means higher costs as well as higher output, and that more output is never the only effect of any action we might take. To decide whether steps to accelerate growth are sensible requires comparison of costs, the size of the effect on growth, and side effects.

This leads to the first of two conditions I deem essential for any program to stimulate growth a great deal beyond what it will be if we have no such objective. It is that the public be persuaded that acceleration of growth must be made an overriding national goal. Moreover, it must probably be persuaded of this for reasons other than the increase in individual welfare—probably reasons related to the external situation facing the country. This is necessary because there is a presumption that the more important steps required impose costs that exceed the income benefits and thus reduce welfare. Otherwise they presumably would be taken anyway. Even where the benefits may exceed the costs for the country as a whole, we are usually dealing with some deep-seated condition, often of long standing, that is likely to be changed only for some new and overpowering reason.

The presumption that the costs of a proposed change exceed the benefits may be refuted in specific instances. We need not suppose that we now act rationally on the basis of full information in reaching all of our individual and collective decisions, so we need not assume that every step that would increase growth would reduce individual welfare. In putting together my own package of proposals, I try to stress those where I think the possibility is greatest—I do not mean that it is necessarily great—that present practices derive from ignorance and would be changed by greater knowledge and understanding. This may imply a certain arrogance on my part, but without some such approach this paper could not be written.

The second condition necessary for any large effort to stimulate growth is full ultilization of resources. It will hardly be possible to obtain support for a broad program to increase our productive potential unless we use rather fully the potential that we do have. Indeed, if unemployment is persistently high, we can look forward to actions that will reduce growth, including greater public and private restriction on efficient production, and reduction of hours intended to spread employment rather than to increase leisure.

To add one percentage point to the growth rate I shall suggest a thirteen-part program that seems to me to combine feasibility, in the sense of avoiding things no one knows how to do, with minimization of sacrifice. The expected contribution from each proposal to the growth rate over twenty years will be stated in hundredths of a percentage point. Thus we need means of adding 100 hundredths of a percentage point to the growth rate.

Let me now indicate the general approach I use to assess the effect of each proposal on the growth rate. To raise the growth rate over twenty years by one hundredth of a percentage point requires some action not now in prospect that would make the 1980 national income .2 per cent, or nearly 2 billion dollars, larger than it would be in the absence of that action. The action must serve either to increase the quantity or quality of labor, land, or capital going into the productive system, or else to increase their productivity.

Because of the presence of economies of scale, an increment of slightly less than .2 per cent to total factor input in 1980 would probably suffice to raise the 1980 national income .2 per cent. I assume the addition to output would exceed that in total input by one-eleventh. Hence an increase in total input of slightly over .18 per cent would raise output by .2 per cent. This could, in principle, be accomplished by increasing all kinds of input by .18 per cent or only one kind of input by a larger percentage. From national income data

I estimate that labor comprises 77 per cent of total input, capital 20 per cent, and land 3 per cent. Hence we could raise total input by slightly over .18 per cent in 1980 if we could raise labor input alone by .24 per cent over what it would otherwise be, or capital input alone by .93 per cent, or land input alone by 6.10 per cent. My proposals would not change the ratio of capital to labor input very much, so the problem of diminishing returns is not acute.

I shall first suggest some ways to increase inputs, indicating the contribution expected from each and sketching the basis of the estimate, and then turn to ways of raising productivity.

1. Yearly net immigration currently equals .2 per cent of our population. As recently as 1911-15 it averaged .6 per cent. Immigration could be increased simply by changing the law. I assume the additional immigrants would make a per capita contribution of labor two-thirds as large, after adjustment for quality differences, as does the existing population. On this assumption, doubling the present immigration rate would raise labor input in 1980 by about $2\frac{1}{2}$ per cent, enough to add .10 to the growth rate of national income. Extra immigration probably would not lower the per capita income of the existing population, but it would impose some other costs. It would also benefit our international relations. More immigration seems to me among the most sensible means of stimulating growth.

2. By working three hours a week, or about $8\frac{1}{3}$ per cent, longer than we otherwise would in 1980, we could add .28 to the growth rate.

My projection of a $3\frac{1}{3}$ per cent growth rate assumed that normal annual working hours will drop the equivalent of four hours a week from 1960 to 1980. This is about the rate at which they dropped during the fifties and much less than they dropped during the thirties and forties. Had I assumed a drop of only one hour instead of four, my projected growth rate would have been .28 higher. The calculation that we could add .28 to the growth rate by working three hours a week longer assumes that, in the range within which we will then be operating, more than three-fourths of the impact of shorter hours falls on output rather than being offset in labor efficiency. A decline of only one hour a week in twenty years would allow some leveling down where hours are especially long and some additional holidays, vacations, or coffee breaks, but no change in the standard forty-hour week.

Longer hours are in my list partly because it would be hard to obtain the desired total effect on the growth rate without them. But it is at least possible that we tend to arrive at a level of hours too short to maximize welfare. I say this partly because so little is known about the amount of income that actually is sacrificed for more leisure, and partly because hours have sometimes been shortened in order to spread employment.

Acceptance of this proposal requires employment opportunities so abundant that work spreading disappears as a reason for shortening standard hours, no reduction in legal standards for hours, and probably general acceptance by labor and employers of the need to maintain present hours. Since the AFL-CIO has already established the thirty-five hour week as an objective, this means a change in the present policy of labor.

3. I call upon additional education to raise the quality of labor enough to add .07 to the growth rate. I estimate that this requires addition of one year to the average amount of schooling that would otherwise be received by everyone leaving school between now and 1980. This estimate is derived from existing income differentials among groups with different amounts of education, and the assumption that three-fifths of these differentials result from more education rather than reflect associated variables such as natural ability. It allows for the loss of work by those who will be in school in 1980 rather than working, on the assumption that if they were working their labor would be of half the average quality. Provision of the extra schooling would absorb .3 or .4 per cent of the national income.

My national income projection already assumes a considerable increase from the present age at which young people leave school. This trend can be confidently anticipated. To add still another year, without adversely affecting the quality of education, would place great strain on educational resources and require a major effort to secure teachers and facilities. Noneconomic benefits of extra schooling seem to me large, and this is another case where we might do more than we will be doing if the public had complete information on which to base decisions.

4. I estimate that we could add .03 to the twenty-year rate if we could cut in half structural unemployment and underemployment that results from long-term declines in labor requirements in individual areas and industries, including agriculture.

To contribute to growth in any real sense this must be done by speeding re-employment in expanding industries and areas, not by curtailing the displacement of workers that results from demand shifts or technological progress. If we have a bouyant economy in which unfilled jobs at least match the number unemployed, there

ought to be ways to cut these types of structural unemployment in half. Swedish experience can be drawn upon in devising means.

5. I look to increased capital input for a contribution of .20 to the growth rate. This requires capital input in 1980 to be 19 per cent larger than it would be otherwise. Whereas my projection assumes a 64 per cent increase in capital input from 1960 to 1980, capital input must nearly double in the same period to provide this additional contribution to growth.

I look for this to be made possible by the other measures proposed to raise growth. I assume here that the crucial difficulty in accelerating growth by increasing the rate of capital formation concerns the possibility of providing attractive investment opportunities rather than of changing saving propensities. Hopefully, the other means of accelerating growth that I am suggesting would bring about the required broadening of investment opportunities. The capital-output ratio will be the same in 1980 if real national income increases $4\frac{1}{4}$ per cent a year and capital input doubles or if national income increases $3\frac{1}{3}$ per cent a year and capital input increases 64 per cent.

To raise capital formation this much requires a higher fraction of national income to be saved during the next twenty years, even though income would itself be larger with a higher growth rate. Hence it would require the sacrifice of consumption that could otherwise be made. If net private savings proves inadequate for so high a rate of net investment, as it may, additional saving could be provided by a surplus in the federal budget.

These five ways of increasing labor and capital input would provide 68 of the required 100 hundredths of a point in the growth rate. For the remaining 32 hundredths, I turn to ways of increasing output per unit of input.

6. From estimates by Gary S. Becker, it can be inferred that employment discrimination against Negroes, taking their qualifications as given, costs us .8 per cent of the national income. If discrimination could be abolished within twenty years by a concerted natural effort, this would add .04 to the growth rate. To the extent that progress will be made anyway the economic costs of discrimination twenty years hence will be less than now, and the opportunity for further growth stimulation is overstated.

7. For nearly two centuries most economists have held that restrictions on international trade reduce output and living standards while most the public has believed the exact opposite to be true. The economists are right, but I am not sure how they can become more persuasive in the

future than in the past. The cost to us of misallocation of resources resulting from barriers to international trade is not easy to estimate, but I have put it at about $1\frac{1}{2}$ per cent of the national income. My projection assumes this percentage will not change. A serious program to stimulate growth would sweep away all barriers to imports and use our willingness to do so as leverage to get foreign nations to eliminate barriers to our exports. If we could eliminate all barriers far enough in advance of our twenty-year deadline to allow basic readjustments in production and trading patterns to be made throughout the world, this would add .07 to the growth rate.

8. Resale price maintenance laws result in the use of more resources in trade than are required to perform the function. Their cost is very hard to estimate, but I believe it to be large. If, as I have guessed, fair trade costs us 1 per cent of the national income, repeal of fair-trade laws could add .05 to the growth rate.

9. Formal obstacles imposed by labor unions in some industries against the most efficient use of resources costs us output, although again it is very difficult to say how much. My guess is that the cost here might also be 1 per cent of the national income. It seems to me possible that a determined program to adopt better ways of meeting labor's needs might cut this cost in half. This would add .02 to the growth rate.

10. The effectiveness of labor incentives is important to productivity. Close correspondence between each employee's individual contribution to production and his individual reward, and employee awareness of the correspondence, are crucial. Shifts from time rates to piecework have sometimes been accompanied by large increases in productivity. Greater use of incentive pay systems where they are or can be made feasible is the obvious way to obtain substantial improvement. Better evaluation of individual performance for use in setting pay differentials among salaried employees and others paid by time, and in promotion, and more honest letters of recommendation, would be helpful. Certain changes in the tax laws might also help. It strikes me as possible that an intensive effort to improve incentives along these lines could contribute .05 to the growth rate. This could be done, for example, if the efficiency of one-tenth of the work force could be raised 11 per cent.

11. We could add to output by permitting consolidation in the regulated industries where this would mean greater efficiency. If claims that as many as 200,000 employees could be eliminated by railroad consolidation are correct and some minor economies are possible in other regulated industries, consolidation could add about .02 to the growth rate.

12. We could increase output by shortening the lag of average business practice behind the best known. My projection assumes that knowledge will be advancing fast enough to contribute .8 percentage points to the growth rate of real product, as measured, in the next twenty years. This exceeds my estimate of its rate of advance in the past. If we could shorten the lag of average practice behind the best known by nine months, which I consider a large reduction for the whole economy, output in 1980 would therefore be .6 per cent larger than otherwise and the twenty-year growth rate .03 higher. My projection of national product already assumes a reduction of nine months in the lag; thus I am calling for an additional nine-months reduction.

Sweeping away all barriers to international trade, aside from the benefits previously taken into account, would put pressure for modernization upon protected industries that are not now highly competitive, and some of the other steps I have suggested would be slightly helpful in this respect. For the rest, we should have to look to better means of disseminating information and alertness in adopting it. I may note in passing that there is nothing to be added on this account to the contribution of additional investment to growth that I have already computed.

13. For the final .04 required to reach my goal of a full point in the growth rate I look to the advance of knowledge itself. This requires that the state of knowledge in 1980 be where it would otherwise be in 1981. I would be uncomfortable in looking for a large contribution because we know too little about how to alter the rate at which knowledge relevant to production advances to feel sure we know how to get much more out of this source of growth. There is little evidence that the big postwar increase in research and development expenditures has had much effect on the rate of increase in measured productivity. Moreover, present prospects are that we shall absorb into research and development all the qualified personnel that will be available and be expanding these human resources as fast as is likely to be fruitful. But something can probably be done about the distribution of effect. There is extreme concentration of research expenditures in a few product lines and industries. In 1956, industries accounting for only 31 per cent of the national income made 96 per cent of research and development expenditures. Moreover, most of the effort, by far, is devoted to development of new

and better products rather than cost reduction. It seems likely that greater dispersion of research effort might get us ahead faster, and it is to steps to bring this about that I would look for the additional contribution to growth.

I suspect there are important possibilities of raising productivity in research. But in the absence of agreement even on whether we should move toward more or less organization and planning of research, I cannot very well recommend what should be done that would not otherwise be done.

This completes my prescription for raising the growth rate by one percentage point. The contributions to be obtained from the individual elements obviously are crude estimates, but with any luck over-estimates will be offset by underestimates and the package should achieve the assigned target.

Many alternative packages of proposals could be put together to arrive at the same effect on the growth rate. The study from which this list is drawn tries to provide a rather complete menu of the choices available to stimulate growth. From that list anyone can make his own combination. This particular package is fairly concrete and practical in the sense that the principal steps required do not exceed our knowledge. I have tried to put together as attractive a package as I could. In my view it would not impose intolerable burdens. But this does not mean I am advocating it or think the country would necessarily be better off for adopting it. This depends mainly on a judgment as to how important it is to raise the rate at which output grows, and why.

# Inflation

*C*ONFLICTING EXPLANATIONS OF various increases in the general
level of commodity prices have been put forward by different economists.
Some of these are discussed in this section. The first selection is an extract
from Charles Schultze's 1959 classic, "Recent Inflation in the United States."
In this article Schultze registers his disagreement with other explanations of
the United States 1955–57 inflation and suggests that a major factor causing
the inflation was a shift in demand from one type of commodity to another.
The second article, by Fritz Machlup, is of a more general nature; it considers
the cost-push and demand-pull theories of inflation and the tests which
economists have used in an effort to determine which of these situations
occurred during a particular period of time. The final selection is Depodwin
and Selden's examination of business pricing practices as a cause of inflation.

*Part*

*6*

CHARLES L. SCHULTZE

# Recent Inflation in the United States

*22*

## The Current Controversy: Demand-Pull versus Cost-Push

The purpose of this study is to examine the nature of the gradual inflation to which the American economy has been subject in recent years. There is relatively little controversy over the basic features of a wartime or reconversion inflation; rising prices are attributed to an increase in the effective demand for goods and services over and above the capacity of the economy to furnish them. There is wide disagreement, however, about the nature of and remedies for the more gradual rise in prices which has occurred during the postwar period. Most of the discussion has centered on the merits of the "cost-push" versus the "demand-pull" theories of inflation. Proponents of the cost-push thesis attribute the major blame for the price increases, particularly those of the 1955–57 period, to autonomous upward movements in either wage rates or administered prices or both. The demand-pull theorists on the other hand, assert that price

increases currently, as always, are the reflection of aggregate excess demand for goods and services, including the services of the factors of production.

We have been and shall be using the concept of excess demand throughout this study in a dynamic sense. In an economy characterized by steadily improving technology and substantial net investment, the supply of goods and services forthcoming at full employment is continually growing. Hence an absolutely stable demand could only be consistent with full employment if prices declined. Excess aggregate demand, in a dynamic context, only exists, therefore, when monetary demands for goods and services are rising *faster* than the constant dollar value of supplies of goods and services at full employment. The degree of excess demand will, of course, be influenced by the composition of the aggregate: an increased output in some industries can more easily be supplied than in others. Moreover, as chapter 4 points out, we can have a situation in which output is below its potential even though the labor force is fully employed. If, for example, there is large-scale hiring of salaried employees, those employees may be retained even when

Reprinted from "Recent Inflation in The United States" (Study Paper No. 1; Joint Economic Committee, *Study of Employment, Growth, and Price Levels,* 1959), pp. 4–16, by permission of the author. Charles Schultze is Director, Bureau of the Budget.

output does not rise as expected—we have under-employment. But these refinements aside, the essential point to remember is that the term "excess aggregate demand" is used throughout in the context of a growing full employment supply.

In analyzing the process by which price increases are generated there are two major sets of factors to be considered:

1. The impact of rising prices and wages on aggregate demand for goods and services.
2. The impact of changes in the demand for goods and for factors of production on prices and wage rates. Put more simply, how does the growth of excess capacity and unemployment affect prices and wages?

Prices and wages have a dual nature when considered in the aggregate: they are costs to buyers and incomes to sellers. Thus an increase in the general level of prices does not automatically mean a reduction in the quantity of goods and services demanded as it normally would in the case of a single commodity. The increased cost of purchasing any article or any factor of production is matched by the higher incomes received by the seller. So long as the increase in prices is accompanied by an equal increase in money expenditures, *real* purchases of goods and services will not be affected and employment will not be reduced. There are, however, indirect influences on the level of real demand exerted by a rising price level. If the tax system is progressive, the higher money incomes lead to a higher proportion of income taken in taxes. With a constant money supply, higher prices normally lead to a tighter money market, which in turn has some depressing influence on investment demand. If these and other indirect effects are important, their depressing influence on demand must continually be offset by demand increases from other sources, if the rising price level is not to result in rapidly growing unemployment. If, on the other hand, these indirect effects are relatively unimportant, then a rising price level will not bring about excess capacity and unemployment, or at least will do so only very slowly.

If prices and wages are *sensitive* to changes in demand, then no inflation can continue unless aggregate excess demand is constantly being renewed. The appearance of unemployment and excess capacity would quickly halt any price rise. Consequently the strength of the indirect influences discussed above determines how large an inflation will result from a given initial excess demand. There can be no inflation without the excess demand, however. Hence monetary and fiscal policy, appropriately handled, can achieve

full employment and price stability; all that needs to be done is to prevent the excess demand, without which wages and prices would cease to rise. If, on the other hand wages and prices are relatively *insensitive* to changes in demand, then the indirect influences of the price level on aggregate demand will determine not how large the price rise will be but how much unemployment it will generate. For if prices and wages do not respond to growing excess capacity and unemployment, then the limitation of aggregate demand will not halt the inflation—it will only lead to unemployment.

The responsiveness of prices and wages to changes in demand is thus the central issue. Let us call prices and wages which are sensitive to changes in demand "flexible" and those which do not respond to demand, "cost-determined." The latter category includes both those cases in which prices and wages adjust solely to changes in costs[1] and those in which there occur autonomous increases in prices and wages. We can distinguish four types of situations, depending on the nature of price and wage behavior and the impact of rising prices and wages on demand.

I. Rising prices and wages tend to reduce demand and employment:
    1. Prices and wages *flexible*.
    2. Prices and wages *cost-determined*.
II. Rising prices and wages do not tend to reduce demand and employment:
    1. Prices and wages *flexible*.
    2. Prices and wages *cost-determined*.

So long as prices and wages are cost-determined, then a cost-push inflation is possible, regardless of whether case I or case II holds. If the direct effects of a cost-push inflation are relatively weak, so that real aggregate demand is not reduced (case II), then the inflation is self-validating—a cost-push inflation will not, of itself, lead to unemployment. If the indirect effects of rising prices and wages on aggregate demand are significant (case I), then unemployment and excess capacity will result. But since prices and wages are not flexible, the inflation will continue. In this situation, the maintenance of full employment requires a positive Government monetary and fiscal policy to provide the validating demand. In either situation the failure of aggregate demand to keep pace with a growing full employment output would not eliminate the inflation, so long as price and wage decision making does not respond to demand conditions.

[1] Changes in consumer prices are equivalent to changes in costs for the purpose of wage determination.

If, on the other hand, prices and wages vary in response to changes in demand as well as costs, then the failure of demand to match full employment supply will quickly bring an inflation to a halt. The effect of rising prices and wages on aggregate demand determines how much of an inflation will result from a given initial excess demand. If a general price and wage rise leads to a large reduction in demand, then the economic system has a built-in self-correction factor. The Government need only exercise self-restraint; so long as excessive deficits and money supply increases are avoided, inflation is not a serious problem. If, on the other hand, the self-corrective influence of a rising price level is weak, then positive government counterinflationary policy may be a recurrent necessity. In either event, the flexibility of prices and wages implies that full employment can be maintained without price inflation. If prices and wages start to rise, a restriction of aggregate demand will lead to a cessation of price and wage gains rather than a growth in unemployment.

The controversy between the demand-pull and cost-push theorists is in reality, therefore, a debate about the consistency of full employment and price stability.

> Given an appropriate monetary-fiscal policy, the answer to the question whether we can continue to enjoy a large, growing, and reasonably stable volume of production and employment * * * lies in the relations of prices, costs, and profits.[2]

Do labor unions and monopolistic firms largely disregard the state of the market in setting prices and wages? Are prices marked up as costs rise with little regard for demand conditions? Does a rise in the cost of living lead to an equivalent wage increase even in periods of unemployment? Few would take an extreme position on these questions. There is rather a spectrum of opinion. Toward the one end of the spectrum are those who feel that prices and wages do respond rather quickly to changes in demand. The possibility that strongly organized groups can push up their cost prices in the absence of ex ante excess aggregate demand is not "an empirically important possibility,"[3] according to these demand-pull theorists. Further, according to this theoretical approach, the existence of inflation implies that the excess demand must be an *aggregate* excess.

If prices and wages are responsive to demand conditions, excess demands in particular areas of the economy, balanced by deficient demands in other sectors, will merely lead to a realinement of relative prices. Only if demands in the aggregate are too high will the general level of prices rise.

Toward the other end of the spectrum are those who feel that prices and wages are, within a substantial range, set independently of demand conditions. No one would deny that there is some level of unemployment and excess capacity which would halt a price-wage spiral. But the cost-push theorists feel that the degree of unemployment and excess capacity required to break through the cost-determined nature of wages and prices is quite large. The power of big business and big labor to determine prices and wages is so great, that under conditions of relatively full employment, even without excess demand, a secular rise in the price level is unavoidable.

The validity of either approach in this controversy cannot be discovered from the historical relationship of a few large aggregates. The fact that in recent years wages have risen faster than productivity, for example, is often cited as evidence that we have been experiencing a cost-push inflation. But this relationship tells us absolutely nothing about the nature of inflation. In the purest sort of demand-pull inflation, wages would also rise more rapidly than productivity. By the same sort of "reasoning" we could cite the fact than money expenditures rose more rapidly than output as a proof of demand-pull inflation. An equally strong condemnation applies to demonstrations which point to the rise in the money supply or its velocity as proof of the demand-pull nature of inflation.

Even the timing of wage and price increases cannot be offered, by itself, as evidence of the nature of the inflationary process. Suppose, for example, that prices are marked up mainly in response to rising wages. Then an excess demand inflation will first lead to a rise in wage rates through its impact on the labor market, and only thereafter in a price rise. The historical data would indicate that the increase in wages preceded the rise in prices, yet the inflation would be one which was initiated by excess demands.

A cost-push inflation need not arise solely from an *autonomous* upward push of administered wages or prices. If prices are set by applying a constant margin to costs, and if wages are determined by movements in the level of consumer prices, then an initial general price rise, stemming from any source, can perpetuate itself, as wages

[2] Edward Mason, "Essays in Honor of John H. Williams," p. 189.
[3] Milton Friedman, in "The Impact of the Union," edited by D. M. Wright, p. 244.

and prices successively adjust upward to each other. The greater the insensitivity of the price and wage "markups" over cost to unemployment or excess capacity, the greater the inflationary possibilities. The shorter the lag between the mutual adjustment of prices to wages and wages to prices, the faster the inflation will proceed.

The response of prices and wages to changes in demand cannot, in reality, be forced into the simple categories of "flexible" and "cost-determined." The most important fact about their behavior, for the purpose of analyzing creeping inflation, is its asymmetry. Prices and wages tend to be more flexible upward in response to increases in demand than they are in a downward direction in response to decreases in demand. As a consequence, the composition of demand as well as its aggregate magnitude, takes on a central role in the generation of inflation. The further development of this point is one of the major features of the present study.

## The Nature of the Recent Inflation

An examination of recent economic history suggests that creeping inflation is not a phenomenon which can be dealt with in aggregate terms. In particular the price increases from 1955 to 1957 stemmed, in the main, neither from autonomous upward "pushes" of administered prices or wages nor from the existence of an aggregate excess demand. Neither of these explanations can satisfactorily account for a number of apparent paradoxes during this period: The dissipation of a relatively modest 5 per cent per annum rise in money expenditures in a $3\frac{1}{2}$ per cent price rise and only $1\frac{1}{2}$ per cent output gain; the apparent correlation of price increases with demand increases industry by industry, but with an upward bias, so that the overall level of prices rose while the overall level of demand was not excessive; the fact that prices rose more rapidly than unit wage costs, while at the same time net profit margins were shrinking; and finally the high level of investment activity followed by disappointing gains in productivity and consequent increases in unit costs.

The theoretical and empirical analysis of the economic processes which lead to creeping inflation is not easily summarized. It is not a relatively simple matter which can be condensed into a short formula, like the popular "too much money chasing too few goods." Nor is it a "devil" theory in which abound the villains of most cost-push

theories—the union boss and the greedy monopolist. We shall attempt in the remainder of this chapter however, to sketch the characteristics of economic behavior which lead to creeping inflation and indicate briefly the application of the analysis to the 1955–57 period.

### The Importance of the Composition of Demands

Prices and wages in the modern American economy are generally flexible upward in response to excess demand, but they tend to be rigid downward. There is, as we noted earlier, an asymmetry in their behavior. Even if demands in the aggregate are not excessive, a situation of excess demand in some sectors of the economy balanced by deficient demand in other sectors will still lead to a rise in the general level of prices. The rise in prices in markets characterized by excess demand will not be balanced by falling prices in other markets.

Excess demand in particular industries transmits its impact to the rest of the economy through its influence on the prices of materials and the wages of labor. Crude materials prices are normally quite sensitive to changes in demand, and are unlikely to rise significantly unless demands for them in the aggregate are excessive. Prices of intermediate materials supplies and components, on the other hand, are more likely to be rigid downward, but flexible upward in response to an increase in demand or costs. Prices of those materials chiefly consumed by industries with excess demand rise, since excess demand for the final goods usually implies excess demand for specialized materials. Materials used mainly in industries with deficient demand will not fall in price, unless the demand deficiency is quite large. Thus excess demand in particular sectors of the economy will result in a general rise in the prices of intermediate materials, supplies, and components; industries which are not experiencing excess demands will find themselves confronted with rising materials costs.

Wages will also be bid up in excess demand industries. Wages in other industries will tend to follow. Even though demand for labor is not excessive, firms cannot allow the wage differential between themselves and other firms to get too large; this is not because they fear the wholesale desertion of their work force, but because they do not wish to experience the inefficiencies and lowered productivity which result from dissatisfaction over widening differentials. Rising wage rates, originating in the excess demand sectors thus spread throughout the economy. Because productivity gains in the short run are greatest where demand and output are increasing, firms in those sectors where demand is rising slower than capacity will often be faced with even larger increases in unit wage costs than firms in the areas of excess demand. In some cases the size of wage increases will be determined by long-term contracts concluded in earlier periods. Except as such increases are modified by changes in the cost of living (through escalator clauses) they will have little relationship to the current state of the market.

The spread of wage increases from excess demand sectors to other parts of the economy accentuates the rise in the price of semifabricated materials and components. Thus the influence of rising costs and the resistance of prices to declining demands will be larger at the later stages of the production process, other things being equal. The opportunities for rigidities to build up and for rising costs, particularly labor costs, to affect prices are multiplied as products approach the finished state.

Producers of finished goods will be confronted with a general rise in the level of costs, even when the demand for their products and their own demands for materials and labor are not excessive. The more cost determined are the pricing policies of the industries involved, the greater will be the price rise. In competitive sectors of the economy the rising costs will be at least partly absorbed. But in very many industries they will be more fully passed on in higher prices. Markups will of course be shaded when excess capacity begins to rise. As inflationary pressures spread out from excess demand sectors, their force will be somewhat damped in the absence of excess aggregate demand. Similarly the tendency of wages to follow the pattern set in the rapidly expanding industries will be modified as unemployment rises. But so long as markups and wages are more sensitive in an upward than in a downward direction, a rise in the general level of prices can be initiated by excess demand in particular industries.

This kind of inflationary process cannot be neatly labelled. It arises initially out of excess demand in particular industries. But it results in a general price rise only because of the downward rigidities and cost oriented nature of prices and wages. It is not characterized by an autonomous upward push of costs nor by an *aggregate* excess demand. Indeed its basic nature is that it cannot be understood in terms of aggregates alone. Such inflation is the necessary result of sharp changes in the composition of demand, given the structure of prices and wages in our economy.

The downward rigidities and cost-oriented nature of prices and wages act like a ratchet on the price level. Most maladjustments of prices relative to each other and of prices relative to wages tend to be corrected by upward movements in the out-of-line prices or wages rather than by a mutual adjustment to a common center. The short-run inflationary mechanism which we have been describing thus imparts a longrun secular bias to the price level. A floor is placed under each higher level, from which later increases take off. During earlier periods in our history, the recurrence of substantial and lengthy depressions broke through these rigidities and forced large declines in the levels of prices and wages. The widespread bankruptcies and reorganizations of depression periods also led to massive writedowns in the value of fixed assets. This removed an additional feature of the ratchet mechanism. Moreover, a much larger proportion of total value produced originated in the demand sensitive raw materials industries—particularly agriculture. Even if rigidities in the industrial sector were as great then as now, they played a smaller role in the overall economy.

### Overhead Costs

A second major factor influencing the determination of prices and the movement in the general price level in recent years has been the rapid growth in the proportion of overhead or fixed costs in total costs. This development played a particularly important role in the 1955–57 period.

Between 1947 and 1955 a very large part of the rise in total costs was accounted for by the rise in relatively fixed costs. Of the total increase in employment during those years, 65 per cent represented employment of professional managerial, clerical, sales, and similar personnel. Only 20 per cent of the increase was accounted for by operatives, laborers, and craftsmen. In manufacturing, nonproduction worker employment rose 40 per cent and production worker employment only 2 per cent. During this same period fixed capital costs per unit increased very rapidly. Prices of capital goods rose relative to other prices, and the proportion of short-lived equipment to long-lived plant rose sharply. Depreciation charges thus expanded very substantially. Depreciation and salary costs per unit, taken together accounted for more than 40 per cent of the increase in total unit costs in manufacturing between 1947 and 1955. Adding profits per unit we account for two-thirds of the cost increase.

The period between 1955 and 1957 was characterized by a very sharp rise in investment outlays

## Table 1. Changes in Manufacturing Costs and Prices

*(in per cent points)*

|  | 1947-55 | 1955-57 |
|---|---|---|
| "Price" of value added in manufacturing | 29.8 | 9.6 |
| Unit wage cost | 9.0 | 3.9 |
| Unit salary cost | 7.7 | 5.6 |
| Depreciation per unit | 4.2 | 1.0 |
| Profits per unit | 7.2 | −2.2 |
| Indirect taxes per unit | 1.6 | 1.3 |

*Source:* App. A.

accompanied by a quite modest growth in aggregate demand and output. Not only was capacity expanded rapidly but there was a continuation, indeed an acceleration, of the postwar growth in the number of overhead employees. Unlike earlier postwar booms however, the expansion in these relative fixed inputs was not matched by a corresponding rise in output (table 2). Fixed

## Table 2. Indexes of Capacity, Employment, and Output in Manufacturing Industries

*(1947 = 100)*

|  | 1955 | 1957 |
|---|---|---|
| Capacity: |  |  |
| A[a] | 156 | 175 |
| B[b] | 146 | 163 |
| Nonproduction worker employment | 140 | 155 |
| Production worker man-hours | 103 | 100 |
| Output | 140 | 145 |

[a]A—McGraw-Hill Department of Economics estimates.
[b]B—Fortune magazine estimates.

costs per unit of output therefore rose sharply, not because output was falling but because it did not rise rapidly enough. Prices were raised almost, but not quite enough to cover these higher costs. Of the total rise in unit costs (including profit margins) some 55 per cent was accounted for by higher salary costs per unit as compared to 40 per cent by higher wage costs. Book depreciation charges are unreliable for most purposes; nevertheless, in combination with other costs, they put pressure on profit margins and to some extent on prices.

The fact that a large part of the increased employment during the period was in the nature of overhead employment helps explain why the general price rise, during a period in which

monetary demands were not excessive, did not lead to significant unemployment. By the same token the lack of rise in output relative to fixed inputs accounts for the disappointing gain in productivity. The rise in prices was accompanied by a relatively moderate increase in money expenditures. Real expenditures and output rose by substantially less than the "normal" postwar rise to be expected from growth in the labor force and productivity gain. Yet instead of a rise in unemployment, there occurred a shortfall of productivity below its potential. Output per production worker man-hour continued to increase fairly sharply throughout the period—indeed production worker employment declined. But the failure of output to match the rise in overhead labor input substantially moderated the overall gain in productivity. In general, the more important fixed costs become, the more sensitive productivity will be to changes in output.

The failure of output to rise toward the levels implicit in the expansion of fixed inputs was partly due to the fact that declining demand in particular sectors of the economy—housing and automobiles—largely offset the rising demands for investment goods. But in addition the attempt to recapture in prices a substantial expansion in fixed costs at existing levels of output tended to raise the level of prices relative to any given money income; the gross saving rate at any given level of output was increased. This in itself damped the rise in output, so that the process tended to be self-defeating. Had output risen along with capacity, overhead costs would have been spread over a larger volume of output. But, by restricting the growth in real demand, the very pricing policies which attempted to recover fixed costs at low levels of output, led to a rise in fixed costs per unit. To some extent a kind of "vicious circle" occurred. The failure of aggregate output to increase raised fixed costs per unit. Insofar as prices were marked up relative to wage and salary rates in order to recover these higher unit costs, the forces impeding the growth in output were strengthened. This kept fixed unit costs high, and so on around the circle again.

The major part of the general rise in prices during recent years may thus be attributed to two sets of factors:

1. The downward rigidity and cost oriented nature of prices and wages in most of industry. During a period in which dynamically stable *aggregate* demand veils a fairly violent shift in the composition of demands, such market characteristics will result in a general rise in the level of prices. This rise cannot be said to result either from excess *aggregate* demand or from autonomous upward adjustments of administered

prices and union wages. Rather it stems from excess demand in particular markets, and is propagated throughout the rest of the economy by a cost mechanism.

2. The attempt to recapture in prices at least some of the increase in fixed unit costs which occurred when a vigorous investment boom and a rapid substitution of fixed for variable labor input impinged on a situation of sluggish growth in output. Further, the fact that most of the employment rise was in overhead labor helps explain why the subnormal growth in output did not involve a rise in unemployment. It did however lead to the growth of excess capacity.

None of the foregoing is designed to indicate that all inflations are mainly the result of these processes. Excess aggregate demand has been the basic cause of all of our *major* inflations, including the postwar reconversion inflation. And for a short while in late 1955 there seemed to be some excess aggregate demand. But the major thesis of this study is that the creeping inflation of 1955–57 is different in kind from such classical inflations, and that mild inflation may be expected in a dynamic economy whenever there occur rapid shifts in the mix of final demands. It is, in effect, a feature of the dynamics of resource adjustment where prices and wages tend to be rigid downward. Moreover, it gives a secular upward bias to the price level so long as the major depressions which "broke" the ratchet in the past are avoided in the future.

Similarly there is no attempt here to prove that *autonomous* upward pressures of wage rates have had no impact on the price structure. Such pressures may have played a role in recent inflation. But the role was not a major one. The mere showing that wage rate increases exceeded productivity gains proves anything at all with respect to the magnitude of this role. (It is interesting to note, however, that the substitution of overhead for direct labor implies that wage rates cannot rise as fast as the statistical number called output per production worker if total unit costs are to be stable.)

## A Detailed Analysis of the 1955–57 Period

. . . In this summary it is impossible to do more than list some of the more important characteristics of the general rise in prices which occurred during those years.

### Demands and Prices

1. As the economy recovered from the 1954 recession it reached a situation of aggregate excess demand in late 1955. Demands in all sectors of the economy were high and rising. The three major volatile sectors—capital goods, automobiles, and housing—were expanding particularly sharply. Production rose even more rapidly than sales, as inventory accumulation speeded up. Raw materials prices, which are especially sensitive to the state of existing and expected demand, rose steeply during the last half of the year. This aggregate excess lasted only briefly however. After the end of the year purchases of automobiles and houses fell rapidly, and remained at reduced levels in 1956 and 1957. Business demand for capital goods, on the other hand, continued to boom throughout the period.

2. On balance aggregate money outlays, after mid-1955, rose at a rate of about 5 per cent per year. Prices rose at a $3\frac{1}{2}$ per cent annual rate and output by only $1\frac{1}{2}$ per cent. The normal postwar rate of growth in output during prosperity periods has been about 4 per cent per year.

3. The slow rate of growth in output and productivity cannot be explained by the "indigestion" hypothesis—(i.e., the very size of the investment boom itself caused such dislocations that normal productivity gains were temporarily impossible). Output per man-hour of production workers *did* rise significantly; producers *were* able to substitute overhead for fixed labor; most importantly there was a strong interindustry correlation between output and output per man-hour. Those industries whose output rose also achieved substantial productivity gains.

4. Thus the difference between the rise in aggregate money expenditures and output did not represent aggregate excess demand. The output rise was clearly less than the economy's potential. The growth of widespread excess capacity is a good commonsense indicator of this.

5. The magnitude of price rises among different sectors of the economy and among different industries was associated with the magnitude of the rise in demand in each sector or industry. On the average, however, prices rose, even though demand, in the aggregate, was not excessive. There was, in other words, a substantial upward bias in the relationship of price changes to demand changes.

6. The magnitude of price rises among industrial commodities was related to two major factors: In general, commodities which experienced the largest price rises were those which had the largest increases in demand. With some important exceptions, most commodities with large price rises were those associated with the boom in capital goods. The frequency of price declines

and the magnitude of average price increases among different groups of commodities differed also according to the stage of fabrication. Very few finished commodities were reduced in price; price increases were, on the average, somewhat smaller and the evidence of price flexibility slightly greater for semi-manufactured materials; the smallest average price rise, after late 1955, and the most flexibility occurred among crude materials.

7. Steel and automobiles were the major exceptions to the pattern described in the preceding paragraph. Relative to the change in demand and output price increases were much larger than those associated with similar changes in demand and output in other industries.

### Wages

1. Wage rate increases were fairly uniform among different industries. Wages in industries with stable or declining output rose by the same amount as they did in rapidly expanding industries. A United Nations study has found this uniformity of behavior to exist among industrial countries generally.

2. Productivity gains were closely associated with the degree of rise in output. Industries with rising output tended to have larger productivity gains than other industries, and vice versa.

3. As a consequence of these characteristics of wage and productivity behavior, wage costs per unit of output rose less in expanding than in contracting industries.

4. Price increases in the capital goods and associated industries accounted for two-thirds of the rise in the industrial wholesale price index between 1955 and 1957. Their prices rose 15 per cent compared with an average increase of 4 per cent for all other industries. Yet wage rate increases in the two groups were almost identical. Because of the relationship between productivity and output mentioned above, unit wage costs in the industries with large price increases averaged less than in other industries. Prices in industries which accounted for the bulk of the overall inflation also rose substantially more than wage costs. In other industries unit wage costs rose proportionately (but not absolutely) more than prices.

### Overhead Costs

1. All of the employment rise during the period was in overhead type employment. In

fact the employment of direct labor fell substantially.

2. More than 50 per cent of the rise in total units costs in manufacturing was accounted for by rising unit salary costs, and an additional 20 per cent by rising depreciation. Net profit margins declined from the high levels reached in late 1955.

3. The rise in salary costs per unit was not only due to an increase in salary rates—which rose by about the same amount as wage rates—but also by the rising ratio of salaried employment to output. The increase in this ratio stemmed chiefly from the failure of output to rise along with capacity. Had it done so, evidence from other postwar years indicates that the salaried employment-output ratio would not have increased.

4. Since productivity of both direct and overhead labor is output sensitive, it is clear that, within moderate limits, a further rise in output could have resulted in lower unit costs. The data suggest an elasticity of minus one-half; i.e., a 1 per cent further rise in output in industries operating below capacity could have yielded a one-half-per cent decline in total unit costs.[4]

### Consumer Prices

1. In the Consumer Price Index, food, nonfood commodities, and services each account for approximately one-third of the total weight. Even among nonfood commodities manufacturers' prices make up not much more than half of the total price, the rest being transportation, wholesaling, and retailing costs. The service component of the CPI is made up of a long list of heterogeneous items, including such things as auto, real estate, and medical insurance, public utility rates, haircuts, postage, and interest rates. Thus it would seem that the direct impact of changes in industrial prices and wages on the Consumer Price Index is relatively limited. Yet an increase in the prices of manufactured products diffuses itself throughout the economy by many indirect routes. Steel prices rise, school construction costs go up, and property tax rates are adjusted upwards; an initial rise in the CPI on account of an increase in industrial prices leads, with some time lag, to rising wages in the service industries and e.g., auto-repair charges rise; and the examples could be multiplied ad infinitum.

[4] This assumes that the additional demand for production labor would not have led to even more rapid wage increases. Considering the reductions in production worker employment during the period, this is a most reasonable assumption.

2. About one-third of the rise in the Consumer Price Index was contributed by increasing food prices. In turn, half of the rise in food prices was attributable to rising farm prices for livestock and half to increased marketing costs. The livestock rise chiefly reflected changing supply conditions. But an examination of the details of the increase in marketing costs shows that the same factors were operative as in the industrial sector generally.

3. The heterogeneity and institutional character of service prices make any simple characterization suspect. The rise in consumer prices generated in other sectors of the economy, and the general rise in wage rates, however, did lead after some time lag to a significant speedup in the rate of increase in service prices after mid-1956. And the rise in service prices in turn had repercussions on the increase in wages and prices in the industrial sector of the economy.

## Some Implications

Although it may not be obvious at first, this analysis is fairly optimistic with respect to its implications for the magnitude of the potential secular upward drift in the price level. In particular the size of the price increases between 1955 and 1957 are not a good indicator of the kind of problem which may be confronting us (assuming, of course, we do not allow classical excess aggregate demand inflation to get started).

The magnitude of the shifts in demands between mid-1955 and mid-1957 were unusually great, even for a dynamic economy. We should not be continually subject, for example, to a 2-year increase in expenditures for fixed business investment of some 25 per cent (and a much larger rise in order backlogs) accompanied by 20 per cent decline in residential construction and automobile sales.

The upward price pressure arising out of attempts to recapture fixed costs at reduced "standard volume" is not a continuing phenomena. It is unlikely, indeed impossible, for the average operating rate at which entrepreneurs attempt to recapture fixed costs to fall indefinitely. Indeed the very size of the current ex ante profit margin, at full utilization of capacity, which resulted from this reduction in standard volume should become a moderating factor, offsetting price pressures from other sources as output rises toward full utilization of capacity.

This study does not attempt to evaluate the policy aspects of creeping inflation. It does, however, lead to certain general conclusions which are relevant in the formulation of anti-inflationary policy.

In the first place it is quite obvious that monetary and fiscal policies designed to combat an inflation arising out of excess *aggregate* demand are not suitable to a situation in which demand in the aggregate is not excessive. When, as in recent years, a rise in the general level of prices accompanies a growth in excess capacity, further restriction of the general level of demand may be positively harmful. Since productivity is sensitive to changes in output when output is running below capacity, a general reduction in demand is more likely to raise unit costs by its effects on productivity than to lower them by its effects on wage rates. This will be particularly true if the restriction of aggregate demand continues to leave the booming sectors of the economy relatively unaffected.

Monetary and fiscal policies which do not restrain aggregate demand, but impinge only on the sectors where demand is excessive may indeed limit the inflationary forces during a period of creeping inflation. Had investment demand risen more slowly between 1955 and 1957, and automobile and housing demand more evenly, we would have experienced a larger rise in aggregate output and a smaller rise in prices. The question of selective tax and credit controls is far too broad to be discussed here; their application involves a host of economic and social questions which cannot be casually answered. At the same time however, our analysis does indicate that counter-inflationary monetary and fiscal policies must take into account the composition as well as the magnitude of demand. The use of monetary and fiscal policy to prevent the emergence of aggregate excess demand can prevent one type of inflation—indeed the most harmful type. But inflation can still arise in a situation of dynamically stable aggregate demand. Under these circumstances we can either attempt to alter the composition of demand by using *selective* monetary and fiscal policy or we can accept the moderate price increases which take place. This is our choice. We cannot solve the problem, indeed we shall do positive harm, by a further restriction of aggregate demand through *general* monetary and fiscal restraint.

There is one final implication of this analysis. The moderate inflation of recent years was part of the process of resource allocation. Simply because it is called inflation, one cannot attribute to it the dire consequences associated with classical hyperinflation. It does indeed benefit some individuals and harm others—like many other aspects of the resource allocation process. In fact it is, in part, a reflection of the attempt by individuals and groups in society to ease the adjustments in relative incomes which result from a shift in the composition of demand. Such an inflation probably disturbs the social structure less than do the rapid changes in technology, the shift of income between industries, and the movement of industries from one region to the other, which we take to be the marks of a dynamic economy.

*FRITZ MACHLUP*

# Another View of Cost-Push and Demand-Pull Inflation

*23* It is with some hesitation that I join the discussion and thus contribute to the galloping inflation of the literature on the creeping inflation of prices. My excuse is probably the same as that of most of my fellow writers: dissatisfied with much of what others have written, I have, perhaps presumptuously, decided that my way of thinking would be more successful. Hence, I am presenting another view of cost-push and demand-pull inflation.

## The Current Debate

Before I set forth the controversial issue and the most widely held views, I shall indulge in a few preliminaries by referring briefly to the old squabble about what should be meant by inflation.

Reprinted from the *Review of Economics and Statistics,* Vol. XLII (1960), pp. 125–139, by permission of the author and publisher, Harvard University Press. Copyright 1960 by the President and Fellows of Harvard College. Fritz Machlup is a professor at Princeton University.

### Inflation of What?

Some people regard "inflation" as a *cause* (explanation) of a general rise in prices (and of some other things too), while others use the word as a *synonym* (equivalent) for a general rise in prices. In times when governments undertake to control prices by prohibitions with threats of sanctions against unauthorized price rising, many writers realize how awkward it is to use the term inflation to signify price increase, because then they want to discuss the "latent" or "repressed" inflation—one that does not show up in a general price index, or does not show up adequately. Also when one talks about inflation and deflation as apparent opposites, a definition in terms of general prices is quite inconvenient, inasmuch as the problem of deflation is so serious largely because it shows up in falling volumes of production and employment instead of falling prices.

One solution would be to use the word inflation always with a modifying word that tells exactly *what* is blown up: currency, credit, spending, demand, wages, prices, etc. This would be a great help; indeed some controversial problems would disappear, because the disputants would find out that they were talking about different things, and other problems would be greatly clarified. The most lively issue of our times, whether "our" inflation in the last four years has been due to a demand-pull or to a cost-push, would lose some of its muddiness if the analysts had to qualify all their pronouncements with regard to the inflation of credit, spending, demand, wholesale prices, consumer prices, and so forth.

A search of the learned literature would yield scores of definitions of inflation, differing from one another in essentials or in nuances. A search of the popular literature, however, reveals no realization of the differences in the meanings experts give to the term. The differences apparently have been reserved for the treatises and the quarterlies; the daily papers and the weeklies were not to be encumbered with "technicalities." Now that inflation has become such a widely debated topic, with many scholars participating in the debates, the popular meaning of inflation, denoting an increase in the consumer price index, has been increasingly adopted by the professional economists. Although this is probably bad for analysis, we may have to accept it. But at the risk of appearing pedantic I shall continue to speak of various kinds of inflation and to specify which I happen to be speaking about.

### The Controversial Issue

Opinion is divided on whether consumer prices in recent years have increased chiefly (1) because industry has invested too much and government has spent too much (relative to the nation's thrift) or (2) because big business has raised material prices and/or big labor has raised wage rates too high (relative to the nation's increase in productivity). The issue is partly who is to be "blamed" for the past rise in consumer prices, and partly what policies should be pursued to avoid a continued increase.

If demand-pull inflation is the correct diagnosis, the Treasury is to be blamed for spending too much and taxing too little, and the Federal Reserve Banks are to be blamed for keeping interest rates too low and for creating or tolerating too large a volume of free reserves, which enable member banks to extend too much credit.

If cost-push inflation is the correct diagnosis, trade unions are to be blamed for demanding excessive wage increases, and industry is to be blamed for granting them, big business may be blamed for raising "administered prices" of materials and other producers goods to yield ever-increasing profit rates, and government may be

assigned the task of persuading or forcing labor unions and industry to abstain from attempts to raise their incomes, or at least to be more moderate.

Not everybody draws the appropriate conclusions from the theory which he espouses. And not everybody is willing to adopt policies to correct the undesirable situation. (Nor does everybody find the situation sufficiently undesirable to get seriously worried.)[1] The ambivalent position of many partisans of labor unions is noteworthy. They reject the wage-push diagnosis because, understandably, they do not wish to take the blame for the inflation. But they also reject the demand-pull diagnosis, because this diagnosis would militate against the use of fiscal and monetary policies to bolster employment. They want effective demand to be increased at a rate fast enough to permit full employment at rapidly increasing wage rates; but they do not want to attribute increasing prices either to the increase in demand or to the increase in wage rates. The only way out of this logical squeeze is to blame the consumer-price increase on prices "administered" by big business; but in order to support this hypothesis one would have to prove that the profit margins and profit rates of the industries in question have been rising year after year—which they have not.[2] But we shall see later that matters are not quite so simple and cannot be analyzed exclusively in these terms.

Our first task is to deal with the contention that the distinction between cost-push and demand-pull inflation is unworkable, irrelevant, or even meaningless.

### "Cost-Push No Cause of Inflation"

There is a group of outstanding economists contending that there cannot be such a thing as

---

[1] Cf. "Argument for Creeping Inflation," *New York Times*, March 3, 1959; "Slow Inflation: An Inescapable Cost of Maximum Growth Rate," *Commercial and Financial Chronicle*, March 26, 1959; "Inflation— A Problem of Shrinking Importance," *Commercial and Financial Chronicle*, April 23, 1959—all by Sumner H. Slichter.

[2] "The period 1947 to 1958 was a time of decreasing profit margins. This fact is important because it shows that the initiative in raising prices was not being taken by employers. In the four years 1947 to 1950 inclusive the net income of non-financial corporations after taxes per dollar of sales averaged 4.45 cents. In the next four years the average net income was 4.10 [cents] per dollar of sales; and in the three years 1955 to 1957 inclusive, it was about 3.3 cents per dollar of sales." Slichter, *Commercial and Financial Chronicle*, April 23, 1959.

a cost-push inflation because, without an increase in purchasing power and demand, cost increases would lead to unemployment and depression, not to inflation.

On their own terms, these economists are correct. The rules of inductive logic say that if A and B together cause M; and if A without B cannot cause M, whereas B without A can cause M; then B, and not A, should be called the cause of M. Make A the wage-raising power of the unions and the price-raising power of the corporations; make B the credit-creating and money-creating power of the monetary system; make M the successive price increases. It should be quite clear that without the creation of new purchasing power a continuing price increase would be impossible. Hold the amount of money and bank credit constant (relative to real national product) and all that the most powerful unions and corporations can do is to price themselves out of the market.

Having admitted all this to the economists who reject the possibility of cost-push inflation, we can shift the weight of the argument to the question whether, given the power of the monetary system to create money and credit, this power would be exercised to the same extent if strong trade unions and strong corporations desisted from raising wages and prices as it actually is exercised when wages and prices are being pushed up. There would probably be quick agreement that, given our present system, the exercise of the wage-raising power of strong unions and the price-raising power of strong corporations induces, or adds impetus to, the exercise of the ability of the banking system to create purchasing power.

The point then is that an increase in effective demand is a necessary condition for a continuing increase in general prices, but that a cost-push under present conditions will regularly lead to an expansion of credit and to that increase in effective demand which will permit the increase in consumer prices.

There remains, however, an important question of fact. Assume it is decided not to exercise the power to create money and credit—more than is needed to maintain a constant ratio to real national product—even at the risk of severe unemployment that might result if wages and prices increased; would we then have to expect that the strong unions and corporations would continue to make use of their wage-raising and price-raising powers? Some economists are convinced that unions and business firms would adopt much more moderate policies if they had

to fear that any lack of moderation would lead to unemployment and stagnation. This does not mean that a considerable level of unemployment would be required to impress industry and unions with the desirability of moderation. Industrial firms would know that, under an unyielding monetary policy, they could not hope to pass increases in labor cost on to consumers and they would therefore refuse to yield to union pressure. Unions, in turn, would not strike for higher wages if they were sure that industry could not afford to give in, Hence, no cost-push and no extra unemployment.

Acceptance of this view by any number of economists would not yet make it a practicable policy. It could not work unless the monetary authorities embraced it without reservation, since any indication of a lack of faith and determination on the part of the authorities would remove the premise: unions could hope that industries would hope that an eventual relaxation of the monetary brake would "bail them out" and by means of an expansion of demand avert the business losses and the unemployment that would threaten to arise in consequence of wage and price increases.

## "Demand-Pull No Cause of Inflation"

Having shown that there is a sense in which the contention is correct that "cost-push is no cause of inflation, it takes a demand-pull to produce it," we shall now attempt to show that the opposite contention may likewise be correct. There are indeed assumptions for which it would be appropriate to say that "demand-pull is no cause of inflation, it takes a cost-push to produce it." What are these assumptions and how do they differ from those of the traditional model?

In the traditional model, prices rise or fall under the impact of anonymous market forces. They rise when at their existing level the quantity of goods demanded exceeds the quantity supplied. Not that producers, noticing the increased demand, would decide that they could do better if they "charged" more; rather the mechanism of a "perfect market" would automatically lift prices to the level where the consumers would not want to purchase any more than was supplied. Sellers, in this model, don't ask higher prices, they just get them. The same thing happens in the model of the perfect labor market. When the demand for labor increases, workers don't ask for higher wages, they just get them as a result of competition.

In a large part of our present economy, prices and wages do not "rise" as if lifted by the invisible hand, but are "raised" by formal and explicit managerial decisions. Assume now that prices and wage rates are administered everywhere in the economy in such a way that changes in demand are not taken into account; instead, they are set in accordance with some "rules of thumb." Prices and wages may then be so high (relative to demand) that inventories accumulate, production is cut, and labor is unemployed; or they may be so low (relative to demand) that inventories are depleted, production is raised, customers must patiently wait for delivery or their orders are rejected, and there are plenty of vacancies, but no workers to fill them. If the rules of thumb are universally observed by producers, distributors, and labor unions and take full account of increased cost of production and increased cost of living, but disregard all changes in demand, then there can be no demand-pull upon prices. In such circumstances an increase in effective demand leads to unfilled orders and unfilled vacancies, but not to higher prices.[3]

One may object, of course, that such a model cannot possibly apply to all markets; that there exist numerous competitive markets in which no producer has enough power to "set" or "charge" a price; that in many markets in which prices are administered the would-be buyers, in periods of increased demand, offer higher prices in order to be served and sellers are glad to accept them even though they exceed their list prices; and that this regularly happens when the demand for labor is brisk, so that wages paid can be higher than the rates agreed in collective bargaining. Thus, demand-pull is likely to work despite the existence of administered prices and wages.

Although the objection may be sustained on practical grounds, this does not destroy the value of the model. If there are, in actual fact, *many* industries where backlogs of orders accumulate while prices fail to rise and where job vacancies grow in number while wages fail to rise, then the model has some relevance, and it is legitimate to speculate about the functioning of an economic system in which *all* prices and wages are administered on the basis of cost calculations and held at the set levels even in the face of excess demand. It is not easy to decide whether on balance the institutions in our economy are such that a model featuring "market-clearing prices"

or a model featuring "cost-plus prices" fits better the purposes of speculating about the over-all performance of the entire economy.

In any case, the contention must be granted that there may be conditions under which "effective demand" is not effective and won't pull up prices, and when it takes a cost-push to produce price inflation. But this position disregards an important distinction, namely, whether the cost-push is "equilibrating" in the sense that it "absorbs" a previously existing excess demand or whether it is "disequilibrating" in the sense that it creates an excess supply (of labor and productive capacity) that will have to be prevented or removed by an increase in effective demand. Thus we are back at the crucial issue; a "monistic" interpretation cannot do justice to it.

## Statistical Tests

It is possible to grant the usefulness of the distinction between cost-push and demand-pull in building theoretical models for speculative reasoning, and yet to deny its usefulness in identifying the causes of general price increases in concrete situations. It may be that the concepts are not operational, that statistical tests are either unavailable or unreliable.

Some have proposed to answer the question, whether wage-push or demand-pull had "initiated" the upward movement of prices, by looking to see which has *increased first*, prices or wages. But "first" since what time? If prices and wages have risen in turn, in successive steps, the choice of a base period is quite arbitrary, and a conclusion assigning the leading or initiating role to one factor or the other would be equally arbitrary. (This is especially so if our statistical information is limited to annual data.)

Not much better is the idea of looking to see which of the two, money-wage rates or consumer prices, has *increased more*. The arbitrary choice of the base period for this comparison is again a serious difficulty. But even more important is the fact that the annual rise in productivity (output per labor hour) normally secures increases in real wages over the years. Hence it is to be expected that wage rates increase relative to consumer prices regardless of whether there is inflation, and regardless of whether prices are pulled up by demand or pushed up by wages. Even some highly-seasoned economists have fallen victim to another logical snare: that any increase in money-wage rates that *exceeded the increase in labor productivity* was a sure sign of a wage-push. Yet, even if there were no labor

---

[3] ". . . if all prices were administered on the basis of markup over direct cost—then excess demand might exist in all markets, yet without effect on the price level." Gardner Ackley, "Administered Prices and the Inflationary Process," *American Economic Review,* Papers and Proceedings, XLIX (May 1959), 421.

union in the country and no worker ever asked for higher wages, a demand-pull inflation would eventually pull up the wage level; and if the demand-pull were such that prices and wages rose by any percentage above two or three a year—and it may well be five or ten or twenty per cent—money-wage rates would be up by more than the rate of increase in productivity. This, then, would have been the result of demand-pull only, without any wage-push at all. Hence the proposed statistical test is completely inconclusive.

A test which is based on a fundamentally correct chain of reasoning would compare profit rates with wage rates, and diagnose demand-pull when *profit rates increase faster than wage rates*. A slight variant of this test uses the relative shares of profits and wages in national income. The theory behind these tests is simply this: when an expansion of effective demand—without a wage-push—pulls up product prices, an increase in profits and profit rates would result until wage rates are pulled up by the derived demand for labor. On this theory, an increase in consumer prices associated with increased profit rates, but with wage rates lagging, would reliably indicate the existence of a demand-pull inflation. The operational difficulties with a test based on this theory are the same as those connected with other statistical tests: the arbitrary selection of the time periods. The theory, moreover, applies to an economy in which most prices are the result of anonymous market forces, not of administrative decisions. If most prices were administered and the price setters decided to raise their "profit targets" (perhaps at the same time that trade unions were out to engineer a wage boost, but a little faster or by a bigger jump) we could find—given the present monetary regime guided by the high-level-employment goal—that prices and profit rates increase ahead of wage rates even though the movement was not started by an autonomous expansion of demand. Hence, the lead of profit rates is not a reliable indication of demand-pull; it may occur also in conjunction with a cost-push in which price setters take a leading part.

Widely accepted as reliable symptoms of demand-pull inflation are over-employment and over-time payments. The statistical operations proposed to establish these symptoms are, for over-employment, to see whether *job vacancies exceed job applications* and, for over-time pay, to see whether *average hourly earnings have increased faster than wage rates*. Some critics rightly point out that the presence of these symptoms does not rule out that some cost-push has contributed to the inflation of prices. Indeed it would have been possible that a cost-push actually initiated the process and that the compensatory monetary injection, expanding demand to avoid the threatening unemployment, turned out to be heavier than necessary. Thus while these tests can verify the existence of an inflation of demand, they cannot prove that it was excess demand that precipitated the inflation of consumer prices.

## Proposed Concepts and Distinctions

The diversity of expert opinion and the absence of any good statistical tests to support a diagnosis may in part be due to the lack of precise definitions. It is clear that an inflation of effective demand is a necessary condition not only for a demand-pull inflation of consumer prices but also for a cost-push inflation. Without an expansion of demand the cost boost would result in less production and less employment, not in a continuing rise of the level of consumer prices. Should one then speak of a demand-pull inflation only when the expansion in demand is clearly the initiating factor and any administrative cost increases are clearly induced? Or should one also speak of a demand-pull inflation if administrative wage and material-price increases start and lead the procession of events, but are then joined and overtaken by induced or compensatory expansions of demand?

### Autonomous, Induced, and Supportive Demand Inflation

It is useful to distinguish autonomous from induced and supportive expansions of demand. *Autonomous* would be expansions which are not linked to previous or to expected cost increases; hence, disbursements which would also occur if no cost increases had been experienced or anticipated. *Induced* expansions of demand are direct consequences of a cost increase, in that those who receive the increased cost-prices or those who pay them will make larger disbursements than they would have made otherwise. For example, the industrial firms yielding to union pressure for a wage increase may borrow from banks (or dig into cash reserves) in order to pay the higher wage bill; or the recipients of higher wages may increase installment purchases and induce an expansion of consumer credit. *Supportive* (compensatory) expansions of demand would be those which are engineered by monetary or fiscal policy designed to reduce the unemployment arising, or threatening to arise, from cost increases. For example, the monetary authorities may reduce reserve requirements or create reserves in order to allow banks to extend loans, or the fiscal authorities may increase government expenditures in an attempt to expand effective demand and employment.

Without wishing to restrict the freedom of choice of those who formulate definitions, I submit that the choice should be appropriate to the purposes for which the concept is used. If the concept of a demand-induced inflation, or demand-pull inflation, is to serve for diagnostic and prognostic purposes in the development of economic policies, it would seem preferable to confine it to autonomous expansions of demand. This would not obstruct but rather aid the analysis of instances in which cost-induced expansions or supportive expansions of demand should turn out to be excessive in the sense that they create more employment opportunities than are destroyed by the cost increases, and hence give rise to some of the symptoms of a demand-induced inflation.

### Aggressive, Defensive, and Responsive Cost Inflation

Similar obscurities due to a lack of essential distinctions surround the concept of the cost-induced inflation. Perhaps so much is clear that the term refers to increases in consumer prices that are the (direct or indirect) result of cost increases—labor cost, material cost, or any other cost. But it is not clear whether these cost increases have to be *autonomous* in the sense that they would not have come about in the absence of any monopoly power (price-making power), merely as a result of competitive demand. For it is quite possible that formal administrative decisions are behind cost increases which, however, do not go beyond what would have occurred without such decisions. For example, a trade union may achieve a "victory" in its negotiations with an employer group bringing home the same raise in pay which the individual employers would have offered (without collective bargaining) in trying to get or keep the labor force they want. Let us decide to call these cost increases *responsive* (or competitive) to distinguish them from those that could *not* be obtained in a purely competitive market.

It would be misleading to denote all non-responsive (non-competitive) price or wage increases as "autonomous," since they may well be "induced" by some changes in the economic situation. (And the adjectives "autonomous" and "induced" are usually used as opposites.) A wage-rate increase, for example, is not responsive unless it is in response to an excess demand (short supply) in the particular labor market; but an increase which is not "demand-induced" (and which therefore presupposes some "autonomy" with respect to competitive market forces) may yet be induced by (a) an increase in the employer's profits, (b) an increase in wage rates obtained by other labor groups, or (c) an increase in the cost of living. I propose to call (a) a "profit-induced" wage increase, (b) an "imitative" (or "spill-over") wage increase, and (c) a "defensive" wage increase. Any one of these increases may act as either an "impulse" or a "propagation" factor in the inflationary process.

Profit-induced and imitative increases as well as spontaneous increases may be called *aggressive* because they are designed to achieve a net advance in the real wage rate. A *defensive* increase merely restores real earnings which the group in question has long been enjoying; an aggressive increase raises real earnings above that level. The specification of a time interval is necessary in the definition so that one avoids calling "defensive" what really is a battle to defend the ground just gained in an aggressive action. For example, an aggressive wage-rate increase of ten per cent is likely to be partially eroded within less than a year through the resulting cost-push inflation (aided by induced and supportive expansions of demand). If the same trade unions then demand "cost-of-living raises" to restore their real wages, it would be somewhat ironic to call these new wage adjustments "defensive." But there will always be a wide range in which cost increases may as legitimately be considered defensive as aggressive, especially since trade unions take turns in their actions, each defending the real earnings of its own members that have suffered in consequence of the aggressive actions of other unions, and at the same time attempting to obtain a net improvement.

Administrative price increases by industries producing materials and other producers goods which enter as significant cost items into the prices of many other products can likewise be characterized as responsive (competitive), defensive, or aggressive. Purely responsive increases cannot occur in an industry with much unused productive capacity; only when plants are working at capacity and orders are piling up can administrative price increases be merely responsive; in such circumstances it is economically irrelevant that these prices are administered. Defensive increases leave real profit rates substantially unchanged; these increases take account of increased production cost and no more. Needless to say, the rates of return must be calculated on the basis of the reproduction cost of the required capacity; that is to say, the book values of the fixed capital may be too low if reproduction cost of building and equipment is higher than at the time of their acquisition, or too high if assets are included which are not required for current production, Thus, price increases designed to defend, in periods of falling production, a profit rate that is calculated on the basis of the value of assets inclusive of unused capacity are really aggressive; and price increases designed to raise the money rate of return on capital just enough to take care of increased replacement costs are really defensive.

Should all kinds of wage increase and price increase be included in the concept of a cost-push inflation whenever they are collectively negotiated, unilaterally announced, or otherwise the result of administrative action? I submit that increases which are merely responsive (competitive) do not belong there at all. Defensive increases do of course play an important role in the process of price inflation and the economist will surely not leave them out of his analysis. But in an explanation of an inflationary process going on year-in year-out the aggressive increases have a more substantive role to play than defensive increases; and when it comes to assign "blame" for an inflation of consumer prices, the aggressive cost boosts will obviously be the more eligible candidates.

## The Basic Model Sequences

With the help of the proposed concepts the two basic model sequences of consumer-price inflation can be easily described.

(A) *Demand-pull infla-tion:* Autonomous expansions of demand (government spending, business spending, consumer spending) are followed by responsive (competitive) price and wage increases.

(B) *Cost-push infla-tion:* Aggressive increases of wage rates and/or material prices are followed by induced and/or supportive (compensatory) demand expansions.

Cost-push models are relatively simple as long as they contain only a single impulse—either wage or price increases—with all sequential changes in the nature of adjustments.

(B-1) *"Pure" wage-push inflation:* Aggressive increases of wage rates are followed by induced and/or supportive demand expansions, and by responsive increases of material prices and other wage rates.

(B-2) *"Pure" price-push inflation:* Aggressive increases of material prices are followed by induced and/or supportive demand expansions, and by responsive increases of other material prices and wage rates.

Models become more complicated as more discretionary actions are included in the sequence of events, especially imitative and defensive increases of cost elements, or even aggressive increases, requiring further adjustments. For example, an autonomous demand expansion may be followed by administered wage and price increases more drastic than merely competitive increases would be; thus, the increases would be partly responsive and partly aggressive, requiring further demand expansions, induced or supportive, if unemployment is to be avoided. Or, aggressive wage and price increases may be followed by excessive demand expansions, perhaps because a nervous government rushes in with overdoses of supportive injections of buying power; some of the effective demand thus created would then be in the nature of an autonomous expansion, resulting in further (responsive) upward adjustments of costs.

## Attempted Application

Even the most complicated model sequence will probably still be much simpler than the actual course of events as reflected in the data at our disposal. Since reality is so messy that no neat and simple model will fit at all closely, whereas various complex models will fit approximately, it is not surprising that even impartial analysts arrive at divergent interpretations of the so-called facts.

## The Postwar Inflation

In the narrow scope of this article no attempt can be made to sift the data, to assess the comparative applicability of the various models, and to award first prize to the best-fitting model. But I shall not dodge this question and shall indicate briefly what impressions I have derived from the data presented by governmental and private researchers.

I believe that for an explanation of the consumer-price inflation from 1945 to 1948, and from 1950 to 1952, the basic model of the demand-pull inflation does as well as, or better than, any of the other models, simple or complicated. On the other hand, for the period 1955–59 several cost-push models appear to do better, and I am prepared to regard the consumer-price increases of these four years as a result of a cost-push inflation.

The choice among the various cost-push models is a hard one, especially in view of the controversy about the behavior of administered material prices. The periodic increases in steel prices have sometimes been regarded as the most strategic impulse factor in the inflationary process. A special theory of "profit-target pricing" assuming "periodic raising of the target" has been devised in support of this diagnosis and an array of empirical material has been added in its support.

### Wage or Profit Push?

Neither this theory nor the statistical data seem to me to make the model of the "material-price-push inflation" a plausible explanation of the period in question. While many of the administered price increases may have hampered the performance of our economy and accelerated the inflationary process, I doubt that all or most of them have been "aggressive" in the sense defined. The reported data on profit rates and profit margins do not, in my judgment, indicate that the price increases were aggressive. Of course, few, if any, of the increases since 1955 have been in the nature of responsive adjustments to excess demand—but probably most of them were defensive in nature, taking account of cost increases without raising real profit rates. I cannot verify this impression of mine to everybody's satisfaction, and perhaps not even to my own. But my impression is strengthened by the deduced consequences of certain assumptions, which I consider plausible, concerning the policies and objectives of business managers.

There is, in my opinion, nothing invidious in contending that there are essential differences between most wage increases obtained by strong labor unions and most increases of material prices announced by strong corporations. Nor is it meant to be critical of union policies or

uncritical of business policies if many wage increases are held to be aggressive, and many administered price increases defensive. The point is that the situation of most businesses is such that a series of aggressive price increases would be either injurious to them in the long run or downright impossible. A series of aggressive wage increases, on the other hand, may be both possible and beneficial to the labor groups concerned.

To hold that most administered price increases have been defensive rather than aggressive, does not mean (a) that the prices in question were not too high—they probably were, (b) that the increases did not speed up the inflationary process —they certainly did, or (c) that they were "justified"—which they were not if a competitive market model is used as the standard. But if the question is only whether these price increases were the "impulse factors," the "initiating forces" of the price inflation, then I believe the answer is negative.

## Wage Increases and Productivity

I do not expect serious exception to the proposition that most of the wage increases obtained by strong trade unions in the last four years, whether spontaneous or profit-induced or imitative, have been aggressive in the sense defined. (This is in contrast to most wage increases between 1945 and 1952, which were responsive.) We must now inquire whether aggressive wage increases are inflationary if they do not exceed the relative rate at which productivity increases.

### Aggressive Wage Increases to Capture Average Productivity Gains

According to accepted doctrine, the consumer price level can be held approximately stable, and full employment maintained, if the average increase in money-wage rates does not exceed the average increase in productivity in the economy as a whole. Some of the necessary qualifications to this proposition are not relevant to the issues under discussion. For interested readers they are presented in a footnote.[4] One qualifica-

---

[4] There is the first qualification for the sacrifice of fixed-income recipients. The existence of contractual payments in fixed money amounts makes it possible for wage rates to increase a little more than productivity. Assume, for the sake of a simple arithmetical illustration, that of a national product of $1,000 a share of $700 is distributed in the form of

tion, however, that may matter here to some extent concerns the additional profits needed as returns on the additional investments required for the increase in national product. It is sometimes possible for total product per worker to increase thanks to a progress of technology, organization, or skills, without any increase in capital investment. More often, however, it takes some additional investment to achieve an increase in productivity. If such investments were not allowed to earn a return, progress might be stopped short; but if they are to earn a return, total profits must increase lest the rates of return on capital are cut, which could lead to reduced investment and employment. Hence, as a rule,

wages, $100 in the form of profits, and $200 in the form of fixed interest, rent, and pension payments. If now net national product rises by $20 (or 2 per cent) and the recipients of fixed money incomes get no share in the increased product (because prices are held stable), 20 per cent of the increased product, i.e., $4, becomes available as a possible bonus for labor in addition to their 70 per cent share of $14. Total wage payments can thus increase by $18 or 2.57 per cent.

A second qualification relates to possible improvements in the terms of trade. Assume that the price of imports (relative to the price of exports) falls by 2 per cent and that imports had amounted to 10 per cent of the net national product, or $100. If the entire gain of $2 is seized as another bonus for labor, wages can rise by $20 or 2.86 per cent.

A third qualification concerns the possible effects of increased tax revenues. Assume that the effective tax rate on profits (distributed plus undistributed) is 50 per cent while the marginal tax rate on wages is 20 per cent. The additional profits are (10 per cent of $20 = ) $2 and the taxes on this are $1. The taxes on additional wages are (20 per cent of $20 = ) $4. If the government kept expenditures constant despite increased revenues, another bonus of $5 could be distributed in the form of wages, bringing the total addition to $25 before taxes, or more than the entire increase in net national product. (We neglect now the tax on the third bonus.) Wages before taxes could with all three bonuses be increased by 3.57 per cent, compared with a 2 per cent increase in national income.

The second and third bonuses, however, cannot be counted upon; the second bonus may just as likely be negative since the terms of trade may deteriorate rather than improve. Even the first bonus is likely to disappear in an economy with perpetual inflation, because contractual incomes might gradually be made subject to automatic cost-of-living adjustments. All three qualifications are probably less important than the one presented in the text and this one works in the opposite direction.

This exposition has been freely adapted from Friedrich A. Lutz, "Cost- and Demand-Induced Inflation," *Banca Nazionale del Lavoro*, No. 44 (March 1958), 9–10. The adaptations were necessary because I believe Lutz's argument to be partly erroneous.

wage increases must not absorb the entire increase in output. And if the additional investment were so large that capital per worker has increased at a percentage rate greater than that of output per worker, wage rates cannot even increase by as much as output per worker and still allow price stability with full employment.[5]

The following formulation will steer clear of such technicalities and express the essential points. Apart from a few modifying influences, such as a squeezing of quasi-rents in stagnant industries, a whittling down of the real claims of recipients of contractual incomes, or a lucky improvement in the terms of foreign trade, real wages per worker cannot increase faster than product per worker. If *money*-wage rates are raised faster than productivity, and the monetary authorities supply the money needed to pay the increased wages without unemployment, prices will rise enough to keep *real*-wage rates from rising faster than productivity. To say that the price inflation has the "function" of keeping the increase in real wages down to the rate at which productivity increases may help some to understand the mechanism. But it is not really an appropriate expression, for nothing has to "function" to "prevent from occurring" what cannot occur anyway. Either prices rise (with the help of supportive expansion of demand) to cut the real wage rates to the level made possible by the productivity increase, or unemployment occurs (if demand expansion is prevented or restrained) and cuts total real wages even lower.

If money wages were not increased at all and all increments to the net national product that are due to technological progress were distributed to consumers in the form of lower prices, *all* income recipients—wage earners, owners of businesses, and fixed-income recipients—would share in the increased product. If money wages all over the economy are increased approximately by the rate at which average productivity has increased, prices on the average will neither fall nor rise and hence the fixed-income recipients (bondholders, landlords, pensioners, perhaps also civil servants, teachers, etc.) will be cut out of their share in the increment. Thus, aggressive money wage increases which, on the average, equal the average increase in productivity in the economy will improve the relative income share

[5] If wage rates were to increase as much as output per worker while prices were kept from rising, total output would not be large enough to allow any return to be earned by the new capital; employers, then, might not want to maintain the level of investment and employment. See Lutz, *loc. cit.*, 4.

of labor at the expense of the receivers of contractual income.

## Aggressive Wage Increases to Capture Individual Productivity Gains

The "rule" that price stability and full employment can be maintained if all money wage rates are increased by the same percentage by which average productivity has increased in the economy as a whole is frequently misunderstood and mistakenly applied to advocate increases in money-wage rates in individual firms or industries by the same percentage by which productivity has increased in these firms or industries. In other words, the rule is perverted to the proposal that the benefits of advancing productivity should accrue to the workers in the industries in which the advances take place. It is twisted into a proposition justifying

> . . . union demands in those industries, which, because of improved technology and consequent cost reductions, can afford to pay higher wages without charging higher prices for their products. This proposition is thoroughly unsound. It misses completely the economic function of prices and wages; its realization would sabotage the economic allocation of resources without serving any purpose that could be justified from any ethical or political point of view.[6]

A sensible allocation of resources requires that the same factors of production are offered at the same prices to all industries. It causes misallocations if industries in which technology has improved are forced to pay higher wages for the same type of labor that gets lower pay in industries where technology has not changed. Wage rates should be temporarily higher in fields into which labor is to be attracted, not in fields where labor is released by labor-saving techniques. It is economic nonsense to advocate that wage rates should be forced up precisely where labor becomes relatively abundant.

> One might accept an economically unsound arrangement if it were ethically much superior. But no one could claim that the proposition in question satisfied any ethical norm. If five industries, let us call them A, B, C, D, and E, employ the same type of labor; if any of them, say Industry A, develops a new production process and is now able to make the same product as before with half the amount of labor; then this Industry A could afford to raise its wage rates without raising its selling prices. Should now workers in Industry A get a wage increase of 100 per cent while their fellow workers in Industries B, C, D, and E get nothing? Should the coincidence that the technological advance took place in A give the workers there the windfall of the entire benefit, raising them above the rest of the people? I can see no ethical argument that could be made in favor of such a scheme.
>
> But as a matter of practical fact, apart from economics and ethics, the scheme could never be consistently applied, because the workers in other industries would not stand for it, . . . similar wage increases would have to be given in all . . . firms and industries regardless of their ability to pay, regardless of whether their selling prices would remain stable or go up slightly or a great deal. It simply would not be fair if a favored group were to be the sole beneficiary of progress while the rest of the population would have to sit back and wait for better luck.[7]

No fair-minded person would ask them to sit back and wait; every labor union with any power at all would press the claims of its members, and where no unions existed workers would eventually appeal to their employers and to the public to end the injustice. Yet, any "equalizing" wage increases would be clearly of the cost-push type and would, if unemployment is prevented, lead to consumer price increases which take away from the originally privileged worker groups some of the real gains they were first awarded (with the approval of short-sighted commentators and politicians).

This spill-over of money-wage increases and the cost-push inflation which it produces (with the help of a supportive demand inflation) serve to redistribute some of the productivity gains first captured by the workers in the industries where the gains occurred. This redistribution by means of consumer-price inflation cuts back the real wages of the first-successful labor groups, whose unions will then complain about the erosion of their incomes and will call for seemingly defensive wage increases to regain the ground lost through inflation (though they rarely lose all of their gain in real income and often keep a large part of it).

In short, a policy that condones wage increases in industries which, because of increased productivity, can afford to pay increased wages without charging increased prices, is actually a policy that accepts a rising cost-price spiral without end.

[6] Fritz Machlup, *The Political Economy of Monopoly* (Baltimore, 1952), 403.

[7] *Ibid.*, 404–5.

## Price Reductions Essential for Stability

A wage increase obtained by a particular labor group may initiate an inflationary process, but the speed of this process will depend largely on the incidence of defensive price increases and of imitative and defensive wage increases. If nothing but responsive (competitive) price and wage increases were to occur, the rate of inflation initiated by an isolated wage boost would be very small, perhaps negligible. It is, nevertheless, interesting to examine models of price inflation that include neither defensive nor imitative increases.

### Inflation Without Spill-Over Wage-Push

In the inflationary process described in the last section, the industries that were forced to pay the increased wages (out of the economies provided by improved techniques) were assumed for the sake of the argument not to increase their selling prices. The price inflation was chiefly the work of a spill-over of the wage increases into fields where productivity had increased less or not at all. But even in the absence of any spill-over, even if no worker in the country were to receive a raise that did not come from economies in production, some degree of consumer-price inflation would be inevitable in an economy in which (a) wage rates are never reduced in any sector, even in the face of unemployment, (b) wage rates are increased to capture productivity gains entirely in the industries where they accrue, and (c) full employment is secured, if necessary, through expansion of effective demand. Now when workers are released in the industries where productivity increases, but production, with unchanged prices and unchanged demand, is not increased, it will take an inflation of demand to create employment for the workers set free by the advance of technology. In other words, the "technological unemployment" will have to be cured by an expansion of demand, which in turn will cause a rise in consumer prices.

Does not this argument overlook the increase in demand on the part of workers who receive wage increases? It does not. Since the wage increases were granted just to offset the cost reduction made possible by the increase in output per worker, the workers who stay employed receive their raise out of funds no longer paid out as wages to the workers who lost their jobs. A little arithmetic may clarify this point. If 90 workers can now produce the output previously produced by 100, and are now paid the total wage that was previously paid to 100, the total purchasing power in the hands of the workers stays the same. The 10 workers who were released get nothing, and what was saved on them is being paid to the "more productive" 90. The firm, paying the same wage bill (though to fewer workers), finds its costs neither increased nor reduced and keeps its selling prices unchanged. Since at these prices demand is the same as before, the firm has no use for the 10 workers; nor has anybody else if wages rates are nowhere reduced. If the authorities want them reemployed, a demand inflation has to be engineered. True, the 10 workers will produce something once they are employed, but only after increased prices have created incentives for employers "to use more labor; or they will have to be employed (and paid for with new money) in the production of public services not sold in the market.

The assumptions built into the model underlying this chain of reasoning have excluded growth (of labor force and capital stock) and excess capacity. If there were adequate excess capacity in each and every line of production, the demand created (in order to re-employ the labor released by the more productive industries) could be satisfied without price increases anywhere. But no inflation model can reasonably include the assumption of ubiquitous excess capacity; limited facilities (bottlenecks) are implied in any explanation of inflation. Thus, no exception should be taken to the assumption that the new wages paid to the re-employed workers will not all be spent for their own products, but largely for other things, and that prices will be bid up in the process.

The exclusion of a growing labor force and a growing capital stock have served merely to simplify the reasoning. When inputs and outputs are increasing, a certain increase in the money supply and in aggregate spending will be required to manage the increase in output and trade at given prices. An expansion of money demand to effect a re-absorption of technological unemployment would be over and above the money demand required to take care of the growth in labor force and capital stock. To combine the analyses of such growth and of technological unemployment would be an unnecessary complication; the other growth factors can be disregarded without vitiating the conclusions derived in an isolated treatment of technological unemployment.

The price inflation to be expected from a demand inflation engineered to absorb "technological unemployment" will of course be quite moderate in this case, where all the spill-over wage increases are ruled out. Here is a type of inflation that cannot be characterized as a cost-push inflation, and not as a demand-pull inflation either, if that term is reserved for autonomous expansions of demand. To be sure, aggressive wage increases are involved in the process, but these increases, merely offsetting the growth of productivity, will push up only the cost per labor hour, not the cost per unit of output, and thus no price increases can be said to result from cost increases.

### Inflation Without Any Wage Increases

One may easily jump to the conclusion that technological unemployment, and the need to resort to demand inflation as its only cure, is entirely due to the aggressive wage increases, giving to the workers in the technically advancing industries the entire benefit of the productivity gain. This conclusion would be wrong. The consequences will be the same if in the absence of any wage increase the firms in question find their profits increased but for some reason fail to let consumers benefit in the form of lower selling prices.

Does this argument rely on lower marginal propensities to spend, or on insufficient investment opportunities, or on excessive liquidity preferences? It does not. Even if it is assumed that corporations spend all of their retained profits and stockholders spend all their dividends —just as the workers would have spent their wages—the workers released in the industries where technology has advanced will not be re-employed without the help of demand inflation unless prices to consumers are lowered. The case is almost the same as that in which the workers captured the productivity gain, except that now the corporations and their owners pocket the entire benefit.

Why "almost" the same, why not exactly the same? Because there is the possibility that an increase in retained earnings, as an increase in capital supply, raises the marginal productivity of labor and thus the demand for labor at given wage rates. But it would be absurd to expect that this would suffice to re-employ all the released labor. Assume that the entire amount saved on the wage bill is spent on new machinery; this new demand for machinery (and indirectly for the labor that goes into its manufacture) merely takes the place of the former workers' demand for consumer goods (and indirectly for the labor

that went into their production). Thus the spending of the retained profits—earned by reducing the wage bill—constitutes no increased demand for labor. Only the resulting increase in productive facilities may eventually help the demand for labor to the extent of a small fraction of the technological unemployment created by the (labor-saving) increase in productivity. Hence the conclusion is the same as it was in the case of wage increase: only if consumers get a chance through lower prices to buy more product with their given money incomes will the released workers get a chance to find jobs in the absence of demand inflation.[8]

But why should firms refuse to lower their prices when production costs fall? The well-known theoretical models of a monopolist responding to a lowering of his cost curve show with no reasonable exceptions that he would reduce his selling price and increase his output. If firms can be observed acting otherwise, what is wrong with the model or what is wrong with the firms? One possible hypothesis would be that the firms of the real world had been in "disequilibrium," charging less than profit-maximizing monopoly prices and waiting for a good occasion to adjust their position. If now their costs are reduced, inaction, failure to reduce their prices, may be an easy way to adjust. Another hypothesis would be that the firms of the real world are in positions of not firmly coordinated oligopoly, where the safest rule is always "not to rock the boat," that is, never to reduce prices lest a rival mistake it for an outbreak of price competition. A third hypothesis would be that the "administered" prices in modern business cannot be explained by any models based on intelligent considerations, but are set by some fixed rules of thumb, and that one of these rules is never to reduce a price. There are perhaps still other hypotheses to explain the fact of "downward inflexibility" of prices—if indeed it is a fact. But no matter which hypothesis is accepted, the conclusion remains valid that if prices are not reduced when productivity has increased,

---

[8]This does not mean that the entire increase in productivity must be passed on to consumers in the form of reduced prices. Technological unemployment will neither be perpetuated nor require a price-inflating demand expansion for its cure if wage rates are raised by the national average increase in productivity. This will still permit price reductions in the industries where productivity has increased. The money the consumers save in buying these products at reduced prices will be spent on other goods and will drive up some other prices, without however raising consumer prices on the average.

technological unemployment arises and cannot be absorbed except through demand inflation and consequent consumer-price inflation.

### Stabilization of Individual Prices Necessitates Inflation

The argument of the preceding pages was designed to demonstrate that the failure to reduce prices in industries where productivity has increased will result in an inflationary increase of general prices, which

(a) will be most rapid if the productivity gains are captured by the workers of these industries by way of wage rate increases—because of the practically inevitable spill-over of the wage increases to other worker groups; but

(b) will also occur, though much more slowly, in the absence of such spill-over, because it will take a demand expansion to re-employ the workers released when the wage bill of the progressive industries is distributed over fewer workers; and

(c) will not be avoided even in the absence of any wage increases, because a demand expansion will be required to re-employ the workers released when the entire part of the wage bill that is saved through the technological advance is transformed into profits without giving consumers a chance to buy more product.

An economist willing to rely on the most abstract and general principles of economic theory can derive this "inevitability" of inflation from a simple set of theorems. He can deduce from the equilibrium conditions in a system of general equilibrium that general prices must rise if individual prices are maintained in industries where productivity increases. For a fall of production cost in one industry will call forth a reduction of the price of its product relative to the prices of all other products; this adjustment of relative prices will, in a money economy, proceed either through a fall in the money price of the product that now requires less labour per unit than before or through an increase in all other money prices (or through a combination of both); hence, stabilization of the money price of the more economically produced product implies that equilibrium will be restored through a general increase in money prices.

I do not propose to use this technical way of reasoning to convince trade union leaders, business executives, or members of Congress. But the previous argument was, I trust, understandable before I added the sophisticated demonstration of its conclusion.

### The O'Mahoney Plan to Check Inflation

It should now be clear that the only way to prevent inflation of consumer prices, and prevent unemployment too, is to make prices more flexible in the downward direction and, in particular, to encourage price reductions in industries where productivity has increased. Senator O'Mahoney's plan, partly incorporated in Senate Bill 215 of April 1959, and receiving serious consideration by several members of Congress, would achieve exactly the opposite. According to the preamble of the Bill, its author believes that "inflation will be checked if the pricing policies of these [dominant] corporations are publicly reviewed before increased prices may be made effective." On this theory the Bill provides for public hearings and investigations of large corporations whenever they want to raise prices. But the harder it is made for firms to raise prices the more surely will they avoid ever reducing their prices.

If a nation is committed to a full-employment policy, that is, to a policy of using demand inflation to create employment, it can avoid inflation only be avoiding anything that may create unemployment. Since economic growth proceeds chiefly through technological progress, and technological unemployment can only be avoided through price reductions, the prime requirement of a non-inflationary full-employment policy is to prevent the workers, owners, and managers of the progressing industries from capturing all the productivity gains accruing in these industries in the form of increased money wages and increased profits, respectively, and to encourage the dispersion of most of these gains to consumers in the form of reduced prices.

The O'Mahoney policy in effect encourages the trade unions in the industries in question to get out and capture the entire productivity gains for their workers. It does so implicitly because, if the firms are prevented from raising prices after the aggressive wage increases have absorbed "only" the new economies, the labor unions will no longer be blamed by the public for causing or precipitating higher prices. The "visible link" between these wage increases and price inflation is removed, and the union leaders will have even less compunction in pressing for these supposedly non-inflationary wage increases. The firms, losing all or most of the productivity gains to their workers, will hardly be eager to reduce prices. But even if they should, by means of tough bargaining, succeed in keeping a good deal of the gains, they will surely not dream of sharing any part of them with the consumers, because they would consider it foolish to reduce prices that cannot be raised again except after expensive, cumbersome, and perhaps embarrassing public inquisitions.

The O'Mahoney plan to check inflation would actually tend to make inflation perennial and perpetual. The only thing that can be said for the proposed policy is that it might in the short run, perhaps for a couple of years, slow down the progress of the price inflation. But even this is doubtful since, apart from encouraging trade unions to fight for the productivity gains accruing in their industries, it does nothing to check the spill-over wage increases, which in genuine cost-push fashion engender many chains of defensive, "approvable" price increases and necessitate continual resort to supportive demand inflation.

## Conclusion

It was not the purpose of this article to lead up to a critique of a proposed policy; this was a mere by-product. The intention was to examine the conceptual framework employed in recent discussions and, in view of its inadequacies, to propose some improved theoretical tools that may serve better in the analysis of the inflationary process of our time.

Analysis requires the following distinctions: an administered cost increase may be "equilibrating" in the sense that it merely "absorbs" a previously existing excess demand, or it may be "disequilibrating" in the sense that it creates an excess supply that may be prevented or removed only by an expansion of demand. To facilitate the analysis, three kinds of demand expansion are distinguished: *autonomous*, *in-duced*, and *supportive*. Likewise three kinds of cost increase are distinguished: *responsive*, *defensive*, and *aggressive*. Any one of these cost increases may be "administered"; but the responsive ones would also occur in a fully competitive market. Neither defensive not aggressive increases are in response to excess demand, and both therefore presuppose monopolistic power; defensive increases, however, attempt merely to restore previous real earnings of the group concerned, while aggressive increases raise real earnings above previous levels.

With the aid of these new concepts one can construct models of the inflationary process of various degrees of complexity. It may be possible to develop empirical tests for the choice of the model that fits best the recorded data of particular periods. The author believes that the price inflations of the periods 1945–48 and 1950–52 were of the demand-pull type, but that for 1955–59 a cost-push model would fit better. He tentatively suggests that wage-push was more effective than profit-push.

Finally the relation of inflation to increases in productivity was examined. The popular idea of a "non-inflationary" distribution of productivity gains by way of wage increases to the workers employed in the industries in which technology has advanced was found to be untenable. Imitative wage increases would lead to a brisk inflation. But some degree of inflation would occur even without such "spill-over" wage increases, because the distribution of the productivity gains to the workers or owners in the progressing industries would result in technological unemployment, and remedial full-employment measures would inflate the price level.

*HORACE J. DEPODWIN AND RICHARD T. SELDEN*

# Business Pricing Policies and Inflation[1]

*24* The notion that "administered prices" play a major role in determining the course of aggregate economic activity has served for nearly three decades as a rallying point for those who believe the economy is improperly dominated by business. Sired by Gardiner C. Means in the 1930's, the notion gained wide currency as an explanation of the sharp fall in employment and of the failure of the economy to snap back to full production.[2]

The popularity of the theory, however, was not due to the quality of evidence presented to support it. Quite the contrary, the major studies undertaken to test the theory dismissed it.[3] Yet the theory remained popular. Frederick C. Mills, in his introduction to Alfred C. Neal's study of the purported relationship between administered prices and recession, observed: "One of the serious disabilities from which the social sciences suffer arises from their failure to give prompt and effective quietus to useless, meaningless, even to false theories."[4]

Although the evidence failed to support his original theory, Means has recently revived the "administered price" theory and put it to another use. Whereas concentrated industries formerly were accused of aggravating the unemployment

---

[1] We acknowledge with gratitude helpful suggestions received on an early version of this paper from Charles R. Dean, Irvine Grossack, Ralph L. Nelson, Harvey S. Segal, George J. Stigler, and Hans Thorelli. Robert Harris provided valuable assistance.

[2] Means first stated his views in *Industrial Prices and Their Relative Inflexibility* (Senate Document No. 13, January 17, 1935 [Washington: Government Printing Office, 1935]). They were treated at greater length in National Resources Committee, *The Structure of the American Economy*, Part I. (Washington: Government Printing Office, 1939), prepared under the direction of Means.

Reprinted from the *Journal of Political Economy*, Vol. LXXI (1963), pp. 116–126 by permission of the authors and the University of Chicago Press. Copyright 1963 by the University of Chicago. Horace DePodwin and Richard Selden are respectively professors at New York University and Cornell University.

[3] See Alfred C. Neal, *Industrial Concentration and Price Inflexibility* (Washington: American Council on Public Affairs, 1942), p. vii; Edward S. Mason, "Price Inflexibility," *Review of Economics and Statistics*, May, 1938; Willard L. Thorp and Walter F. Crowder, *The Structure of Industry* (Temporary National Economic Committee, Monograph No. 27 [Washington: Government Printing Office, 1941]); and Rufus Tucker, "The Essential Historical Facts about 'Sensitive' and 'Administered' Prices," *The Annalist*, February 4, 1938.

[4] Neal, *op. cit.*, p. vii.

problem, because they allegedly maintained prices in the face of falling demand, Means now blames them for the inflationary trends in the United States during the 1950's. Prices that were supposed to have displayed downward inflexibility are now asserted to be characterized by upward flexibility, independently of demand and cost changes.

This paper has one modest aim: to present some empirical evidence that bears on Means's theory of inflation. For the most part we leave to others such interesting questions as the nature and extent of price administration, the degree to which Means's administrative inflation hypothesis is internally consistent, and the formulation of explanations of the inflation of the 1950's that can withstand empirical tests.[5] We are aware that "administered prices" may be relevant to theories of inflation other than the simple one propounded by Means. An example of such theorizing is Charles L. Schultze's study, "Recent Inflation in the United States."[6] While we find that the Schultze interpretation is no more convincing than the Means hypothesis, we emphasize that only the latter is tested here.

## Means's Evidence

Means has summarized his administrative inflation hypothesis in a series of bar charts, one of which we have reproduced (see Fig. 1 below).[7] In these charts Means shows percentage change in prices from 1953 to 1957 for each of the fifteen major industry groups that comprise the United States Bureau of Labor Statistics' Wholesale Price Index (WPI). The groups are ordered by amount of price change, those with the greatest rises being placed to the left. The vertical bars on Means's charts vary in width according to each group's weight in the WPI. The bars also vary in shading; groups in which production is

[5] In this context see George J. Stigler, "Administered Prices and Oligopolistic Inflation," *Journal of Business*, XXXV (1962), 1–13, where reference is made to an earlier draft of this paper.

[6] Study Paper No. 1, *Study of Employment, Growth, and Price Levels*, United States Congress, Joint Economic Committee, September 1959.

[7] Means developed these charts for use in a presentation before the Kefauver Committee in 1959 (see Subcommittee on Antitrust and Monopoloy, United States Senate, *Administered Prices, Hearings*, Part 9 [86th Cong., 1st sess. (1959)]). This presentation was revised and published privately for free distribution to economists and others under the title *Administrative Inflation and Public Policy* (Washington: Anderson Kramer Associates, 1959).

(according to Means) highly concentrated are shown in black, competitive groups in white, and "mixed" groups in gray. The concentrated groups (Means uses "concentrated" and "administration-dominated" interchangeably) fall to the left, the mixed groups occupy the middle ground, and the competitive groups are mainly on the right. In view of the greater price increases characteristic of the concentrated product groups and in view of their greater importance in the WPI, Means concludes that the inflation between 1953 and 1957 consisted fundamentally of—and was caused by—increases in administered prices.

> The administered price groups marked in black account for 85 per cent of the gross increase in the wholesale price index.
>
> If these groups had not gone up in price, the wholesale price index would have risen less than one per cent and, so far as the wholesale price index is concerned, there would have been no inflation. Anyone who thinks the recent inflation is not an administrative inflation had better study the record.[8]

Administrative inflation is a new phenomenon according to Means. In his testimony before the Senate Subcommittee on Antitrust and Monopoly he stated that the prior period, 1942–53, was a period of "classical" inflation characterized by excess demands with "market" or "competitive" prices rising faster than "administered" prices. The reverse is alleged to be characteristic of the period 1953–58. Means has concluded:

> It is because this type of inflation arises from the exercise of this administrative power over prices and wage rates that I have christened it an administrative inflation in contrast to the monetary inflation which comes from an excess of demand and in contrast to the inflation which accompanies the recovery from a serious depression.[9]

## Obvious Weaknesses

Even a cursory analysis of Means's statistical procedures reveals serious flaws. The most glaring defect is its extreme crudeness. The WPI is based on prices for about 1,900 items, and in its regular publications the BLS presents not only the overall price index but detailed indexes by 15 major product groups, 86 subgroups, 250 product

[8] *Administered Prices*, p. 4760.

[9] *Ibid.*, p. 4746. See also Gardiner C. Means's *Pricing Power and the Public Interest: A Study Based on Steel* (New York: Harper & Bros., 1962), pp. 112–50.

classes, and 1,789 individual items. (Risk of disclosure is the main factor accounting for the difference between the number of price series used in the WPI and the number of price series reported in BLS publications.) Despite the availability of finer classifications, Means used data only for the fifteen major product groups—groups that are far from homogeneous in terms of price behavior. Every major product group contains important examples of both flexible and inflexible prices and examples of items that are produced in concentrated as well as non-concentrated industries.[10]

Another major defect is the complete absence of objective criteria for assigning particular product categories to the three market groups— administered, mixed, or competitive. Despite the large body of evidence on market structures that might have been used, Means simply uses his own judgment to classify product categories along these lines. Even if one is willing to accept his judgment, one is never sure whether his subjective criteria are influenced mainly by degree of price flexibility or by degree of industrial concentration. Obviously the two need not coincide, though Means and his supporters tend to regard these criteria as the same.

Finally, it should be noted that Means accepts BLS price data at face value despite well-known shortcomings in them. Sellers often report catalogue prices to the BLS rather than actual prices prevailing in the market place. It has been amply demonstrated that there may be dramatic differences between the two. Actual prices are often far more flexible and may be substantially lower than catalogue prices. It appears that such departures from catalogue prices were considerably more common in 1957 and 1958 than in 1953, with the result that BLS data exaggerate the degree of price rise over this period.[11]

Still another limitation of BLS price series is their failure to take full account of product improvements over time, particularly for complex equipment. As product quality improves and as special features become standard, available price series may not reflect these changes. Therefore, price increases are overstated.[12]

Furthermore, one would expect these statistical shortcomings to show up more frequently in the sectors Means regards as having administered prices.

Thus, in addition to its extreme crudeness and its subjective nature, Means's analysis rests to an unknown extent on biased data.

## Concept of Administered Price

From the foregoing comments it is obvious that we must clarify the "administered price" concept before carrying out a test of Means' hypothesis. Three definitions follow:

Gardiner C. Means states: "I would define an administered price as a price which is set and maintained for a period of time and a series of transactions. That is a very precise definition."[13] And from earlier testimony: "The opposite of an administered price is a market price, a price that fluctuates on the basis of supply and demand as these forces are felt in the market."[14]

J. K. Galbraith relies on fewness of firms and price leadership: "In one form or another the firms of an industry will enjoy measurable discretion over their prices whenever the number of such firms in the particular market is fairly small or where one or two firms have a large

[10] See statement by Walter D. Fackler and Padraic P. Frucht in Subcommittee on Antitrust and Monopoly, Committee on the Judiciary, U.S. Senate, *Hearings*, Part 11 (86th Cong., 1st sess. [1959]), pp. 5221–83. It contains the results of a detailed examination of other aspects of Means's evidence and those interested in this subject should consider it in conjunction with this paper.

[11] See the evidence on heavy electrical equipment prices presented by Charles R. Dean and Horace J. DePodwin, "Product Variation and Price Indexes: A Case Study of Electrical Apparatus," in American Statistical Association, *1961 Proceedings of the Business and Economics Section* (Washington: American Statistical Association, 1961), pp. 271–79. For a wide range of other examples of discrepancies between reported and actual prices see Harry E. McAllister, "Statistical Factors Affecting the Stability

of the Wholesale and Consumers' Price Indexes," and John Flueck, "A Study in Validity: BLS Wholesale Price Quotations," Staff Papers 8 and 9, in Price Statistics Review Committee, *The Price Statistics of the Federal Government* (New York: National Bureau of Economic Research, 1961). The committee's conclusion on this point is worth quoting. "In summary, the evidence that the BLS company price quotations are not valid transaction prices is highly persuasive. The quotations now collected are at best the initial base for negotiation in many cases, and often represent only the hopes of sellers or the snares of inexperienced buyers" (*ibid.*, p. 70).

[12] See the work on hedonic price indexes by Z. Griliches, Staff Paper 3 in Price Statistics Review Committee, *op. cit.*; Dean and DePodwin *op. cit.*; and the earlier work of A. T. Court, "Hedonic Price Indexes with Automobile Examples," in *The Dynamics of Automobile Demand* (New York: General Motors Corp., 1939).

[13] *Administered Prices*, p. 4759.

[14] *Administered Prices, Hearings*, Part 1 (85th Cong., 1st sess.), p. 75.

share of that market and are able to exercise a strong price leadership that other firms follow."[15]

Jules Backman relates administered pricing to the process of price making: "When a price is established by a company and the company offers to meet all demands (within its capacity to do so) at that price, it is administered. This is so whether the company sets the price for one week or for four months."[16]

These quotations do not begin to cover the whole range of semantic confusion that has arisen over the term "administered prices." However, the Galbraith definition and the Means analysis as depicted by his charts suggest an operational basis for testing Means's theory. For this purpose we will assume that the "administrativeness" of a price varies directly with the degree of industrial concentration. From their testimony and writings, it would appear that industrial concentration is only *one* dimension for measuring the degree of price administration. It is apparently, however, the dimension that Means used subjectively in drawing up his charts of price changes for WPI products and its use seems consistent with the purpose at hand.

## Industrial Concentration and Amplitude of Price Change: Some New Evidence

The major pillar of the administrative inflation argument is that prices in concentrated markets are more susceptible to "administration" and to discretionary increase than prices in less concentrated markets. And, according to Means, the pattern of price increases in recent years "is clearly that of an administrative inflation—with the administered prices dominating the prices increases."[17] This statement, assuming that degree of price administration is measured by industrial concentration, presents a clear-cut testable hypothesis, although it is stated as though it were an incontrovertible fact. To test this hypothesis, the authors ran a large number of regressions between measures of industrial concentration for several hundred Standard Industrial Classification (SIC) product classes and percentage change in price between 1953 and 1959. The remainder of this paper will discuss the findings and the data on which they are based.

15 *Ibid.*, p. 34.
16 Jules Backman, "Administered Prices" in *Steel and Inflation, Fact or Fiction* (New York: U.S. Steel Co., 1958), p. 207.
17 *Administered Prices*, Part 9, p. 4759.

### The Data on Prices

The price indexes constructed for purposes of these tests are based on individual commodity price series available in BLS Wholesale Price Index monthly reports. The first step in the procedure consisted of constructing price indexes for as many five-digit SIC product classes as WPI price data allowed. A modified Laspeyres index form with 1954 Census of Manufactures value of shipment weights was used. The formula is:

$$I_{59,\,53} = \frac{\Sigma \dfrac{I_{59}}{I_{53}}(p_{54}q_{54})}{\Sigma\,(p_{54}q_{54})}$$

where

$I_{59}$ = BLS Wholesale Price Index for an individual product, July, 1959
$I_{53}$ = BLS Wholesale Price Index for an individual product, July, 1953
$p_{54}q_{54}$ = value of shipments, 1954.

The summation covers all seven-digit SIC product categories within the five-digit product class for which a price index could be constructed. $I_{59,53}$, then, is a weighted average percentage increase in prices from July, 1953, to July, 1959, for a five-digit SIC product class. Although 1953 weights might have been preferable, 1953 value-of-shipment figures are not available in the same detail as data for 1954. Since indexes were computed for individual five-digit SIC product classes, any bias introduced by the use of 1954 rather than 1953 value of shipment weights should be negligible inasmuch as the product classes are designed to consist of homogeneous groupings of products.

In all, price indexes were constructed for 322 five-digit product classes. Since there are over 1,000 classes in the SIC classification system, some explanation for the elimination of over 700 classes is warranted. The reasons are almost entirely related to problems of availability of data, and comparability of BLS and Census data.

There are no indications that the price series constructed and used in this study have any biases disadvantageous to the hypothesis being tested. Indeed, if there are biases they work in favor of the Means hypothesis. The average increase in the WPI (all commodities) between 1953 and 1959 was 7.8 per cent, whereas the aggregate index covering price series used in this study (using WPI weights) rose 11.5 per cent. Furthermore, as we indicated earlier, the use of prices reported to BLS rather than actual market prices probably introduces an additional bias in favor of the Means hypothesis.

Detailed discussion of the problems encountered in gathering and preparing the data, and of the coverage of the study, are relegated to the Appendix.

## The Data on Concentration

The data on concentration include conventional concentration ratios based on proportions of shipments accounted for by the four and eight largest producers plus unpublished "Herfindahl Indexes."[18] Conventional concentration ratios, for each of the 322 five-digit product classes for which price indexes were computed, were obtained from *Concentration in American Industry*, U.S. Senate, 1957, which presents such data based on the 1954 *Census of Manufactures*.

## The Time Period

Means's analyses of administrative inflation cover two time periods. One analysis traces increases in annual average prices for fifteen major WPI product groups between 1953 and 1957. The results appear in Figure 1. The second analysis traces increases in prices for fourteen major product groups and three subgroups, using annual average price for 1953 as the initial point and price in October, 1958, as the terminal point.

The analyses of this paper cover price changes over a single longer period, July, 1953–July, 1959, for the following reasons: (*a*) the longer period decreases the chance of random influences, (*b*) no historical occurrences between 1957 and 1959

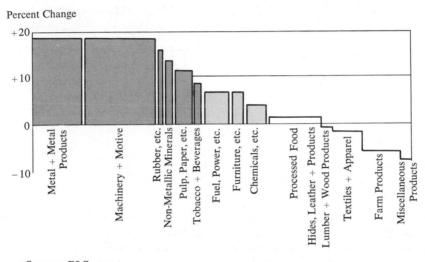

Source: BLS

Figure 1. Wholesale Price Changes by Product Groups, 1953-57 (Average Increase, 6.8 Per Cent).

Herfindahl concentration indexes based on 1954 data were made available for 159 five-digit product classes by Dr. Ralph L. Nelson, who had computed them in an independent study. Herfindahl's index, the sum of the squared ratios of each individual firm's shipments to total industry shipments, was used because it is generally superior to the conventional ratios. It includes all firms rather than an arbitrary number of leading producers and takes into account the distribution of market shares among firms. Thus, the Herfindahl index is both a more comprehensive and a more sensitive measure of concentration.

[18] Orris C. Herfindahl, "Concentration in the Steel Industry" (unpublished Ph.D. dissertation, Columbia University, 1950).

appear to invalidate this test of the Means thesis, (*c*) July in both years lay in a period of relatively high prosperity, and (*d*) the data extending into 1959 are more current and more relevant.

## Administered Price-Inflation Tests

1. *Results of five-digit product class tests.* To test the hypothesis that price rises have been greater in the more highly concentrated (that is, more "administered") industries, twelve regressions were run on the five-digit SIC class data. Equations of the form $Y = a + bx$ and $Y = a + bx + cx^2$ were fitted, where $Y$ is price increase and $x$ the index of concentration. The observations to be correlated were both unweighted and

## Table 1. Regression Equations and Correlation Coefficients for Change in Wholesale Prices and Indexes of Industrial Concentration, Five-Digit SIC Product Classes

| Type of Relation | Coefficient of Correlation (r) | DETERMINANTS OF REGRESSION EQUATION | | | Standard Error of Estimate |
|---|---|---|---|---|---|
| | | a | b | c | |
| | | Unweighted | | | |
| Linear: | | | | | |
| Concentration ratio: | | | | | |
| Four largest producers | .1210 | 107.5548 | .0895 | ... | 17.1707 |
| Eight largest producers | .0977 | 107.4719 | .0703 | ... | 17.2151 |
| Herfindahl Index | .0165 | 113.3588 | 2.5133 | ... | 17.9401 |
| Curvilinear: | | | | | |
| Concentration ratio: | | | | | |
| Four largest producers | .1231 | 106.1663 | .1571 | − .0007 | 17.1931 |
| Eight largest producers | .1077 | 103.6680 | .2247 | − .0013 | 17.2243 |
| Herfindahl Index | .1349 | 110.1565 | 48.1714 | − 84.9724 | 17.8354 |
| | | Weighted | | | |
| Linear: | | | | | |
| Concentration ratio: | | | | | |
| Four largest producers | .2969 | 100.3828 | .1969 | ... | 16.8251 |
| Eight largest producers | .2451 | 99.3930 | .1727 | ... | 17.0823 |
| Herfindahl Index | .2134 | 107.4726 | 25.0975 | ... | 16.7024 |
| Curvilinear: | | | | | |
| Concentration ratio: | | | | | |
| Four largest producers | .3021 | 103.9636 | .0327 | .0015 | 16.7964 |
| Eight largest producers | .2711 | 109.4846 | − .2235 | .0032 | 16.9597 |
| Herfindahl Index | .3074 | 193.1118 | 89.9973 | − 128.7604 | 16.2689 |

weighted by 1955 value of shipments.[19] (Weights derived from *1955 Annual Survey of Manufactures* were used since 1954 was a recession year, and many durable goods industries had inordinately low shipments.) The results of these twelve tests are shown in Table 1. Figure 2 shows a scatter plot of the five-digit concentration ratios and price indexes.

The wide dispersion of the plotted points across the entire chart, and particularly above the 50 per cent concentration level, suggests that the administered price-inflation thesis need not be considered seriously. Attempts to measure the degree of association yielded results that are equally unimpressive. The strongest of the relationships—that between per cent price changes and the Herfindahl index, weighted by

[19] The correlation coefficients with observations weighted by value of shipments in effect allow those product classes with more weight in the economy to exert a greater effect on the value of *r* and the regression equation. The authors have not stressed the weighted results in the text because they have some reservation about the statistical appropriateness of the technique.

1955 value of shipments—yielded a correlation coefficient of + .31. At most, degree of industrial concentration had a minor (about 9 per cent) influence on interproduct differences in price changes during the 1953–59 period. The relationships are even weaker for the other two indexes of concentration on a curvilinear basis. On an unweighted basis all three relationships are substantially weaker. There seems to be no indication that administered prices, as measured by degree of industrial concentration, increased appreciably more in the 1953–59 period than prices determined under supposedly more competitive conditions.

As a further test, the five-digit product class data were divided into groups depending on the first two digits of their SIC code. These basic manufacturing sectors—major industry groups— were then analyzed separately and for each sector where price data were available for at least twelve product classes, a separate linear regression was run between the price change and the eight-company concentration ratio. The results for eleven groups are shown in Table 2.

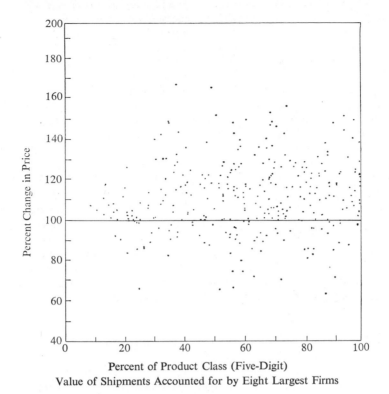

Figure 2. Changes in Wholesale Prices, 1953-59, and Degrees of Industrial Concentration in 1954 for 322 Five-Digit Product Classes.

## Table 2. Regression Equations and Correlation Coefficients for Change in Wholesale Prices and Eight-Company Concentration Ratio, Five-Digit SIC Product Classes, by Major Industry Group

| SIC Major Industry Group | Coefficient of Correlation (r) | DETERMINANTS OF REGRESSION EQUATION | | Value of t | No. of Classes |
|---|---|---|---|---|---|
| | | a | b | | |
| 20. Food and kindred products | −.0285 | 102.18 | −.0295 | .1778 | 41 |
| 22. Textile mill products | .2780 | 91.60 | .1020 | 1.2790 | 23 |
| 23. Apparel and other fabricated textile products | −.2156 | 103.17 | −.0512 | .9874 | 22 |
| 25. Furniture and fixtures | .3773 | 104.33 | .2095 | 1.4110 | 14 |
| 26. Paper and allied products | −.3627 | 120.31 | −.1887 | 1.2910 | 13 |
| 28. Chemicals and allied products | −.2291 | 123.07 | −.2150 | 1.4320 | 39 |
| 32. Stone, clay, and glass products | −.5549 | 157.83 | −.2493 | 2.6690 | 18 |
| 33. Primary metal industries | −.0924 | 131.99 | −.1177 | .3918 | 20 |
| 34. Fabricated metal products | .0466 | 120.05 | .0325 | .2190 | 24 |
| 35. Machinery, except electrical | −.2660 | 133.69 | −.1548 | 1.8720 | 48 |
| 36. Electrical machinery | .1849 | 97.39 | .2699 | .7525 | 18 |

Again, the results do not support Means's hypothesis. In fact, we observe here that there are more negative than positive correlations when the data are subdivided into major manufacturing industry groups. The strongest positive result is for Group 25, furniture and fixtures, $r = + .38$. Thus for the group that gives greatest support to the Means hypothesis, only 14 per cent of the variation in price can be accounted for by degree of concentration. Ironically, this major industry group is one of the least concentrated segments of manufacturing, using conventional concentration ratios.

When sample size is taken into account the coefficient of correlation for the furniture and fixtures group, $+ .38$, is not statistically significant. In fact, only one of these values of $r$ is significant at the .05 level, that for Group 32, which is negative. (Values of $t$, computed to test whether the coefficients of correlation for the product classes of the major industry group differ significantly from zero, appear in Table 2.)

2. *Results of four-digit industry class tests.* Price indexes for four-digit SIC industry classes were computed from the basic seven-digit price series using methods similar to those described for five-digit classes. These price indexes, along with concentration ratios for four-digit industry classes, formed the basis for eight further tests of the Means hypothesis. These tests were

identical to the tests summarized in Table 1, except they did not include the Herfindahl measure of concentration since it was not available for four-digit industry classes. The four-digit classes included numbered 155, or 34.7 per cent of all four-digit classes, accounted for 47.6 per cent of the total value of shipments for manufacturing. Table 3 summarizes the results of these additional tests. (These are not considered to rest on as good a statistical foundation as the tests on five-digit product classes reported above.)

Here again the coefficients of correlation are of low order, indicating that there is little relationship between change in price and degree of industrial concentration. Only about 10 per cent of the increase in price for these industry classes over this six-year period can be explained by degree of industrial concentration. On balance there is no reason to believe that industries characterized by high economic concentration realized substantially higher price increases than industries of lower concentration.

## Conclusions

The investigation reported in this paper was undertaken to test one simple hypothesis—that inflation since 1953 can be traced to industries with the power to "administer" their prices.

## Table 3. Regression Equations and Correlation Coefficients for Change in Wholesale Prices and Indexes of Industrial Concentration, Four-Digit SIC Industry Classes

| Type of Relation | Coefficient of Correlation (r) | DETERMINANTS OF REGRESSION EQUATION | | | Standard Error of Estimate |
|---|---|---|---|---|---|
| | | a | b | c | |
| Unweighted | | | | | |
| Linear: concentration ratio: | | | | | |
| Four largest producers | .1551 | 106.7751 | .1001 | ... | 14.8637 |
| Eight largest producers | .1490 | 106.1320 | .0886 | ... | 14.8779 |
| Curvilinear: concentration ratio: | | | | | |
| Four largest producers | .1558 | 106.1033 | .1380 | −.0004 | 14.9109 |
| Eight largest producers | .1609 | 102.3467 | .2590 | −.0015 | 14.8984 |
| Weighted | | | | | |
| Linear: concentration ratio: | | | | | |
| Four largest producers | .3150 | 101.5417 | .1964 | ... | 13.2879 |
| Eight largest producers | .2466 | 101.7209 | .1497 | ... | 13.5684 |
| Curvilinear: concentration ratio: | | | | | |
| Four largest producers | .3208 | 104.5942 | .0263 | .0018 | 13.2606 |
| Eight largest producers | .2532 | 105.3068 | −.0100 | .0015 | 13.5445 |

Using concentration as our measure of degree of administration and BLS wholesale price data to measure price increases, we found the following:

1. The relationship between price change and concentration for 322 five-digit SIC product classes is extremely low. Of eight possible tests made on these data, the best one can do is to explain 9 per cent of price variation by referring to economic concentration.

2. When the data on five-digit product classes are combined and analyzed by major industry groups, only one group yields a significant coefficient of correlation, and more than half of the groups yield negative coefficients.

3. On a four-digit industry class basis the best that one can do is to explain 10 per cent of price variation in terms of economic concentration.

The principal ground on which the administrative inflation hypothesis has gained widespread reputation is its repeated assertion. Despite the crude and subjective analyses presented to support it, the alleged relationship was used to advance proposals for federal legislation, and congressional hearings on these were held in the late 1950's. In the course of these hearings early in 1959, Means testified on the new version of his administered price theory and it was then that he unveiled his black and white bar charts.

While he took note of some of the inadequacies of his evidence he ignored contradictory findings with which Jules Backman had confronted him nearly two years earlier.[20]

The most recent presentation of the new theory —the administrative inflation hypothesis—appears in Means's new book, *Pricing and the Public Interest*.[21] It also lacks detailed documentation, as did earlier presentations, and its argumentation is no more convincing. In the light of the findings presented in this article, we suggest that it is time to put administrative inflation hypothesis to rest.

---

[20] In late 1957, both men addressed a conference on "Administered Prices, Administered Wages, and Inflation." Means advanced his theory, and Backman presented some compelling contrary evidence drawn from the metals and metal products component of the WPI. The results were summarized in a scatter diagram, and the scatter is highly dispersed (see Fig. 2).
See Jules Backman, "Administered Prices, Administered Wages, and Inflation," in *Current Business Studies*, No. 28 (published by the Society of Business Advisory Professions, Inc., in co-operation with the Graduate School of Business Administration of New York University, 1957). In the same publication is a talk by Means entitled "Administrative Inflation."

[21] *Op. cit.*

# General Policy Considerations

*V*ARIOUS MONETARY AND fiscal policies have long been advocated by economists as being means to eliminate or reduce conditions of inflation or unemployment that might arise in an economy. Despite this advocacy, the policies of the United States federal government and its central bank, the Federal Reserve System, have not always been appropriate and sometimes have even been detrimental to the existence of a prosperous, market-oriented economy.

In this first article of this section Paul Samuelson and Robert Solow discuss the cause of inflation and the problems associated with identifying these causes so that appropriate anti-inflation policies might be implemented. The Samuelson and Solow article emphasizing inflation is followed by an extract from the Council of Economic Advisors' 1965 annual report, which emphasizes unemployment and idle productive capacity. Then Robert H. Scott and John R. McKean consider the effect of inflation on an economy's rate of growth, and Robert Mundell discusses the policy implications of fixed exchange rates.

Next, Harry G. Johnson discusses some of the issues and considerations related to the implementation of monetary and fiscal policies, and the Council of Economic Advisors reviews United States experience since 1946 when Congress declared that it was the policy and responsibility of the federal government to maintain full employment.

In the final selection Milton Friedman proposes, as a result of the past failures of discretionary monetary and fiscal policies, a series of reforms designed to eliminate them.

*Part*

*7*

*PAUL A. SAMUELSON AND ROBERT M. SOLOW*

# Analytical Aspects of Anti-Inflation Policy

*25*

I

Just as generals are said to be always fighting the wrong war, economists have been accused of fighting the wrong inflation. Thus, at the time of the 1946–48 rise in American prices, much attention was focused on the successive rounds of wage increases resulting from collective bargaining. Yet probably most economists are now agreed that this first postwar rise in prices was primarily attributable to the pull of demand that resulted from wartime accumulations of liquid assets and deferred needs.

This emphasis on demand-pull was somewhat reinforced by the Korean war run-up of prices after mid-1950. But just by the time that cost-push was becoming discredited as a theory of inflation, we ran into the rather puzzling phenomenon of the 1955–58 upward creep of prices, which seemed to take place in the last part of the period despite growing overcapacity, slack labor markets,

slow real growth, and no apparent great buoyancy in over-all demand.

It is no wonder then that economists have been debating the possible causations involved in inflation: demand-pull versus cost-push; wage-push versus more general Lerner "seller's inflation"; and the new Charles Schultze theory of "demand-shift" inflation. We propose to give a brief survey of the issues. Rather than pronounce on the terribly difficult question as to exactly which is the best model to use in explaining the recent past and predicting the likely future, we shall try to emphasize the types of evidence which can help decide between the conflicting theories. And we shall be concerned with some policy implications that arise from the different analytical hypotheses.

## History of the Debate: The Quantity Theory and Demand-Pull

The preclassical economists grew up in an environment of secularly rising prices. And even prior to Adam Smith there had grown up the

Reprinted from the *American Economic Review: Papers and Proceedings*, Vol. L (1960), pp. 177–194, by permission of the authors and publisher. Paul Samuelson and Robert Solow are professors at the Massachusetts Institute of Technology.

belief in at least a simplified quantity theory. But it was in the neoclassical thought of Walras, Marshall, Fisher, and others that this special version of demand determination of the absolute level of money prices and costs reached its most developed form.

We can oversimplify the doctrine as follows. The real outputs, inputs, and relative prices of goods and factors can be thought of as determined by a set of competitive equations which are independent of the absolute level of prices. As in a barter system, the absolute level of all prices is indeterminate and inessential because of the "relative homogeneity" properties of these market relations. To fix the absolute scale factor, we can if we like bring in a neutral money. Such money, unlike coffee or soap, being valued only for what it will buy and not for its intrinsic utility, will be exactly doubled in demand if there is an exact doubling of all prices. Because of this important "scale homogeneity," fixing the total of such money will, when applied to our already determined real system of outputs, factors, and relative prices, fix the absolute level of all prices; and changes in the total of such money must necessarily correspond to new equilibria of absolute prices that have moved in exact proportion, with relative prices and all real magnitudes being quite unaffected.[1]

As Patinkin and others have shown, the above doctrines are rather oversimplified, for they do not fully analyze the intricacies involved in the demand for money; instead they ignore important (and predictable) changes in such proportionally coefficients as velocity of circulation. But by World War I, this particular, narrow version of demand-pull inflation had more or less triumphed. The wartime rise in prices was usually analyzed in terms of rises in the over-all money supply. And the postwar German inflation was understood by non-German economists in similar terms.

But not all economists ever agree on anything. Just as Tooke had eclectically explained the Napoleonic rise in prices partially in terms of the war-induced increase in tax, shipping, and other costs, so did Harold G. Moulton and others choose to attribute the World War I price rises to prior rises in cost of production. And it is not without significance that the great neoclassical Wicksell expressed in the last years of his life some misgivings over the usual version of wartime price movements, placing great emphasis on movements in money's velocity induced by wartime shortages of goods.

Of course, the neoclassical writers would not have denied the necessary equality of competitive costs and prices. But they would have regarded it as superficial to take the level of money costs as a predetermined variable. Instead, they would argue, prices and factor costs are simultaneously determinable in interdependent competitive markets; and if the level of over-all money supply were kept sufficiently in check, then the price level could be stabilized, with any increases in real costs or any decreases in output being offset by enough backward pressure on factor prices so as to leave final money costs and prices on the average unchanged.

Many writers have gone erroneously beyond the above argument to untenable conclusions such as the following: A rise in defense expenditure matched by, say, excise taxes cannot raise the price level if the quantity of money is held constant; instead it must result in enough decrease in wage and other factor costs to offset exactly the rise in tax costs. Actually, however, such a fiscal policy change could be interpreted as a reduction in the combined public and private thriftiness; with $M$ constant, it would tend to swell the volume of total spending, putting upward pressure on interest rates and inducing a rise in money velocity, and presumably resulting in a higher equilibrium level of prices. To roll back prices to their previous level would take, even within the framework of a strictly competitive neoclassical model, a determined reduction in previous money supply. (This illustrates the danger of going from the innocent hypothesis, that a balanced change in all prices might in the long run be consistent with no substantive changes in real relations, to an overly simple interpretation of a complicated change that is actually taking place in historical reality.)

While the above example of a tax-induced price rise that takes place within a strict neoclassical model might be termed a case of cost-push rather than demand-pull, it does not really represent quite the same phenomena that we shall meet in our later discussion of cost-push. This can perhaps be most easily seen from the remark that, if one insisted on holding prices steady, con-

---

[1] But as Hume had early recognized, the periods of rising prices seemed to give rise to at least transient stimulus to the economy as active profit seekers gained an advantage at the expense of the more inert fixed-income, creditor, and wage sectors. The other side of this Hume thesis is perhaps exemplified by the fact that the post-Civil War decades of deflation were also periods of strong social unrest and of relatively weak booms and long periods of heavier-than-average depressions—as earlier National Bureau studies have suggested.

ventional demand reduction methods would work very well, within the neoclassical model, to offset such cost-push.

*Demand-Pull à la Keynes.* Aside from the neoclassical quantity theory, there is a second version of demand-pull associated with the theories of Keynes. Before and during the Great Depression, economists had become impressed with the institutional frictions and rigidities that made for downward inflexibilities in wages and prices and which made any such deflationary movements socially painful. Keynes's *General Theory* can, if we are willing to oversimplify, be thought of as a systematic model which uses downward inflexibility of wages and prices to convert any reduction in money spending into a real reduction in output and employment rather than a balanced reduction in all prices and factor costs. (This is overly simple for at least the following reasons: in the pessimistic, depression version of some Keynesians, a hyperdeflation of wages and prices would not have had substantive effects in restoring employment and output, because of infinite elasticity of liquidity preference and/or zero elasticity of investment demand; in the general form of the *General Theory*, and particularly after Pigou effects of the real value of money had been built in, if you could engineer a massive reduction in wages and costs, there would have been some stimulating effects on consumption, investment, and on real output; finally, a careful neoclassical theory, which took proper account of rigidities and which analyzed induced shifts of velocity in a sophisticated way, might also have emerged with similar valid conclusions.)

While the Keynesian theories can be said to differ from the neoclassical theories with respect to analysis of deflation, Keynes himself was willing to asume that attainment of full employment would make prices and wages flexible upward. In *How to Pay for the War* (1939), he developed a theory of inflation which was quite like the neoclassical theory in its emphasis upon the demand-pull of aggregate spending even though it differed from that theory in its emphasis on total spending flow rather than on the stock of money. His theory of "demanders' inflation" stemmed primarily from the fact that government plus investors plus consumers want, in real terms among them, more than 100 per cent of the wartime or boomtime available produceable output. So prices have to rise to cheat the slow-to-spend of their desired shares. But the price rise closes the inflationary gap only temporarily, as the higher price level breeds higher incomes all

around and the real gap reopens itself continually. And so the inflation goes on, at a rate determined by the degree of shifts to profit, the rapidity and extent of wage adjustments to the rising cost of living, and ultimately by the extent to which progressive tax receipts rise enough to close the gap. And, we may add, that firmness by the central bank in limiting the money supply might ultimately so increase credit tightness and so lower real balances as to bring consumption and investment spending into equilibrium with available civilian resources at some higher plateau of prices.

*Cost-Push and Demand-Shift Theories of Inflation.* In its most rigid form, the neoclassical model would require that wages fall whenever there is unemployment of labor and that prices fall whenever excess capacity exists in the sense that marginal cost of the output that firms sell is less than the prices they receive. A more eclectic model of imperfect competition in the factor and commodity markets is needed to explain the fact of price and wage rises before full employment and full capacity have been reached.

Similarly, the Keynes model, which assumes stickiness of wages even in the face of underemployment equilibrium, rests on various assumptions of imperfect competition. And when we recognize that, considerably before full employment of labor and plants has been reached, modern prices and wages seem to show a tendency to drift upward irreversibly, we see that the simple Keynesian system must be modified even further in the direction of an imperfect competition model.

Now the fact that an economic model in some degree involves imperfect competition does not necessarily imply that the concepts of competitive markets give little insight into the behavior of relative prices, resources allocations, and profitabilities. To some degree of approximation, the competitive model may cast light on these important real magnitudes, and for this purpose we might be content to use the competitive model. But to explain possible cost-push inflation, it would seem more economical from the very beginning to recognize that imperfect competition is the essence of the problem and to drop the perfect competition assumptions.

Once this is done, we recognize the qualitative possibility of cost-push inflation. Just as wages and prices may be sticky in the face of unemployment and overcapacity, so may they be pushing upward beyond what can be explained in terms of levels and shifts in demand. But to what degree these elements are important in explaining price behavior of any period becomes an important quantitative question. It is by no means always to be expected that by observing an economy's behavior over a given period will we be able to make a very good separation of its price rise into demand and cost elements. We simply cannot perform the controlled experiments necessary to make such a separation; and Mother Nature may not have economically given us the scatter and variation needed as a substitute for controlled experiments if we are to make approximate identification of the causal forces at work.

Many economists have argued that cost-push was important in the prosperous 1951–53 period, but that its effects on average prices were masked by the drop in flexible raw material prices. But again in 1955–58, it showed itself despite the fact that in a good deal of this period there seemed little evidence of over-all high employment and excess demand. Some holders of this view attribute the push to wage boosts engineered unilaterally by strong unions. But others give as much or more weight to the co-operative action of all sellers—organized and unorganized labor, semimonopsonistic managements, oligopolistic sellers in imperfect commodity markets—who raise prices and costs in an attempt by each to maintain or raise his share of national income, and who, among themselves, by trying to get more than 100 per cent of the available output, create "seller's inflation."

A variant of cost-push is provided by Charles Schultze's "demand-shift" theory of inflation. Strength of demand in certain sectors of the economy—e.g., capital goods industries in 1955–57—raises prices and wages there. But elsewhere, even though demand is not particularly strong, downward inflexibility keeps prices from falling, and market power may even engineer a price-wage movement imitative in a degree of the sectors with strong demand. The result is an upward drift in average prices—with the suggestion that monetary and fiscal policies restrictive enough to prevent an average price rise would have to be so very restrictive as to produce a considerable level of unemployment and a significant drop in production.

## II

### Truths and Consequences: The Problem of Identification

The competing (although imperfectly competing) theories of inflation appear to be genuinely different hypotheses about observable facts. In that case one ought to be able to distinguish empirically between cost and demand inflation. What are the earmarks? If I believe in cost-push, what should I expect to find in the facts that I would not expect to find were I a believer in demand-pull? The last clause is important. It will not do to point to circumstances which will accompany any inflation, however caused. A test must have what statisticians call power against the main alternative hypotheses.

Trite as these remarks may seem, they need to be made. The clichés of popular discussion fall into the trap again and again. Although they have been trampled often enough by experts, the errors revive. We will take the time to point the finger once more. We do this because we want to go one stop further and argue that this problem of identification is exceedingly difficult. What appear at first to be subtle and reliable ways of distinguishing cost-induced from demand-induced inflation turn out to be far from airtight. In fact we are driven to the belief that aggregate data, recording the *ex post* details of completed transactions, may in most circumstances be quite insufficient. It may be necessary first to disaggregate.

### Common Fallacies

The simplest mistake—to be found in almost any newspaper discussion of the subject—is the belief that if money wages rise faster than productivity, we have a sure sign of cost-inflation. Of course the truth is that in the purest of excess-demand inflation wages will rise faster than productivity; the only alternative is for the full increase in the value of fixed output to be siphoned off into profits, without this spilling over into the labor market to drive wages up still further. This error is sometimes mixed with the belief that it is possible over long periods for industries with rapid productivity increase to pay higher and increasingly higher wages than those where output per man-hour grows slowly. Such a persistent and growing differential is likely eventually to alter the skill- or quality-mix of the labor force in the different industries, which casts doubt on the original productivity comparison.

One sometimes sees statements to the effect that increases in expenditure more rapid than increases in real output necessarily spell demand inflation. It is simple arithmetic that expenditure outrunning output by itself spells only price increases and provides no evidence at all about the source or cause of the inflation. Much of the talk about "too much money chasing too few goods" is of this kind.

A more solemn version of the fallacy goes: An increase in expenditure can come about only through an increase in the stock of money or an increase in the velocity of circulation. Therefore the only possible causes of inflation are $M$ and $V$ and we need look no further.

### Further Difficulties

It is more disconcerting to realize that even some of the empirical tests suggested in the professional literature may have little or no cutting power in distinguishing cost from demand inflation.

One thinks automatically of looking at the timing relationships. Do wage increases seem to precede price increases? Then the general rise in prices is caused by the wage-push. Do price increases seem to precede wage increases? Then more likely the inflation is of the excess-demand variety, and wages are being pulled up by a brisk demand for labor or they are responding to prior increases in the cost of living. There are at least three difficulties with this argument. The first is suggested by replacing "wage increase" by "chicken" and "price increase" by "egg." The trouble is that we have no normal initial standard from which to measure, no price level which has always existed and to which everyone has adjusted; so that a wage increase, if one occurs, must be autonomous and not a response to some prior change in the demand for labor. As an illustration of the difficulty of inference, consider average hourly earnings in the basic steel industry. They rose, relative to all manufacturing from 1950 on, including some periods when labor markets were not tight. Did this represent an autonomous wage-push? Or was it rather a delayed adjustment to the decline in steel wages relative to all manufacturing, which took place during the war, presumably as a consequence of the differential efficiency of wage control? And why should we take 1939 or 1941 as a standard for relative wages? And so on.

A related problem is that in a closely interdependent economy, effects can precede causes. Prices may begin to ease up because wage rates are expected to. And more important, as wage and price increases ripple through the economy, aggregation may easily distort the apparent timing relations.

But even if we could find the appearance of a controlled experiment, if after a period of stability in both we were to notice a wage increase to a new plateau followed by a price increase, what could we safely conclude? It would be immensely tempting to make the obvious diagnosis of wage-push. But consider the following hypothetical chain of events: Prices in imperfect commodity markets respond only to changes in costs. Labor markets are perfectly competitive in effect, and the money wage moves rapidly in response to shifts in the demand for labor. So any burst of excess demand, government expenditure, say, would cause an increased demand for labor; wages would be pulled up; and only then would prices of commodities rise in response to the cost increase. So the obvious diagnosis might be wrong. In between, if we were clever, we might notice a temporary narrowing of margins, and with this information we might piece together the story.

Consider another sophisticated inference. In a single market, price may rise either because the demand curve shifts to the right or because the supply curve shifts to the left in consequence of cost increases. But in the first case, output should increase; in the second case, decline. Could we not reason, then, that if prices rise, sector by sector, with outputs, demand-pull must be at work? Very likely we can, but not with certainty. In the first place, as Schultze has argued, it is possible that certain sectors face excess demand, without there being aggregate pressure; those sectors will indeed show strong price increases and increases in output (or pressure on capacity). But in a real sense, the source of inflation is the failure of other sectors, in which excess capacity develops, to decrease their prices sufficiently. And this may be a consequence of "administered pricing," rigid markups, rigid wages and all the paraphernalia of the "new" inflation.

To go deeper, the reasoning we are scrutinizing may fail because it is illegitimate, even in this industry-by-industry way, to use partial equilibrium reasoning. Suppose wages rise. We are led to expect a decrease in output. But in the modern world, all or most wages are increasing. Nor is this the first time they have done so. And in the past, general wage and price increases have not resulted in any decrease in aggregate real demand—perhaps the contrary. So that even in a single industry supply and demand curves may not be independent. The shift in costs is accompanied by, indeed may bring about, a compensating shift in the subjectively-viewed demand curve facing the industry. And so prices may rise with no decline and possibly an increase in output. If there is anything in this line of thought, it may be that one of the important causes of inflation is—inflation.

## The Need for Detail

In these last few paragraphs we have been arguing against the attempt to diagnose the source of inflation from aggregates. We have also suggested that sometimes the tell-tale symptoms can be discovered if we look not at the totals but at the parts. This suggestion gains force when we recognize, as we must, that the same general price increase can easily be the consequence of different causes in different sectors. A monolithic theory may have its simplicity and style riddled by exceptions. Is there any reason, other than a desire for symmetry, for us to believe that the same reasoning must account for the above-average increase in the price of services and the above-average increase in the price of machinery since 1951 or since 1949? Public-utility prices undoubtedly were held down during the war, by the regulatory process; and services ride along on income-elastic demand accompanied by a slower-than-average recorded productivity increase. A faster-than-average price increase amounts to the corrective relative-price change one would expect. The main factor in the machinery case, according to a recent Joint Economic Committee study, appears to have been a burst of excess demand occasioned by the investment boom of the mid-fifties. And to give a still third variant, Eckstein and Fromm in another Joint Economic Committee study suggest that the above-average rise in the wages of steel-workers and the prices of steel products took place in the face of a somewhat less tight labor and product market than in machinery. They attribute it to a joint exercise of market power by the union and the industry. Right or wrong, it is mistaken theoretical tactics to deny this possibility on the grounds that it cannot account for the price history in other sectors.

## Some Things It Would Be Good to Know

There are at least two classical questions which are relevant to our problem and on which surprisingly little work has been done: One is the behavior of real demand under inflationary conditions and the other is the behavior of money wages with respect to the level of employment. We comment briefly on these two questions because there seems to us to be some doubt that ordinary reversible behavior equations can be found, and this very difficulty points up an important question we have mentioned earlier: that a period of high demand and rising prices molds attitudes, expectations, even institutions in such a way as to bias the future in favor of further inflation. Unlike some other economists, we do not draw the firm conclusion that unless a firm stop is put, the rate of price increase must accelerate. We leave it as an open question: It may be that creeping inflation leads only to creeping inflation.

The standard way for an inflationary gap to burn itself out short of hyperinflation is for the very process of inflation to reduce real demands. The mechanisms, some dubious, some not, are well known: the shift to profit, real-balance effects, tax progression, squeeze on fixed incomes. If price and wage increases have this effect, then a cost-push inflation in the absence of excess demand inflicts unemployment and excess capacity on the system. The willingness to bear the reduced real demand is a measure of the imperfectness of markets permitting the cost-push. But suppose real demands do not behave in this way? Suppose a wage-price rise has no effect on real demand, or a negligible one, or even a slight positive one? Then not only will the infliction not materialize, but the whole distinction between cost-push and demand-pull begins to evaporate. But is this possible? The older quantity theorists would certainly have denied it; but the increase in velocity between 1955 and 1957 would have surprised an older quantity theorist.

We do not know whether real demand behaves this way or not. But we think it important to realize that the more the recent past is dominated by inflation, by high employment, and by the belief that both will continue, the more likely is it that the process of inflation will preserve or even increase real demand, or the more heavily the monetary and fiscal authorities may have to bear down on demand in the interests of price stabilization. Real-income consciousness is a powerful force. The pressure on real balances from high prices will be partly relieved by the expectation of rising prices, as long as interest rates in an imperfect capital market fail to keep pace. The same expectations will induce schoolteachers, pensioners, and others to try to devise institutions to protect their real incomes from erosion by higher prices. To the extent that they succeed, their real demands will be unimpaired. As the fear of prolonged unemployment disappears and the experience of past full employment builds up accumulated savings, wage earners may also maintain their real expenditures; and the same forces may substantially increase the marginal propensity to spend out of profits, including retained earnings. If there is anything to this line of thought, the empirical problem of verification may be very difficult, because much of the experience of the past is irrelevant to the hypothesis. But it would be good to know.

### The Fundamental Phillips Schedule Relating Unemployment and Wage Changes

Consider also the question of the relation between money wage changes and the degree of unemployment. We have A. W. Phillips' interesting paper on the U.K. history since the Civil War (our Civil War, that is!). His findings are remarkable, even if one disagrees with his interpretations.

In the first place, the period 1861–1913, during which the trade-union movement was rather weak, shows a fairly close relationship between the per cent change in wage rates and the fraction of the labor force unemployed. Due allowance must be made for sharp import-price-induced changes in the cost of living, and for the normal expectation that wages will be rising faster when an unemployment rate of 5 per cent is reached on the upswing than when it is reached on the downswing. In the second place, with minor exceptions, the same relationship that fits for 1861–1913 also seems to fit about as well for 1913–48 and 1948–57. And finally Phillips concludes that the money wage level would stabilize with 5 per cent unemployment; and the rate of increase of money wages would be held down to the 2–3 per cent rate of productivity increase with about $2\frac{1}{2}$ per cent of the labor force unemployed.

Strangely enough, no comparably careful study has been made for the U.S. Garbarino's 1950 note is hardly a full-scale analysis, and Schultze's treatment in his first-class Joint Committee monograph is much too casual. There is some evidence that the U.S. differs from the U.K. on at least two counts. If there is any such relationship characterizing the American labor market, it may have shifted somewhat in the last fifty to sixty years. Secondly, there is a suggestion that in this country it might take 8 to 10 per cent unemployment to stabilize money wages.

But would it take 8 to 10 per cent unemployment forever to stabilize the money wage? Is not this kind of relationship also one which depends heavily on remembered experience? We suspect that this is another way in which a past characterized by rising prices, high employment, and mild, short recessions is likely to breed an inflationary

bias—by making the money wage more rigid downward, maybe even perversely inclined to rise during recessions on the grounds that things will soon be different.

There may be no such relation for this country. If there is, why does it not seem to have the same degree of long-run invariance as Phillips' curve for the U.K.? What geographical, economic, sociological facts account for the difference between the two countries? Is there a difference in labor mobility in the two countries? Do the different tolerances for unemployment reflect differences in income level, union organization, or what? What policy decisions might conceivably lead to a decrease in the critical unemployment rate at which wages begin to rise or to rise too fast? Clearly a careful study of this problem might pay handsome dividends.

### III

### A Closer Look at the American Data

In spite of all its deficiencies, we think the accompanying scatter diagram in Figure 1 is useful. Where it does not provide answers, it at least asks interesting questions. We have plotted the yearly percentage changes of average hourly earnings in manufacturing, including supplements (Rees's data) against the annual average percentage of the labor force unemployed.

The first defect to note is the different coverages represented in the two axes. Duesenberry has argued that postwar wage increases in manufacturing on the one hand and in trade, services, etc., on the other, may have quite different explanations: union power in manufacturing and simple excess demand in the other sectors. It is probably true that if we had an unemployment rate for manufacturing alone, it would be somewhat higher during the postwar years than the aggregate figure shown. Even if a qualitative statement like this held true over the whole period, the increasing weight of services in the total might still create a bias. Another defect is our use of annual increments and averages, when a full-scale study would have to look carefully into the nuances of timing.

A first look at the scatter is discouraging; there are points all over the place. But perhaps one can notice some systematic effects. In the first place, the years from 1933 to 1941 appear to be *sui generis*: money wages rose or failed to fall in the face of massive unemployment. One may attribute this to the workings of the New Deal (the 20 per cent wage increase of 1934 must

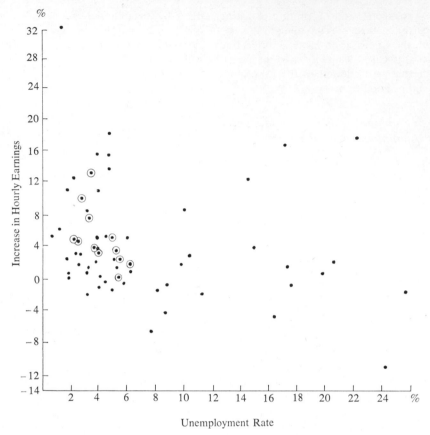

Figure 1. Phillips Scatter Diagram for U.S. (The Circled Points Are for Recent Years).

represent the NRA codes); or alternatively one could argue that by 1933 much of the unemployment had become structural, insulated from the functioning labor market, so that in effect the vertical axis ought to be moved over to the right. This would leave something more like the normal pattern.

The early years of the first World War also behave atypically although not so much so as 1933–39. This may reflect cost-of-living increases, the rapidity of the increase in demand, a special tightness in manufacturing, or all three.

But the bulk of the observations—the period between the turn of the century and the first war, the decade between the end of that war and the Great Depression, and the most recent ten or twelve years—all show a rather consistent pattern. Wage rates do tend to rise when the labor market is tight, and the tighter the faster. What is most interesting is the strong suggestion that the relation, such as it is, has shifted upward slightly but noticeably in the forties and fifties. On the one hand, the first decade of the century and the twenties seem to fit the same pattern. Manufacturing wages seem to stabilize absolutely when

4 or 5 per cent of the labor force is unemployed; and wage increases equal to the productivity increase of 2 to 3 per cent per year is the normal pattern at about 3 per cent unemployment. This is not so terribly different from Phillips' results for the U.K., although the relation holds there with a greater consistency. We comment on this below.

On the other hand, from 1946 to the present, the pattern is fairly consistent and consistently different from the earlier period. The annual unemployment rate ranged only narrowly, from 2.5 per cent in 1953 to 6.2 per cent in 1958. Within that range, as might be expected, wages rose faster the lower the unemployment rate. But one would judge now that it would take more like 8 per cent unemployment to keep money wages from rising. And they would rise at 2 to 3 per cent per year with 5 or 6 per cent of the labor force unemployed.

It would be overhasty to conclude that the relation we have been discussing represents a reversible supply curve for labor along which an aggregate demand curve slides. If that were so, then movements along the curve might be dubbed standard demand-pull, and shifts of the curve might represent the institutional changes on which cost-push theories rest. The apparent shift in our Phillips' curve might be attributed by some economists to the new market power of trade-unions. Others might be more inclined to believe that the expectation of continued full employment, or at least high employment, is enough to explain both the shift in the supply curve, if it is that, and the willingness of employers (conscious that what they get from a work force is partly dependent on its morale and its turnover) to pay wage increases in periods of temporarily slack demand.

This latter consideration, however, casts real doubt on the facile identification of the relationship as merely a supply-of-labor phenomenon. There are two parties to a wage bargain.

## U.S. and U.K. Compared

A comparison of the American position with Phillips' findings for the U.K. is interesting for itself and also as a possible guide to policy. Anything which will shift the relationship downward decreases the price in unemployment that must be paid when a policy is followed of holding down the rate of wage and price increase by pressure on aggregate demand.

One possibility is that the trade-union leadership is more "responsible" in the U.K.; indeed the postwar policy of wage restraint seems visible in Phillips' data. But there are other interpretations. It is clear that the more fractionated and imperfect a labor market is, the higher the over-all excess supply of labor may have to be before the average wage rate becomes stable and the less tight the relation will be in any case. Even a touch of downward inflexibility (and trade-unionism and administered wages surely mean at least this) will make this immobility effect more pronounced. It would seem plausible that the sheer geographical compactness of the English economy makes its labor market more perfect than ours in this sense. Moreover, the British have pursued a more deliberate policy of relocation of industry to mop up pockets of structural unemployment.

This suggests that any governmental policy which increases the mobility of labor (geographical and industrial) or improves the flow of information in the labor market will have anti-inflationary effects as well as being desirable for other reasons. A quicker but in the long run probably less efficient approach might be for the government to direct the regional distribution of

its expenditures more deliberately in terms of the existence of local unemployment and excess capacity.

The English data show a quite clearly non-linear (hyperbolic) relation between wage changes and unemployment, reflecting the much discussed downward inflexibility. Our American figures do not contradict this, although they do not tell as plain a story as the English. To the extent that this nonlinearity exists, as Duesenberry has remarked, a given average level of unemployment over the cycle will be compatible with a slower rate of wage increase (and presumably price increase) the less wide the cyclical swings from top to bottom.

A less obvious implication of this point of view is that a deliberate low-pressure policy to stabilize the price level may have a certain self-defeating aspect. It is clear from experience that interregional and inter-industrial mobility of labor depends heavily on the pull of job opportunities elsewhere, more so than on the push of local unemployment. In effect the imperfection of the labor market is increased, with the consequences we have sketched.

## IV

We have concluded that it is not possible on the basis of a priori reasoning to reject either the demand-pull or cost-push hypothesis, or the variants of the latter such as demand-shift. We have also argued that the empirical identifications needed to distinguish between these hypotheses may be quite impossible from the experience of macrodata that is available to us; and that, while use of microdata might throw additional light on the problem, even here identification is fraught with difficulties and ambiguities.

Nevertheless, there is one area where policy interest and the desire for scientific understanding for its own sake come together. If by deliberate policy one engineered a sizable reduction of demand or refused to permit the increase in demand that would be needed to preserve high employment, one would have an experiment that could hope to distinguish between the validity of the demand-pull and the cost-push theory as we would operationally reformulate those theories. If a small relaxation of demand were followed by great moderations in the march of wages and other costs so that the social cost of a stable price index turned out to be very small in terms of sacrificed high-level employment and output, then the demand-pull hypothesis would have received its most important confirmation. On the other hand, if mild demand repression checked cost and price increases not at all or only mildly, so that considerable unemployment would have to be engineered before the price level updrift could be prevented, then the cost-push hypothesis would have received its most important confirmation. If the outcome of this experience turned out to be in between these extreme cases—as we ourselves would rather expect—then an element of validity would have to be conceded to both views; and dull as it is to have to embrace eclectic theories, scholars who wished to be realistic would have to steel themselves to doing so.

Of course, we have been talking glibly of a vast experiment. Actually such an operation would be fraught with implications for social welfare. Naturally, since they are confident that it would be a success, the believers in demand-pull ought to welcome such an experiment. But, equally naturally, the believers in cost-push would be dead set against such an engineered low-pressure economy, since they are equally convinced that it will be a dismal failure involving much needless social pain. (A third school, who believes in cost-push but think it can be cured or minimized by orthodox depressing of demand, think that our failure to make this experiment would be fraught with social evil by virtue of the fact that they expect a creep in prices to snowball into a trot and then a gallop.)

Our own view will by now have become evident. When we translate the Phillips' diagram showing the American pattern of wage increase against degree of unemployment into a related diagram showing the different levels of unemployment that would be "needed" for each degree of price level change, we come out with guesses like the following:

1. In order to have wages increase at no more than the $2\frac{1}{2}$ per cent per annum characteristic of our productivity growth, the American economy would seem on the basis of twentieth-century and postwar experience to have to undergo something like 5 to 6 per cent of the civilian labor force's being unemployed. That much unemployment would appear to be the cost of price stability in the years immediately ahead.

2. In order to achieve the nonperfectionist's goal of high enough output to give us no more than 3 per cent unemployment, the price index might have to rise by as much as 4 to 5 per cent per year. That much price rise would seem to be

the necessary cost of high employment and production in the years immediately ahead.

All this is shown in our price-level modification of the Phillips curve, Figure 2. The point $A$, corresponding to price stability, is seen to involve about $5\frac{1}{2}$ per cent unemployment; whereas the point $B$, corresponding to 3 per cent unemployment, is seen to involve a price rise of about $4\frac{1}{2}$ per cent per annum. We rather expect that the

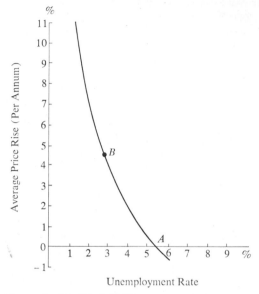

Figure 2. Modified Phillips Curve for U.S. This Shows the Menu of Choice Between Different Degrees of Unemployment and Price Stability, as Roughly Estimated from Last Twenty-Five Years of American Data.

tug of war of politics will end us up in the next few years somewhere in between these selected points. We shall probably have some price rise and some excess unemployment.

Aside from the usual warning that these are simply our best guesses we must give another caution. All of our discussion has been phrased in short-run terms, dealing with what might happen in the next few years. It would be wrong, though, to think that our Figure 2 menu that relates obtainable price and unemployment behavior will maintain its same shape in the longer run. What we do in a policy way during the next few years might cause it to shift in a definite way.

Thus, it is conceivable that after they had produced a low-pressure economy, the believers in demand-pull might be disappointed in the short run; i.e., prices might continue to rise even though unemployment was considerable. Nevertheless, it might be that the low-pressure demand would so act upon wage and other expectations as to shift the curve downward in the longer run—so that over a decade, the economy might enjoy higher employment with price stability than our present-day estimate would indicate.

But also the opposite is conceivable. A low-pressure economy might build up within itself over the years larger and larger amounts of structural unemployment (the reverse of what happened from 1941 to 1953 as a result of strong war and postwar demands). The result would be an upward shift of our menu of choice, with more and more unemployment being needed just to keep prices stable.

Since we have no conclusive or suggestive evidence on these conflicting issues, we shall not attempt to give judgment on them. Instead we venture the reminder that, in the years just ahead, the level of attained growth will be highly correlated with the degree of full employment and high-capacity output.

But what about the longer run? If the per annum rate of technical progress were about the same in a low- and high-pressure economy, then the initial loss in output in going to the low-pressure state would never be made up; however, in relative terms, the initial gap would not grow but would remain constant as time goes by. If a low-pressure economy could succeed in improving the efficiency of our productive factors, some of the loss of growth might be gradually made up and could in long enough time even be more than wiped out. On the other hand, if such an economy produced class warfare and social conflict and depressed the level of research and technical progress, the loss in growth would be compounded in the long run.

A final disclaimer is in order. We have not here entered upon the important question of what feasible institutional reforms might be introduced to lessen the degree of disharmony between full employment and price stability. These could of course involve such wide-ranging issues as direct price and wage controls, antiunion and antitrust legislation, and a host of other measures hopefully designed to move the American Phillips' curves downward and to the left.

# The Gap Between Actual and Potential GNP

*26* The economy today has room for—and need for—more employment and more production. The Employment Act's objectives of "maximum production" and "maximum employment" can only be achieved together. Unemployment is wasted manpower. Moreover, idle men are generally accompanied by idle machines. Thus, when the economy is marked by excessive unemployment, it is producing below its full potential. The distance between our actual and our potential gross national product (GNP) is one measure of the cost of high unemployment to the whole Nation.

The potential GNP of the U.S. economy measures the volume of goods and services that our economy could produce if the unemployment rate were at the interim target of 4 per cent. Potential GNP cannot actually be observed when unemployment is above 4 per cent; and to estimate it is an inherently difficult task. Even the best use of available data and of statistical and economic techniques will leave a margin of error in the calculation. Nevertheless, decisions on policies to stimulate or restrain the over-all

level of economic activity require a judgment on the gap between current and potential production.

The Council has continuously examined the current and prospective growth of potential in light of new data and emerging developments in the economy. In its past three Annual Reports, the growth of potential GNP since mid-1955 has been approximated by a trend line rising at a rate of $3\frac{1}{2}$ per cent a year. It now appears that the growth of potential has recently stepped up: A real growth rate of actual GNP somewhat greater than $3\frac{1}{2}$ per cent has been required to prevent a rise in the unemployment rate.

The precise causes of the recent pattern are not definitely established. We may have already begun to experience a more rapid growth of the labor force; the growth trend of productivity may have increased modestly; or these two factors may have operated in combination. Nor is it yet clear just when the recent pattern began. Despite these unsettled issues, the best estimate of recent potential growth must be placed somewhat above $3\frac{1}{2}$ per cent and below 4 per cent. In line with this conclusion, Figure 1 shows the growth rate of potential GNP as $3\frac{1}{2}$ per cent from 1955 through 1962 and $3\frac{3}{4}$ per cent thereafter.

Reprinted from the 1965 *Annual Report of the Council of Economic Advisors,* pp. 81–84.

Potential GNP includes the output that could be produced by people who would leave the ranks of the unemployed and also by many who are not currently counted in the labor force but who would be at work if unemployment were reduced to 4 per cent. Some people who are ready and willing to work have concluded that jobs are not available; they are not actively seeking employment and are therefore not counted as unemployed. According to past evidence, such "hidden unemployment" is concentrated among women, young males, and older men. Men in the 25–54 age bracket have a permanent attachment to the labor force; their labor force participation rates remain close to 97 per cent regardless of changes in the availability of jobs. Participation rates of all the remaining age-sex groups are substantially lower and are sensitive to changes in employment opportunities. These relationships are indicated in Chart 13 which shows labor force participation rates and the corresponding employment-population ratios each year since 1952 for males aged 25–54 and for all age-sex groups combined.

Furthermore, productivity would be higher in

Figure 1. Gross National Product, Actual and Potential, and Unemployment Rate.

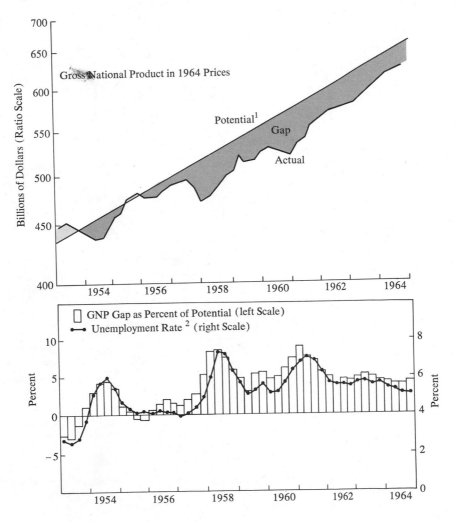

*Seasonally Adjusted Annual Rates

[1] 3½ % Trend Line Through Middle of 1955 to 1962 IV 3¼ % Trend Line Thereafter

[2] Unemployment as Percent of Civilian Labor Force; Seasonally Adjusted

Sources: Department of Commerce, Department of Labor, and Council of Economic Advisers

Figure 2. Labor Force Response to Employment.

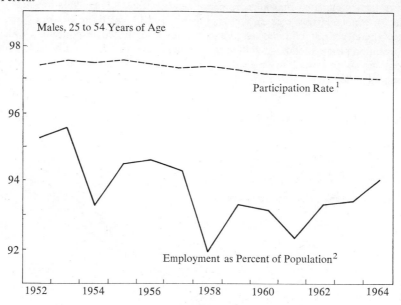

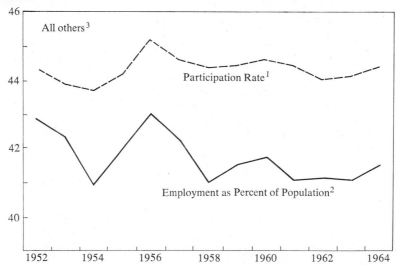

1 Percent of Non-Institutional Population in the Labor Force (Includes Armed Forces).
2 Percent of Non-Institutional Population Having Employment (Includes Armed Forces).
3 Includes Females, 14 Years of Age and Over. Males 14-24 Years and 55 Years and Over

Source: Department of Labor

a full-employment economy than it actually is today; this is also reflected in the estimate of potential GNP. In periods of underutilization, output per worker is depressed because of the overhead nature of some clerical, professional, and managerial employment and because plant and equipment are being operated at inefficient rates. During periods of movement toward full employment, rapid gains in productivity reflect the fact that both workers and machines are operating more fully and more efficiently.

Actual GNP for 1964, at $622 billion, was $27 billion or 4 per cent below estimated potential. In the first quarter of 1961, the gap was $51 billion (in 1964 prices) or 9 per cent of potential. Thus, the current expansion has substantially narrowed the gap; its present size indicates the remaining distance to full realization of potential.

The Council's estimate of potential GNP reflects the belief that the economy could operate at a 4 per cent unemployment rate today without substantial strains on either labor supplies or plant capacity. Operating rates in industry show the presence of capacity to fill additional demands. Labor supplies are generally abundant in most labor markets. While unemployment rates vary widely among different age-sex groups in the population, rates are consistently above those of 1956, when the over-all unemployment rate was 4.2 per cent.

The ease of attaining a given global unemployment rate can be affected by major shifts in the composition of the labor force. Some groups, like teenagers and uneducated adults, typically have relatively high unemployment rates; a large increase in their numbers relative to the total labor force would be expected to make the attainment of a given over-all unemployment goal more difficult. In fact, there have been moderate shifts in the composition of the labor force in the direction of *age-sex groups* with typically higher unemployment rates. But there have also been shifts toward *education groups* with lower unemployment rates. If every *age-sex group* now had the same unemployment rate it experienced in March 1957, the over-all unemployment rate would be 0.2 per cent *higher* than it was then. On the other hand, if every *education group* now had the same unemployment rate it experienced in March 1957, the global unemployment rate would be 0.3 per cent *lower* than it was then.

The interim target of a 4 per cent unemployment rate is attainable, given the required level of demand for goods and services. By improving labor market information, skills, and formal education, the manpower policies can facilitate the transition to a 4 per cent unemployment rate and can, in the future, let us attain even lower rates.

*ROBERT HANEY SCOTT AND JOHN R. McKEAN*

# A "Cross-Section" Look at Employment, Growth, and Inflation

*27* This paper contains evidence that supports the hypothesis that rates of inflation greater than 2 per cent annually deter growth. Additional evidence supports the existence of the "Phillips" curve that relates achievable rates of unemployment with various rates of inflation.

Spiraling inflation leading to the breakdown of an exchange economy hardly constitutes a climate beneficial to economic growth. On this nearly everyone agrees. But, many economists apologize for "controlled" inflation and some even suggest that "creeping inflation" should be an objective of policy because of its stimulating effects on

the economy.[1] Theoretical attacks on the inflationist's position often center on supposed adverse distribution effects of inflation. Federal Reserve System spokesmen sometimes oppose inflationary policies because of potential adverse effects on the balance of payments. But, operationally minded economists have gone directly to the heart of the problem and examined the correlation of rates of growth with rates of inflation for different countries and different periods of time. Upon finding that some countries have had inflation and growth and that others have had no inflation and growth, these empiricists contend that no discernible relationship exists between these two phenomena.[2]

This is a revised version of an article by the same title which initially appeared in the *Western Economic Journal*, Vol. III (1964), pp. 1–6. It appears here by permission of the authors and publisher. Robert Haney Scott and John McKean are professors at the University of Washington. The authors were assisted in the preparation of this revision by the comments of Professor John W. Birch of the University of Wyoming. The authors wish to thank the Faculty Research Committee of the College of Business Administration for financial support for this study. Also, they wish to thank Harry G. Johnson for helpful comments on an earlier draft.

[1] See Sumner H. Slichter, "On the Side of Inflation," *Harvard Business Review*, May–June 1957, pp. 15 ff.; and for a reply to his position, see Neil H. Jacoby, "The Threat of Inflation," *Harvard Business Review*, September–October 1957, pp. 15 ff.

[2] See part of a staff paper prepared for the Commission on Money and Credit and published as an addendum to the testimony by J. Cameron Thomson in "Review of the Report of the Commission on Money and Credit," *Hearings, Joint Economic Committee*, 87th Cong., 1st Sess., August 1961, pp. 374–87; Thomas Wilson, "Inflation and Growth,"

Another group of economists apologizes for inflation for a related but different reason. Presumably, if a society wants to achieve "adequately" high employment levels in the face of "cost-push" forces it must yield, to an extent, to inflationary forces. Within a given institutional framework characteristic of most Western societies, full employment and price stability are alternative goals of policy. The "Phillips" curve describes the relationship between rates of inflation and rates of unemployment, and each point on the curve represents a combination of these two rates that policymakers might choose if their instruments of control are confined to those that determine the level of aggregate demand.[3]

There is an abundance of literature on the relationship between inflation and unemployment, and somewhat less but still an abundant volume on the relationship between inflation and growth; but there is only slight mention of the relationship that exists between growth and unemployment.[4]

There are, of course, three variables, and three ways of combining them two at a time, and most analyses of these target variables are explicit only in bivariate terms. Even in the voluminous papers published by the Joint Economic Committee of Congress on "Employment, Growth, and Price Levels," one never finds the trio treated simultaneously in a single place. Nor did the Commission on Money and Credit treat them other than in pairs. Three-way relationships are only implicit in these studies.

With three target variables in mind the range of possible empirical investigation expands considerably. Multiple regression suggests itself as an experimental tool. To test the hypothesis that inflation stimulates growth, one might let growth be the dependent variable and inflation and unemployment be independent variables. Of course, if it were found that inflation "explains" growth, some economists might challenge the results with the contention that high rates of

growth generated by exogenous forces often give rise to inflationary pressures. Thus, inflation really is not a spur to growth, it is the other way around: growth brings on inflation and the correlation observed merely reveals this.[5] To test the hypothesis that growth leads to inflation, therefore, one might let inflation be the dependent variable, and growth and unemployment be independent variables.

A "cross section" approach helps overcome questions relating to tests of significance, autocorrelated errors, and multicollinearity that sometimes spoil the fruit of time series studies. Hence, data on inflation, national income, and unemployment were obtained for 13 countries for an 11-year period, 1949–1959, inclusive. The average rate of unemployment was reported by each country for each of the 11 years, and these averages were then averaged to obtain an average rate of unemployment, $U$, over the 11-year period as a whole for each of the 13 countries. Average rates of growth, $G$, for each country were obtained simply by taking 1959 real national income as a percentage of 1949 real national income and dividing the total percentage increase in income by 11 to arrive at an average annual increase for the 11-year period for each country. Similarly, average annual rates of inflation were found by taking 1949 as a base period and dividing the percentage increase in the price level over the 11 years by 11 to obtain an average annual percentage for each of the 13 countries. The data used are presented in Table 1. Coefficients of determination between pairs of variables are shown in Table 2.

The correlation between $P$ and $U$ improves somewhat when the curvilinear logarithmic form is used. But the significance of the coefficients remains so low that it is easy to understand why investigators of this subject have been led to the conclusion that there is little identifiable relationship among these variables.

Equation (1) describes a "Phillips" curve for the Western countries of the sample with curvature introduced by adoption of the parabolic form of regression. Its multiple coefficient of determination is .872.

$$P = -2.689\ U + .224\ U^2 + 9.73 \qquad (1)$$
$$\phantom{P = } (.328) \quad\ (.027)$$

Standard errors of the estimates of the regression coefficients are given in parentheses. A selected sample of $(U, P)$ solutions are (2, 5.2), (3, 3.6),

*Three Banks Review*, September 1961, pp. 3–21; Otto Eckstein "Inflation, the Wage-Price Spiral and Economic Growth," *The Relationships of Price to Economic Stability and Growth*, papers presented to the Joint Economic Committee, 85th Cong., 2d Sess., March 1958, pp. 361–74.

[3] For an excellent exposition of this relation, see A. C. L. Day and S. T. Beza, *Money and Income* (New York: Oxford University Press, 1960), pp. 400—405; P. A. Samuelson and R. M. Solow, "Analytical Aspects of Anti-Inflation Policy," *American Economic Review*, May 1960, pp. 177–94.

[4] See, for example, A. W. Phillips, "Employment, Inflation and Growth," *Economica*, February 1962, pp. 1–16.

[5] Eckstein discusses the impact of growth on inflation in his paper "Inflation, the Wage-Price Spiral and Economic Growth," *op. cit.*

## Table 1. Data Used in Regressions

| Country | P | G | U |
|---|---|---|---|
| Australia | 8.55 | 2.94 | 11.53 |
| Belgium | 1.96 | 3.67 | 6.76 |
| Canada | 2.64 | 5.80 | 4.07 |
| Denmark | 4.27 | 2.06 | 9.83 |
| Finland | 9.12 | 6.59 | 0.78 |
| Ireland | 4.63 | −0.56 | 8.29 |
| Italy | 3.45 | 6.62 | 9.24 |
| Netherlands | 4.34 | 5.70 | 1.95 |
| Norway | 6.22 | 2.11 | 1.39 |
| Sweden | 5.38 | 3.97 | 2.27 |
| Switzerland | 1.16 | 6.11 | 4.72 |
| United Kingdom | 5.19 | 1.22 | 1.56 |
| United States | 2.25 | 4.98 | 4.66 |

*Source:* Data derived from those found in the *United Nations Statistical Yearbooks* and *International Labor Review, Statistical Supplement,* December 1957 and September 1961. For Sweden and the United Kingdom real gross national product was used in place of real national income. Data on inflation for Australia and Denmark are based on a 10-year period instead of an 11-year one. Data for Western Germany and Austria were omitted because of their extreme values. Only incomplete data were available for France and New Zealand and these countries were omitted from the sample. See text for a description of the computation of the 11-year averages.

(4, 2.5) and (5, 1.8). Samuelson and Solow present a "Phillips" curve for the American economy,[6] and Figure 1 shows portions of the curve they estimated for comparison with the curve of Eq. (1). The minimum position of the curve occurs at around 6 per cent unemployment with 1.5 per cent inflation, and some observations lie beyond this minimum as the scatter diagram shows.

The fit of regressions that relate $P$ and $U$ improves greatly when the parabolic form is used in place of linear or logarithmic forms. Three interesting observations may be made. The first is that a nonlinear form improves the fit. The second is that the signs of the coefficients of

and this is well within the 5 per cent level of significance for 8 degrees of freedom.

$$P = -.597 \ G + .074 \ G^2 -$$
$$(.408) \quad (.057)$$
$$-2.734 \ U + .227 \ U^2 + 10.702 \quad (2)$$
$$(.330) \quad (.030)$$

Sample values of $(P, U)$ when $G$ is 3 are (4.17, 2), (2.57, 3) and (1.44, 4). These numbers appear quite reasonable. Thus, allowing growth to enter the experiment helps validate the arguments of those who posit the existence of a "Phillips" curve in their analysis of problems of unemployment and inflation. When $G$ is 3, the parabolic form of the "Phillips" curve is lowered

## Table 2. Simple Correlation Coefficients, Squared

| | A | | | B | |
|---|---|---|---|---|---|
| | U | G | | log of U | log of G |
| P | −.009 | −.036 | log P | −.123 | −.032 |
| U | | −.050 | log U | | −.058 |

regression are "correct" for levels of unemployment below the level of 6 per cent. The third is that rates of unemployment above 6 per cent are accompanied by inflation, and there is no theoretical explanation for this phenomenon.

When growth is introduced alongside unemployment as a determinant of inflation, as shown in Eq. (2), a slight improvement in fit appears. The multiple coefficient of determination is .900

[6] Samuelson and Solow, *op. cit.*, p. 192.

(by approximately a percentage point throughout) below its position when growth is omitted from the regression estimates.

The coefficient of $G$ in Eq. (2) is not so significant, but still it is significant enough to be interesting. Its negative sign indicates that as growth increases inflationary pressures subside. At least this is true up to rates of growth of between 8 and 9 per cent, at which levels the influence of the squared term takes over. Since these rates lie beyond the range of observations

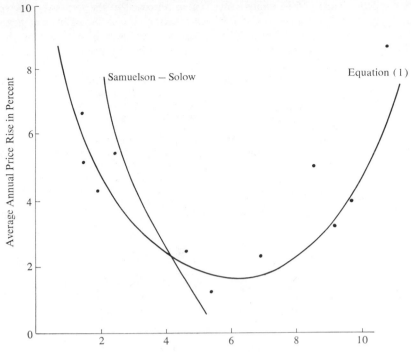

Figure 1. Average Annual Unemployment in Percentage.

this matter lacks seriousness. Thus, this regression supports the argument of those who believe better growth rates will help offset inflationary pressures.

Of course, this same evidence also supports the argument of those who believe inflation hinders growth. But, to ask this question more directly it may be preferable to restructure the regression in the form found in Eq. (3). Here, the multiple coefficient of determination is .43, and, while this falls considerably below the significance of that recorded for Eq. (2), it still merits attention. The size of the standard errors in relation to their coefficients indicates that

$$G = -2.809 \ P + .207 \ P^2 -$$
$$(1.298) \quad (.097)$$

$$-1.575 \ U + .118 \ U^2 + 14.926 \quad (3)$$
$$(1.982) \quad (.164)$$

and unemployment makes little contribution to the explanation of growth, but that inflation probably does contribute to growth—that is, to negative growth. Unfortunately, however, while this evidence may be used as ammunition for the anti-inflationist it casts little light on the question of "creeping" inflation of around 2 per cent per year simply because only two observations in the sample used were this low. Since nearly all the observations showed inflation of more than 2 per

cent, there is really no estimate of growth rates that might have followed from no inflation at all.[7]

## Conclusions

Empirical analysis is always only indicative, never conclusive. But certain observations seem to be worth pointing up. First, an analysis of the relation between inflation and unemployment suffers if growth is left out of the picture. Similarly, an analysis of inflation and growth suffers when unemployment is omitted. Thus, it seem-better to treat the trio together if at all possible. Second, curvilinear structures offer an improve-ment over linear ones, and, after all, the curvi-linear form fits some of the theory better. Third, the closeness of fit obtained in Eq. (2) is really astonishing when one reflects on the many

[7] A regression with unemployment as the dependent variable is presented in Eq. (4). Its multiple coefficient of determination is .12, a value so low that it merits no consideration.

$$U = -1.888 \ P + .157 \ P^2 - .822 \ G +$$
$$(2.580) \quad (.238) \quad (2.336)$$
$$+ .023 \ G^2 + 12.473 \quad (4)$$
$$(.305)$$

It is interesting, however, to note the tremendous difference it makes in the significance of the regres-sions when the problem is structured differently.

differences in the economies of the countries in the sample and on the many differences in the manner of measurement of economic variables in these countries. Fourth, the evidence supports the existence of a "Phillips" curve phenomenon for the economies of the Western countries. Fifth, for reasons unknown, the evidence shows that *high* rates of unemployment as well as *low* rates are accompanied by inflation. Sixth, the evidence supports two divergent arguments: (a) that greater growth helps hold the lid on inflationary pressures, and (b) that inflation greater than 2 per cent per year inhibits growth. A testing of further hypotheses deduced from these is necessary to enable one to infer which relationship is being observed in the regressions. Seventh, there is little or no indication of any significant relationship between growth and unemployment in the evidence offered above.[8]

[8] Some suggestions for further investigation seem appropriate. Time series studies including a third variable might prove to be profitable. The choice of the form of regression is always to some extent arbitrary, and many other possibilities exist. For example, one might wish to leave out the squared term for growth while leaving in the squared term for unemployment when inflation constitutes the dependent variable. Also, the choice of data may vary. For example, data on industrial production might supplant national income data in estimates of growth.

*ROBERT A. MUNDELL*

# The Appropriate Use of Monetary and Fiscal Policy for Internal and External Stability

## 28

This paper deals with the problem of achieving internal stability and balance of payments equilibrium in a country which considers it inadvisable to alter the exchange rate or to impose trade controls. It is assumed that monetary and fiscal policy can be used as independent instruments to attain the two objectives if capital flows are responsive to interest rate differentials, but it is concluded that it is a matter of extreme importance how the policies are paired with the objectives. Specifically, it is argued that monetary policy ought to be aimed at external objectives and fiscal policy at internal objectives, and that failure to follow this prescription can make the disequilibrium situation worse than before the policy changes were introduced.

The practical implication of the theory, when stabilization measures are limited to monetary policy and fiscal policy, is that a surplus country experiencing inflationary pressure should ease monetary conditions and raise taxes (or reduce government spending), and that a deficit country suffering from unemployment should tighten interest rates and lower taxes (or increase government spending).[1]

## The Conditions of Equilibrium

Internal balance requires that aggregate demand for domestic output be equal to aggregate supply of domestic output at full employment. If this condition is not fulfilled, there will be inflationary pressure or recessionary potential according to whether aggregate demand exceeds or falls short of, respectively, full employment output. It will be assumed here that, during transitory periods of disequilibrium, inventories are running down, or accumulating, in excess of desired changes, according to whether the disequilibrium reflects a state of inflationary or recessionary potential.

External balance implies that the balance of

---

Reprinted from the *International Monetary Fund Staff Papers,* Vol. IX (1962), pp. 70–77, by permission of the author and publisher. Robert Mundell is a professor at the University of Chicago.

[1] This possibility has been suggested, and to a limited extent implemented, elsewhere. See, for example, De Nederlandsche Bank N.V., *Report for the Year 1960* (Amsterdam, 1961).

trade equals (net) capital exports at the fixed exchange parity. If the balance of trade exceeds capital exports, there will be a balance of payments surplus and a tendency for the exchange rate to appreciate, which the central bank restrains by accumulating stocks of foreign exchange. And likewise, if the balance of trade falls short of capital exports, there will be a balance of payments deficit and a tendency for the exchange rate to depreciate, which the central bank prevents by dispensing with stocks of foreign exchange.

In what follows it is assumed that all foreign policies and export demand are given, that the balance of trade worsens as the level of domestic expenditure increases, and that capital flows are responsive to interest rate differentials. Then domestic expenditure can be assumed to depend only on fiscal policy (the budget surplus) and monetary policy (the interest rate) at the full employment level of output. The complete system can thus be given a geometric interpretation in the two policy variables, the interest rate and the budget surplus[2] (Figure 1).

In the diagram, the *FF* line, which will be referred to as the "foreign-balance schedule," traces the locus of pairs of interest rates and budget surpluses (at the level of income compatible with full employment) along which the balance of payments is in equilibrium. This schedule has a negative slope because an increase in the interest rate, by reducing capital exports and lowering domestic expenditure and hence imports, improves the balance of payments; while a decrease in the budget surplus, by raising domestic expenditure and hence imports, worsens

the balance of payments. Thus, from any point on the schedule an increase in the rate of interest would cause an external surplus, which would have to be compensated by a reduction in the budget surplus in order to restore equilibrium. Points above and to the right of the foreign-balance schedule refer to balance of payments surpluses, while points below and to the left of the schedule represent balance of payments deficits.

A similar construction can be applied to the conditions representing internal balance. The *XX* line, or "internal-balance schedule," is the locus of pairs of interest rates and budget surpluses which permits continuing full employment equilibrium in the market for goods and services. Along this schedule, full employment output is equal to aggregate demand for output, or, what amounts to the same condition, home demand for domestic goods is equal to full employment output less exports. There is, therefore, only one level of home demand for domestic goods consistent with full employment and the given level of exports, and this implies that expenditure must be constant along *XX*. The internal-balance line must therefore have a negative slope, since increases in the interest rate are associated with decreases in the budget surplus, in order to maintain domestic expenditure constant.

Both the internal-balance and the foreign-balance schedules thus have negative slopes. But it is necessary also to compare the steepness of the slopes. Which of the schedules is steeper?

It can be demonstrated that *FF* must be steeper than *XX* if capital is even slightly mobile, and by an amount which depends both on the responsiveness of international capital flows to the rate of interest and on the marginal propensity to import. The absolute slope of the internal-balance schedule *XX* is the ratio between the responsiveness of domestic expenditure to the rate of interest and the responsiveness of domestic expenditure to the budget surplus. Now, if it is assumed for a moment that capital exports are constant, the balance of payments depends only on expenditure, since exports are assumed constant and imports depend only on expenditure. In other words, if capital exports are constant, the slope *FF* also is the ratio between the responsiveness of domestic expenditure to the rate of interest and the responsiveness of such expenditure to the budget surplus. Therefore, apart from the effects of changes in capital exports, the two slopes are the same. It is then possible to see that the responsiveness of capital exports to the rate of interest

---

[2] The assumptions could be made less restrictive without detracting from the generality of the conclusions. Thus, an assumption that capital imports directly affect domestic expenditure, as in theoretical transfer analysis, would tend to reinforce the conclusions. Even the (plausible) assumption that, in addition to capital flows, capital indebtedness is responsive to the rate of interest (to take account of the "stock" nature of much of international floating capital) would not change the conclusions, although it may affect the quantitative extent of the policy changes required.

Notice, however, that I have implicitly assumed away strong "Pigou" effects, speculation on international markets that is related to the size of the (positive or negative) budget surplus, forward rate movements that more than offset interest-rate-differential changes (an unlikely occurrence), and concern about the precise composition of the balance of payments; the last assumption may mean that the method of achieving equilibrium suggested below is desirable only in the short run.

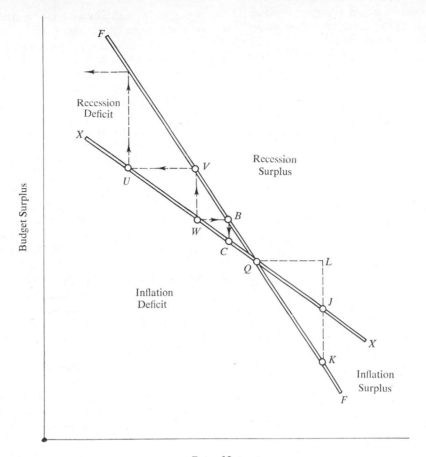

**Figure 1.**

makes the slope of *FF* greater in absolute value than the slope of *XX*.[3]

Consider, for example, what happens to an initial situation of over-all equilibrium at *Q* as this equilibrium is disturbed by an increase in the rate of interest equal to *QL*. Because of the higher rate of interest, there would be deflationary pressure and a balance of payments surplus at the point *L*. If the budget surplus is now lowered, the deflationary pressure can be eliminated at a point like *J* on the internal-balance schedule. But at *J*,

expenditure is the same as it was at *Q*, and this means that imports, and hence the balance of *trade*, must be the same as at *Q*. The balance of *payments* is therefore in surplus at *J* because of capital imports attracted by the higher rate of interest; this makes necessary a further reduction in the budget surplus in order to bring the balance of payments again into equilibrium. It follows, then, that the point *K* on the foreign-balance schedule is below the point *J* on the internal-balance schedule, and that *FF* is steeper than *XX*. It can then also be concluded that the absolute difference in slopes is greater, the more mobile is capital (because this causes a larger external surplus at *J*) and the lower is the marginal propensity to import (because this necessitates a larger budget deficit to correct any given external surplus).[4].

---

[3] Both the absolute and relative values of the slopes depend on the particular fiscal policy in question. The discussion in the text applies to income tax reductions because that instrument tends to be neutral as between home and foreign spending. The conclusions would be strengthened or weakened, respectively, as the particular fiscal policy was biased toward or against home goods; the more the change in the budget surplus results from a change in spending on home goods, the greater is the difference between the slopes of *XX* and *FF*.

[4] The assumption that imports depend only on expenditure, while the latter depends partly on the rate of interest, means that imports are affected by

In Figure 1, the two schedules separate four quandrants, distinguished from one another by the conditions of internal imbalance and external disequilibrium. Only at the point where the schedules intersect are the policy variables in equilibrium.

## Two Systems of Policy Response

Consider now two possible policy systems determining the behavior of fiscal policy and monetary policy when internal and external balance have not been simultaneously achieved. The government can adjust monetary policy to the requirements of internal stability, and fiscal policy to the needs of external balance, or it can use fiscal policy for purposes of internal stability and monetary policy for purposes of external balance.

It will be demonstrated first that the policy system in which the interest rate is used for internal stability, and fiscal policy is used for external equilibrium, is an unstable system. Consider, for example, a situation of full employment combined with a balance of payments deficit, represented by the point W. To correct the deficit by fiscal policy, the budget surplus must be raised from that indicated by W to that given by V. At V there will be equilibrium in the balance of payments, but the increased budget surplus will have caused recessionary pressure. If now the threatening unemployment is to be prevented by monetary policy, the rate of interest must be lowered from that indicated by V to that described by U. But at U there is again a balance of payments deficit, which in turn necessitates a further increase in the budget surplus. The process

continues with the interest rate and the budget surplus moving ever further from equilibrium.[5]

To show formally that the system is unstable, it is sufficient to note that the payments deficit at U, after the first round of policy changes, exceeds the deficit at W. This is evident since it is known that the balance of *trade* at U and W is the same but, because of the lower rate of interest, the balance of *payments* at U is worse. It follows that this type of policy reaction is unstable.

On the other hand, the opposite type of policy response is stable. Suppose that the authorities adjust the interest rate to correspond to the needs of external equilibrium and adjust fiscal policy to maintain internal stability. Then from the same disequilibrium point W, the rate of interest would be raised to B, thereby correcting the external deficit. But the tendency toward unemployment generated by the restrictive credit policy must now be corrected by a reduction in the budget surplus or increase in the budget deficit. At C there is again internal balance and a balance of payments deficit, as at W. But it is now possible to see that the deficit at C is *less* than the deficit at W. This follows, as before, because the balance of *trade* at C is identical with that at W but, since the rate of interest is higher at C, the balance of *payments* deficit must be less. The system is therefore stable.

The diagrammatic argument can be absorbed at once when it is realized that at W—or anywhere in the quadrant representing a deficit and recession—the interest rate is lower, and the budget surplus is higher, than is appropriate to the overall equilibrium at Q. The use of fiscal policy for external balance, and monetary policy for internal balance, drives the interest rate and budget surplus further away from equilibrium while the alternative system moves the instruments closer to equilibrium.

The same argument applies to an initial disequilibrium in the opposite quadrant, representing inflationary pressure and external surplus. To restore equilibrium, the interest rate must be reduced, and fiscal policy must be made more restrictive. Only if monetary policy is used for

---

the rate of interest, although the *share* of imports in expenditure is not. This assumption could be relaxed without fundamentally altering the results, although an exception—remote in practice but possible in theory—does arise, if import goods are highly responsive to the rate of interest while home goods are not, capital flows are only slightly responsive to the rate of interest, and the marginal propensity to buy imports is high relative to the marginal propensity to buy home goods. Under these conditions, it is possible that XX may be steeper than FF. More formally, then, it is necessary to limit the present conclusions to countries in which the ratio of the effect of budget policy on the balance of payments to its effect on domestic excess demand is less than the ratio of the effect of the interest rate on the balance of payments to its effect on excess demand.

[5] It need hardly be mentioned that the demonstration of instability in this instance (or of stability in the subsequent analysis) is not dependent upon the particular assumption that the government corrects imbalance first in one sector and then in the other, an assumption which is made only for expositional convenience. The conclusions follow, for example, even if the authorities simultaneously adjust fiscal and monetary policies.

the external purpose, and fiscal policy for the internal purpose, will correction of the disequilibrium automatically ensue.[6]

In the other two quadrants, monetary and fiscal policies will be moving in the same direction under either system of policy response, because both tighter monetary policy and an increased budget surplus correct inflationary pressure and external deficit, and both easier monetary policy and a reduced budget surplus tend to alleviate recession and external surplus. The distinction between the two policy systems appears less important in these phases of the international trade cycle; it nevertheless remains, since inaccurate information about the exact location of the point $Q$ could propel the situation into one of the quadrants involving either recession and deficit or inflation and surplus.[7]

## Conclusions

It has been demonstrated that, in countries where employment and balance of payments policies are restricted to monetary and fiscal

instruments, monetary policy should be reserved for attaining the desired level of the balance of payments, and fiscal policy for preserving internal stability under the conditions assumed here. The opposite system would lead to a progressively worsening unemployment and balance of payments situation.

The explanation can be related to what I have elsewhere called the Principle of Effective Market Classification: policies should be paired with the objectives on which they have the most influence.[8] If this principle is not followed, there will develop a tendency either for a cyclical approach to equilibrium or for instability.

The use of fiscal policy for external purposes and monetary policy for internal stability violates the principle of effective market classification, because the ratio of the effect of the rate of interest on internal stability to its effect on the balance of payments is less than the ratio of the effect of fiscal policy on internal stability to its effect on the balance of payments. And for precisely this reason the opposite set of policy responses is consistent with the principle.

On a still more general level, we have the principle that Tinbergen has made famous: that to attain a given number of independent targets there must be at least an equal number of instruments.[9] Tinbergen's Principle is concerned with the *existence* and location of a solution to the system. It does not assert that any given set of policy responses will in fact lead to that solution. To assert this, it is necessary to investigate the stability properties of a dynamic system. In this respect, the Principle of Effective Market Classification is a necessary companion to Tinbergen's Principle.

[6] Even if the authorities do not wish to pair instruments and targets, they can use the information provided by the analysis to determine the relation between *actual* policies and *equilibrium* policies. Thus, situations of deficit and recession imply that the budget surplus is too high and the interest rate is too low, while situations of surplus and inflation imply the opposite. In this manner, appropriate policies can be determined by observable situations of target disequilibria.

[7] The system can be generalized for a two-country world by assuming that the other country adjusts fiscal policy to maintain internal stability. The only difference in the conclusion is that the conditions of dynamic stability of the adjustment process are slightly more restrictive, requiring that the marginal propensities to import be, *on the average*, no greater than one half; this is the usual assumption necessary to rule out any "reverse transfer" that is due to policies affecting expenditure.

[8] "The Monetary Dynamics of International Adjustment Under Fixed and Flexible Exchange Rates," *Quarterly Journal of Economics*, Vol. LXXIV (1960), pp. 249–50.

[9] J. Tinbergen, *On the Theory of Economic Policy* (Amsterdam, 1952).

# Domestic Issues in Monetary and Fiscal Policies

*29*

## The Shift to Fiscal Policy

The emergence of the United States as a reserve-currency country with a chronic balance of payments deficit has forced a major change in the conception of the respective roles of fiscal and monetary instruments in carrying out U.S. economic policy. This change is more apparent in the successive annual reports of the Council of Economic Advisers than in the views and attitudes of the general public. At some cost in terms of longer-run historical accuracy, notably with respect to the early 1930's, it can be said that the United States in the past has relied in large part on monetary policy as its major instrument for achieving price stability and high employment. While fiscal policy has been used from time to time since the beginning of the New Deal, and especially during World War II, for the pursuit of macroeconomic objectives, the prolonged period of dollar shortage prevented any serious conflict between the objectives of internal and external

balance and made it unnecessary to work out a coherent and publicly accepted philosophy of the coordinated use of fiscal and monetary policy. In particular, it was not necessary to educate the public, including the legislators, in the use of fiscal policy to achieve short-run economic stability.

But with the appearance of a chronic deficit and balance of payments problem, it was no longer possible to use monetary policy for purely domestic purposes. Instead, monetary policy has had to be governed increasingly by the requirements of the balance of payments, and especially by the need to control international capital movements. Correspondingly, it has become necessary to put increasing emphasis on fiscal policy as the primary instrument for accomplishing domestic objectives.

## Problems and Requirements of the Transition

The transition has not been without strain. Nor is it yet complete. One aspect of the strains involved has been the continued criticism of

Reprinted from "Major Issues in Monetary and Fiscal Policies," *Federal Reserve Bulletin,* Vol. L (1964), pp. 1405–1412 by permission of the author and publisher. Harry Johnson is a professor at the University of Chicago.

Federal Reserves policies by economists and others who have been dissatisfied with the performance of the domestic economy but who have been unwilling—or have refused—to recommend alternatives to monetary stringency as a way of coping with the balance of payments deficit. In other words, many professionals have continued to think of monetary policy as a purely domestic instrument in circumstances in which it cannot be so.

A more important aspect was the long delay in getting the tax cut through Congress and the need ultimately to sell it by the promise of government economy, both of which reflected the attachment of important sections of the public and of the Congress to orthodox notions of the necessity of balanced budgeting. While it is true that the apparent success of the tax cut has enabled the President to promise further tax cuts in the near future without exciting anything like the degree of opposition encountered before the recent tax bill was passed, there is certainly no proof that the country has mastered and accepted the theory of countercyclical fiscal policy.

I would maintain, on the contrary, that one of the major issues in monetary and fiscal policy in this country at the present time is the development of concious public acceptance and official use of fiscal policy as a countercyclical device. It is one thing to concur in a tax cut after years of preaching by a conservative press that taxes are too high, and to do so after paying appropriate lipservice to the need for economy in government spending. It is quite another to set up machinery allowing the administration to cut taxes without a gesture in the direction of cutting spending, and to allow the administration to do so on the basis of its own judgment of what the economy requires. And it would be a still more demanding test to empower the administration to raise taxes when it felt that fiscal restraint was necessary to prevent inflationary developments.

To put the problem in another way, the tax cut has been only a first, and a relatively easy, step toward the efficient use of fiscal policy as a major instrument of domestic economic stabilization. The next step required is one that would give the budgeting authority discretionary control of fiscal policy. Such control would be comparable to the discretionary control that the monetary authority has long enjoyed over the money supply. This will be a difficult step. One reason is that it will be necessary to establish the idea of countercyclical fiscal policy as an operating principle of public finance. Another is that the step will require either a surrender of some congressional control over the taxing power or a revolutionary change in the

methods by which Congress conducts fiscal business.

The former appears to be the more probable avenue of change. At the technical level, it would require the selection of those taxes whose variation will have the most predictable and substantial effects on expenditures—a matter important both for the use of tax variation as a policy instrument and for the feasibility of transfer of power over taxes from legislative to executive control—and the framing of rules for discretionary variation in tax rates that would be adequate to the needs of policy-making without departing too far from the principle of separation of powers in the Government of the United States.

As a preliminary, it would probably be necessary—and would be desirable on other grounds—to effect the rationalization of the tax structure that the experts have been urging for years but that was sacrificed in the pursuit of over-all reduction in taxes. It would also be helpful to keep the macroeconomic impact of the tax expenditure structure in the forefront of the discussion, as the Council of Economic Advisers did in its report for January 1964, with a view to more frequent adjustment of tax rates to the increasing yield potentials created by the growth of the economy.

## Specific Issues of Monetary and Fiscal Policy

### General Effectiveness

Let me now turn from the broad issues raised for the deployment of the instruments of fiscal and monetary policy by recent changes in the world monetary environment and the international position of the U.S. economy to some of the more specific issues that have been raised by the use of these instruments in recent years.

It will be generally agreed, I think, that one issue has been conclusively settled by recent experience. This is the capacity of fiscal and monetary policy, in cooperation, to raise the level of economic activity and to reduce the level of unemployment. The current expansion has continued longer than any previous expansion in this century. Indeed, it shows no clear indications of an early relapse, but rather of continuation at least into 1965. It has truly confounded those who believe that a "natural" business cycle is inevitable and that economic policy can exercise no major influence over it. The expansion has exceeded the forecasts. It has reduced the budget deficit below the level that had been predicted. And it has permitted the administration to hold out the promise of further tax cuts next year, earlier than could have been expected.

The unemployment rate has fallen to 4.9 per cent, and this without any serious upward pressure on prices. This last fact is of special importance, in view of the hypothesis so widely advanced in recent years that economic policy has been faced with an entirely new problem—that of structural unemployment caused by automation. Traditional macro-economic policies, it was alleged, were incapable of coping with this problem. The evidence presented in support of this hypothesis was usually no more than the observation that a rise in unemployment has a differential impact on different sectors of the labor force, and it should be noted that empirical research on the problem has tended to reject the hypothesis as uncorroborated by the evidence.

The recent reduction in the unemployment rate provides much more direct and convincing evidence against the hypothesis. But it is not likely that this evidence will convince those who are overly impressed by the labor-saving effects of technical progress and who are unable to appreciate the capacity of a buoyant labor market to reabsorb displaced labor: indeed, a group calling itself the Ad Hoc Committee on the Triple Revolution has been making a great splash in Chicago recently with the notion that cybernation—not automation; that term is old fashioned—threatens unemployment in the near future on a scale so great as to demand both the public revision of incomes to a large part of the labor force and the redefinition of the term "work" to include education, voluntary political activity, and social welfare work.

To argue that the recent reduction in the unemployment rate demonstrates the efficacy of macroeconomic policies is not, of course, to argue that the present level of unemployment is satisfactory. Still less does it imply that there is no need for policies to improve the mobility of labor, if lower levels of unemployment are to be achieved with reasonable price stability. Nor does it imply that unemployment policy will be free of problems in the future, especially those associated with the impending flood of new entrants to the labor market; however, it does suggest that macroeconomic policy, properly managed, can make a greater contribution to the solution of those problems than most noneconomist commentators on automation, education, and related phenomena seem to believe. Finally, it does not imply that we have no need for a program to deal with problems stemming from poverty, since the roots of most poverty lie in one form or other of incapacity to participate in the labor force, or to provide labor services valuable enough to earn a socially decent wage.

## Relative Effectiveness: Fiscal Versus Monetary Policy

While recent experience demonstrates the efficacy of fiscal and monetary policy in stimulating aggregate demand and employment, it raises the issue of the relative contributions of fiscal and monetary policy to the expansion. And this issue in turn involves perennial and deeper questions concerning the importance of money and the effectiveness of monetary policy.

A variety of factors make it difficult to interpret the experience of the past few years. One of these relates to the changes in Regulation Q in 1962 and 1963. These changes, designed to allow rates on time and savings deposits to rise enough to attract and hold short-term capital, caused these deposits to rise much faster than demand deposits and currency. The possibilities of substitution between demand and time deposits on the one hand, and between time and savings deposits and competing savings media provided by other financial intermediaries on the other hand, in response to the rise in deposit rates, make it impossible to determine exactly how expansionary monetary policy has been over the period, according to quantity theory standards. Such as determination would require a more detailed analysis of the magnitudes of the relevant cross-effects than is currently available.

If the question is approached in terms of movements in interest rates, other complications are encountered. One of particular relevance is the effect of the new depreciation guidelines and investment tax credit adopted in 1962 in raising the net return on investment, and so in effect making any given level of long-term interest rates less restrictive than before. E. M. Bernstein has estimated the effects of these changes as equivalent to a reduction of 1 percentage point in interest rates.[1]

Another is the standard point that the restrictiveness of a given level of interest rates varies with the circumstances. The importance of this point has been emphasized in certain theoretical papers that have reached me recently in advance of publication and that have been written with the current policy situation in view.[2]

---

[1] This information was obtained in private conversation with Mr. Bernstein.

[2] The authors in question are David Meiselman, R. A. Mundell, and Arnold Collery.

Essentially, these papers question the standard diagrammatic assumption that the investment-saving (*IS*) curve slopes downward, so that monetary expansion necessarily reduces interest rates. The contrary assumption that the *IS* curve slopes upward can be reached by a variety of routes: (1) an income-investment relation stronger than the income-saving relation; (2) a static translation of the accelerator; (3) the application of marginal productivity theory to the effects of increased employment on the marginal productivity of capital in an aggregated Keynesian model; (4) the application of the relation between relative production quantities and factor prices in a two-goods model on the assumption that the capital goods sector is capital-intensive. And this assumption implies both that monetary expansion will raise interest rates and that the effort to stabilize interest rates in the face of shifts in the *IS* curve will be destabilizing.

Even without the assumption of an upward-sloping *IS* curve, the effort to stabilize rates may involve substantial expansion of the money supply, depending on the interest-sensitivity of the *IS* curve. And it may well be that both the critics and the defenders of recent monetary policy, in their concentration on interest rates, have been misled into understating the expansiveness of monetary policy and overstating the restraints imposed on it by balance of payments considerations.

In explaining changes in the U.S. economy in recent years, the 1964 report of the Council of Economic Advisers gives the impression of assigning relatively greater weight to tax reductions and a lesser and complementary role to monetary policy conducted, as it has been, within the limits set by the policy of raising short-term rates and twisting the yield structure to reduce out-flows of short-term capital.

Milton Friedman, on the other hand, in reporting on his research in the 44th annual report of the National Bureau of Economic Research, demonstrates that in the period 1957–63 there was a fairly close connection between rates of change in the money supply (on the standard and his own definitions of money) and subsequent rates of change in the index of industrial production, when the changes in each series were calculated for homogeneous subperiods. This demonstration indicates that the otherwise mysterious slackening of the pace of economic expansion in the latter part of 1962, which is difficult to explain in terms of fiscal developments, appears to have been linked to a reduction earlier that year in the rate of growth of the money stock. The comparative timing of these changes also makes them difficult to explain in terms of a response of the money supply to prior changes in income.

In view of this evidence, of the considerations previously outlined, and of a variety of other evidence not worth citing in detail, I am inclined to attach a greater importance to monetary policy in generating and sustaining the expansion than the Council does, though I would not be prepared to accept the monetary explanation of growth in economic activity to the point of denying that fiscal policy was an important influence on income and employment. But while I believe that monetary policy was an important influence, I am not convinced that the monetary stimulation that has occurred has been fully intended. There is reason to suspect that it has been, to some extent, the unintended consequence of a policy intended to be modestly restrictive in the sense of raising the level of interest rates, but one that actually turned out to be quite expansionary in its effects on the money supply.

## Effectiveness of the "Twist"

A related but subsidiary question about recent monetary policy relates to the effectiveness of the policy of twisting the rate structure. This issue involves the broader question of the empirical validity of the liquidity-preference theory. When this policy was initiated, the results of contemporary research suggested that changes in the composition of the public debt would have relatively trivial effects on interest rates. In fact, David Meiselman's work on the expectations theory of term structure implied that it would be negligible. Meiselman's work has since been found defective by R. Kessel and John H. Wood, who have discovered some evidence of liquidity preference.

Meanwhile, the twist policy has apparently had more influence on the rate structure than was earlier predicted for it. A recently completed doctoral dissertation by Neil Wallace which attempts to combine term-structure theory with liquidity preference in a more general theory of forward interest rates, finds that the term structure has been twisted to a greater extent than the liquidity-preference element in his formulation would predict. As a result of the balance of payments problem, this question of the manipulatability of the yield structure has gained new significance, and further research is evidently called for. A plausible line of explanation, but one difficult to explore, is that Federal Reserve policy pronouncements have a direct effect on the market's expectations.

## The Performance of the Federal Reserve: Independence and Competence

The issues just discussed relate to the potency of monetary policy as an instrument, first, for controlling aggregate demand, and second, for achieving differential effects on the pattern of interest rates. Issues of quite a different kind have been raised by the performance and pronouncements of the Federal Reserve in the period since 1957. These issues relate to the control over the monetary instrument, as contrasted with the control of that instrument over the economy, and are concerned with two broad questions, which may be loosely described as the external and the internal aspects of control over monetary policy.

By the external aspect I mean the question of co-ordination of monetary policy with the other instruments of policy—fiscal policy and debt management. This is really a question of the external relation of the Federal Reserve System to the other agencies of economic policy-making and more broadly to the political processes of government. By the internal aspect I mean the question of the efficiency with which the Federal Reserve manages monetary policy in pursuit of the objectives of that policy. This is really a question of the internal organization and operating procedures of the System.

The former is in essence a political problem or a problem of political organization. The latter is a problem on which economic theory and scientific economic research can be brought to bear—and in fact have recently been brought to bear. But it too is ultimately a political problem—or perhaps it would be more accurately described as a sociological problem. The economist does not have the skills to provide the answers to these problems, but in view of his alternative role as a political economist, he is naturally concerned with them.

These issues became active as a result of the Federal Reserve System's adoption of a sharply contractionary monetary policy in 1950–60 and of the resulting premature choking-off of the recovery from the 1957–58 recession. At that stage, I think it is fair to say, the major part of the professional comment was directed at the first issue. The Federal Reserve was widely criticized for being too concerned about resisting inflation and for having too little concern for promoting full employment and growth. And it was generally believed that the constitution of the System needed to be revised to give the administration a stronger and tighter control over the formulation and conduct of monetary policy.

While some commentators directed their criticisms at the System's methods rather than at its objectives, they were very much in a minority. And it was the majority view that found expression in the report of the Commission on Money and Credit. The report's discussion of the potentialities of monetary policy was bland and conventional; and the report made extensive recommendations for reforming the constitution of the Federal Reserve System, without paying much attention to how the System actually operates policy.

The issues have recently been thrashed out again in the *Hearings* before the Sub-Committee on Domestic Finance of the Committee on Banking and Currency of the House of Representatives on "The Federal Reserve System After Fifty Years". These *Hearings* were in many respects an odd production, in which the popular concern about the monopoly power of the money trust inherited from the late nineteenth century confronted the mid-twentieth century professional economists' concern about the failure of the country's central banking arrangements to apply sophisticated new developments in monetary theory. The two concerns found very uncertain common ground in an onslaught on the independence of the Federal Reserve in the Government structure and on its organization and methods of performing its functions.

In contrast to the proceedings of the Commission on Money and Credit, the purpose of the *Hearings* has been deliberately to encourage the airing of criticisms of the Federal Reserve—and criticisms have been recorded in abundance. The Keynesians have had their revenge on the System for the monetary policies of 1959–60. And the quantity theorists have had their revenge on both the System and the Keynesians for past insults and neglect.

Moreover, the quantity theorists' attack has been extended beyond past charges of ignorance of how money influences the economy—charges based on recent research on the theory of the demand for money—to charges of ignorance of how the System itself influences money. These charges are based on still more recent research on the theory of the supply of money.

Here I refer not to the *Hearings* themselves, but to the staff study by Karl Brunner and Allan Meltzer on "The Federal Reserve's Attachment to the Free Reserve Concept". This study follows earlier works by Alexander J. Meigs and William G. Dewald, which pinpointed the fallacies of the theory of monetary control originated by Winfield

W. Riefler and underlined the inadequacies of this theory as a guide to the conduct of monetary control.

The result of the *Hearings* has been to dramatize both the unpopularity of the Federal Reserve System and its methods with a large number of monetary economists and the extent to which it has lost touch with new developments in monetary theory and new empirical research on monetary phenomena. The report of the Commission on Money and Credit and the discussions of monetary policy surrounding it had already revealed the gap between the Federal Reserve and the academic economists. But the *Hearings*—and especially the threat of legislation emanating from Representative Patman's Committee—are undoubtedly the main influence behind the efforts that Chairman Martin has recently initiated to modernize the Federal Reserve System.

As already mentioned, there are two distinct issues involved here, the external and the internal. So far as the first is concerned, I would judge that few economists now would be prepared to advocate an "independent" central bank, as propounded in the literature published between the two World Wars; that is, a bank whose first duty is to protect the value of money against the inflationary propensities of the elected politicians. Such a function is consistent with neither political democracy nor modern concepts of the economic responsibilities of government. And even if it were, the historical record provides little evidence of the capacity of central banks to perform it wisely [24]. However, there are some subtle issues relating to precisely how the central bank should be integrated into the organization of the government's economic policy-making, and specifically whether the central bank should be coordinate with the Treasury under the executive department, or should be subordinate to the Treasury.

In Canada this issue was recently decided in favor of making the Governor of the Bank responsible to the Minister of Finance, with the latter determining the broad outlines of monetary policy. This is the system that has ruled in England since 1945. Such a system of organization assumes that the Treasury makes macro-economic policy.

In this country, however, there is historical reason to fear that the Treasury might be excessively concerned with minimizing the interest cost of public debt. This problem is part of a larger problem mentioned earlier: the need to develop among our people, including the legislative and executive branches of government themselves, a better understanding of the techniques and implications of fiscal policy.

With regard to the second issue—the application of modern economic theory and scientific research methods in the conduct of monetary policy—it is worth making the obvious point that the problem is not to get the central bank to employ and use economists. The Federal Reserve has done that for a long time, as have most other central banks. The real problem, which has close analogies with the problem of the use of scientists in industry, or of economists in economic planning, is to establish and maintain an organizational structure within which a scientific and research-oriented approach can be maintained in the face of the continual pressure of decisions that must be made on matters only remotely connected with scientific fundamentals.

A central bank operates in the markets for credit, and there is an inevitable tendency for it to conduct its analysis and formulate and rationalize its policies in terms of how they affect credit markets. There is an equally inevitable tendency for economists who get involved in central bank policy-making to think and talk in the same terms, if only to be able to communicate and command attention. As the Brunner-Meltzer study shows, for example, the prevalence of the free-reserve concept in Federal Reserve thinking is intimately associated with the necessity of formulating and communicating decisions to be implemented by the Manager of the System Open Market Account.

What internal institutional arrangements in the central bank would suffice to prevent this I cannot say: any major improvement in the theory of policy adopted by the bank is likely to harden into a dogma offensive to subsequent theorists, as indeed happened to the Riefler theory. Perhaps the best that can be hoped for is that more active and sustained criticisms by academic economists will accelerate the rate of adoption of theoretical innovations.

# The Employment Act: Twenty Years of Policy Experience

*30* There were great expectations and not a few qualms when the Employment Act was signed into law on February 20, 1946, following enactment by heavy bipartisan majorities in both houses of Congress. This year, which marks the 20th anniversary of that enactment, is a suitable occasion to review our experience under the Act, to take stock of where we stand today, and to consider the challenges ahead.

## The Act and its Background

The legislation of 1946 set forth the following declaration of policy:

The Congress declares that it is the continuing policy and responsibility of the Federal Government to use all practicable means consistent with its needs and obligations and other essential considerations of national policy, with the assistance and cooperation of industry, agriculture, labor, and State and local governments, to coordinate and utilize all its plans, functions, and resources for the purpose of creating and maintaining, in a manner calculated to foster and promote free competitive enterprise and the general welfare, conditions under which there will be afforded useful employment opportunities, including self-employment, for those able, willing, and seeking to work, and to promote maximum employment, production, and purchasing power.

In making this declaration, the Congress recognized that the billions of independent spending and saving decisions of a free economy could well result in levels of total demand either short of full employment or in excess of productive capacity. Futhermore, it took the view that Government policies could play a constructive role in improving the stability and balance of the economy.

The Act was a product of the experiences of the Great Depression and World War II. The Depression shook but did not destroy the faith in an automatic tendency of the economy to find its proper level of operation. In the early 1930's, public works and other antidepression programs were justified as temporary "pump priming," to help the private economy get back on its track after an unusual and catastrophic derailment. And the departure from orthodox fiscal principles was made with regret and without complete consistency. The Government expenditures explicitly

Reprinted from the 1966 *Annual Report of the Council of Economic Advisors*, pp. 170–186.

264

designed to combat depression necessarily increased budget deficits; but this implication was veiled by financing these outlays through an "extraordinary" budget. Meanwhile, taxes were raised, and salaries and housekeeping expenditures cut in the regular budget, thereby reducing the over-all stimulation of Government measures.

The relapse of the economy in 1937 into a sharp decline from a level still far below full employment gave rise to conflicting interpretations. To some, it proved that pump priming and Government deficits had undermined the confidence of the business community and thereby only worsened the situation. Others, however, concluded that it pointed to the need for larger and more sustained fiscal and monetary actions to revive the economy. In drawing this conclusion, economists were buttressed by the writings of J. M. Keynes, who offered a theoretical explanation of the disastrous depression. The Keynesian conclusions received additional support during World War II because they offered a satisfactory explanation of why the high deficit-financed expenditures of that period not only wiped out unemployment but went beyond to create inflationary pressures.

Memories of the disastrous 1930's were very much in the public mind as World War II was drawing to an end. Many active proponents of "full employment" legislation in 1945 and 1946 feared a relapse into depressed levels of economic activity like those of the 1930's, once military spending ended. They looked toward Federal public works spending as a peacetime replacement —at least, in part—for the wartime defense outlays.

The opponents of "full employment" legislation had several reservations and objections. Some feared that it would mean a statutory blessing for perpetual budgetary deficits, soaring public expenditures, and massive redistribution of income from upper to lower income groups. There were doubts that Government actions could and would on balance raise employment; and there were fears that these actions would lead to regimentation and would jeopardize the free enterprise system. The proponents of legislation, on the other hand, argued that the Act would merely provide a setting essential to the proper functioning of the free enterprise system because a depressed economy heightened social tensions, discouraged innovation and initiative, dulled competition, and undermined confidence.

The legislation which finally emerged from this discussion wisely abstained from diagnosing depression as the disease and public works as the cure, but instead concentrated on establishing the principle of continuing Government responsibility to review and appraise economic developments, diagnose problems, and prescribe appropriate remedies. And it placed major responsibility squarely upon the President, who was asked to discuss his execution of that responsibility in an Economic Report to be transmitted to the Congress at the start of each year.

The Act also established two agencies—the Council of Economic Advisers in the Executive Branch and the Joint Committee on the Economic Report (later named the Joint Economic Committee) of the Congress—with inter-related but separate responsibilities. These institutions have each filled a vital and previously missing role in their respective branches of Government—they have provided a coordinated overview of the economic impact of the entire spectrum of Government tax, expenditure, monetary, and other activities. To maintain the emphasis on advice and coordination, the Joint Economic Committee was not given any substantive legislative responsibility nor the Council any policy-executing duties. Both agencies have participated actively in the counsels of Government; both have conscientiously striven for a thoroughly professional economic competence and approach in their respective reports and recommendations; and both have contributed to the public understanding of economic issues.

Today's economic policies reflect the continuing impact of the Employment Act in all the years since its inception. And our accumulating experience is certain to be reflected in the policies of the future. This chapter reviews the development of policy in the past 20 years and outlines the present relationship between economic analysis and economic policy.

## Avoiding Depressions and Booms

The Congress proved wise in its decisions to state goals broadly and to concentrate on continuing review, analysis, and proposals, since the specific problems that actually arose were somewhat different from those which many supporters of the Employment Act had anticipated.

Although an important part of the impetus for the Employment Act derived from the prolonged depression of the 1930's and the resulting fear of stagnation in the American economy, this problem did not prove to be the primary challenge to economic policymaking under the Act. Indeed, immediately after World War II, excess-demand inflation proved to be the key problem. Subsequently, policy was focused on the age-old problem of limiting the size and duration of cyclical swings. Only much later and in a much different and milder form did stagnation arise as a live issue.

Thus, much of our experience under the Act consisted of policy actions to combat recession— lest it turn into depression—and to contain excess demand pressure—lest it generate inflationary boom.

## Combating Recessions

A series of relatively short and mild recessions required Government attention in the postwar period. The problem of cyclical declines was not unexpected by the framers of the Employment Act, nor was it new to the American economy. In the period between 1854 (the beginning of the business cycle annals of the National Bureau of Economic Research) and World War II, we had experienced 21 periods of recession or depression. Our post-war record is blemished by 4 additional periods of contracting economic activity—1948–49, 1953–54, 1957–58, and 1960–61.

Compared with the previous cyclical record, the postwar recessions have been far shorter, consider-ably milder, and substantially less frequent. Post-war recessions ranged in duration from 8 to 13 months; the average duration of previous declines had been 21 months, and only 3 had been shorter than 13 months in length. Measured by the dec-line in industrial production from peak to trough, postwar recessions ranged in magnitude from 8 per cent to 14 per cent. By comparison, in the inter-war period, the declines ranged from 6 to 52 per cent; three of the five contractions exceeded 30 per cent and only one was less than the 14 per cent maximum of the postwar period. During the past 20 years, the economy has spent a total of 42 months, or 18 per cent of the time, in periods of recessions, far less than the 43 per cent applicable to the 1854–1939 era.

*Discretionary Policies.* This improvement in the postwar record of the economy was aided by the deliberate discretionary steps taken by the Govern-ment to modify the impact of business downturns and thereby to prevent cumulating declines into depression. The speed and force of these actions —in both the fiscal and monetary areas—varied among the recessions. Thus, in 1949 little new fiscal action was taken, partly because inflation was viewed as a key problem even during the decline, and partly because Government meas-ures taken the previous year were expected to have a considerable impact on the economy: the tax reductions of 1948 were supplying large refunds, and large expenditure increases were

forthcoming under the recently enacted Marshall Plan. The Federal Reserve did act to reduce reserve requirements in a series of steps during the spring and summer of 1949, reversing a two-year rise in short-term interest rates.

In 1953–54, as military outlays declined and aggregate activity retreated, the principal expan-sionary influence came from previously scheduled reductions of corporate and personal income taxes. But some new action was taken to reduce excise taxes and to speed up expenditures. All three major instruments of monetary policy— reserve requirements, the discount rate, and open market operations—were used to encourage the expansion of credit-financed expenditures. Mean-while, the Administration planned larger fiscal steps that might be taken if the recession seemed likely to be prolonged. Significantly, in 1954, the bipartisan character of expansionary fiscal policies was established for the first time, as the Republican Administration of President Eisenhower adopted measures that had previously been linked to the New Deal and Keynesian economics.

In 1958, the recession was considerably deeper than its two postwar predecessors and both the Eisenhower Administration and the Congress were more vigorous in taking action. An important concern of earlier years—that business confidence might be disturbed by Government recognition of a recession—seemed insignificant since the sharp recession was obvious to all.

Several important measures were taken. The benefit period for unemployment compensation was temporarily extended. Grants to States under the Federal highway program were enlarged and accelerated, and other programs in the budget also were expanded or rescheduled to provide an earlier stimulative effect. The Government also acted to spur housing activity by financial opera-tions in the mortgage market and by altering terms on Government-guaranteed home mort-gages. The important measures were launched near, or after, the trough of the recession. Thus, in retrospect, policy helped most to strengthen the early recovery rather than to contain or shorten the recession. Nevertheless, in view of the general recognition that the Government would be run-ning a substantial deficit in any case, these ad-ditions to Federal outlays were a significant reflection of changed attitudes toward the role of fiscal policy.

Monetary policy also played a constructive role in the 1957–58 recession, once the monetary authorities moved to ease credit 3 months after the peak in economic activity. Thereafter, Federal Reserve actions contributed to a revival in housing and other investment by promoting a sharp reduction in interest rates, both short- and long-term.

The first fiscal measures to deal with the 1960–61 recession were taken with the inauguration of President Kennedy in January 1961, when the recession had just about run its course. Nevertheless, improvements in the social insurance system, rescheduling of Federal expenditures, and expanded programs (including defense and space) were an important stimulus to the recovery during 1961. In contrast to the delay in taking fiscal measures, the Federal Reserve reversed a tight money policy early in 1960, prior to the downturn.

Not all discretionary changes in taxes or expenditures have contributed to economic stability. Indeed, some steps taken to pursue national security or social goals had destabilizing economic impacts, which were not always appropriately offset. Previously scheduled payroll tax increases took effect in 1954, 1959, and 1962, and drained off purchasing power in recession or in initial recovery. In 1953, defense outlays declined and triggered a recession before offsetting expansionary policies were adopted.

*Structural Changes for Stability.* On the whole, discretionary fiscal and monetary actions made a distinct positive contribution in limiting declines. Even more important in this respect was the strengthened inherent stability of the postwar economy.

In large measure, this can be traced simply to the greater size of the Government relative to the total economy: that is, the increased importance of Government expenditures—both purchases of goods and services and transfer payments. Government outlays do not participate in the downward spiral of recession; because of its borrowing capacity, the Federal Government—unlike businesses and households—can maintain its spending in the face of declining income receipts. Although State and local governments do not have equal immunity from the need to tighten their belts, they have been able to maintain their growing spending programs relatively unaffected during the mild postwar recessions.

The increased relative importance of Government outlays is shown in Figure 1. Social insurance and national defense have added especially to the postwar totals of Federal outlays. State and local outlays have been rising rapidly in an effort to catch up with neglected needs and to keep up with the desires of a wealthier society for improved public services.

The contribution to the stability of the economy resulting from a high level of Government expenditures, insulated from revenue declines, has been augmented by the cushions to private purchasing power provided by the built-in fiscal stabilizers.

When private incomes and employment decline, purchasing power is automatically supported by both a decline of Federal revenues and an increase in unemployment compensation payments. Transmission of the virus of deflation is thus impeded. During postwar recessions, the progressive Federal personal income tax has not had to demonstrate its full stabilizing effectiveness because of the mildness of dips in personal earnings. There have, however, been sharp declines in corporate incomes; the Federal Treasury has shared about half of the drop in profits, thereby helping to bolster dividends and to cushion cash flow, and hence investment outlays.

A number of improvements in our financial structure were developed in the 1930's to assure that financial collapse and declines in economic activity would not generate a vicious downward spiral as they did after 1929. These important financial mechanisms include Federal insurance of private deposits; the separation of commercial and investment banking functions; the Federal Reserve's increased ability to provide banks with reserves in time of crisis; and the joint work of the Federal Reserve and the Securities and Exchange Commission to reduce harmful speculation in the stock market. The very existence of these structural changes has contributed to stability by improving confidence.

With the help of the more stable structure of the economy, recessions in the postwar era have been limited to declines in investment spending (and, in 1953–54, Federal outlays). Consumer incomes have not declined significantly, and hence households have maintained their spending in recession. With the nearly two-thirds of GNP represented by consumer expenditures insulated from decline and with a solid foundation of public outlays, declines in private investment have not cumulated. In contrast, the Great Depression generated a decline of consumer outlays of 40 per cent from 1929 to 1933, and the shrinkage of consumer markets aggravated and reinforced the collapse in investment spending.

## Containing Inflationary Pressures

The desirability of price stability was clearly recognized in the legislative discussion of the Employment Act. But few considered the danger of postwar inflation nearly as great as the opposite danger of relapse into depression. The legislation itself emphasized the objectives of using resources

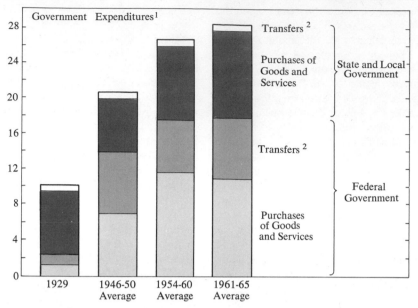

Percent of GNP

<sup></sup>

¹ National Income Accounts Basis

² Transfer Payments, Net Interest, and Subsidies Less Current
Surplus of Government Enterprises

Figure 1. Role of Federal and State and Local Governments in the Economy.

fully and attaining high employment. It did not explicitly label price stability an objective of policy, although this was implicit in the Act and fully reflected in the policies of every Administration. Nevertheless, concern has been expressed at times that policies for "maximum employment" might allow demand to press too hard on available resources, thus biasing the American economy toward inflation.

In the wartime environment, inflationary pressures of excess demand had been suppressed by direct controls on prices and by rationing. It turned out, however, during the years immediately following World War II that these measures had served partly to postpone—rather than to eliminate—significant demand pressures. Substantial backlogs of demand emerged in the 1946–48 period. Consumers and businesses possessed large accumulations of liquid assets to finance the rebuilding of their depleted stocks of household appliances, machinery and equipment, and their houses and plants.

Thus, contrary to expectations, the initial years of the postwar era were marked by excessive rather than inadequate demand. In this environment, living standards of consumers, the productivity of labor, and the capacity of businesses rose rapidly. But so did the price level, with a jump of

31 per cent in consumer prices from June 1946 to August 1948. Automatic fiscal stabilizers helped to contain the growth of private after-tax incomes, and were reflected in budgetary surpluses during the period. The economic policymaking machinery set up under the Employment Act may have moderated pressures to cut taxes drastically. Meanwhile, monetary policy was tied to a policy of supporting Government bond prices and was not free to combat inflation.

During the Korean war, however, the Government acted vigorously to counter inflationary tendencies close to their source. The March 1951 Federal Reserve-Treasury "accord" unleashed monetary policy. Selective controls on consumer instalment credit and on home mortgages were instituted. The enactment of three large increases in income and profits tax rates in 1950 and 1951 is one of the better examples of timely fiscal policy. These actions reflected, in part, recommendations by the Council of Economic Advisers and hearings and reports of the Joint Economic Committee.

Right after the outbreak of hostilities, prices had risen sharply in a flurry of consumer and business buying and, as a result, prices and wage ceilings had been imposed early in 1951. Once the restraining influence of over-all fiscal and monetary policies was fully felt, there was little pressure on the ceilings, and the economy was able to meet the peak defense demands of the emergency without inflationary strain.

The immediate postwar period and the early months of the Korean war are the two blemishes of clearly excessive demand on our postwar record. Apart from these two intervals, wholesale prices have shown a net increase of only two per cent in the postwar era. In 1956 and 1957, the only other periods of marked price increases, over-all demand was not generally excessive. That inflation raised new issues, which are discussed below. In view of the whole postwar record, it can hardly be said that the Employment Act has biased policy toward inflation.

## Evolving Problems and Policies

During the postwar era, the American economy has remained free of the malignant diseases of depression and run-away inflation. And the rate of economic growth has considerably exceeded its long-term average. The objectives of the Employment Act, however, have not always been fully met. In particular, experience has demonstrated that the avoidance of depression did not guarantee the achievement of "maximum employment" and the avoidance of excess-demand booms did not assure the maintenance of price stability.

### Inadequate Demand in Expansion

The strength of private demand in the early postwar years and then again immediately after the Korean war led to a reassessment of the tasks of stabilization policy. After a decade of postwar experience, suspicions arose that the typical problem would be to contain rather than to stimulate private demand.

Any such conclusion was soundly refuted by the facts of the ensuing years. With the backlogs met, and with a marked decline in the rate of family formation, private demand weakened in the late 1950's. The economy's performance weakened correspondingly because Government did not act to compensate. Thus, while unemployment had averaged 4.2 per cent of the civilian labor force in the first postwar decade, it remained above that level every month between late 1957 and October 1965, averaging 5.7 per cent.

The problem of inadequate demand in expansion, which became the primary focus of fiscal action in the 1960's, was a new challenge to policy-making under the Employment Act. In the first postwar decade, each time the economy advanced or rebounded from a recession, it reached the neighborhood of full employment. The policy-makers had been ready in the early postwar years to deal with noncyclical problems of submerged prosperity or stagnating production. They had seen maximum employment as a moving target which could be maintained only through a substantial growth of output. Both the Council of Economic Advisers and the Joint Economic Committee had given these issues repeated attention in the late 1940's and early 1950's. But until the late 1950's no experience had been encountered to distinguish the problem of full employment from that of cyclical prosperity.

Then came a sequence of disturbing events: the 1957–58 recession followed a year of slow advance; the 1960–61 recession began from a peak far below full employment; and the expansion that began in 1961 seemed to be running out of steam after little more than a year.

During the initial years of this period, Government policy maintained vigilance against excessive buoyancy of demand when that was no longer the problem. Restrictive fiscal and monetary actions choked off the recovery of 1958–60. The shift to an expansionary fiscal policy by the Kennedy Administration early in 1961 was designed primarily to initiate a thriving recovery. A determined policy strategy to assure complete recovery was first formulated when the economy faltered in 1962.

The combination of fiscal stimuli to consumer demand and direct tax incentives to investment, together with monetary actions permitting an ample rise in credit, promoted a vigorous and sustained expansion after 1963. The inherent strength of both consumption and investment demand appeared in a new light, once the Revenue Act of 1964 exerted its invigorating influence.

### Inflation at Less Than Full Employment

Another problem encountered at times during the postwar era has been the tendency of prices to rise even in the absence of over-all excess demand pressures. This tendency reflects structural characteristics of the American economy. The economy is not made up of fully competitive labor and product markets in which large numbers of buyers and sellers interact and respond passively to prices. On the contrary, in many industries both unions and businesses exercise a considerable degree of market power. As a first result, wages and prices are both somewhat rigid in a downward direction. To the extent that prices rise more readily in response to excess demand than they decline in the face of excess supply, the price level is given an upward bias, which can become particularly acute if there are sharp shifts in demand among various sectors of the economy. Secondly, because of market power, some firms augment increases in costs originating elsewhere and unions can escalate their wage demands if prices begin to rise. Third, firms can use a strong market position to widen margins in a period of prosperity even if there are no upward pressures on their costs. Fourth, in the nature of the collective bargaining process, key wage bargains in some industries may tend to establish a pattern applied elsewhere. In particular, if the industries with key wage bargains happen to have excess demands and very strong profits, the pattern will tend to pull wages upward more rapidly throughout the economy.

An important, broadly oriented study by the Joint Economic Committee analyzed the workings of these important influences in the 1956–57 inflation. In that period, excess demands that were present in machinery and equipment, automobile, and metals industries led to price increases that were not offset elsewhere. Large wage settlements in these industries with high demand and high profits had pattern-setting effects on many other contracts, thus adding to costs on a broad front.

Rising prices that originate from such a process can affect expectations, jeopardize the stability and balance of an expansion, and create inequities and distortions just as readily as demand inflation. But measures to restrain these price increases by reducing over-all demand will enlarge unemployment and impair the productivity record so important to cost-price stability over the longer run. Policies to improve the operations of markets, increase resource mobility and accelerate technical change can help to increase the economy's resistance to rising prices. But in a world where large firms and large unions play an essential role, the cost-price record will depend heavily upon the responsibility with which they exercise the market power that society entrusts to them.

The need for responsible private action was brought to public attention in the Economic Reports of President Eisenhower's second Administration. Through the major innovation of the guideposts in the Kennedy and Johnson Administrations, this need has since been focused and developed into a national policy to enlist the force of public opinion to maintain cost-price stability. The emergence of such a policy has been all the more important in recent years because of the balance of payments problem that has persisted alongside the domestic need for more expansion.

## Economic Policy Today

Two decades of economic analysis and policy experience have shaped the development of a revised economic policy. By some, current policy has been labeled the "new economics." It draws heavily on the experience and lessons of the past, and it combines both new and old elements. Current policy represents a coordinated and consistent effort to promote balance of overall supply and aggregate demand—to sustain steady balanced growth at high employment levels with essential price stability.

This approach to policy has several key aspects, not entirely novel by any means. First, it emphasizes a continuous, rather than a cyclical, framework for analyzing economic developments and formulating policies. Stimulus to demand is not confined to avoiding or correcting recessions, but rather is applied whenever needed for the promotion of full-utilization and prosperity. Second, in this way, it emphasizes a preventive strategy against the onset of recession. Third, in focusing on balance of the economy, this policy strategy cannot give top priority to balance in the budget. When private investment threatens to outrun saving at full employment, a Government surplus is needed to increase total saving in the economy while restrictive monetary policy may also be called for to restrain investment outlays. When, as in recent years, private saving at full employment tends to outrun actual private investment, the balance should be corrected by budget deficits and expansionary monetary policy. Fourth, it considers the budget and monetary conditions in the framework of a growing economy, recognizing that revenues expand and thereby exert a fiscal drag on demand unless expansionary actions are taken; similarly, it recognizes that money and credit must expand just to keep interest rates from rising. Fifth, this strategy emphasizes the use of a variety of tools to support expansion while simultaneously pursuing other objectives. Manpower policies, selective approaches to control capital outflows, as well as general fiscal and monetary measures, are all part of the arsenal. Sixth, it calls for responsible price-wage actions by labor and management to prevent cost-inflation from impeding the pursuit of full employment. Finally, it makes greater demands on economic forecasting and analysis. The job of the economist is not merely to predict the upturn or downturn but to judge continuously the prospects for demand in relation to a growing productive capacity.

## The Nature of Cyclical Instability

An industrial economy is vulnerable to cumulative upward and downward movements in activity, so evident in our long-term record. While they can have diverse specific causes, these cyclical fluctuations can be explained as the result of imbalances between the rate of growth of productive capacity and the rate of growth of final demands that make use of productive capacity.

During periods of prosperity, a considerable part of the Nation's output is used to increase productive capacity through investment in plant and equipment and business inventories. If demand keeps pace, sales expand and the new capacity turns out to be profitable. Businessmen find that their decisions to increase capacity have been validated and they continue to pursue expansionary investment policies. If, on the other hand, inventory stocks are built up far in advance of need—on the basis of overly optimistic sales forecasts or as an inflation-hedge—businessmen will subsequently wish to cut back their rate of accumulation. Similarly, if outlays for business fixed investment add to productive capacity faster than demand expands, overheads on new capital cut into profits, inducing firms to trim their capital outlays. Even if businessmen continue to add somewhat to their productive capacity, the mere decline in the rate of expansion can mean an absolute reduction in the demand for capital goods and for output to go into inventories. Payrolls and purchasing power are thereby curtailed and a decline in total demand can result. Thus a slowdown in economic activity is converted into a definite downturn—a recession or depression.

Imbalance can arise because businessmen in the aggregate invest too much and overbuild, creating more capacity than the economy can—even at best—put to productive use. Or alternatively it can stem from "underbuying," a growth of final demand to slow to make use of even moderate additions to capacity. In principle, cyclical movements can also be triggered by over-building of new homes and consumer durables.

Overbuilding of inventories—partly encouraged by expectations of rising prices—was probably the key factor in the first postwar downturn, which occurred in 1948. That experience demonstrated that a situation of high total demand could deteriorate rapidly into recession without any change in the basic underlying factors in the private economy or any restraining shift in public policy. In 1953, the sharp decline in defense outlays reduced final demands and precipitated recession; productive capacity became temporarily excessive and investment spending declined. In 1956–57, rapid growth of productive capacity was associated with an investment boom; meanwhile, final demands grew very slowly. It is not possible to deliver a clear verdict on whether more vigorous growth of final demand would have justified the high investment levels then obtaining. But with the slow growth of demand that actually occurred, there was an abrupt decline in plant and equipment spending as well as inventory investment in 1957. In 1959–60, the rate of expansion of capacity (including inventories) was not excessive measured against the capabilities of the economy; the failure of the economy to support that growth of capacity must be attributed to "underbuying," the inadequate expansion of final demand, in an environment of restrictive fiscal and monetary policies.

In the future as in the past, policies to avert recession cannot wait until imbalances develop and the signs of a downturn are clear. The fact that economic activity is rising cannot be an assurance of continued growth if the expansion is too slow to match the growth of productive capacity. Nor can a strong level of investment be relied on to sustain expansion if it threatens an excessive growth of productive capacity. Recognizing these tasks, Government must apply its fiscal and monetary policies continuously to sustain and support a balanced expansion, sometimes by moderating the strength of an excessive investment boom, sometimes by adding to the strength of lagging final demand. The best defense against recession is a policy to sustain continued expansion. In a free economy, fluctuations in private demand will inevitably occur, and the Government will not always have the wisdom or the ability to counteract them. Continued expansion cannot be guaranteed, but recurrent recession need not be accepted as a necessary fact of economic life.

## Policy for a Growing Economy

In order to achieve the goal of maximum employment, the Government must coordinate all its policies to take account of the persistent growth of the economy's potential output.

*The Problem of Fiscal Drag.* One consequence of economic growth is that budgetary policies become more restrictive if they stand still. If tax rates are unchanged, Federal revenues will grow continuously as the economy expands. Meanwhile, if Federal expenditures are held constant in the face of growing revenues, the Federal budget will exert a continuing "fiscal drag" on private demand.

Either increased expenditures or reduced tax rates can offset this influence. A total of these two types of stimulative actions which exactly matched the dollar amount of normal revenue growth would provide a precise offset to fiscal drag (and would leave unchanged the high-employment surplus, discussed in Chapter 1).

A simple mechanical offset to fiscal drag is not, however, a satisfactory rule for fiscal policy. When aggregate demand threatens to exceed the supply capacity of the economy, some fiscal drag should be allowed to operate. On the other hand, waning strength in private demand points to fiscal action that would more than offset the drag, effecting a desirable decline in the high-employment surplus.

Furthermore, tightness or ease of monetary policy is important in determining appropriate fiscal actions. There is an analog to drag in the monetary area: A growing economy generates rising demands for liquid assets and increasing needs for borrowing. If monetary policies stand still in the sense of holding supplies unchanged, continually tighter credit conditions and higher interest rates will be the result.

*Accelerating Growth.* The growth of the economy is a major influence on policy; the opposite side of the coin is the major role of policy in influencing potential economic growth. The larger the amount of current output invested in physical and human resources, the more rapidly productivity and the productive capacity of the economy will increase.

A number of policy choices can speed growth by shifting resources into various types of investment. Public investment in human and physical resources can yield rich returns in more rapid economic growth. Some public investments, such as those on research and development, encourage complementary private investment. Outlays for manpower training improve labor skills and productivity. Throughout our history, investment in education has been one of the key contributors to growth. Private investment in plant and equipment is a key determinant of our industrial capacity. It can be stimulated by easing monetary policies. It can also be encouraged by selective tax reductions, such as the investment credit and depreciation reform of 1962 and the reductions in corporate tax rates in 1964 and 1965.

When the economy is below full employment, any stimulative measure is likely to add to private investment, thereby contributing to the growth of potential, as well as to actual, output. But, at full employment, more resources can be devoted to capital formation only if current consumption is restrained. A policy strategy to accelerate growth may therefore point to higher personal income taxes or similar measures to hold consumption below what would otherwise be appropriate.

*Choices of Tools.* Economic policy has many tools available in pursuing the goals of full employment, rapid growth, price stability, and balance of international payments. The full range of economic objectives must be reflected in the selection of policies to meet particular circumstances.

Policy instruments differ in their impact. Sometimes policy tools can advance the economy toward more than one goal. For example, manpower policies help to maintain price stability at high employment and to promote economic growth. Conflicts may occur, however. For example, high interest rates impinge particularly on investment both at home and abroad, hence somewhat reducing foreign capital outflows but also reducing aggregate demand and slowing economic growth. In the case of potential conflicts, instruments must be used more selectively; for example, moderate changes in interest rates can be supplemented by taxes on foreign investment, like the Interest Equalization Tax.

The potential for timely results differs for various policy instruments. Monetary policy can be altered readily, although its full economic impact will not be immediate. While some restraint or speedup in Federal outlays can be applied by Executive authority alone, tax rate changes must, of course, be approved by the Congress. The speed of Congressional action on tax changes has varied. It acted rapidly to increase taxes in 1950, and to reduce excise taxes both in 1954 and 1965. On the other hand, it took 13 months to enact the comprehensive Revenue Act of 1964. Tax revision can help to avoid the necessity for abrupt changes in Federal expenditures, which could require stopping a project before its conclusion or starting a new one with inadequate planning.

Given the possibility for achieving needed short-run stimulus or restraint through changes in taxes, transfer payments, or monetary policy, decisions on expenditures for public services can rest on basic judgments of costs and benefits of public and private spending. The availability of this choice permits resources to be devoted to the highest priority uses.

## Prerequisites of Successful Policy

Choice of the right policy action demands full information about the state of the economy and understanding of its workings. And execution of stabilizing policy requires public understanding and acceptance.

### Information

An important requirement of economic policy-making is a firm and timely knowledge of where the economy stands. Spurred by the need for prompt and enlightened decisions, the Federal statistics program has made rapid forward strides in the postwar period, and now provides a much better gauge of current economic developments. Of the 369 monthly series now carried in *Economic Indicators*, the statistical summary prepared by the Council and issued by the Joint Economic Committee, only 60 per cent would have been available by the monthly publication date at the time *Economic Indicators* was launched in the late 1940's.

In addition to the information on current developments, a number of anticipatory surveys have been instituted which provide important information on the probable future course of the economy. Outstanding among these is the Commerce-Securities and Exchange Commission survey on plant and equipment; additional important clues to future developments come from the Commerce inventory survey and the Census quarterly survey of consumer buying intentions. Important information also is obtained from private sources including the University of Michigan's Survey Research Center, the National Industrial Conference Board, and McGraw-Hill, Inc.

Yet, our data are not completely satisfactory. The revisions of the national accounts last summer gave evidence of how much we learn later that could have been helpful on a current basis. There are any number of areas—capital stock and capacity, productivity, employee fringe benefits, job vacancies, among them—where there are important gaps and weaknesses in our quantitative information which can be remedied only by expansion of our statistical programs.

Not all the information useful to the Council comes from published sources or takes the form of numbers. The Council, as enjoined by the Act, finds it most useful to consult regularly with business and labor. These consultations provide valuable information and opinions, and also allow the Council to explain and clarify Administration views.

### Professional Knowledge

Facts are the essential raw materials for analysis, but they require intelligent processing to be useful in guiding policy. The ability of economists to diagnose and forecast on the basis of current facts and to evaluate the impact of alternative policy measures is a key determinant of what policy can do to maintain stable balanced growth.

Our economic knowledge has made great advances in the past generation, but many important questions remain, answers to which should be and can be improved through further research.

There are many quantitative uncertainties in forecasting the strength of private demands. Some of these were illustrated in 1965 when the improvement in profits and sales—coupled with the shifting defense picture—generated a more rapid and greater surge in investment demand than was foreseen initially. Furthermore, the linkage between monetary policy actions and changes in ultimate spending also require more exploration. And even in areas that are more readily quantified, such as the impact on GNP of changes in Government purchases and personal tax reductions, there remains a considerable range of doubt about the timing of the impacts and the specific influences on consumption and investment.

Departing from the domain of aggregative output effects, we need a better understanding of many more specialized problems, such as the functioning of labor markets—how job vacancies are filled, how skill shortages are met, and how excess supplies in one area are ultimately absorbed elsewhere. Such knowledge can be a useful guide to the possibilities for expanding output and employment while avoiding bottlenecks.

But while much remains to be learned about our economy, it would be a disservice to understate the power of economic analysis, and to underrate the substantial contribution of the profession to the successful course of our economy in the postwar period. The Employment Act provided the framework in which this professional contribution could be rendered and be given its proper place in the framing of public policy.

### Public Understanding

Not all the needed improvements in knowledge and understanding are of technical character. Even though viewed as correct by the professional analyst, policies cannot be applied effectively unless the Congress and the public at large understand how the proposed measures intend to further desirable objectives.

If policy proposals of the Administration are to be converted into legislation, they must be convincing to the Congress. Twenty Annual Economic Reports have explained the rationale for the programs of four Presidents. And the Joint Economic Committee has rendered invaluable service in contributing to an understanding of general economic policy and specific proposals. The principles of fiscal policy and their implications for tax and expenditure legislation have been central to the Nation's economic education in the past 20 years. The great increase in understanding is best seen in the sophisticated current level of public discussion.

Proper understanding of policies by the public, moreover, contributes to the very success of the policy measures. In the absence of public understanding, there can be perverse reactions. If people read policies to maintain price stability as an announcement that inflation has arrived, rather than an exercise of determination to avoid it, destabilized prices may be the result. If people see steps to combat recession as a sign of panic rather than a support to the economy, this too can have adverse psychological effects. In particular, a firm appreciation by the American people of the rationale of wage-price guideposts is essential to make them effective and to limit the need for active participation by Government. It is the public that gets hurt by irresponsible wage-price decisions, and public reaction can be the best reminder to those with market power of their social responsibility.

## Conclusion

As the primary objective set by the Employment Act is being reached, new problems move to the fore and are receiving increasing attention in public policy. These include the efficient use of the Nation's human and natural resources, the conquest of poverty and suffering, the reconstruction of our cities, and the many other tasks set forth in the preceding pages of this Report. And undoubtedly in the pursuit of the goals of the Employment Act during the next 20 years, policymakers will encounter a new range of problems, no more completely foreseeable now than were the issues of today in 1946.

While important problems remain, we are nonetheless at an historic point of accomplishment and promise. Twenty years of experience have demonstrated our ability to avoid ruinous inflations and severe depressions. It is now within our capabilities to set more ambitious goals. We strive to avoid recurrent recessions, to keep unemployment far below rates of the past decade, to maintain essential price stability at full employment, to move toward the Great Society, and, indeed, to make full prosperity the normal state of the American Economy. It is a tribute to our success under the Employment Act that we now have not only the economic understanding but also the will and determination to use economic policy as an effective tool for progress.

MILTON FRIEDMAN

# A Monetary and Fiscal Framework for Economic Stability

*31* During the late 19th and early 20th centuries, the problems of the day were of a kind that led economists to concentrate on the allocation of resources and, to a lesser extent, economic growth, and to pay little attention to short-run fluctuations of a cyclical character. Since the Great Depression of the 1930's, this emphasis has been reversed. Economists now tend to concentrate on cyclical movements, to act and talk as if any improvement, however slight, in control of the cycle justified any sacrifice, however large, in the long-run efficiency, or prospects for growth, of the economic system. Proposals for the control of the cycle thus tend to be developed almost as if there were no other

Reprinted from the *American Economic Review*, Vol. XXXVIII (1948), pp. 245–264, by permission of the author and publisher. An earlier version of this paper was presented before the Econometric Society on September 17, 1947, at a meeting held in conjunction with the International Statistical Conferences in Washington, D.C. The author is a professor at The University of Chicago. He is deeply indebted for helpful criticisms and constructive suggestions to Arthur F. Burns, Aaron Director, Albert G. Hart, H. Gregg Lewis, Lloyd W. Mints, Don Patinkin, and George J. Stigler.

objectives and as if it made no difference within what general framework cyclical fluctuations take place. A consequence of this attitude is that inadequate attention is given to the possibility of satisfying both sets of objectives simultaneously.

In constructing the monetary and fiscal framework proposed in this paper, I deliberately gave primary consideration to long-run objectives. That is, I tried to design a framework that would be appropriate for a world in which cyclical movements, other than those introduced by "bad" monetary and fiscal arrangements, were of no consequence. I then examined the resulting proposal to see how it would behave in respect of cyclical fluctuations. It behaves surprisingly well; not only might it be expected not to contribute to cyclical fluctuations, it tends to offset them and therefore seems to offer considerable promise of providing a tolerable degree of short-run economic stability.

This paper is devoted to presenting the part of the analysis dealing with the implications of the proposal for cyclical stability. Nonetheless, in view of the motivation of the proposal it seems well to begin by indicating the long-run objectives adopted as a guide, even though a reasonably full discussion of these long-run objectives would not be appropriate here.

The basic long-run objectives, shared I am sure by most economists, are political freedom, economic efficiency, and substantial equality of economic power. These objectives are not, of course, entirely consistent and some compromise among them may be required. Moreover, objectives stated on this level of generality can hardly guide proximate policy choices. We must take the next step and specify the general institutional arrangements we regard best suited for the attainment of these objectives. I believe—and at this stage agreement will be far less widespread—that all three objectives can best be realized by relying, as far as possible, on a market mechanism within a "competitive order" to organize the utilization of economic resources. Among the specific propositions that follow from this general position, three are particularly relevant: (1) Government must provide a monetary framework for a competitive order since the competitive order cannot provide one for itself. (2) This monetary framework should operate under the "rule of law" rather than the discretionary authority of administrators. (3) While a truly free market in a "competitive order" would yield far less inequality than currently exists, I should hope that the community would desire to reduce inequality even further. Moreover, measures to supplement the market would need to be taken in the interim. For both purposes, general fiscal measures (as contrasted with specific intervention) are the most desirable non-free-market means of decreasing inequality.

The extremely simple proposal which these long-run objectives lead me to advance contains no new elements. Indeed, in view of the number of proposals that have been made for altering one or another part of the present monetary or fiscal framework, it is hard to believe that anything completely new remains to be added. The combination of elements that emerges is somewhat less hackneyed; yet no claim of originality can be made even for this. As is perhaps not surprising from what has already been said, the proposal is something like the greatest common denominator of many different proposals. This is perhaps the chief justification for presenting it and urging that it receive full professional discussion. Perhaps it, or some variant, can approach a minimum program for which economists of the less extreme shades of opinion can make common cause.

This paper deals only with the broad outlines of the monetary and fiscal framework and neglects, or deals superficially with, many difficult, important, and closely related problems. In particular, it neglects almost entirely the transition from the present framework to that outlined here; the implications of the adoption of the recommended framework for international monetary arrangements; and the special requirements of war finance. These associated problems are numerous and serious and are likely to justify compromise at some points. It seems well, however, to set forth the ultimate ideal as clearly as possible before beginning to compromise.

## I. The Proposal

The particular proposal outlined below involves four main elements: the first relates to the monetary system; the second, to government expenditures on goods and services; the third, to government transfer payments; and the fourth, to the tax structure. Throughout, it pertains entirely to the federal government and all references to "government" should be so interpreted.[1]

1. A reform of the monetary and banking system to eliminate both the private creation or destruction of money and discretionary control of the quantity of money by central bank authority. The private creation of money can perhaps best be eliminated by adopting the 100 per cent reserve proposal, thereby separating the depositary from the lending function of the banking system.[2] The adoption of 100 per cent reserves would also reduce the discretionary powers of the reserve system by eliminating rediscounting and existing powers over reserve requirements. To complete the elimination of the major weapons of discretionary authority, the existing

---

[1] The reason for restricting the discussion to the federal government is simply that it alone has ultimate monetary powers, not any desire to minimize the role of smaller governmental units. Indeed, for the achievement of the long-run objectives stated above it is highly desirable that the maximum amount of government activity be in the hands of the smaller governmental units to achieve as much decentralization of political power as possible.

[2] This proposal was advanced by Henry C. Simons. See his *A Positive Program for Laissez-Faire: Some Proposals for a Liberal Economic Policy*, Public Policy Pamphlet No. 15 (Univ. of Chicago Press, 1934); "Rules *vs.* Authorities in Monetary Policy," *Jour. Pol. Econ.*, Vol. XLIV (Feb., 1936), pp. 1–30. Both of these are reprinted in Henry C. Simons, *Economic Policy for a Free Society* (Chicago, Univ. of Chicago Press, 1948).

powers to engage in open market operations and the existing direct controls over stock market and consumer credit should be abolished.

These modifications would leave as the chief monetary functions of the banking system the provision of depositary facilities, the facilitation of check clearance, and the like; and as the chief function of the monetary authorities, the creation of money to meet government deficits or the retirement of money when the government has a surplus.[3]

2. A policy of determining the volume of government expenditures on goods and services—defined to exclude transfer expenditures of all kinds—entirely on the basis of the community's desire, need, and willingness to pay for public services. Changes in the level of expenditure should be made solely in response to alterations in the relative value attached by the community to public services and private consumption. No attempt should be made to vary expenditures, either directly or inversely, in response to cyclical fluctuations in business activity. Since the community's basic objectives would presumably change only slowly—except in time of war or immediate threat of war—this policy would, with the same exception, lead to a relatively stable volume of expenditures on goods and services.[4]

3. A predetermined program of transfer expenditures, consisting of a statement of the conditions and terms under which relief and assistance and other transfer payments will be granted.[5] Such a program is exemplified by the present system of social security under which

rules exist for the payment of old-age and unemployment insurance. The program should be changed only in response to alterations in the kind and level of transfer payments the community feels it should and can afford to make. The program should not be changed in response to cyclical fluctuations in business activity. Absolute outlays, however, will vary automatically over the cycle. They will tend to be high when unemployment is high and low when unemployment is low.[6]

4. A progressive tax system which places primary reliance on the personal income tax. Every effort should be made to collect as much of the tax bill as possible at source and to minimize the delay between the accrual of the tax liability and the actual collection of the tax. Rates, exemptions, etc., should be set in light of the expected yield at a level of income corresponding to reasonably full employment at a predetermined price level. The budget principle might be either that the hypothetical yield should balance government expenditure, including transfer payments (at the same hypothetical level of income) or that it should lead to a deficit sufficient to provide some specified secular increase in the quantity of money.[7]

---

[3] The adoption of 100 per cent reserves is essential if the proposed framework is to be entirely automatic. It should be noted, however, that the same results could, in principle, be achieved in a fractional reserve system through discretionary authority. In order to accomplish this, the monetary authorities would have to adopt the rule that the quantity of money should be increased only when the government has a deficit, and then by the amount of the deficit, and should be decreased only when the government has a surplus, and then by the amount of the surplus.

[4] The volume of expenditures might remain stable either in money or real terms. The principle of determining the volume of expenditures by the community's objectives would lead to a stable real volume of expenditures on current goods and services. On the other hand, the usual legislative procedure in budget making is to grant fixed sums of money, which would lead to stability of money expenditures and provides a slight automatic contra-cyclical flexibility. If the volume of real expenditures were stablized, money expenditures would vary directly with prices.

[5] These transfer payments might perhaps more appropriately be regarded as negative revenue.

[6] It may be hoped that the present complex structure of transfer payments will be integrated into a single scheme co-ordinated with the income tax and designed to provide a universal floor to personal incomes. But this is a separate issue.

[7] These specifications about the hypothetical level of income to be used and the budget principle to be followed are more definite and dogmatic than is justified. In principle, the economic system could ultimately adjust to any tax structure and expenditure policy, no matter what level of income or what budget principle they were initially based on, provided that the tax structure and expenditure policy remained stable. That is, there corresponds some secular position appropriate to each possible tax structure and expenditure policy. The best level of income and the best budget principle to choose depend therefore on short-run adjustment considerations: what choice would require the least difficult adjustment? Moreover, the level of income and budget principle must be chosen jointly: the same final result can obviously be obtained by combining a high hypothetical income with a surplus budget principle or a low hypothetical income with a deficit budget principle or by any number of intermediate combinations. My own conjecture is that the particular level of income and budget principles suggested above are unlikely to lead to results that would require radical short-run adjustments to attain the corresponding secular position. Unfortunately, our knowledge about the relevant economic interrelationships is too meager to permit more than reasonably informed conjecture. See Section IV below, especially footnote 22.

The tax structure should not be varied in response to cyclical fluctuations in business activity, though actual receipts will, of course, vary automatically.[8] Changes in the tax structure should reflect changes in the level of public services or transfer payments the community chooses to have. A decision to undertake additional public expenditures should be accompanied by a revenue measure increasing taxes. Calculations of both the cost of additional public services or transfer payments and the yield of additional taxes should be made at the hypothetical level of income suggested above rather than at the actual level of income. The government would thus keep two budgets: the stable budget, in which all figures refer to the hypothetical income, and the actual budget. The principle of balancing outlays and receipts at a hypothetical income level would be substituted for the principle of balancing actual outlays and receipts.

## II. Operation of the Proposal

The essence of this fourfold proposal is that it uses automatic adaptations in the government contribution to the current income stream to offset, at least in part, changes in other segments of aggregate demand and to change appropriately the supply of money. It eliminates discretionary action in response to cyclical movements as well as some extraneous or perverse reactions of our

[8] The principle of setting taxes so as to balance the budget at a high level of employment was suggested by Beardsley Ruml and H. Chr. Sonne, *Fiscal and Monetary Policy*, National Planning Pamphlet no. 35 (July, 1944).

Since the present paper was written, the Committee for Economic Development has issued a policy statement in which it makes essentially the same tax and expenditure recommendations—that is, it calls for adoption of a stable tax structure capable of balancing the budget at a high level of employment, a stable expenditure policy, and primary reliance on automatic adjustments of absolute revenue and expenditures to provide cyclical stability. They call this policy the "stabilizing budget policy." The chief difference between the present proposal and the C.E.D. proposal is that the C.E.D. is silent on the monetary framework and almost silent on public debt policy, whereas the present proposal covers both. Presumably the C.E.D. plans to cover monetary and debt policy in separate statements still to be issued. See *Taxes and the Budget: A Program for Prosperity in a Free Economy*, a statement on national policy by the Research and Policy Committee of the Committee for Economic Development (Nov., 1947).

present monetary and fiscal structure.[9] Discretionary action is limited to the determination of the hypothetical level of income underlying the stable budget; that is, essentially to the determination of a reasonably attainable objective. Some decision of this kind is unavoidable in drawing up the government's budget; the proposal involves a particular decision and makes it explicit. The determination of the income goal admittedly cannot be made entirely objective or mechanical. At the same time, this determination would need to be made only at rather long intervals—perhaps every five or ten years—and involves a minimum of forecasting. Further, as will be indicated later, errors in the income goal tend to be automatically neutralized and do not require a redetermination of the goal.

Under the proposal, government expenditures would be financed entirely by either tax revenues or the creation of money, that is, the issue of non-interest-bearing securities. Government would not issue interest-bearing securities to the public; the Federal Reserve System would not operate in the open market. This restriction of the sources of government funds seems reasonable for peacetime. The chief valid ground for paying interest to the public on government debt is to offset the inflationary pressure of abnormally high government expenditures when, for one reason or another, it is not feasible or desirable to levy sufficient taxes to do so. This was the justification for wartime issuance of interest-bearing securities, though, perversely, the rate of interest on these securities was pegged at a low level. It seems inapplicable in peacetime, especially if, as suggested, the volume of government expenditures on goods and services is kept relatively stable. Another reason sometimes given for issuing interest-bearing securities is that in a period of unemployment it is less deflationary to issue securities than to levy taxes. This is true. But it is still less deflationary to issue money.[10]

[9] For example, the tendency under the existing system of fractional reserve banking for the total volume of money to change when there is a change in the proportion of its total stock of money the community wishes to hold in the form of deposits; the tendency to reduce tax rates and increase government expenditures in booms and to do the reverse in depressions; and the tendency for the government to borrow from individuals at the same time as the Federal Reserve System is buying government bonds on the open market.

[10] See Henry C. Simons, "On Debt Policy," *Jour. Pol. Econ.*, Vol. LII (Dec., 1944), pp. 356–61.

This paragraph deliberately avoids the question of the payment of interest to banks on special issues of government bonds, as has been proposed in some

Deficits or surpluses in the government budget would be reflected dollar for dollar in changes in the quantity of money; and, conversely, the quantity of money would change only as a consequence of deficits or surpluses. A deficit means an increase in the quantity of money; a surplus, a decrease.[11]

Deficits or surpluses themselves become automatic consequences of changes in the level of business activity. When national money income is high, tax receipts will be large and transfer payments small; so a surplus will tend to be created, and the higher the level of income, the larger the surplus. This extraction of funds from the current income stream makes aggregate demand lower than it otherwise would be and reduces the volume of money, thereby tending to offset the factors making for a further increase in income. When national money income is low, tax receipts will be small and transfer payments large, so a deficit will tend to be created, and the lower the level of income, the larger the deficit. This addition of funds to the current income stream makes aggregate demand higher than it otherwise would be and increases the quantity of money, thereby tending to offset the factors making for a further decline in income.

The size of the effects automatically produced

versions of the 100 per cent reserve proposal. The fundamental issue involved in judging such proposals is whether government should subsidize the use of deposit money and a system of check clearance and if so, what form the subsidy should take.

The large volume of government bonds now outstanding raises one of the most serious problems in accomplishing the transition from the present framework. This problem would be eased somewhat by the monetization of bonds that would occur in the process of going over to 100 per cent reserves. But there would still remain a substantial volume. Two alternatives suggest themselves: (1) freeze the volume of debt at some figure, preferably by converting it into perpetuities ("consols"); (2) use the monetization of the debt as a means of providing a secular increase in the quantity of money. Under the second plan, which, on a first view, seems more attractive, the principle of balancing the stable budget would be adopted and the government would commit itself to retiring, through the issuance of new money, a predetermined amount of the public debt annually. The amount to be retired would be determined so as to achieve whatever secular increase in the quantity of money seemed desirable. This problem, however, requires much additional study.

[11] These statements refer, of course, to the ultimate operation of the proposal. Under the second of the alternatives suggested in the preceding footnote, the change in the quantity of money during the transitional period would equal the excess of government expenditures over receipts plus the predetermined amount of money issued to retire debt.

by changes in national income obviously depends on the range of activities government undertakes, since this will in turn determine the general order of magnitude of the government budget. Nonetheless, an essential element of the proposal is that the activities to be undertaken by government be determined entirely on other grounds. In part, this element is an immediate consequence of the motivation of the proposal. The motivation aside, however, it seems a desirable element of any proposal to promote stability. First, there is and can be no simple, reasonably objective, rule to determine the optimum share of activity that should be assigned to government —short of complete socialization—even if stability were the only objective. Changes in circumstances are likely to produce rapid and erratic variations in the share that seems desirable. But changes in the share assigned government are themselves likely to be destabilizing, both directly and through their adverse effects on anticipations. The attempt to adapt the magnitude of government operations to the requirements of stability may therefore easily introduce more instability than it corrects. Second, the share of activity assigned government is likely to have far more important consequences for other objectives— particularly political freedom and economic efficiency—than for stability.[12] Third, means other than changes in the share of activity assigned government are readily available for changing the size of the reaction to changes in income, if experience under the proposal should prove this desirable. And some of these means need not have anything like the same consequences for other objects.

Under the proposal, the aggregate quantity of money is automatically determined by the requirements of domestic stability. It follows that changes in the quantity of money cannot also be used—as they are in a fully operative gold standard—to achieve equilibrium in international trade. The two criteria will by no means always require the same changes in the quantity of money; when they conflict, one or the other must dominate. The decision, implicit in the framework recommended, to select domestic stability means that some other technique must

[12] An example of the relevance of these two points is provided by the tendency during the 'thirties to recommend an increase in the progressiveness of the tax structure as a means of increasing the propensity to consume and hence, it was argued, employment. Applied to the postwar period, the same argument would call for a shift to regressive taxes, yet I wonder if many economists would wish to recommend regressive taxes on these grounds.

be used to bring about adjustments to changes in the conditions of international trade. The international arrangement that seems the logical counterpart of the proposed framework is flexible exchange rates, freely determined in foreign exchange markets, preferably entirely by private dealings.[13]

## III. Effect of Proposal under Present Institutional Conditions

The fluctuations in the government contribution to the income stream under the proposed monetary and fiscal framework are clearly in the "right" direction. Nonetheless, it is not at all clear that they would, without additional institutional modifications, necessarily lead either to reasonably full employment or to a reasonable degree of stability. Rigidities in prices are likely to make this proposal, and indeed most if not all other proposals for attaining cyclical stability, inconsistent with reasonably full employment; and, when combined with lags in other types of response, to render extremely uncertain their effectiveness in stabilizing economic activity.

### A. Price Rigidities

Under existing circumstances, when many prices are moderately rigid, at least against declines, the monetary and fiscal framework described above cannot be expected to lead to reasonably full employment of resources, even though lags in other kinds of response are minor. The most that can be expected under such circumstances is a reasonably stable or moderately rising level of money income. As an extreme example, suppose that the economy is in a relatively stable position at reasonably full employment and with a roughly balanced actual government budget and that the great bulk of wage rates are rigid against downward pressure. Now, let there be a substantial rise in the wage rates of a particular group of workers as a consequence either of trade union action or of a sharp but temporary increase in the demand for that type of labor or decrease in

its supply, and let this higher wage rate be rigid against downward pressure. Employment of resources as full as previously would imply a higher aggregate money income since, under the assumed conditions of rigidity, other resources would receive the same amount as previously whereas the workers whose wage rates rose would receive a larger aggregate amount if fully employed. But if this higher money income, which also of course would imply a higher price structure, were attained, the government would tend to have a surplus since receipts would rise by more than expenditures. There is nothing that has occurred that would, in the absence of other independent changes, offset the deflationary effect of the surplus. The assumed full employment position would not therefore be an equilibrium position. If attained by accident, the resultant budgetary surplus would reduce effective demand and, since prices are assumed rigid, the outcome could only be unemployment. The equilibrium level of income will be somewhat higher than before, primarily because transfer payments to the unemployed will be larger, so that some of the unemployment will be offset. But there is no mechanism for offsetting the rest. The only escape from this situation is to permit inflation.

As is widely recognized, the difficulty just described is present also in most other monetary and fiscal proposals; they, too, can produce full employment under such circumstances only by inflation. This dilemma often tends, however, to be concealed in their formulation, and, in practice, it seems fairly likely that inflation would result. The brute fact is that a rational economic program for a free enterprise system (and perhaps even for a collectivist system) must have flexibility of prices (including wages) as one of its cornerstones. This need is made clear by a proposal like the present. Moreover, the adoption of such a proposal would provide some assurance against cumulative deflation and thereby tend to make flexibility of prices a good deal easier to achieve since government support for monopolistic practices of special occupational and industrial groups derives in large measure from the obvious waste of general deflation and the need for protection against it.

### B. Lags in Response

Our economy is characterized not only by price rigidities but also by significant lags in other types of response. These lags make impossible any definitive statement about the actual degree

[13] Though here presented as a byproduct of the proposed domestic framework, flexible exchange rates can be defended directly. Indeed, it would be equally appropriate to present the proposed domestic framework as a means of implementing flexible exchange rates. The heart of the matter is that domestic and international monetary and trade arrangements are part of one whole.

of stability likely to result from the operation of the monetary and fiscal framework described above. One could reasonably expect smaller fluctuations than currently exist; though our ignorance about lags and about the fundamental causes of business fluctuations prevents complete confidence even in this outcome. The lag between the creation of a government deficit and its effects on the behavior of consumers and producers could conceivably be so long and variable that the stimulating effects of the deficit were often operative only after other factors had already brought about a recovery rather than when the initial decline was in progress. Despite intuitive feelings to the contrary, I do not believe we know enough to rule out completely this possibility. If it were realized, the proposed framework could intensify rather than mitigate cyclical fluctuations; that is, long and variable lags could convert the fluctuations in the government contribution to the income stream into the equivalent of an additional random disturbance.[14]

About all one can say about this possibility is that the completely automatic proposal outlined above seems likely to do less harm under the circumstances envisaged than alternative proposals which provide for discretionary action in addition to automatic reactions. There is a strong presumption that these discretionary actions will in general be subject to longer lags than the automatic reactions and hence will be destabilizing even more frequently.

The basis for this presumption can best be seen by subdividing into three parts the total lag involved in any action to offset a disturbance: (1) the lag between the need for action and the recognition of this need; (2) the lag between recognition of the need for action and the taking of action; and (3) the lag between the action and its effects.

The first lag, which is nonexistent for automatic reactions of the kind here proposed, could be negative for discretionary proposals if it were possible to forecast accurately the economic changes that would occur in the absence of government action. In view of the record of forecasters, it hardly needs to be argued that it would be better to shun forecasting and rely instead on as prompt an evaluation of the current situation as possible. The lag between the need for action and the recognition of that need then becomes positive. Its exact magnitude depends on the particular discretionary proposal, though

the past record of contemporary interpreters of business conditions indicates that it is not likely to be negligible.[15]

The second lag is present even for automatic reactions because all taxes will not or cannot be collected at source simultaneously with the associated payments, and transfer payments will not or cannot be made immediately without some kind of a waiting period or processing period. It is clear, however, that this lag can be reduced to a negligible time by appropriate construction and administration of the system of taxes and transfer payments. For discretionary action, the length of the lag between the recognition of the need for action and the taking of action depends very much on the kind of action taken. Action can be taken very promptly to change the form or amount of the community's holdings of assets by open market purchases or sales of securities or by changes in rediscount rates or reserve requirements. A considerably longer time is required to change the net contribution of the government to the income stream by changing the tax structure. Even though advance prescription for alternative possibilities eliminates any delay in deciding what changes to make in tax rates, exemptions, kinds of taxes levied, or the like, administrative considerations will enforce a substantial delay before the change becomes effective. Taxpayers, businesses or individuals acting as intermediaries in collecting the taxes, and tax administrators must all be informed of the change and be given an opportunity to make the appropriate adjustments in their procedures; new forms must be printed or at least circulated; and so on.

The longest delay of all is likely to be involved in changing the net contribution of government to the income stream by changing government expenditure policy, particularly for goods and services. No matter how much advance planning may have been done, the rate of expenditure cannot be stepped up or curtailed overnight unless the number of names on the payroll is to be the only basis in terms of which the expenditure is to be controlled or judged. Time is involved in getting projects under way with any degree of efficiency; and considerable waste in ceasing work on projects abruptly.

The third lag, that between the action and its effects, is present and significant both for automatic reactions and discretionary actions, and little if anything can be done about it by either legal or administrative reform of the fiscal and

---

[14] See Milton Friedman, "Lerner on the Economics of Control," *Jour. Pol. Econ.*, Vol. LV, No. 5 (Oct., 1947), p. 414, especially footnote 12.

[15] *Ibid.*, p. 414, especially footnote 11.

monetary structure.[16] We have no trustworthy empirical evidence on the length of this lag for various kinds of action, and much further study of this problem is clearly called for. Some clues about the direction such study should take are furnished by *a priori* considerations which suggest, as a first approximation, that the order of the various policies with respect to the length of this lag is the reverse of their order with respect to the length of the lag between the recognition of the need for action and the taking of action. Changes in government expenditures on goods and services lead to almost immediate changes in the employment of the resources used to produce those goods and services. They have secondary effects through the changes thereby induced in the expenditures of the individuals owning the resources so employed.

The lag in these induced changes might be expected to be less than the lag in the adjustment of expenditures to changed taxes or to a changed amount or form of asset holdings. Changes in taxes make the disposable incomes of individuals larger or smaller than they would otherwise be. Individuals might be expected to react to a change in disposable income as a result of a tax change only slightly less rapidly than to a change in disposable income as a result of a change in aggregate income.

These indications are, however, none too trustworthy. These are likely to be important indirect effects that depend on such things as the kinds of goods and services directly affected by changed government expenditures, the incidence of the changes in disposable income that result from changed expenditures or taxes, and the means employed to finance government deficits. For example, if deficits are financed through increases in the quantity of money and surpluses are used to reduce the quantity of money, part of the effect of changes in government expenditures or taxes will be produced by changes in interest rates and the kind and volume of assets held by the community. The entire effect of open-market operations, changes in rediscount rates and reserve requirements, and the like will be produced in this way, and it seems likely that these effects would take the longest to make themselves felt.

The automatic reactions embodied in the proposal here advanced operate in part like tax changes—in so far as tax receipts vary—and in part like expenditure changes—in so far as

transfer payments vary; and like both of these, some part of their effect is through changes in the quantity of money. One might expect, therefore, that the lag between action and its effects would be roughly the same for automatic reactions as for discretionary tax changes, a good deal shorter for automatic reactions than for discretionary monetary changes, and somewhat longer for automatic reactions than for discretionary changes in government expenditures on goods and services.

This analysis, much of which is admittedly highly conjectural, suggests that the total lag is definitely longer for discretionary monetary or tax changes than for automatic reactions, since each of the three parts into which the total lag has been subdivided is longer. There is doubt about the relative length of the total lag only for discretionary expenditure changes. Even for these, however, it seems doubtful that the shorter lag between action and its effects can more than offset the longer lag between the need for action and the taking of action.

Given less extreme conditions than those required to convert the present proposal into a destabilizing influence, the reduction achieved in the severity of fluctuations would depend on the extent and rapidity of price adjustments, the nature of the responses of individuals to these price changes and to the changes in their incomes and asset holdings resulting from the induced surpluses or deficits, and the lags in such responses. If these were such as to make the system operate reasonably well, the improvement would tend to be cumulative, since the experience of damped fluctuations would lead to patterns of expectations on the part of both businessmen and consumers that would make it rational for them to take action that would damp fluctuations still more. This favorable result would occur, however, only if the proposed system operated reasonably well without such aid; hence, in my view, this proposal, and all others as well, should be judged primarily on their direct effects, not on their indirect effects in stimulating a psychological climate favorable to stability. It must be granted, however, that the present proposal is less likely to stimulate such a favorable psychological climate than a proposal which has a simpler and more easily understood goal, for example, a proposal which sets a stable price level as its announced goal. *If the business world were sufficiently confident of the ability of the government to achieve the goal*, it would have a strong incentive to behave in such a way as greatly to simplify the government's task.

[16] Reforms of other types, for example, reforms increasing the flexibility of prices, might affect this lag.

## IV. Implications of the Proposal if Prices Are Flexible and Lags in Response Minor

The ideal possibilities of the monetary and fiscal framework proposed in this paper, and the stabilizing economic forces on which these possibilities depend, can be seen best if we put aside the difficulties that have been detaining us and examine the implications of the proposal in an economy in which prices of both products and factors of production are flexible[17] and lags in other types of response are minor. In such an economy, the monetary and fiscal system described above would tend toward an equilibrium characterized by reasonably full employment.

To describe the forces at work, let us suppose that the economy is initially in a position of reasonably full employment with a balanced actual budget and is subjected to a disturbance producing a decline in aggregate money demand that would be permanent if no other changes occurred.[18] The initial effect of the decline in aggregate demand will be a decline in sales and the piling up of inventories in at least some parts of the economy, followed shortly by unemployment and price declines caused by the attempt to reduce inventories to the desired level. The lengthening of the list of unemployed will increase government transfer payments; the loss of income by the unemployed will reduce government tax receipts. The deficit created in this way is a net contribution by the government to the income stream which directly offsets some of the decline in aggregate demand, thereby preventing unemployment from becoming as large as it otherwise would and serving as a shock absorber while more fundamental correctives come into play.

These more fundamental correctives, aside from changes in relative prices and interest rates, are (1) a decline in the general level of prices which affects (a) the real value of the community's assets and (b) the government contribution to the income stream, and (2) an increase in the stock of money.

The decline in the general level of prices that follows the initial decline in aggregate demand will clearly raise the real value of the community's stock of money and government bonds since the nominal value of these assets will not decrease. The real value of the remainder of the community's assets may be expected to remain roughly the same, so the real value of the total stock of assets will rise.[19] The rise in the real value of assets will lessen the need for additional saving and hence increase the fraction of any given level of real income that the community will wish to consume. This force, in principle, would alone be sufficient to assure full employment even if the government maintained a rigidly balanced actual budget and kept the quantity of money constant, since there would presumably always be some price level at which the community could be made to feel rich enough to spend on consumption whatever fraction or multiple of its current income is required to yield an aggregate demand sufficient to permit full employment.

This effect of a lower price level in increasing the fraction of current private (disposable) income devoted to consumption is reinforced by its effect on the government's contribution to the income stream. So long as the price level, and with it money income, is below its initial level, the government will continue to run a deficit. This will be true even if employment is restored

---

[17] The concept of flexible prices, though one we use continually and can hardly avoid using, is extremely difficult to define precisely. Fortunately, a precise definition is not required for the argument that follows. All that is necessary for the argument is that there be a "substantial" range of prices that are not "rigid" because of long-term contracts or organized noncontractual agreements to maintain price and that these prices should react reasonably quickly to changes in long-run conditions of demand or supply. It is not necessary that there be "perfect" flexibility of prices, however that might be defined, or that contracts involving prices be subject to change at will, or that every change in long-run conditions of demand or supply be reflected instantaneously in market price.

[18] The same analysis would apply to disturbances producing only a temporary decline. The reason for assuming a permanent decline is to trace through the entire process of adjustment to a new equilibrium position.

[19] If the real value of other assets of the community should fall, this would simply mean that the price level would have to fall farther in order to raise the real value of the community's total stock of assets. Note that under the proposed framework, all money in the community is either a direct government obligation (nondeposit currency) or is backed one hundred per cent by a direct government obligation (deposits in the central bank). If this analysis were to be applied to a fractional reserve system, the assets whose aggregate real value could be guaranteed to rise with no directly offsetting fall in the real value of private assets would be the total amount of government obligations (currency and bonds) held outside the treasury and central bank. On this and what follows, see A. C. Pigou, "The Classical Stationary State," *Econ. Jour.*, Vol. LIII (Dec., 1943), pp. 342–51, and "Economic Progress in a Stable Environment," *Economica*, n.s. XIV (Aug., 1947), pp. 180–90; and Don Patinkin, "Price Flexibility and Full Employment," to be published in the September, 1948 number of this *Review*.

to its initial level, so that transfer payments and loss in tax receipts on account of unemployment are eliminated. The tax structure is progressive, and exemptions, rates, etc., are expressed in absolute dollar amounts. Receipts will therefore fall more than in proportion to the fall in the price level; expenditures, at most, proportionately.[20] Because of the emergence of such a deficit, the price decline required to restore employment will be smaller than if the government were to maintain a rigidly balanced actual budget, and this will be true even aside from the influence of the deficit on the stock of money. The reason is that the price level will have to fall only to the point at which the amount the community desires to add to its hoards equals the government deficit, rather than to the point at which the community desires to add nothing to its hoards.[21]

[20] The effect of the lower price level on expenditures depends somewhat on the precise expenditure and transfer policy adopted. If, as is called for by the principle of determining the expenditure program by the community's objectives, the real volume of government expenditures on goods and services is kept cyclically stable and if the program of transfer payments is also stated in real terms, expenditures will decline proportionately. If government expenditures on goods and services are kept cyclically stable in dollar terms, or the program of transfer expenditures is stated in dollar terms, expenditures will decline less than proportionately.

[21] If the real volume of government expenditures on goods and services is kept cyclically stable and the transfer program is also stated in real terms, the aggregate expenditures of government under fixed expenditure and transfer programs would tend to be the same fraction of the full-employment income of society no matter what the price level. This fraction would be the maximum net contribution the government could make to the income stream no matter how low prices, and with them money income and government receipts, fell. Consequently, this force alone would be limited in magnitude and might not, even in principle, be able to offset every disturbance. If either program is in absolute terms, there would be no limit to the fraction that the government contribution could constitute of the total income stream.

An alternative way to describe this effect is in terms of the relation between the expected expenditures and receipts of consumers, business, and government. It is a condition of equilibrium that the sum of the desired expenditures of these groups equal the sum of their receipts. If the government maintains a rigidly balanced budget, equilibrium requires that consumers and business together plan to spend what they receive (*i.e.*, not seek to add to their money hoards). If the government runs a deficit, consumers and business together need not plan to spend all they receive; equilibrium requires that their planned expenditures fall short of their receipts by the amount of the deficit (*i.e.*, that they seek to add to their hoards per period the amount of the deficit).

The decline in the price level may restore the initial level of employment through the combined effects of the increased average propensity to consume and the government deficit. But so long as a deficit exists, the position attained is not an equilibrium position. The deficit is financed by the issue of money. The resultant increase in the aggregate stock of money must further raise the real value of the community's stock of assets and hence the average propensity to consume. This is the same effect as that discussed above except that it is brought about by an increase in the absolute stock of money rather than by a decline in prices. Like the corresponding effect produced by a decline in prices, the magnitude of this effect is, in principle, unlimited. The rise in the stock of money and hence in the average propensity to consume will tend to raise prices and reduce the deficit. If we suppose no change to occur other than the one introduced to start the analysis going, the final adjustment would be attained when prices had risen sufficiently to yield a roughly balanced actual budget.

A disturbance increasing aggregate money demand would bring into play the same forces operating in the reverse direction: the increase in employment would reduce transfer payments and raise tax receipts, thus creating a surplus to offset part of the increase in aggregate demand; the rise in prices would decrease the real value of the community's stock of money and hence the fraction of current income spent on consumption; the rise in prices would also mean that even after "overemployment" was eliminated, the government would run a surplus that would tend to offset further the initial increase in aggregate demand;[22] and, finally, the surplus would reduce the stock of money.

As this analysis indicates, the proposed fiscal and monetary framework provides defense in depth against changes in aggregate demand. The first line of defense is the adjustment of transfer payments and tax receipts to changes in employment.[23] This eases the shock while the defense is

[22] The limit to the possible effect of the surplus on the current income stream would be set by the character of the tax structure, since there would probably be some maximum percentage of the aggregate income that could be taken by taxes no matter how high the price level and the aggregate income.

[23] It should be noted that this is the only effect taken into account by Musgrave and Miller in their calculations of the possible magnitude of the effect of automatic variations in government receipts and expenditures. (R. A. Musgrave and M. H. Miller, "Built-in Flexibility," this *Review*, March, 1948, pp. 122–28.) They conclude that "the analysis here pro-

taken over by changes in prices. These raise or lower the real value of the community's assets and thereby raise or lower the fraction of income consumed. They also produce a government deficit or surplus in addition to the initial deficit or surplus resulting from the effect of changes in employment on transfer payments and tax receipts. The final line of defense is the cumulative effect of the deficits or surpluses on the stock of money. These changes in the stock of money tend to restore prices to their initial level. In some measure, of course, these defenses all operate simultaneously; yet their main effects are likely to occur in the temporal order suggested in the preceding discussion.

Even given flexible prices, the existence of the equilibrating mechanism described does not of course mean that the economy will in fact achieve relative stability. This depends in addition on the number and magnitude of the disturbances to which the economy is subject, the speed with which the equilibrating forces operate, and the importance of such disequilibrating forces as adverse price expectations. If the lags of response are minor, and initial perverse reactions unimportant, adjustments would be completed rapidly and there would be no opportunity for disequilibria to cumulate, so that relative stability would be attained. Even in this most favorable case, however, the equilibrating mechanism does not prevent disturbances from arising and does not counteract their effects instantaneously—as, indeed, no system can in the absence of ability to predict everything in advance with perfect accuracy. What the equilibrating mechanism does accomplish is, first, to keep governmental monetary and fiscal operations from themselves contributing disturbances and, second, to provide an automatic mechanism for adapting the system to the disturbances that occur.

Given flexible prices, there would be a tendency for automatic neutralization of any errors in the hypothetical income level assumed or in the calculations of the volume of expenditures and revenues at the hypothetical income level. Further, it would ultimately be of no great importance exactly what decision was reached about the relation to establish between expenditures and

revenue at the hypothetical income level (*i.e.*, whether exactly to balance, to strive for a deficit sufficient to provide a predetermined secular increase in the quantity of money, etc.). Suppose, for example, that errors in the assumed income level, the calculated volume of expenditures and receipts, and the relation established between expenditures and receipts combined to produce a deficit larger than was consistent with stable prices. The resulting inflationary pressure would be analogous to that produced by an external disturbance and the same forces would come into play to counteract it. The result would be that prices would rise and the level of income tend to stabilize at a higher level than the hypothetical level initially assumed.

Similarly, the monetary and fiscal framework described above provides for adjustment not only to cyclical changes but also to secular changes. I do not put much credence in the doctrine of secular stagnation or economic maturity that is now so widely held. But let us assume for the sake of argument that this doctrine is correct, that there has been such a sharp secular decline in the demand for capital that, at the minimum rate of interest technically feasible, the volume of investment at a full-employment level of income would be very much less than the volume of savings that would be forthcoming at this level of income and at the current price.[24] The result would simply be that the equilibrium position would involve a recurrent deficit sufficient to provide the hoards being demanded by savers. Of course, this would not really be a long-run equilibrium position, since the gradual increase in the quantity of money would increase the aggregate real value of the community's stock of money and thereby of assets, and this would tend to increase the fraction of any given level of real income consumed. As a result, there would tend to be a gradual rise in prices and the

---

vided lends no justification to the view now growing in popularity that 'built-in flexibility' can do the job alone and that deliberate countercyclical fiscal policy can be dispensed with." While this is a valid conclusion, it does not justify rejecting the view that "built-in flexibility" can do the job alone, since the "analysis here provided" takes no account of what have been termed above the "more fundamental correctives."

24 Because of the effect discussed above of price changes on the real value of assets, and in this way on the average propensity to consume, it seems to me that such a state of affairs would not lead to secular unemployment even if the quantity of money were kept constant, provided that prices are flexible (which is the reason for including the qualifications "at the current price level" in the sentence to which this footnote is attached). But I am for the moment accepting the point of view of those who deny the existence or importance of this equilibrating force. Moreover, if the quantity of money were constant, the adjustment would be made entirely through a secular decline in prices, admittedly a difficult adjustment. Once again changes in the government contribution to the income stream and through this in the quantity of money can reduce the extent of the required price change.

level of money income and a gradual reduction in the deficit.[25]

## V. Conclusion

In conclusion, I should like to emphasize the modest aim of the proposal. It does not claim to provide full employment in the absence of successful measures to make prices of final goods and of factors of production flexible. It does not claim to eliminate entirely cyclical fluctuations in output and employment. Its claim to serious consideration is that it provides a stable framework of fiscal and monetary action, that it largely eliminates the uncertainty and undesirable political implications of discretionary action by governmental authorities, that it provides for adaptation of the governmental sector to changes occurring in other sectors of the economy of a kind designed to offset the effects of these changes, and that the proposed fiscal and monetary framework is consistent with the long-run considerations stated at the outset of this paper. It is not perhaps a proposal that one would consider at all optimum if our knowledge of the fundamental causes of cyclical fluctuations were considerably greater than I, for one, think it to be; it is a proposal that involves minimum reliance on uncertain and untested knowledge.

The proposal has of course its dangers. Explicit control of the quantity of money by government and explicit creation of money to meet actual government deficits may establish a climate favorable to irresponsible government action and to inflation. The principle of a balanced stable budget may not be strong enough to offset these tendencies. This danger may well be greater for this proposal than for some others, yet in some measure it is common to most proposals to mitigate cyclical fluctuations. It can probably be avoided only by moving in a completely different direction, namely, toward an entirely metallic currency, elimination of any governmental control of the quantity of money, and the re-enthronement of the principle of a balanced actual budget.

The proposal may not succeed in reducing cyclical fluctuations to tolerable proportions. The forces making for cyclical fluctuations may be so stubborn and strong that the kind of automatic adaptations contained in the proposal are insufficient to offset them to a tolerable degree. I do not see how it is possible to know now whether this is the case. But even if it should prove to be, the changes suggested are almost certain to be in the right direction and, in addition, to provide a more satisfactory framework on which to build further action.

A proposal like the present one, which is concerned not with short-run policy but with structural reform, should not be urged on the public unless and until it has withstood the test of professional criticism. It is in this spirit that the present paper is published.

[25] This and the preceding paragraph, in particular, and this entire section, in general, suggest a problem that deserves investigation and to which I have no satisfactory answer, namely, the characteristics of the system of equations implicit in the proposal and of their equilibrium solution. It is obvious that under strictly stationary conditions, including a stationary population, the equilibrium solution would involve constancy of prices, income per head, etc., and a balanced actual budget. The interesting question is whether there is any simple description of the equilibrium solution under specified dynamic situations. For example, are there circumstances, and if so what are they, under which the equilibrium solution will tend to involve constant money income per head with declining prices, or constant prices with rising money income per head, etc? It is obvious that no such simple description will suffice in general, but there may well be broad classes of circumstances under which one or another will.

# *Monetary Policy*

*T*HE POLITICAL PROBLEMS inherent in changing fiscal activities in the United States economy have resulted in stabilization efforts to a large extent being left by default to the implementation of monetary policies. But will monetary policies work and, if they will, what form should they take? In the first article in this section, Warren L. Smith discusses the various monetary techniques which might be used in the United States economy. In the next two articles, James R. Schlesinger considers some of the criticisms which have been raised regarding the use of monetary policies for stabilization purposes and James Galbraith discusses the effects on monetary policies of the existence of financial institutions which are outside of the control of the Federal Reserve System. Then George Horwich examines the possibility that the higher interest-rate levels resulting from the use of monetary policies might themselves cause inflation. Finally Thomas Beard discusses the relationship between the management of the United States national debt and the implementation of monetary policies, and Milton Friedman reviews the changes which he feels have occurred in monetary theory and policy during the postwar era.

*WARREN L. SMITH*

# The Instruments of General Monetary Control

# *32*

## I. Introduction

At present, the Federal Reserve System possesses three major instruments of general monetary control: the power to buy and sell securities in the open market; the power to fix discount rates and regulate other conditions of member bank borrowing; and the power to change within specified limits the reserve requirements of member banks. This paper deals with the relative usefulness of these three credit-control instruments and with problems of their proper co-ordination.[1]

---

[1] In addition to the three general credit control instruments, the System has from time to time employed selective controls, including the regulation of consumer and real estate credit. At the present time, however, the only important selective control power that the System has is the authority to regulate margin requirements applicable to loans for purchasing and carrying securities. This paper makes no effort to deal with the use of selective controls or their co-ordination with general controls.

---

Reprinted from the *National Banking Review,* Vol. I (1963), pp. 47–76, by permission of the author and publisher. Warren Smith is a professor at the University of Michigan.

## II. The Primacy of Open Market Operations

Nearly all students of American monetary affairs would probably agree that open market operations constitute the primary weapon of monetary policy. The initiative with respect to such operations lies firmly in the hands of the Federal Reserve System, and the weapon possesses great flexibility with respect to both timing and magnitude. That is, operations can be used to produce large or small changes in credit conditions, and the direction of operations can be changed almost instantaneously.

In addition to their use to control credit in the interest of economic stability and growth, open market operations are carried on continuously for the purpose of offsetting the short-run effects on member bank reserves resulting from factors outside the control of the Federal Reserve—changes in float, currency in circulation, gold stock, Treasury and foreign deposits at the Reserve banks, and so on. These operations, which have been increasingly perfected in recent years, serve the important function of maintaining an even keel in the central money market. They also act as a kind of camouflage which frequently makes it rather difficult to discern and interpret the longer-run objectives of System policy as reflected in open market operations. Thus, since open market operations are generally going on continuously and are directed at the accomplishment of a rather complex variety of objectives, they are relatively free from the psychological overtones (sometimes called "announcement effects") that frequently accompany changes in discount rates or in reserve requirements. For reasons that will be explained below, I believe this absence of psychological implications is a rather important advantage of open market operations.

To the extent of its net purchases or sales of Government securities, the Federal Reserve changes not only the supply of bank reserves but the amount of interest-bearing Federal debt held by the public. In addition, by varying its purchases and sales in various maturity sectors of the market, it can influence the maturity composition of the publicly-held debt and, to some extent at least, the term-structure of interest rates. Thus, open market operations are a form of debt management. They should be closely coordinated with the Treasury's debt management decisions concerning the maturities of securities to issue or retire in its cash borrowing, refunding, and debt retirement operations.

For a period of about eight years beginning in March 1953, the Federal Open Market Committee, which is responsible for the conduct of System open market operations, adhered to the so-called "bills-only" policy, the key feature of which was that open market operations for the purpose of effectuating stabilizing monetary policy were confined to short-term securities, chiefly Treasury bills. Early in 1961, this policy was altered to a more flexible one which permitted operations in all maturity ranges of the U.S. Government securities market.[2] The primary reason for the 1961 change in policy was the emergence of a serious balance of payments deficit partly caused by substantial outflows of short-term capital to foreign money centers at a time when the domestic economy was suffering

from substantial unemployment and underutilization of productive capacity.

Although System open market purchases of longer-term securities have actually been quite modest since early 1961, the greater flexibility of open market policy, together with associated shifts in the conduct of Treasury debt management activities, has undoubtedly helped to make it possible to maintain and even increase U.S. short-term interest rates in line with those abroad, thus preventing excessive outflows of short-term funds, while at the same time preventing increases in the long-term bond yields and mortgage interest rates which influence plant and equipment expenditures, capital outlays of State and local governments, and housing construction.[3]

Open market operations are firmly established as the fundamental weapon of monetary policy in the United States. Accordingly, the important questions concerning the proper co-ordination of monetary control instruments really have to do with the extent to which the other weapons— discount policy and reserve requirements policy— should be used to supplement (and perhaps in certain special circumstances to replace) open market operations. Let us begin by considering discount policy.

## III. The Role of Discount Policy

For many years prior to the Treasury–Federal Reserve Accord of March 1951, the amount of member bank borrowing from the Reserve banks was negligible. Throughout the later 1930's, the volume of excess reserves was continuously so large that it was seldom necessary for member banks to borrow. And during World War II, the Federal Reserve kept the banks amply supplied

---

[2] The changes were made at the meetings of the Federal Open Market Committee on February 7 and March 28, 1961. See the Record of Policy Actions of the Federal Open Market Committee in the *Annual Report* of the Board of Governors of the Federal Reserve System covering the year 1961, pp. 39–43 and 54–55.

[3] In addition to open market operations and debt management, other policy actions have helped to "twist" the interest-rate structure; i.e., to raise short-term rates while exerting as much downward pressure as possible on long-term rates. The increase in interest rate ceilings applicable to time deposits by the Federal Reserve and the FDIC at the beginning of 1962 enabled U.S. commercial banks to compete more effectively with foreign banks for deposits and also attracted an enlarged supply of funds into time deposits—funds which were largely channelled into mortgages and State and local government securities, thus bringing down yields on such securities. And the reduction of reserve requirements on time deposits from 5 to 4 per cent in October and November 1962, combined with action to sustain Treasury bill yields, undoubtedly also helped to some extent.

with reserves through open market operations so that there was little occasion for borrowing. The atrophied state of the discount mechanism is indicated by the fact that, for the entire period 1934 to 1943, member bank borrowing averaged less than one-tenth of one per cent of total member bank reserves.

Since the Accord, the volume of borrowing has increased, especially during periods of credit restraint when the reserves of member banks have been under pressure. The Federal Reserve has encouraged this revival of the discount mechanism and has attempted to restore the discount rate to the important role it is supposed to have played in monetary policy prior to the 1930's.[4] But while member bank borrowing has increased in magnitude since the Accord, it is still very much less important as a source of reserves than it was in the 1920's. From 1951 to 1959, borrowing averaged 3.2 per cent of total member bank reserves with average borrowings reaching peak levels of approximately $4\frac{1}{2}$ per cent of total reserves in the years 1957 and 1959, when monetary policy was relatively tight. In contrast, during the period 1922 to 1929, borrowing averaged 30.0 per cent of total reserves, with the ratio rising as high as 40 per cent in 1923 and 1929.

## A. The Discount Rate as a Cost Factor

It is possible to distinguish two main facets of Federal Reserve discount policy. In the first place, the discount rate represents the cost of borrowed reserves, and the rate is changed from time to time for the purpose of regulating member bank borrowing. Changes in the rate for this purpose should be co-ordinated as closely as possible with open market operations. In addition, however, the discount rate at times plays an independent role in monetary policy, serving as a signal to the economy of changes in Federal Reserve policy. Let us first consider the discount rate as a regulator of member bank borrowing.

[4] In connection with the Accord itself, the Treasury and the Federal Reserve agreed upon the desirability of reviving the discount mechanism as a means for making adjustments in bank reserve positions. See the identical statements concerning the Accord by the Secretary of the Treasury and the Chairman of the Board of Governors in *Monetary Policy and Management of the Public Debt—Replies to Questions and Other Materials for the Use of the Subcommittee on General Credit Control and Debt Management*, Joint Committee on the Economic Report, 82nd Congress, 2d Session, Washington: U. S. Government Printing Office, 1952, Part I, pp. 74–76 and 349–51.

### 1. COST VERSUS "RELUCTANCE" AS A REGULATOR OF BORROWING

Due to the organization of the banking and financial system in the United States, it has not been feasible to establish the discount rate as a "penalty rate" in the sense in which this has been the case in Britain. There a penalty rate has been possible because the discount houses rather than the banks have customarily done the borrowing from the Bank of England. Since the discount houses have made a practice of carrying quite homogeneous portfolios of commercial bills and, in recent years, Treasury bills, it has been feasible to keep the Bank rate above the yield on such bills, so that when the discount houses are "forced into the bank" (as the phrase goes), they lose money on their borrowings. Traditionally, this penalty rate has served to keep borrowing from the Bank of England to a minimum and to make the interest rate structure highly sensitive to monetary action carried out through the co-ordinated use of open market operations and the discount rate.[5]

In the United States, member banks borrow directly from the Reserve banks, and since there are very many member banks operating in numerous local and regional, as well as national, credit markets and investing in a great variety of earning assets bearing a wide range of yields, it is not feasible to maintain a true penalty rate.[6]

Since the 1920's, it has come to be widely accepted doctrine that use of the System's dis-

[5] For a good recent discussion, see R. S. Sayers, *Modern Banking* (4th ed.; Oxford: Clarendon Press, 1958), pp. 104–14. As indicated by Sayers, both the indirect nature of the relation between the commercial banks and the Bank of England and the penal Bank rate have become somewhat attenuated in recent years, as the Bank has developed the alternative practice of supplying funds to the discount houses and in some cases to the commercial banks themselves by purchasing Treasury bills at the market rate.

[6] In order to be a penalty rate with respect to a particular bank, the rate does not need to be higher than the expected return on all of the bank's earning assets. In fact, in a sense, it is a penalty rate if it is higher than the expected return on the lowest yielding assets in the bank's portfolio. However, the discount rate can be a penalty rate in this sense in relation to some banks and not others, due to differences in the composition of the banks' portfolios.

[7] This argument was advanced in W. W. Riefler, *Money Rates and Money Markets in the United States*, New York: Harper & Bros., 1930, esp. Chap. II. According to Riefler, the tradition against borrowing existed among commercial banks prior to the formation of the Federal Reserve System and was strengthened during the 1920's by the System's discouragement of borrowing for other than temporary purposes.

count facilities is restrained by a tradition against borrowing on the part of member banks.[7] As evidence in support of this view, which has come to be known as the "reluctance theory," it was pointed out that in the 1920's open market interest rates were more closely related to the amount of outstanding member bank borrowing than they were to the discount rate, suggesting that member banks did not like to be in debt and, when they were, tended to liquidate secondary reserve assets in order to repay their borrowings, thus forcing up open market interest rates.[8]

Although the purposes for which banks borrow —to maintain their reserve positions in the face of customer withdrawals or clearing drains and to meet temporary (e.g. seasonal) increases in their customers' demands for loans—are commonly so pressing as probably to be quite cost-inelastic, it does not follow that member bank borrowing is insensitive to the discount rate. Banks have a choice of obtaining additional funds by borrowing at the Federal Reserve or by liquidating secondary reserves or other investment securities. Given a certain "reluctance to borrow," the major factor influencing the choice will presumably be the relevant cost of funds obtained by the various methods, and this depends chiefly on the relation between the discount rate and the yield on assets that the bank might liquidate. In principle, the relevant comparison is between the discount rate and the expected yield on the asset whose liquidation is being considered over the period of time for which the funds will be needed, taking account of any capital gains or losses that may be involved. For instance, if interest rates are expected to fall during the period, the relevant interest rate for comparison with the discount rate may be higher than the current interest rate on the asset. This factor will be more important the longer the maturity of the asset.[9]

Thus, there is little doubt that commercial banks are "reluctant" to borrow in the sense that borrowing is felt to involve a form of disutility. However, the banks' reluctance can be overcome provided that the profits to be obtained from

borrowing (as compared with other means of obtaining reserves) are sufficiently attractive— that is, banks balance the disutility of borrowing against the utility of further profits.[10] Moreover, not all banks are equally reluctant to borrow:[11] this is evidenced by the fact that the Federal Reserve has found it necessary to discourage "continuous borrowing" and to bolster the banks reluctance in its regulations covering discounts and advances.[12] In addition, the System keeps the borrowing practices of individual member banks under constant surveillance and in this way attempts to reinforce the banks' reluctance to borrow. At the same time, the System apparently does not unequivocally refuse to lend to member banks, despite the fact that it has authority to do so under the Federal Reserve Act.[13]

## 2. CO-ORDINATION OF OPEN MARKET OPERATIONS AND DISCOUNT POLICY

It used to be said with reference to monetary policy in the 1920's that open market operations served the function of making the discount rate effective.[14] In order to implement a restrictive monetary policy, the Federal Reserve would sell Government securities in the open market; this would put pressure on member bank reserve positions and cause them to increase their borrowings. At this point the discount rate would be raised, and the increase in borrowings was supposed to help to insure that the discount rate

[8] Ibid., pp. 25–28; also W. R. Burgess, The Reserve Banks and the Money Market, Rev. ed.; New York: Harper & Bros., 1946, pp. 219–21.

[9] See W. L. Smith, "The Discount Rate as a Credit-Control Weapon," Journal of Political Economy, LXVI, April 1958, pp. 171–77; Ralph Young, "Tools and Processes of Monetary Policy," in N. H. Jacoby, United States Monetary Policy, The American Assembly, Columbia University, 1958, pp. 13–48, esp. pp. 26–27.

[10] For a systematic development of this point of view, together with some evidence to support it, see the interesting article by M. E. Polakoff, "Reluctance Elasticity, Least Cost, and Member-Bank Borrowing: A Suggested Integration," Journal of Finance, XV, March 1960, pp. 1–18.

[11] On this, see Lauchlin Currie, The Supply and Control of Money in the United States, Cambridge: Harvard University Press, 1935, Chap. VIII.

[12] See Regulation A of the Board of Governors regulating member bank borrowing as revised effective February 15, 1955, (Federal Reserve Bulletin, January 1955, pp. 8–14). The Foreword to the revised Regulation contains a statement of "General Principles" (pp. 8–9) which attempts to delineate in a general way the purposes for which member banks should and should not use the System's discount facilities.

[13] On the subtleties of non-price rationing in the administration of the discount window, see C. R. Whittlesey, "Credit Policy at the Discount Window"; R. V. Rossa, "Credit Policy at the Discount Window: Comment;" and Whittlesey, "Reply," Quarterly Journal of Economics, LXXIII, May 1959, pp. 207–16, and 333–38.

[14] Burgess, op. cit., p. 239.

increase would be transmitted through into an increase in other interest rates.[15]

In view of the primary role of open market operations under present conditions, it is better to look at the matter the other way around and to say that the discount rate can be used to support and strengthen the effectiveness of open market operations. Thus, when the System, for example, wishes to implement a restrictive policy during a period of inflation, it uses open market operations to keep down the supply of reserves in relation to the swelling demands for credit. As a result, interest rates rise and member banks, finding their reserve positions under increased pressure, tend to increase their borrowings from the Reserve banks. In order to discourage the creation of additional reserves through borrowing, the System can raise the discount rate in pace with the increase of other interest rates. Thus the discount rate can be used to supplement and strengthen open market operations. Conversely, when the System desires to ease credit conditions, it provides additional reserves through open market operations, and in order to discourage members banks from using a portion of the new reserves to repay indebtedness at the Reserve banks, the discount rate can be lowered.[16]

A variant of this reasoning which stresses the reluctance of member banks rather than the discount rate has also been expressed by persons connected with the Federal Reserve System. According to this view, most member bank borrowing arises out of the fact that in a unit banking system such as ours with a very large number of banks, individual banks often find their reserve positions unexpectedly depleted as a result of unfavorable clearing balances associated with redistribution of reserves among the banks. Borrowing is a handy means of making temporary adjustments in reserve positions; if the depletion of a bank's reserve position lasts very long, the bank may later adjust by liquidating secondary reserves, using the proceeds to repay its borrowing at the Reserve bank.[17] The pressure on banks to make prompt adjustments in portfolios in order to repay borrowing depends on the level of the discount rate in relation to other interest rates.

At times when monetary policy is tight and the Federal Reserve is maintaining pressure on bank reserve positions in the interest of limiting excessive growth of bank credit, more banks will be managing their reserve positions closely, reserve deficiencies will occur more frequently, and member bank borrowing will increase.[18] Due to the fact that the banks are reluctant to borrow, the increase in borrowing causes them to adopt more cautious lending policies and to reduce the availability of credit. However, since banks balance the disutility of borrowing against the utility of increased profits, it is necessary to make successive upward adjustments in the discount rate as interest rates rise due to the effects of the restrictive policy, in order to stiffen the banks' reluctance to remain in debt and to encourage them to contract their loans and investments.

It may be noted, however, that short-term open market interest rates are subject to a considerable amount of random variation in the short run and that, under present arrangements, the discount rate is only changed at irregular and rather infrequent intervals. For this reason, the differential between the discount rate and other interest rates varies rather erratically. This is apparent from Figure 1, which shows the movements of the discount rate and the yield on outstanding Treasury bills since 1953. As a result of the continuously shifting relation between the

---

[15] This is rather similar to the classical British practice of selling in the open market to reduce the cash reserves of the commercial banks. To replenish their cash reserves, the banks would call some of their loans to the discount houses. The discount houses, in turn, would be forced to borrow from the Bank of England at the (penalty) Bank rate, and as a result of the ensuing adjustments bill rates would be forced up. Thus, open market operations were said to have the function of "forcing the market into the Bank."

[16] See the statement of the Chairman of the Board of Governors concerning the relation between the discount rate and open market operations in *United States Monetary Policy: Recent Thinking and Experience*, Hearings before the Subcommittee on Economic Stabilization of the Joint Committee on the Economic Report 83d Congress, 2d Session, Washington: U. S. Government Printing Office, 1954, p. 11. A similar view is suggested in C. E. Walker, "Discount Policy in the Light of Recent Experience," *Journal of Finance*, XII, May 1957, pp. 223–37, esp. pp. 232–34.

[17] Roosa, *op. cit.*, p. 335.

[18] *Ibid.*, p. 336. A similar argument is presented by Young, *op. cit.*, who says (p. 34): "As a policy of monetary restraint continues or is accentuated, there will be more frequent and more widespread reserve drains among member banks. This will lead an increasing number of banks to borrow temporarily at the discount window of the Reserve Banks in order to maintain their legal reserve positions. For each bank, the borrowing will be temporary, but the repayment by one bank draws reserves from other banks, which in turn will have need to borrow at a Reserve Bank. Thus, restrictive monetary action leads to a larger volume of member bank borrowings, as more banks find their reserve positions under pressure more often."

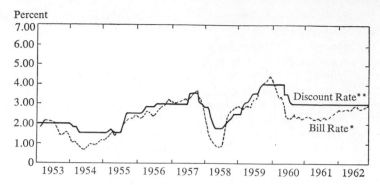

* Monthly average of daily yields on outstanding issues
** Average of discount rates at all Federal Reserve banks

Source: Board of Governors of the Federal Reserve System.

Figure 1. Federal Reserve Discount Rates and Market Yield on Treasury Bills, 1953-1962.

discount rate and other interest rates, the willingness of banks to borrow presumably undergoes considerable erratic variation.

### 3. DOES BORROWING REINFORCE OR OFFSET OPEN MARKET OPERATIONS?

There has been some discussion as to whether the increase in member bank borrowing that occurs during a period of credit restriction is a factor which intensifies the restrictive effects or a loophole which weakens the effectiveness of monetary policy.[19] It is almost certainly true that, as a result of the reluctance of member banks to borrow, banks tend to follow somewhat more restrictive and cautious policies as far as loans are concerned when they are in debt to the Reserve banks than when they are not in debt. However, the important thing to bear in mind is that if banks were constrained not to borrow when their reserve positions were impaired by a restrictive policy, they would have to adjust their reserve positions in some other way. This would ordinarily mean contraction of loans or investments.[20] Thus, in the absence of borrowing, the

adjustment would itself *consist in* restricting credit. On the other hand, to the extent that borrowing occurs, restrictive effects are postponed and banks are merely put in such a position that they are somewhat more likely to restrict credit at some future time. Moreover, it should be noted that borrowing by one member bank for the purpose of adjusting its reserve position adds to the *aggregate* reserves of all member banks and thus indirectly takes some of the pressure off other banks. Adjustment of reserve positions through liquidations of securities, on the other hand, does not add to the reserves of the system of banks.[21]

Thus, it seems clear that the effect of increased member bank borrowing at a time when a restrictive policy is being applied is to offset rather than to reinforce the restrictive policy. The effect may not be very important in itself, since the induced increase in borrowing is not likely to be large enough to pose a serious problem for the authorities; it merely means that a somewhat more restrictive open market policy is required than would otherwise be necessary. However, there are a number of other offsetting reactions in the banking and financial system—such as shifts in the composition of bank portfolios from Government securities to loans, adjustments by

[19] Roosa seems to imply that it has an intensifying effect ("Credit Policy at the Discount Window," *op. cit.*). Whittlesey ("Credit Policy at the Discount Window," and "Reply" [to Roosa's comment], *op. cit.*) contends that it is an offset, although not, under present conditions, a very important one.

[20] Another possibility is that banks might make greater use of the Federal funds market to adjust their reserves. Although use of this market has increased in recent years, the number of participating banks is still rather small, and there are technical impediments to a substantial increase. (See *The Federal Funds Market*, Washington: Board of Governors of the Federal Reserve System, 1959. Increased use of the Federal funds market during periods when credit is being restricted economizes the use of existing reserves,

reduces excess reserves, and thereby constitutes an offset to the initial restrictive action (see H. P. Minsky, "Central Banking and Money Market Changes," *Quarterly Journal of Economics*, LXXI, May 1957, pp. 171–87). Thus, resort to the Federal funds market has effects similar to member bank borrowing (as explained below).

[21] Smith, "The Discount Rate as a Credit-Control Weapon," *op. cit.*, p. 172–73; also P. A. Samuelson, "Recent American Monetary Controversy," *Three Banks Review*, March 1956, pp. 10–11.

financial intermediaries, and so on—and the addition of one more such reaction, even though not quantitatively very large, may not be wholly without significance.

Another point of view that has been expressed concerning the discount mechanism is that, while it has an offsetting effect, this effect is actually helpful to the monetary authorities, because it can be likened to a brake on an automobile. It is said that brakes, by making it possible to control the car more effectively, permit one to drive at a higher rate of speed than would otherwise be possible.[22] Similarly, the discount mechanism, although seeming to weaken monetary controls, actually strengthens them by making it possible to use other controls (chiefly open market operations) more vigorously. However, this is not a proper analogy. If the automobile simile is retained, the discount mechanism is more like a defective clutch than a brake, and few would argue that a slipping clutch makes it possible to drive at a higher rate of speed.[23] A brake is a discretionary weapon and not a device that automatically operates more intensively, the harder one pushes on the accelerator.

### 4. A CRITIQUE OF THE CONCEPT OF "FREE RESERVES"

A by-product of the revival of the discount mechanism since the Accord is the emphasis that has been placed on the level of "free reserves" as an immediate guide to System policy. "Free reserves," of course, is simply the difference between aggregate member bank excess reserves and aggregate member bank borrowings. It appears that, increasingly in the last few years, the System has been setting its proximate goals of monetary policy in terms of "target" levels of free reserves. As can be seen from Figure 2, free reserves have been positive (excess reserves greater than borrowings) during periods of credit ease, as in 1953–54, 1958, and 1960–63, while during periods of credit restriction, free reserves have been negative (i.e., borrowings have been greater than excess reserves, or there have been "net borrowed reserves"). It has become commonplace to judge the objectives and

[22] P. A. Samuelson, "Reflections on Monetary Policy," *Review of Economics and Statistics*, XLII, August 1960, p. 266.

[23] If the motor were too powerful for the car—e.g., if a Cadillac motor were mounted in a Volkswagen—I suppose a clutch that slipped might be helpful. But the proper analogy for the relation between monetary policy and the stability of the economy may well be just the reverse; i.e., monetary policy can be likened to a Volkswagen motor which has been assigned the task of operating a heavy Cadillac.

direction of monetary policy to a considerable extent by the changes that take in free reserves.[24]

The first thing to notice about free reserves is that the two components that compose it—excess reserves and borrowings—are distributed quite differently among member banks. Excess

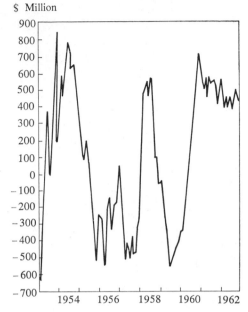

Source: Board of Governors of the Federal Reserve System.

Figure 2. Free Reserves of Member Banks, 1953-1962.

reserves tend to be heavily concentrated in the hands of country banks, while most of the borrowing is ordinarily done by reserve city banks. (See Figures 3 and 4.) Country banks tend to hold fairly substantial amounts of excess reserves most of the time, and are able to absorb pressure by drawing down such excess reserves. Reserve city banks, on the other hand, manage their reserve positions more closely, hold relatively small amounts of excess reserves, and borrow more frequently from the Federal Reserve when they are placed under pressure. Of course, these behavior patterns do not coincide exactly with the arbitrary classifications of banks for reserve requirement purposes—some reserve city banks, for example, undoubtedly hold large excess reserves, while some

[24] No matter what the shortcomings of free reserves as a guide to monetary policy, it is appropriate for those who are attempting to judge the character of System policy to pay close attention to this magnitude simply because the System does seem to use it as a guide.

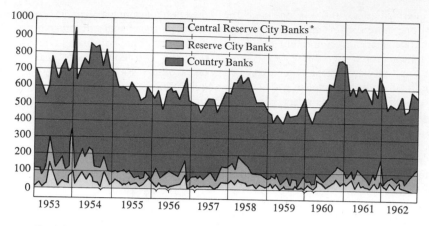

* Central Reserve City Classification terminated July 28, 1962

Source: Board of Governors of the Federal Reserve System.

Figure 3. Excess Reserves of Member Banks by Reserve Requirement Classifications, 1953-1962.

country banks manage their reserve positions closely. Nevertheless, it is quite clear that there are substantial differences among banks with respect to holdings of excess reserves and reliance on borrowing from the Federal Reserve. And there is no reason to suppose that an increase in borrowings on the part of one group of banks would be exactly offset, insofar as effects on credit conditions are concerned, by an equal increase in holdings of excess reserves by another group of banks. That is to say, for example, that $500 million of net borrowed reserves might have quite different implications depending upon whether it was the resultant of $1.5 billion of borrowings and $1 billion of excess reserves or the resultant of $700 million of borrowings and $200 million of excess reserves.

It should be noted, however, that in practise a very large proportion of the variation in free reserves is attributable to variation in borrowings.[25] The amount of excess reserves is negatively correlated with member bank borrowing; consequently, an increase (decrease) in free reserves is likely to be attributable partly to a decrease (increase) in borrowings and partly to an increase (decrease) in excess reserves. However, as a comparison of Figures 3 and 4 indicates, the variation in borrowings is much greater than the variation in excess reserves; in fact, the variance of borrowings accounts for about 62 per cent of the variance of free reserves, whereas the variance of excess reserves accounts for only 7.7 per cent, the remainder being attributable to the effects of the negative correlation that exists

[25] Young, op. cit., p. 35.

between borrowings and excess reserves.[26] This suggests that the behavior of free reserves is largely explained by the behavior of borrowings and that excess reserves are not ordinarily a very important factor.

It was pointed out earlier that the amount of borrowing that member banks will want to do can be expected to depend, among other things, on the relation between the discount rate and other interest rates, which can for our present purposes be represented by the Treasury bill rate. Since borrowing is the main element in free reserves, this suggests that the amount of free reserves member banks will desire to hold will vary inversely with the difference between the bill rate and the discount rate. As the bill rate rises relative to the discount rate, banks will tend to increase their borrowings and desired free reserves will fall; conversely, as the

[26] Free reserves ($R$) is given by

$$R = X - B,$$

where $X$ = excess reserves and $B$ = borrowings from Federal Reserve banks. The variance of $R$ is given by

$$\sigma_r{}^2 = \sigma_x{}^2 + \sigma_b{}^2 - 2r_{xb}\sigma_x\sigma_b, \qquad (1)$$

where $\sigma_x{}^2$ = variance of excess reserves, $\sigma_b{}^2$ = variance of borrowings, and $r_{xb}$ is the coefficient of correlation between excess reserves and borrowings. Based on monthly data (averages of daily figures) for the period January 1953, through March 1960, $r_{xb}$ is $-.697$. Using expression (1) the variance of excess reserves accounts for 7.7 per cent of the variance of free reserves, the variance of borrowings accounts for 61.8 per cent, and the remaining 30.5 per cent is accounted for by the tendency for borrowings to vary inversely with excess reserves (as reflected in the term $-2r_{xb}\sigma_x\sigma_b$).

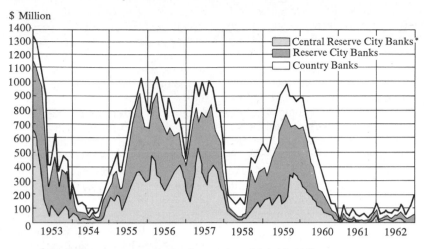

* Central Reserve City Classification terminated July 28, 1962

Source: Board of Governors of the Federal Reserve System.

Figure 4. Discounts and Advances of Member Banks by Reserve Requirements Classifications, 1953-1962.

bill rate falls in relation to the discount rate, they will tend to repay existing indebtedness to the System, and desired free reserves will rise.[27]

Thus, during a period of credit restriction, as market interest rates rise with the discount rate lagging behind, desired free reserves will decline, and the banks will attempt to reduce actual free reserves. If the Federal Reserve attempts to hold free reserves constant, it will have to adjust its open-market policy to increase total reserves, thereby weakening the over-all restrictive effect of its policy. Conversely, when economic activity begins to level off in the late stages of an expansion, market interest rates may begin to fall. Under these circumstances, with a given or lagging discount rate, desired free reserves will increase, and if the Federal Reserve attempts to hold free reserves constant, it will have to tighten its open-market policy, and the over-all restrictive effect of monetary policy is likely to become stronger.[28]

This suggests that it is wrong to believe that a constant level of free reserves means a constant degree of credit tightness or ease. At the very least, it would be necessary to adjust the discount rate continuously to the changing level of market rates. Even if this were done, changes in other

factors would mean that the effective degree of credit restriction could vary substantially while the level of free reserves was held constant.

Nor is an increase (decrease) in free reserves an unambiguous indication that credit has become easier (tighter). For example, if credit is tightened by raising the discount rate, the rise in the cost of borrowed reserves will cause the banks to reduce their borrowings, making offsetting adjustments in their reserve positions perhaps by selling Treasury bills. Total reserves will decline and interest rates will rise. But this tightening of credit will be accompanied by an increase in free reserves—indeed the increase in free reserves will be the means through which credit-tightening comes about.

On the other hand, if credit is tightened by open market sales of securities while the discount rate remains constant, the resulting rise in the bill rate (and other short-term open market interest rates) will make borrowing relatively more attractive as a means of obtaining reserves. The resulting increase in borrowing will reduce free reserves—thus, a tightening of credit will be associated with a decline in free reserves. But even in this case, the increased borrowing that is reflected in declining free reserves tends to increase total reserves and thereby to offset a portion of the restrictive effect of the initial open market sales.

"Free reserves" is an artificial construct, which has had the unfortunate effect of providing a spuriously exact guide to the monetary authorities—or at least has been so interpreted by

[27] This is pointed out by Milton Friedman in *A Program for Monetary Stability*, New York: Fordham University Press, 1959, pp. 41–43. See also the excellent study by R. J. Meigs, *Free Reserves and the Money Supply*, Chicago: University of Chicago Press, 1962.

[28] Friedman, *op. cit.*, p. 42.

persons outside the Federal Reserve System.[29] If the discount rate were regulated in such a way as to maintain a constant differential between it and the Treasury bill rate (a possibility that is discussed below), the amount of free reserves might perhaps become a somewhat better index of credit conditions than it is at present. Even in that case, however, it would commonly be a mistake to assume that a constant level of free reserves would necessarily mean a constant degree of credit tightness or ease. It would be better under most circumstances for the System to set its proximate goals in terms of interest rate behavior and growth of total reserves and to allow free reserves to seek the levels required to achieve these goals.

## B. The Discount Rate as a Signal

Thus far, we have been considering changes in the discount rate as an adjunct to open market operations, the purpose of which is to serve as a partial governor of member bank indebtedness by regulating the cost of obtaining reserves by borrowing as compared with sales of secondary reserves.

To some extent, the discount rate also plays an independent role in monetary policy by serving as a signal of the intentions of the monetary authorities. Particularly at turning points in business conditions, a change in the discount rate is often the first clear indication of a basic alteration in monetary policy. Discount rate changes of this kind are said to have psychological effects or "announcement effects," which may influence business conditions by altering the expectations of businessmen and financial institutions.[30]

### 1. DIFFICULTIES OF INTERPRETING DISCOUNT RATE ADJUSTMENTS

It is commonly taken for granted that the announcement effects of discount rate changes are normally such as to strengthen the impact of monetary policy. However, those who advance the expectations argument have not explained in any detail the way in which the expectational

effects are supposed to work. Actually, there are several different possible expectational effects, and in the case of each of them there is some uncertainty concerning even the direction (let alone the magnitude) of the effects.

One of the difficulties is that many changes in the discount rate are merely technical adjustments designed to restore or maintain an appropriate relationship between the discount rate and other rates of interest, as indicated above. Most of the periodic adjustments that are made during periods when interest rates are gradually rising or falling are of this nature. However, the interpretation placed on even these rather routine changes is sometimes unpredictable, because their timing may be affected by various considerations not directly related to stabilization policy. Sometimes, for example, discount rate adjustments may be accelerated in order to get the possible accompanying disruptive effects on the securities markets out of the way before an important Treasury debt management operation is scheduled. Or, on the other hand, action may be postponed until the repercussions of a forthcoming debt management operation are out of the way. Furthermore, the very fact that technical adjustments are sometimes interpreted by the public as having policy implications may affect System decisions concerning the timing of such adjustments. Such factors as these not only tend to make the interpretation of discount rate changes difficult, but are also partly responsible for the System's difficulties, referred to earlier, in adjusting the discount rate frequently enough to maintain a reasonably stable relation between that rate and other interest rates.[31]

Partly as a result of erratic timing and partly due to the fact that the business situation is usually fraught with some uncertainty, discount rate changes that are in fact meant to be merely routine adjustments are sometimes endowed with importance as "straws in the wind" regarding System policy by the press and by students of financial and economic affairs. And sometimes even a *failure* to change the discount rate so as to maintain "normal" interest rate relationships is taken as a sign of change of System policy. More-

---

[29] The fact that the System officials are aware of the shortcomings of the free reserves concept is apparent from the criticisms directed at it by Ralph Young, (*op. cit.*, pp. 35–36). Young points out one defect not referred to above—the fact that the amount of free reserves is subject to considerable day-to-day and week-to-week variations, due to unpredictable changes in factors outside the control of the Federal Reserve authorities.

[30] See, for example, Burgess, *op. cit.*, pp. 221–230.

[31] As Friedman puts it (*op. cit.*, p. 40): "The discount rate is something that the Federal Reserve must continually change in order to keep the effect of its monetary policy unchanged. But changes in the rate are interpreted as if they meant changes in policy. Consequently, both the System and outsiders are led to misinterpret the System's actions and the System is led to follow policies different from those it intends to follow."

over it is quite common for different commentators to place different interpretations on System action—or even lack of action—with respect to the discount rate.

The truth is that changes in the discount rate constitute the crudest kind of sign language.[32] Why this Stone Age form of communication should be regarded as superior to ordinary English is really quite difficult to understand. And, in this particular case, the use of such crude signals is subject to a special disadvantage arising from the fact that the signal itself has an objective effect on the situation in addition to serving as a means of communication. That is, changes in the discount rate combine action and communication, and there may be times when it is proper to act and not speak and other times when it is proper to speak and not act.

It is possible that some of the disadvantages of discretionary discount rate changes could be overcome, if the changes that were made were accompanied, at least under some circumstances, by statements explaining the reasons underlying the action. However, a change in the discount rate requires action by the boards of directors of the Federal Reserve banks and approval by the Board of Governors.[33] As a result, a very large number of persons are involved and the reasons for the action may vary among the different participants—some of whom may not thoroughly approve of the action—thus making it difficult to agree upon a generally acceptable accompanying statement.[34] This raises an interesting question: how can the general public and the business community help but be confused in their interpretations of a change in the discount rate when the persons who are responsible for making the change are not themselves entirely clear about the reasons for it?

## 2. ANNOUNCEMENT EFFECTS OF DISCOUNT RATE ADJUSTMENTS

In addition to the confusion resulting from the fact that some discount rate adjustments are meant to be signals of a change in monetary policy while others are not, there is a further question whether the resulting announcement effects, even when they are intended, will help to stabilize the economy. Announcement effects work through expectations, and the relationships involved are quite complex. It is possible to break down expectational reactions into reactions of lenders, reactions of borrowers, and reactions of spenders.[35]

a. *Expectational Effects on Lenders and Borrowers.* A discount rate change may cause shifts in lenders' supply curves of funds and/or in borrowers' demand curves, the nature of these shifts depending upon the kind of expectations prevailing among lenders and borrowers. If interest rate expectations are elastic, a rise (fall) in present interest rates creates expectations of an even larger proportionate rise (fall) in future interest rates, whereas, with inelastic expectations, a rise (fall) in present interest rates induces the

---

[32] Some writers seem to show no realization of the difficulties involved in this peculiar form of communication. For example, Walker (*op. cit.*, pp. 229–30) says: "Discount policy—particularly with respect to changes in the rate—is a simple and easily understandable technique for informing the market of the monetary authorities' views on the economic and credit situation. Open-market operations, which are used to cushion the effects of seasonal influences as well as for cyclical and growth purposes, may at times be confusing to some observers because the System may be supplying funds to the market . . . when cyclical developments clearly dictate a restrictive monetary policy, or vice versa. The time-honored device of raising or lowering discount rates, however, can hardly be susceptible to misinterpretation by even the most uninformed observers."

[33] In this connection, see the interesting paper by H. C. Carr, "A Note on Regional Differences in Discount Rates," *Journal of Finance*, XV, March 1960, pp. 62–68, which uses differences in the timing of discount rate changes on the part of different Reserve banks as a means of classifying the banks as "leaders," "follow-the-leaders," "middle-of-the-roaders," and "dissenters." By studying rate increases and rate decreases separately, he also tries to discern differences in the banks' attitudes toward inflation and deflation.

[34] This is pointed out by Burgess (*op. cit.*), who says: "No reasons for the action are ordinarily given out at the time, partly because the decision represents the views of many people, who have perhaps acted for somewhat diverse reasons, so that it would be an extremely difficult task to phrase a statement which would fairly represent the views of all the directors of the Reserve Bank concerned and the Washington Board; and partly because it would be equally difficult to make any statement which did not either exaggerate or minimize the importance of the change. Such a statement is always subject to misinterpretation, as has been repeatedly illustrated." This statement was written a number of years ago, but it probably still reflects rather accurately the problem involved and the attitudes of those responsible for the administration of the discount rate.

[35] Our approach follows that adopted in dealing with the exceptional effects of monetary policy in general by Assar Lindbeck in his study entitled *The "New" Theory of Credit Control in the United States*, Stockholm Economics Studies, Pamphlet Series, No. 1, Stockholm: Almquist & Wiksell, 1959, pp. 25–29, and 38–39. To a considerable extent, borrowers and spenders are the same people, of course, but it is useful to consider the two activities separately.

expectation of a smaller proportionate rise (fall) in future interest rates.[36]

Let us take the case of a discount rate increase and suppose that initially it causes a rise in market interest rates. If lenders have elastic expectations, they may reduce their present commitments of funds in order to have more funds available to invest later on, when interest rates are expected to be relatively more favorable. Conversely, if lenders have inelastic expectations, they may increase the amounts of funds they are willing to supply at the present time. Borrowers, on the other hand, may postpone their borrowing if they have inelastic expectations and accelerate it if they have elastic expectations. For a reduction in the discount rate, all of these reactions are reversed.

According to this view, the announcement effects of a discount rate adjustment will be clearly of a stabilizing nature if lenders have elastic expectations and borrowers have inelastic expectations, since in this case an increase in the discount rate will reduce both the demand for and the supply of funds, while a reduction in the discount rate will increase both demand and supply. On the other hand, if lenders have inelastic and borrowers elastic expectations, the effects will be clearly destabilizing, while if both groups have elastic or both have inelastic expectations, the outcome is uncertain and will depend on the relative strengths of the two reactions.[37]

Thus, in order to get favorable reactions on both sides of the market, it is necessary for lenders and borrowers to have the opposite kinds of expectations—a phenomenon that does not seem very likely. However, the significance of all of these considerations is considerably reduced due to the fact that, in practice, their main effects may be confined to producing changes in the interest rate structure. That is, a lender who has elastic interest rate expectations is not very likely to reduce the total supply of funds offered in the market; rather, he is likely to reduce his supply of funds in the longer-term sectors of the market, putting the funds into the short-term sector, while he awaits the expected rise in yields. Or, if he has inelastic expectations, he may shift funds from the short- to the long-term sector. Conversely, a borrower who has elastic expectations may not accelerate his total borrowings, but instead merely increase the proportion of his borrowing in the long-term market. Or, if he has inelastic expectations, he may shift a portion of his borrowings from the long- to the short-term market.[38] With our present limited knowledge concerning the effects of changes in the structure of interest rates on the level of expenditures, it is impossible to judge the effects of such shifts in the supply and demand for funds between the long- and short-term markets. It does seem safe to conclude, however, that the effects would not be very important.

b. *Expectational Effects on Spenders.* A discount rate adjustment may affect not only interest rate expectations of lenders and borrowers but also the sales and price expectations of businessmen on which spending plans are based. However, it is not entirely clear what the nature of these effects would be or how they would

[36] We are using the Hicksian concept of the elasticity of expectations, defined as

$$N = \frac{r_2^e - r_1^e}{r_1^e} \bigg/ \frac{r_2 - r_1}{r_1},$$

where $r_1$ and $r_2$ stand for the present interest rate before and after the change, $r_1^e$ and $r_2^e$ stand for the expected future interest rate before and after the change. Elastic expectations, as the term is used above, means $N > 1$, while inelastic expectations means $N < 1$. See J. R. Hicks, *Value and Capital*, 2d ed.; Oxford: Clarendon Press, 1946, Chap. xvi.

[37] In the case of an increase in the discount rate, if both lenders and borrowers have elastic expectations, lenders will reduce their offerings of funds while borrowers will increase their demands. If both have inelastic expectations, lenders will increase their supplies and borrowers will reduce their demands. In each of these cases, the outcome will depend upon the relative magnitudes of the respective shifts of demand and supply, as well as on the interest elasticities of demand and of supply.

[38] If lenders have elastic and borrowers inelastic expectations, both demand and supply will tend to shift from the long- to the short-term market following a rise in the discount rate, and the shifts will tend to cancel each other out as far as their effects on the interest rate structure are concerned. It may be noted that the typical behavior of the interest rate structure is consistent with the hypothesis that both borrowers and lenders have inelastic expectations, since in this case (with a rise in the discount rate), demand would shift from the long- to the short-term market while supply would shift from the short- to the long-term market and these reactions would cause a rise in short-term interest rates relative to long-term rates. When rates are generally high, short-term rates actually do often tend to be higher than long-term rates. This is also consistent with the behavior postulated by the general expectational theory of the interest rate structure when expectations are inelastic, as set forth in Tibor Scitovsky, "A Study of Interest and Capital," *Economica*, VII, n.s., August 1940, pp. 293–317; see also F. A. Lutz, "The Structure of Interest Rates," *Quarterly Journal of Economics*, LV, November 1940, pp. 36–63, reprinted in W. Fellner and B. F. Haley (eds.), *Readings in the Theory of Income Distribution*, Philadelphia: Blakiston Co., 1946, pp. 499–529.

affect economic stability. Taking the case of an increase in the discount rate, two situations (doubtless there are many variants of these) may be distinguished to illustrate the possibilities.

First, if inflationary expectations were already widespread and quite firmly established, if the possibility of restrictive anti-inflationary action by the Federal Reserve had not adequately been taken into account in the formation of these expectations, and if there was widespread confidence that monetary policy was capable of bringing inflation promptly and firmly under control, then a rise in the discount rate heralding the onset of a vigorously anti-inflationary monetary policy might have a bearish effect on sales and price expectations and thereby cause cutbacks and cancellations of expenditure plans. In this case the announcement effects would be helpful to the authorities.

Second, if the outlook was somewhat uncertain but shifting in an inflationary direction, if observers were aware of the Federal Reserve's concern about the situation and were waiting to see whether the System would act, and if—perhaps on the basis of past experience—it was felt that monetary policy (even though potentially effective) would take considerable time to be brought to bear effectively enough to check the inflation then a rise in the discount rate might have a bullish effect by confirming the emerging view that the near-term outlook was inflationary. In this case the announcement effects would be destabilizing.

Similar alternative expectational reactions could be postulated in the case of a reduction in the discount rate for the purpose of stimulating business activity. Although it is difficult to generalize concerning such matters and the effects might differ considerably from one situation to another, the second of the possible patterns of reaction outlined above seems, in general, considerably more plausible than the first. That is, it seems likely that the announcement effects of discount rate changes on the expectations of businessmen may frequently be of such a nature as to weaken rather than strengthen the effectiveness of monetary policy. At the same time the actions of the Federal Reserve are only one of the factors—and ordinarily not a major one—on which business expectations are based, and it is therefore doubtful whether the announcement effects of discount rate changes are really very important one way or the other.

We may conclude that the "psychological" effects of discount rate changes on the domestic economy—like all expectational phenomena in economics—are highly uncertain and that the discount rate as a weapon of "psychological warfare" is of very dubious value to the Federal Reserve.

A change in the discount rate has traditionally been used as a "signal" by some countries in an entirely different connection. In time of balance of payments crisis, a sharp increase in the discount rate may be used to communicate to the rest of the world a country's determination to defend by whatever means may be necessary the external value of its currency. Britain has used discount rate changes for this purpose on occasion since World War II, and this was a major reason why Canada abandoned the "floating discount rate" system (discussed below) and raised the rate to 6 per cent at the time of the Canadian balance of payments crisis in June 1962. While a long tradition has perhaps made discount rate increases a reasonably effective means of international communication in some situations of this kind, there are surely other equally satisfactory means available; e.g., English, French, Latin, or Zulu.

## C. Conclusions Concerning Present Discount Policy

The above analysis suggests that the discount rate as presently handled is not a very effective element in Federal Reserve policy. At times when a restrictive policy is applied, the induced increase in member bank borrowing constitutes a minor "leakage" in the controls, since it permits member banks to postpone contraction of their loans and investments and also adds to the total supply of member bank reserves. For the purpose of controlling the amount of borrowing, the Federal Reserve relies on adjustments in the discount rate together with a tradition against borrowing that prevails among member banks and System surveillance of the borrowing practices of the banks. Due to the fact that open market interest rates fluctuate continuously while the discount rate is changed only at somewhat unpredictable discrete intervals, the relation between the discount rate and open market rates (which largely determines the incentive to borrow) behaves in a very erratic fashion. The System relies on "free reserves" as an immediate short-run guide for monetary policy; however, the restrictive effect of a given amount of free reserves varies with (among other things) the relation between the discount rate and the yields on assets—especially

Treasury bills—that banks might alternatively liquidate to adjust their reserve positions.

Discretionary changes in the discount rate may at times have rather unpredictable effects on the business and financial situation, partly because it is often uncertain whether such changes are meant to be passive adjustments to keep the discount rate in line with other interest rates or whether they represent independent moves to tighten or ease credit. To the extent that changes in the discount rate do influence business conditions directly, they do so chiefly through psychological or "announcement" effects, the nature of which depends upon the kinds of expectations held by lenders, borrowers, and spenders. Although these announcement effects are quite complex and probably not of great importance in most cases, it seems likely that on occasion they may tend to increase economic instability.

## D. Possible Reforms in Discount Policy

A number of students of monetary affairs have expressed discontent with the present discount policy of the Federal Reserve, although some of them have not made specific suggestions for a change.[39] However, at least three fairly specific proposals for reform have been suggested. Two of these would de-emphasize discount policy— one by getting rid of the discount mechanism entirely and the other by tying the discount rate to market interest rates and thereby eliminating discretionary changes in it. The third would move in the opposite direction by trying to reform the discount mechanism in such a way as to make the discount rate a much more powerful weapon of credit control. We shall discuss each of these proposals in turn.

### 1. ABOLITION OF THE DISCOUNT MECHANISM

The proposal has been advanced quite forcefully by Professor Milton Friedman that the discount mechanism should be abolished altogether.[40] Friedman argues that the legitimate

function of the central bank is to control the stock of money and that the discount rate is an ineffective instrument for this purpose. Many of his arguments are similar to the ones set forth above, and his analysis was cited at several points in our discussion.

One difficulty with the complete elimination of discounting is that the discount mechanism serves a useful function as a "safety valve" by which banks are able to make adjustments in their reserve positions and the Federal Reserve is able to come to the aid of the banking system— or individual banks—in case of a liquidity crisis. In order to provide a means for individual banks to make short-run adjustments in their reserve positions, Friedman proposes the establishment of a fixed "fine" to be assessed on reserve deficiencies; the fine to be set high enough to be above likely levels of market interest rates, in order to prevent the device from becoming an indirect form of borrowing from the Federal Reserve.[41] As far as liquidity crises are concerned, he contends that, due to the success of deposit insurances in practically eliminating bank failures, such crises are now scarcely conceivable and that the "lender of last resort" function of the Federal Reserve is now obsolete, so that we need not worry about its elimination. It may be noted that if the discount mechanism were eliminated, it would be possible to use the repurchase agreement technique as a means of providing emergency assistance to the banking system in times of crisis.[42]

### 2. TYING THE DISCOUNT RATE TO THE TREASURY BILL RATE

An alternative to the complete abolition of borrowing would be to change the discount rate at frequent intervals in such a way as to maintain an approximately constant relation between it and some open market interest rate, such as the Treasury bill rate. For example, each week as soon as the average rate of interest on Treasury bills at the Monday auction became known, the discount rate could be adjusted so as to

[39] See, for example, E. C. Simmons, "A Note on the Revival of Federal Reserve Discount Policy," *Journal of Finance*, XI, December 1956, pp. 413–31.

[40] Friedman, *A Program for Monetary Stability*, *op. cit.*, pp. 35–45; see also his testimony in *Employment, Growth, and Price Levels*, Hearings before the Joint Economic Committee, Part 9A, Washington: U. S. Government Printing Office, 1959, pp. 3019–28. A. G. Hart also suggested the possibility of abolishing discounting a quarter of a century ago in connection with a discussion of the 100 per cent reserve plan;

see his "The 'Chicago' Plan of Banking Reform," *Review of Economic Studies*, II, February 1935, pp. 104–16, reprinted in F. A. Lutz and L. W. Mints (eds.), *Readings in Monetary Theory*, Philadelphia: Blakiston Co., 1951, pp. 437–56.

[41] Friedman, *A Program for Monetary Stability*, *op. cit.*, pp. 44–45.

[42] This possibility was mentioned by Hart in connection with his suggestion for the elimination of the discount mechanism (*op. cit.*, p. 110 in original, p. 447 in *Readings in Monetary Theory*).

preserve a constant differential between the two rates.[43]

Under this arrangement, the discount rate would no longer be a discretionary credit control weapon, and the unpredictable and often perverse announcement effects on the expectations of businessmen and financial institutions would be done away with. To the extent that the Federal Reserve wanted to influence expectations and felt that it could manage such effects so as to contribute to economic stability, it could implement these effects through the issuance of statements concerning its intentions, the economic outlook, and so on. While the present writer is rather dubious about the value of such activities, it is surely true that to the extent that they can contribute anything useful they can be handled better by verbal means than through reliance on such a crude signal as the discount rate.

The major question involved in the adoption of an arrangement for tying the discount rate to the bill rate would be the choice of the proper differential between the two. Obviously, the discount rate should be above the bill rate; beyond this the establishment of the differential is a matter of judgment. The larger the differential, the smaller would be (a) the average amount of borrowing and (b) the swings in borrowing that would occur as credit conditions changed. In view of the wide variations among individual banks with respect to both portfolio composition and expectations, the present writer feels that a fairly large differential of perhaps one per cent would be desirable, in order to keep down the amount of borrowing, which, for reasons discussed earlier, represents a minor leakage in monetary controls. But there does not seem to be any analytical principle that provides a basis for selecting the proper differential. Doubtless the best procedure would be to experiment with various differentials, retaining each one long enough to observe its effectiveness.

Under this arrangement, in contrast to the complete elimination of discounting, the discount mechanism would continue to be available to serve as a means of making temporary adjustments in bank reserve positions and as a "safety valve" that could be used in times of crises. If this approach were adopted, it would probably be desirable to give up the efforts to rely on such an intangible and unreliable means of controlling discounting as the traditional "reluctance" of member banks and the so-called "surveillance" of the Federal Reserve, recognizing borrowing as a "right" rather than a "privilege" of member banks, and relying entirely on the discount rate (in relation to the bill rate) as a means of controlling it.[44]

A procedure of the kind discussed above was employed in Canada from November 1956 to June 1962. During this period, the Bank of Canada adjusted its lending rate each week so as to keep it $\frac{1}{4}$ of 1 per cent above the average rate on treasury bills at the most recent weekly auction. The reasons given for adopting such an arrangement in 1956 were similar to those set forth above.[45] The policy was abandoned at the time of the Canadian balance of payment crisis in June 1962, when, as part of a program for dealing with the crisis, the discount rate was raised to 6 per cent as a signal to the rest of the world of Canada's determination to defend the external value of the Canadian dollar.[46] The traditional discretionary discount rate policy has been employed in Canada since that time.

3. INCREASING THE EFFECTIVENESS OF THE DISCOUNT RATE

A proposal for reform of the discount mechanism very different from the two discussed above

---

[43] See Smith, "The Discount Rate as a Credit-Control Weapon," *op. cit.* Friedman (*A Program for Monetary Stability, op. cit.*, p. 45) refers to such an arrangement as an alternative (albeit a less desirable one in his opinion) to complete abolition of discounting. He points out, quite correctly, that if the differential between the discount rate and the bill rate were made large enough, the plan would be equivalent to abolishing discounting. Professor J. M. Culbertson ("Timing Changes in Monetary Policy," *Journal of Finance*, XIV, May 1959, pp. 145–60, esp. 157–158) concludes with respect to discount policy that the Federal Reserve "should subordinate the discount rate by making adjustments in it routinely in response to changes in market rates and should seek a less ambiguous vehicle for such communication with the public as may be useful."

[44] In this connection, Friedman (*A Program for Monetary Stability, op. cit.*) says: "If rediscounting is retained, it should be a right, not a privilege, freely available to all member banks on specified terms." It appears that Friedman exaggerates the amount of discretion exercised by the System with respect to lending to individual banks, although the views expressed by System officials, concerning the "administration of the discount window"—such as Roosa's attempt ("Credit Policy as the Discount Window: Comment," *op. cit.*, pp. 333–34) to draw a distinction between saying "No," and refusing to say "Yes"—are so ambiguous that it is very difficult to judge the amount of discretion employed.

[45] See Bank of Canada, *Annual Report of the Governor to the Minister of Finance*, 1956, pp. 45–46.

[46] See Bank of Canada, *Annual Report of the Governor to the Minister of Finance*, 1962, pp. 3–4 and 72–73.

has recently been advanced by Professor James Tobin.[47] Instead of dismantling the discount mechanism entirely or abolishing discretionary changes in the discount rate, Tobin would greatly increase the importance of the rate and turn it into a major weapon of credit control.

The Tobin proposal calls for two changes in present procedures:

1. The Federal Reserve would pay interest at the discount rate on member bank reserve balances in excess of requirements.

2. The prohibitions against payments of interest on demand deposits and the ceilings on the payment of interest on time and savings deposits would be repealed.

These changes would greatly increase the leverage of the discount rate by making it an important consideration for banks that are not in debt to the Federal Reserve as well as for those that are. The opportunity cost to a bank of increasing its loans and investments would be the return it could earn by holding excess reserves, and this cost would be firmly under the control of the Federal Reserve. Moreover, the interest rate offered by the banks to holders of idle deposits would presumably be linked rather closely to the rate paid on excess reserves, since the bank could always earn a return on its deposits at least equal to one minus its reserve requirement times the discount rate. Thus, if the Federal Reserve wished to tighten credit, it could raise the discount rate, and this would increase the opportunity cost of lending for all of the member banks (whether they were in debt or not) and would, therefore, make them willing to lend only at higher interest rates than previously, while at the same time causing the banks to raise interest rates on deposits, thereby increasing the attractiveness of bank deposits relative to other assets on the part of the public.[48] The discount

rate could be used independently to control credit, or it could be combined with open market operations. It is not clear, however, what principle should govern the division of responsibility between the two weapons.

The proposal is ingenious and would certainly be practical and capable of being put in operation without causing disruption. And it might have the incidental advantage that the payment of interest on excess reserves might encourage more banks to become members of the Federal Reserve System. What is not clear, however, is why a flexible monetary policy could be implemented more effectively by means of the discount rate under this proposal than is now possible by means of open market operations. It is true that the proposal would presumably permit the Federal Reserve to control the cost of bank credit very effectively, but this can already be done—in principle at least—by open market operations. In part, the problems of monetary policy seem to stem from the fact that the demand for bank credit is not very sensitive to changes in interest rates and other monetary variables, so that it has proved to be difficult to operate forcefully enough to produce prompt changes of the degree necessary for effective stabilization. Perhaps it would be possible to bring the forces of monetary policy to bear more rapidly by means of the Tobin proposal, but this is by no means obvious. If the proposal merely provides another way of doing what is already possible, it hardly seems worthwhile.

The repeal of the existing restrictions relating to payment of interest on deposits is in no way dependent upon provision for the payment of interest on excess reserves, and there is much to be said for the repeal of these restrictions, even if the remainder of the Tobin proposal is not adopted.

---

[47] James Tobin, "Towards Improving the Efficiency of the Monetary Mechanism," *Review of Economics and Statistics*, XLII, August 1960, pp. 276–79.

[48] Allowing the banks to pay interest on deposits would have two related advantages. One is that it would probably reduce the propensity for the velocity of deposits to increase when a restrictive policy was applied, since the banks would be able to raise interest rates on deposits making them more attractive and weakening the tendency for rising interest rates on other claims to induce shifts of deposits into the hands of persons having a high propensity to spend. The other advantage is that it should reduce the amount of real resources devoted to the task of economizing the use of cash balances. Since the revival of flexible monetary policy, many large corporations, as well as state and local governments, have developed extensive facilities for handling short-term investments in order to

minimize their holdings of sterile cash balances, and the amount of skilled personnel devoting its time to this kind of activity at present is certainly not trivial (see C. E. Silberman, "The Big Corporate Lenders," *Fortune*, August 1956, pp. 111–114, 162–70). Resources devoted to this purpose represent a form of economic waste, since the real cost of creating deposits is virtually zero so that there is no economic gain from exercising economy in their use. This is pointed out by Tobin and is emphasized even more strongly by Friedman (*A Program of Monetary Stability*, *op. cit.*, pp. 71–75). The two advantages (reducing destabilizing velocity changes and discouraging efforts to economize in the use of costless deposits) are related in the sense that the propensity to waste resources in economizing cash balances tends to increase during periods of credit restriction and rising interest rates, and this increased application of resources helps to permit a destabilizing rise in velocity.

## 4. CONCLUSIONS

Of the three proposals for reforming the discount mechanism, the present writer feels that the strongest case can be made for the procedure of changing the discount rate each week in such a way as to maintain a constant spread between the discount rate and the Treasury bill rate. This would be a less drastic reform than the complete elimination of discounting, would eliminate the unpredictable effects of discretionary changes in the discount rate, would preserve the discount mechanism as a safety valve, and would eliminate the effects on credit conditions that now result from erratic variations in the relation between the discount rate and open market rates. The Tobin proposal for increasing the potency of the discount rate as a credit-control weapon is worthy of careful study, but it is not yet clear that the proposal would greatly strengthen the hand of the Federal Reserve.

If the present system of making discretionary adjustments in the discount rate at irregular intervals is retained, it would be desirable to reform the administration of the discount mechanism, perhaps by shifting the authority for making changes in the rate from the individual Reserve banks to the Federal Open Market Committee. The purpose of such a change would be to reduce the number of persons involved in decisions regarding the discount rate so that it would be easier to agree on the reasons for making changes. This would facilitate the issuance of explanatory statements at the time changes are made, in order to eliminate the confusion that often results due to the varying interpretations that are frequently placed on rate changes in the absence of explanations. It should then be feasible to make more frequent technical adjustments in the rate with less need to worry about the danger of disruptive effects on the credit situation, thereby permitting closer co-ordination of the discount rate with open market operations.

# IV. The Role of Variable Reserve Requirements[49]

Since the accord with the Treasury in March 1951, the Federal Reserve has made no systematic anti-cyclical use of changes in member bank

[49] Much of the discussion in this section is based upon the author's study entitled "Reserve Requirements in the American Monetary System," in *Monetary Management*, prepared for the Commission on Money and Credit, Englewood Cliffs, N. J.: Prentice-Hall, Inc., 1963, pp. 175–315.

reserve requirements. Reductions in the reserve requirement percentages applicable to demand deposits were made in the recessions of 1953–54 (reductions in July 1953 and June–August 1954) and 1957–58 (reductions in February–April 1958). In the recession of 1960–61, reserves were released by permitting member banks to count vault cash as reserves—to a limited extent beginning in December 1959, and without limitation beginning in November, 1960. And, finally, reserve requirements applicable to time deposits were reduced from 5 to 4 per cent in October–November 1962, at a time when output was expanding but unemployment remained high.

Under present provisions, the Board of Governors can change requirements on demand deposits between 10 and 22 per cent for reserve city banks and between 7 and 14 per cent for country banks, while it can change requirements on time deposits between 3 and 6 per cent; as this is written (July 1963) the requirements are $16\frac{1}{2}$ per cent and 12 per cent for demand deposits at reserve city and country banks, respectively, and 4 per cent for time deposits.[50] The Board may permit member banks to count all or part of their vault cash as required reserves; at the present time vault cash may be counted in full.

## A. Variable Reserve Requirements as a Credit Control Weapon

A change in reserve requirements alters both the amount of excess reserves available and the credit expansion multiplier, which determines the amount of potential credit expansion per dollar of excess reserves. For relatively small changes in reserve requirements, the first of these effects is much more important than the second—with net demand deposits amounting to roughly $100 billion, a reduction of one percentage point in requirements releases approximately $1 billion of excess reserves.

However, changes in reserve requirements have harsh and rather indiscriminate effects, at least when the changes made amount to as much as one-half or one percentage point, as has been customary in recent years. This does not cause serious problems in the case of reductions in requirements, because, as explained below, excessive bank liquidity generated by such reductions can be—and in practice has been—sopped up by open market sales of securities. Increases in requirements, however, have trouble-

[50] Under legislation passed in July 1959, the "central reserve city" classification of member banks was eliminated effective July 28, 1962.

some side effects which are not quite so easily dealt with.

Increases in requirements affect all banks—or at least all the banks in a particular reserve requirement classification—including some banks that are plentifully supplied with liquid assets which permit them to make easy adjustments in their reserve positions, as well as banks whose liquidity positions are less comfortable. To the extent that banks are forced to carry out troublesome portfolio readjustments, they are able to see clearly that these adjustments were forced upon them by Federal Reserve action; whereas the adjustments resulting from open market operations are either voluntary or, to the extent that they are involuntary, appear to be the result of impersonal market forces. Thus, frequent reserve requirement increases are likely to cause resentment among member banks and, under present conditions, might even be a significant deterrent to membership in the Federal Reserve System. Moreover, while the initial effect of reserve requirement increases is felt by all the banks, it is likely that there will be substantial secondary effects which will be concentrated on banks in the larger money centers as interior banks draw down correspondent balances and sell Government securities in the central money market in order to restore their reserve positions.

## B. Co-ordination of Reserve Requirement Changes and Open Market Operations

To some extent, it is possible to soften the unduly harsh impact of changes in reserve requirements by proper co-ordination with open market operations. The open market operations associated with the mid-1954 reductions in reserve requirements, which were designed to encourage continuing recovery from the recession of 1953–54, provide a good example of this co-ordination. The reserve requirement reductions that were made resulted in the injection of what the Federal Reserve authorities felt was an unduly large amount of excess reserves within a short period of time.[51] Accordingly the Federal Reserve sold securities in the open market at about the same time the reserve requirement reductions were made, in order to absorb a portion

---

[51] In a succession of changes in June, July, and August, 1954, demand deposit reserve requirements were reduced by 2 percentage points at central reserve city banks and 1 percentage point at reserve city and country banks, while time deposit reserve requirements were reduced by 1 percentage point at all classes of banks. These adjustments released about $1.5 billion of reserves.

of the released reserves: then, over a period of several months, it purchased securities in order to feed reserves back into the economy at times when additional reserves appeared to be needed in the interest of orderly recovery.[52] Thus, a skillful blending of reserve requirement changes and open market operations produced a smooth and gradual adjustment.

Similar recent examples of the use of open market operations to soften the impact of reserve requirement increases during periods of inflation are not available, since the Federal Reserve has not made use of reserve requirement increases since the Accord.[53] The blending of open market operations with reserve requirement adjustments would probably not result in quite such a smooth adjustment in this case, because the problem here is not only to prevent an unduly sharp impact on the total supply of money and credit, but to alleviate harsh impacts on individual banks. Since some banks which were squeezed especially hard might not possess securities of the maturities being purchased by the System, these banks might not be helped directly by open market operations.

If reserve requirement changes have important advantages as a means of controlling credit, the

---

[52] Between June and August 1954, the Federal Reserve reduced its holding of Government securities (average of daily figures) by $1.0 billion, while the net effect of factors outside the control of the Federal Reserve was to reduce member bank reserves by another $200 million. Thus, total reserves declined by $1.2 billion, and required reserves fell by the same amount, leaving excess reserves unchanged. From August to December 1954, the Federal Reserve increased its portfolio of Government securities by $0.9 billion as it fed reserves back to the banking system to meet seasonal demands. (Calculations based on data from *Federal Reserve Bulletin*, February 1955, p. 149.)

[53] During the immediate postwar inflation in 1948 while the Federal Reserve was "pegging" the market for Government securities, reserve requirement increases were used on several occasions in an effort to implement a policy of credit restraint. In this situation, however, member banks were plentifully supplied with Government securities, which were saleable at virtually fixed prices. Consequently, the banks tended merely to sell more securities than they otherwise would have sold, and these securities had to be purchased by the System to prevent securities prices from falling. Thus, banks were able to replenish their reserves readily, and there was little effect on the cost or availability of credit. In this situation, open market purchases were, in effect, used to offset more or less permanently the effects of reserve requirement increases. Such operations did tend to reduce bank liquidity somewhat, since the banks were giving up liquid securities for less liquid required reserves; however, the operations were not on a sufficiently large scale to make this a significant factor.

technical difficulties in making two-way adjustments could be greatly reduced by making smaller changes in the requirements than have been customary in the past and by smoothing the impact by means of open market operations. It has been suggested that more frequent and smaller changes be made, and there is no technical reason why this could not be done.[54] And if more frequent use of reserve requirement changes would clearly permit the Federal Reserve to conduct monetary policy more efficiently than would otherwise be possible, the fact that such adjustments might be somewhat unpopular with commercial bankers should not be taken too seriously. The real question is: What advantages do reserve requirement adjustments have in comparison with other credit-control weapons, especially open market operations? To this question we now turn.

## C. Possible Usefulness of Reserve Requirement Changes

Under most circumstances, the effects of (for example) expanding credit by lowering reserve requirements will almost surely be different in detail from those produced by the same amount of expansion (measured in terms of the increase in income-generating expenditures) produced by open market purchases. That is, the spending units which will be induced to increase their expenditures will be different in the two cases, as will the types of expenditures affected. Unfortunately, however, our knowledge of relative "incidence" of the two weapons is very poor, so that, while we may be sure that there are differences, there is very little that can be said about them. For this reason, we can scarcely even discuss intelligently the "mix" of the two that should be used to accomplish particular objectives. The best we can do is to indicate some rather general considerations which differentiate reserve requirement adjustments from open market operations and some special situations in which the reserve requirements weapon may be especially appropriate.

### 1. NEUTRALITY

The Federal Reserve authorities in recent years have shown a strong antipathy toward selective credit controls and have taken the position that the central bank should confine its efforts to the control of the total supply of money and credit, leaving the task of allocating credit to market forces. This attitude has been reflected for example in the System's opposition to the establishment of consumer credit controls even on a stand-by basis. Although there are other considerations involved also, this philosophy seems to be one of the bases for the Federal Reserve's adherence to the "bills-only" policy between 1953 and 1961. During this period, the System carefully eschewed efforts to control the maturity structure of interest rates, leaving this to the determination of market forces.

If such a philosophy of "neutrality" were to be pushed to its logical conclusion, it would lead to reliance on reserve requirement adjustments as a means of monetary control. Even bills-only is not entirely neutral in its effects on the interest rate structure, since changes in the money stock produced by this method involve, as a by-product, changes in the stock of securities of a particular maturity (namely, Treasury bills) and have a special impact on short-term interest rates. Reserve requirement changes, on the other hand, have no direct effects on interest rates or on stocks of securities—all such effects are produced by the decisions and activities of borrowers and lenders (including commercial banks).

The "neutrality" argument for reliance on reserve requirement changes would carry weight only with those who accept the "neutrality" philosophy. Moreover, its implementation would require that all monetary adjustments be accomplished by reserve requirement changes. This would include the day-to-day operations of the Federal Reserve designed to counteract the effects of uncontrollable factors (float, currency in circulation, etc.) affecting member bank reserves. These operations seem clearly to serve a useful, if not indispensable, function in keeping the money market on an even keel and are now quite efficiently carried out by means of open market operations. While it would undoubtedly be possible to make smaller and more frequent adjustments in reserve requirements than have been employed in the past, it would surely be wholly impracticable to employ reserve requirement changes on a day-to-day basis. For this, as well as other reasons, the "neutrality" argument for the use of reserve requirement adjustments appears to be purely academic and of no practical importance.

### 2. ANNOUNCEMENT EFFECTS

Like discount rate adjustments and unlike open market operations, changes in reserve

---

[54] See C. R. Whittlesey, "Reserve Requirements and the Integration of Credit Policies," *Quarterly Journal of Economics*, LVIII, August 1944, pp. 553–70.

requirements are overt actions of the Federal Reserve which are widely reported and commented upon in the press. As such, they are likely to have "announcement effects" through their influence on the expectations of businessmen and financial institutions. In fact, it seems quite likely that the reductions in reserve requirements that were made in 1953 and 1958 were motivated partly by a desire to convince the public that the System intended to take vigorous anti-recession action.

The question of announcement effects was discussed at some length in connection with discount rate changes, and the conclusion of that discussion was that such effects are uncertain and unpredictable. This conclusion seems to apply also to reserve requirement changes. For example, it seems at least as plausible to suppose that a dramatic reduction in reserve requirements in the early stages of a recession will strengthen the feeling that business conditions are worsening, as to suppose that it will make people optimistic by showing that the Federal Reserve is actively on the job trying to maintain stability.

I believe the fact that reserve requirement changes tend to have announcement effects is a disadvantage rather than an advantage. The best way to produce announcement effects—if and when such effects seem likely to be desirable—is by means of carefully-worded public statements explaining the views or intentions of the authorities. Action and communication should, in general, be carefully separated rather than rigidly linked together.

## 3. SPEED OF REACTIONS

It has been argued that reserve requirements changes have more widely diffused effects than open market operations and therefore may affect economic conditions more promptly. The reasoning behind this argument is that open market operations are consummated in the central money market of the country in New York and therefore have their initial impact chiefly on the reserve positions of the money market banks. Effects are gradually diffused throughout the country, primarily by means of interregional flows of funds set in motion by the adjustments of these banks to the initial changes in their reserve positions—a process which takes some time to carry through. Reserve requirement changes, on the other hand, instantaneously affect the reserve positions of all banks and therefore produce more rapid effects on credit conditions outside the central money markets. Federal Reserve officials apparently accept this argument and think it is

especially relevant with respect to anti-recession policies, since Chairman Martin of the Board of Governors has used it to explain why the System used reserve requirement reductions as a means of attacking the recessions of 1953–54 and 1957–58.[55]

One study covering the period from mid-1951 to mid-1953, when the Federal Reserve relied on open market operations to tighten credit rather gently at first and then with increasing intensity, suggests that the effects were felt first in New York and that there were noticeable lags in their transmission to the rest of the country.[56] The free reserve position of central reserve city banks appears to have been affected earlier and more strongly than that of other banks, and New York City banks showed an earlier and more pronounced tendency to shift the composition of their portfolios from investments to loans than did banks outside New York City. The author of this study suggests more frequent use of changes in reserve requirements, in order to shorten the lags in the regional transmission of monetary policy.

While this study is somewhat suggestive, it is not clearly convincing, since the statistical series involved are so ragged in their behavior as to be difficult to interpret, and because one cannot be sure that such differences in regional reactions as were present were not due to factors unrelated to monetary policy. There are several reasons for doubting whether the difference in the reaction speeds of the two weapons is great enough to be an important consideration. In the first place, as noted above, while the initial impact of reserve requirement changes is widely diffused, adjustments of interior banks via changes in correspondent balances and security transactions are likely to pass a disproportionate share of it back to the central money markets. Furthermore, to the extent that the initial effects of open market operations are more concentrated, the fact that central money market banks are very sensitive to changes in their reserve positions and prompt in reacting thereto would suggest that the transmission of effects to other parts of the economy is likely to get under way quickly and proceed rapidly. And finally, the other lags in monetary policy appear to be so long that it is doubtful

[55] See Martin's testimony in *January 1960 Economic Report of the President,* Hearings before the Joint Economic Committee, 86th Congress, 2d Session, Washington: U. S. Government Printing Office, 1960, pp. 163–212.

[56] I. O. Scott, Jr., "The Regional Impact of Monetary Policy," *Quarterly Journal of Economics,* LXIX, May 1955, pp. 269–84.

whether such differences as do exist between the two weapons are of appreciable importance in the overall picture. In fact, one cannot even be sure that there is not frequently some advantage in open market operations, because commercial banks all over the country adjust their reserves through sales of securities (which largely clear through the central money market) so that purchases (for example) of securities may have some tendency to direct the flow of new reserves to the points where they are most needed, instead of scattering them indiscriminately over the map.[57]

### 4. NATIONAL EMERGENCIES

One circumstance in which the power to raise reserve requirements might be used to good purpose is in times of a war or major national defense emergency, which requires the expenditure of large amounts of borrowed funds by the Government during a period of full employment. Under such conditions, there is much to be said for the Treasury's obtaining such funds as it needs but cannot raise through taxation or through borrowing from the nonbank public by selling securities directly to the Federal Reserve, with the System raising reserve requirements to immobilize the excess reserves that are created when the Treasury spends the money. This process would avoid the accumulation of excessive liquidity in the hands of the commercial banks and the accompanying threat of post-emergency inflation and would save the Treasury some interest costs. It would, of course, require that the Federal Reserve be given virtually unlimited power to raise reserve requirements.

### 5. CONCLUSIONS

The upshot of the above discussion is that there appear to be few if any circumstances in

normal times when reserve requirement changes are clearly superior to open market operations as a means of controlling credit. Reserve requirement changes have "announcement effects" while open market operations do not, but these may frequently turn out to be a nuisance rather than an aid to the Federal Reserve and, to the extent that they are desirable, can be produced more effectively by other methods. Conceivably, reserve requirement changes may affect business conditions more promptly than open market operations; however, this is not certain, and in any case the advantage is unlikely to be great enough to be of much significance. In view of the superior administrative efficiency of the open market operations, together with the unpopularity among commercial bankers of frequent two-way adjustments of reserve requirements, there is much to be said for relying exclusively on open market operations under normal circumstances.[58]

## V. Concluding Comments

As they are used at the present time, open market policy, discount policy, and reserve requirements policy are three instruments of monetary control with essentially a single purpose—the regulation of the total supply of money and bank credit. Open market policy is powerful, effective, and administratively flexible; it is unquestionably the key weapon of general monetary control. Discount policy, as reflected in changes in the discount rate, has a weak and to some extent even perverse effect on the total supply of money and credit and is, at the same time, a rather inept and confusing device for waging "psychological warfare" against economic

---

[57] Chairman Martin of the Board of Governors has stated his belief that an increase in reserve requirements would be the best way to offset the effects on member bank reserves of a substantial gold inflow, if circumstances required such offsetting (see his testimony in *January 1960 Economic Report of the President*, Hearings before the Joint Economic Committee, *op. cit.*, p. 187). Perhaps this would be true in some circumstances, but the present writer is inclined to believe that open market sales of securities might often be the more appropriate weapon for this purpose, since the funds resulting from the sale of gold to the Treasury by foreign governments are often likely to find their way to the central money market, so that the way to offset the effects of these flows with the minimum impact on domestic business activity might be through the sale of Treasury bills, which would, in the main, withdraw funds from the central money market.

[58] Another issue that has come up recently relating to the choice between open market operations and reserve requirement changes is the differing effects that these two weapons have on the Treasury's interest costs on the profits of commercial banks. For example, the creation of a given amount of additional money by open market purchases will result in lower costs to the Treasury and lower profits to the banking system than would be the creation of the same amount of money by lowering reserve requirements. (For an extensive discussion, see Smith, "Reserve Requirements in the American Monetary System," *op. cit.*, pp. 216–49.) However, this matter is relevant chiefly in connection with long-term developments related to the choice between open market purchases and reserve requirement reductions as alternative means of providing reserves to support the secular growth of the money supply. It has little bearing on the relative merits of the two weapons as alternative means of producing two-way anti-cyclical changes in credit conditions.

instability via the public's expectations. Reserve requirements policy is a powerful weapon but too cumbersome for frequent use and not clearly capable of accomplishing anything under ordinary circumstances that cannot be done at least as well by means of open market operations.

Doubtless the three weapons have somewhat different economic effects; however, detailed knowledge of the impact of monetary changes is inadequate to permit a meaningful differentiation. Consequently, it is not possible to specify the circumstances in which one of these weapons rather than the others should be used. They are all designed to serve the same purposes—one effectively and the other two rather ineptly.

Accordingly, I would favor placing complete reliance on open market operations, under ordinary circumstances, as the means of conducting general monetary policy. The best way of handling the discount rate would probably be to tie it to the Treasury bill rate as explained earlier in this paper. Reserve requirements should probably be fixed at an appropriate level and kept there.[59] I would also favor the elimination of the present threefold classification of banks for reserve requirement purposes and the establishment of uniform reserve requirements for demand deposits at all banks, including non-member banks. There does not appear to be any logical basis for differentiating among banks as far as reserve requirements are concerned, and uniform requirements would increase somewhat the precision of open market policy as a means

of controlling the total supply of money and bank credit.[60]

There may be circumstances under which the Federal Reserve should try to affect economic activity by influencing the public's expectations, although this is clearly a tricky and possibly even dangerous form of activity. To the extent that it is employed, it should be divorced from actions designed to control bank reserves and should take advantage of the subtleties of everyday language. One of the advantages of open market operations is that they are necessarily being carried out continuously and are largely devoid of so-called "announcement effects."

One final question should perhaps be raised: Does not the situation of the last three years or so when monetary policy has had to be directed simultaneously at stimulation of the domestic economy and protection of the balance of payments against excessive outflows of short-term capital argue for the retention of all of the traditional credit control weapons, in order to maximize the flexibility of the monetary authorities? I do not believe so. It is true that, for example, by lowering reserve requirements and simultaneously selling enough Treasury bills to keep the bill rate from falling, the authorities could presumably stimulate the domestic economy to some extent without increasing outflows of short-term capital. But such a result could equally well be brought about by requisite purchases of longer-term securities combined with sales of bills. It is difficult to see that adjustments in reserve requirements and the discount rate give the authorities any ability to change the structure of interest rates and the total credit supply that could not equally well be accomplished by sufficiently flexible use of Federal Reserve open market and Treasury debt management operations.

[59] The question of what is the "appropriate" level of reserve requirements is beyond the scope of this paper and, in any case, is a matter of judgment. It is in connection with this question that the effects of reserve requirements on bank profits and Treasury interest costs referred to in footnote 58 become relevant.

[60] *Ibid.*, pp. 175–99.

*JAMES R. SCHLESINGER*

# Monetary Policy and Its Critics

*33*    In assessing the import of the criticisms of monetary policy which seemingly have flowed in an unending stream during the last three decades, it is wise to recognize at the outset that some people simply do not *like* monetary policy. This antipathy arises from non-logical policy judgments concerning the *suitability* of monetary restraints, but it is reflected in a continuously evolving set of charges concerning the *operation* of monetary policy. Whenever one argument appears defective, these critics readily turn to another—one which may or may not be consistent with what was previously espoused. It is this underlying emotional response which helps to explain the quality of changeableness that has characterized the debate over monetary policy.

Much of the antagonism to monetary policy stems from its reliance on the price mechanism. A rationing process that operates through the

Reprinted from the *Journal of Political Economy*, Vol. LXVIII (1960), pp. 601–616, by permission of the author and the University of Chicago Press. Copyright 1960 by the University of Chicago. James Schlesinger is on the staff of the Rand Corporation.

market seems inhuman to many people, and the results are regarded as unfair or harmful. In addition, the impact of monetary policy on spending decisions is so subtle that many doubt that it is there at all. Influencing total spending by bringing about changes in the value, the volume, or the composition of the financial assets of the community strikes some observers as a mechanism too weak or too indirect to be relied upon. Thus there are doubts about the effectiveness of monetary policy as well as about its appropriateness, and, of course, legitimate doubts along these lines inevitably are seized upon by self-interested groups to attain monetary conditions more satisfactory from their point of view. Still, the genuine misgivings do raise certain issues of public policy which ought to be considered explicitly.

A substantial portion of the recent debate has been concerned not with the monetary mechanism itself but with a particular monetary policy. For example, it has been argued that the level of demand consistent with a stable price level is somewhat lower than that necessary to achieve full employment. Much of the present criticism of Federal Reserve policies consists of assertions that the System has chosen the wrong monetary goal—preventing cost inflation—and that its attempt to influence aggregate supply conditions through its control over the money stock is foolhardy. Such criticisms do not imply that the critic necessarily distrusts or disapproves of the use of monetary controls; they are simply disagreements over details of monetary policy. To cite one prominent example, Sumner Slichter was a vigorous critic of Federal Reserve policies, yet nowhere in his writings is there any indication that he felt any doubt that some degree of monetary restraint is necessary for the proper functioning of the economy. Other observers, especially quantity theorists, have argued that the Federal Reserve is at fault for permitting rises in the price level. By the very nature of their position, such critics cannot be taken to believe that monetary controls are either unnecessary or inappropriate.

In this paper we shall not be concerned with such surface disputes over goals but with the much more fundamental criticisms of those who argue that monetary policy is, for one reason or another, *inherently defective*. Put into three general categories, these charges maintain that monetary policy is (1) ineffective, (2) discriminatory, and (3) contrary to sound social policy. Each will be considered in turn.

## I. The Question of Effectiveness

Although it is almost a truism that to question the effectiveness of monetary policy is potentially the most devastating of the criticisms, the neo-classical economists never appeared to entertain such doubts. From Wicksell to Keynes (of the *Treatise*) is was generally believed that monetary policy, by lowering interest rates and, concurrently, the supply prices of capital goods, could induce investment demand sufficient to maintain the constancy of the price level or, to stress a more modern consideration, sufficient to achieve the utilization of all factors of production. Conversely, it was believed that a rise in interest rates would serve to deter enough marginal borrowers to contain total spending within the limits of total supply at the prevailing price level. The investment-demand schedule was assumed to be sufficiently elastic so that correct monetary policy, in the long run if not in the business cycle, would insure the absorption of full-employment savings. Yet this Age of Faith was soon to be followed by an Age of Despair.

### (a) The 1930's

The deep and seemingly unshakable depression of the thirties simultaneously dragged monetary policy down from the position of honor that it had occupied and raised doubts as to whether it had any influence on spending at all. Skeptics questioned whether so minor an item in the total cost picture as a small rise in the interest rate was sufficient to alter the spending decisions of borrowers. For short-lived investments such as those in machinery and equipment, the period of investment was too brief for changes in the interest rate to have any substantial influence on costs. (Such considerations were reinforced by corporate rules of thumb which required every piece of machinery to pay for itself in some arbitrary time period.) On the other hand, it was argued that, for long-lived investments, where it is obvious that even a small change in the rate of interest will have a substantial impact on costs, the risk allowance was so large that variations in the cost of borrowing would be swallowed up by the allowance for risk. Consequently, investment demand could be considered insensitive to interest-rate variation. Of course, the abler critics, such as the late Sir Hubert Henderson, who was the guiding figure in the iconoclastic Oxford studies of the price mechanism, did recognize that there were certain long-lived, relatively riskless investments—in housing, public utilities, and public investments—which were extremely sensitive to interest-rate changes. They argued, however, that population growth in most Western nations had either slowed down or ceased entirely and that it was toward population growth that the interest-sensitive categories of long-lived investment were oriented.[1] The fact that this area of investment activity had shrunk further reduced the impact of interest-rate changes.

Empirical studies during the period tended to confirm this skeptical appraisal of monetary policy. Investigators,[2] using either questionnaires or case studies, reached the conclusion that perhaps half the firms studied paid no attention whatsoever to interest rates and that only a

[1] H. D. Henderson, "The Significance of the Rate of Interest," *Oxford Economic Papers*, No. 1 (January, 1938), reprinted in *Oxford Studies in the Price Mechanism*, ed. T. Wilson and P. W. S. Andrews (New York: Oxford University Press, 1951), pp. 20–22.

[2] See the articles by J. E. Meade and P. W. S. Andrews reprinted in *Oxford Studies in the Price Mechanism*, pp. 27–30, 51–66; also J. F. Ebersole, "The Influence of Interest Rates upon Entrepreneurial Decisions in Business—a Case Study," *Harvard Business Review*, XVII, No. 1 (Autumn, 1938), 35–39.

small minority considered them to be significant. Of course, it is necessary to make allowance for the period in which these studies were made; nevertheless, the number of relevant issues which the investigators *failed* to consider is noteworthy.

1. Since the bulk of investment activity is concentrated in the largest firms, is not the percentage - of - firms criterion misleading? Were the minority of firms that borrowed heavily and invested heavily the ones that were sensitive to interest-rate changes, as seems likely?

2. Does not the responsiveness of firms to monetary policy vary with the time and the economic climate? Consequently, will conclusions drawn in a depressed period characterized by excess capacity be applicable under other conditions—particularly periods of expansion?

3. If interest rates do not control the investment decision, do they influence the *timing* of the expenditures which follow from that decision?

4. Do interest rates affect corporate dividend policy (that is, corporate savings), thus providing non-credit sources of expenditures?

5. Are expenditures influenced by credit conditions other than interest rates or by the general tone of the money market of which the interest rate is simply a symptom?

6. Are businessmen actually able to appraise the determinants of their own decisions; is it not likely that they are constitutionally far more alert to positive inducements such as sales than to (negative) inhibitors like interest rates?

7. Finally—and perhaps most important of all —do not investigations of this sort, which make inquiries of individual businessmen and then argue from the specific to the general, ignore the *indirect* influence of interest rates on spending decisions? Cannot an all-round process of expansion be generated from slender beginnings? If even a few businesses are induced by cheaper credit to expand outlays, may not other concerns also be persuaded to increase expenditures as their sales rise?

To raise questions of this sort is to underscore the conceptual defects of the empirical investigations. Nevertheless, at the time, these studies did tend to confirm the new analytical presupposition that investment decisions were insensitive to changes in the interest rate. Moreover, difficulties posed by the inelasticity of the investment-demand schedule were compounded by the Keynesian view of liquidity preference, which hinted that monetary policy has little effect on interest rates anyway. Even with limited demand

for investment funds, the long-term interest rate, it was believed, would not fall below some positive level, say 2 per cent, because the threat of capital loss at lower interest rates was so great that the public would absorb in cash balances more and more money without bidding up bond prices or lowering interest rates. Buttressed by such conceptions, dominant opinion in the late thirties in the government and in academic circles held that monetary policy was ineffective.

Nevertheless, it remains a distinct possibility that the sensitivity of investment to interest-rate changes and the strength of liquidity preference may vary substantially with changes in the over-all economic climate. If we recall the influences bearing on the effectiveness of monetary policy, it seems plausible to argue that the observers of the thirties erred in generalizing from conditions prevailing in the deepest depression ever experienced. When national income has at one point fallen by almost 50 per cent, when many industries are operating at 20–30 per cent of capacity, when new investment is deterred by excess capacity, when no new markets are foreseen and business confidence has ebbed, low interest rates are unlikely to have much stimulative effect, no matter how low they fall. Such conditions may well be described by an inelastic investment-demand schedule.

In addition, consider the strong desire for liquidity then prevailing, the willingness of the public and the banks to hoard rather than to commit funds (the theory of credit expansion precludes excess reserves). In the period after 1929 there was a run to liquidity. By 1933 the banking system had reached a state of collapse. Many banks were forced to shut their doors because of illiquidity at the same time that the financial community was still being blamed for the speculative excesses of the twenties. Is it surprising that both the public and the banking community exhibited under these conditions a strong liquidity preference, reflected in excess reserves and in the astonishing gap between long-term and short-term interest rates?

Moreover, the economic difficulties were reinforced by political conditions that were hardly conducive to business confidence. Monetary policy attempts to influence business decisions at the margin; yet such considerations become insignificant when the social system appears to be in chaos. Labor conditions were unsettled. Businessmen, who were widely used as scapegoats, were apprehensive. Neither the path to an effective monetary policy nor the path to recovery lies in the direction of alarming those who make investment decisions. Plainly, it would be unwise to regard monetary policy as *generally ineffective* on the basis either of the analysis or of the conditions of the thirties.

### (b) The 1940's

Financial developments of the forties provided an institutional rationalization for the skepticism concerning monetary policy, yet at the same time gave rise to the inflationary pressures which eventually were to strike the wartime chains from monetary policy. At the end of World War II, however, the heritage of control, associated with fear of the consequences of the use of the traditional weapons provoked by the enormously expanded public debt, reinforced the anti-monetary attitudes of the thirties.[3] Rising interest rates, it was argued, would not inhibit spending, yet would increase the cost of debt service to the taxpayer—failure to reckon the costs of inflation, of course, tended to lead to undue stress on the cost of debt service. Perhaps more important was the belief that the bulk of the debt was infirmly held and that rising interest rates would provoke a panic, in the course of which a substantial part of the debt, perhaps including even savings bonds, would be jettisoned. If, eventually, the Federal Reserve were forced to intervene to pick up the pieces, why not prevent such a cataclysm by an initial policy of support to the government securities market? Periodic Treasury refunding operations which would require Federal Reserve support were held to reinforce such considerations. These arguments were so widely accepted that for a time even the Federal Reserve System readily acquiesced in its own Babylonian captivity.[4]

In view of the excess liquidity which characterized the postwar period, it is certainly arguable that monetary controls would have had little

immediate effect, even though, as a general proposition, monetary policy is more effective in coping with inflationary pressures than with depression. There may always be an interest high enough or monetary pressure severe enough to check investment demand, but, in conditions already characterized by monetary redundancy, it may not be practicable to bring this about. When anything that is bought can be sold, when inflation will justify any investment, when markets appear overwhelmingly promising, money expenditures will rise as the circulation of money increases, even though the supply be held constant. Some inflation is inevitable as a phase of the process of reducing excess liquidity. Yet, even if monetary restraint could not have dissipated the inflation potential in 1945–46, there is clearly no long-run case against monetary control. Moreover, events have demonstrated that fears of the collapse of the government securities market, understandable as they may have been in light of our lack of experience in handling so large a debt, have been excessive. The market for governments is normally stable in the sense that when some holders wish to sell securities, purchasers other than the central bank stand ready to buy. There is no *cumulative unloading* of securities but rather a *transfer* of securities among holders without the intervention of the Federal Reserve system. Nevertheless, the "loose-cargo" argument did cling curiously to life. As the years passed, the Federal Reserve System became increasingly restive under conditions such that its open-market operations accentuated, first, the inflation of 1946–48, then the recession of 1949, and then the renewed inflation of 1950–51. Yet down to the Accord of 1951 and later, a substantial body of academic opinion regarded monetary restraint as unnecessary, monetary policy as ineffective, and general credit controls as obsolete.[5]

### (c) The 1950's

With the revival of monetary policy, far greater stress was placed upon the *availability* of credit as opposed to its *cost* than would have been deemed appropriate in neoclassical thought. But

[3] Cf. Lawrence H. Seltzer, "Is a Rise in Interest Rates Desirable or Inevitable?" *American Economic Review*, Vol. XXXV, No. 5 (December, 1945). One interesting aspect of Seltzer's article is that it contains an early expression of the belief that monetary policy remains utterly useless up to the point that it becomes potentially disastrous and that there are no intermediate effects. This view has been modified by more recent writers, but (for other reasons) it is still with us. Today it is argued that sizable interest-rate changes may precipitate a depression, but that, up to the point that it becomes dangerous, monetary policy is ineffective. Based on the presupposition that even a small rise in the interest rate would provoke a panic in the government securities market, Seltzer's formulation was far more coherent than the more recent one.

[4] See the 32d, 33d, 34th, 35th, and 36th *Annual Report of the Board of Governors of the Federal Reserve System* (1945–49).

[5] Consider the comments of the various contributors to the "Symposium on Monetary Policy," *Review of Economics and Statistics*, Vol. XXXIII, No. 3 (August, 1951), at the time of the revival of monetary policy in this country and also those of the contributors to "Monetary Policy: A Symposium," *Bulletin of the Oxford University Institute of Statistics* Vol. XIV, Nos. 4, 5, and 8 (April, May, and August, 1952), when British monetary policy was revived.

interest rates move sluggishly. Debt instruments are imperfect substitutes for each other. Save in the open market, lenders are subject to a sense of restraint. Consequently, it seems clear that it is more than the price of credit itself that limits borrowing. The willingness of lenders to lend is an important consideration; lenders may prefer to curtail requests for credit without increasing rates.[6] Borrowers themselves may become reluctant to borrow when they do not feel assured about their long-run liquidity position, even if they are undeterred by the cost of borrowing per se. It is the availability of credit that is most important, and rising interest rates may merely be symptomatic of the several forces at work during periods of monetary stringency.

In response to the renewed emphasis upon monetary policy, a third type of criticism has developed, drawing on the older arguments, yet transposing or inverting the elements contained therein.[7] Basically, it is contended that the

---

[6] The new emphasis on the lender as opposed to the borrower was stressed by Robert V. Roosa as a part of what came to be called "the availability doctrine" (see "Interest Rates and the Central Bank," in *Money, Trade, and Economic Growth*: *In Honor of John Henry Williams* [New York: Macmillan Co., 1951]; also I. O. Scott, Jr., "The Availability Doctrine: Development and Implications," *Canadian Journal of Economics and Political Science*, Vol. XXIII, No. 4 [November, 1957]). One aspect of the doctrine upon which Roosa laid some stress was the belief that a small rise in the rate of interest might bring about a curtailment of lending on the part of conservative financial institutions. Such a rise might generate caution in disposing of liquid assets like bills and at the same time lock these institutions into their portfolios of long-term governments on account of the reluctance to take capital losses. From the vantage point of the late fifties, it appears that this restraining influence was a phase of the transition from the kept markets of the forties to the free markets of the fifties. In recent years, financial institutions have not been at all reluctant to dispose of government securities in the face of rising interest rates.

[7] The most vigorous exponent is W. L. Smith. See his "On the Effectiveness of Monetary Policy," *American Economic Review*, Vol. XLVI, No. 4 (September, 1956); his "Monetary Policy and the Structure of Markets," in *The Relationship of Prices to Economic Stability and Growth*: *Compendium of Papers Submitted by Panelists Appearing before the Joint Economic Committee* (Washington, D.C., 1958), pp. 493–98; and his "Some Unsettled Issues in Monetary Policy," in *United States Monetary Policy* (Durham, N.C.: American Assembly, Duke University, 1959), pp. 14–30; see also W. W. Heller, "CED's Stabilizing Budget Policy after Ten Years," *American Economic Review*, XLVII, No. 3 (September, 1957), 646–49; and L. S. Ritter, "Income Velocity and Monetary Policy," *American Economic Review*, Vol. XLIX, No. 1 (March, 1959).

nation's financial machinery, through the lubricating medium of the government debt, can effectively and automatically mobilize idle balances to maintain monetary expenditures whenever pressure is applied. Rising interest rates, which are a consequence of monetary restraint, supply the incentive and the mechanism through which such idle balances are mobilized. During boom periods, banks are subjected to pressure to expand business loans. As they attempt to sell bonds, interest rates rise, and this increase induces those who held idle or excessive balances at lower interest rates to purchase securities. The sale of securities by the banks frees reserves and permits the expansion of business loans. This process of replacing investments by business loans is considered to be inflationary, even though the liabilities side of the banks' balance sheets is left unaffected. The exchange of assets permits the activation of the money supply. As velocity increases, so do monetary expenditures, even though the money stock is held constant. Thus "mere" control of the money supply will not seriously limit expenditures in the short run; monetary policy is ineffective.

It is interesting to compare the ingredients of the current critique with those of the older arguments. First, it is believed that rising interest rates in themselves have little deterrent effect on expenditures—this is, of course, a necessary element in any questioning of the effectiveness of monetary policy. Second, Keynes's notion of liquidity preference has, more or less, been turned on its head. Initially designed to demonstrate that increases in the money stock would not serve to lower interest rates in depression and therefore were an ineffective stimulus, it is now used to demonstrate that rising interest rates are the means through which monetary hoards are mobilized and consequently that control over the monetary stock in inflation is an ineffective restraint. Third, the government debt is seen not as an incubus making interest-rate variation risky but as the lubricating element in the financial structure. It is a point of historical irony that some of those who support the new criticism previously held the "loose-cargo" view of the government debt. Nevertheless, it would be folly—despite some rather abrupt changes in the positions of the critics—not to recognize that the new indictment is the most profound criticism of monetary policy yet devised, not at all dependent on the peculiarities of deep depression or the vagaries of wartime finance. There is, no doubt, some element of truth in the argument. Increasing velocity, by activating idle balances, does reduce the *immediate* effectiveness of monetary policy. But there is some limit to the increase of velocity, so that in the intermediate period,[8] at least, monetary restraint does imply the ability to limit money expenditures. The problem is how rapidly. If there is a *substantial* lag before monetary restraints take hold, then, by their nature, monetary controls may be a weak tool to *rely* upon in dealing with *short-run* fluctuations.

Even in the short run, one should recognize the limits of the argument. First, investment demand is probably more sensitive to interest rates than the critics admit, and the declining liquidity associated with the growing pressure for bank loans undoubtedly plays some role in deterring expenditures. Second, the possibility of *substantial* loan expansion through the sale of securities may have been in part a temporary manifestation associated with the high proportion of governments in commercial bank portfolios after the war. The higher the ratio of loans to total bank credit becomes, the more limited is the possibility of further expansion through exchange. Third, the effect of the long-term decline in the securities ratio on the willingness of banks to dispose of investments may be reinforced by a debt-management policy which during recession (unlike the Treasury policy in 1954) prevents the excessive accumulation of highly liquid, short-term items which serve as the basis of loan expansion on the return of prosperity. Finally, it can be argued that increasing velocity is a part of the mechanism of restraint.[9] The Federal Reserve does not wish

to close off spending from borrowed sums but merely to encourage reconsideration of spending decisions. Unless velocity is perfectly elastic in its response to monetary pressure, some restraint will occur. Although the argument based on loan expansion and variable velocity is the most reasonable of the criticisms of the effectiveness of monetary policy, it should be emphasized that the argument does not imply any doubt concerning the necessity for monetary control; it asserts only that monetary policy should not be *exclusively* relied upon for dealing with short-term fluctuations. This position is perfectly consistent with advocating monetary restraint in boom times for the purpose of alarming potential spenders about their future liquidity positions. Monetary policy, although it should be employed, may not be *sufficiently* effective by itself; therefore, it should be strengthened and supplemented by other devices.

## II. The Question of Discrimination

The broad charge of discrimination implies that monetary restraint is unfair because of its disproportionate impact on certain categories of borrowers who either lose access to funds or else become subject to *exceptionally* onerous terms of borrowing.[10] The ordinary indictment implies that monetary restraint affects the *allocation of resources* in a way that drastically and inappropriately affects the interests of certain categories of borrowers and at the same time is potentially damaging to the national economy. Plainly, this charge is wholly inconsistent with the preceding argument, for if monetary policy can affect the allocation of resources and the volume of expenditures, it cannot at the same time be *ineffective*. Yet resource allocation is inextricably meshed with the *distribution of income*, so that sometimes the charge becomes the assertion that monetary restraint unfairly alters the income distribution.

[8] In the short run, velocity might rise because of the activation of idle balances. In the long run, in principle at least, velocity might rise because of an adjustment in the community's methods of completing financial transactions (frequency of receipts and expenditures, etc.); this is particularly pertinent in the age of the credit card. It is an intermediate period that monetary controls can take hold, that is, after idle balances have been exhausted but before the habits of the community have time to change.

[9] Since velocity is regarded as a constant, increases in velocity could not be expected to be *part* of the mechanism of restraint in a rudimentary quantity theory such as the one based on the Fisherine equation. Milton Friedman has argued, however, that in a more sophisticated version of the quantity theory one would not expect velocity to be a constant but rather to vary with interest rates (*Studies in the Quantity Theory of Money* [Chicago: University of Chicago Press, 1956], pp. 12–13). Without considering one's self a quantity theorist, one can surely accept this position with regard to the effect of restraint on velocity.

[10] The most prominent proponent of this position is Leon H. Keyserling, see *inter alia*, his statement, *January 1957 Economic Report of the President: Hearings before the Joint Economic Committee* (Washington: Government Printing Office, 1957). It has also been indorsed by J. K. Galbraith and S. E. Harris, see Galbraith's statement, *January 1958 Economic Report of the President: Hearings before the Joint Economic Committee* (Washington: Government Printing Office, 1958), and the joint communication, "The Failure of Monetary Policy," which is included. This position has also been reiterated perenially by countless representatives of affected groups.

This is a traditional political refrain among legislators whose constituents include a large number of farmers or small businessmen—the charge having overtones of "the people" versus "the interests." It is essentially a protest against higher interest rates which ignores both the change in the demand for borrowed funds and the possible costs of inflation. To be valid, it has to be assumed that those who need borrowed funds are somehow more deserving than those who supply them. Some of the current cries of discrimination do involve such a notion—consumer credit is almost a pure case in point—yet, for the most part, charges of discrimination are concerned with the effect on resource allocation.

It must be recognized at the outset that monetary policy cannot fail to affect different citizens differently. Since it affects the availability of credit, the impact of monetary policy must be "disproportionate" in that it is as asymmetrical in its consequences. Such inherent asymmetry may be traced to two causes: (1) Some institutions are more dependent on borrowed funds than are others; of those dependent on borrowed funds, some are especially dependent on bank credit, whereas others have access to other sources— that is, security markets. (2) Within the camp of borrowers, the strength of the demand will vary among the several groups. Those whose demand is not so inelastic will be unwilling to pay as high a price as will others, and consequently, as interest rates rise, their share of the funds will fall. Now surely it would be trivial if those who charge discrimination had these kinds of disparities in mind. It is hardly logical to charge discrimination simply because the cost of borrowing has risen, even though those who are forced to pay higher rates are likely to be resentful. Nor would it appear logical to charge discrimination because those who use borrowed funds more than others are more damaged by increased competition (that is, demand) for such funds or a reduction in supply. (Is it contended that the available funds be allotted by some sort of parity system based on historical norms?) Nor would it appear logical to charge discrimination when those whose demand is less intense receive a smaller share of the available funds.[11] (Would it then be fairer or less discriminatory for those whose demand is less intense to share equally with those whose demand is more intense?)

Plainly, those who argue that monetary policy is discriminatory must have something more than these banalities in mind. After all, in a market *not characterized by discrimination*, one may anticipate that, with the tightening of credit, interest rates will rise most and borrowings fall least in money submarkets in which demand is most inelastic and that interests rates will rise least but borrowings will fall most in money submarkets in which demand is most elastic.[12] Any results other than these would constitute a prima facie case of discrimination. Critics of monetary policy, however, must have in mind situations in which the market does not behave in this normal way—that is, situations in which some borrowers are faced with a more-than-to-be-anticipated increase in rates or decrease in funds. Complaints of this type are put forward by, or on behalf of, five categories of borrowers —homebuilders, municipalities and state governments, small businesses, consumer borrowers, and affected industries. Each type of complaint will be examined in turn.[13]

### (a) Homebuilding

In periods of tight money, new housing starts sometimes show an extraordinary rapid decline. For example, from 1955 to 1957—years of intensifying boom and rising interest rates— housing starts actually dropped from 1.3 million to 1.0 million per year, although housing starts had risen by some 20 per cent in the preceding period of recession. Such changes may in large degree reflect the elasticity of demand for housing credit—housing is a long-lived asset, so that a small rise in the interest rate means a sharp rise in the supply price. Nevertheless, other factors may help to account for the decline —in particular, the entire fall may be attributed to the decrease in Veterans Administration and Federal Housing Authority mortgages. While government-underwritten new housing starts

[11] If this were not so, the charge of discrimination could be raised in behalf of any and all borrowers. When money becomes tight, some borrowers will pay substantially higher rates; all others will discover substantial reductions in their volume of borrowings. Since all pay higher rates or suffer from a reduction in funds, all may charge discrimination, according to the above logic.

[12] Those categories of borrowers who are unwilling to pay higher rates will probably not have their borrowings fall to zero because of the desire for the diversification of holdings on the part of lenders.

[13] In the discussion which follows I am very much indebted to the investigations of Harmon H. Haymes ("An Investigation of the Alleged Discriminatory Impact of General Credit Controls in Periods of Monetary Stringency" [unpublished Ph.D. dissertation, University of Virginia, 1959]).

fell by 400 thousand units, those with conventional mortgages rose moderately by some 70 thousand.[14] Congress has set a maximum rate on mortgages, beyond which the Veterans Administration and Federal Housing Authority cannot insure. Is the sharp drop in government-underwritten mortgages a type of discrimination attributable to monetary policy? When credit grows tight, what other result could be expected than that those who are restrained by legal restrictions from bidding emphatically will be eliminated from the market? Clearly, it is the law that discriminates, implying that homebuilders should not be encouraged in an unwise inclination to sign a mortgage bearing (at that time) more than $4\frac{3}{4}$ per cent interest. In any event, the charge that it is monetary restraint which is discriminatory should be dropped.

### (b) Local Government Borrowing

During the boom, 1955–57, complaints were heard from both municipalities and state governments that they were unable to raise the funds that they needed. Despite rising demand for funds, new-security issues of state and municipal governments fell from $7.0 billion in 1954 to $5.4 billion in 1956. Yet, during the mid-fifties, interest rates rose proportionately more rapidly for municipal bonds than for corporate bonds or for United States government bonds. To put the issue another way, the premium which municipals had previously enjoyed over competing bonds disappeared during the same period. Is this not a case of discrimination, with both volume falling and interest rates rising sharply? The fall in volume is largely explicable in terms of the attitudes of local governments. Many municipalities have ordinances prohibiting the paying of more than, say, 4 per cent on debt issues; when market rates rise, they are unable to borrow and are eliminated from the market. The same results follow in other municipalities because of the unwillingness of officials to pay more than some stipulated rate. Apparently,

the citizens in the localities have examined the intensity of their demand for local improvements and their willingness to pay taxes and have correspondingly limited their bids for funds. Consequently, during periods of tight money, the volume of borrowing falls. The reluctance to pay higher taxes may be shortsighted, to be sure, but the fall in volume cannot be charged to the discriminatory impact of monetary policy.[15]

The proportionally more rapid rise of interest rates on municipal bonds may be attributed to another structural characteristic of the market —the response to the tax-exemption privilege. As long as demand is small enough to be satisfied by the supply of funds from those who benefit sufficiently to pay a premium for tax-exempt returns, interest rates will remain low. When, however, the demand rises (as it has in the fifties) or the supply of funds from those willing to pay a premium drops, interest rates will rise suddenly to a competitive level, since the municipalities will have to pay enough at the margin to fulfil their requirements. Such results can hardly be charged to the discriminatory impact of monetary policy but rather to the evaporation of a tax feature designed to aid (discriminate in favor of) local governments.[16]

### (c) Small Business

During periods of credit restraint the accusation is invariably made that tight money discriminates against small business vis-à-vis large business. Of all the charges of discrimination, it is here that the evidence seems best to substantiate the charge. "True" discrimination—a failure of ordinary market forces—occurs when certain categories of borrowers lose access to credit, although they are willing to pay competitive rates. Large business concerns usually maintain substantial lines of credit which may normally be unused. In boom periods they will draw upon these lines of credit; so that banks

---

[14] The *Federal Reserve Bulletin* provides the following data on new housing starts:

| | New Housing Starts (Thousands) | Mortgages Gov't-Underwritten | Conventional |
|---|---|---|---|
| 1955......... | 1,329 | 670 | 659 |
| 1957......... | 1,042 | 313 | 729 |

Since the value of construction as opposed to the number of starts fell relatively little, it may be argued that the effect of the law was to encourage the building of fewer but bigger houses.

[15] The niggardliness of local governments has come in for considerable criticism lately. The underlying notion that the citizen-consumer is foolish or misguided, although difficult to express publicly, is really somewhat different from the charge that there has been discrimination.

[16] This does not eliminate the equity problem posed by the fact that certain well-to-do people have been obtaining high tax-free returns while the municipalities have not been obtaining any compensating advantage in the terms of borrowing. The justification that municipalities could get cheaper financing without dispensing much in the way of ill-gotten gains seems to have worn thin in recent years.

may be forced to reject loan requests by small businesses willing to pay market rates or higher. In the main this appears to be a problem of small businesses located in larger communities where banks are likely to have "big business" customers. Of course, during boom periods small businesses can and do turn to other sources of credit—open-book accounts, factors, etc. Such substitutes are inferior to bank credit and frequently far more costly. Much bank credit is siphoned to small business through the accounts receivable of large business borrowers. Small businesses do get by, but this does not solve the problem posed by the fact that our financial system discourages small business, while it is public policy to encourage it. Action by the Small Business Administration and the recently formed investment companies under the Small Business Investment Act seems desirable in counteracting such tendencies.

### (d) Consumer Credit

Sometimes it is argued that tight money discriminates against users of consumer credit. In fact, consumer credit rises rapidly during periods of boom (tight money) and tends to contract mildly in periods of recession, so that the charge of discrimination must relate to its allegedly unfair impact on income distribution rather than resource allocation. A leading congressional critic is fond of rhetorically informing Federal Reserve officials that they are forcing the ordinary man to pay more for his house, for his car, and for any other purchase on time. With respect to consumer credit, at least, this charge seems to be inaccurate. Interest rates on consumer credit are normally very high and rigid, some of them pressing against state maximums; the demand for this credit is highly inelastic. Thus, during prosperity, rates rise little, if at all. Because of the relatively high rates, lenders, including banks, are always ready to satisfy any demand for consumer credit. In prosperity the rise of other rates reduces the relative attractiveness of consumer credit, but not enough to divert funds to other uses. In a market in which tight money barely affects the volume of funds lent and has only a slight effect on interest rates, the charge of discrimination would appear to be at its wildest.

### (e) Affected Industries

As might easily be anticipated, industries especially sensitive to monetary restraint are likely to see themselves as victims of discrimination. This is especially true of the construction and railroad industries. The late Robert R. Young, for example, was one of industry's most persistent, if not most perceptive, critics of tight money, ready to explain to interested congressional committees how many more box-cars the New York Central could have bought, had interest rates not been so unwarrantedly high.[17] On occasion similar criticisms are heard from the electric-power, natural-gas-transmission, and automobile industries as—for other reasons—from the farming and small-business sectors of the economy. Most of such complaints use the word "discrimination" in the sense that a general control bears down more heavily on those sectors of the economy which are sensitive to it than on those sections which are not, rather than that there are discriminatory standards for the several industries. It should be understood that such complaints do bring to the surface grave policy issues. How fair is it, for example, to help stabilize the general economy by forcing a particular industry like housing through wider fluctuations, using monetary policy reinforced by Veterans Administration and Federal Housing Authority controls? But, for the most part, the policy issues raised by the affected industries verge upon the third general criticism of monetary policy—that its results are contrary to sound social policy.

## III. The Question of Social Policy

Even if monetary policy is effective, even if it is non-discriminatory, it may be argued that its consequences are in conflict with either long-run welfare considerations or the national interest. In particular, restrictive monetary policy operates by cutting down on investment activity and thus

[17] In his statement (*Monetary Policy: 1955–56: Hearings before the Subcommittee on Economic Stabilization of the Joint Economic Committee* [Washington: Government Printing Office, 1957], p. 54), he comments: "We have slowed down the scheduling of our building of boxcars just because we cannot afford to pay $5\frac{1}{2}$ per cent for money when the Interstate Commerce Commission gives us a 3 per cent return. It is just that simple. . . . If the figures were reversed, we would start building; if we paid 3 per cent for money and we were allowed to earn 5 per cent, we would cure the boxcar shortage overnight."

Young was, no doubt, correct in his last assessment. The problems of the regulated industries, in which investment tends to be long-lived and riskless, cannot simply be laid at the door of monetary policy, however.

militates against economic growth.[18] Monetary policy may be all too effective in reducing what may be referred to as "social investment" and for this reason may be less attractive than certain forms of fiscal policy. By its nature, monetary policy is particularly effective in deterring the long-lived, relatively riskless investment that can be considered especially conducive to progress (business investment in plant, electric-power production, transportation, including pipelines, and educational facilities) or conducive to social health (housing, municipal and other public services). Even if monetary policy is not discriminatory in the technical sense, it works by curtailing those expenditures which are in the public interest. The affected categories of borrowers (in effect, those charging discrimination) do not have to be protected against discrimination; they should nevertheless be encouraged in the long-run interests of the society.

Reliance on monetary policy, so the argument runs, means that national resources are wasted on additional consumption goods or on "silly" investment in neon lighting and amusement parks rather than being devoted to "worth-while" purposes. This view of consumer expenditures as superfluous is plainly at the opposite pole from the one maintaining that the defect of monetary policy is that it discriminates against the poor man who must use consumer credit to lift his standard of living, since the chief defect alleged in this case is that credit resources are "wasted" on consumption goods and other fripperies. It may readily be understood how the appeal of an argument stating that our social values are wrong and that we are not sacrificing enough for economic growth has been reinforced by concern over the menacing posture of the Soviet Union.

It is difficult not to have some immediate sympathy for this position. Our scale of social priorities may indeed be askew. Many are affronted by the current "boom psychology" and its accompanying orgy of materialism. Surely we ought not to permit credit to be wasted on consumer goods when it might be used to create additional productive capacity. Still, if this orgy of materialism is so vicious, what is the purpose of additional economic progress? Why should consumers not buy automobiles now, so that plants may be built to produce more automobiles in the future? Why should resources be diverted from washing machines to electric-power facilities at the present time, so that future generations of consumers have electric power for their washing machines? Viewed in this way, the criterion of more investment for more rapid growth becomes somewhat less compelling. Even in regard to social services, particularly those provided by municipalities, it seems perfectly apparent that the higher interest costs of new schools, new sewerage systems, and the like could be met without inducing a lower interest rate, if citizens saw a compelling social reason. The taxpayers have decided, rightly or wrongly, that they do not wish to bear the cost. Stern Galbraithian denunciations of "the unseemly economics of opulence" notwithstanding, the American people seem to like more, shiny, tasteless consumer goods. In monetary policy as elsewhere, responsibility for unsound social standards should be placed where it belongs and not attributed to the conventional wisdom of economists.[19]

Still, it may be that our scale of social priorities is distorted and that reliance on monetary policy tends to aggravate such perversions. Assuming that the American people could be converted to this way of thinking, what kinds of alternative policies seem appropriate? What remedies can be suggested by those who argue that restrictive monetary policy is inconsistent with a desirable level of social investment? Disregarding those who explicitly or implicitly argue that there are no limits to the nation's resources and all that need be done to increase production is to increase demand, it seems plain that if restrictive monetary policies are de-emphasized, some substitute method of restricting total expenditures must be employed. The likeliest choice is a more restrictive fiscal policy. If the protests against the

---

[18] Keyserling and others have argued in these terms but have failed to recognize the implications of the argument, in that some alternative restraint on spending must be employed. Of those economists concerned with the growth issue, Arthur Smithies has been most forthright and consistent in urging not only fiscal restraints but the use of selective controls to restrict consumption (see his "Uses of Selective Credit Controls," *United States Monetary Policy* [New York: American Assembly, Columbia University, 1958], esp. pp. 73–81).

[19] Economists as a group can no more be accused of discouraging the public from paying for public services than they can of urging the public to litter the national parks. (Despite the entreaties of billboards and broadcasts, the public seems to regard littering as a constitutional right, not to be compromised by the penalty of paying for the picking-up of the beer cans they have been unwilling to refrain from discarding. "The fault, dear Brutus, lies not in our stars but in ourselves that we are underlings.") Cf. J. K. Galbraith, *The Affluent Society* (New York: Houghton Mifflin Co., 1958), p. 253.

social implications of restrictive monetary policy are to be anything more than the futile whine that it is unpleasant to have the nation's aspirations limited by its resources, those who make such criticisms must in all consistency demand more rigorous fiscal restraints, particularly those which bear down heavily on consumption. Failing in this, if the argument is to make any sense at all, it represents a plea for direct controls over investment activities (and other activities?), and, until now, the American people have given no indication that they would permit such powers to be exercised in peacetime. If one abandons general controls, there is no alternative save direct controls to rapid inflation. Selective controls, particularly on consumer spending, may ease the problem somewhat, but selective controls have in the past revealed administrative, political, and economic weaknesses that have inevitably led to their breakdown. If the argument that monetary restraint leads to undesirable social consequences is accepted, the nation must be assured that some alternative form of control will, in fact, be substituted for such restraint before it can be abandoned.

## IV.  Implications for Monetary Control

It should be clear that the various strands of criticism cannot be woven together to form a well-meshed case against monetary policy. Each line of argument is discrete, and sometimes inconsistent with other lines. Plainly, if monetary policy is ineffective, if it has no impact on total expenditures and resource allocation, then it cannot be undesirable because it brings about an allocation of resources which is contrary to sound social policy or because it squeezes particular sectors of the economy in a discriminatory manner. Monetary policy can hardly be defective *both* because it discriminates against consumer credit *and* because it permits credit that could be used "productively" to be diverted into frivolous consumption. Much of the criticism of monetary policy reflects the desire of the critic to substitute his own judgment for what he regards to be the defective results of the market process. Since individual judgments vary widely, clearly the critics are likely to disapprove as vehemently of each other's diagnoses and prescriptions as they are of monetary restraint itself.

Any single criticism may quite reasonably be defended. Most of the more perceptive critics do confine themselves to one line of attack—that is, in-

effectiveness or discrimination. Others, with much less logic, attempt simultaneously to maintain several contradictory lines of criticism. Such attitudes can only be ascribed to the emotional, rather than the critical, faculties. Some of the inconsistencies may be attributed to the fact that the defects of monetary policy have varied with economic circumstances over the last three decades. Since the arguments have emerged fortuitously, they could not be expected to form a logical whole.[20] At one time monetary policy might be ineffective, at another it might be effective but discriminatory, etc. Nevertheless, the simultaneous employment of contradictory arguments can hardly be defended, and the rapidity with which new arguments emerged as the debate shifted over the years can be attributed to the antagonism felt by many professional and lay observers toward monetary policy.

Monetary policy is surviving the debate, albeit

[20] The views of Seymour E. Harris, who has frequently been a penetrating critic of monetary policy, may be one example. Over the years they have undergone various metamorphoses. In *Twenty Years of Federal Reserve Policy* (Cambridge, Mass.: Harvard University Press, 1933), he argued that monetary policy failed in the twenties because the Federal Reserve officials invariably were timid in the face of political pressure. To this theme he returned after a Keynesian interlude (*The New Economics* [New York: Alfred A. Knopf, 1948], pp. 50–51) in his comments in the "Symposium on Monetary Policy" (*op. cit.*, pp. 179–84, 198–200), arguing that it is the lack of courage on the part of the central bank rather than the weakness of its weapons that frustrates monetary policy. At various points in the argument he makes the following observations: "The problem [of monetary policy] has certainly not been one of impotency of weapons. . . . The Federal Reserve . . . is surely in a position to deny the economy the money without which a large inflation could not be carried on" (p. 183), and "monetary restraints are the easiest approach to inflation control—much less painful than more taxes or less public expenditures. . . . [T]heir atrophy is the result not of ignorance, but of the determination not to fight inflation which prevails in the country" (p. 180), in the *January 1959 Economic Report of the President: Hearings before the Joint Economic Committee* (Washington; Government Printing Office, 1959), he readily admits, though with mixed feelings, that this generation of Federal Reserve officials has not yielded to political pressure and has in his view been altogether too courageous in defending its convictions. All this is understandable. But in the communication with Galbraith ("The Failure of Monetary Policy," *loc. cit.*), he argues that monetary policy simultaneously is ineffective, discriminatory, and dangerous. How the view that tight money is ineffective can be reconciled with his views of 1951 is not made clear, nor is it explained to the reader how monetary policy can be so ineffective in dealing with inflationary pressure, yet curtail demand sufficiently to bring on a depression.

somewhat scarred in places. Plainly, the Arcadian view of monetary policy of the twenties has departed. Various institutional changes—the rise of liquidity, the declining importance of bank credit in the spending decisions of large corporations, the problems of debt management, and the removal of certain spending decisions from the market—have reduced somewhat the immediate effectiveness of monetary policy. But the major attacks on monetary policy have also been blunted. The technical charge of discrimination is, for the most part, fallacious, save in the case of small versus large businesses, and even here the importance should not be exaggerated. With regard to effectiveness, the extreme, depression-born doubts that monetary policy could have little influence on spending decisions have disappeared, along with the war-born refusal to use credit policy for any purpose other than maintenance of the interest-rate pattern on the government debt. What remains is a reasoned critique of monetary restraint, not so much a case *against* monetary control as a case *for* recognizing its limitations and its defects and for searching for alternative policies and tools. This critique consists of two parts:

1. In boom periods, monetary controls may "take hold" only after an operational lag of substantial duration. The integration of the financial community in association with the widespread holding of government securities permits rapid mobilization of idle balances during periods of pressure. A restructuring of the assets of the banking system may permit rising money expenditures through rising velocity, though the money supply is held constant. But this *does not imply that monetary control is unnecessary.* Control over the money stock is essential in the long run. Even in the short run, rising interest rates, rising velocity, and falling liquidity are all parts of the mechanism of restraint. Even if it operates slowly, monetary control operates in the right direction. At worst, all that this argument implies is that the nation should not rely upon monetary restraint as its sole instrument for combating short-term fluctuations. Monetary control cannot be dispensed with, but the search should continue for other instruments of general control.

2. Monetary restraint, as it becomes effective, may lead to results which we would not prefer on other grounds—national interests, economic progress, welfare considerations, etc. But this does not imply that monetary restraint in itself is undesirable, it merely hints that the results of alternative policies might be better. It imposes upon the critics the obligation of proposing and of obtaining public acceptance of alternative instruments of control. The use of alternative instruments may permit the alleviation of monetary restraint; it will never permit dispensing with monetary control.

From the standpoint of the more dramatic charges, the above critique is very modest indeed, representing a plea for de-emphasizing monetary policy, while accepting the necessity of monetary control. Needless to say, it would not be accepted by all economists, particularly those who feel that maximum welfare is invariably obtained through the market process. For the latter, monetary policy has additional advantages in that it reflects the current savings decisions by individuals in a way that fiscal restraints cannot. Yet, supposing the critique is accepted, it is clear even then that there is a residue of monetary policy which must be used. Until such time that fiscal restraints and other alternative controls have been perfected to the point that over-all demand can be precisely controlled, there will be minimal need for monetary policy at the fringes. To argue to the contrary is to imply that fiscal policy is more flexible, less crude, than we have experienced it to be in fact—a Beveridge Plan type of utopianism. In democracies, particularly those in which authority is divided, fiscal controls have proved to be incapable of achieving a delicate adjustment of demand. Since a free economy is prone to periodic surges of spending, inevitably, in the quest for stability, a minimal use of monetary policy cannot be avoided.

Much of the public criticism of monetary policy arises from restlessness under any form of restraint, a restlessness that reflects a natural and inevitable human distress at the fact that resources are limited. Economists should try to counteract such tendencies. In order to achieve maximum impact on public policy, it is necessary that economists ocasionally coalesce on fundamentals. With the exception of a few ultra-moderns,[21] virtually all economists do agree that

---

[21] It is somewhat ironical that the recent arguments that monetary policy is ineffective in the short run but potentially dangerous in the long run *because of the existence of lags* (as in the Galbraith-Harris communication cited in nn. 11 and 20) run exactly parallel to criticisms directed against discretionary fiscal policy (see Milton Friedman, "A Monetary and Fiscal Framework for Economic Stability," *American Economic Review*, XXXVIII, No. 3 [June, 1948], esp. 254–58). Friedman has consistently adhered to the logically impeccable position that lags constitute an argument against all forms of discretionary authority.

monetary policy must be used to some extent in the attempt to stabilize the economy. True, under some conditions monetary policy may

But many of those who currently criticize monetary policy on the basis of lags can hardly be described as skeptics about discretionary *fiscal* policy. To me, it appears true that lags do complicate the work of using either the fiscal or the monetary instrument and place limits on the effectiveness of both. This represents, however, an argument for greater flexibility rather than the abandonment of either instrument. That is tantamount to throwing out the baby with the bath water.

not be effective, particularly in the short run; in any given case, however, the only way to learn how effective it is, is to use it. In discussing the need for co-ordinating monetary policy and fiscal policy, economists have come to recognize that neither of these instruments is necessarily either immediately or precisely effective; that is the nature of instruments which seek to influence *voluntary* spending decisions on the part of the public. But both instruments have their roles to play; neither can be disregarded.

*J. A. GALBRAITH*

# Monetary Policy and Nonbank Financial Intermediaries

## 34

There are some who believe that the functioning of nonbank financial intermediaries and commercial banks have comparable effects on the economy and hence are of equal concern for monetary policy.[1] There is, however, a sharp division of opinion on the question whether nonbank financial intermediaries (hereafter described as near banks) expand or contract with the banking system.

Monetary policy may operate more effectively, if near banks move with rather than against the policy. However, there are some who argue that near banks are able to slip away from monetary policy, that is to expand when monetary policy contracts the banking system.[2]

These differences of view, we propose to show, may be explained by the connection between monetary policy and the size of near banks.[3] For this purpose, we explore three aspects of policy: its direct effect on the cash base of near banks; its effect on the size of the market for the claims of near banks; and its effect on interest rates.

---

[1] Cf. the remarks of Irwin Friend in "The Effects of Monetary Policies on Nonmonetary Financial Institutions and Capital Markets," *Private Capital Markets*, pp. 8–9, 108–109, 120, for a contrary view. Prepared for the Commission on Money and Credit. Englewood Cliffs, N.J.: Prentice-Hall, Inc., 1964.

---

Reprinted from the *National Banking Review*, Vol. IV (1966) pp. 53–60, by permission of the author and publisher. The author has taken advantage of this reprinting to make minor changes in the original article. J. A. Galbraith is Economist, The Royal Bank of Canada, Montreal. The views expressed do not necessarily reflect those of The Royal Bank of Canada. The author has profited greatly from discussions with Professor J. C. Weldon, McGill University.

[2] Cf. the survey article by Harry G. Johnson, "Monetary Theory and Policy," *American Economic Review*, 52, June 1962, pp. 373–374. James Tobin and William C. Brainard, "Financial Intermediaries and the Effectiveness of Monetary Controls," *American Economic Review, Papers and Proceedings*, 53, May 1963, pp. 384, 386, are concerned with the effect of near banks on the "rate of return on ownership of real capital" and not with the manner in which these financial intermediaries move with monetary policy.

[3] Edward C. Ettin, "A Note on the Growth of Nonbank Financial Intermediaries and Interest Rate Determination," *Quarterly Journal of Economics*, 78, November 1964, pp. 649–652, endeavors to explain the debate in terms of the effect of near banks on interest rates.

# I. Cash Base

It is generally assumed that monetary policy does not directly affect the cash base of near banks as it does that of banks. This is most apparent with respect to the open-market operations of the monetary authorities. Since the purchases and sales of securities by the monetary authorities are generally carried out with security dealers, which are either customers of the banks or banks themselves, there is no direct effect on the outstanding claims of near banks, as there is on the deposits of commercial banks.

Of course, open-market sales will reduce near bank claims if purchasers of the securities, sold by the central bank, carry working balances with near banks which are drawn down in making payment to the central bank. Similarly, open-market purchases will expand near bank claims if sellers of the securities, bought by the central bank, deposit the proceeds directly with near banks.[4] Probably, however, any such direct effects of open-market operations on near bank claims are negligible, and would be so even if near banks carried their working cash balances with the central bank instead of with commercial banks.

If buyers of securities from the central bank finance their purchases with loans from near banks, the effect is simply to alter the composition of the assets of the near banks. Their liabilities remain constant. The near banks merely have less cash and more loans outstanding. And if sellers of securities to the central bank use the proceeds to pay off near bank loans, the effect is to increase near bank cash and reduce near bank loans. There is no direct effect on near bank liabilities. Therefore the direct effect of monetary policy on near banks may be assumed to be negligible.

# II. Market Size

When monetary policy expands the banking system, the amount of bank deposits held by the public increases. This means that, if nothing else has changed, the total amount of financial intermediary claims outstanding—bank and nonbank—has been increased. If near banks maintain their share of the total market, they will expand as monetary policy expands the banking system, and they will contract as monetary policy contracts the banking system.

For this to be so, the amount of near bank claims held by the public ($MP$) must be a function of the amount of bank deposits held by the public ($DP$), such that

$$MP = f(DP) = n(DP) \qquad (1)$$

The behavioral relation (1) assumes an attempt by the public to keep a constant ratio ($n$) between holdings of near bank claims and bank deposits. This relationship is assumed by those who hold that near banks expand and contract with the banking system, and so are affected by monetary policy in the same way as banks. Thus, D. A. Alhadeff points out that monetary policy will affect the near bank sector in the same way as the banking system only if the public holds constant the ratio of bank deposits to near bank liabilities.[5] The ratio can then be incorporated into multiplier analysis in much the same way as the currency ratio is included in banking multipliers, to show that near banks expand when banks expand, and contract when banks contract.[6]

Those who use the ratio or multiplier approach to reach this conclusion usually assume, as a simple fact, that a stable relationship exists between bank deposits and near bank claims. Thus, D. Shelby holds that the public will, in fact, divide its holdings of claims on financial institutions in some given ratio between banks and near banks.[7] *The Report of the Royal Commission on Banking and Finance* speaks of near banks obtaining a given share of the public's total business with financial institutions, with the public's preference for different types of financial assets being one of the determinants of the share obtained.[8] The Bank of Canada argues that, *ceteris paribus*, when the banking system is expanding "there is no reason to suppose that the public could be

[4] The Bank of Canada, *Evidence of the Governor before the Royal Commission on Banking and Finance*, Ottawa, May 1964, p. 125, paragraph 41, suggests that a seller of securities to the central bank might deposit the proceeds with a near bank.

[5] "Credit Controls and Financial Intermediaries," *American Economic Review*, 50, September, 1960, p. 661.

[6] Cf. D. Shelby, "Some Implications of the Growth of Financial Intermediaries," *Journal of Finance*, 13, December 1958, pp. 529–532; also compare Assar Lindbeck, *A Study in Monetary Analysis*, Stockholm, 1963, pp. 188–198, D. I. Fand, "Intermediary Claims and the Adequacy of Our Monetary Controls," *Banking and Monetary Studies*, Deane Carson ed., Homewood, Illinois, 1963, pp. 241–242, and, W. P. Yohe, "The Derivation of Certain Financial Multipliers," *Southern Economic Journal*, 29, July 1962, pp. 26, 28–29.

[7] *Op. cit.*, pp. 524, 533–534.

[8] Ottawa: Queen's Printer, 1964, pp. 93–102, 111–112. A simplified interpretation of the Commission's approach is given by J. A. Galbraith in, "Near Banks and Monetary Policy: Views of the Royal Commission on Banking and Finance," *The Canadian Banker*, 71, Autumn 1964, pp. 23–31.

induced to add to its holdings of chartered bank deposits without adding to its holdings of these other types of liquid assets (near bank liabilities) as well."[9]

Irwin Friend works with a more unusual relationship in which the public demands a fixed total of deposits supplied by banks and near banks.[10] Monetary policy that reduces the amount of bank deposits causes the public to acquire additional deposits from near banks in order to keep constant total deposits held by the public. However, additional funds are required for a contracting banking system to pay off loans and to buy the securities being sold by the banking system. Therefore, the total amount of deposits desired by the public should fall with a banking contraction.

If no relationship exists between bank deposits and near bank claims, however, changes in the size of the banking system as such have no effect on the near banks. Even if a relationship exists, it may be a lagged one and may depend more on income effects than on an "asset" or balance-sheet effect. Near bank claims may move with bank deposits because changes in bank deposits alter total expenditures, incomes, and savings, which in turn affect the holdings of near bank claims. W. L. Smith argues that this is the connection, and that, as a result, the time period of an expansion or contraction for near banks is entirely different from that of the banking system.[11] For this reason, he doubts whether a "credit expansion approach" to near banks is "desirable or useful." Assar Lindbeck points out that if changes in the public's holdings of near bank claims are related to changes in savings, a change in size of the banking system that does not alter savings will not affect the size of the near bank sector.[12] D. I. Fand categorically states that "in the short run the public's preference for increments of intermediary claims may be close to zero."[13]

Futhermore, to the extent that near bank claims are not redeemable on demand, or transferable, the public will be able to withdraw funds from near banks in response to a contraction in bank deposits only as their near bank liabilities mature. It is possible that no change can occur in near bank claims outstanding during the period that bank deposits are being contracted.

In the absence of a definitive empirical testing of the hypothesis, one can only conclude at present that near banks will expand and contract as a direct result of a corresponding expansion and contraction of the banking system if the public attempts to maintain a given ratio between holdings of bank deposits and of near bank claims, given constant relative interest rates. For policy purposes, as pointed out in Part V, it is immaterial whether such a relationship exists.

## III. Interest Rates

Monetary policy, in addition to altering the size of the banking system, may also change interest rates. A contractionary monetary policy is likely to raise interest rates. In the absence of rigidities, rates paid by borrowers, as well as those received by lenders, will rise. This will include the rates paid and received by banks and near banks. If bank and near bank rates are not equally flexible, the relative change in rates may induce the public to shift funds between banks and near banks.

This will be the case if the amount of near bank claims held by the public ($MP$) is a function of the difference between the rate of return on near bank claims ($i_n$) and the over-all rate of return on bank deposits ($i_b$). Thus,

$$MP = f(i_n - i_b) \qquad (2)$$

with the property $\partial MP / \partial f (i_n - i_b) > 0$

The rate of return paid on bank deposits can be considered an over-all net rate of return on all deposits, which takes into account the fact that demand deposits may yield no explicit rate of interest and that service charges and similar fees levied for the maintenance of deposit accounts reduce the over-all rate of return. Banks, therefore, by adjusting the rate paid on interest-bearing deposits, but also service charges and compensating balance requirements (in banking systems having these requirements) can alter the over-all rate of return yielded by bank deposits.[14]

For convenience, it is assumed that $i_n > i_b$, so that an increase in $(i_n - i_b)$ represents a widening of the prevailing differential between the two rates of return. This widening makes near bank claims

---

[9] *Evidence of the Governor before the Royal Commission on Banking and Finance*, p. 125, paragraph 41.

[10] "The Effects of Monetary Policies on Nonmonetary Financial Institutions and Capital Markets," pp. 8–9.

[11] "Financial Intermediaries and Monetary Controls," *Quarterly Journal of Economics*, 73, November 1959, pp. 536–538.

[12] *Op. cit.*, p. 198.

[13] *Op. cit.*, p. 239.

[14] Cf. A. D. Alhadeff, "Credit Controls and Financial Intermediaries," pp. 662–665.

more attractive relative to bank deposits, causing the public to demand more near bank claims in accordance with relation (2). On the contrary, a reduction in $(i_n - i_b)$, representing a narrowing of the differential between the two rates, which makes near bank claims less attractive relative to bank deposits, may cause the public to reduce its demand for near bank claims. However, the shift from banks to near banks may be nonreversible. While the public may shift from banks to near banks when the differential in rates widens, they may not, however, shift back when the differential narrows—people once becoming customers of near banks may continue to remain customers even after the additional rate differential that initially attracted them to near banks disappears.

Matching changes in $i_n$ and $i_b$ that leave $(i_n - i_b)$ constant should have no effect on the public's demand for near bank claims. However, if the public think in real terms, a rise in the absolute level of interest rates, even with a constant differential between bank and near bank rates, would change the public's holdings of near bank claims if these claims were not fixed (nominal) price claims as are most bank deposits. Even if all intermediary claims were fixed-price, which most are, an absolute change in interest rates, by producing a wealth effect, might cause the public to change its holdings of near bank claims despite a constant differential in rates between bank and near bank claims. Such an effect, however, is unlikely to be large. When it exists, it means that bank rates must be more flexible than near bank rates—the differential between the two must narrow—in order to prevent funds from shifting to near banks when interest rates rise.

It follows that if the relationship in (2) exists, there could be an interest rate effect on near banks associated with monetary policy. And the rate effect could cause near banks to move perversely with the movement of the banking system. A perverse movement would result if near bank interest rates were more flexible than bank rates. If near bank rates were less flexible than bank rates, the rate effect of monetary policy would cause near banks to move with, not against, monetary policy. However, the rate of return on bank deposits is likely to be less flexible than that on near bank claims, because of special restrictions usually imposed on banks. The restrictions may be indirect, as in Canada, where for many years, a 6 per cent effective maximum on most bank lending rates limited the extent to which interest rates on bank deposits could be raised. In the United States, of course, the legal restraint on deposit rates is direct.

If bank rates were denied as much upward flexibility as near bank rates, in a tight money situation with the banking system contracting and interest rates rising, near bank rates would rise more than bank rates. The widening of the rate differential between near banks and banks would favor a shift of funds to the near banks, which would enable near banks to expand when the banking system was contracting. This represents a slippage from monetary control.

In a deposit expansion, however, rate rigidities will not result in any offset to monetary policy if the public shifts to near banks only when the rate differential widens but does not shift again when it narrows. In that case, near bank claims move to offset monetary policy when bank deposits are contracted, but remain neutral when bank deposits are expanded. Monetary policy then favors a growth of near banks during a period of tight money, growth that is not lost during a period of easy money.

If a category of near bank suffers from a rate rigidity not shared by other types of near banks, that near bank category will find funds flowing from it during periods of tight money, and to it in times of easy money. Its claims will then be found to be moving in the same direction as monetary policy. Thus, J. R. Vernon found that U. S. savings and loan associations were responsive to monetary policy because the rates they paid for funds were relatively less flexible than the rates paid by competing users of funds.[15] The lack of flexibility in this case may partly result from elastic demand for mortgage loans, If, as interest rates rise, the demand for particular types of loans falls, then any category of near bank specializing in these types of loans will be unable to pass on to borrowers higher rates paid for funds. Such near banks will then be adversely affected by a restrictive monetary policy. Near banks locked into long-term loans acquired at lower interest rates in easier money periods will also be unable to recoup higher borrowing rates by upward adjustments in their lending rates. This seems to be the situation facing U. S. savings and loan associations today.[16]

Many writers assume that near bank rates are more flexible than bank rates and so derive an interest-rate effect. Their analysis runs in terms of interest-induced shifts of funds be-

---

[15] "Savings and Loan Association Response to Monetary Policies, 1953–61: A Case Study on 'Availability'," *Southern Economic Journal*, 31, January 1965, pp. 229, 232, 234, 237.

[16] Cf. John Davenport, "The Strain Is on the Banks," *Fortune*, July 1, 1966, p. 168.

tween banks and near banks, which is seen as offsetting monetary policy.[17] This approach is often implicit in the discussion of the effect of near banks on monetary policy that runs in terms of the demand for money being shifted, and its interest elasticity altered, as a result of interest-induced shifts of funds from banks to other intermediaries.[18] If the demand for money becomes more elastic as near banks grow, a given amount of open-market operations will have less effect on interest rates than otherwise,[19] Thus, by concentrating on the interest-rate effect alone, and assuming, often explicitly, an interest rate rigidity for banks, these writers arrive at the conclusion that near banks offset monetary policy.

## IV. Reconciliation

We have seen that those who analyze the problem in terms of market size easily conclude that near banks are affected by monetary policy in the same directions as banks. Those who concentrate on interest rates reach the opposite conclusion. A reconciliation is simply a matter of combining both effects, which may exist side by side.

A combination of the two effects can be illustrated by a diagram showing the relationship

[17] Those who adopt this approach include R. S. Thorn, "Nonbank Financial Intermediaries, Credit Expansion, and Monetary Policy," *International Monetary Fund Staff Papers*, 6, November 1958, pp. 376–377, 380; Assar Lindbeck, *op. cit.*, pp. 228–229; D. I. Fand, *op. cit.*, pp. 244–249; W. L. Smith, "Financial Intermediaries and Monetary Controls," pp. 539–540; idem, "Reserve Requirements in the American Monetary System," *Monetary Management*, pp. 309–312, prepared for the Commission on Money and Credit, Englewood Cliffs, N.J.: Prentice-Hall Inc., 1963; *Money and Credit: Their Influence on Jobs, Prices, and Growth*, p. 78. Report of the Commission on Money and Credit, Englewood Cliffs, N.J.: Prentice-Hall Inc., 1961.

[18] This is one of the arguments found in J. G. Gurley and E. S. Shaw, *Money in a Theory of Finance*, Washington, D.C., 1960, pp. 207–208, 216–218, 239–241. Also cf. the interpretation of Gurley and Shaw in the review article by Don Patinkin, "Financial Intermediaries and the Logical Structure of Monetary Theory," *American Economic Review*, 51, March 1961, p. 110.

[19] J. G. Gurley and E. S. Shaw, *loc. cit.*, and Don Patinkin, *loc. cit.*, imply near banks impart greater elasticity to the demand for money; A. L. Marty in "Gurley and Shaw on Money in a Theory of Finance," *Journal of Political Economy*, 69, February 1961, pp. 59–60, and Assar Lindbeck in *op. cit.*, p. 184, hold that near banks might make the elasticity less. Harry G. Johnson, *op. cit.*, p. 373, states that the central issue for monetary policy of "financial development" is whether near banks "substantially increase the interest-elasticity of demand for money."

between the public's holdings of near bank claims and bank deposits. In Figure 1, the relationship between the two is depicted by the line $ci_1$, which may be called the near bank function. Bank deposits are measured along the horizontal axis and near

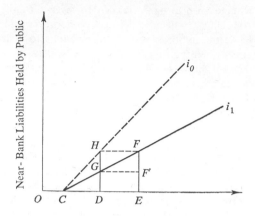

Figure 1. Near Bank Function

bank claims along the vertical axis, both in dollar amounts. The function $ci_1$, is drawn for a given differential between the rates of return on near bank claims and bank deposits. It is also based on the simplifying assumptions that the marginal currency ratio of the public is zero and has a zero interest elasticity, and that the marginal cash ratio of all near banks is zero and remains constant. From Figure 1, it is apparent that as open-market operations expand bank deposits, near bank claims held by the public rise. And as open-market operations contract bank deposits, near bank claims fall. This is on the assumption that the interest differential between the two rates of return remains unchanged as bank deposits expand and contract.

A widening of the differential, however, shifts the function $ci_1$, upward to a new position. Thus, if in Figure 1 a contraction in bank deposits from $E$ to $D$ is accompanied by a shift of $ci_1$ to $ci_0$, because of relative rate movements, near bank claims will not fall but will remain equal to $EF$, which equals $DH$. And if the rate movement is such as to shift $ci_1$ beyond $ci_0$, near bank claims will actually rise as bank deposits fall by $DE$. The opposite conclusions result for a narrowing of the rate differential between banks and near banks which causes the near bank function to shift downward. The function will not shift downward if new customers attracted by near banks, as a result of a widening in the normal differential between banks and near banks, do not shift back to the banks again when the differential is restored to its normal level. And, of course, if near bank rates are less flexible than bank rates, the function will fall as the banking system is contracted, causing near bank claims to decline with bank deposits.

If no relationship exists between the public's holdings of near bank claims and bank deposits, such that the public does not attempt to maintain a constant ratio between the two, the situation could be represented in the Figure by a straight line parallel to the horizontal axis. This line would intercept the vertical axis at the point representing the amount of near bank claims the public chooses to hold. *Ceteris paribus*, changes in deposits would not result in the public trying to alter the amount of near bank claims held. The line would shift up and down, however, as the rate differential between deposits and near bank claims widened or narrowed.

If there is no interest-rate rigidity, so that bank deposit rates and rates on near bank claims are both equally flexible, there is no interest-induced shift of the near bank function, so that near bank claims either expand and contract with bank deposits or remain constant. If the former is true, monetary policy is reinforced; if the latter occurs, it is because the public does not try to shift between bank deposits and near bank claims when the amount of deposits is changing. In that case, there is no interference with the effectiveness of monetary policy.

Of course, if near bank claims can be made to expand and contract along with the banking system, it would spread the direct influence of monetary policy more widely. This, however, would not necessarily make monetary policy more effective. It would take additional administrative controls (and effort) to get a near bank reaction from monetary policy, and there would be no net gain for monetary policy if all objectives were previously being obtained simply through the banking system.[20]

## V. Policy Implications

In the debate on near banks and monetary policy, policy recommendations have been as varied as the analyses of how monetary policy affects near banks. Participants to the debate, despite the absence of hard facts, have not been slow to draw policy recommendations from their analyses. Those who concentrate on the interest-rate effect have favored the prevention of interest-induced shifts of funds to near banks during periods of tight money, through direct controls such as reserve requirements on near banks and ceilings on their interest rates.[21] Some, such as W. L. Smith, who see no evidence of "systematic destablizing shifts" of funds between banks and near banks, only venture to say that "if such shifts should raise difficulties in the future, their destabilizing effects can be eliminated" by applying direct controls to near banks.[22] And, of course, those who concentrate on the market-share effect are equally quick to dismiss the need for imposing monetary policy forms of control on near banks.

This analysis suggests that, from the policy point of view, it is immaterial whether a constant ratio exists between the public's holdings of bank deposits and near bank claims. If such a ratio exists, it helps monetary policy; but if it does not exist, monetary policy is not directly harmed. Less flexible rates of return on bank deposits than on near bank claims, however, may create difficulties for monetary policy. The monetary authorities should take care, in imposing any administrative or legal restraints on bank interest rates, that bank rates do not become less flexible than near bank rates. Flexibility in bank rates should, in fact, be encouraged so as to avoid interest-induced destabilizing shifts of funds from banks and near banks.[23]

---

[20] Assar Lindbeck, *op. cit.*, pp. 208, 289, appears to take the opposite view. He sees the question of the effects of near banks on the efficiency of monetary policy to be whether the monetary authorities can "achieve a reduction in the supply of credit" by imposing cash reserve requirements, or other direct controls, on near banks.

[21] J. G. Gurley and E. S. Shaw, *op. cit.*, pp. 289–290, list a large number of direct control measures that may be imposed on near banks to soften adverse effects of monetary policy on the banking system.

[22] W. L. Smith, "Financial Intermediaries and Monetary Controls," p. 552; also compare R. S. Thorn, "Nonbank Financial Intermediaries, Credit Expansion, and Monetary Policy," *International Monetary Fund Staff Papers*, 6, November 1958, pp. 373–381.

[23] W. P. Hogan, "Monetary Policy and the Financial Intermediaries," *Economic Record*, 36, December 1960, p. 529, advocates a more flexible interest rate policy for banks to reduce the transfer of funds to near banks in Australia. In "Catching the Non-banks," *Economist*, London, November 21, 1964, p. 582, it is suggested that "the prime reason why the rival financial institutions have fared so much better than the banks in periods of tight money may not after all lie in their freedom from official controls as such but in the fact that their interest rates are usually far more flexible than those of the banks."

*GEORGE HORWICH*

# Tight Money, Monetary Restraint, and the Price Level

# *35*

## I. Introduction

In recent years a substantial body of public opinion has opposed monetary restraint on the ground that higher interest rates, designed to curb inflation, raise prices by raising business costs. The net effect of monetary policy in controlling inflation would thus be negligible, if not actually perverse. This point of view has been particularly prevalent in official policy statements and public pronouncements by members of the Democratic party.[1]

However, it is not limited to the latter group, for even Republicans, as well as nonpartisan monetary officials, have accepted the argument in principle.

The stock reply of the proponents of monetary

[1] As might be expected, these pronouncements were more in evidence before the party came to power in 1961. See, for example, the statements of Democratic senators in Hearings before the Committee on Finance, United States Senate (85th Cong., 1st Sess.), *Investigation of the Financial Condition of the United States*, June–August 1957, pp. 68, 323, 342, 345, 390–91, 733, 739, 785, 952, 1093, 1402–03. In the summer of 1959, Senator William Proxmire, of the

Senate Banking and Currency Committee, circulated a questionnaire to a large number of economists in which the opening question was:

> What evidence is there to support a conclusion that "tight money" serves to limit inflation enough to off-set the rising costs of borrowing and the higher total cost of everything that is paid for "on time?" (I am seeking evidence to determine the extent to which credit restraint counteracts over-all inflationary pressure, on the one hand, and the extent to which it channels the price increases into the time payment segment of the economy on the other.)

A more recent statement of Senator Proxmire's views is contained in Hearings before the Joint Economic Committee (87th Cong., 1st Sess.), *Review of Report of the Commission on Money and Credit*, August 1961, p. 256. Representatives of organized labor take a similar position. See Hearings before the Joint Economic Committee (85th Cong., 2nd Sess.), *The Relationship of Prices to Economic Stability and Growth: Commentaries*, October 1958, pp. 33 and 248.

The opinion among Democratic senators (and

Reprinted from the *Journal of Finance*, Vol. XXI (1966), pp. 15–33, by permission of the author and publisher. George Horwich is a professor at Purdue University. The author has benefited from comments and suggestions by M. June Flanders, A. P. Lerner, and the editorial reader, none of whom is responsible for any remaining flaws in the analysis.

policy is simply that interest is a small and un-important element in total business costs.[2] But this is a fatal concession. For the rate of interest, narrowly defined (as it usually is) as the return on borrowings, is only one of many varieties of rent paid on the existing stock of capital. The relevant economic variable is in fact all property income, which constitutes as much as a third of the national income. As a first approximation, the various components of the property return, in-cluding bond interest, stock dividends, and building rentals, would be expected to rise and fall together over time.

The belief that higher interest as a cost might contribute to inflation has not been seriously discussed by contemporary economists, in spite of the widespread popularity of the argument. The failure to offer an analysis is due, I think, to our own incomplete integration of the theoretical role of interest as a production cost, as a return to the claimants of capital, and as a variable in monetary policy.

This paper outlines a framework within which the impact of interest on prices may be analyzed. There are two main building blocks in the approach, both Keynesian. One is a concept of monetary restraint, which derives from the *Treatise*. It is essentially Wicksellian: interest rates are fundamentally determined by internal forces, rather than by the monetary authority. The other building block is the assumed nature of the return to capital, which is advanced in the *General Theory*. This is the marginal efficiency relationship, which links interest movements closely to changes in the productivity of real

capital. The Keynesian monetary and capital structure is set forth in Sections II and III, respectively. They are combined in Section IV, which examines the impact of tight money on the price level. Section V considers an alternative concept of monetary restraint, in which the monetary authority assumes a more independent role in setting interest rates. Section VI is a summary and conclusion. An Appendix offers a theoretical foundation for the determination of the price and output of capital and consumption goods.

## II. Monetary Restraint: The Keynes-Wicksell Framework

"Tight money" is the appellation generally applied to an economy experiencing rising interest rates and rising income.[3] In the Wicksellian-Keynesian view, interest rates rise because of an excess demand for loanable funds caused by an increase in desired investment or a decrease in desired saving. This constitutes an increase in the natural rate of interest, which the market rate follows with a lag. Simultaneously money income rises, according to Wicksell, because the quantity of money supplied rises with the rate of interest (the money supply is "elastic"); or, according to Keynes, the quantity of money demanded falls with the rise of the rate of interest. In either case, there is a higher equilibrium interest rate, which is associated with a higher equilibrium level of prices and income.

In this context monetary restraint, which raises interest rates, accelerates an adjustment that would occur in any case. In the language of Wicksell, the monetary authority raises the market rate to the level of the higher natural rate.[4] The nature of the disturbance and the role

---

presidents) the higher interest rates are inflationary has an historical precedent in the writings of Thomas Tooke and the "Banking School." See, for example, Albert Feaveryear, *The Pound Sterling*, Oxford: The Clarendon Press, 1962, 2nd edition (edited and revised by Victor Morgan), p. 266, who quotes Tooke: "A high rate of interest had no effect upon prices, except perhaps to raise them, in the long period, by raising the cost of production." This "heretical" view was supported by William New-march's investigation into the circulation of bills of exchange for the period 1830–1853. He found no evidence that commercial credit was limited at all by rising interest rates. See Tooke and Newmarch, *History of Prices*, New York: Adelphi Co., 1857, Vol. VI. For a survey of this whole controversy, see J. R. T. Hughes, *Fluctuations in Trade, Industry and Finance*, Oxford: The Clarendon Press, 1960, pp. 228–36.

[2] See the remarks by Treasury Secretary Humphrey, Hearings before the Committee on Finance, *op. cit.*, pp. 390–91; Under Secretary of the Treasury Burgess, *ibid.*, p. 733; and Chairman Martin of the Board Governors, *ibid.*, pp. 1268–69, 1402.

[3] Rising interest rates are rarely accompanied by falling income. Hendershott and Murphy ("The Monetary Cycle and The Business Cycle: The Flow of Funds Re-examined," *National Banking Review*, I, June 1964, p. 535) were able to find only one quarter in the entire period 1952–62 during which interest rose while economic activity declined.

[4] This view of monetary policy is advanced by Keynes in a *Treatise on Money*, London: Macmillan and Co., Ltd., 1950, Vol. I, p. 273, and Vol. II, pp. 351–52 and 362. See also D. H. Robertson, who bases similar policy prescriptions on a more purely Wicksellian model, in which the inflation is due to elasticity of the money supply: "Industrial Fluctuation and the Natural Rate of Interest," *Economic Journal*, XLIV, December 1934, pp. 650–56 (reprinted as Ch. V in *Essays in Monetary Theory*, Staples Press, Ltd., 1940). For recent treatments, see M. J. Bailey,

of monetary policy is shown with the aid of Figure 1.

In the left diagram are the real flow functions, saving (*S*), which is the complement of consumption, and investment demand (*I*). Desired investment increases with lower interest rates, while saving decreases. Unlike the investment-interest relation, the dependency of saving on the rate of interest is not essential to our argument. In the right diagram are the stock or existing-asset functions, the demand (*L*) and the supply of real balances (*M/P*), which are the complements of the demand and supply, respectively, of all nonmonetary assets (typically financial claims or securities). The demand for real balances (liquidity preference) is a downward function of the

equilibrium) rate of interest *r″* is created by a decrease in the saving schedule from *S′* to *S″*. At *r″* asset-holders want a lower quantity of real balances and, by implication, a greater quantity of nonmonetary assets or securities. These desires are measured by the movement from *A* to *B* along the liquidity preference schedule. In the absence of outside interference, the reduction in real balances will be obtained through an internally generated inflationary process.[5] Immediately following the decrease of saving, we have at *r′*, the initial—and, momentarily, still prevailing—rate of interest, *I > S″*, an excess of ex ante investment over desired saving. This is the spur to both higher prices and the higher market rate of interest. Given the level of real income and

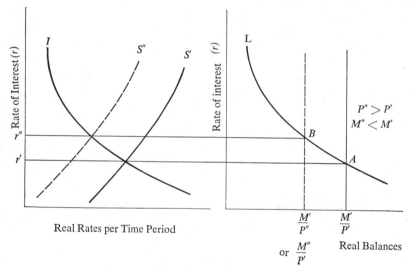

Figure 1.

rate of interest. The supply of real balances is assumed, for simplicity, to be insensitive to the interest rate. Both saving and the demand for money also depend on the level of real income, which we assume, for the present, is constant at the full employment level. Each pair of schedules in the diagram is in equilibrium at a common rate of interest *r′*, the natural rate. The equilibrium quantity of real balances (at point *A*) is the ratio of *M′*, which is the nominal stock of money, to *P′*, the index of all prices.

Now suppose that a higher natural (i.e.,

National Income and The Price Level, New York: McGraw-Hill Book Co., Inc., 1962, pp. 156–57; and G. Horwich, *Money, Capital, and Prices*, Homewood: Richard D. Irwin, Inc., 1964, pp. 450–51.

stock of money *M′*, *I > S″* persists until the market rate is *r″* and prices are *P″*. The higher price level establishes the quantity of real balances desired at *B*, *M′/P″*.[6]

However, from the viewpoint of asset-holders, the new equilibrium at *B* could also be reached by reducing the quantity of money, the price level remaining constant. More precisely, there is a

[5] Cf. Horwich, *op. cit.*, Ch. IV and pp. 277–79.

[6] If there are any unemployed resources or excess capacity in the economy, the adjustment will raise output along with prices. The real saving schedule and the demand for real balances both shift to the right. This will lower the natural rate somewhat below *r″* and raise the equilibrium level of real balances above *M′/P″*. The adjustment thus terminates earlier and prices rise less than if output were constant.

quantity $M'' < M'$ such that $M''/P' = M'/P''$. Restrictive monetary policy accordingly takes the form of an open-market sale conducted by the central bank, which reduces the quantity of money to $M''$ and raises the market rate of interest to $r''$. This establishes swiftly and directly the new equilibrium interest rate and real balances, both of which are otherwise achieved internally through a prolonged inflationary adjustment.

The goal of a tight monetary policy is thus the avoidance of inflation, accomplished by "raising" interest rates along a course they would naturally follow. The criticism of this policy, referred to in Section I, is that the higher interest rate nevertheless contributes to inflation by raising the interest costs of production. We are now ready to analyze this argument by considering in more detail the real forces that give rise to an increase in the equilibrium (natural) rate of interest. We assume that the monetary authority is completely successful in offsetting inflationary pressures due to a reduction in the quantity of real balances demanded. The only disturbances to the system are thus in the rate of interest, the rate of saving and investment, and any other variables that are necessary concomitants of these three.

## III.  The Marginal Efficiency of Investment

The role of interest as a cost of production depends upon the nature of the investment demand function. The most widely accepted investment theory is the Keynesian marginal efficiency concept, as elaborated by Lerner and Robertson.[7] In this view investment demand (ex ante investment), a downward function of interest, is derived from a short-run inverse relation between the return to (the marginal efficiency of) investment and the rate of ex post investment. This latter relationship is represented by the *MEI* line in Figure 2. The entire line is based upon a given gross marginal product of capital, which is effectively a constant in any one- or two-year

period.[8] Thus the downward slope of the line is due not to changes in the gross product, but rather to variations in the net product remaining after subtraction of variable depreciation charges. The latter in turn depend upon the marginal cost and supply price of new capital goods, which in the short run vary directly with their rate of output. The greater the rate of ex post investment, the greater therefore are the output and supply price of capital. Given that the capital stock is valued at replacement, rather than historical cost, the greater are the depreciation allowances and the smaller is the net available return to the claimants of the capital stock. The rate of return, defined as the ratio of net earnings to the supply price of capital, thus falls both because of the decrease in the numerator and the increase in the denominator.[9]

Assuming that firms are rational and competitive, they will equate the percentage return on investment to the market rate of interest. That is, at any rate of interest, investment expenditures will be an amount, which, if realized ex post, will result in a return to investment just equal to the interest rate. Given accurate knowledge of the return corresponding to each rate of ex post investment, ex ante investment ($I$)—a function of interest—thus coincides exactly with the *MEI* schedule.[10]

In utilizing the Keynesian investment theory, we assume, for simplicity, that there exists only one variety of capital, the return on which is equated to "the" rate of interest. We assume also that the price of the capital stock and the direction of investment is such that the return on all existing capital units and all new investment projects is the same. Finally, we assume that all claims to capital held in the form of fixed-value financial instruments are renegotiated con-

[7] See Keynes, *The General Theory of Employment, Interest and Money*, New York: Harcourt, Brace and Co., 1936, Ch. 11; A. P. Lerner, *The Economics of Control*, New York: The Macmillan Co., 1944, Chs. 21 and 25, and "On Some Recent Developments in Capital Theory," *American Economic Review*, LV, May 1965, pp. 284–95; D. H. Robertson, *Lectures on Economic Principles*, Vol. II, London: Staples Press, Ltd., 1958, pp. 61–68; and Horwich, *op. cit.*, pp. 40–43.

[8] In any individual firm, changes in capital may, of course, create substantial changes in its marginal product in any period of time. But the marginal product of capital, *averaged* over all firms in the economy, is not likely to move very much in the short run.

[9] A detailed two-sector account of the derivation of the marginal efficiency and investment demand schedules is presented in the Appendix, Section A.

[10] The assumption of competitive behavior among firms is not essential to the analysis. In the absence of perfect competition, the ex post marginal efficiency schedule will lie above the ex ante investment demand function. The vertical distance between the schedules will be monopoly profit. This can be handled by the subsequent analysis (Sections IV and V) by simply requiring that the two schedules shift together simultaneously in the same direction.

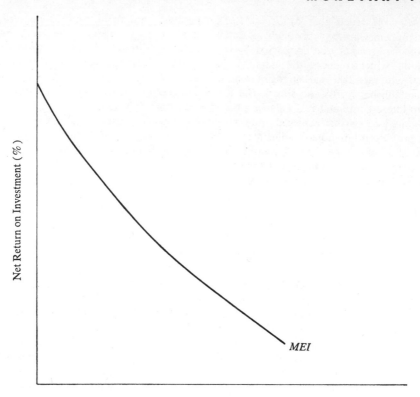

Figure 2.

tinuously in order to equate the coupon rate to the market rate of interest. This assumption maximizes the possible impact of higher interest rates on current business costs and the general price level.

## IV. Two Disturbances

Within the framework of Sections II and III let us analyze a rise in the equilibrium rate of interest due to an autonomous (i) decrease in saving, and (ii) increase in investment.

### A. Saving

A decrease in saving entails a leftward shift in the saving schedule and an upward movement along the I function. The monetary authority immediately carries out an open-market sale, which reduces the nominal supply of money and raises the market rate to the higher natural level (see Figure 1). Resources flow into consumption industries, ex ante saving and investment are maintained in constant equality, and the price level, up to this point, is unchanged.

The movement along the investment demand schedule coincides with an upward real movement along the MEI line. This implies that the increase in the rate of interest is accompanied by an increase in the net return to capital. The return rises as ex post investment and the marginal cost and supply price of capital-goods output all decline to lower equilibrium levels. All firms employing capital find that they may reduce their current depreciation charges, thereby financing the higher coupon rates created by the higher rate of interest. Thus, while interest costs are higher, there is for every firm an added revenue available to meet this cost. Under these circumstances, there are no forces on the side of cost and production tending to alter the average price of commodities. (Any change in the price level due to the lower price of capital goods is offset by a correspondingly higher price of consumption goods, which results when consumption demand increases at the expense of saving.[11])

Given the Keynesian "interest-equalization" monetary policy and the capital-investment

[11] See the Appendix, Section B, for a fuller description of the impact of a shift in saving on both the investment-goods and consumption-goods sectors.

decision process, there are thus neither monetary nor nonmonetary sources of inflation. The only qualification to this hinges on the possibility that the transfer of resources from investment to consumption industries might be facilitated by a given increase or rate of increase in the price level. If this were true, the Keynesian monetary action would contribute to a degree of immobility, unemployment, and temporary reduction of aggregate output. Prices, as a result, would rise. One can only speculate how this would compare quantitatively, or—from a public policy viewpoint—how it should be evaluated, relative to the *permanent* inflation due to an internally stimulated movement along the liquidity preference schedule. Notice, moreover, that inflation attributable to resource immobility in this case cannot be characterized as resulting from higher interest "costs." Rather, the inflation is due to immobility originating in a decrease in demand and *revenues* in investment-goods industries.

## B. Investment

An independent increase in investment results from an increase in the gross marginal product of capital. This implies that aggregate output $y$ has also increased. The monetary disturbance is now somewhat more complex and is described with reference to Figure 3.

The initial schedules, drawn with solid lines, all meet at $r'$, the natural rate. In the left diagram the predisturbance functions are $I'$ and $S(y')$, which is saving based on output $y'$. The equilibrium is at point $A$. In the right diagram the beginning equilibrium is at point $C$, at which real balances are $M'/P'$, the quantity determined by $r'$ along the initial schedule $L(y')$. The investment curve increases to $I''$ and is accompanied by a simultaneous increase in output to $y''$.[12] This causes three simultaneous shifts: (i) real saving moves to the right to $S(y'')$, establishing a new saving-investment equilibrium at point $B$; (ii) the demand for real balances increases to $L(y'')$; (iii) given price flexibility, the increase in $L$ lowers the general price level from $P'$ to $P''$, raising the supply of real balances to $M'/P''$. Assuming that

the demand and supply of real balances increase synchronously, the equilibrium in this market moves horizontally to point $D$. Now, if left to its own devices, the economy will establish a new money-market equilibrium at point $E$, at which the interest rate, determined by $S(y'')$ and $I''$, is $r'' > r'$; real balances are $M'/P'''$; and, since the money stock is constant throughout, the price level is higher at $P''' > P'$.[13]

The monetary authority can again perform its catalytic role of raising the market rate to the natural rate. If it assumes full responsibility for doing so, it will conduct an instantaneous open-market sale, moving the equilibrium from $D$ to $E$ by reducing the money supply to $M'' < M'$ and real balances to $M''/P'' = M'/P'''$. However, at point $D$ prices are $P'' < P'$, and at $E$ the economy is thus left with a net reduction in the price level due to the increase in output. Since we are only interested in evaluating the role of monetary policy in raising interest rates, we shall assume for analytical purposes that the lower price level is allowed to remain. We assume that prices are perfectly flexible downward in response to the rise of output, which, for the moment, is constant at $y''$. Under these "pure" circumstances, does the higher interest rate, viewed as a *cost* phenomenon, promise to raise prices?

Let the productivity increase, which gave rise to the increase in investment, be distributed uniformly among all firms. There are thus throughout the economy greater revenues with which to meet higher interest payments. The increased interest rate has no independent influence on costs, output, or prices, which remain at the levels described in the preceding paragraphs. Now suppose, more realistically, that some firms fail to share in the greater productivity of capital. The latter typically stems from an increase in the labor force or an innovation, neither of which will be experienced by every producer. Nevertheless, the greater interest charges on existing capital must be met by all firms, and those not sharing in the productivity rise will undergo an increase in costs unmatched by greater revenues. These firms must retrench, releasing resources. If the resources are mobile and find employment elsewhere, then aggregate output is constant and the price level again is not directly affected by the higher interest rate.

---

[12] The increase in the marginal efficiency schedule may reflect an anticipated future increase, rather than a de facto current increase in output and the productivity of capital. In this event firms may have to resort to additional finance, including new money and the dishoarding of existing balances, in order to service new borrowings or security issues. However, as a source of inflation, this can only be a temporary, reversible phenomenon.

[13] It is possible (though unlikely) for point $E$ to lie directly above or to the right of point $C$, implying that the final price level is equal to or less than the beginning one. This could be the result of a greater income coefficient in saving or in the demand for money, shifting either schedule farther to the right.

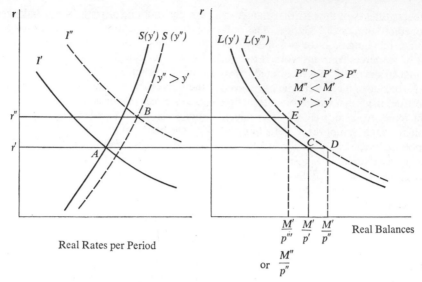

Figure 3.

However, if in the short run the necessary re-allocation creates unemployment and a net reduction of output, prices will tend to rise. In the actual context of an increase in capital productivity, unemployment may simply prevent output from rising and prices from falling by their maximum amounts. It is in this sense that an increase in investment and the rate of interest—"tight money"—is a force tending to raise costs and also prices.[14]

A further possible source of inflation is again the required transfer of resources between consumption and investment industries: In the present disturbance the movement along $S(y'')$ from $r'$ to $r''$ is an increase in the proportion of income saved; resources must accordingly move from consumption to investment-goods output.[15] If this transfer is in any way dependent upon

inflation, then the Keynesian monetary policy will delay it. Output will fall below $y''$ and prices will rise above $P''$.

## V. Monetary Restraint: An Alternative View

Let us now modify the analysis by assuming that monetary restriction does not coincide with an increase in the natural rate of interest. The monetary authority reduces money and raises interest in order to offset inflationary disturbances which do not themselves operate through, or entail a change in, the rate of interest. An example of such a disturbance is a direct movement from cash balances into goods—i.e., a leftward shift in the demand schedule for money—or money creation via a fiscal deficit which does not raise bank reserves.[16] The impact of tight money against such a background is discussed with reference to Figure 4. For simplicity, we describe the disturbance and the monetary response separately, though in fact they may coincide.

The system initially is in stock-flow equilibrium at interest rate $r'$ and real balances $M'/P'$. The existing-asset equilibrium is at point $A$. Suppose that the inflationary disturbance to which the

---

[14] See Appendix, Section C, for the two-sector account of an increase in investment.

[15] The increase in saving at $r'$ due to the shift of the schedule from $S(y')$ to $S(y'')$ will also require a movement of resources from consumption to investment industries, provided that (i) the spontaneous increase in output from $y'$ to $y''$ is distributed between consumption and investment goods in the pre-disturbance ratio; (ii) the marginal rate of saving is greater than the average rate. If, for example, the marginal saving rate were less than the average, the de facto increase in investment goods due to the more productive capital stock would exceed the increase desired by savers, and resources would have to leave investment industries. However, (ii) is in fact widely accepted on both theoretical and empirical grounds. (i) is difficult to justify. I know of no commonly accepted production functions or types of technological change that guarantee this result.

[16] This is the kind of disturbance (though generally it is the opposite case of hoarding) that Robertson typically is concerned with. See, e.g., *Banking Policy and the Price Level*, London: Staples Press, Ltd., 1949, pp. 53–54; and "Saving and Hoarding," *Economic Journal*, XLIII, September 1933, pp. 401–2 (reprinted as Ch. IV in *Essays in Monetary Theory, op. cit.*).

monetary authority reacts is a once-for-all decrease in the demand-for-money schedule relative to goods. In the diagram $L$ shifts leftward from $L'$ to $L''$. Assuming a fixed level of output, commodity prices rise directly to, say, $P''$.[17] The supply of real balances falls to $M'/P''$ and the existing-asset equilibrium moves horizontally from $A$ to $B$.

The central bank now strives, through open-market action, to offset the higher price level. It conducts an instantaneous open-market sale, which reduces $M$ to $M''$ and raises $r$ to $r''$. This entails an instantaneous movement in the stock equilibrium from $B$ to $C$ along $L''$. The price

to an open-market sale, and then falls through the internal adaptive mechanism. This is in contrast to the Keynesian-Wicksellian framework in which tight money entailed an interest rate rising monotonically from one equilibrium level to another. The role of the central bank was to facilitate and accelerate that movement. In both cases the monetary policy serves to curtail simultaneously occurring inflationary pressures. In the Keynesian case the inflation was a built-in response to the movement of the rate of interest. In the present action the inflation is an autonomous disturbance which the bank-induced change in money and interest endeavours to offset.

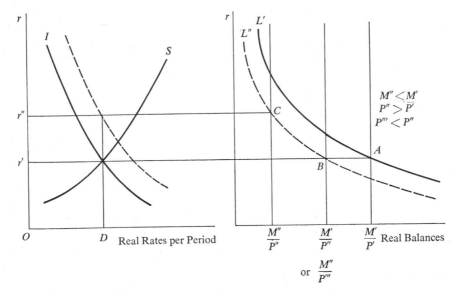

Figure 4.

level remains, for the moment, unchanged at $P''$. But at the higher market rate $r''$, ex ante saving exceeds investment. This causes both prices and interest to fall over time via a stock-flow dynamic adjustment (output is still constant).[18] The final equilibrium is at point $B$, at which the market rate is again $r'$, prices are $P'\,'' < P''$, and real balances are $M''/P'\,'' = M'/P''$. If the bank's objective were to stabilize the price level, then $M''$ would be a quantity such that $P'\,'' = P'$.

Tight money is thus now characterized by a market rate of interest whose average level is temporarily raised. The rate rises first in response

Once again, in order to evaluate any impact on the price level of the higher interest rate as a cost phenomenon, we must turn to the underlying real variables. We have seen that the capacity of firms to absorb higher interest costs depends on the net return to capital, which is a function of the level of ex post investment. In Section IV monetary tightness, as imposed by the central bank, was accompanied by constant equality between desired saving and investment, to which ex post investment corresponded. But now desired saving and investment are unequal throughout the period of higher interest rates. Neither the disturbances nor the adjustment process indicate in themselves what the level of ex post investment will be. However, we will consider several possibilities lying between the blades of the ex ante saving-investment scissors and generalize from there. We continue to assume,

---

[17] The increase in the demand for goods is assumed to be across the board, with no effect on relative prices or the rate of interest. Thus real saving and investment remain unchanged at their initial level of equality.

[18] See Horwich, *op. cit.*, pp. 179–187.

for the present, that total output and employment are constant.

Perhaps the simplest assumption is that ex ante and ex post investment are equal. Beginning at the initial equilibrium yield $r'$, ex post investment moves up along the ex ante investment demand schedule $I$ to the height of the tight money rate $r''$, and then down again to the unchanged equilibrium yield $r'$. On our assumptions, this coincides with an identical movement along the schedule of the marginal efficiency of investment. The return to investment thus moves exactly, and finances the production costs associated, with changes in the market rate of interest. The return first rises as resources move out of capital production, lowering the relative price of investment goods and the necessary depreciation allowances held against capital. Then the return falls to its original level as the sequence is reversed. This analysis parallels that of the decrease in saving (Section IV-A). In both cases the variable interest costs are accompanied by equal variations in net revenues for all firms. Profits, output, and prices are unaffected by the adjustment process.[19]

Perhaps a more realistic assumption is that resources are completely immobile. This would tend to be true the briefer is the time interval of the tight money period. Ex post investment would then remain at the predisturbance level, $OD$ in Figure 4, which is above the ex ante levels indicated by the $I$ schedule. It appears thus that the return to investment will remain equal to $r'$, below the prevailing interest rates. But the only way in which unwanted capital goods can be sold to firms is by lowering their price. In the face of falling demand, this implies that the entire investment-goods supply schedule drops, reflecting a reduction in the compensation paid to resources in that industry. The supply price of capital output falls—both absolutely and relatively—and the $MEI$ schedule (based on a given investment-goods supply function) rises initially to the location of the dashed (unlabeled) curve in Figure 4. In brief, resources stay on in the investment industry by accepting lower real returns, thereby raising the profitability of each investment-output level; the ex ante $I$ schedule follows the movement of the $MEI$ line.[20] As the market

rate of interest falls (owing to the continuing excess of ex ante $S$ over ex ante $I$), investment demand rises along the dashed curve. This permits resource payments and the supply price of capital to increase by whatever amount is required to maintain $OD$ as the profitable investment. Thus the movement to equilibrium is one in which the $I$ and $MEI$ schedules gradually shift downward to their original positions. The return to investment is always at least as great as the market rate of interest. Hence, there is no independent upward pressure on costs and prices originating in the higher rate of interest.[21]

Any tendency for ex post investment to exceed the ex ante amount would be analyzed in the manner of the preceding paragraph. The marginal efficiency schedule would shift along the locus of marginal efficiency-ex post investment points, financing the higher interest rates of the adjustment period. As shown in the Appendix, the precise location of the ex post points, and thus the $MEI$ schedule, depends on the relative shifts of the marginal cost schedules of investment and consumption industries. These shifts determine the ex post levels of output and the relative prices of the two commodities, which together determine the return to real capital.

The assumption of fixed total output and employment in a deflationary process is apt to be quite unrealistic, owing to cost and price rigidities. However, the present monetary policy is designed to offset an inflationary disturbance, and the *net* movement of the price level over time may not actually be great. The total demand for output would thereby be relatively stable, even though interest rises and stimulates an excess of saving over investment, as described.[22] But even with a stable price level, the adjustment will require a temporary reallocation of resources, except in the limiting case of constant output in each sector, noted above. Given less-than-perfect mobility between sectors, unemployment and a decline in aggregate output would thus generally occur. This would reduce aggregate saving and raise the natural rate of interest, terminating the deflationary adjustment at a higher price level and market rate of interest.

The development of unemployment and reduced

---

[19] See the description in the Appendix, Section D.

[20] The upward shift in the $I$ schedule reduces the magnitude of the saving-investment gap and consequently the fall over time of the rate of interest and the speed of the deflationary adjustment. For a similar point in his criticism of Keynes' *Treatise*, see D. H. Robertson, "Mr. Keynes' Theory of Money," *Economic Journal*, XLI, September 1931, p. 401.

[21] Cf. also Appendix, Section E.

[22] The inflationary disturbance was assumed in n.17 to have no effect on interest or real saving and investment. Hence these variables are influenced only by the monetary contraction. Given more or less stability of the general price level, the relevant aspects of the sectoral price changes described in the Appendix, Sections D and E, are thus the relative, rather than the absolute movements.

output does not itself alter the basic analysis regarding the ability of firms to finance interest on capital. Whatever the degree of employment or unemployment, this ability depends on the location of the marginal efficiency schedule, which the ex ante *I* function will tend to follow. This is equivalent to saying that firms will not commit themselves to the payment of interest on new (and old) capital above what the return on investment promises to be.[23] And this has nothing to do, per se, with the degree of unemployment or the constancy of output. Conceivably, even though resources are idled, the movement of output and prices in the two sectors might be consistent with a movement along the predisturbance *MEI* schedule and with equality between ex ante and ex post investment, as previously described. But unemployment ought certainly to increase the range of possibilities with respect to the shift of *MEI*. To the cases already considered, we might wish to add the possibility that the movement of variables will drive *MEI* and *I below* their predisturbance location.

## VI. Summary and Conclusion

Sections II-IV advanced a model of money and capital in which (i) policy increases in market interest rates are merely a response to prior independent increases in the natural rate of interest, and (ii) higher interest cost—or, more generally, higher rent on the existing capital stock—is financed by an increase in the net productivity of capital. If tight money (defined as simultaneous rising interest rates and inflationary pressures) is due to a decrease of saving, the greater capital productivity is provided by an allowable reduction in depreciation charges. All firms share in this

productivity rise, which finances the higher interest costs. Restrictive monetary policy, aimed at raising interest rates to the natural level, tends to stabilize the price level, unless the movement of resources from investment to consumption is delayed by price stability. For then unemployment and a reduction of aggregate output might furnish a nonmonetary source of inflation.

If tight money is caused by an independent increase in investment, the gross product of capital and the level of output rise directly. Interest-equalizing monetary policy is thus consistent with a decline in prices. However, the more bountiful capital stock is not likely to be distributed evenly throughout the economy. Resource reallocation within the given industrial structure (and also, possibly, between consumption and investment industries) is required. Unemployment may again result, reducing output and raising prices. Since capital productivity has increased, output may simply rise, and prices fall, less than otherwise. But just as in the decrease of saving, the monetary authority in this case is not responsible for the necessary movements of the interest rate or of resources. These would occur in any event. Only if, in curtailing the monetary inflation, the authority removes what happens to be a stimulus to resource mobility, is it guilty in any degree of causing unemployment and nonmonetary inflation.

In Section V tight money is caused by monetary contraction designed to offset inflationary disturbances which do not involve a movement in the market or natural rate of interest. The monetary authority is thus solely responsible for the higher interest rate. However, the rise in interest is only temporary, since the forces which counteract the rise in prices tend at the same time to return the interest rate to its original level. During the deflationary—or better, anti-inflationary—adjustment, ex ante saving exceeds ex ante investment. Ex post investment is thereby indeterminate and may take on a wide range of values. It is shown that any particular level of ex post investment, entailing the purchase of new capital goods, can only be effected by raising the return on investment to the level of the higher interest rate. This is accomplished by appropriate shifts in the marginal cost and supply price of both investment and consumption output. The interest costs are thus always covered by productivity changes. But the adjustment very likely will require some reallocation of resources; imperfect mobility will again cause unemployment, reduced output, and a nonmonetary source of inflation.

The tendency of tight money (defined most

[23] We have been assuming that firms know what the marginal efficiency of various investment levels is, and that the ex ante *I* schedule invariably coincides with the *MEI* function. In Section IV, where the schedules undergo a once-for-all shift, and monetary policy contributes an element of stability to the adjustment process, this is not an unreasonable assumption. However, in the present context, where *MEI* may shift constantly, entrepreneurial error as to the return on investment is a more serious possibility. (Keynes himself stressed the underlying role of expectations in the marginal efficiency concept; cf. *The General Theory, op. cit.*, pp. 138–144.) Thus, if firms in the aggregate overestimate the return, offering to pay more interest than the de facto marginal efficiency on the investment justifies, *I* is above *MEI*. Costs, including interest, will exceed revenues, and output will be reduced, provoking unemployment and nonmonetary inflation.

generally as a tendency to rising income and
rising, or higher average, interest rates), in the
face of monetary restraint, to raise the price level
thus depends on the ease with which associated
resource movements are accomplished. Only in
one case can the necessary reallocation be said in
some sense to result from an increase in interest
"costs." That is the case of an independent
increase in the investment demand schedule. The
increased costs are those of a limited number of
firms whose share in the greater productivity of
capital is below average, and who will, accordingly,
lose resources. In all other cases of tight money
the resource movements, while induced by the
interest rise, are not directly attributable to an
increase in interest costs as such, but rather to a
decline of revenues in affected industries.

The claim that higher interest rates raise prices
by raising costs is thus, within our analytical
framework, without much substance. Whether the
natural rate is constant or increasing, greater
interest payments tend to be financed by greater
net productivity of real capital. The single case in
which higher interest rates raise costs—that of an
increase in investment demand—is one in which
the overall cost structure and price level are falling
because of a more productive capital stock. The
real thrust of the interest rate in this case is thus
only to limit a deflationary movement, not
literally to create inflation.

# Appendix

This appendix presents the theoretical under
pinnings for the relationship between the stock
and flow capital-goods markets, the marginal
efficiency schedule, and the market for consumption goods. The model, which is an extension of
the analysis of Witte,[24] is presented in Section A.
Following this, successive sections apply the
framework to the analysis of a decrease in saving;
an increase in investment; the equality of ex ante
and ex post investment, and the excess of ex post
over ex ante investment in deflationary processes.

[24] J. G. Witte, Jr., "The Microfoundations of the
Social Investment Function," *Journal of Political
Economy*, LXXI, October 1963, pp. 441–56. Witte
draws on the work of R. W. Clower, "An Investigation
into the Dynamics of Investment," *American
Economic Review*, XLIV, March 1954, pp. 64–81. Cf.
also W. T. Newlyn, *Theory of Money*, Oxford University Press, 1962, pp. 93–95. I have been influenced
in the treatment of the consumption-goods sector by
the work of S. B. Chase, Jr., *Asset Prices in Economic
Analysis*, Berkeley: University of California Press,
1963, Ch. III.

## A. The Model

The capital-goods sector is described by means
of three connected diagrams in Figure 5(a-c). The
upper left drawing, Figure 5(a), is that of the
existing or "stock" capital-goods market. On the
vertical axis is $P_K$, the dollar price of capital goods.
Also indicated on the vertical axis is $1/p$, the ratio
of $P_K$ to the net earnings on a unit of capital.
$P_K$ and $1/p$ move in the same direction, both
because of the direct presence of $P_K$ in the numerator, and the influence of $P_K$ in determining the
denominator, of $1/p$ (cf. page 333). The vertical
line in the diagram represents the existing stock
of capital, $K'$. The stock demand schedule is $D_K$,
an inverse function of both $P_K$, and the interest
rate, $r$. The latter variable is entered as a parameter
of the schedule. Given $r$, the resulting $D_K$ schedule
will determine a price (and net earnings) at which
the rate of return is $p = r$.

In the upper right diagram, Figure 5(b), is the
flow or production market for new capital. $S_K$ is
the marginal cost supply schedule. $\Delta K$ on the
horizontal axis represents the quantity of capital
or investment goods produced per period $t$.

Finally, in the lower right diagram, Figure 5(c),
$p$ and $\Delta K$ and $r$ and $I$ are linked up to form the
marginal efficiency and investment demand
schedules, respectively. Plotting $\Delta K$ (ex post
investment), as indicated in the upper right
diagram, against the corresponding values of $p$,
as taken from the upper left diagram, we obtain
the *MEI* schedule. Plotting $I$, the flow *demand*
(ex ante investment) for the same quantities, $\Delta K$,
and associating it with the values of $r = p$, we
obtain the coinciding $I$ schedule.

Consider the impact of a change in the rate of
interest, the gross marginal product of capital
remaining constant. The system is initially in
equilibrium at point $A$ in all three diagrams. The
interest rate is increased from $r'$ to $r''$. In Figure
5(a) the $D_K$ schedule falls from $D'_K$ to $D''_K$, reducing
$P_K$ from $P'_K$ to $P''_K$ and $1/p$ from $1/p'$ to $1/p'' = 1/r''$.
Moving to the right to Figure 5(b), the desired
output at $P''_K$ is $\Delta K'' < \Delta K'$ (at point $B$). Combining $\Delta K''$ with $p''$ and $r''$ in Figure 5(c) gives us
a higher point, $B$, on the marginal efficiency-
investment demand schedules.

What the three-way diagram makes clear is that
(i) the *MEI* and $I$ schedules are "market equilibrium" curves, derived from the stock and flow
capital-goods markets, and are not demand
schedules in the Marshallian sense;[25] and (ii) the
price of capital goods is effectively determined in
the stock market, where the rate of interest is
equated to the percentage return on the existing

[25] Witte, *op. cit.*, p. 447.

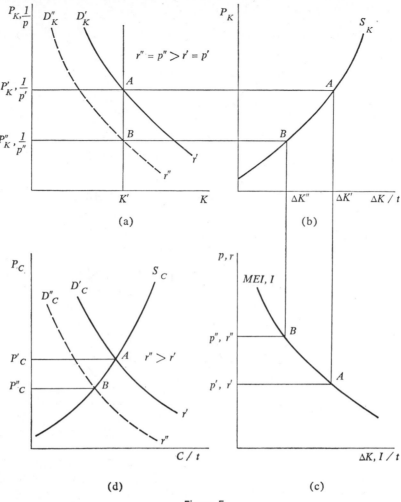

Figure 5.

capital stock. In the latter connection, the reader will recall our assumption of equality in the return on all new and existing investments. Thus the action that equates $p$ and $r$ in the upper left diagram has the same effect in the lower right diagram.

The analysis ignores the role of new capital goods in the determination of price; i.e., the stock is held constant at $K'$, ignoring the increments forthcoming from points along $S_K$. For our short-run purposes, I think this is a realistic assumption. However, it can easily be relaxed. Adding the increments to $K'$ would lower both the price and the gross marginal product of capital over time. Thus the value of $p$ corresponding to a given $P_K$ would be lowered, and the entire $MEI$ and $I$ schedules would drop.[26] I would argue that shifting the $I$ schedule in this way (i) overstates the short-run influence of the growth of the capital

stock on its gross product, and (ii) is one-sided, in that it ignores constantly occurring technological and population changes that simultaneously tend to raise $MEI$ and $I$.

Figure 5(d), a diagram of the consumption-goods market, completes our sectoral representation of the system. $D_C$ and $S_C$ are, respectively, the demand and supply of new consumption goods, $C$, per unit time. $P_C$ is the money price of $C$. Since saving is a rising function of $r$, $D_C$, based on a given real income, varies inversely with $r$. Thus the increase in $r$ referred to a moment ago shifts $D_C$ downward and lowers the equilibrium from $A$ to $B$, as indicated.

### B. Saving

The decrease in saving, analyzed in Section IV-A, can be illustrated by the $A$-$B$ movements in Figures 5(a-c) and 6. The initial saving schedule, a rising curve, would pass through point $A$ in

[26] Lerner, *The Economics of Control, op. cit.*, p. 335.

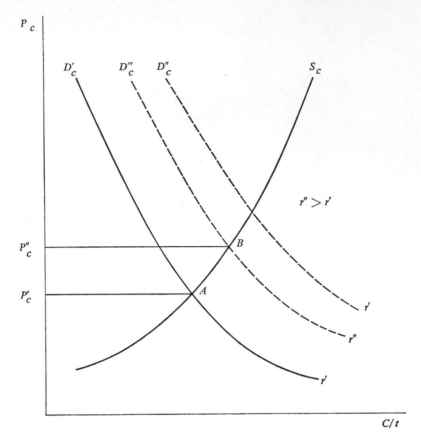

Figure 6.

Figure 5(c). The subsequent schedule would pass through point $B$. In Figure 6, the consumption market, the decrease of saving is offset by an initial increase in consumption demand from $D'_C$ to $D''_C$. The latter schedule is based upon the initial interest rate $r'$. However, the increase in interest reduces demand to $D'''_C$, which determines the final equilibrium at point $B$.[27]

We assume that on net the average price of commodities and total output, measured by appropriate indexes, are unchanged. However, the relative decline in $P_K$ enables the marginal efficiency of investment to rise.

### C. Investment

The increase in investment, described in Section IV-B, is a simultaneous increase in the gross

[27] Strictly speaking $P_C$ should be entered as a parameter of the saving schedule, paralleling the use of $r$ in determining $D_C$. However, taking account of this additional relationship would complicate the model considerably, requiring a full treatment of stability conditions. We avoid doing so, since the basic analysis and conclusions can, on further plausible simplifying assumptions, be retained intact.

marginal product of capital and real output of the economy. *All* schedules in the investment-consumption complex shift to the right. $S_K$ and $S_C$ shift because of the greater productivity, and hence lower supply price, in the output of both capital and consumption goods. The shifts in $S$ and $D_C$ are a response to the greater real income available to both savers and consumers. $MEI$ and thus $I$ shift because of the reduction in $S_K$. The shift of $I$ is assumed to exceed that of $S$, creating a higher equilibrium interest rate $r''$. $S_C$ is assumed to shift more than $D_C$, lowering $P_C$.

At the predisturbance interest rate $r'$, $D_K$ increases because of the spontaneous increase in the numerator of $p$, and hence $p$ itself, due to the rise of capital's gross (and net) marginal product. In order to maintain equality between $r'$ and $p$, $D_K$ and thus $P_K$ rise until a sufficiently higher price restores $p$ to $p' = r'$. (In a word, the relationship between the $1/p$ and $P_K$ scales is altered: at each $P_K$ the corresponding $1/p$ is less.)

When $r$ rises to its new equilibrium $r''$, $D_C$, $D_K$, and $P_K$ fall somewhat below their initially higher levels. It is neither inconceivable nor inconsistent for $P_K$ to fall below its predisturbance value. But whether it does so or not, the downward movement of $P_C$ is assumed to dominate the general price index.

### D. Ex Ante and Ex Post Investment Equal

The sequence described on page 338 entails an upward movement along a given marginal efficiency schedule from interest rate $r'$ to $r''$, followed by a reverse movement back to $r'$. $r''$ is imposed from outside the system by a monetary contraction. The restoration to $r'$ is accompanied by a fall in the general price level.

Holding the interest rate momentarily at $r''$ and investment at $I(r'')$, the increase in interest reduces $D_K$ and $D_C$. The general deflation in prices and costs lowers $D_K$ and $D_C$ further, while also reducing $S_K$ and $S_C$. This is because these schedules are functions of money prices. On net, $D_K$ and $S_K$ fall so as to determine jointly a price $P_K$ and investment level consistent with the new point $I(r'')$ on the unchanged *MEI-I* schedule. By assumption, $S_C$ drops more than $D_C$, raising consumption output and absorbing labor released from the investment sector. In order to raise $p$ to the level of $r''$, $P_K$ must drop relative to $P_C$. If this was not true in the first instance, $D_K$ and $S_K$ can be lowered further to accomplish it. Since $D_K$ and $S_K$ are lowered *equally*, they remain consistent with the given investment point $I(r'')$.

As $r$ returns to $r'$ and prices continue to fall, the relative price and resource shifts of the above paragraph are reversed. Ex post investment rises, consumption falls, $P_K/P_C$ rises and hence $p$ falls with $r$.

### E. Ex Post Investment Exceeds Ex Ante Investment

In this case the initial disturbance is again an independent monetary contraction which raises $r$ to $r''$. In the ensuing adjustment the general price level again falls and $r$ returns to $r'$. But as this occurs, ex post investment exceeds ex ante investment, as indicated by the predisturbance $I$ schedule, owing to complete resource immobility (see page 338). Thus, while $r''$ lowers $D_K$ and $D_C$, and general deflation lowers $D_K$, $D_C$, $S_K$, and $S_C$, the combined shifts are such as to maintain investment and consumption output at their predisturbance levels. In order to raise $p$ to $r''$, $P_K/P_C$ must decline, and once again there will always be a combination of shifts to accomplish this. Since $I(r'')$ now corresponds to the predisturbance level, while both $r$ and $p$ have increased, investment lies on a higher marginal efficiency and investment demand schedule, as drawn in Figure 4.

The relative shifts are gradually reversed as $r$ return to $r'$ and the price level falls.

THOMAS R. BEARD

# Debt Management: Its Relationship to Monetary Policy, 1951-1962

## 36
Since the famous Treasury-Federal Reserve Accord, the relationship between debt management and monetary policy has undergone certain basic changes.[1] In general,

three major periods may be distinguished: (1) the 1951–1952 period of the "transition to free markets"; (2) the 1953–1960 era of "free markets"; and (3) the most recent period of "twisting" or "nudging." In view of the continuing controversy over the proper role of debt management,[2] it is instructive to review the debt management policies followed and their relationship to monetary policies during each of these three periods. Some tentative conclusions can be drawn con-

[1] For the purposes of this paper, debt management is distinguished as clearly as possible from monetary and fiscal policy. All actions of the Federal government which directly affect the composition and terms of the publicly held Federal debt (debt held outside the Federal Reserve and U.S. Government trust funds and agency accounts), whether initiated by the Treasury or by the Federal Reserve, are included within this definition. However, debt management does not involve the size of the debt (which is a matter of fiscal policy) or the net amount of debt bought and sold by the central bank in the conduct of its open market operations (which is a matter of monetary policy). Our definition of debt management does not include so-called non-interest bearing

"debt," either in the form of currency held outside the Federal government or non-Federal government deposits at the Federal Reserve banks. Rather, these latter items are related to monetary policy.

A similar definition of debt management has frequently been utilized. See, for example, Warren L. Smith, *Debt Management in the United States*, Study Paper No. 19 for the Joint Economic Committee, Washington, D.C.: Government Printing Office, 1960. By way of contrast, a broader definition which includes non-interest bearing "debt" has recently been suggested by James Tobin, "An Essay on Principles of Debt Management," *Fiscal and Debt Management Policies*, Englewood Cliffs, N.J.: Prentice-Hall, 1963, pp. 143–218.

[2] For a brief summary of alternative views on debt management, see William E. Laird, "The Changing Views on Debt Management," *Quarterly Review of Economics and Business*, III, Autumn, 1963, pp. 7–17.

Reprinted from the *National Banking Review*, Vol. II (1964), pp. 61–76, by permission of the author and publisher. Thomas Beard is a professor at Louisiana State University. The author wishes to acknowledge the earlier financial assistance of the Ford Foundation and the more recent financial assistance of the L. S. U. Foundation during the preparation of this paper. Miss Janice Krummack and Mr. Normand Bernard offered several helpful suggestions. Of course, the author alone is responsible for the views expressed.

cerning the probable impact of debt management in each period.

## I. The Background

Prior to March 1951, considerations of debt management effectively tied the hands of the monetary authorities. At the end of World War II, it was widely feared that the large war debt might not be held willingly by investors and that debt markets were highly susceptible to destabilizing speculative fluctuations. In some quarters it was feared that instability of security prices would destroy public confidence in the government's credit and undermine investment incentives. These fears at first led to the view that even moderately small increases in interest rates could not be permitted. With the passage of time, the views of Federal Reserve spokesmen changed. While they felt unpegging could take place only gradually, they wished to move steadily in the direction of greater reliance on flexible monetary policy. Treasury officials, however, fought a delaying action.[3]

Continuously pegged long-term interest rates persisted well into the post-war years—long after any legitimate need for rigid pegs had seemingly disappeared. While central bank officials may have been guilty of overemphasizing the extent of debt monetization that took place,[4] effective central bank control over the money supply was greatly hampered.[5] In effect, monetary

[3] An excellent account of the evolving positions of Treasury and Federal Reserve officials during the war and early post-war years is found in Henry C. Murphy, *The National Debt in War and Transition*, New York: McGraw-Hill, 1950.

[4] For comments along this line, see Alvin Hansen, "Monetary Policy," *Review of Economics and Statistics*, XXXVII, May 1955, especially pp. 116–117. Kareken has argued that the large scale investor selling of certain maturities which at times did take place—particularly from June 1950, to March 1951 —cannot be disassociated from the Treasury-Federal Reserve struggle and the effect of this conflict on market expectations. He has suggested that the actions of the monetary authorities resulted in a more rapid debt monetization than would otherwise have taken place. John H. Kareken, "Monetary Policy and the Public Debt: An Appraisal of Post-War Developments in the U.S.A.," *Kyklos*, X, Fasc. 4, 1957, especially pp. 418–423.

[5] Numerous critical views on pre-Accord monetary-debt management policies can be found in United States Congress, Subcommittee on Monetary, Credit, and Fiscal Policies of the Joint Committee on the Economic Report, *Monetary, Credit, and Fiscal Policies, Hearings, Statements, and Report*, 81st Congress, 1st Session, 1949–1950, and United States

policy was largely relegated to the task of insuring the liquidity of the public debt. The stabilization of government security prices rendered all maturities virtually as liquid as the shortest-term instruments. At the same time, the initiative in changing bank reserves was transferred to holders of government securities.

Finally, in the Accord of March 1951, the advocates of flexible monetary policy were triumphant. This victory, however, was only one step in the gradual process of regaining central bank "independence."

## II. The Transition to Free Markets, 1951–1952

The first major period following the Accord lasted for roughly two years. During most of this period, the predominant atmosphere was one of uncertainty. The Federal Reserve as well as the Treasury wished to avoid any actions that might precipitate disorderly conditions in the securities market. At the same time, it was widely felt that inflation, rather than depression, was the important danger.

A reconciliation of these conflicting claims on central bank policy was facilitated by a new theory of credit control. In short, the theory had been developed within the Federal Reserve that central bank policy could be an effective stabilizer even though fluctuations in interest rates were moderate.[6] The impact of Federal Reserve policy was said to be transmitted primarily through direct effects on lenders and the "availability of credit," rather than through variations in interest rates or in the money supply. Large-scale central bank operations were unnecessary in an environment characterized by a large and widely held public debt spread over a wide range of maturities. Such a debt facilitated the rapid transmission of credit policies between the various segments of the market. Other institutional developments, such as the growth of non-bank financial institutions

Congress, Subcommittee on General Credit Control and Debt Management of the Joint Committee on the Economic Report, *Monetary Policy and the Management of the Public Debt, Their Role in Achieving Price Stability and High Level Employment, Replies, Hearings, and Report*, 82nd Congress, 2nd Session, 1952. These volumes are referred to, respectively, as the Douglas and Patman Documents.

[6] See, in particular, R. V. Roosa, "Interest Rates and the Central Bank," *Money, Trade, and Economic Growth*, New York: The Macmillan Co., 1951, pp. 270–295, and portions of the testimony of Chairman Martin in *Patman Replies*, pp. 207–632.

characterized by conservative portfolio management, were also seen as giving open market
operations a significant impact with relatively
small changes in interest rates.[7]

As part of the transition to free markets, the
Federal Reserve continued until the last refunding
of 1952, its previous policy of lending direct
support to Treasury refunding operations. This
support took the form of central bank purchases
of "rights" to new issues, new issues on a "when
issued" basis, and outstanding securities in the
market comparable to the new issues. Despite the
availability of central bank underwriting, there
was little enthusiasm for debt lengthening by the
Treasury. Treasury spokesmen contended that
"no significant volume" of long-term funds was
available for the purchase of government bonds.
In addition, they continued to emphasize the
importance of maintaining "confidence in the
Government's credit" and a "sound" securities
market—both objectives being correlated with
relatively stable security prices.[8]. This emphasis
worked to discourage all but a few minor
attempts at financing outside the short-term
(under 1-year) area. Consequently, the maturity

structure of the debt continued its sharp downward drift, as had been the case continuously
since the end of the Second World War.

Even after monetary policy tightened in the
spring and summer of 1952, attrition (cash-ins of
maturing securities) never became especially
serious, owing primarily to the rather sizable
support purchases by the central bank. Although
the debt managers' problems were clearly eased
by central bank underwriting, it appears that the
monetary authorities were anxious to abandon
such support as quickly as feasible. As it was
later argued in a subcommittee report on the
functioning of the government securities market,
a firm commitment to support refundings
"seriously hampers freedom of action in effectuating general credit policy."[9] The most persuasive
arguments seemed to be that the ability of the
Federal Reserve to contain credit expansion is
limited by the necessity of making frequent and
often substantial support purchases and that
support purchases at least temporarily establish
a "pegged" market.[10]

The importance of these arguments has been

---

[7] For an analytical discussion of this theory,
including the so-called "locking-in" effect, "value-
of-portfolio" effect, "credit rationing" effect, etc.,
see Assar Lindbeck, *The "New" Theory of Credit
Control in the United States*, Stockholm; Almqvist
and Wiksell, 1959. See, also, Warren L. Smith, "On
the Effectiveness of Monetary Policy," *American
Economic Review*, XLVI, September 1956, pp.
588–606, and John H. Kareken, "Lenders' Preferences, Credit Rationing, and the Effectiveness of
Monetary Policy," *Review of Economics and Statistics*,
XXXIX, August 1957, pp. 292–302.

It is evident that central bank reliance on the
"availability doctrine" in its original form has
diminished with the passage of time. For a documentation of this change in emphasis as reflected in
one significant publication of the Board of Governors,
see Lawrence S. Ritter, "Official Central Banking
Theory in the United States, 1939–61: Four Editions
of *The Federal Reserve System: Purposes and Functions*," *Journal of Political Economy*, LXX, February
1962, pp. 14–29. Ritter notes a number of changes
with respect to the theory of monetary control from
the 1954 to the 1961 editions. Among these changes
were the following: the large and widely distributed
Federal debt and highly developed financial system
were no longer viewed as "unmixed blessings" since
they facilitate mobilization of idle balances and
credit creation; the lending behavior of non-bank
financial institutions was no longer viewed as "highly
susceptible" to System control; the "locking-in"
effect had been downgraded, etc.

[8] See portions of the report submitted by Secretary
Snyder in *Patman Replies*, pp. 1–206, and the *Annual
Report of the Secretary of the Treasury, 1952*, pp.
1–13.

[9] Report of the three member subcommittee
appointed to investigate the impact of open market
techniques on the functioning of the government
securities market in: United States Congress, Subcommittee on Economic Stabilization of the Joint
Committee on the Economic Report, *United States
Monetary Policy: Recent Thinking and Experience,
Hearings*, 83rd Congress, 2nd Session, 1954, p. 303.
This document is called the *Flanders Hearings*.

[10] The full text of the subcommittee report is
included in the *Flanders Hearings*, pp. 257–307. The
subcommittee also argued that support purchases
encourage unrealistic (low) rates on new Treasury
issues and result in a "frozen" central bank portfolio
heavily weighed with the securities acquired in the
support operations.

Neither argument appears persuasive. It is possible
that a general commitment to support all refunding
operations regardless of the terms set by the Treasury
could force massive purchases on the central bank.
However, there is no reason why the Federal Reserve
should agree to support any operation in which the
Treasury insisted on terms that were unrealistically
low in the System's view. In such cases—which
would undoubtedly become infrequent—the Treasury
would have to assume full responsibility. Similarly,
the "frozen" portfolio argument is less than completely convincing. The System is not forced to
maintain any given security in its portfolio over
time. Securities purchased in support operations can
later be sold, though perhaps gradually, with the
potential effect on bank reserves being offset by
purchases of Treasury bills if necessary. This argument
reduces to the more basic desire to minimize market
intervention, whatever the purpose. For a similar
emphasis, see Deane Carson, "Federal Reserve
Support of Treasury Refunding Operations," *Journal
of Finance*, XII, March 1957, pp. 51–63.

questioned, however.[11] While free reserves often registered sizable increases (or net borrowed reserves registered decreases) for a period of several weeks following large support operations, the seriousness of this situation depended both upon the use made of the additional reserves and the speed with which these reserves were utilized. In general, in any period of refunding support, if banks rapidly utilize their new reserves to make loans rather than to reduce their indebtedness to the central bank, it is probably more difficult for the monetary authorities to offset the initial effect of the support purchases. When banks make new loans before the System has had time to reabsorb the reserves, conditions in the money market, if measured by free reserves,[12] may appear as tight as the conditions existing before the support operation was undertaken. But loan expansion has occurred. On the other hand, commercial banks may consider reserves created in support operations as extremely temporary—especially if the System could make it known that reserves created under such circumstances do not reflect a permanent easing of monetary policy. The "traditional" view of discounting, i.e., that banks are reluctant to remain in debt to the central bank, suggests that the bulk of the newly created reserves would be used to reduce bank indebtedness. In this case, figures for free reserves reflect the easing conditions brought about by support operations, and therefore the easing conditions are more readily offset.

Furthermore, one should distinguish sharply between so-called "temporary pegs" during a period of refunding support, and a policy of rigid, continuous support of security prices.[13] With temporary pegs, interest rates are free to

move between major Treasury operations. It is essential, however, that the Federal Reserve does not purchase securities over a period much longer than the subscription period—as might be done if the purpose were to guarantee purchasers that they could not better their return for an appreciable period of time. If the period of market stabilization is short and support purchases are limited, the bulk of the funds released could be reabsorbed quickly. During the transition period, the Open Market Committee was able to accomplish a certain volume of offsetting sales of other securities concurrently with support purchases, and to mop up substantial reserves between refundings.[14] Apparently, however, the monetary authorities were not satisfied with the net result. It is problematical to what degree their dissatisfaction was attributable to an aversion to interference with the "free market."[15]

## III. The Era of Free Markets, 1953–1960

The second major period of debt management corresponds roughly to the eight years of the Eisenhower administration. With the inauguration of "bills only" in March 1953, the Federal Reserve completed its move toward "central bank independence" and "free markets"—a policy which, as one critic put it, came to represent the "fetish of laissez-faire."[16] In addition to the elimination of Treasury refunding support, swapping operations were specifically disallowed. Open market operations were to be confined, except in the correction of disorderly markets, to short-term securities, preferably bills.[17] "Bills

[11] See, in particular, Carson, *op. cit.* Hansen argued that the subsequent decision to abandon support operations amounted to "a partial abdication of the Reserve System with respect to one of its functions. Private flotations have the benefit of underwriting support, and one should imagine that a central bank would have as one of its primary functions the obligation to act as the underwriter for Treasury flotations." Hansen, *op. cit.*, p. 111.

[12] It is, of course, difficult to estimate the importance of the free reserves concept in the formulation and interpretation of central bank policy. It is evident, however, from various pronouncements that the concept does carry substantial weight. See, for example, "The Significance and Limitations of Free Reserves," *Federal Reserve Bank of New York Monthly Review*, XL, November 1958, pp. 162–167.

[13] For an excellent discussion of various approaches to "pegs," see R. V. Roosa, "Integrating Debt Management and Open Market Operations," *American Economic Review, Papers and Proceedings*, XLII, May 1952, especially pp. 218–223.

[14] A tabulation of Federal Reserve transactions in Treasury securities both during periods of refundings and between refunding periods is found in the *Flanders Hearings*, p. 265.

[15] Carson argued that while more market intervention was required and the timing of credit policy was occasionally disrupted because of the support policy, the central bank was able to maintain a "reasonably effective" degree of restraint. By "traditional standards," monetary policy was successful. Carson, *op. cit.*

[16] Ervin Miller, "Monetary Policies in the United States since 1950: Some Implications of the Retreat to Orthodoxy," *Canadian Journal of Economics and Political Science*, XXVII, May 1961, p. 218.

[17] See the record of operating policy statements in *Annual Report of the Board of Governors of the Federal Reserve System, 1953*, pp. 86–105. Until its discontinuance in 1961, the "bills only" policy was reaffirmed annually by the Open Market Committee.

only" was felt to be consistent with the objectives of "neutrality" and "minimum intervention." By confining its operations under normal conditions to Treasury bills, the central bank would keep the impact of its activities as broad and impersonal as possible—neither influencing prices of particular securities directly, nor attempting to maintain any particular rate structure.[18]

At roughly the same time, a distinct change in the philosophy and objectives of Treasury debt management was evidenced as the new Administration assumed office. The necessity of lengthening the debt structure was emphasized re-

peatedly.[19] This objective was primarily (although not entirely) placed in the context of anti-inflationary policy. Excessive short-term maturities were considered dis-advantageous primarily for three reasons: (1) frequent trips to the market by the Treasury would restrict the freedom of the central bank to pursue credit restraint;[20] (2) shorter-term issues were more likely to be purchased by commercial banks, thus resulting in an inflationary expansion in the money supply;[21] and (3) short-term securities, even when purchased by non-banks, would provide close money substitutes, thus adding to inflationary pressures.

In this new atmosphere, debt management assumed a secondary role. Debt management

[18] In addition to its rather specific objections to support of Treasury refunding operations, the subcommittee's major concern was that all central bank operations outside the shortest end of the market (except those necessary in the correction of disorderly conditions) interfered unduly with the operational excellence of the market, i.e., its "depth, breadth, and resiliency." Perhaps the two best defenses of "bills only" have been given by Winfield W. Riefler, "Open Market Operations in Long-Term Securities," *Federal Reserve Bulletin*, XLIV, November 1958, pp. 1260–1274, and Ralph A. Young and Charles A. Yager, "The Economics of 'Bills Preferably,'" *Quarterly Journal of Economics*, LXXIV, August 1960, pp. 341–373. Young and Yager carefully developed the argument that such a policy contributes to a well-performing securities market. Riefler emphasized the argument that the initial effects of monetary policy on short-term interest rates are rapidly transmitted to the long-term market by a process of arbitrage. It makes little difference for the structure of interest rates whether operations are conducted in Treasury bills or directly in long-term securities.

Criticism of the "bills only" policy and of its theoretical and philosophical underpinnings has apparently constituted one of the favorite pursuits of academic economists. For a brief sample of a vast critical literature, see Joseph Aschheim, *Techniques of Monetary Control*, Baltimore: John Hopkins Press, 1961, chapter 4; Deane Carson, "Recent Open Market Committee Policy and Technique," *Quarterly Journal of Economics*, LXIX, August 1955, pp. 321–342; Dudley Luckett, " 'Bills Only': A Critical Appraisal," *Review of Economics and Statistics*, XLII, August 1960, pp. 301–306; Warren L. Smith, *Debt Management in the United States*, especially pp. 118–134; and Sidney Weintraub, "The Theory of Open Market Operations: A Comment," *Review of Economics and Statistics*, XLI, August 1959, pp. 308–312. In his survey of monetary theory and policy, Harry Johnson suggested, "The bills-only policy . . . appeared to most academic economists as an undesirable renunciation by the central bank of an important technique of monetary control, and the reason given for it . . . as a shallow excuse masking the unwillingness of the Federal Reserve to risk unpopularity with the financial community by overtly subjecting it to capital losses." Harry G. Johnson, "Monetary Theory and Policy," *American Economic Review*, LII, June 1962, p. 374.

[19] For example, see the addresses and statements made during 1953 by Secretary Humphrey and Deputy to the Secretary Burgess that are published in the *Annual Report of the Secretary of the Treasury, 1953*, especially pp. 239–242, 255, and 260–266. The debt lengthening objective was frequently reiterated throughout the entire 1953–1960 period, even during those times when few long-term bonds were actually issued.

[20] Even if the central bank does not underwrite the Treasury, it must inevitably adjust somewhat to the Treasury's financing requirements. The Federal Reserve follows a policy of attempting to maintain an "even keel" in the market during periods of Treasury finance. This policy precludes any actions that might alter basic market relationships or market expectations, and thus is felt to prevent the central bank from making independent policy decisions during periods of large Treasury operations.

[21] The argument that sales of securities to commercial banks are inflationary because of the resulting money creation is clearly invalid. Banks which have no excess reserves can purchase government securities only by disposing of other investments or by reducing outstanding loans. If banks have excess reserves, they are either not in equilibrium or they desire to hold excess reserves for liquidity purposes. Banks in disequilibrium would purchase other assets even if they did not buy the government securities, while banks that hold excess reserves for liquidity purposes would buy the government securities only if they could sell other assets. Thus, in no case are sales to commercial banks inflationary in the sense of money creation. Furthermore, when the proceeds of security sales to banks are added to Treasury balances at the Federal Reserve, bank reserves are decreased.

The Treasury's fear of debt monetization leads to a confusion about the respective roles of the Treasury and Federal Reserve. Changes in total commercial bank assets, which include government securities, are more closely regulated by central bank policy than by Treasury debt management. On the question of debt monetization, see Milton Friedman, *A Program for Monetary Stability*, New York: Fordham University Press, 1960, especially pp. 52–55, and Tilford C. Gaines, *Techniques of Treasury Debt Management*, New York: The Free Press, 1962, pp. 249–251.

operations were to be conducted so as to contribute to the effectiveness of monetary policy—thus, in effect, largely reversing their pre-Accord roles. At first, it appeared that the public debt might be managed counter-cyclically as a supplement to counter-cyclical monetary policy. A counter-cyclical debt management policy would involve lengthening the debt structure during periods of monetary restraint and placing only minimum reliance on bond issues during periods of recession. Therefore, debt management would alternately reduce liquidity when monetary policy was tight and expand liquidity when monetary policy was easy. Such a policy was not forthcoming, however.

Initial attempts at debt lengthening in the first half of 1953 encountered serious difficulties.[22] After monetary policy shifted in mid-year to combat the ensuing recession, the Treasury judiciously refrained from selling long-term (over 10-year) bonds so as to avoid competition with private demands for long-term funds. However, the policy of monetary ease created a highly receptive market for government securities outside the short-term area. The Treasury's newly adopted program of optional exchange offerings[23] allowed the public, especially commercial banks, to purchase substantial quantities of intermediate-term (5–10 year) bonds. On balance, debt management was at least mildly pro-cyclical. From the end of June 1953, to December 1954, publicly held marketable Treasury debt in the 5–10 year category rose from $16.9 billion to $32.2 billion, while that under 1 year fell by $5.6 billion.[24]

With the passage of time, Treasury debt management became progressively more, rather than less, pro-cyclical. In mid-1955, the Federal Reserve moved toward a more restrictive policy and, in general, maintained restraint on commercial bank reserves until the last quarter of 1957. However, from March 1955, to September 1957, the Treasury made only a single offering of bonds. Consequently, public holdings of Treasury issues with less than 1-year to maturity rose by $16.0 billion; 1–5 year issues rose by $11.7 billion; and 5–10 year issues declined by $18.5 billion.[25] In view of its long-standing objective to lengthen the debt structure, the Treasury's failure to sell more long-term bonds during these years was undoubtedly an important factor leading to the excessive reliance on bond financing after the recession began in late 1957. In an 8-month period —from November 1957, through June 1958— there were 6 new issues of bonds. Some $3.2 billion of over 15-year bonds and $12.2 billion of intermediate-term bonds were sold to the public in cash and refunding operations. This vigorous debt lengthening program eventually resulted in the speculative market collapse following the issue of $2\frac{5}{8}$ per cent bonds in June.[26] Both the Treasury and Federal Reserve intervened on a limited scale to stabilize the market. However, by the end of the summer, at a very early stage of the recovery, long-term bond yields were back at approximately the same levels that

---

[22] In April 1953, the Treasury announced a cash issue of $3\frac{1}{4}$ per cent bonds of 1978–83. Approximately $1.1 billion of these long-term securities were sold to the public. However, the government securities market became somewhat disorganized after this issue. The Treasury was criticized in certain quarters for its decision to press for debt lengthening at that time and for the "excessive" rate of interest paid.

[23] In optional exchange offerings, holders of maturing issues are given an option between at least two new issues of varying maturities. While this technique reduces cash-ins of maturing issues, it is subject to the disadvantage of partially transferring control over the maturity structure of the debt to the public.

[24] These and subsequent figures on the maturity structure of the debt are taken from various issues of the *Federal Reserve Bulletin*. Admittedly, these figures are only broadly indicative of the liquidity impact of debt management and must be used with discretion. The use of maturity categories for liquidity analysis is subject to notorious shortcomings; i.e., all securities within a given category are not equivalent with respect to liquidity and there is likely to be a greater substitutability between certain issues in different categories than between certain issues in the same category.

[25] Treasury spokesmen stressed the difficulty of selling intermediate- and long-term bonds in the face of restrictive monetary policy and prevailing expectations of rising interest rates. Expectational forces are said to be so strong during such times that buyers cannot be found. Attempts to "force" longer-term securities on unwilling investors could result in chaotic markets. In addition to the practical difficulties of issuing longer-term securities, the higher interest costs involved may have also acted as a deterrent to debt lengthening. For an emphasis on the practical difficulties of selling government bonds, see the remarks by Under Secretary of the Treasury Baird published in *Annual Report of the Secretary of the Treasury, 1958*, pp. 275–279; the testimony of Secretary Anderson in United States Congress, Joint Economic Committee, *Employment, Growth, and Price Levels Hearings*, Part 6C, 86th Congress, 1st Session, 1959, especially pp. 1721–1729; and Secretary Anderson, "Financial Policies for Sustainable Growth," *Journal of Finance*, XV, May 1960, especially pp. 133–139.

[26] For a detailed description of this episode, see the *Treasury-Federal Reserve Study of the Government Securities Market*, Parts I–III, Washington, D.C.: Government Printing Office, 1959–1960.

had prevailed at the previous cyclical peak. The extent to which these events contributed to the unsatisfactory character of the 1958–1960 economic expansion is problematical. After the upturn in economic activity, monetary policy changed—too quickly according to many critics—[27] to "fostering . . . balanced economic recovery" (August 1958) and finally to "restraining inflationary credit expansion . . . " (May 1959).[28] During this economic expansion, the Treasury, for reasons somewhat beyond its control, again concentrated on short-term financing.[29]

During a large part of the 1953–1960 period, for whatever reasons, debt management operations exerted a pro-cyclical liquidity impact. Thus, whatever contribution the Treasury made with respect to the effectiveness of monetary policy must have taken the form of minimizing interference with central bank operations. Partly for this reason, Treasury officials continued to emphasize the importance of "tailoring" issues to the needs of the market and, beginning in 1958 and 1959, extended the auction technique to 6-month and 1-year bills and instituted non-par pricing of new issues. Following the withdrawal of direct underwriting support by the central bank, however, average attrition rates rose during successive phases of rising interest rates.[30] Based

on this evidence, it has been suggested that in appraising the effects of attrition, the Treasury widened its limits of tolerance in order to avoid direct assistance from the central bank.[31]

In retrospect, the Federal Reserve's "bills only" policy contributed to pro-cyclical debt management in two respects; yet, ironically, it is likely that the effectiveness of monetary policy was hampered at times by the pro-cyclical liquidity impact of debt management operations.[32] First, except in rare cases, the central bank restricted its own operations in public debt to the short end of the market. By this decision, the Federal Reserve voluntarily passed up opportunities to buy intermediate and long-term issues during recessions and to sell similar maturities during inflationary periods. Second, and more important because of the much larger scale of the Treasury's operations, the lack of dependable underwriting support from the central bank may have led the Treasury into undue conservatism in its choice of securities. During periods of rising interest rates, especially in 1955–1957, the Treasury was reluctant to experiment with new bond issues in the face of prevailing market expectations. By attempting to "force" bond issues on the market, the Treasury felt that it would risk a very substantial attrition. In turn, this reluctance led to exploitation of market expectations in the following recession. While it is quite unrealistic to assume that direct underwriting support by the Federal Reserve would have solved all of the Treasury's problems, it is also quite likely that the performance of debt management would have been somewhat better with such support.

[27] See, for example, Warren L. Smith, "Monetary Policy, 1957–1960: An Appraisal," *Review of Economics and Statistics*, XLII, August 1960, pp. 269–272, and Sidney Weintraub, "Monetary Policy, 1957–1959: Too Tight, Too Often," *Review of Economics and Statistics*, XLII, August 1960, pp. 279–282.

[28] *Annual Report of the Board of Governors of the Federal Reserve System, 1958*, p. 59; *Annual Report, 1959*, p. 44. In December 1958, the wording of the Open Market Committee's directive had been changed to indicate a greater degree of restraint than that indicated in August 1958.

[29] In particular, the Treasury's hands were tied for a significant part of this period by the legal interest rate ceiling of $4\frac{1}{4}$ per cent on new issues of bonds. In addition, cash requirements were exceptionally large because of the large cash deficits and the net redemption of non-marketable Treasury issues.

[30] As one study found, average attrition rates were higher from December 1954, to August 1957, than from October 1952, to June 1953, and highest of all from August 1958, to August 1959 (the cut-off date). Burton C. Hallowell and Kossuth M. Williamson, "Debt Management's Contribution to Monetary Policy," *Review of Economics and Statistics*, XLIII, February 1961, pp. 81–84.

Carson has pointed out that debt management was more "successful" in minimizing attrition from June 1951, to September 1952, when Federal Reserve support was utilized, than in the "comparable

period" of monetary restraint, November 1955, to July 1957, when Treasury support through purchases for the trust funds was utilized. Deane Carson, "Treasury Open Market Operations," *Review of Economics and Statistics*, XLI, November 1959, pp. 438–442.

[31] Hallowell and Williamson, *op. cit.*

[32] For an emphasis on the desirability of counter-cyclical debt management, see J. M. Culbertson, "A Positive Debt Management Program," *Review of Economics and Statistics*, XLI, May 1959, pp. 89–98; R. L. Bunting, "A Debt Management Proposal," *Southern Economic Journal*, XXV, January 1959, pp. 338–342; and Thomas R. Beard, "Counter-Cyclical Debt Management—A Suggested Interpretation," *Southern Economic Journal*, XXX, January 1964, pp. 244–252.

Both Gaines and Friedman, for somewhat different reasons, have proposed a "neutral" debt management policy. "Neutrality" involves maintaining a constant maturity structure of the debt regardless of economic conditions. Gaines, *op. cit.*, especially chapter 8, and Friedman, *op. cit.*, especially pp. 52–65.

## IV. The Twisting or Nudging of the Interest Rate Structure

The most recent of the three post-Accord periods of debt management policy should include, perhaps, the final portion of the 1960–61 recession as well as the low-level recovery and expansion of 1961–62.[33] Although the 1960–61 decline was relatively mild, it was especially disturbing because the economy has never completely recovered from the 1957–58 recession. While the rise in unemployment was more moderate than in the two preceding recessions, this increase was superimposed on the already high level of unemployment that had persisted at the peak of the previous expansion. Even after the trough of February 1961, unemployment remained disappointingly high—a situation apparently requiring expansionary policies of greater strength and duration than those utilized following the previous upturns in economic activity. On the other hand, the recession developed against the background of a persistent deficit in the balance of payments, a condition considerably aggravated in both 1960 and 1961 by large outflows of short-term capital. The authorities felt that the international differentials in short-term interest rates that developed in 1960 contributed to this state of affairs. Therefore, international considerations began to influence monetary and debt management policies to an extraordinary extent.[34] The main focus of these policies concerned finding methods of combatting the persistent balance of payments deficits, including the outflows of short-term capital, while, at the same time, maintaining conditions conductive to more rapid recovery and expansion.[35]

A major result of this dual concern was the inauguration of "operation nudge," which involved official attempts at "twisting" the interest rate structure. Upward pressure on short-term rates (but not the establishment of a particular floor) was considered desirable for external purposes. Downward pressure on long-term rates was sanctioned for domestic purposes. Debt management was thus elevated to a new level of importance as the major instrument of economic policy most capable of twisting the rate structure in the desired manner. This new approach to debt management presumably involved the cooperation of both the Treasury and the Federal Reserve. The decision by the Federal Reserve to conduct open market operations outside the short-term area constituted a partial abandonment of the "free market" doctrine—but only partial in the direct support of Treasury refunding was not resumed. This decision also represented some apparent change in official thinking with respect to the Federal Reserve's ability to alter the rate structure.[36]

Partly because of the unusual economic conditions, it is not surprising to find considerable debate concerning the degree of ease or tightness of monetary policy in both recession and recovery. According to public statements and testimony, the intentions of the monetary authorities were on the side of relative ease.[37] Supporters of the "easy money" interpretation have pointed to a number of indicators: the continuation of positive free reserves throughout 1961 and 1962; the usual stability of intermediate- and long-term interest rates during the recovery and expansion; the rapid rate of growth in time and savings

---

[33] While operations in longer-term issues were not sanctioned until February 1961, open market operations were extended to include issues in the 9–15 month range in the fall of 1960 in order to avoid downward pressure on bill rates. Also, in the last half of 1960 there was some expansion in short-term issues by the Treasury.

[34] The extraordinary degree of importance attached to international considerations by historical standards is emphasized in the *Annual Report of the Federal Reserve Bank of New York, 1961*, pp. 6–7. It is stated, for example,

"The hard facts of recent balance-of-payments developments, in the context of the international role of the dollar, have revised the basic framework for monetary policy in the United States. As an objective of monetary policy, the defense of the international value of the dollar has come to occupy a position alongside the goal of stable domestic growth" (p. 7).

[35] See, for example, R. V. Roosa, "Reconciling Internal and External Financial Policies," *Journal of Finance*, XVII, March 1962, pp. 1–16.

[36] In contrasting the new position with previous statements as to the System's inability to alter the rate structure, one critic was prompted to remark, "How can the Fed influence the interest rate structure for international purposes, if it cannot do so for domestic purposes?" James R. Schlesinger, "The Sequel to Bills Only," *Review of Economics and Statistics*, XLIV, May 1962, p. 185, fn. 3.

[37] See, for example, the testimony of Chairman Martin in United States Congress, Joint Economic Committee, *State of the Economy and Policies for Full Employment*, Hearings, 87th Congress, 2nd Session, 1962, pp. 601–648, and in United States Congress, Joint Economic Committee, *January 1963 Economic Report of the President*, Hearings, 88th Congress, 1st Session, 1963, pp. 337–379.

deposits in commercial banks; etc. Those who support the "tightness" view have emphasized an allegedly inadequate rate of growth in the money supply (demand deposits plus currency);[38] the high level of long-term interest rates, especially during the recession; etc.

Similarly, the impact of debt management on liquidity and the structure of interest rates is debatable. Analyzing the impact of debt management is especially difficult for at least two reasons. First, during this period, the public's holdings of marketable debt in *both* the shortest-term (under 1-year) and the longest-term (over 20-years) maturity categories registered increases. Second, the debt management operations of both the Treasury and the Federal Reserve must be considered, and this creates uncertainties. Treasury and Federal Reserve operations which have identical impacts on the maturity structure of the publicly held debt could still differ in their respective impacts on the interest rate structure. This differential impact can exist if the central bank's operations have a more pronounced effect on market expectations, and if expectations are important in determining the term structure of rates.

With respect to short-term issues, the public's holdings of under 1-year securities rose by roughly $8.6 billion (including tax anticipation issues) in the last half of 1960, by a significant $8.4 billion in 1961, and by another $2.4 billion in 1962. While increases in 1962 were moderate, the authorities emphasized the fact that public holdings of Treasury bills rose by $5.2 billion, being only partially offset by declines in coupon-bearing issues with less than one year to maturity. The bulk of the expansion in short-term issues resulted from Treasury operations. However, the central bank also made a significant contribution, especially from the point of view of the short-term interest rate objective. If the Federal Reserve had followed earlier procedures of supplying reserves only through purchasing bills, it would have been a net buyer of $3.5 billion of short-term issues in 1961–62, rather than a net seller of about $950 million.[39]

With respect to the capital market, a considerable amount of debt extension was under-

taken.[40] Due largely to the Treasury's "senior" advance refunding operations—a debt management technique first utilized in October 1960—outstanding maturities in excess of 20 years rose in the range of $1.5 billion to $2.5 billion per year from 1960–62. For largely the same reason, the arithmetic average maturity of the total marketable debt rose slightly in both 1960 and 1962, while remaining roughly unchanged in 1961. In these "senior" advance refundings, holders of outstanding $2\frac{1}{2}$ per cent bonds with from roughly $6\frac{1}{2}$–11 years to maturity were given the option of exchanging them for new issues in the range of 19–38 years to maturity.[41]

What was the impact of "senior" advance refunding on liquidity and long-term interest rates? While little analysis of advance refunding has yet appeared, it is quite possible that the impact of debt lengthening could be either overestimated or underestimated.

The sale of long-term debt is likely to have a more *immediate* impact on liquidity and long-term interest rates in a cash or regular refunding operation than in a "senior" advance refunding. When the Treasury sells long-term government bonds for cash, the total amount of bonds is increased and additional long-term funds must be found for their purchase—funds which would otherwise be available for the purchase of alternative types of long-term private issues. Likewise, the immediate market impact of regular refundings is similar even though the total volume of government debt is not increased. The maturing securities are held in large measure by short-term investors who are not interested in purchasing long-term bonds. Therefore, investors who wish to exchange for the long-term bonds will ordinarily purchase "rights" to the new issues or "when-issued" securities from dealers (who in turn acquire "rights"), and this transfer of ownership involves a considerable amount of

---

[38] See, for example, the testimony of J. M. Culbertson in *State of the Economy and Policies for Full Employment, Hearings*, pp. 417–430, and the testimony of Allan H. Meltzer in *January 1963 Economic Report of the President, Hearings*, especially pp. 595–605.

[39] "Changes in Structure of the Federal Debt," *Federal Reserve Bulletin*, XLIX, March 1963, p. 305.

[40] One of the most persistent critics of debt lengthening operations during this period has been J. M. Culbertson. In addition to his testimony cited earlier, see his paper, "The Recent Policy Mix and Its Implications," *Proceedings of the Business and Economic Statistics Section of the American Statistical Association, 1963*, pp. 362–366.

[41] The Treasury has also conducted "junior" advance refundings and pre-refunding operations. "Junior" advance refundings involve outstanding issues with 1–5 years to maturity and pre-refundings involve issues with less than 1-year to maturity. Normally, a significantly smaller extension in average maturity is accomplished in these operations than is accomplished in advance refundings of the "senior" variety.

market "churning." The "senior" advance refunding operations, however, minimize changes in ownership and the amount of new cash funds required to purchase the long-term bonds. Presumably, a large portion of the long-term bonds taken in "senior" advance refundings are substituted for the eligible issues of shorter maturity which are held by the typically long-term investors—thus minimizing the *immediate* market impact of the operation.[42]

On the other hand, the above argument tends to understate the impact of "senior" advance refundings by concentrating narrowly on the immediate market reaction. Even if the purchase of long-term governments does not immediately reduce (significantly) the flow of funds into corporates, municipals and mortgages, this undesirable effect may only be delayed or spread out over time. As the passage of time moves outstanding government bonds toward the intermediate-term range, "long-term" investors normally dispose of many of these securities in order to lengthen their portfolios through the purchase of corporates, municipals, and mortgages. By inducing investors to lengthen their portfolios through the purchase of long-term government bonds, it is likely that over a period of time the flow of funds from the intermediate sector into private long-term securities is reduced.

A related issue concerns the impact of the Federal Reserve's operations in intermediate- and long-term securities. Despite the celebrated abandonment of "bills only," it is clear that the volume of central bank operations outside the short-term area was not large. In both 1961 and 1962 combined, the Federal Reserve made net purchases outside the short-term area of only $4.4 billion, of which less than $1.2 billion were in over 5-year maturities.[43] By way of contrast, the Treasury engaged in substantial bond sales to the public in both regular and advance refundings. It is unlikely that the Federal Reserve can exert much downward pressure on interest rates—even if that were its intention—in those market sectors in which the Treasury is greatly expanding its debt operations. Furthermore, there is good evidence that the relatively small amount of bond purchases by the Federal Reserve was not normally undertaken with the specific purpose of exerting downward pressure on rates, but rather was conducted "in a manner intended to exert minimum direct influence on prevailing prices and yields."[44] Typically, the Trading Desk did not solicit offerings from dealers, but only purchased some of the securities offered at the dealers' initiative. Purchases of longer-term issues were geared largely to the objective of cushioning downward pressures on short-term rates,[45] rather than creating direct downward pressures on intermediate- and long-term rates.

For these various reasons, the extent of debt management's contribution to the remarkable stability of intermediate- and long-term rates over the 1961-62 expansion is somewhat questionable. Clearly, during the latter year, the impact of the weak recovery on expectations and the desire of commercial banks for longer-term assets[46] were both significant developments in exerting downward pressure on long-term rates. Likewise, the precise impact of debt management on liquidity is difficult to assess. Nevertheless, even with these uncertainties, one conclusion seems readily apparent—that debt management made a greater contribution to the objectives of monetary policy than was the case in the earlier era of "free markets" when debt management operations were decidedly pro-cyclical. Even if our present international difficulties should largely (and perhaps miraculously) disappear, it would be unwise for debt management to retreat to the policies of the "free market" era.

[42] Secretary Dillon has defended advance refunding as an important technique for improving the debt structure with a minimum impact on long-term rates and the flow of funds into long-term private investment. See the testimony of Secretary Dillon in United States Senate, Committee on Finance, *Advance Refunding and Debt Management, Hearings*, 87th Congress, 2nd Session, 1962, pp. 1-86, and in *State of the Economy and Policies for Full Employment*, especially pp. 666-668, 677-681, and 685-686. See, also, "Debt Management and Advance Refunding," U.S. Treasury Department, September 1960, and "Advance Refunding: A Technique of Debt Management," *Federal Reserve Bank of New York Monthly Review*, XLIV, December 1962, pp. 169-175.

[43] "Changes in Structure of the Federal Debt," *Federal Reserve Bulletin*, March 1963, p. 307.

[44] "Federal Reserve Open Market Operations in 1962," *Federal Reserve Bulletin*, XLIX, April 1963, p. 432.

[45] Apparently, the System bought intermediate- and long-term issues for two major reasons: (1) to supply reserves without exerting direct downward pressure on short-term rates; and (2) to offset the reserve effect of bill sales made to cushion downward pressure on short-term rates.

[46] Higher interest rates on time and savings deposits channeled a large volume of short-term funds into the banking system. Banks tended to invest these funds in medium- and long-term assets, thereby contributing to the actual declines in intermediate- and long-term rates during 1962.

## V. Concluding Observations

Admittedly, we do not have complete answers to all the important questions bearing on the proper relationship of debt management and monetary policy. In recent years, debt management has often been heralded as offering a unique tool for combatting external balance of payments problems without sacrificing the domestic objective of more rapid growth. Clearly, the actions of the authorities with respect to short-term rates were taken largely for external purposes. With respect to international considerations, the important questions are two-fold: (1) the extent to which debt management can push up short-term rates (especially bill rates) to higher levels than would otherwise exist; and (2) the significance of international interest rate differentials with respect to short-term capital flows.

Perhaps even more important, we need to know more about whether a *genuine* policy of "twisting" by both the Treasury and Federal Reserve is desirable for *purely domestic* purposes. Consider an expansionary debt management policy. Increasing the public's holdings of highly liquid short-term issues (to exert upward pressure on short-term rates) while reducing the public's holdings of less liquid longer-term issues (to exert downward pressure on longer-term rates) would have a desirable liquidity effect and reduce the demand for cash balances. But the strength of this effect depends upon the relative "degree of moneyness" of government securities of varying maturities—about which little is known of a precise nature.

Similarly, the extent to which debt management can actually "twist" the interest rate structure is important.[47] A policy of attempting to twist the rate structure for domestic purposes will be more desirable to the extent that: (1) long-term rates can be reduced even in the presence of higher short-term rates; (2) short-term rates are much less important than long-term rates with respect to private investment decisions; and (3) higher short-term rates discourage the holding of cash balances while lower long-term rates encourage credit expansion by financial institutions because of the greater capital values of their asset holdings.

One final observation seems relevant. The advance refunding technique has enhanced the flexibility of Treasury debt management and increased the Treasury's ability to sell long-term bonds. It is far from certain, however, what course the Treasury would pursue in the event of a future resurgence of inflationary pressures coupled with generally rising interest rates. Past experience suggests that it may become necessary for the central bank to extend limited underwriting support to the Treasury in an attempt to avoid the consequences of a serious shortening of the debt structure.[48] In such circumstances, the Federal Reserve would face a dilemma that could be framed in the following terms. To what extent would the central bank's ability to contain monetary and credit expansion be negated by a policy of supporting Treasury debt management operations? But on the other hand, in the absence of support operations, would a decidedly procyclical Treasury debt management policy seriously complicate the task of monetary restraint through the piling up of highly liquid money substitutes?

---

[47] The degree to which changes in the debt structure affect the structure of interest rates partly depends on the strength of other forces that influence the pattern of rates. Some economists consider expectations about future rates to be the predominant influence. If the expectational factor is dominant, a change in the maturity structure of the debt would by itself have little effect on the structure of interest rates. Recent empirical work by Meiselman supports the expectations approach. David Meiselman, *The Term Structure of Interest Rates*, Englewood Cliffs, N. J.: Prentice-Hall, 1962. Meiselman's approach, however, does not completely rule out any effect of debt management on the interest rate structure. Changes in the amounts of various maturities outstanding can cause expectations to change, and thus affect the prevailing interest rate structure. See John H. Wood, "Expectations, Errors, and the Term Structure of Interest Rates," *Journal of Political Economy*, LXXI, April 1963, pp. 160–171.

Some recent empirical work by Okun for the Commission on Money and Credit indicates that the effect of changes in relative supplies of various securities on the rate pattern was small for the period 1946–1959. Arthur M. Okun, "Monetary Policy, Debt Management and Interest Rates: A Quantitative Appraisal," *Stabilization Policies*, Englewood Cliffs, N. J.: Prentice-Hall, 1963, pp. 331–380. However, for an approach which gives considerable weight to the relative supplies of various securities in the market, see J. M. Culbertson, "The Term Structure of Interest Rates," *Quarterly Journal of Economics*, LXXI, November 1957, pp. 485–517. For a discussion of the great variety of factors which can shape the interest rate structure, see Stephen H. Axilrod and Ralph A. Young, "Interest Rates and Monetary Policy," *Federal Reserve Bulletin*, XLVIII, September 1962, pp. 1110–1137.

[48] Central bank underwriting, of course, cannot solve the problems created by the legal interest rate ceiling on government bonds in periods when market rates reach the critical level. The solution to this problem lies in either one of two directions. Either Congress must remove this artificial barrier to flexible debt management policy, or the Treasury must be willing to risk unpopularity and circumvent the ceiling by issuing bonds at a sufficient discount to be in line with existing market rates.

*MILTON FRIEDMAN*

# Postwar Trends in Monetary Theory and Policy

*37* The postwar period has seen a dramatic change in the views of academic students of economics about monetary theory and of governmental officials about monetary policy. At the end of the war most professional economists and most governmental officials concerned with economic policy took it for granted that money did not matter, that it was a subject of minor importance. Since then there has been something of a counter-revolution in both theory and policy.

In theory, the direction of change has been toward the earlier attitudes associated with the quantity theory of money, but with a different emphasis, derived from the Keynesian analysis, on the role of money as an asset rather than as a medium of exchange. In the field of policy, the direction of change has been away from what we might call "credit policy," i.e., policy which emphasizes rates of interest and availability of credit, and toward monetary policy, i.e., policy

Reprinted from the *National Banking Review*, Vol. II, (1964), pp. 1–9, by permission of the author and publisher. Milton Friedman is a professor at the University of Chicago. This paper is adapted from a talk given in Athens in January 1963, under the auspices of the Center for Economic Research.

which is concerned with the quantity of money. The emphasis has been away from qualitative controls and toward quantitative controls. And, finally, in the field of policy there has been renewed attention to the problem of relating internal stability to external stability. In examining these changes I shall outline briefly what the situation was at the end of the war; I shall then discuss in more detail the changes in theory that I have just sketched, and finally analyze the changes in policy.

## I. The Postwar Situation

Economic thought at the end of the war was greatly affected by the Keynesian revolution which occurred in the 1930's. Keynes himself was much less extreme in rejecting the importance of money than were some of his later disciples. Keynes stressed the particular problem of under-employment equilibrium. He argued that under such circumstances one might run into something he called absolute liquidity preference. His analysis concentrated on the relation between money, on the one hand, and bonds or other fixed interest securities, on the other. He argued that bonds were the closest substitute for money, and that in the first instance one could regard people as choosing between holding their wealth in the form of money or holding it in the form of bonds. The cost of holding wealth in the form of money was the interest that could otherwise be received on bonds. The higher the rate of interest, the less money people would want to hold and vice versa. But, Keynes said, there exists some rate of interest so low that if the rate were forced still lower nobody would hold any bonds.

At that interest rate, liquidity preference is absolute. At that rate of interest, if more money were introduced into the economy people would try to get rid of the money by buying bonds. This, however, would tend to lower the rate of interest. But even the slightest decline in the rate of interest would lead people to hold money instead. So, said Keynes, under such circumstances, with the interest rate so low that people were indifferent whether they held money or bonds, no matter what quantity of the one they held or what quantity of the other, changes in the stock of money would have no effect on anything. If the quantity of money were increased by buying bonds, for example, the only effect would be that people would substitute money for bonds. If the quantity of money were decreased by selling bonds, then the opposite effect would occur.

Keynes did not of course deny the validity of the famous quantity equation, $MV = PT$. That is an identity which is a question of arithmetic not of theory. What he said, in effect, was that in conditions of under-employment, $V$ (velocity) is a very unstable, passive magnitude. If $M$ (quantity of money) increases, $V$ will go down and the product will not change. If $M$ decreases, $V$ will go up and the product will not change. I emphasize this point in order to make clear that the question at issue is an empirical question and not a theoretical question. There was never any dispute on a purely theoretical level in this respect between Keynes and the quantity theorists.

Keynes himself felt that such a position of unstable velocity would occur only under conditions of under-employment equilibrium. He said that under conditions of inflation the quantity theory comes into its own. But some of his disciples went much farther. They argued that even under conditions less extreme than those of absolute liquidity preference, changes in the stock of money would not have any significant effect. It is true, they said, that under such

circumstances changes in the stock of money would lead to changes in interest rates. But, changes in interest rates, they argued, would have little effect on real flows of spending: the amount of money people want to invest in projects is determined by considerations other than the rate of the interest they have to pay; in technical language, the demand for investment is highly inelastic with respect to the interest rate. And consequently, they argued that, even under conditions of full employment or of inflation, changes in the quantity of money are of minor importance. An increase in $M$ would tend to lower the interest rate a little, but this in turn would have very slight effect in expanding investment. And hence, they argued, one would find again that $V$ of the $MV$ equation fluctuated widely, tending to offset changes in $M$.

The general presumption among most economists at the end of the war was that the postwar problem was going to be depression and unemployment. The problem was going to be to stimulate sufficient investment and sufficient consumption to prevent substantial unemployment. The appropriate monetary policy in their view was very simple. The monetary authorities should keep money plentiful so as to keep interest rates low. Of course, interest rates according to this view did not make much difference, but insofar as they had any effect it would be in the direction of expanding investment slightly and hence contributing to the investment that would be urgently needed to offset deficiencies of demand. Nearly two decades have elapsed since then, and it is hard now to remember how widespread these views were and how strongly they were held by people in responsible positions, as well as by economists in general. For example, in 1945, E. A. Goldenweiser who at the time was the Director of Research of the Federal Reserve Board's Division of Research and Statistics wrote:

> This country will have to adjust itself to a $2\frac{1}{2}$ per cent interest rate as the return on safe, long-time money, because the time has come when returns on pioneering capital can no longer be unlimited as they were in the past.[1]

This whole approach was shattered by the brute evidence of experience. In the first place, and most important, the problem of the postwar world turned out to be inflation and not deflation. Country after country which adopted an easy money policy because of the views I just described

[1] "Postwar Problems and Policies," *Federal Reserve Bulletin*, February 1945, p. 117.

discovered that it was faced with rising prices. Equally important, no country succeeded in stopping inflation without taking measures which had the effect of controlling the quantity of money. Italy stopped inflation in 1947. How? By measures designed to hold down the quantity of money. The experience was repeated in Germany after the monetary reform in 1948; in the U.S., after the Federal Reserve-Treasury Accord in 1951; in Britain, when it restored orthodox monetary policy in 1951 to keep prices down; in Greece; and in France, a recent (1960) addition to the list. Those countries which continued to follow low interest rate policies or continued to increase the quantity of money rapidly, continued to suffer inflation, whatever other measures they took.

Though this experience was in many ways the most important single factor that produced a radical change in attitudes toward money, it was reinforced by several other factors. One was the developments which were proceeding in the world of economic theory in the analysis and re-examination of the body of doctrine which had emerged out of the Keynesian revolution. The most important element here was the emphasis on the role of real cash balances in affecting flows of expenditures, first pointed out by Haberler and then by Pigou in several articles which received more attention. An essential element of the Keynesian approach has been the view that only substitution between money and bonds is important, that real goods or real expenditures are not an important substitute for cash balances, and that when cash balances are larger than people desire to hold, they alter solely their desired holdings of other securities. The intellectual importance of the forces brought to the fore by Haberler and Pigou was the emphasis they placed on the possibility of substitution between cash on the one hand and real flows of expenditures on the other. This contributed to a re-emphasis on the role of money.

Another development that had the same effect, in a negative way, was the disillusionment with fiscal policy. The counterpart of the Keynesian disregard for money was the emphasis placed on fiscal policy as the key element in controlling the level of aggregate demand. In the U.S. in particular, governmental expenditures have proved to be the most unstable element in the economy in the postwar years, and they have been unstable in a way that has tended to increase fluctuations rather than to decrease them. It has proved to be extremely hard to change expenditures and receipts in advance in such a way as to offset other forces making for fluctuations. This led to re-emphasis on monetary policy as a more flexible instrument which could be used in a sensitive way.

## II. Developments in Monetary Theory

Let me turn now to the developments in monetary theory that have followed this postwar experience and the re-emphasis on money as an important economic magnitude. One development has been that many economists who continue to use the Keynesian apparatus have revised their empirical presumptions. These economists now say that liquidity preference is seldom absolute, that there is some elasticity in the demand for cash balances, and that if there are changes in the stock of money there will be changes in interest rates. They say also that investment is not completely insensitive to interest rates, that when borrowing becomes more expensive, the amount spent on investment is reduced, and conversely. This view goes along with the attitude that, while money is more important than these economists used to think it was, monetary policy still can influence income only indirectly. A change in the stock of money may affect the interest rate, the interest rate may affect investment, the change in investment may affect income, but it is only by this indirect route, the argument runs that monetary changes have an effect on economic change.

This is purely a semantic question of how one wants to describe the channels of influence. The crucial issue is the empirical one of whether in fact the links between money and income are more stable and more regular than the links between investment and income. And it is on this empirical issue that the postwar evidence spoke very strongly and led to a re-examination of the role of money.

A more fundamental and more basic development in monetary theory has been the reformulation of the quantity theory of money in a way much influenced by the Keynesian liquidity preference analysis. That analysis emphasizes money as an asset that can be compared with other assets; its emphasis is on what is called "portfolio analysis," analysis of the structure of peoples' balance sheets, of the kinds of assets they want to hold. This emphasis looks at monetary theory as part of capital theory, or the theory of wealth. This is a rather different emphasis than that derived from earlier approaches, particularly that of Irving Fisher, which put major emphasis on transactions and on money as a mechanical medium of exchange somehow connected with the transactions process.

The emphasis on money as an asset has gone in two different directions. On the one hand, it has led to emphasis on *near moneys*, as an alternative source of liquidity. One example is the work of Gurley and Shaw and their analysis of financial intermediaries as providing money substitutes. Another example, in its most extreme form, is in the Radcliffe Committee report which attempts to widen the concept of money to make it synonymous with the concept of liquidity, itself an undefined term which covers the universe. My own view is that this particular trail toward widening the range of reference of the concept of money is a false trail. It will peter out and will not in fact be followed. The reaction which the Radcliffe Committee analysis has received among academic economists and others seems to suggest that my opinion is widely shared.

The other direction in which the emphasis on money as an asset has led is toward the development of a theory of the demand for money along the same lines as the theory of the demand for other assets and for commodities and services. In such a theory, one asks what determines the amount of cash balances that people want to hold. Here it is essential to distinguish between cash balances in two senses: nominal cash balances, the nominal quantity of money as defined in terms of monetary units such as drachmas, dollars, and so forth; and real cash balances, the real stock of money as defined in terms of command over goods and services.

The essential feature of the quantity theory of money in both its older versions and its more recent and modern version is the assertion that what really matters to people is not the number of things called drachmas or dollars they hold but the real stock of money they have, the command which those pieces of paper give them over goods and services. In talking about the demand for money, one must ask what determines the command over goods and services that people want to keep in the form of money. For example, take a very simple definition of money as consisting only of currency, of the pieces of paper we carry in our pockets. We must then ask what determines whether the amount that people hold is on the average equal to a little over six weeks' income, as it is in Greece, or a little over four weeks' income, as it is in the U.S., or five weeks' income, as it is in Turkey. Thus, when we talk

about the demand for money, we must be talking about the demand for real balances in the sense of command over goods and services, and not about nominal balances.

In the theory of demand as it has been developed, the key variables include *first*, wealth or some counterpart of wealth, for example, income or, preferably, something like permanent income which is a better index of wealth than measured income. Because the problem is one of balance sheet, the first restriction is that there is a certain total amount of wealth which must be held in the form of money, or bonds, or other securities, or houses, or automobiles, or other physical goods, or in the form of human earning capacity. Hence, income or wealth acts as a restraint in determining the demand for money in exactly the same way that the total income people have operates to determine their demand for shoes or hats or coats by setting a limit to aggregate expenditures. The *second* set of variables that is important is the rates of return on substitute forms of holding money. Here, the most important thing that has happened has been a tendency to move away from the division of assets into money and bonds that Keynes emphasized, into a more pluralistic division of wealth, not only into bonds but also into equities and real assets. The relevant variables therefore are the excepted rate of return on bonds, the expected rate of return on equities and the expected rate of return on real property, and each of these may of course be multiplied by considering different specific assets of each type. A major component of the expected rate of return on real property is the rate of change in prices. It is of primary importance when there is extensive inflation or deflation.

I should like to stress the significance of the emphasis on money as one among many assets, not only for the kinds of variables that people consider as affecting the demand for money, but also for the process of adjustment. According to the earlier view of money as primarily a medium of exchange, as something which is used to facilitate transactions between people, it was fairly natural to think of a short link between changes in the stock of money and changes in expenditure and to think of the effects of changes in the stock of money as occurring very promptly. On the other hand, according to the more recent emphasis, money is something more basic than a medium of transactions; it is something which enables people to separate the act of purchase from the act of sale. From this point of view, the role of money is to serve as a temporary abode of purchasing power. It is this view that is fostered by considering money as an asset or as part of wealth.

Looked at in this way, it is plausible that there will be a more indirect and complicated process of adjustment to a change in the stock of money than looked at the other way. Moreover, it seems plausible that it will take a much longer time for the adjustment to be completed. Suppose there is a change in the stock of money. This is a change in the balance sheet. It takes time for people to readjust their balance sheets. The first thing people will do is to try to purchase other assets. As they make these purchases, they change the prices of those assets. As they change the prices of those assets, there is a tendency for the effect to spread further. The ripples spread out as they do on a lake. But as prices of assets change, the *relative* price of assets, on the one hand, and flows, on the other hand, also change. And now people may adjust their portfolios not only by exchanging assets but by using current income to add to, or current expenditures to subtract from, certain of their assets and liabilities. In consequence, I think that this reformulation of monetary theory with its emphasis on monetary theory as a branch of the theory of wealth has very important implications for the process of adjustment and for the problem of time lags.

## III. Developments in Monetary Policy

Policy does not always have a close relation to theory. The world of the academic halls and the world of policy makers often seem to move on two wholly different levels with little contact· between them. The developments in postwar monetary policy have not been the same throughout the world. However, the makers of monetary policy in different countries have been in closer and more systematic touch with one another than the monetary theorists. As a result, I think one can speak to some extent of general trends in policy without necessarily referring to the country.

As I indicated earlier, I think two features dominate and characterize the trends in postwar monetary policy. The first is the shift of emphasis away from credit policy and toward monetary policy. I think this is a distinction of first rate importance, and yet one which is much neglected. Therefore let me say a word about the meaning of this distinction. When I refer to credit policy, I mean the effect of the actions of monetary authorities on rates of interest, terms of lending, the ease with which people can borrow, and conditions in the credit markets. When I refer to monetary policy, I mean the effect of the actions of monetary authorities on the stock of money— on the number of pieces of paper in people's pockets, or the quantity of deposits on the books of banks.

Policy makers, and central bankers in particular, have for centuries concentrated on credit policy and paid little attention to monetary policy. The Keynesian analysis, emphasizing interest rates as opposed to the stock of money, is only the latest rationalization of that concentration. The most important earlier rationalization was the so-called real bills doctrine. The belief is still common among central bankers today that, if credit were somehow issued in relation to productive business activities, then the quantity of money could be left to itself. This notion of the real bills doctrine goes back hundreds of years; it is endemic with central bankers today. It understandably derives from their close connection with commercial banking, but it is basically fallacious.

The emphasis on credit policy was closely linked with the emphasis at the end of the war on qualitative controls. If what matters is who borrows and at what rate, then it is quite natural to be concerned with controlling the specific use of credit and the specific application of it. In the U.S., for example, emphasis on credit policy was linked with emphasis on margin controls on the stock market, and with controls over real estate credit and installment credit. In Britain, it was linked with controls over hire purchase credit. In each of these cases, there was a qualitative policy concerned with credit conditions. The failure of the easy money policy and of these techniques of qualitative control promoted a shift both toward less emphasis on controlling specific rates of return and toward more emphasis on controlling the total quantity of money.

The distinction that I am making between credit and monetary policy may seem like a purely academic one of no great practical importance. Nothing could be farther from the truth. Let me cite the most striking example that I know; namely, U.S. experience in the great depression from 1929 to 1933. Throughout that period the Federal Reserve System was never concerned with the quantity of money. It did not in fact publish monthly figures of the quantity of money until the 1940's. Indeed, the first mention in Federal Reserve literature of the quantity of money as a criterion of policy was in the 1950's. Prior to that time there was much emphasis upon easy or tight money, by which was meant low or high interest rates. There was much emphasis on the availability of loans, but there was no emphasis and no concern with the quantity of money.

If there had been concern with the quantity of money *as such*, we could not have had the great depression of 1929–33 in the form in which we had it. If the Federal Reserve System had been concerned with monetary policy in the sense in which I have just defined it, it literally would have been impossible for the System to have allowed the quantity of money in the U.S. to decline from 1929 to 1933 by a third, the largest decline in the history of the U.S. in that length of time. In reading many of the internal papers of the Federal Reserve Board during that period, the communications between the various governors of the Federal Reserve Banks and the Board of Governors, and so forth, I have been struck with the lack of any quantitative criterion of policy. There are vague expressions about letting the market forces operate. There are comments about "easy" money or "tight" money but no indication of precisely how a determination is to be made whether money is "easy" or "tight." This distinction between emphasis on credit policy and emphasis on monetary policy is a distinction of great importance in the monetary history of the U.S., and I think also in the monetary history of other countries.

The failure of the easy money policy was reinforced by another factor which promoted a shift in policy away from qualitative measures involving control of particular forms of credit, and toward quantitative measures involving concern with changes in the stock of money. This other factor was a reduction of exchange controls and quantitative restrictions on international trade, as in the postwar period one country after another began to improve its international position. There was a move toward convertibility in international payments. This shift toward convertibility led to a reduction of emphasis on qualitative direct controls and toward increased emphasis on general measures that would affect the course of events through altering the conditions under which people engaged in trade. In turn, this led to a final development in monetary policy—the renewed concern about the relation between internal monetary policy and external policy, the problem of the balance of payments. In this area we have had, most surprisingly of all I think, a return to an earlier era of something approximating a gold standard.

In the immediate postwar period, concern with the balance of payments tended to be centered in the countries of Western Europe that were having a so-called dollar shortage. Those countries were at that time facing the problem of recurrent drains of their international reserves. They were in the position of having somehow to restrain their residents from converting their local currencies into foreign currencies. Those were also the countries that emerged from the war with fairly extensive exchange controls and direct restrictions on trade. And thus in the first years after the war the solution to this problem took the form of direct control rather than of monetary policy.

At that time the U.S. was in a very different position. It was gaining gold and it was able to take the position that it could conduct its monetary policy entirely in terms of internal conditions and need pay no attention to the effects that its policies had abroad. Of course, that was not what happened. There is little doubt that during the immediate postwar period the ease in the U.S. gold position contributed toward a greater readiness to accept inflation than would otherwise have prevailed, so that the ease in the international balance produced a relatively easier monetary policy than we otherwise would have had. But once the U.S. started selling gold on net instead of buying gold on net, to use a more accurate term than the term "losing gold," the situation changed drastically and the U.S. itself became much more concerned with the effect of monetary policy and much more driven toward a pre-World War I gold standard approach.

In recent years, the concern with the international balance of payments has given rise to greater co-operation among central banks. They have tried to develop techniques which will assure that any temporary drains on the reserves of one country will be matched by offsetting movements by central banks in the other countries. Despite the immense amount of good will and of human ingenuity that has gone into this effort to avoid payments difficulties through central bank co-operation, I must confess that I regard the tendency as an exceedingly dangerous one. The danger is that the arrangements developed will provide an effective system for smoothing minor difficulties but only at the cost of permitting them to develop into major ones.

I am much struck by the analogy between what is now happening in this respect and what happened in the U.S. between 1919 and 1939. The U.S. in that earlier period developed a monetary system which turned out to be an effective device for smoothing minor difficulties. The system was highly successful in helping to make the years from 1922 to 1929 relatively stable. But this stability was purchased at the cost of major difficulties from 1920 to 1921, from 1929 to 1933, and again from 1937 to 1938. I very much fear that the same results may emerge from present trends toward international co-operation among central banks, because these measures do not go to the root of the problem of international adjustment.

In international financial arrangements, as in personal finances, the problem of having enough liquid assets to meet temporary drains must be sharply distinguished from the adjustment to changed circumstances. The central bank arrangements look only to providing liquidity for temporary drains. More fundamental adjustment to changed circumstances can come only through either: (1) domestic monetary and fiscal policy directed toward holding down or reducing domestic prices relative to foreign prices when the country is experiencing a deficit, or toward permitting domestic prices to rise relative to foreign prices when the country is experiencing a surplus; (2) changes in exchange rates to achieve a similar alteration in the relative level of domestic and foreign prices when expressed in the same currency; or (3) direct measures designed to alter the flows of receipts or expenditures, such as changes in tariffs, subsidies, and quotas, direct or indirect control of capital movements, restrictions on foreign aid or other governmental expenditures, extending ultimately to that full panoply of foreign exchange controls that strangled Western Europe after the war and remains today one of our most unfortunate gifts to many underdeveloped countries.

The great danger is that central bank co-operation and other means to enlarge liquidity, by providing palliatives that can at best smooth over temporary imbalances, will encourage countries to postpone undertaking such fundamental adjustments to changed circumstances. The consequence will be to allow minor imbalances to accumulate into major ones; to convert situations that could have been corrected by gradual and minor monetary tightness or ease, or by small

movements in exchange rates, into situations that would require major changes in monetary policy or exchange rates. The consequence is likely to be not only international financial crises, but also the encouragement of the use of the third method of adjustment, direct controls. Paradoxically, most economists and most policy makers would agree that it is the worst of the three; yet it is the one that has most regularly been resorted to in the postwar period.

These developments in monetary policy are much more difficult to pin down precisely than the developments in monetary theory, as may be expected from the fact that monetary policy is and must be much more a matter of opportunism, of day-to-day adjustment, of meeting the particular problems of the time. The theorist can sit in his ivory tower and make sure that his structure is coherent and consistent. This is, I must say, an advantage of the theorist and a great disadvantage of the policy maker, and not the other way around. But I think it is clear that we are likely to see in the future still further developments in monetary policy.

There is almost invariably a long cultural lag before developments in theory manifest themselves in policy. If you were to look at what is being proposed today in domestic policy in the U.S., you would say that my analysis of changes in the field of monetary theory must be a figment of my imagination. The policy proposals that are being made in the U.S. today are all reflections of the ideas of the late 1930's, or at the latest of the early 1940's. That is natural and widespread. The people who make policy, who are involved in policy formation, are inevitably people who got their training and their education and their attitudes some 20 or more years earlier. This is a special case of a much more general phenomenon. I am sure all are aware of that famous book by A. V. Dicey on *Law and Public Opinion in the 19th Century*, the main thesis of which is precisely that trends in ideas take about 20 years before they are effective in the world of action. What is happening in the U.S. today is a dramatic illustration of his thesis. And so I expect that monetary policy will in the course of the next 20 years show some radical changes as a result of the changes I have described in monetary theory.

# *Fiscal Policy*

*N*OWHERE IN THE realm of macroeconomics is there as much controversy and public misinformation as in the area of fiscal policy. Argument and indecision seem to rage continually at the highest political levels regarding the desirability of employing fiscal policies in an effort to avoid inflation and unemployment. One of the most controversial subjects involves the budgets of the United States government and whether or not one or another of them should be balanced over some period of time.

This group of articles opens with Arthur Smithies' discussion of the balanced budget controversy. The Smithies article is followed by two selections in which Daniel Hamberg and the Council of Economic Advisors examine past United States fiscal activities in relation to the conditions which existed in the economy. Then D. J. Smyth considers the effectiveness, for stabilization purposes, of the automatic changes in the levels of an economy's taxes and other fiscal activities which occur where there are changes in the economy's level of income. The section is concluded with three articles on the subject of government budgets. In the first, Joseph Scherer describes the present form of the government's budgets. Then Richard Musgrave discusses the possibility of the United States adopting a capital budget, and Francis Bator considers some aspects of budgetary reform.

*ARTHUR SMITHIES*

# The Balanced Budget

38

**I**

For over a quarter of a century, economists, or the majority of them, have been protesting against the dogma that the annually balanced budget is the path of financial virtue. I regret to have to report that we have made remarkably little headway at the high political levels. Depite the economists, or perhaps because of them, every President has clung tenaciously to the dogma. President Roosevelt's papers clearly reveal that he regarded budget deficits as an evil that had to be tolerated in order to achieve a greater good. The published views of President Truman make his views on the subject abundantly clear. The spoken utterances of President Eisenhower leave no doubt about where he stands on the matter. But despite our failure to demolish this pillar of the financial temple, there seems to be general acceptance of the view that deficits, though evil, are inevitable during depressions. The 12 billion dollar deficit in 1958 does not seem to have been grist to anyone's

political mill—perhaps because everyone participated in creating it. But 1959 and 1960 have seen desperate if not ruthless efforts not only to achieve a balanced budget but to achieve balance at the pre-existing level of taxation. I can easily visualize the tortured sessions in the Budget Bureau and the Treasury that produced a surplus of 100 million dollars in the President's budget for fiscal 1960. I imagine similar sessions are going on this minute with respect to fiscal 1961.

Adherence to the dogma is so strong that we are prepared to delay vital defense programs in order to pay lip service to it. The government is also willing to impair the budgetary process itself in order to preserve the semblance of balance. As one spectacular example, I can find no indication of the capital cost of post office construction in the President's 1959 budget. Even though the government has decided to buy its post offices on time, surely the public is entitled to know how many post offices are being bought. If rationality rather than dogma dictated attitudes towards the budget, there might be less incentive for deception.

The survival of the balanced budget rule, however, is not entirely a matter of dogma. Indivi-

Reprinted from the *American Economic Review: Papers and Proceedings*, Vol. L (1960), pp. 301–309, by permission of the author and publisher. Arthur Smithies is a professor at Harvard University.

duals and groups with no dogmatic convictions have a strong interest in keeping the dogma alive. The classical objection to government debt was a natural reaction to the consequences of government extravagance during the seventeenth and eighteenth centuries.[1]

The requirement of a balanced budget was and still is the simplest and clearest rule to impose "fiscal discipline" and to hold government functions and expenditure to a minimum. Those who still entertain this desire as an overriding objective may be well advised not to retreat from the general rule until they are reasonably sure that the retreat will not become a rout.

The advocates of unbalanced budgets have not been reassuring from the conservative point of view. The unbalanced budget usually means fiscal freedom, borrowing, and deficits, and not deficits or surpluses as the occasion demands. The New Deal deficits were associated not simply with recovery but with recovery and reform; and when the New Deal was in full flower, the President took pains to insist that recovery was inseparable from reform.

Even an avowedly countercyclical fiscal policy is believed to give rise to an upward trend in expenditures that might not otherwise occur. The expenditures undertaken to counteract a depression are unlikely to be discontinued in the succeeding boom. If the boom is countered at all, the measures taken will be credit restriction or increased taxation; and then further expenditure programs will be taken to offset the next depression. The increased expenditures hastily undertaken to meet the 1958 recession indicate that this possibility is by no means academic.

The discipline of the balanced budget is not necessarily the right degree of discipline. It is generally agreed that in time of war the unwilling taxpayer should not be allowed to hamper the defense of the country. The taxpayer is supposed to come into his own in times of peace. But the present situation is neither peace nor war. Despite amiable conversations among heads of state, a permanent state of military readiness for the indefinite future will be imperative. Organized groups of taxpayers have not shown a clear appreciation of the situation. The President and the leaders of Congress must have some freedom to act even though they cannot pay the bills from current revenue. But if all notions of fiscal discipline and budget balance were removed and no alternative was provided, there can be no

doubt that expenditures would increase to a level that was economically undesirable and politically demoralizing. However rich we become, public and private wants are likely to increase more rapidly than the means of satisfying them; and in our complex political system some rules of financial conduct that are simple enough to survive in a political context seem to me to be desirable.

## II

Nevertheless, the rule that the budget should be balanced annually is inadequate to secure the proper allocation of resources between the public and the private sectors. The objections to it have been stated time and again. I shall therefore confine myself to a brief summary of those I consider the most important.

First, to attempt to balance the budget on an annual basis is inconsistent with the long-range character of many government programs. Research, development, and procurement for defense purposes inevitably involve activities extending over a number of years. If the programs are well conceived in the first place, waste and inefficiency will result from disrupting them in order to achieve particular budget results. I remember that on one occasion during the Korean war the government deferred payments to contractors for the sake of the appearance on the budget and naturally had to pay a high rate of interest to them as compensation for waiting for their money. Again, it is wasteful to suspend work on a battleship for the sake of avoiding disbursements at a particular time. Perhaps the battleship should not have been started; but to leave it half-finished for a time simply adds to its cost.

Another case where the requirement of annual balance is disruptive is the foreign aid program. This program is the favorite target for indignant charges of waste and inefficiency. But there is no surer way to waste and ineffectiveness than to expose our own program to such vicissitudes and uncertainties that the receiving countries are unable to mesh their own activities with it. Everyone who has examined the problem with understanding and sympathy has stressed the need for continuity.

With respect to the question of "annuality," the economists and the accountants are in league against effective government operations. The accountants like to clean up their books every year and hence stress the need for annual control. The economists take the same point of view because they want a flexible fiscal system whose

[1] For an admirable survey of the history of the balanced budget doctrine, see Jesse V. Burkhead, "The Balanced Budget," reprinted in *Readings in Fiscal Policy* (A.E.A., 1955).

impact on the economy can be varied from year to year as a contribution to general economic stability. Some compromise between the programming and the annual points of view is clearly needed. Neither can be ignored. But a satisfactory compromise, in my opinion, requires less strict adherence than we now attempt to the annual point of view.

A second objection to the balanced budget rule is that stress on the balanced budget as a criterion tends to give the misleading impression that the government is well managed if the budget is balanced. The examples I have just given illustrate this point, but, more generally, there is no indication that some over-all rule will secure efficiency down the line. When budget requests are cut to conform to the rule, the programs most likely to suffer are the new ones designed to meet new situations; and those most likely to survive are those that have acquired the support of powerful vested interests inside or outside the government. Not all new activities are necessarily more meritorious than the old, but some of them are. The way we now seem to be placidly accepting the Russian lead in space exploration—presumably for budgetary reasons—is a vivid illustration of my point.

Government efficiency cannot be achieved by budget ceilings imposed at the behest of hard-headed budget directors and appropriations committees. While some discipline of this kind is probably inevitable, the solution must lie in application of the economics of choice, subject to budget constraints, at every level of government. Public administrators traditionally do not learn economics, and vested interests have a strong interest in avoiding the application of economic principles.

The third objection relates to the effect of the balanced budget on economic fluctuations. Surely it is now agreed by economists that attempts, especially successful ones, to balance the budget every year worsen economic fluctuations. If governments curtail their expenditures when they are short of revenues and expand them when yields rise as a result of economic prosperity, their activities will be cyclical rather than counter-cyclical. It may be argued that I am stressing income effects and ignoring the monetary consequences of the balanced budget. The pre-Keynesian view was that depression cuts of expenditures released funds for the private economy. But the decisive objection to this point of view is that a central bank can do the same thing, so that the country can have the benefit of both income and monetary effects.

My final objection is that the balanced budget will not necessarily be the policy needed for achieving desired rates of economic growth. One of the unhappy ironies of the present time is that although the country is richer than it has ever been, further growth is becoming an explicit objective of policy—at a time when we should be enjoying the euphoria of John Stuart Mill's stationary state. We are not prepared to get the additional resources needed for national security and social welfare by cutting back on consumption. That would mean higher taxes. We must therefore grow in order to obtain more resources. Some eminent authorities maintain that the American economy must grow at 5 per cent a year instead of its traditional 3 per cent. If accelerated growth is required, it seems to me very likely that the total rate of national saving must be increased, and the only practicable way to increase total saving is through the generation of budget surpluses. Budgetary doctrine in this country has hardly begun to contemplate this possibility.

### III

A more general objection to the balanced budget or any other budgetary rule is that it places unnecessary restrictions on ability to achieve a variety of economic policy objectives. In terms of Tinbergen's now famous proposition, the requirement of balance may leave the government with fewer instruments than it has targets; and consequently may mean that objectives more important than balance must be ignored or that new instruments must be discovered.

The point can be illustrated very simply. Let us ignore for the moment pressing issues such as inflation and the balance of payments and assume that the government has only three policy objectives: first, it must spend enough to give effect to foreign and domestic policy objectives; second, it must maintain full employment; and, third, it must ensure that private investment will, in each year, be carried out at the rate required to maintain a given rate of economic growth for the economy as a whole. Thus every year it has three fixed targets: national income or output, private investment, and government expenditures. With present institutional arrangements, convictions, and predilections, it is virtually restricted to three instruments; namely, appropriations, taxation, and general credit expansion or contraction.

If the government has freedom to use these three instruments, it can attain the three objectives. If in addition it must balance the budget or maintain any prescribed relationship between expenditures and revenues, it has set for itself a fourth objective and is consequently one instrument short.

So long as it possesses only the three instruments, some other must give way: growth, full employment, or the government's own programs. As a matter of fact, during the last few years the government has placed even more severe restrictions on itself. It has attempted not only to balance the budget but to balance it at existing levels of taxation. This means that it has denied itself the use of one instrument. The expenditure objective necessarily gives way to this requirement (insofar as the requirement is met), and the government is left with general credit policy to achieve both full employment and a satisfactory rate of growth—a task that it is logically and practically impossible for the harassed monetary authorities to perform. Their difficulties are compounded when in addition they are expected to help correct the balance of payments and to prevent inflation.

If the government is short of instruments, it must acquire new instruments if it is to attain its objectives. Such new instruments could be selective credit controls, selective tax measures, and various kinds of direct controls. It would take me too far afield to discuss these possibilities in detail. Suffice it to say that many of them are pure anathema to those who must vehemently support the balanced budget doctrine. They are likely to be required to pay a high price for the dogma.

## IV

We are unlikely to achieve full coherence in the formation of fiscal and budget policy. Some incoherence is likely to remain so long as there is separation of powers between the President and Congress and between the powerful committees of the Congress. Nevertheless, considerable improvement is possible and feasible. To be optimistic about that, one only has to reflect on the extent to which economic thinking has penetrated the government since World War II, largely as an outcome of the Employment Act of 1946 and the institutions set up under it. I therefore consider it worth while to offer some suggestions concerning the directions that improvement might take.

First of all, the President should transmit his budget to Congress as part of a comprehensive economic program. This is not done at the present time. The present Budget Message is notable for its lack of economic analysis. The President's Economic Report, on the other hand, is equally notable for its lack of an analysis of the economic impact of the budget. However much they may consort in private, the Budget Bureau and the Council of Economic Advisers do not embrace in public. The President's program would analyze economic policy as a whole in terms of the variety of objectives to be attained and the instruments to be employed.

With respect to the budget itself, the President would recommend a surplus, balance, or a deficit, depending on economic conditions. If a deficit were proposed, this should be proposed as a positive recommendation, not as a confession of failure to balance the budget combined with a wistful hope that balance will be achieved next year.

This approach could have the same disciplinary value as the balanced budget. If the President were prepared to give the weight of his authority to the need for a surplus or a deficit of a certain amount, that should have the same disciplinary value as balance from the point of view of the Congress and the executive departments.

For this suggestion to be as effective as possible, the Congress would have to co-operate. In particular, the Joint Economic Committee should join with the Appropriations Committee and the Ways and Means Committee in considering the President's program and in formulating Congressional economic and budgetary policy. But such a change in Congressional procedure is unlikely to come about unless the President takes the lead.

Second, the President's economic program should distinguish between long-run economic policy and the policy needed to counteract particular episodes of boom and recession. The long-run policy should contemplate continuity in government operations and continued growth of the economy. Budgetary policy in particular should be designed to conform with the requirements of long-run growth.

Of course long-run policy would be revised from year to year, to take account of changing circumstances and to correct errors in diagnosis. But in the absence of violent changes, say in defense requirements, it seems unlikely that abrupt changes in the relation of government expenditures to revenues would be required. Consequently, some simple budgetary rule that should apply in normal circumstances may be feasible. In times of full employment without inflation, it could be said that the budget should have a surplus or a deficit of some known order of magnitude.

It follows that the basic revenue and expenditure estimates should be made and published with reference to a full employment situation rather than to the situation actually predicted. This is the stabilizing budget approach that has long been advocated by the Committee for Economic Development, but which has made very little headway in official circles.

I suggest, also, that if the government's policy is to keep a stable price level, the expenditure and revenue estimates should be made in stable prices. This procedure provides an automatic check on inflation. It would tend to prevent inflationary increase in revenues from being regarded as a substitute for taxation. It would also put some pressure on the spending agencies in the event of inflation. They should make some contribution by attempting to curtail their activities. But if they consider that impossible, they should demonstrate the fact in requests for supplemental appropriations.

Thirdly, the question of countercyclical policy should be dealt with in a separate chapter of the President's program. This would include a discussion of the effects of recessions or booms on the budget and recommendations concerning the budgetary measures needed as correctives.

In view of what I said above, long-range government procurement programs should be interfered with as little as possible for cyclical policies. Nor should new programs that will last for a number of years be hastily adopted merely for the sake of relieving a single recession. This, however, does not mean that all public works should be continued at the same rate regardless of booms and depressions. Highway construction and many items authorized by the Rivers and Harbors Bill can be adjusted to short-term economic needs.

However, if the main emphasis were placed on charges in taxation and transfer payments for purposes of short-run stability, the inefficiencies connected with abrupt alterations in expenditure programs could be avoided. The 1958 recession furnishes a good example. The government refused to use tax reduction as its fiscal weapon, and consequently got large and ill-considered increases in expenditures which will continue long after the antidepression need for them has passed. Nevertheless, I believe at the time and still believe that the tax route would have been wrong. Taxes once reduced are notoriously hard to restore. In fact it is hard to think of any tax increases during the last thirty years that were not undertaken in response to emergency situations. Even the tax increases of the New Deal come under that

category. If the existing tax rates are likely to be needed for long-run purposes, it is of questionable wisdom to reduce them for short-run reasons, unless the reduction can be of an explicitly temporary character.

This leads me, and has led many others, to the conclusion that short-run stability should be achieved as far as possible through "built-in flexibility" of the budget and through monetary measures that can be readily reversed.

Built-in flexibility has increased appreciably as a result of social security, unemployment compensation, and agricultural support on the expenditure side and through the automatic operation of the tax system. But such measures—even in conjunction with vigorous credit measures—are unlikely to meet the requirements of a severe recession. There is need for further automatic measures. Consequently, I venture to repeat a proposal in which I participated some years ago.[2] Under certain specified signs of recession, there should be an automatic reduction in the first bracket of the income tax. The reduction should be restored automatically when recovery has reached a prescribed point. To guard against inappropriate use of the remedy, its application should be subject to veto by the President. Devices such as this could give reasonable assurance that anything but the deepest depression would be corrected and would help materially to avoid the psychological conditions that might produce depressions of the catastrophic kind.

Our proposal was considered in the chancelleries of the world and was unanimously rejected by respectable opinion. Had it been in effect it would have been very serviceable in 1958. Automatic reversible devices are the most effective way to avoid the radical political consequences of a flexible fiscal policy, and thus to allay the fears of those who cling to the balanced budget rule on rational rather than superstitious grounds.

To return finally to the long-run question. I have suggested that surpluses rather than deficits may be needed in the future—if the government pursues an economic policy that is consonant with national and international needs. But surpluses are hard to achieve. Senator Taft once remarked that in his long experience, surpluses and debt retirement occurred only through inadvertence. If that is true, perhaps the balanced budget doctrine has some long-run merit after all.

---

[2] See the United Nations Report, *National and International Measures for Full Employment* (1950).

D. HAMBERG

# Fiscal Policy and Stagnation Since 1957

*39* Since 1957 the economy of the United States has been marked by an alarmingly slow rate of growth, deficient demand, and growing unemployment. As has happened before, the specter of secular inflation has been replaced by the specter of secular stagnation. Recent events have started many wondering whether the U. S. economy is saving too much—at least relative to the investment outlets available in the private sector of the economy. In a sense, this appears to have been the case, but largely because of budgetary behavior in the Federal sector. This source of the recent slowdown in the growth of our economy will be examined in the main part of this paper, Section II. Before doing so, however, to provide an analytical framework for this discussion, we shall present an adaptation of a set of tools, familiar to economists, which is designed to provide the basis for determining the nature of secular trends. Generally, the difficulties involved in efforts to analyze these trends seem to be associated with an inability to say something concrete about potential (private) investment outlets. It is this gap which the model presented below is meant to fill—in a rough way.

Reprinted from the *National Banking Review*, Vol. II (1964), pp. 1–9, by permission of the author and publisher. Milton Friedman is a professor at the University of Chicago.

## I. Saving vs. Investment Outlets in a Growing Economy

We begin by defining the well-known *natural*, or ceiling, growth rate. The natural rate of growth is that growth rate which, in the presence of full employment, is permitted by the growth in the labor force and the rate of technological progress (measured in terms of advances in output per worker). It is this growth rate that provides the basis for estimating capital requirements or investment outlets in the private sector of the economy (with certain qualifications set forth below).

Specifically, this natural growth rate is one whose capital requirements are, at a given rate of interest, set by the combined growth in labor force and production techniques. For example, assume that a 1.5 per cent annual growth in labor force and a 2 per cent annual growth in output per worker determine a potential growth in national income of (approximately) 3.5 per cent a year. If the (marginal) capital-output ratio is 3, then the demand for capital will approximate 10.5 per cent of national income. Algebraically, this proposition may be written as:

$$\frac{\Delta Y}{Y_n} \times \frac{\Delta K}{\Delta Y} = \frac{\Delta K}{Y_n} = \frac{I}{Y_n} \qquad (1)$$

where $\Delta Y/Y_n$ represents the natural (percentage)

rate of growth of national income and output, as determined by the growth rates of labor force and productivity, and $\Delta K/\Delta Y$ represents the marginal capital-output ratio, where $\Delta K$ stands for the increase in capital stock, or net investment, I.

With the possible exception, equation (1) gives the long-run demand for capital, at a given rate of interest, in complete or exhaustive fashion. Ultimately, there are only three sources of demand for capital: (1) to equip a growing labor force at a given capital-labor ratio; (2) to provide for the implementation of new techniques; and (3) to provide additional capital per head of working population and hence per unit of output in response to a fall in (long-term) interest rates.[1] Thus it will be seen that a variation in labor force growth, or technological progress as it affects the growth in labor productivity, as well as the value of the capital coefficient, or changes in the rate of interest, as these affect this coefficient, will alter the capital requirements associated with the natural growth rate. From the small and slow changes in the capital-output ratio (at full utilization) over long periods of time, it appears that the assumption of constancy in this ratio for periods of five years or so will serve as a fairly good approximation to reality.

One possible source of investment demand not covered by the above analysis derives from shifts in the composition of the national product in favor of industries with capital-output ratios larger than those of the industries from which demand has shifted. However, on the one hand, this factor can work both ways; that is, shifts in the composition of output can move in favor of industries with capital coefficients smaller than those of the lagging industries. On the other hand, in principle this factor can be handled in the above model by viewing the capital-output ratio as a weighted average for the private sector as a whole.

In opposition, as it were, to the natural growth rate, we have one which, with a given capital-output ratio, will fulfill the standard equilibrium condition of equating planned saving and investment. Given the (full employment) saving ratio, $S/Y$, and the capital coefficient, $\Delta K/\Delta Y$, we can write

$$\frac{\Delta Y}{Y} \times \frac{\Delta K}{\Delta Y} = \frac{S}{Y} \qquad (2)$$

or

$$\frac{\Delta K}{Y} = \frac{S}{Y} \qquad (3)$$

or since by definition $\Delta K = I$,

$$\frac{I}{Y} = \frac{S}{Y} \qquad (4)$$

Thus it is that rate of income growth, $\Delta Y/Y$, in (2) is with the given saving and capital-output ratios an equilibrium growth rate in the sense of equating planned saving and investment. This growth rate may also be called the full-capacity growth rate, because in equalizing planned saving and investment its realization assures that aggregate demand will grow apace with the growth in productive capacity (incremental capital stock) originating in the net investment associated with it.

We now have before us a tool for rendering (rough) judgments about whether an economy is saving and investing too little or too much, whether, in other words, it is faced with secular exhilaration or secular stagnation. From equation (4) we find that associated with equilibrium or full-capacity growth is a certain rate of capital accumulation or net investment. From equation (1) we find that associated with the natural growth rate (or *full employment* growth rate, because in the nature of it, the natural growth rate assures full employment of the growing labor force and those tending to be released from production through advances in productivity) is a certain rate of demand for capital. If the ratio $I/Y$ exceeds the ratio $I/Y_n$, the economy is indeed saving and investing too much, relative, that is, to the capital requirements of long-run growth. Persistence of this condition over long periods implies that the economy's secular capital requirements are inadequate to its saving propensities. Unless either the saving coefficient is lowered, and/or the growth in labor force or productivity are speeded up, the economy will display the characteristics of secular stagnation.[2]

---

[1] If it be asked what has happened to the demand for additional capital originating in the need to produce, simply, a larger output, along the lines usually expressed by the acceleration principle, the answer is that the first source of demand listed above is concealed in the acceleration principle. To say that the demand for capital is a function of the level of output assumes that the labor force is growing fast enough to produce the output at given interest rates and techniques of production. Therefore, the acceleration principle (or incremental output) is not an additional source of demand for capital over and above the three sources listed above; it is simply a variant of (1).

[2] Incidentally, contrary to the beliefs of some economists, stagnation does not necessarily imply the absence of growth. In the absence of stabilizing fiscal devices, stagnation would probably take the form of deep and prolonged depressions and upswings that persistently fell short of full capacity and full employment growth. But it is very well

In like manner, if $I/Y$ is less than $I/Y_n$, the economy is saving and investing too little—relative to the secular capital requirements of a growing labor force and advancing technology. The demand for capital originating in these growth factors will outrun the rate of capital accumulation associated with full capacity or equilibrium growth; a condition of excess demand is implied, as in a condition of secular exhilaration. As society chooses, this condition may be dealt with either by raising the saving coefficient and/or reducing the rates of labor force growth and technological advance.

## II. Fiscal Policy and Recent Stagnation

Can we adduce an excess of private saving and investment over long-run capital requirements in explanation of the low rate of U. S. economic growth since 1957? This is a possibility, but I believe that it is not yet necessary to look for this kind of explanation. Instead, I think the explanation lies mainly in fiscal policies that have tended to generate large Federal budget surpluses at full employment, thereby crippling our upswings and causing them to die aborning.

It is a simple matter to modify the earlier model to allow for the influence of fiscal policy. Equation (2) can be rewritten in the form

$$\frac{\Delta Y}{Y} \times \frac{\Delta K}{\Delta Y} = \frac{S}{Y} + \frac{B}{Y} \qquad (5)$$

Whence equation (4) appears now as

$$\frac{I}{Y} = \frac{S}{Y} + \frac{B}{Y} \qquad (6)$$

where $B$ stands for the budget balance or, more exactly, the (algebraic) budget surplus; like saving and investment, $B$ is expressed as a proportion of the national income.[3] A budget surplus, of course,

possible that the cyclical peaks might be successively higher, indicating a long-run upward trend. And if income is growing faster than population, even per capita income will grow. In the presence of fiscal stabilizers, the depressions need not be deep and prolonged. However, in this case, we are confronted with the potential danger that the same stabilizers that limit contractions also act to retard the ensuing upswings and keep the latter from reaching full employment. As I shall argue below, in Section II, this threat has actually been realized in the U. S. economy.

[3] $B/Y$, of course, is the algebraic excess of $T_n/Y$ over $G/Y$, where $T_n$ stands for taxes net of Government transfer payments and $G$ for Government purchases of goods and services. It is thus evident that $B$ refers to the Government budget balance on national income and product account.

represents additional saving for the economy at large, saving that, as a condition of equilibrium, must be absorbed by a higher rate of (planned) investment; the opposite is true of a budget deficit. In other words, a budget surplus tends to raise the investment ratio $I/Y$ (and implicitly the equilibrium growth rate), while a budget deficit tends to reduce these variables.

However, although I may be belaboring the obvious, let me emphasize that what is important for the present analysis is not so much absolute surpluses and deficits as such, but algebraic changes in their size. A smaller deficit, for example, has just the same effect on $I/Y$ (and the equilibrium growth rate) as a larger surplus. In certain instances during the period under review, it has been this kind of phenomenon, as well as budget surpluses *per se*, that have enfeebled our upswings.

Turning to specifics, I think it is fair to say that we may have purchased stability at the expense of economic growth. We have become quite proud of the capacity of our economy to limit downswings to rather minor recessions, and we point to our powerful automatic stabilizers as perhaps the chief reason for this new-found stability. In the area of fiscal policy, these economic gyroscopes consist of the familiar, more-than-proportionate decline in taxes when the national income and product decline, thereby holding up after-tax incomes and thus spending in the face of falling production and employment; bolstering the automatic stabilizing effects of taxes have also been the automatic increases in outlays for unemployment compensation. On the other side of the budget, we have found Government purchases of goods and services displaying remarkable stability during recessions (even in those cases when earlier reductions in such spending have played a prime role in initiating the recessions) in the face of sharply falling tax receipts, thereby helping strongly to maintain total spending, private and public, as production contracts.

What seems to have been largely overlooked, however, particularly from the standpoint of economic growth, is that these stabilizers, functioning as good gyroscopes should, stabilize in both directions—upwards and downwards! With a very progressive income-tax structure, taxes in the United States also *rise* more than proportionately during periods of economic expansion, thereby causing after-tax incomes and thus private spending to rise less than proportionately in the face of expanding production; these deflationary effects are reinforced by the decline in outlays for unemployment compensation as unemployment drops. At the same time for various reasons, mostly shortsighted, Federal spending has also been held relatively stable or even reduced somewhat, thus reinforcing the retardation in the growth of total spending as the national product rises.

The significance of this fiscal behavior is that large chunks of incremental income have been removed from the stream of private expenditures in the form of taxes (and reduced unemployment compensation) without being offset by sufficient increments in Government spending. Hence, since 1957, total spending has tended to lag badly behind rising production, leading to unintended inventory accumulation, excess capacity, and therefore too slow a rise in business capital expenditures.

The foregoing can be briefly rephrased in terms of our model. What we now have in the United States is a relatively high Federal marginal propensity to tax (net of government transfer payments), $\Delta T_n/\Delta Y$, accompanied by a comparatively small Federal marginal propensity to spend on goods and services, $\Delta G/\Delta Y$. The result is that the algebraic value of $B/Y$ rises sharply in the course of expansions in the national income, thereby eventually raising $I/Y$ sharply above $I/Y_n$.[4]

In illustration of these strictures, the table below presents data on Federal marginal tax and spending ratios, marginal changes in the algebraic value of the Federal budget surplus, as well as changes in the absolute dollar value of the latter—all for the four quarters following the one in which GNP turned up in the aftermath of the four post-World War II recessions. Because of both apparent tax lags and lags in changes in Federal spending, the phenomena in question do not show up in the first quarters of upswings. At the same time, in the absence of strong fortuitous or exogenous developments later on, it is clear that what happens in the early stages of upswings exercises a powerful influence on the behavior of upswings at later stages. Moreover, these data emphasize how rapidly the deflationary swings in the Federal budget have set in. Although there has been some recent awareness of this phenomenon, the data show that it has been characteristic of upswings throughout the postwar period.

While the data contained in the table speak more or less for themselves, we may briefly point up a few highlights. To begin with, a glance down the first column shows that with a few exceptions the Federal marginal spending ratio has been remarkably low during the initial stages of postwar upswings. In contrast, Federal marginal tax collections net of transfer payments have been consistently on the high side. And only a small share of the explanation can be traced to the contraction of transfer payments; as the figures in the third column attest, the marginal tax ratio gross of transfer payments ($\Delta T/\Delta GNP$) has also been consistently on the high side.[5]

Not unexpectedly, the result of these disparities in marginal spending and tax ratios has been, as the fourth column shows, comparatively large increases in the (algebraic) Federal budget surpluses, expressed as a proportion of change in GNP; in other words, $B/Y$ in our model has tended to rise rather sharply in the early stages of every postwar upturn, starting with that of 1949. On a year-to-year basis, the increase in the algebraic value of the Federal budget surpluses relative to GNP for each of the first three upturns was 40 per cent, 23 per cent, and 30 per cent, respectively. This same point may be driven home with greater thrust by observing the figures on the absolute dollar change in the algebraic Federal surplus during these upturns. Note that in the year following the 1949 upturn, there was a \$24 billion swing in the direction of a budget surplus; for the same period following the next two upturns, the swings were approximately \$11 and \$13 billions.

Although it is too early yet to observe the actual behavior of the Federal budget (on income and product account) during the 1961–62 upturn, some portents of the future are clearly present, and they hold forth the promise of continued

---

4 The same point may be expressed in terms of more conventional multiplier analysis. A high marginal propensity to tax, like a high marginal propensity to save, means a small national-income multiplier: thus the multiplier effects of exogenous increases in private and Government spending on the national income and product are smaller than they would be with a smaller $\Delta T_n/\Delta Y$. At the same time, there have been relatively small rises in multiplicands, especially Federal spending. The result has been slow growth in the "product," *viz.*, the *national* product.

5 With a progressive income-tax structure, one would have expected a rising trend in the marginal propensity to tax. We have been "saved" from this fate very probably by the changes in the Internal Revenue Code of 1954. One of the least publicized of these changes, but probably one of the most important, was the provision for accelerated depreciation by use of sum-of-years'-digits or declining-balance methods in place of the straight-line formula. Although the high postwar rates of investment in new plant and equipment, particularly the latter, have played some role, unquestionably the major explanation of the more-than-doubling in the ratio of corporate depreciation allowances to GNP since 1950, and hence the corresponding decline in corporate taxable net income and taxes, is to be found in these tax-law changes.

## Table 1. Behavior of Federal Marginal Tax and Spending Ratios and Algebraic Changes in the Federal Budget Surplus on Income and Product Account in Four Quarters of Cyclical Upturns Following Quarter in Which Gross National Product Turned Up, 1949-1961

| Period | (1) $\dfrac{\Delta G}{\Delta GNP}$ | (2) $\dfrac{\Delta Tn}{\Delta GNP}$ | (3) $\dfrac{\Delta T}{\Delta GNP}$ | (2-1) $\dfrac{\Delta B}{\Delta GNP}$ | (4) Change in Federal Surplus |
|---|---|---|---|---|---|
| | | | | | (in $ billion) |
| 1950$_{II}$ | − .22 | 1.23 | .49 | 1.45 | $12.4 |
| 1950$_{III}$ | .06 | .52 | .35 | .46 | 8.5 |
| 1950$_{IV}$ | .39 | .23 | .30 | − .16 | − 1.7 |
| 1951$_{I}$ | .44 | .82 | .80 | .38 | 5.1 |
| | | | | | |
| 1954$_{IV}$ | − .20 | .15 | .27 | .35 | 3.1 |
| 1955$_{I}$ | .07 | .28 | .28 | .21 | 2.8 |
| 1955$_{II}$ | − .05 | .28 | .28 | .33 | 2.8 |
| 1955$_{III}$ | .06 | .27 | .25 | .21 | 2.2 |
| | | | | | |
| 1958$_{III}$ | .19 | .26 | .31 | .07 | 0.6 |
| 1958$_{IV}$ | .04 | .28 | .29 | .24 | 3.2 |
| 1959$_{I}$ | − .09 | .41 | .36 | .50 | 5.8 |
| 1959$_{II}$ | .04 | .25 | .26 | .21 | 3.3 |
| | | | | | |
| 1961$_{III}$ | .08 | .17 | .26 | .09 | 0.8 |
| 1961$_{IV}$ | .15 | .28 | .29 | .13 | 2.1 |

Source: U. S. Department of Commerce, *U. S. Income and Output: A Supplement to the Survey of Current Business* (Washington, D.C., 1959), Table III, 3; *idem., Survey of Current Business*, July, 1961, Table 22, p. 17; and *Survey of Current Business*, May 1962, Table 5, p. 9. The above table is derived from data representing seasonably adjusted annual rates.

retarding effects on U.S. economic growth. According to recently-published figures,[6] the Federal deficit, in the administrative budget, of fiscal 1962 was some $5.5 billion less than the $12.4 billion deficit of fiscal 1959 (both deficits reflecting the effects on tax receipts of years of recessions). This was true despite a $9 billion greater total of expenditures in the former fiscal year! With unemployment running, if anything, a bit higher in the more recent recession, this is potentially bad news. For the smaller deficit of the last recession, despite the 11 per cent higher expenditures, implies a relation between taxes and expenditures such that there has been a big increase in the budget surplus that would be generated at full employment currently, compared to the full employment surplus of earlier years. This is the only way to account for the much smaller recent deficit with virtually the same levels of unemployment. Since the earlier

[6] *The Budget of the United States Government for the Fiscal Year Ending June 30, 1963* (Washington, D. C., 1962), p. 42.

tendencies to generate large surpluses during expansion "choked off" the 1958–59 recovery short of full employment, even stronger tendencies in this direction are filled with foreboding.

Possibly, a skeptical reader might observe in the table that the tendencies toward big and rapid swings in the direction of Federal budget surpluses were evidently more pronounced during earlier upswings than more recent ones; yet sustained periods of full-employment growth were achieved. The explanation is, of course, that for war and postwar reasons the demands for capital were exceptionally high prior to 1957.[7] Before the huge backlogs from the Depression and World War II were exhausted, the Korean War produced a large increase in Federal spending (offsetting the high marginal tax ratios and leading to large budget deficits) and another large increase in investment

[7] Or, in the terms of footnote 4, the multiplicand(s) in the multiplier formula were expanding rapidly. Much of demand for capital referred to in the text below lies outside the model of equation (1), which is essentially a peacetime theory of capital demand.

spending in defense-connected industries. Abetted by the continued boom in residential construction through 1957, the enormous "automobile" year in 1955, the subsequent capital-goods boom in 1955–56, and the "Suez" export boom of 1956–57, plus the spurt in Government spending over the same period, these war and postwar stimuli were enough, evidently, either to keep the tendencies toward large budget surpluses from being realized or else to offset them with large demands for capital in the private sector until 1957.

There is no evidence at present of any basic long-term weakness in private investment, but neither is there any basis for expecting large and mounting levels of such expenditures, comparable to those of the post-World War II era, such as would once more offset the damping effects of the high marginal tax bite. If this is correct, it is clear that, unless the people of the United States are prepared to undertake large increases in Government spending, larger than are currently contemplated, the increasing clamor for sharp reductions in income-tax rates is well-taken, indeed. Otherwise, we must be prepared to witness a continuation of the large and abrupt swings towards the Federal budget surpluses that have been severely retarding our economic growth in recent years.[8]

In closing, it might be worth while examining the question how, in the event of a general cut in income-tax rates, such a cut should be apportioned, especially between personal and corporate taxes. Obviously, a reasonably exact and detailed answer to this question would occupy another paper by itself, but a step in this direction may be made by a brief report on marginal tax ratios in the personal and corporate sectors of the economy, for the same periods included in the table above.

The most striking observation that results from such a breakdown is that, with three exceptions, the marginal ratio of corporate profits taxes to GNP exceeds the marginal ratio of personal income taxes to GNP. This is true despite the

(not-unexpected) fact that the marginal ratio of corporate profits to GNP is ordinarily less than the marginal ratio of personal income to GNP. Now the marginal tax ratios in relation to GNP are the products of these marginal income ratios times the marginal ratios of corporate profits taxes to corporate profits and personal income taxes to personal income, respectively.[9] Hence the marginal ratio of corporate profits taxes to corporate profits should exceed the marginal ratio of personal income taxes to personal income, and it does, by a very substantial margin, in all but one instance.

The implication of this information is that, by and large, the relatively large marginal, total tax bites shown in the table above may be traced to the high, but virtually proportionate, rate of corporate profits taxation, and only in a distinctly secondary way to the progressive personal income tax.[10]

Of course, it does not necessarily follow from all this that it is the corporate profits tax that should be lowered, or even given principal emphasis in a program of general income tax reduction. A reduction in the total marginal tax rate could be effected just as well through a cut in personal income taxes. Nevertheless, other data suggest that, from the standpoint of promoting faster economic growth, at least, a substantial decrease in the corporate profits tax may be desirable. In particular, the fact that business fixed investment has remained virtually unchanged from its 1956 and 1957 levels and has fallen from 10.7 per cent to 8.9 per cent (in 1961) of GNP indicates that this variable is in need of a strong shot in the arm. It is true that lagging growth in aggregate demand has been a major factor underlying the depressing behavior of business fixed investment, and that a boost to consumer spending could provide the needed stimulus. However, there are strong indications that the investment component has itself been a drag on aggregate demand, and

---

[8] To a lesser extent, part of the blame for the recent stagnation must be placed at the feet of the Federal Reserve System for its insistence on fighting inflation by means of tight money policies long after it became clear that inflation was a thing of the past. But this point has been so thoroughly explored in the literature that it hardly needs further elaboration here. Nevertheless, it is worth pointing out that easy money policies conducted during the upswing that began in March 1961, have not prevented the same sluggishness in the rate of expansion from reappearing, whereas Federal budget behavior shows strong signs of maintaining its postwar pattern.

[9] I.e., $\Delta T_c/\Delta \text{GNP} = \Delta Pr./\Delta \text{GNP} \times \Delta T_c/\Delta Pr.$, and $\Delta T_p/\Delta \text{GNP} = \Delta Y_p/\Delta \text{GNP} \times \Delta T_p/\Delta Y_p$, where $T_c$ stands for corporate profits taxes, $Pr.$, for corporate profits, $T_p$ for personal income taxes, and $Y_p$ for personal income.

[10] Whether or not the above information will surprise a reader is problematical. In any case, it squares with the fact that virtually all corporate profits are taxed at the 52 per cent rate, whereas according to Federal tax and personal income distribution data (*Survey of Current Business*, April 1962, pp. 11 and 15), the vast bulk of personal income is taxed in a range of average rates of about 6–13 per cent, with the $50,000 and over income bracket (the highest shown) being taxed at the average rate of 33 per cent of personal income.

for reasons independent of the behavior of the latter variable.

Between 1950 and 1961 before-tax corporate profits rose some $5.5 billion, whereas after-tax profits rose a mere $0.5 billion; in the interval 1957–61, a $3 billion rise in before-tax profits was accompanied by a $1 billion increase in after-tax profits (and the latter was from a figure that reflected a $0.5 billion *drop* from the 1950 level in the face of a $2.5 billion increase in before-tax profits). Whatever was happening to aggregate demand and other influences on profits clearly was reflected in before-tax profits; in contrast, the virtual constancy of after-tax profits can be explained only in terms of the high corporate profits tax. Not unexpectedly, there has also occurred a noticeable downward trend in after-

tax rates of return.[11] Similarly, between 1950 and 1961 corporate retained profits fell from 63 to 24 per cent of corporate cash flows (depreciation allowances plus retained earnings), and in the same period corporate cash flows fell from 15 to 12 per cent of corporate gross product (defined as equal to corporate income originating plus corporate depreciation allowances).

The stultifying effect of these important influences on investment demand, all the apparent outcome of the high corporate profits tax, would seem to make a rather strong case for a large cut in this tax in any program of general tax reduction.

---

[11] On stockholders' equity; see *Economic Report of the President* (Washington, D. C., 1962), p. 280.

# Fiscal Policy in Perspective

*40* Tax revision is the principal instrument of U.S. economic policy to achieve prosperity and more rapid economic growth in the mid-1960's. The nature of that revision and the means by which it will accomplish its objectives have been described in the preceding chapter.

The aim and expectation of this program is to restore full prosperity, which, in the last analysis, is the only sure path to budgetary balance. Since this will, at least temporarily, involve large budgetary deficits, it is important also to examine what deficits mean in modern economic society. Government deficits are not a new fiscal experience for Americans. The first part of this chapter reviews several relevant aspects of that experience, and in particular distinguishes two kinds of deficits and their economic effects—deficits that grow passively out of economic recession or inadequate growth, and deficits that grow out of positive fiscal action, such as tax reduction, to invigorate the economy. The perspective is further widened by placing the Federal deficit or

surplus in the context of balancing and offsetting deficits and surpluses in the other major sectors of the national economy.

Since deficits increase the national debt, it is important also to appraise that debt in relation to the Nation's wealth and the Nation's income. The national balance sheet allows us to view the Federal debt as one of a set of interrelated assets and liabilities.

Expansionary tax policy must be considered also in terms of the possible effects it may have on the stability of our price level. Not only is inflation unjust and disruptive, but it would interfere with our progress toward achieving balance in our international financial accounts.

These are some of the problems discussed in this chapter. They are problems which have been considered at length in the technical literature of finance and economics. But they become problems for all Americans to consider as the Nation prepares to take bold steps to invigorate its economy—steps involving large interim Federal deficits. Both experience and analysis confirm that this positive use of fiscal policy in 1963 will make a significant contribution to the achievement of our employment and growth goals and

Reprinted from the 1963 *Annual Report of the Council of Economic Advisors*.

incur minimum risks of interfering with continued price stability and progress toward balance of payments equilibrium.

## Passive Fiscal Policy and Automatic Stabilization

Any weakening in private spending will reduce incomes, causing tax revenues to fall and transfer payments to rise. Thus disposable incomes will decline less than pre-tax incomes, and will be partly cushioned against the decline in private demand. In effect, the impact of the decline in private income is shared with the Federal Government, which does not shrink its purchases when its income falls. The greater the extent to which a fall in government revenues cushions the decline in private incomes, the less the flow of spending for output will be curtailed.

Automatic stabilization operates in reverse when private demand increases. Additional income is generated, but part of it is siphoned out of the spending stream in higher tax payments and lower transfers. Disposable incomes therefore rise less than incomes before taxes, and the spending and re-spending is limited and damped.

Thus the tax-and-transfer response narrows fluctuations in income caused by irregularities in the strength of demand. The sharper the response of tax collections to changes in GNP, the stronger the stabilization effect. Although the tax-and-transfer response cannot prevent or reverse a movement in GNP, it can and does limit the extent of cumulative expansions and contractions. At least with respect to contractions, this is clearly an important service to the economy.

Automatic fiscal stabilizers have made a major contribution in limiting the length and severity of postwar recessions. Each of the four postwar recessions—1948–49, 1953–54, 1957–58, and 1960–61—has been both short and mild. The decline in real GNP from its peak to its trough has ranged from a high of 4.4 per cent in 1957–58 to a low of 2.1 per cent in 1960–61, and the duration of the recessions has varied from 9 to 13 months. Figure 1 demonstrates that changes in disposable personal income from quarter to quarter have been much smaller than changes in GNP. Although GNP changes were frequently negative (in each of the postwar recessions), disposable income fell in only one quarter in the entire postwar period. This relative stability of personal disposable income has been mainly due to the automatic fiscal stabilizers, together with

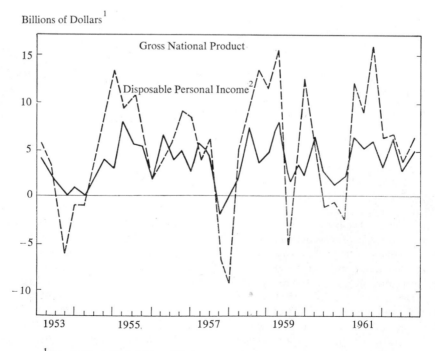

Billions of Dollars[1]

Gross National Product

Disposable Personal Income[2]

1953    1955    1957    1959    1961

[1] Seasonally Adjusted Annual Rates

[2] Personal Income Less Personal Taxes

Figure 1. Quarterly Changes in Gross National Product and Disposable Personal Income.

the tendency of corporations to maintain their dividends at the expense of retained earnings during recessions. The maintenance of disposable incomes has prevented sharp declines in consumer expenditures. The resulting stability in markets for consumer goods, which constitute by far the largest component of final demand, has prevented any drastic collapse in business investment in fixed capital.

Automatic fiscal stabilizers increase the stability of the economy. Stability is a desirable thing for an economy that is balanced where it wants to be. Thus, an economy operating, on the average, at high levels of output and employment benefits from a tax-and-transfer system highly responsive to changes in output and income, as a cushion against sharp movements of aggregate demand either toward inflation or toward recession.

However, in the present situation—with the American economy laboring for over five years well below its potential rate of output—automatic stabilization becomes an ambiguous blessing. The protection it gives against cumulative downward movements of output and employment is all the more welcome. But its symmetrical "protection" against upward movements becomes an obstacle on the path to full employment, throttling expansion well before full employment is reached.

Under such conditions, high employment can be restored—as is being proposed under the 1963 tax program—by a reduction in taxes. When this is done the need is not primarily to lessen the responsiveness of tax receipts to changes in GNP. Rather the whole schedule of taxes should be lowered—so that, at any given GNP, taxes siphon off less private purchasing power—while leaving the response of tax receipts to *changes* in GNP about as great as before. To be sure, it is almost impossible to lower taxes without lessening to some degree their sensitivity to changes in GNP. But the purpose of such a change should be to lower the level of taxes—and hence their persistent drag on purchasing power—rather than to reduce their automatic countercyclical response.

## Tax Cuts to Aid Recovery

Just as we have had postwar experience with automatic stabilization, we have had experience with active tax cuts which served positively to increase demand. These experiences are of interest in the present context.

In two of the postwar recessions—1948–49 and 1953–54—tax cuts helped to check the decline and to spur the ensuing recovery. Neither of the tax cuts is an example of deliberate counter-cyclical fiscal action, but both had important expansionary effects which came when they were needed.

Under the Revenue Act of 1948, which was passed by the Congress in April, taxes were reduced by $4.7 billion. While at the time, the tax cut appeared inappropriately timed—few observers were predicting recession—when the recession of 1949 in fact occurred, it turned out to be fortunate that the tax cut had been legislated. The cut was retroactive to January 1, 1948, and as a result refunds were exceptionally large in mid-1949. The upturn began in October 1949. In addition to the tax cut, there was a significant increase in Federal expenditures in late 1948 associated with the introduction of the Marshall Plan. This also helped to mitigate the recession. The economy was further stimulated in the expansion phase by the heavy increases in placement of military orders associated with the Korean War, which began in June 1950. As a result of the tax cut and the increased expenditures, together with the effects of the automatic stabilizers, the recession was short and mild, and the ensuing expansion was strong. By the first quarter of 1951, unemployment had been reduced to 3.5 per cent of the labor force.

As a result of the rapid expansion, by the second quarter of 1950, Federal tax liabilities as shown in the national income accounts had risen substantially above the levels that prevailed at the time taxes were cut in the second quarter of 1948.

Taxes also were cut during the recession of 1953–54. Effective January 1, 1954, the excess profits tax was repealed, and personal income tax rates were reduced. Excise taxes were reduced on April 1, and further tax reductions for both individuals and corporations were embodied in the Internal Revenue Code of 1954. These measures are estimated to have reduced Federal revenues by about $6.1 billion (seasonally adjusted annual rate) in the first half of 1954. Further cuts which went into effect later brought the revenue loss on a full-year basis to about $7.4 billion. These cuts in personal and corporate income and excise taxes were partially offset, however, by an increase of about $1.4 billion (annual rate) in OASI contributions, which became effective on January 1, 1954. For the most part, the tax reductions in 1954 were part of a program of tax reform and were not viewed primarily as fiscal policy measures aimed at countering the recession. Yet as a result of the tax cuts that became effective at the beginning of 1954, disposable personal income and personal consumption expenditures turned up in the first quarter, while personal income and GNP were still declining. It is generally agreed that the recession ended in August. Tax reduction, together with an easy monetary policy which made a plentiful supply of funds available to finance a strong expansion of housing and automobile demand, helped to shorten the recession and to invigorate the ensuing expansion which brought unemployment down to 4.2 per cent of the labor force by the third quarter of 1955.

As a result of the expansion, by the first quarter of 1955 total Federal tax liabilities, as shown in the national income accounts, had risen significantly above the level that prevailed in the fourth quarter of 1953 before the tax cuts were put into effect.

While the tax cuts of 1954 helped considerably in rescuing the economy from the recession, it should be recognized that had they gone into effect earlier, the recession of 1953–54 might have been completely avoided. Government expenditures (principally defense spending) were cut by nearly $11 billion between mid-1953 and mid-1954. The tax cuts took effect 6 months after expenditures began to fall. As it was, fiscal policy, taken as a whole, was contractionary in this period and was a major cause of the recession. The Federal deficit as shown in the national income and product accounts was $7.0 billion (seasonally adjusted annual rate) in the second quarter of 1953 when the recession began. By the fourth quarter the operation of the automatic stabilizers associated with the decline in economic activity had increased the deficit to $11.8 billion despite significant cuts in expenditures. The deficit dropped to $10.6 billion in the first quarter of 1954, and as a result of sharp cuts in expenditures, to $5.4 billion in the second quarter despite the tax reductions that went into effect in the first half of 1954.

Private scholars who have studied the period have estimated that if the economy had continued to operate as the same rate of unemployment that prevailed in the second quarter of 1953, the budget deficit would have dropped from $7.0 billion in that quarter to $3.8 billion in the fourth quarter of 1953 and would have shifted to a surplus of $3.0 billion by the second quarter of 1954. This represents a shift of $10 billion between the peak of the previous recovery and the trough of the recession. It is an approximate measure of the net contractive effect of active fiscal policy during this period.

## Fiscal Policy in the 1930's

During the 1930's, America had its longest uninterrupted experience with budget deficits. Their persistence, their relatively large size in comparison with GNP, and their association with an unprecedented unemployment rate (averaging 18.2 per cent from 1930–39) have sometimes been interpreted as demonstrating the futility of expansionary fiscal policy.

The 1930's were a tragic period in the Nation's history. The "Great Depression," the causes of which are still not fully diagnosed, produced a tremendous "gap" between actual and potential output—not the 6 per cent average of recent years but about 40 per cent during much of the period. In such an abnormal situation, it is perhaps too much to expect that fiscal policy alone could have fully offset a prolonged failure of the private economy to generate strong expansionary forces.

But in fact, active fiscal policy was not employed vigorously, consistently, or with proper timing. And whatever constructive impact fiscal policy may have had was largely offset by restrictive monetary policies and by institutional failures—failures that could never again occur because of fundamental changes made during and since the 1930's.

Briefly summarized, the facts are these:

(1) Fiscal policy was moderately expansionary for the decade as a whole. Federal expenditures increased substantially, adding to total demand. But most of the effect of this expenditure growth was offset by a series of very heavy tax rate increases, especially in the Revenue Acts of 1932 and 1936. Federal revenues increased by 77 per cent over the decade even with a terribly depressed tax base. If the unemployment rate had stayed at the 1929 level, revenues would have more than doubled. The Federal budget changed from a surplus of slightly over $1 billion in 1929 to deficits that would have averaged less than $1 billion over the decade had unemployment been at the same level as in 1929. Of course, because of the collapse of the revenue base, actual deficits were much larger; but these were partly the passive product of depression and partly the reflection of an actively expansionary policy.

(2) At two crucial periods, fiscal policy shifted sharply in a contractionary direction: in 1932–33, and again in 1937–38 In the first period the contractionary policy coincided with and intensified the monetary collapse, and in the second choked off the 1937 recovery.

(3) State and local government budgets were then much larger than the Federal budget, and they were changed in a highly restrictive manner, shifting from a deficit in 1929 to surpluses after 1934.

(4) Unemployment melted away very rapidly when military needs began in 1941 to lead to large budget

deficits. Of course, as these expenditures and deficits grew during the war, they not only restored full employment but became a serious inflationary danger. But this wartime overdose of expansionary fiscal medicine should not obscure the fact that more moderate dosages in the early stages quickly solved an unemployment problem which had seemed insoluble for 10 years. This was not because the expenditures happened to be military in nature—any expenditures, private or public, on the same scale would have expanded demand and put men back to work.

## Some Conclusions from Past Experience

Several conclusions emerge from the preceding review.

The automatic stabilization which our present fiscal system provides is a powerful weapon to damp cyclical movements of output and employment. It is one of the factors that has kept the U.S. economy free from major depressions in the postwar period.

The postwar record shows that deliberate tax cuts can have a counter-cyclical impact, encouraging recovery by stimulating private demand. The experience reviewed above shows how in two cases tax reduction contributed in this manner to recovery from recession. The fact that these tax changes came at times when they helped to check recession and encourage recovery was, however, largely accidental.

The 1948 tax reduction was intended as a permanent one, reflecting the postwar decline of military expenditures. The 1954 tax cuts were also intended as a permanent adjustment to the sharp reductions in government expenditures at the end of the Korean emergency. But a recession will not always coincide with the need for permanent tax reduction. The temporary fluctuations in private demand that are commonly responsible for cyclical movements in business activity thus may call for temporary adjustments in fiscal policy that can be reversed as the need for them recedes.

Last year the President proposed two measures for greater fiscal flexibility to meet recessions. These were (a) a proposal that the Congress grant to the President limited authority to initiate temporary reductions in personal income tax rates, subject to Congressional approval; and (b) a proposal that the Congress give the President stand-by authority to accelerate and initiate appropriately timed public capital improvements in times of serious unemployment. In his Economic Report the President has reaffirmed his support of the principle underlying these two proposals.

A weak private economy can generate very large deficits without receiving a positively stimulating effect from those deficits. The large passive deficits of the 1930's provide examples. More recent examples appear in the experience of the past 5 years. Although the administrative budgets presented for the fiscal years 1958–63 foresaw a surplus in every year, averaging $1.4 billion, the actual outcome has been a deficit in all but one of these years, averaging $5.5 billion. This record is summarized in Table 1. The discrepancy between the Administration's proposed budget and the actual fiscal outcome is, of course, accounted for by two factors: variance between actual and anticipated GNP, and Congressional action modifying both expenditures and taxes. But the major factor explaining these discrepancies was the failure of the economy to attain the GNP that had been anticipated.

Passive deficits are largest when the economy experiences recession. A recession which would reduce the expected GNP gains in fiscal year 1964 by even $15 billion below what they would otherwise be would add almost $5 billion to the deficit.

The experience of the last few years should make it clear that merely to incur deficits is not an appropriate objective of policy. For it is not the deficits as such that provide stimulus. Only reductions in tax rates or increases in expenditures have an actively stimulating role. The passive deficits which are the product of recession or slack, however, have a valuable cushioning function. Nevertheless, it is an appropriate objective of policy to eliminate the deficits that are the product of a recession or a sluggish economy—because of the human and economic waste that is involved in recessions and slack. The proper objectives of policy are full employment and growth, and recessions and slack are the opposites of these.

It is clear that the deficit which a slack economy or recession produces cannot realistically be eliminated by raising tax rates or by reducing government expenditures. Its source is not excessive spending or tax rates that are too low. The attempt to eliminate a deficit by these means would be largely self-defeating. Such a policy would be disastrous for employment, incomes, profits; the deficit would remain; and the role of the dollar as an international currency would be undermined.

Expenditures that are wasteful or represent improper fields for government action (something which only the public, acting through elected representatives, can determine) should surely be eliminated. But unless taxes were simultaneously reduced by more than expenditures decline, the effect would be contractionary on the economy. The beneficial effect on incentives through lower tax rates might be more than offset by a net loss in demand. A cut in expenditures reduces market demand directly by the full amount of the cut, while an equal reduction in taxes expands market demand by a smaller amount, because a part of the reduction will be added to personal and business saving.

Deficits that result from recession or slack can be eliminated only by restoring and maintaining a vigorous, rapidly growing economy. If the tax

## Deficits and Surpluses—Private and Public

For the economy as a whole, expenditures on final output in any past period must necessarily add up to the value of total gross product or income. Therefore, if any one sector in the economy has incurred a deficit by spending more than it has received in income, some other sector must have incurred a surplus by spending less than it has received. Putting it differently, the sum of all sectoral deficits must be identical with the sum of all surpluses. The problem is to maintain a relationship between the deficits and surpluses of the various sectors that will permit this balance

### Table 1. Federal Government Surplus or Deficit: Comparison of Estimate and Actual, Fiscal Years 1958-63

(millions of dollars)

| Fiscal Year | Date of Estimate[a] | ADMINISTRATIVE BUDGET SURPLUS OR DEFICIT (—) | |
|---|---|---|---|
| | | Estimate[a] | Actual[b] |
| 1958-63 average | ... | 1,411 | − 5,511 |
| 1958 | 1957 | 1,813 | − 2,819 |
| 1959 | 1958 | 466 | − 12,427 |
| 1960 | 1959 | 70 | 1,224 |
| 1961 | 1960 | 4,184 | − 3,856 |
| 1962 | 1961 | 1,468 | − 6,378 |
| 1963 | 1962 | 463 | − 8,811[c] |

Source: Bureau of the Budget.
[a]Estimate in Budget document issued in January of year indicated.
[b]Actual, except for 1963.
[c]Estimate, January 1963.

system imposes an excessive drag on the economy —through its effects on purchasing power and on incentives—tax rates may be too high relative to expenditures, even though the budget is in deficit. Thus, tax revision, involving both reduction and reform, can not only provide stimulus for growth and prosperity, but can even, as a result, balance the budget or produce surpluses. Recession and slack generate deficits; prosperity and growth balance budgets.

The reciprocal relationships among surpluses and deficits in the Federal budget and the strength of the private economy can be clarified by examining the counterparts of the Federal budget for the other sectors of the economy.

to be reached at a satisfactory level of economic activity—and without a prolonged succession of government deficits. The interrelationship between the levels of surplus and deficit of various sectors in the economy has been tabulated in the President's Economic Report each year since 1947. It gives an interesting insight into the cyclical behavior of the economy and places fluctuations in the Federal deficit or surplus in better perspective.

A Federal deficit on national income account means that the Government's injections into the stream of income and expenditures through purchases of goods and services and transfer payments exceed its withdrawals through taxes and social insurance contributions. Conversely, a surplus means that its withdrawals exceed its injections. (The way in which the Government uses its surplus or finances its deficit may have an important bearing on the level of business or even consumer expenditure. These transactions on asset account are not explicitly treated in the present analysis, but these vital considerations of financial policy are dealt with elsewhere in this Report.)

For consumers, receipts of disposable income are withdrawals, and outlays for consumption represent injections. Expenditures on residential construction, though usually treated in the national income accounts as business investment, are here assigned to the consumer sector, and depreciation charges on residential property are treated accordingly as gross consumer saving.

State and local governments, as the Federal Government, withdraw purchasing power from the income stream through taxes, and inject it by purchases of goods and services and by transfer payments. The concept of surplus and deficit is the same as for the Federal Government. In the case of the foreign sector, imports of goods and services drain purchasing power away to other countries, while exports of goods and services for which payments must be made to the United States constitute injections.

For business firms, retained earnings and depreciation allowances (gross saving) are withdrawals from the gross income stream, while expenditures for fixed and inventory investment are injections. A "deficit," in these terms, exists if investment exceeds gross saving. Thus defined, a "deficit" on capital account does not mean that business is unprofitable—quite the contrary. Borrowing to finance investment in productive plant and equipment that yields a return over time lies at the heart of the growth process of the economy. In years of prosperity, when unemployment is low and capacity is fully utilized, business profits are high and the saving from retained earnings and depreciation allowances is relatively large. But in these years, the inducement to invest in new productive facilities is so strong that it substantially outruns even the large supply of internal saving.

The "budget" of the consumer sector characteristically shows a surplus—an excess of disposable income plus depreciation of houses, over the combined total of personal consumption expenditures and residential construction. Indeed, during the period 1947–62, the consumer sector was in surplus in every year except 1947. The average surplus in that period was about $6.5 billion.

State and local governments have had deficits in 8 out of the last 9 years and in 11 of the entire 16 years under review. Their deficits have been relatively small, averaging a little less than a billion dollars in the last few years. The foreign sector has had an excess of current purchases from the United States over sales to the United States in 9 of the 16 years, and for the whole period the excess of purchases averaged a little less than a billion dollars a year. This excess of purchases is a deficit for purposes of the U.S. national income accounts.

Characteristically, the business and Federal Government sectors combined show a deficit, which offsets a consolidated surplus in the remaining sectors. However, the only two sectors whose deficits and surpluses exhibit fluctuations clearly related to changes in the general level of business activity are the business sector and the Federal Government. Figure 2 shows the deficit or surplus in the Federal national income accounts budget and the deficit or surplus of the business sector on capital account for each year from 1947 to 1962. The figure shows clearly that movements in the deficits and surpluses of these two sectors bear a marked inverse relationship. The year-to-year movements of the deficits or surpluses were in opposite direction for these two sectors in 12 of the 15 cases shown.

The budget of the business sector exhibits surpluses or small deficits in years of recession and slack, moves toward deficit as the economy expands, and commonly achieves a substantial deficit in years of prosperity and low unemployment. Consequently, it is in prosperous years, such as 1947, 1948, 1950, 1951, 1952, 1955, 1956, and 1957, that the business sector has had large deficits on capital account. It is in those years that business raises large amounts of funds on the capital market and uses the surpluses of other sectors. On the other hand, when there is substantial unemployment and unutilized capacity, as in the recession years 1949 and 1954 and the years 1958–62, the inducement to invest tends to be so weak that investment spending falls, even relative to the reduced levels of gross retained earnings, and the business sector budget shows only a small deficit or even a surplus.

The Federal budget shows a reverse pattern. It consistently moves toward a surplus as the economy expands and toward a deficit as it contracts. These movements are mainly a passive result of the operation of the automatic fiscal stabilizers, though they reflect also active measures of fiscal policy aimed at minimizing economic fluctuations. As a general rule, the Federal Government has had budget surpluses in years when the unemployment rate has averaged less than $5\frac{1}{2}$ per cent of the labor force and budget deficits in years when the rate has exceeded that figure. The only exceptions to this rule between 1947 and 1962 were the years 1952 and 1953 when the requirements of the Korean war forced very high military expenditures in a time of prosperity and low unemployment, and the year 1960 when a deliberate contraction of

expenditures and hence of economic activity. When capital spending is sluggish, the over-all level of expenditure, and hence income, is likely to be unsatisfactory. A passive deficit in the Federal sector will occur. But this, in itself, cannot provide the new inducement to investment that will restore full employment and in the process permit the Federal Government a surplus in its own accounts.

The business sector cannot, of course, be expected to run large deficits merely in order to maintain high levels of economic activity. General

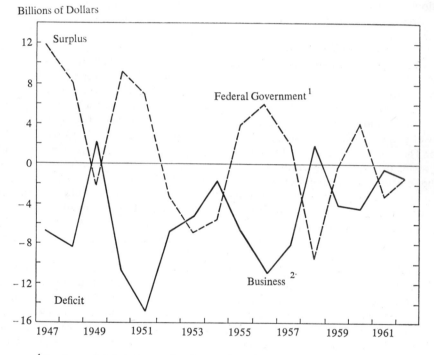

Billions of Dollars

[1] Surplus or deficit ( – ) on national income accounts basis

[2] Excess of gross retained earnings (excluding depreciation on non-farm residential property) over gross private domestic investment (excluding residential construction), or excess of gross private domestic investment over gross retained earnings ( – )

Figure 2. Federal Budget and Business Capital Account: Surpluses or Deficits.

Federal expenditures cut short recovery from the 1957–58 recession while unemployment was still high. On the other hand, in years when unemployment has exceeded $5\frac{1}{2}$ per cent, the business sector has had an average deficit of less than $2 billion, whereas in years in which unemployment has been less than $5\frac{1}{2}$ per cent the business sector deficit has averaged $9 billion.

It is evident that the deficit or surplus in the business sector is related to the surplus or deficit in the Federal Government sector. More important, it is a major determinant of the total level of

economic stabilization is a responsibility of the Federal Government, not of private business organizations. Unavoidable fluctuations in private demand make it almost certain that the Federal budget will show deficits in some years. But the way to avoid chronic Federal deficits and achieve surpluses with reasonable frequency is to pursue active Federal policies—including budget and tax policies—designed to keep the economy operating continuously at high levels of employment and capacity utilization.

## Prospects for the Future

There are many reasons for confidence that, once full employment is restored by fiscal action, the private sectors will once again find it to their advantage to increase investment and incur deficits sufficient to generate a balance in the Federal account—that the private economy will find new buoyancy which will make surpluses possible and appropriate.

The weakness of fixed business investment in recent years has reflected—and in turn reinforced—the slow and uncertain growth of aggregate demand. Greater utilization of existing capacity may not immediately yield a burst of investment activity. Businesses which expanded capacity in 1955–57 in the expectation of expanding markets and reaped only a harvest of higher overhead costs may be hesitant to bet again on sustained prosperity. But as strong markets are restored and maintained, business confidence can and will revive. Private investment will then be once again the primary force for economic growth. Structural factors will favor this development. For example, beginning in the second half of the 1960's demographic conditions will be ripe for one of the strongest and most prolonged booms in residential construction this country has ever known. The vast research and development effort of American industry will yield new techniques and new products which will be profitable to install in steadily expanding markets.

The historical record of the American economy —like that of every industrialized country— exhibits an irregular sequence of periods of strong and buoyant demand, alternating with intervals of weakness and slack. The reasons for this irregularity are many: massive innovations like the automobile or electrification, the opening or closing of new territories, bursts of population growth, the temporary drying-up of profitable investment opportunities. History teaches that all such periods end. The natural tendency to extrapolate the recent past ought not to blind us to the likelihood that the weakness of the past few years will sooner or later be transformed into strength. But if we fail to do what is needed now, the transformation may be long delayed.

*D. J. SMYTH*

# Built-in Flexibility of Taxation and Automatic Stabilization

*41* The effectiveness of a
stabilization measure such as built-in flexibility of
taxation can only be measured in the context of a
dynamic model, whereas the usual approaches
involve the use of static models. The present paper
suggests a measure that may be used with dynamic
systems and applies it to dynamic models of the
Australian and United States economies.

## I

With given tax rates, changes in income lead to
changes in the same direction in tax revenues. In
this way built-in flexibility of taxation arises. The
effect of this built-in flexibility is to lower the
multiplier;[1] the percentage by which the multiplier

[1] Denote income by $Y$, consumption by $C$, autonomous components of expenditure by $A$, taxation

is reduced (or some related measure) is commonly
taken to represent the stabilizing effect of built-in
flexibility.[2]

This approach ignores the dynamic structure of
the system for it merely involves a comparison of
static equilibrium positions. But the problem can

by $T$, the marginal propensity to consume by $c$,
and the marginal rate of taxation by $m$. A simple
aggregative model is

$$\Delta Y = \Delta C + \Delta A,$$
$$\Delta C = c(\Delta Y - \Delta T),$$
$$\Delta T = m\Delta Y.$$

It follows that

$$\Delta Y = \frac{\Delta A}{1 - c + cm}.$$

If there is no built-in flexibility of taxation, $m$ is
zero, in which case

$$\Delta Y = \frac{\Delta A}{1 - c}.$$

As $c$ and $m$ are positive and less than 1 the presence
of built-in flexibility of taxation reduces the multiplier.

[2] This is the measure used in the well-known
article by Musgrave and Miller (1948).

hardly be analyzed in static terms for stabilization policy is concerned with fluctuations and a key feature of fluctuations is that the system is in disequilibrium. Adjustment is not instantaneous and may, in fact, be slow; a system may never reach static equilibrium; and it may be stable according to static formulations but unstable in its adjustment process.[3] Thus a measure of the stabilizing effectiveness of built-in flexibility that specifically takes account of the dynamic structure of the system should be used.[4] I suggest as a suitable measure *the extent by which the standard deviation of income is reduced by the introduction of built-in flexibility of taxation.*[5] Denote the standard deviation of income without built-in flexibility of taxation by $SD(Y)$ and that of income with built-in flexibility by $SD(Y')$. Then the measure, $B$, is

$$B = \frac{SD(Y) - SD(Y')}{SD(Y)} = 1 - \frac{SD(Y')}{SD(Y)}.$$

The standard deviations of the systems with and without built-in flexibility are calculated about the equilibrium of the system concerned so that a pure stabilization effect is distinguished.[6]

If built-in flexibility prevents all fluctuation, then $B = 1$. In general $B$ will be less than 1, not even a marginal rate of taxation of unity being sufficient to make $SD(Y')$ equal to zero. It is possible for $B$ to be negative, in which case built-in flexibility operates perversely to increase fluctuations.[7]

---

[3] For discussion of the possible destabilizing effects of policies aimed at stabilizing the economy see Friedman (1955) and Phillips (1954).

[4] The desirability of a measure taking account of dynamic reactions is pointed out by Goldberger (1959), who, having used the Musgrave and Miller measure, comments: "But . . . a proper measure of built-in stabilization would not be a one dimensional quantity. Not only does the insertion of tax rates reduce the equilibrium multiplier effect on G.N.P., but it also modifies the composition of income and output. Furthermore, it changes the characteristic time pattern of response" (*ibid.*, p. 128).

[5] The use of such a measure is not entirely novel. For instance, Friedman (1955) compared the variance of income without countercyclical policy with the variance of income with countercyclical policy in his investigation of the conditions under which countercyclical policy will actually succeed in reducing instability.

[6] The differences in the equilibrium levels of income depend on the marginal rate of taxation and on the autonomous components in the tax function. This autonomous component could be adjusted so that the same equilibrium level of income is obtained in the two cases.

[7] For an illustration of this possibility see Smyth (1963).

## II

In a recent article (Smyth, 1962) I estimated the following system for Australia:

$$C_t = 94.7$$
$$+ 0.75 \, (Y_{t-1} - T_{t-1} - D_{t-1}) + u_t, \quad (1)$$
$$(0.01)$$

$$I_t = 318.7$$
$$+ 0.48 \, (Y_{t-1} - Y_{t-2}) + 13.7t + v_t, \quad (2)$$
$$(0.04) \qquad\qquad\qquad (1.8)$$

$$Y_t = C_t + I_t + X_t, \quad (3)$$

yielding

$$Y_t = 413.4 + 1.23 \, Y_{t-1} - 0.48 \, Y_{t-2}$$
$$+ 13.7t + u_t + v_t + X_t \quad (4)$$
$$- 0.75 T_{t-1} - 0.75 D_{t-1}.$$

In this system subscript $t$ indicates the time period (year), $Y$ denotes gross national product, $I$ gross private domestic investment, $C$ consumption, $X$ other components of gross national product, $T$ taxation (indirect taxes, less subsidies, plus personal and company taxes, plus estate and gift duties), $D$ (so defined as to be negative) represents transfer payments to obtain gross private income from gross national product, and $u_t$ and $v_t$ are the disturbance terms in the consumption and investment functions, respectively. Quantities are millions of 1946–47 pounds. The figures in parentheses are the standard errors associated with the estimates. In this model $X_t$, $D_t$, and $T_t$ are taken to be determined autonomously. There is, thus, no built-in flexibility of taxation.

Equation (4) consists of three components: constant term and trend; lagged terms in $Y_{t-1}$ and $Y_{t-2}$; and a composite disturbance term $(u_t + v_t + X_t - 0.75 T_{t-1} - 0.75 D_{t-1})$ which is made up of the disturbance terms of the consumption and investment functions and various autonomous components of expenditure. This composite disturbance term has mean 174.2 and standard deviation 61.2, and there is no evidence of either autocorrelation or trend.[8] It is proposed to treat it as a random disturbance.

In equation (4) the term $13.7t$ sets the trend rate of growth or moving equilibrium, and we may concentrate on fluctuations about this equilibrium generated by the interaction of the relationship of $Y_t$ with $Y_{t-1}$ and $Y_{t-2}$ and the disturbance term.

We are interested in obtaining the standard deviation of income measured about the moving equilibrium. Equation (4) is a second-order

---

[8] For this composite disturbance term a Durbin-Watson coefficient of 1.42 is obtained and the correlation between the disturbance and time is $-0.12$.

stochastic difference equation, and use may be made of the properties of such an equation. Consider the equation

$$Y_t + aY_{t-1} + bY_{t-2} = q_t, \qquad (5)$$

where $q_t$ is a non-autocorrelated random variable with standard deviation $\sigma$. Then if the values of $a$ and $b$ are such that the system is stable,[9] the standard deviation of $Y_t$ may be shown (Kendall, 1944; Bartlett, 1955, pp. 144–45) to be

$$\sqrt{\left\{\frac{(1 + b)\sigma^2}{(1 - b)[(1 + b)^2 - a^2]}\right\}}.$$

The values of the parameters in equation (4) are such as to fulfil the stability conditions. The model develops damped oscillations about the growth trend, and these oscillations may be kept alive by erratic shocks such as those generated by the disturbance term (Smyth, 1962). Using the above relationship yields a standard deviation for $Y_t$ of 125.4. This is $SD(Y)$.

Instead of taking taxation as autonomous, an estimate can be made of the marginal rate of taxation. A crude way of doing this is to make taxation a function of gross private income; in a rough way this gives the average marginal rate for the postwar period.[10] This yields

$$T_t = -3.8 + 0.21 (Y_t - D_t) + w_t \qquad (6)$$
$$(0.02)$$

($w_t$ being the disturbance term in the tax function), and substituting this in the consumption function and then substituting for $C_t$, $I_t$, and $X_t$ in equation (3) gives

$$Y_t = 416.3 + 1.07\ Y_{t-1} - 0.48\ Y_{t-2}$$
$$+ 13.7t + u_t + v_t + X_t \qquad (7)$$
$$- 0.75w_{t-1} - 0.59D_{t-1}.$$

Here the composite disturbance term is $(u_t + v_t + X_t - 0.59D_{t-1} - 0.05w_{t-1})$. This composite disturbance term has mean 532.3 and standard deviation 59.5, and there is no evidence of either autocorrelation or trend.[11]

[9] The stability conditions are

   i) $-1 < b < 1$,

   ii) $1 + a + b > 0$,

   iii) $1 - a + b > 0$.

[10] The use of this simple method can be justified by the demonstration below that $B$ is relatively insensitive to changes in the marginal rate of taxation so that errors in estimating the marginal rate are not too significant.

[11] For this composite disturbance term a Durbin-Watson coefficient of 1.48 is obtained, and the correlation between the disturbance and time is 0.36.

Again the properties of equation (5) may be used to obtain an estimate of the standard deviation of income, this time that when built-in flexibility is present.[12] A value of 98.2 is obtained for $SD(Y')$.

The estimated values of $SD(Y)$ and $SD(Y')$ yield a value of 0.22 for $B$. Thus the presence of built-in flexibility of taxation in Australian economy reduces the standard deviation of income fluctuations in the Australian economy by 22 per cent.[13]

In the above it was necessary to calculate the magnitudes of the standard deviations of the two composite disturbance terms, but the whole procedure can be much simplified if it may be assumed that the composite disturbances have the same standard deviation in both cases, for then the standard deviation of the composite disturbance cancels out when the ratio of $SD(Y')$ to $SD(Y)$ is taken, so that it is necessary only to know the parameters of $Y_{t-1}$ and $Y_{t-2}$ in the two cases. Making such an assumption yields a value for $B$ of 0.19 which is close to that obtained by the more laborious method.

In this model $B$ and $m$ are connected by the relationship

$$B = 1 - \sqrt{\left[\frac{0.678}{2.190 - (1.23 - 0.75m)^2}\right]},$$

where $m$ is the marginal tax rate.[14] It is apparent

[12] Like eq. (4), eq. (5) generates damped oscillations above the growth trend.

[13] The present estimate relates to situations in which the share of income going to the farm sector is not highly abnormal for in such situations the fitted model is inappropriate. On this see Smyth (1962, p. 230).

[14] On the assumption that the disturbances are non-autocorrelated and have the same standard deviations:

Without built-in flexibility:

$$Y_t = 0.75\,Y_{t-1} + 0.48(Y_{t-1} - Y_{t-2})$$
$$= 1.23\,Y_{t-1} - 0.48\,Y_{t-2};$$

With built-in flexibility:

$$Y_t = 0.75(Y_{t-1} - T_{t-1}) + 0.48(Y_{t-1} - Y_{t-2})$$
$$= 0.75(Y_{t-1} - m\,Y_{t-1}) + 0.48(X_{t-1} - Y_{t-2})$$
$$= 0.75(1 - m)\,Y_{t-1} + 0.48(Y_{t-1} - Y_{t-2})$$
$$= (1.23 - 0.75m)\,Y_{t-1} - 0.48\,Y_{t-2},$$

where $m$ is the marginal tax rate. Autonomous components are ignored as we are interested in homogeneous forms.

Making use of the relationship given above for stochastic second-order difference equations we get for $SD(Y)$ and $SD(Y')$, where $\sigma$ is the standard deviation of the disturbance terms,

$$SD(Y) = \sqrt{\left\{\frac{(1 + 0.48)\sigma^2}{(1 - 0.48)[(1 + 0.48)^2 - 1.23^2]}\right\}}$$

that $B$ is not very responsive to changes in the marginal rate of taxation—with the estimated value of $m$ of 0.21, the elasticity of $B$ with respect to $m$ (which is $dB/dm[M/B]$) and that indicates the responsiveness of the stabilization measure to changes in the marginal tax rate, is only 0.68, and this elasticity falls as the marginal tax rate rises. Even with a marginal tax rate of unity the standard deviation of income is reduced by only 41 per cent compared with the situation without any built-in flexibility.

It is clear, then, that as far as the Australian economy is concerned, assuming the fitted model to be appropriate, it is not possible to rely upon built-in flexibility of taxation entirely, or even largely, as a stabilization device, and any hopes that the stability of the system may be greatly improved by raising the marginal rate of taxation are misplaced.

In the Australian case just considered it has been possible to make use of a general formula for the standard deviation of income. It becomes increasingly difficult to obtain such formulas as the system becomes more complex,[15] and an alternative approach is to obtain $B$ by means of simulation. This approach may be illustrated using the Klein-Goldberger model of the United States economic system (Klein and Goldberger, 1955).

Goldberger (1959, pp. 122, 126) gives the characteristic equations of the real sector of the Klein-Goldberger model without and with built-in flexibility of taxation as, respectively,

$$x^4 - 2.0886x^3 + 1.5574x^2 - 0.4696x \quad (8)$$
$$+ 0.0567 = 0$$

and

$$x^4 - 1.6837x^3 + 0.9731x^2 - 0.2657x \quad (9)$$
$$+ 0.0354 = 0.$$

The second equation incorporates postwar tax rates. Both the equations yield damped oscillations. The equations, which show the response characteristics of national income to changes in exogenous expenditure, are obtained from systems derived by Goldberger containing four endo-genous variables in four equations. The unit time period is a year.

In the simulation it was assumed that both these systems were subject to the same normally distributed non-autocorrelated random disturbances. The standard deviations of income with and without built-in flexibility were calculated, and so $B$ was obtained. This procedure yielded an estimate of 0.37 for $B$ indicating that the rates of taxation ruling in the postwar period have reduced the standard deviation of U.S. national income by 37 per cent.

The estimates suggest that built-in flexibility of taxation is nearly twice as effective as a stabilization device in the United States as in Australia. There are several possible explanations of this. Cursory inspection does suggest that marginal tax rates are somewhat higher in the United States than in Australia. The values of the other parameters are likely to be different for the two systems. Speeds of adjustment may be different—adjustment is probably faster in the United States. It would, however, require discussion of the whole question of differences in dynamic structures between economies to explain the difference in the estimates, and it is impossible to give that here.

## III

The present paper has suggested that comparative statics conclusions on the automatic stabilizing effects of built-in flexibility of taxation should be regarded as unsatisfactory and inferior to inferences based on analysis taking account of the dynamic structure of the economic system and has put forward a method of analysis that can be applied to dynamic systems. Practical application of the measure to aggregative models of two economies has given some idea of the actual extent to which fluctuations are reduced by built-in flexibility of taxation.

But the models used, especially that for Australia, are fairly simple, and consequently the empirical conclusions should be accepted with a certain amount of reserve and the main emphasis of the paper placed on the suggested *technique* for evaluating the effectiveness of stabilization measures in a dynamic context rather than on the actual empirical results.

The technique suggested—that of looking at the standard deviations of the system with and without the application of a stabilization measure —has been applied here to the particular problem of built-in flexibility of taxation, but clearly the technique can be used to evaluate the effectiveness of any type of stabilization measure.

and

$$SD(Y') = \sqrt{\left\{ \frac{(1 + 0.48)\sigma^2}{(1-0.48)[(1+0.48)^2-(1.23-0.75m)^2]} \right\}}.$$

Substitution in

$$B = 1 - \frac{SD(Y')}{SD(Y)}$$

gives

$$B = 1 - \sqrt{\left[ \frac{0.678}{2.190 - (1.23 - 0.75m)^2} \right]}.$$

[15] For a method see van de Panne (1965).

# REFERENCES

Bartlett, M. S. *An Introduction to Stochastic Processes*. Cambridge, 1955.

Friedman, M. "The Effects of Full Employment Policy on Economic Stability: A Formal Analysis," in *Essays in Positive Economics*. Chicago, 1955.

Goldberger, A. S. *Impact Multipliers and Dynamic Properties of the Klein-Goldberger Model*. Amsterdam, 1959.

Kendall, M. G. "On Autoregressive Time Series," *Biometrika*, XXXIII (August, 1944), 107.

Klein, L. R., and Goldberger, A. S. *An Econometric Model of the United States*, 1929–1952. Amsterdam, 1955.

Musgrave, R. A., and Miller, M. H. "Built-in Flexibility," *A.E.R.*, XXXVIII (March, 1948), 122–28 (reprinted in American Economic Association, *Readings in Fiscal Policy* [Homewood, Ill., 1955]).

Panne, C. van de. "Variances and Stability in Linear Dynamic Models." Discussion Paper, Ser. A, No. 56, Faculty of Commerce and Social Science, University of Birmingham, 1965.

Phillips, A. W. "Stabilization Policy in a Closed Economy," *Econ. J.*, LXIV (June, 1954), 290–323.

Smyth, D. J. "Investment, Growth, and the Trade Cycle: The Post-War Australian Experience," *Econ. Record*, XXXVIII (June, 1962), 226–45.

———. "Can 'Automatic Stabilizers' Be Destabilizing?" *Public Finance*, Nos. 3–4 (1963), pp. 357–64.

*JOSEPH SCHERER*

# A Primer on Federal Budgets

*42*   The Federal budget is a multipurpose document. Its original purpose had been, and its main purpose continues to be, to provide a system of planning and control over Government activities by the executive and legislative branches. In this respect, it serves the same functions that a budget plan performs for an individual or a business. But, unlike the budget of any other single economic unit, the Federal budget because of its sheer size—some $90–120 billion per year, depending upon the particular budget concept used—exerts a potent influence on the nation's economy. This influence, moreover, is being increasingly directed, as a matter of deliberate policy, toward assisting the economy to attain, and sustain, high levels of employment and economic activity. Not only have these growth and stability goals been incorporated in legislation, as in the Employment Act of 1946, but there appears to be a growing consensus among the citizenry that it is appropriate and desirable for the Federal Government to pursue such goals.

Reprinted from the *Federal Reserve Bank of New York Monthly Review* (April, 1965), pp. 79–88, by permission of the author and publisher. Joseph Scherer is an economist on the staff of the Federal Reserve Bank of New York.

In order to evaluate how the Federal Government carries out these housekeeping and policy purposes, it is necessary to examine budget data, totals as well as components. This is not easy, since the needs of analysts have led to the development of a number of concepts that at times appear to provide conflicting data. For example, different dollar magnitudes can be found for categories designated by the same general name. Thus, the data for fiscal 1964 (the year ended June 30, 1964) show the Federal deficit as $8.2 billion in the administrative budget, or $4.8 billion in the consolidated cash budget, or $3.9 billion in the national income account budget. Likewise, for the current year, fiscal 1965, the Bureau of the Budget estimates the deficit will be $6.3 billion in the administrative budget, $4.0 billion in the cash budget, and $5.0 billion in the national income account budget. These three different deficit amounts are, of course, neither arbitrary nor unnecessary. Instead, they reflect an attempt to provide appropriate data for unraveling some exceedingly complicated economic and accounting relationships.

As a very abbreviated summary, each of the three widely used measures of the Federal budget has its own appropriate use. Yet each measure,

**391**

singly, as well as all measures together, still leaves something to be desired in terms of providing a complete picture of the role of the Federal Government in the economy. For example, none of the budgets integrate complete information, on a current basis, about Government lending activities and guarantees of loans, although this information may be assembled from other sources.

The administrative budget provides data which are most useful to the Government itself for housekeeping and control purposes. Because of the detail given for individual agencies and the availability of detailed monthly data, the administrative budget may prove helpful to an analyst focusing on some narrow aspect of the Federal impact on the economy.

The consolidated cash budget provides the most comprehensive view of Federal expenditures and receipts. Changes in these flows have a direct impact on the Government's cash balances and constitute a major determinant of Treasury debt operations with the non-Federal sector.

Finally, the Federal sector in the national income accounts is often used for formulating and analyzing problems primarily in the framework of the national income and product accounts data.

It is the purpose of this article to delineate in broad terms the uses and limitations of the alternative budget series and also to indicate the typical sources where these data can be found. First, the budget process is briefly described. Then an explanation is given of the basic characteristics of each budget concept, of some of the interlocking relationships among the budgets, and of the way in which each budget serves different analytical or administrative purposes.

## The Budget Process

The President's budget message, and its accompanying documents, usually delivered to Congress in the third week of January, present a comprehensive view of Federal spending and receipts for the current and the next fiscal year. (The Federal Government's fiscal year runs from July 1 of one year to June 30 of the following year and is identified by the year in which it ends.) Implementation of the tax and spending programs described in the budget is dependent upon legislation already in effect, as well as on new legislation still to be enacted. The new legislation does not come in a single package, but is intro-

duced and considered by Congress in separately proposed and separately enacted bills. It will be useful to consider for a moment the general process by which a bill is enacted, and then to focus more specifically on what further steps are necessary before a particular agency can actually spend funds for a program.

Each new activity of the Federal Government (or extension of an old activity) must be authorized by a bill which has passed both houses of Congress and has been signed by the President.[1] Such bills are considered first by the appropriate legislative committee responsible for the subject area (true of both the House of Representatives and the Senate), which in turn typically refers the bills to subcommittees specializing in particular segments of the over-all area covered by the full committee. After the relevant legislative subcommittee and committee have approved the bill —including, if necessary, authorization to appropriate up to a given amount of money for the program—the bill is brought to a vote before the full membership of each branch of Congress.

For major legislation in the House of Representatives, the Rules Committee ordinarily acts as an intermediary to determine when legislation can reach the floor for consideration. Failure of the Rules Committee to bring out a bill produces complications since the bill cannot be voted on by the full chamber, except by a cumbersome procedure which is not often tried. If the bills for a particular program passed by the two houses differ in any respect, these differences must be resolved by a conference committee composed of members of the two houses, so that identical bills can be resubmitted for passage in each house and then transmitted to the President for signature.

The above procedure only authorizes the program in a general way. Actual authority to spend funds typically involves a further step—the passage of an appropriations bill again by both houses of Congress, which is then signed by the President. An appropriations bill follows the same general procedure as any substantive legislation, that is, it must pass a subcommittee, then a full committee, and then the full chamber. But for an appropriations bill, no matter what Government agency or subject area is involved, the bill starts its trip in the Appropriations Committee

[1] Some bills, of course, are passed over a Presidential veto, and a few bills have become law without Presidential signature under the Constitutional provision that, if the President does not sign or veto a bill, it becomes law after ten days provided that Congress is in session.

of the House of Representatives before it can be voted upon by the full House and similarly must be passed by the Senate Appropriations Committee before it can be voted on by the full Senate.

In effect, then, legislation requiring the spending of money typically goes through two complete rounds of legislative approval—first, the act authorizing the program (with a bill considered first by the subject area committees) and, secondly, the act providing the funds for the program (with a bill originating in the appropriations committees). And it is important to note that the amount of the appropriations bill need not be the whole amount authorized in the legislation setting up the new program (first round). Since control over the scope of any program is ultimately determined by the amount of money made available, it is obvious that the appropriations committees in the two houses occupy a strategic position. Appropriations bills, however, are not the only avenue by which a Government agency can obtain the right to spend, although it is the most important one.

A government agency acquires the authority to spend money from legislation providing new obligational authority (NOA). The NOA may be given in any of three forms—appropriations, contract authorizations, and authorizations to expend from debt receipts. Only the first two are directly under the control of the appropriations committees of the two houses.

## 1.  Appropriations

These permit an agency to order goods and services and draw funds from the Treasury to pay for these goods and services up to some stated amount. Most spending takes this form. Although appropriations are usually limited to one year, some may cover several years or be "no year" (i.e., available until expended) because of the long-term nature of the project. The Defense Department holds the bulk of the multi-year appropriations. There are also "permanent appropriations", such as for interest on the debt, which do not require new action by Congress when additional funds are needed.

## 2.  Contract Authorizations

These allow an agency to contract for goods and services, but payments cannot be made until Congress passes an appropriation to provide funds for the obligations incurred.

## 3.  Authorizations to Expend from Debt Receipts

These allow agencies to borrow money, generally through the United States Treasury, to contract for the purchase of goods and services, and to pay for them with the borrowed funds. This procedure has been called "back door" financing and has been subjected to criticism by some members of Congress because the appropriations committees have no say in establishing the actual amount of spending by the agency under this system. Instead, the authority to borrow from the Treasury—and the amount—are given in the legislation authorizing the program. Under this arrangement, an agency may carry on its activities indefinitely without recourse to any annual appropriations, unless otherwise specified in the law. Many of the Government loan programs have been set up in this fashion since it is usually expected that such programs will sooner or later be self-supporting.

NOA is generally considered the avenue whereby Congress can control the size of the budget. An increase in NOA for a fiscal year above the amount for previous years suggests that Government spending will grow. The failure of NOA to rise, however, may not be significant since Congress may merely have legislated NOA at levels below the amounts needed to pay for commitments under already existing programs. For example, some veterans' programs specify benefit payments to veterans eligible under specified conditions. If NOA for a program of this type is cut without changing the eligibility requirements and claims under the program are greater than projected, then supplementary appropriations must be voted before the end of the fiscal year in order to prevent default on a commitment made by the Government.

NOA, including carry-overs from prior years, represents the potential level of spending for a particular program. By contrast, obligations are commitments already made which will require spending of funds—funds available to the agency from obligational authority previously granted.[2] Expenditures are the end of the line which runs from NOA to obligations to expenditures.

Spending in any single fiscal year is always

---

[2] Obligations, particularly of the Department of Defense, have sometimes been interpreted as a good approximation of a "new orders" series. Such an interpretation is incorrect, because obligations also include commitments for expected disbursements for the wage and salaries of Government employees.

made up of a combination of spending from appropriations carried over from previous years as well as from appropriations newly legislated. In fiscal 1966, for example, the Administration's recent budget document estimates that $27.6 billion will be spent from the pool of previously authorized NOA—to pay for those parts of long-range programs now under way which will be completed during fiscal 1966. An additional $72 billion will be spent in fiscal 1966 from part of the NOA that the President is asking for in his budget message. Thus, total spending (in the administrative budget) is expected to amount to $99.7 billion—part out of existing multiyear appropriations and part out of new appropriations to be voted this year, which will include some new multiyear appropriations to be spent over several successive fiscal years, roughly at the pace that the programs are carried out.

Expenditures usually take the form of the issuance of a check which, when cashed, will reduce the Treasury's balance at a Federal Reserve Bank. But there are exceptions. Sometimes an expenditure takes the form of the issuance of a security, as in the case of payments of subscriptions to the International Monetary Fund (IMF), which raises the debt but does not reduce the Treasury's cash or bank balances. Since payment by issuance of a security does not affect the Treasury's cash balance, it is therefore not a cash budget expenditure; it is, however, listed as an expenditure in the administrative budget and raises the debt. It does not become a cash expenditure until the security is redeemed (by the IMF in the illustration cited). At that time, the cash balance will be reduced and the transaction will also reduce the amount of outstanding Government debt. Ordinarily, retirement of Federal debt is not counted as an expenditure but as a debt transaction, which is similar to private accounting practice in distinguishing between "current" transactions and balance-sheet transactions.[3]

## Administrative Budget

When reference is made to "*the* budget" in the press or in the halls of Congress, it almost invariably means the administrative budget. The President is required by the Budget and Account-

ing Act of 1921 to submit this budget to Congress every January in order to initiate a new round in the legislative process authorizing funds to support the activities of the regular Government agencies. These agencies are "controlled" by Congress through the power of the purse, i.e., Congress determines how much each agency shall have to spend by specifically approving dollar amounts for various purposes in an appropriations bill (which may lump together a number of agencies).

The administrative budget covers only those agencies for which Congress makes regular appropriations. Prior to the 1930's, this budget was a good measure of total Government activities. However, with the establishment and growth of self-financing agencies—whose operations are not included in the administrative budget—this budget has become an increasingly less adequate measure of the Federal Government sector. Government activities excluded from the administrative budget are the trust funds (of which the best known are the various social insurance funds) and quasi-public agencies, such as the Federal Home Loan Banks. These additional activities in recent years have added some $25 billion to $30 billion a year to Federal receipts and expenditures, as recorded in the cash budget.[4]

In addition to the direct exclusion of certain activities from the administrative budget, there are some accounting conventions in this budget which must be recast in constructing the cash budget and the Federal budget in the national income and product accounts. An example of these conventions can be seen in the treatment of interest payments. Interest payments for fiscal 1964 totaled only $8.0 billion.[5] The bulk of some $3 billion of *noncash* interest is accounted for by "bookkeeping" payments by the Government to itself (intragovernmental transactions) for securities held by the trust funds and by the accrual of interest on outstanding Government securities, most notably savings bonds and Treasury discount bills, which becomes a cash expenditure

---

[3] Of course, debt operations—selling or retirement of securities—will change the level of the Treasury's cash balance but will not be recorded as a receipt or expenditure. In other words, transactions in United States Government debt instruments are usually classified as debt operations and are not included in budget transactions.

[4] Many of these activities (trust accounts) are financed by special earmarked taxes, while others (lending agencies) are financed, at least in part, by borrowing from the Treasury or in the market.

[5] Net interest paid in the Federal sector of the national income accounts for fiscal 1964 was $8.1 billion, compared with $8.0 billion in the cash budget. Usually the difference in levels for interest payments in the cash and national income budgets has been larger than that shown for fiscal 1964. The reason for differences in levels is discussed in the section devoted to the national income version of the budget.

when the savings bonds or Treasury bills are turned in for payment. Other intra-governmental transactions are included in the administrative budget figures, both for receipts and expenditures, in order to allocate these expenses and receipts more properly to the individual agencies concerned. This procedure raises the total of Government receipts and expenditures above the amount shown for the same agencies in the cash budget (described in the next section), because the cash budget eliminates intragovernmental transactions. However, the difference between the cash and the administrative figures for a particular agency in any given year is likely to be relatively small, compared with the total, except for interest payments as just discussed and for those agencies whose operations include trust fund functions, most notably the Department of Health, Education, and Welfare.

Despite its incomplete coverage of the Federal sector, the administrative budget is a source of valuable data to persons interested in knowing how much is spent by a "regular" Government agency and its major divisions. Data for this budget are published in the Treasury's *Monthly Statement of Receipts and Expenditures of the United States Government*, approximately three weeks after the end of each month (see Table 1). To the extent that a Government agency, or activity, can be closely identified with a specific activity or segment of the economy (for example, the National Park Service, Rivers and Harbors and Flood Control, or Military Construction), these outlays as summarized in the *Monthly Statement* indicate the current scope of Government activities in the area concerned. Perhaps the most widely used data in the *Monthly Statement*, other than the summary budget totals, are those which give the breakdown of Defense Department spending by functional category—such as research and development, military construction, etc. (More detailed spending and order data are released directly by the Defense Department but are typically available with a much longer time lag than the administrative budget data.) Annual data classified by broad functional categories are given in the budget itself and usually in the budget review, generally issued after each Congressional session; current data appear in the *Monthly Statement* and in the *Treasury Bulletin*.

## Cash Budget

The cash budget is the most comprehensive budget statement issued by the United States Government and is designed to show the cash flows between the Federal Government and other sectors of the economy. Unlike the administrative budget, it covers not only the activities of the regular Government agencies found in the administrative budget but also the cash flows associated with the activities of the trust funds (such as social security) and Government-sponsored enterprises (such as the Federal Home Loan Bank Board). Like the administrative budget, it also covers the purchase and sale of assets (both "real", such as buildings, and "financial", such as mortgages and other loans). However, as noted earlier, certain items, e.g., interest payments, treated as accrual items in the administrative budget are placed on a cash basis. For many years a substantial number of economists have regarded the cash budget as the best measure of the total impact of the Federal Government on the economy.

Total expenditures and receipts in the cash budget are larger than in the administrative budget, since the cash budget includes a wide range of Government activities omitted from the administrative budget. Nevertheless, because the cash budget eliminates many transactions of Government agencies with each other (intra-governmental transactions), it records certain Government activities at lower levels than the administrative budget (for example, interest payments, as noted previously). The total of cash budget expenditures, however, does understate the full magnitude of the cash flows between the Government and the private sector, as some agencies are listed only on a *net* basis on the expenditures side. The Post Office, for example, is recorded as having spent $600 million in fiscal 1964—but this amount represents only "net expenditures" obtained after deducting postal receipts (sale of stamps, etc.) from total postal expenditures. Government corporations are also typically recorded only on a net basis. The device of netting, incidentally, is not restricted to the cash budget; it also affects some of the data reported in the administrative budget, as mentioned earlier, and in the national income budget.

The cash budget in the form of "receipts from and payments to the public" is also called "the consolidated cash budget". Annual data giving a functional breakdown for receipts and expenditures are published in the budget and in the budget review (with some exceptions). Monthly data are also available (with functional breaks) for this cash budget in the *Federal Reserve Bulletin*, but seasonally adjusted data are available only on a quarterly basis and only for total cash income, total cash outgo, and the resultant cash surplus or deficit.

## Table 1. Federal Budgets and Their Data Sources (Fiscal 1964 and Fiscal 1965)

(billions of dollars)

| Item | ADMINISTRATIVE BUDGET | | CASH BUDGET (DTS BASIS)[a] | | CONSOLIDATED CASH BUDGET— RECEIPTS FROM AND PAYMENTS TO PUBLIC | | NATIONAL INCOME ACCOUNT BUDGET | |
|---|---|---|---|---|---|---|---|---|
| | Fiscal 1964 (actual) | Fiscal 1965 (estimate) | Fiscal 1964 (actual) | Fiscal 1965 (estimate) | Fiscal 1964 (actual) | Fiscal 1965 (estimate) | Fiscal 1964 (actual) | Fiscal 1965 (estimate) |
| Receipts | 89.5 | 91.2 | 121.6 | c | 115.5 | 117.4 | 114.7 | 116.0 |
| Expenditures | 97.7 | 97.5 | 125.6[b] | c | 120.3 | 121.4 | 118.5 | 121.0 |
| Surplus (+) or deficit (−) | − 8.2 | − 6.3 | − 4.0 | c | − 4.8 | − 4.0 | − 3.9 | − 5.0 |
| Type of data | Monthly seasonally unadjusted, available with a three-week lag. The Budget projects annual data for the current fiscal year and the next fiscal year based on the Administration's economic assumptions and proposed programs. | | Daily and monthly seasonally unadjusted, available with a three- to four- day lag. | | Monthly and quarterly unadjusted, quarterly seasonally adjusted, available with a one-month lag. The Budget projects annual data for the current fiscal year and the next fiscal year based on the Administration's economic assumptions and proposed programs. | | Quarterly seasonally adjusted, available with a two-month lag (complete expenditure data and all receipts data except corporate profits tax accruals available with a one-month lag). Quarterly unadjusted, available in February and July. The Budget projects annual data for the current fiscal year and the next fiscal year based on the Administration's economic assumptions and proposed programs. | |
| Sources of data | Treasury Department:   Monthly Statement   Treasury Bulletin Survey of Current Business   Federal Reserve Bulletin   Economic Indicators   The Budget | | Treasury Department:   Daily Statement[a]   Treasury Bulletin | | Treasury Department:   Monthly Statement   Treasury Bulletin Survey of Current Business   Federal Reserve Bulletin   Economic Indicators   The Budget | | Survey of Current Business Economic Indicators The Budget | |

Source: The Budget of the United States Government Fiscal 1966.
Note: Because of rounding figures do not necessarily add to totals.
a Daily Statement of the United States Treasury (DTS).
b Includes clearing account.
c Full reconciliation to DTS basis for estimates is not available.

Detail for some ten categories of receipts and expenditures are available in a variant of the cash budget known as the *Daily Statement of the United States Treasury* (DTS) which excludes a few Government corporations whose accounts are not commingled with the Treasury's. These DTS data, *not* seasonally adjusted, are published for each working day, with a lag of about three or four days and are cumulated to a monthly total and for the fiscal year to date. The DTS data are used by analysts who are particularly interested in the level of, or changes in, the Treasury's cash balances and by those who need current data (daily and monthly totals) for major categories of Government receipts and expenditures and for debt operations.

A comparison of the consolidated cash budget and administrative budget expenditures on a functional basis is shown in Table 2. Differences for the same function, if large, are likely to reflect differences in coverage and in the treatment of intragovernmental transactions in the two budgets. In addition, relatively small differences in amount arise for functions called by the same general name in the two budget accounts because of differences in the accounting techniques used in recording these expenditures for the different budget accounts.

The surplus or deficit of the cash budget (not the administrative budget) will determine how the balances held by the Treasury will change. When a surplus is generated, the balances rise and Government debt held by the public may be retired. On the other hand, cash deficits, depending upon the level of the cash balance, may require that the Government borrow from the public in order to pay its bills. Consequently, the net flows as recorded in the cash budget are one of the major determinants of Government debt operations.

## Table 2. Federal Expenditures and Receipts, Administrative Budget and Consolidated Cash Budget (Fiscal 1964-66)

(billions of dollars)

| Type of Transaction | ADMINISTRATIVE BUDGET | | | CONSOLIDATED CASH BUDGET | | |
|---|---|---|---|---|---|---|
| | Actual | Estimate | | Actual | Estimate | |
| | 1964 | 1965 | 1966 | 1964 | 1965 | 1966 |
| Receipts | | | | | | |
| Individual income taxes | 48.7 | 47.0 | 48.2 | 48.7 | 47.0 | 48.2 |
| Corporation income taxes | 23.5 | 25.6 | 27.6 | 23.5 | 25.6 | 27.6 |
| Excise taxes (net) | 10.2 | 10.7 | 9.8 | 13.7 | 14.4 | 13.7 |
| Employment taxes | — | — | — | 16.8 | 16.7 | 18.7 |
| Estate and gift taxes | 2.4 | 2.8 | 3.2 | 2.4 | 2.8 | 3.2 |
| Customs | 1.3 | 1.4 | 1.5 | 1.3 | 1.4 | 1.5 |
| Deposits by states, unemployment insurance | — | — | — | 3.0 | 3.0 | 2.9 |
| Veterans' life insurance premiums | — | — | — | 0.5 | 0.5 | 0.5 |
| Other budget and trust receipts | — | — | — | 5.6 | 6.1 | 7.1 |
| Miscellaneous budget receipts | 4.1 | 4.5 | 4.7 | — | — | — |
| Interfund transactions | − 0.7 | − 0.8 | − 0.6 | — | — | — |
| Total | 89.5 | 91.2 | 94.4 | 115.5 | 117.4 | 123.5 |
| Expenditures by function | | | | | | |
| National defense | 54.2 | 52.2 | 51.6 | 54.5 | 52.8 | 52.5 |
| International affairs and finance | 3.7 | 4.0 | 4.0 | 3.5 | 3.6 | 4.2 |
| Space research and technology | 4.2 | 4.9 | 5.1 | 4.2 | 4.9 | 5.1 |
| Agriculture and agricultural resources | 5.6 | 4.5 | 3.9 | 5.8 | 4.6 | 4.1 |
| Natural resources | 2.5 | 2.7 | 2.7 | 2.6 | 2.8 | 2.9 |
| Commerce and transportation | 3.0 | 3.4 | 2.8 | 6.5 | 7.4 | 6.5 |
| Housing and community development | − 0.1 | − 0.3 | a | 1.7 | − 0.2 | 0.7 |
| Health, labor and welfare | 5.5 | 6.2 | 8.3 | 27.3 | 28.9 | 34.1 |
| Education | 1.3 | 1.5 | 2.7 | 1.3 | 1.5 | 2.6 |
| Veterans' benefits and services | 5.5 | 5.4 | 4.6 | 6.1 | 6.0 | 5.1 |
| Interest | 10.8 | 11.3 | 11.6 | 8.0 | 8.5 | 8.8 |
| General government | 2.3 | 2.4 | 2.5 | 2.2 | 2.4 | 2.4 |
| Unallocated and interfund transactions | − 0.7 | − 0.7 | − 0.1 | — | — | — |
| Deposit funds (net) | — | — | — | − 0.6 | a | a |
| Undistributed adjustments | — | — | — | − 2.9 | − 1.8 | − 1.6 |
| Total | 97.7 | 97.5 | 99.7 | 120.3 | 121.4 | 127.4 |

Source: *The Budget of the United States Government*, Fiscal 1966.
*Note:* Because of rounding, figures do not necessarily add to totals.
a Less than $50 million.

But there is no one-to-one correspondence between cash deficits and Government debt operations. A deficit can be financed simply by running down the cash balance. Alternatively, the Government may borrow to build up its cash balance rather than to meet a deficit in the cash budget. Moreover, the average level of balances maintained by the Government varies from time to time by substantial amounts which are determined by operating and policy considerations not directly related to the cash surplus or deficit.

## The National Income Account Budget

The Federal budget in the national income and product accounts (NIP) records the receipts and expenditures of the Government sector as an integrated part of the recorded activities of other sectors of the economy. The national income accounts, sometimes called "the GNP accounts", are a measure of current output (both goods and services) in the economy. The Federal sector data have gained wide currency in the last three years, since the President's Council of Economic Advisers has often used this version of the budget for its analyses of Federal fiscal impact.

Like the cash budget, the Federal sector account is a more comprehensive statement than the administrative budget. It differs from the cash budget, however, by restricting itself to receipts and expenditures which reflect the direct impact of Government spending and tax programs on the flow of current income and output, as measured by the national income accounts. A broader measure of the economic impact of the Government would include not only the direct impact but also influences on asset holdings and liquidity—which may indirectly affect income and output. Thus, such a measure would allow for the effect of all transactions involving existing assets, as well as any assets of a purely financial character (bonds, mortgages, loans, etc.).

On the expenditure side, the cash budget records spending at the time of payment, but in the NIP concept spending is typically recorded when delivery is made to the Government sector —which often does not coincide with the time of payment.[6] On the receipts side, the national income budget differs from the cash budget most importantly in recording corporate profits taxes when the tax liability is incurred rather than when the tax payment is made.

Expenditures in the Federal sector account are classified into five categories (see Table 3) which identify the basic economic import of the expenditures. The largest single category, accounting for more than half of the total, is "purchases of goods and services". Such purchases are one of the major components of total GNP as viewed from the product side—the others being personal consumption expenditures, domestic investment, net exports, and state and local government purchases. The next largest category of Federal expenditures, approximately one fourth of the total, is "transfer payments", defined as payments for which no goods or services have been rendered in exchange. These are mainly made to individuals and include such items as old-age pensions and unemployment benefits. Although transfer payments are not directly included in GNP, they do affect GNP indirectly because they add to disposable personal income which in turn strongly affects personal expenditures on goods and services. The other three items, accounting for less than one fifth of total Federal expenditures are (1) "grants-in-aid to state and local governments", which increase the receipts of these governmental units and, in turn, are spent by these units for goods and services or for transfer payments; (2) "net interest paid", which adds to personal income but is not counted as part of GNP;[7] and (3) "subsidies less current surplus of Government enterprises", a category which records the net of subsidy payments to private business offset by any profits made by Government agencies.

This five-part classification is very useful in differentiating broadly, and in a way not available from any other source, between analytically distinct types of Government spending. Moreover, additional details for some of these categories, available on an annual basis only, further enrich our understanding of the composition of Government spending. However, the delivery

---

[6] It should be noted that the "delivery" concept for recording purchases (or spending) is the standard national income accounts treatment for purchases made by all sectors of the economy (and not only the Government sector). Goods produced, but not yet delivered, show up in the inventory component of gross national product (GNP).

[7] Interest paid by the Federal Government is considered as part of personal income, though, unlike private interest payments, it is not included in total GNP because Federal Government interest payments are not viewed as income arising out of current production. Government interest in NIP excludes intragovernmental payments (similar to the cash budget) but treats certain items, such as interest on Treasury bills and savings bonds, on an accrual basis (similar to the administrative budget). Therefore, the interest total in NIP is likely to be different from that in the cash and the administrative budgets.

## Table 3. Federal Receipts and Expenditures in the National Income Accounts (Fiscal 1964-66)

(billions of dollars)

| Type of Transaction | ACTUAL | ESTIMATE | |
|---|---|---|---|
| | 1964 | 1965 | 1966 |

**Receipts**

| | | | |
|---|---|---|---|
| Personal tax and nontax | 51.4 | 50.3 | 52.2 |
| Corporate profits tax accruals | 23.5 | 23.9 | 24.7 |
| Indirect business tax and nontax accruals | 16.0 | 16.8 | 16.1 |
| Contributions for social insurance | 23.8 | 25.0 | 28.0 |
| Total | 114.7 | 116.0 | 121.0 |

**Expenditures**

| | | | |
|---|---|---|---|
| Purchases of goods and services | 66.1 | 65.9 | 66.7 |
| Transfer payments | 30.4 | 31.8 | 35.2 |
| Grants-in-aid to state and local governments | 9.8 | 10.7 | 13.0 |
| Net interest paid | 8.1 | 8.5 | 8.6 |
| Subsidies less current surplus of Government enterprises | 4.1 | 4.1 | 3.5 |
| Total | 118.5 | 121.0 | 127.0 |
| Surplus (+) or deficit (−) | − 3.9 | − 5.0 | − 6.0 |

Source: *The Budget of the United States Government*, Fiscal 1966.
Note: Because of rounding figures do not necessarily add to totals.

basis for recording Government expenditures on goods and services sometimes fails to identify properly the time period when the Government is significantly influencing the level of private employment and output. This is particularly troublesome when the level of Government orders is subject to wide variation, as the case at the beginning and end of the Korean war. This timing problem is one illustration of the need for different budget concepts: it is not possible to construct a single series which is appropriate for all uses.

The Federal sector data are available quarterly on a seasonally adjusted annual rate basis. The figures are released about one month after the quarter is over, except for corporate profit tax accruals which lag by about two months.[8] The

[8] Seasonally unadjusted figures are also available in the February and July issues of the *Survey of Current Business*, United States Department of Commerce.

data are revised as more information is obtained for the period. While individual adjustments of components are generally small, in combination they sometimes shift the budget from an originally estimated deficit to a surplus.

A comprehensive view of how the administrative, cash, and national income budgets are related is shown in Table 4. In summary, moving from the administrative budget to the cash budget primarily entails adding to the administrative budget a total for the trust funds plus Government-sponsored enterprises while eliminating from the administrative budget a total for intragovernmental transactions. The transition from cash to NIP transactions (with some qualifications) primarily involves: (1) timing adjustments (mainly to an accrual basis on the receipts side and to a delivery basis on the expenditures side), (2) the elimination of assets transactions included in the cash figures, and (3) the elimination of lending activities included in the cash figures.

## Table 4. Reconciliation of Administrative Budget and Cash Budget to Federal Receipts and Expenditures in the National Income Accounts (Fiscal 1964)

(billions of dollars)

| Type of Transaction | Administrative Budget Total | Adjustments from Administrative to Cash Budget | Consolidated Cash Budget Total | Adjustments from Cash to National Income Account Budget | National Income Account Budget Total |
|---|---|---|---|---|---|
| **Receipts** | | | | | |
| Administrative budget receipts | 89.5 | — | — | — | — |
| Less: Intragovernmental transactions | — | 4.2 | — | — | — |
| Receipts from exercise of monetary authority | — | 0.1 | — | — | — |
| Plus: Trust fund receipts | — | 30.3 | — | — | — |
| Equals: Federal cash receipts from the public | — | — | 115.5 | — | — |
| Adjustments for agency coverage: | | | | | |
| Less: District of Columbia revenue | — | — | — | 0.3 | — |
| Adjustments for netting and consolidation: | | | | | |
| Less: Interest and other earnings | — | — | — | 1.4 | — |
| Plus: Contributions to Federal employees' retirement funds, etc. | — | — | — | 2.0 | — |
| Adjustments for timing: | | | | | |
| Plus: Excess of corporate tax accruals over collections, personal taxes, etc. | — | — | — | —0.7 | — |
| Adjustments for capital transactions: | | | | | |
| Less: Realization upon loans and investments, sale of Government property, etc. | — | — | — | 0.6 | — |
| Equals: Receipts—national income budget | — | — | — | — | 114.7 |
| **Expenditures** | | | | | |
| Administrative budget expenditures | 97.7 | — | — | — | — |
| Less: Intragovernmental transactions | — | 4.2 | — | — | — |
| Accrued interest and other noncash expenditures | — | 2.0 | — | — | — |
| Plus: Trust fund expenditures (including Government-sponsored enterprise expenditures net) | — | 28.9 | — | — | — |
| Equals: Federal cash payments to the public | — | — | 120.3 | — | — |
| Adjustments for agency coverage: | | | | | |
| Less: District of Columbia expenditures | — | — | — | 0.3 | — |
| Adjustments for netting and consolidation | | | | | |
| Less: Interest received and proceeds of Government sales | — | — | — | 1.4 | — |
| Plus: Contributions to Federal employees' retirement funds, etc. | — | — | — | 2.0 | — |
| Adjustments for timing: | | | | | |
| Plus: Excess interest accruals over payments on savings bonds and Treasury bills | — | — | — | 0.9 | — |
| Excess of deliveries over expenditures and other items | — | — | — | 1.5 | — |
| Less: Commodity Credit Corporation foreign currency exchange | — | — | — | 0.6 | — |
| Adjustments for capital transactions: | | | | | |
| Less: Loans—Federal National Mortgage Association secondary market mortgage purchases, redemption of International Monetary Fund notes, foreign assistance, etc. | — | — | — | 3.4 | — |
| Purchases of land and existing assets | — | — | — | 0.5 | — |
| Equals: Expenditure—national income budget | — | — | — | — | 118.5 |
| Surplus (+) or deficit (−) | − 8.2 | — | −4.8 | — | −3.9 |

Sources: Economic Report of the President, January 1965; The Budget of the United States Government, Fiscal 1966.
Note: Because of rounding, figures do not necessarily add to totals.

## The Budget and the Economy

Because of its sheer size, the Federal Government inevitably exerts a potent influence on the functioning of the economy. Budget data provide the raw material for analyzing this influence, but each form of the budget statement is not equally useful for this purpose. Typically, the administrative budget is not used for assessing the Government's impact on the economy, because it does not cover the full range of Government activities. Instead, the Government sector in the economy is usually analyzed with the data from the cash budget or the NIP budget.

A lively controversy has been going on for a number of years over the relative merits of the cash versus the NIP budget as the best measure of the Government's impact on the economy. When annual data are used, disagreement over the relative merits of the two comprehensive budget statements is not great. Although there are some differences in the levels of receipts and expenditures and the size of the surplus or deficit, the general trends observed in using either of the two comprehensive budget measures by and large will be similar. When quarterly data are used, however, the problems of choosing between the two measures become more troublesome because there are often conflicts both as to the direction and the magnitude of changes. Much depends on the particular problem under investigation, and often data from both budgets are needed to obtain a rounded picture.

The popular view of budget impact is that a surplus is a contractionary influence, that a deficit is an expansionary influence, and that a balanced budget is neutral. This popular view is, at best, only a partial view of the role of fiscal policy in the economy; a fuller perspective of the role of Government impact is somewhat more complex. In its simplest form, this popular view may be called the "cross section" approach. Taking the economy for a fixed period, a balance sheet of each of the sectors is compiled to show how each is affecting the economy. In this view, a Government deficit of $2 billion for the period is expansionary because the Government is adding to the demand side of the economy more than it is taking out in taxes. But this is far from the full story. Another dimension is added by the "time series" approach which looks at the change in budget position between two periods. For example, a deficit of $2 billion may be considered restrictive in the second period if it follows a deficit of $7 billion in the first period, whereas it may be held to be expansionary compared with a previous

surplus. In other words, if the $2 billion deficit followed a period when the budget deficit has been larger, say $7 billion, then the budget is exerting an effect in a contractionary direction. Given the change in strength of the forces at work in other sectors of the economy, this reduction in the amount of stimulus from the Government sector may be just the right amount of restraint for the economy, if high levels of activity are to be maintained and if potential excesses are to be curbed before they develop.

Both of the approaches described above, however, by measuring the fiscal impact of the Government in terms of the over-all budget surplus and deficit ignore the fact that for any given budget structure (the combination of spending programs and tax programs), the budget outcome depends not only on the specific character of these programs but also on the level of operation of the economy itself. Thus, for any particular year, an economy operating at full employment may give a budget surplus, while the same economy operating at 6 per cent unemployment, with the same expenditure and tax programs, will probably show a sizable budget deficit. As a correction for the distortion introduced by the impact of the economy itself on the realized net budget position, the concept of the full-employment budget surplus has been developed.

The full-employment budget surplus is an estimate of the budget outcome for any given budget structure, assuming that the economy is at full employment. (In theory, there could of course be a full-employment deficit.) By estimating the net surplus or deficit of different budget structures for the assumed full-employment level of activity for any year, it is possible to measure the relative restrictiveness of these different structures, i.e., the budget structure with higher full-employment surplus is taken to be more restrictive than budgets with smaller surpluses (or deficits). While the full-employment surplus concept is a highly suggestive addition to the other techniques of analysis, estimates of the precise magnitude of "full employment" and of the budget outcome at that level of activity are not particularly easy, and there are also some problems in the analytical interpretation of the estimates. The development of this concept, however, is indicative of the imaginative way new analytical tools are being forged to advance the art of fiscal analysis.

The full Government impact, of course, depends not only on the absolute levels of its receipts and expenditures, or how they change, but also on the further changes in spending by the private sector induced by the impulses emanating from the Government. Furthermore, different kinds of Government spending may affect the economy differently—for example, increases in Government purchases of goods may not have the same impact on the economy as an equal dollar increase in old-age payments. Similarly, an increase or decrease in income taxes will affect the economy differently from an equal dollar change in excise taxes. But what is not yet known with much certainty is the quantitative extent of these differences and how they may themselves vary under different economic conditions. Thus, a less aggregative approach also will have to be developed eventually to provide greater information.

The Government sector influences the economy in many different ways—by its spending programs, by its tax programs, by its credit programs, by its debt management actions, by its monetary policy, and by other actions which do not fit neatly into any of the foregoing classifications. Only part, although a very important part, of all this economically significant behavior is encompassed by the data typically found in the various budget documents. Much, however, is still to be learned. In part, improved insights will come from advances in the analytical tools applied to the public finance field. In part, advances also will depend on improvements of the kinds and quality of data available, for data provide the raw materials for the application of the analytical tools.

*R. A. MUSGRAVE*

# Should We Have a Capital Budget?

*43* Everyone is agreed that the economic effects of fiscal policy can be measured only by a *comprehensive* budget picture. This is not furnished by the Administrative Budget, but is provided by either the Cash or National Income Base Budget. As between these two, I find no clear preference, each being useful in its own way. A more potent issue is whether budget policy can be improved by the use of a Capital Budget. My comments will be limited to this aspect.

To begin with, one must distinguish between (a) proposals to separate current from capital items on the expenditure side of the budget, including expenditure budgeting for a longer period and appropriate accounting for capital items, but without assigning specific receipts to the current and capital parts, thus retaining the concept of a single, overall balance; and (b) proposals to assign specific types of receipts to specific types of expenditures, and to redefine the

Reprinted from the *Review of Economics and Statistics*, Vol. VL supplement (1963), pp. 134–137, by permission of the author and publisher, Harvard University Press. Copyright 1963 by the President and Fellows of Harvard College. R. A. Musgrave is a professor at Harvard University.

relevant concept of balance as that on current account.

The type of proposal involved under (a) is not controversial and deserves fullest support. There is an excellent case for budgeting capital expenditures over a longer than a one year basis and for improving allowance for capital costs (depreciation and interest) in evaluating the merit of particular programs. Also, it is relevant to know, from the point of view of fiscal prudence, whether budget policy has increased or reduced the public capital stock. Our concern here will not be with these suggestions, but with the more controversial proposals of the (b) type.

Redefinition of budgetary balance as balance between tax receipts and current expenditures is highly tempting politically, since it would result in a more "favorable" budget picture and, in a situation where fiscal policy is too tight, have a beneficial announcement effect. But would it make economic sense, and would it contribute to a more constructive budget discussion over the longer run?

Popular arguments in favor of such proposals frequently draws a mistaken analogy between the corporation and government. As "every farmer in Maine" knows, no one can live on debt forever;

but as "every businessman" knows, business finance justifies borrowing, provided such debt is backed by acquisition of assets. If so, why not apply the same principle to government and offset debt by assets acquired—thus defining deficit as an increase in debt in excess of increase in assets—or putting it another way, a reduction in the government's "net worth"? While possibly useful in making deficit finance politically palatable, this argument involves a complete misreading of the nature of fiscal economics. Government solvency is not a matter of assets held, but of taxable capacity; the reason for incurring debt is not to purchase assets, but to expand income relative to tax finance, and so on. While there is a case for separating out debt incurred in the finance of strictly self-liquidating public enterprises, that is, debt which does not require servicing from general tax receipts, this is where the analogy to business ends. Clearly, it cannot be extended to the larger problem of acquisition of non-fee yielding assets in general.

There is, however, a more sophisticated and valid view of the Capital Budget approach. This is based on the idea of temporal or inter-generation equity: if the government incurs outlays, the benefits from which are spread over a future period, it is unfair to ask the initial generation to sustain the whole cost. Rather, "prudence" requires that finance be based on a "pay-as-you-use" basis, each generation contributing a cost share commensurate with its own share in the benefit stream. The proposition, then, is that tax finance of such outlays is unfair because it places the entire burden on the initial generation, while debt finance (with retirement as the asset is used and the benefits are received) results in an inter-generation distribution of cost which is in line with the corresponding benefit distribution.[1]

This argument bears a superficial resemblance to the net-worth approach, but differs basically in that it deals with all outlays which provide for future benefits, and not only with those which involve acquisition of assets by government. Thus, teachers' salaries as well as school buildings are included, and the bias against investment in

human resources and other forms of intangible capital formation is avoided.

We then come to the major question. Is it true that debt finance (with debt retirement synchronized with the benefit stream) actually serves to achieve the desired objective of pay-as-you-use? This question cannot be answered in general, but depends on the kind of economy in which the budget operates.

*Case 1.* Suppose first that we have a system in which planned investment equals planned saving and full employment is maintained automatically. In this setting, no stabilization policy is needed. When a government purchase is made, the economy must at once release from private employment the required resources, and private outlays must be cut accordingly. This can be done interchangably by either tax or loan finance since, in such a system, $1 of borrowing from the public will reduce private spending by $1, just as does a dollar of tax receipt. But if the outlay is loan financed, the lenders are given a claim to being refunded later, when subsequent beneficiaries are taxed to retire the debt. In this fashion, the burden (in the sense of reduction in the private net worth of particular individuals) may be allocated properly over time for any one consumer, or between overlapping generations.

It may be noted also that substitution of loan for tax finance is likely to reduce private capital formation: depending on the elasticities involved, the increase in the demand for saving (due to increased public demand) under loan finance will drive up the rate of interest. This may raise the total supply of saving somewhat, but chances are that there will be a net increase in the rate of interest and reduction in the level of private investment. But though a reduction in private investment is likely to result, this is incidental to implementing the pay-as-you-use rule among overlapping generations, and not its essence. The mechanism of cost allocation among overlapping generations also works in an economy where there is no private net capital formation. Only if the benefits are shared by non-overlapping generations, does the effect on private capital formation become crucial. In this case, a burden transfer to future generations may result if loan finance retards capital formation, thus reducing the to-be-inherited capital stock.

*Case 2.* Consider now a quite different system, where the supply of saving has no effect on the level of investment, be it because the rate of interest is stuck in the liquidity trap, because investment is wholly inelastic, or for a number of other reasons. Here fiscal policy has the function

[1] The requirement of "comprehensiveness" would hold for the combined dual budget system, but an excess of O.A.S.I. receipts over expenditures would not be recorded as a surplus and be treated as now done in the Administrative rather than the Cash Budget. Since an obligation for the future is incurred (the opposite of providing for future benefits), coverage through tax finance is required. In other words, if one *had* to defend a principle of balance in the present budget system, then the administrative balance is the more meaningful one.

of providing for a full-employment level of demand. A tax dollar now reduces private spending, but a borrowing dollar does not. The level of deficit, required for any given level of public purchases (it being a matter of indifference in this connexion whether they are for capital or current uses) is fixed by considerations of full employment policy. The same instrument (size of deficit), therefore, cannot be used for a second purpose, that is, the accommodation of inter-generation equity. If the latter is given priority, the level of employment (or price level stability) becomes a function of public capital outlays. Unemployment or inflation are likely to result, and neither the objective of stability nor of inter-generation equity is met.

It might be argued that the basic trouble (only one instrument for two objectives) may be met by introducing another instrument, for example, change in the level or composition of public expenditures, or greater reliance on monetary policy. Adjustment in expenditure policy (overall level as well as division between capital and current outlays) offers no solution since efficiency in expenditure planning would be sacrificed in the process. With regard to monetary policy, the basic question is how well the instrument works. In a system where monetary policy is always effective in securing a full employment level of demand, we have essentially our first case. The deficit may be set on inter-generation equity grounds, and the residual stabilization task be met by monetary policy. But in a system where monetary policy is not all powerful, this solution is not available.

The case thus turns on the question of whether the burden for full employment policy can be left with monetary policy, or whether fiscal policy is needed as well. The answer to my mind, is clearly that fiscal policy is needed. Hence, I conclude that the dual budget is justified and desirable on the state and local level, where there is no responsibility for stabilization policy and debt finance frequently involves capital import; but that it is undesirable at the Federal level, where the use of fiscal policy for stabilization is of crucial importance.[2] Given the popular folk-lore on what constitutes sound finance, it could be, of course, that a strategy of counter confusion by appeal to the business analogy could improve the actual performance of fiscal policy (permit a larger deficit when needed) if a Capital Budget were used, but I would rather not bet on such an approach to public policy.

Notwithstanding these conclusions, the rate of public capital formation remains relevant for judging fiscal performance. If the concept of "fiscal prudence" is reinterpreted from "pay-as-you-use" to "providing a net benefit to future generations", then such prudence is measured by the excess of public capital formation over capital use. As before, public capital formation must be interpreted to include investment in human resources as well as acquisition of assets. The budgetary net contribution to capital stock, thus defined, should be assigned a significant place in the budget picture, but the nature of our economy is not such that it should be linked to the question of tax versus loan finance.

[2] Reference is to a Capital Budget system where capital expenditure are excluded in striking the balance in the current budget. There is no objection, of course, to supplementing a single budget, including all expenditures and receipts by a financial statement showing uses and sources of funds in debt transactions.

*F. M. BATOR*

# Budgetary Reform: Notes on Principles and Strategy

**44** The point I wish to make is not concerned with the budget as an aid in program formulation, execution, and control, or as a device for financial planning. It has to do rather with the role of the budget in informing and guiding congressional and public consideration of the large questions of fiscal policy: the balance between total demand and potential output, and the division of output between public and private uses and between consumption and investment.[1]

[1] I would not, of course, deny the importance of the former aspects of budgeting. The budget is a multi-purpose instrument; we must have an integrated system of sub-budgets. If this note appears to ignore that fact, it is only because the suggestion made below is entirely consistent with multi-purpose budget design. There is no conflict.

Reprinted from the *Review of Economics and Statistics,* Vol. VL supplement (1963), pp. 115–120, by permission of the author and publisher, Harvard University Press. Copyright 1963 by the President and Fellows of Harvard College. F. M. Bator is a professor at Harvard University. He was formerly Deputy Special Assistant to the President for National Security Affairs.

It is evident that as regards these large issues, upside-down economics still has the better of it in our public discussions. To be sure, the quality of conversation has improved during the last several years, as shown by the currency, among the more sophisticated people who read and write the nontechnical commentary on economic affairs, of a number of therapeutic notions: for instance, that at times deficits are not a bad thing; that if one cares to assess the fiscal impact of the budget one should look to the "cash" or the "national income and product" (NIP) version and not the "administrative budget"; and—a quite subtle notion—that the "full-employment surplus (deficit)," on NIP or cash account, is a better measure of the weight of the fisc than the actual realized surplus or deficit. However, a little sophistication can be a mixed blessing. None of the above notions shifts attention from the "deficit"—some deficit, perhaps a benign deficit—as the crucial magnitude. Yet, as we know, the beginning of wisdom in these matters is that no deficit, however measured, is an indicator of the expansionary or contractionary effect of the budget on total demand. Even the "full-employment deficit", while it is less misleading than the uncorrected, observed deficit, can easily lead down the garden path.[2]

This is not merely an intellectual quibble. As long as the debate is about which deficit is the true deficit and about when it is and when it is not all right to run a deficit, any weakening of attachment to the strict balance-the-budget rule is likely to be accompanied by the hardening of new doctrine, not quite as rigid but equally arbitrary and possibly, because more readily applied, almost as hobbling. One likely candidate —in some quarters it is already full-fledged dogma—is the proposition that deficits are appropriate in "recession" but not during expansion. Another, less likely to gain immediate acceptance but a good bet if the more knowledgeable members of Congress and the newspaper people begin to take up the notion of the full-employment surplus, is that fiscal policy should assure a full-employment surplus of no less than zero. In a situation where private spending propensities are weak, and public resistance makes it impossible to expand government spending fast enough to take up the slack, such a rule would shift to *monetary* policy much of the burden for keeping total demand from falling behind potential output. If investment and spending on consumer durables should happen to be relatively unresponsive to monetary ease—a likely contingency in a sluggish climate—or if the money managers

are frustrated by a very elastic demand for money (liquidity trap) or feel themselves hobbled by hot (footloose) money, the burden would be too heavy. There would result a chronic shortfall in total demand relative to potential output. Moreover, even if there were no troubles with sticky interest rates and inelastic investment spending or with the balance of payments, and hence if monetary policy could be made to work, there would be no cause for satisfaction. As a community we would be making our choices between investment and consumption blindly, as it were, uninfluenced by the relative desirability and the terms of trade between consumption now *versus* growth for consumption later. By imposing an arbitrary rule on our fiscal and monetary managers we will have lost an important degree of freedom with regard to the allocation of resources and/or, the purist might point out, the distribution of income (perhaps). (Needless to say, the bias of the zero full-employment surplus rule is not necessarily deflationary. In a situation of brisk private demand and fast expanding government spending, it would stack the cards in favor of inflation and/or tight-money-and-low-investment.)

The dilemma is plain. In our current situation a doctrine calling for a zero full-employment surplus would provide support for a badly needed reduction in the net fiscal load carried by the economy: for an increase in expenditures or a cut in tax rates or both. The "deficits are all right in recession" rule, in turn, could turn out to be useful during the next recession. Perhaps, like Churchill, we should welcome help irrespective of pedigree. However, one had better keep reminding oneself of the perils of such alliances. Employing specious crypto-rules in defense of sensible measures today may make it much more difficult to do the things that need to be done tomorrow.

It would be tempting, but wrong, to blame the problem entirely in the national neurosis about deficits. Wrong, because the truth that good fiscal doctrine cannot be based on the difference between expenditures and revenue would pose a thorny problem for fiscal strategy even in the absence of deficit fixation. There would still be a need for budgetary principles which are simple enough to be persuasive at the level of serious newspaper discussion. The President, the Budget Bureau, the Treasury, and the Council can and do work with relatively complicated, unobvious rules; the President, if he will, has the ultimate say. But the Executive has to have a compelling rationale to justify the budget in relation to output, employment, and growth, in the Congress

---

[2] Two budgets with the same full-employment surplus or deficit, and the same revenue structure and expenditure composition, will have markedly different effects on total demand according to whether the level of expenditure (revenue) is $x billion or $2x billion or $1.03x billion. (The "full-employment surplus" notion has the great merit of distinguishing between shifts in schedules and income-change-induced movements along schedules. With a specified level of full-employment income, and if government purchases are constant, changes in the "full-employment surplus" provide a fair, if approximate [one parameter], measure of changes in the "weight" of the net-receipts schedule. For quantitative analysis, however, it is probably better to work directly with the "first-round" effects on the income flow, or, if it is government purchases that are changed, on the flow of spending. If there is a *parallel* shift in the total spending schedule, it makes no difference. If, however, the schedule "twists"—and if as a tentative working assumption one posits exact or near-linearity *nearby* and approximates the result by multiplying the autonomous change by some multiplier—then it is a better strategy, because of lags, to work "forward" and not "backward": later effects come later and the magnitude of subsequent re-spending effects is likely to be more uncertain. Moreover, there is less chance of cumulating error. (If the spending schedule is assumed to exhibit appreciable curvature, then one cannot use a constant multiplier anyway but must re-solve the entire system using the new schedule.)

and the country at large. That need would not vanish even if Poor Richard and the fallacy of composition lost their hold.

Could the budget message be used to provide such a rationale? It is fair to say that the attempt has not been made.[3] Even in the 1963 *Budget*, a much more informative and sophisticated document than its predecessors, the assertion that the projected deficit or surplus is appropriate in terms of the goals of full employment and price stability has to be accepted on its face. In its discussion of the connection between revenues and total output the emphasis of the message is entirely on the revenue-yield of the forecast level of GNP ($570 billion). The much more important inverse relation—what level of taxes will help achieve the desired volume of total demand and output with the given expenditure plans— receives very little attention (see pp. 7–9, 19, 24–25). The budget makes it easy not to discuss that, the critical question, and to talk rather about the rights and wrongs of the surplus or deficit as such.[4]

It would be foolish to think that sensible and explicit treatment of fiscal policy in the budget would be sufficient to assure congressional and public enlightenment. But would it not be a step in the right direction if the President were to present, as the centerpiece of his budget message, a quantitative exposition of the fiscal policy rationale of the budget? This would involve the presentation of the results of a trial-run "nation's economic budget" (NEB) exercise, which would show the expected pattern of net receipts and purchases of households, businesses, the rest of the world, state and local governments, and the federal government, in relation to the target level of "desired" output. The exposition could be relatively brief and refer to a full-length version in the *Economic Report*. It would have to emphasize the tentative, trial-run character of the exercise, its hybrid proposal-program-forecast nature, the large margins of error, the desirability of working with ranges of values (it might give ranges), and the need for revision, month by month, of the estimates, and more often than not, of the proposed policies. But if presented in the right way, such an exercise would make it possible to substitute reasoned discussion for *ex cathedra* pronouncement in the message itself and would help to provide the basis for more intelligent congressional and public consideration of the fiscal policy aspects of the budget.[5]

What are the objections to such a procedure? The objection that an NEB exercise involves illegitimate "planning" is, of course, untenable. If the government is to do an adequate job in terms of almost any widely held notion of the national interest, in terms of the requirements imposed on it by law, or in terms of its political future, it must take into account the fiscal impact of the budget and hence plan in precisely the sense of such an exercise. Arthur Burns could not avoid, any more than can Walter Heller, making estimates about the major components of total demand. He could not even avoid contamination with some notion of desirable, or tolerable, or "potential" output.

The serious objections have to do not at all with the internal use by the executive of such an exercise, but with the wisdom of a strategy of exposure, of publishing the quantitative results and using these to justify the government's fiscal

---

[3] This is written before the publication of the 1964 *Budget*.

[4] In fairness, it should be said that last year the government did publish a sophisticated discussion of the 1962 prospects in the *Economic Report* (pp. 62–68), and that the budget message contains a reference to the *Report* (p. 19). However, it is the budget message which sets the tone and provides the grist for the newspaper people and politicians, and hence we cannot afford to relegate sensible discussion of fiscal policy to the *Report* and leave the budget message to treat fiscal policy as though it had to do primarily with raising money to pay for expenditures. The *Economic Report* should be considered as back-up for the interested few who are willing to read. (Ten pages stuck in the middle of Chapter 1 of the *Economic Report* are not likely to be given much publicity. In contrast, the entire budget message is published in the *New York Times*. To be sure, so is the President's report proper, and last year, for once, that did address the issues right-side up (pp. 11 and 12). Nonetheless, I would think that the point stands.)

[5] It would be superfluous, here, to describe such an exercise, especially since the objections to its use, as proposed, do not generally concern matters of technical detail. (For comments on some technical issues, see the appended *Notes*.) The basis for the exercise would lie in a host of executive decisions about programs and targets, and in a quarter-by-quarter forecast of total demand and its major components. The quantitative results could be summarized in a "G. C. table" (for G. C. read Gerhard Colm and see the first page of any issue of *Economic Indicators*) and presented in the fiscal policy section of the budget message (which should be moved forward to precede the sections on the composition of expenditures and revenues). The text would consist in a commentary on the choice of the target level of output, on the role of the budget in achieving that level of total demand, on the changes in policy that would be required if the projections were to turn out to be too low or too high, etc. Appropriate reference would, of course, have to be made to the fuller discussion in the *Economic Report*.

program. A published NEB exercise will certainly draw fire. It will be attacked as a milestone down the road to serfdom. The target figures for total output and the major components will be attacked as too high, too low, inconsistent, and as reflecting dictatorial tendencies. As forecast, the exercise will be alleged to reflect both technical incompetence and foolish arrogance about the government's ability to predict spending behavior (even its own). Moreover, the betting odds are overwhelming that many of the allegations of inconsistency and bad forecasting will turn out— six or twelve or eighteen months later—to have been justified.

It could be argued, with some truth, that the government cannot hide that it has in fact planned, and cannot avoid revealing many of the specific estimates on which the budget rests, whether or not it publishes an NEB exercise. Even a pure money-raising, Byrd approach to the budget will get involved in the politics of target fixing and target achievement; the revenue estimate implies a target level of GNP. If the $570 billion had not been published, it would almost certainly have "leaked" and provided the basis for jeers by midsummer and for pressure, desirable I think, for a large cut in taxes. Nonetheless, it is a fair guess that the use of an NEB exercise to justify the budget will stimulate rather than quiet controversy.

But would that be bad? The trouble with the present procedure is not that it gives rise to debate but that it fails to pose the true issues and hence makes it difficult to engage in sensible debate. We should welcome controversy about the appropriate balance between personal consumption and various kinds of public consumption, or between consumption and investment for growth, as well as about whether the government's target for total demand is too high or too low in the light of the expected consequences for capacity utilization, the labor market, the price level, and the balance of payments. Vigorous public discussion of these issues, informed by quantitative presentation by the government of its own position in the budget message and the *Economic Report*, would perhaps begin to make inroads on the fixation on deficits and spending and taxes as evil in themselves. Not that sensible presentation of the issues in the budget message will result in miracles. But the current mode of presentation discourages and hinders nonmiraculous, slow improvement.[6]

[6] Nor would it be a bad thing if, as a consequence of greater public exposure, the technical quality of the forecasts and projections underlying the budget

There remains what is perhaps the most serious objection at the level of strategy and tactics: that if the government publishes an NEB exercise, or even if it merely commits itself to a target rate of output, it will thereby impair its freedom of maneuver. This, the flexibility issue, is not without its peculiar side. It not only involves flexibility to adjust policy when off (or on) target, but also flexibility *not* to adjust policy when the economy is off target. One can certainly sympathize with the discomfiture of a Secretary of the Treasury whose own targets and projections of January are being used to pressure him into action in August, action which he may judge undesirable and/or politically unfeasible.

However, the coin has another side. If the government decides in January that, say, $570 billion is a desirable and reasonable target in the light of its estimate of potential output, inflationary pressures, the balance of payments, and a host of political judgments, then it is conceivable that it might even welcome pressure on itself to take corrective action six or nine months later, should performance be substantially off the target. Certainly from the point of view of the national interest, if not the comfort of ministers, it is not evident that the pressure for action which a shortfall or overshoot would generate would be necessarily counter-productive. Moreover, if under such circumstances the President should decide in favor of corrective fiscal action, he would surely find it much easier to make his case with a target and an underlying NEB exercise on the books. Current practice, since it does not exhibit the quantitative links between the budget and the original half-avowed GNP target, does not provide the ingredients for a convincing brief. An intelligently designed exercise published in January, one which takes account of the inevitable margins of error, would be especially helpful at times when the need is for fiscal action which would make large deficits (or surpluses) considerably larger.

were subject to more systematic criticism from the outside. Apart from stimulating improvement in the state of the art, exposure might help to strengthen resistance, in the face of political pressure, against excessive "distortion."

Concerning the danger that an NEB strategy will inflame ideological controversy and divert attention from the true issues, I am prejudiced enough to think that the case for the defense is so strong—and that it can be made so simple, compelling, and even interesting—that one might almost welcome attack and a "great debate" as an opportunity for powerful rebuttal and useful public education about the role of taxes and government spending in relation to price-market institutions.

None of this is to deny the importance of flexibility. Unforeseen price pressures, changes in the balance of payments or in defense requirements, and the like, might well require changes in targets and appropriate adjustments (or non-adjustments) in policy. However, in most such situations it is not only possible but desirable for the Executive to articulate the need for the change. A case can be made that the government should not employ a tactic of comfortable silence even in situations in which it decides to obviate any need for changing policy by passively adopting a change in targets.[7]

All the above is relevant to what may be the real political sticking point. The more explicit is the government's commitment to an output target, and the more explicit are the calculations which underlie such a target, the more clubs one gives away to one's political opponents. Moreover, and quite apart from political warfare, there is always the danger that poor performance—and every now and then performance is bound to be very poor—will be used by the ideologists to discredit systematic quantitative fiscal planning.

Unfortunately, it is not clear that there exists a strategy for the improvement of our fiscal politics which will avoid these dangers. Moreover, sensible and sophisticated presentation of an NEB exercise can do much to blunt irresponsible attack. By emphasizing the tentative quality of the projections and the need to keep re-examining and re-adjusting both the projections and, quite likely, the proposed policies; by avoiding *point* estimates; by scheduling and publishing a re-estimation in June and then quarterly during the entire fiscal year; by indicating the stand-by policies that might have to be invoked, should the gap between performance and target turn out to be large—by all such means the government can both build a strong defense against the charge of naive crystal-ball gazing

---

[7] It could be argued that the requirement to make a public commitment to a target will distort the choice of the target, that is, that the government will want to play safe in January and pick a target which is relatively easy to attain. On its face, it would not appear obvious which way, if at all, the counter-vailing temptations of ambition and caution are likely to bias the choice. In general, if the anticipated pressure to live up to target makes the President and his advisers even more careful and sober about what target they pick than they would be otherwise, that is probably all to the good. Sober seriousness is not, of course, equivalent to a preference for a lower rather than a higher output target. To pick a "low" target is to acquiesce in advance—and, given an NEB exercise, in public—in a loss of output, wages, and profits; in unemployment and sluggish growth.

and, more important, provide for itself a position from which to recommend and undertake changes in policy as circumstances warrant (and pin blame on the Congress when congressional intransigence prevents needed adjustments in policy).[8]

Last, it is perhaps not idle to hope that a strategy of planning and operating fiscal policy rather more in the open will help to create public support for giving the Executive some limited discretion to vary tax rates. As people get used to the notion that taxes and spending are like the brakes and the throttle of a car—that to lock them in place is dangerous, and that small marginal adjustments, made in time, may avoid the need for drastic adjustment—resistance to giving the Executive some freedom of fiscal maneuver is likely to decline.[9]

---

[8] Sensible presentation of an NEB exercise, and especially the use of ranges of values, can help to get around the problem that the executive budget is only a proposal to the legislature and hence contains items on the enactment of which the betting odds are poor.

[9] *Notes on Technical Issues of Budget Design*

(1) Offhand, I can think of no strong reason why the summary NEB exercise—which would appear in the fiscal policy section of the budget message and the purpose of which would be to guide congressional and public discussion—should not follow National Income Division conventions and procedures. Moreover, there is good reason why it should do so, e.g., the need for coherence between the federal sector and the other sectors as regards timing, transactions coverage and exclusions, etc. (My preference for NIP timing [receipts by and large on accrual and purchases on delivery] is not motivated by strategic calculation of how to minimize the damaging effects of deficit-fixation. It is not so motivated because I am not clear on strategic grounds where I would come out. I wish I were more convinced by the Schultze argument—or its opposite.)

(2) When it comes to the use of the budget figures for quantitative analysis of the effects of the budget on total demand, the situation is more complicated:

(a) As regards agency coverage, the administrative budget is inferior to the Cash and NIP Budgets. We need a consolidated statement for the federal government as a whole.

(b) As regards the inclusion or exclusion of "asset-transactions," there is no clear answer and neither the cash nor the NIP version alone will do. Loans and purchases of old assets will have important portfolio-effects on total demand and hence the budget statement should provide information on the government's plans with regard to both categories. The NIP Budget is, on this account, incomplete. On the other hand, it would be a mistake not to try to maintain the distinction between "fiscal" and "monetary" effects and simply to lump, as does the Cash Budget, bona fide loans with expenditures—the more so since much the larger part of the government's capital operations (debt management and Federal Reserve open-market) are anyway not included. Why not add two more non-NIP columns to the five now provided in the NIP version (purchases, transfers, interest, grants-in-aid, subsidies less surplus)? The two new columns could be ignored in the unavoidable calculation of the NIP deficit. (Loan guarantee and other indirect subsidy programs had best be covered in connection with the particular functions and activities they are designed to support.)

(c) On the question of *timing*, it is best to be eclectic and not make a categorical choice between "cash" and "accrual" on the income/receipts side, or for that matter, between "obligations (orders)," "deliveries" and "cash' on the product/expenditure side. All five time-profiles will be significant for the analysis of the effect of the budget on total demand (no doubt differentially so according to cyclical circumstances and, on the expenditure side, according to what is being bought). To the extent feasible, the budget should provide estimates on all five flow-rates. (I suppose if I were made to choose, for purposes of back-of-the-envelope fiscal analysis I should follow NID and use accruals in timing the impact effect on the income stream, and rather more doubtfully, deliveries on the expenditure side. Needless to say, the choice depends on one's notions about the determinants of various components of private expenditure, production lags, and the like.)

(3) It would be useful if the fiscal policy section of the budget message were to point out what the NEB exercise shows to be the estimated effect of the budget on the public share, federal and state-local, in GNP, and on the non-defense public share, and if it were to make some comparisons with prior years. (Appropriate reference would have to be made to subsidies as reflecting some degree of federal absorption of output and also to federal finance of state and local purchases).

(4) The fiscal policy section of the budget message should also point out the implications of the "fiscal policy plan" for the investment-consumption mix in the economy as a whole.

(5) The lead table on budget expenditures by function should be supplemented by a larger table in which the expenditure figure for each function is broken down into purchases of goods and services, outright subsidies, transfer payments to individuals, grants-in-aid, interest, loans, and purchases of old assets.

(6) The above seven-way split should be carried through in the detailed discussion of the "Federal Program by Function."

(7) I would think it a bad idea—on grounds both of concept and of strategy—for the federal government to adopt a two-budget system involving a full-fledged capital account. Such a system would almost certainly result in the enthronement of the shibboleth that it is all right to debt-finance capital expenditures but the current budget should be balanced or in surplus. Except under very strong "classical" assumptions, such a rule would not assure "neutrality" as regards the saving-consumption choice, and would lose us an important degree of freedom, making it much more difficult to achieve through fiscal and monetary measures whatever total demand, income distribution, consumption-investment mix, and public-private balance we might desire. (A related secondary danger is that "investment" would come to be defined as bricks and mortar or the purchase of self-liquidating assets and, in particular, that investment in education, public health, etc., would not qualify.)

(8) The above does not imply that we should continue to lump together public consumption and public investment. It would be most useful to distinguish, on the expenditure side of the budget, between consumption-type expenditures, investment in tangible assets, and what Musgrave calls "expenditures for future benefit not resulting in acquisition of assets." The burden of (7) above is only that we should not associate particular receipts with particular types of expenditure.